Instructional Media

Instructional

AND THE NEW TECHNOLOGIES OF INSTRUCTION

Robert Heinich
Indiana University

Michael Molenda
Indiana University

James D. Russell
Purdue University

John Wiley & Sons
New York
Chichester
Brisbane
Toronto
Singapore

Media

SECOND EDITION

Production Supervisor: Miriam Seda
Photo Research: Elyse Rieder
Copy Editor: Judith Sutton
Cover and Text Design: Kenny Beck
Cover Photo: Geoffrey Gove

Library of Congress Cataloging in Publication Data:

Heinich, Robert.
    Instructional media.

    Includes bibliographies and index.
    1. Educational technology.   I. Molenda, Michael.
II. Russell, James D.   III. Title.
LB1028.3.H45   1985   371.3′07′8   84-20875
ISBN 0–471–87835–9

Printed in the United States of America

10 9 8 7 6 5 4 3 2 1

P R E F A C E

From the Publisher

As publisher of *Instructional Media and the New Technologies of Instruction*, John Wiley & Sons has been very pleased with its acceptance by the field it serves and by the awards it has received.

Its adoption by 250 colleges and universities soon after its introduction in 1982 and the very favorable reviews it received in the professional journals reflected its general reception. The field was obviously ready for a text with up-to-date content, a conceptual point of view, and a format conducive to effective use.

The first award recognition of the text came from Graphic Design U.S.A. The layout, special features, typography, graphics, use of color, and distinctive cover were recognized in the "Desi" award conferred in 1982. Early in 1983 *Instructional Media* won the James W. Brown Publication Award from the Association for Educational Communications and Technology (AECT). Later that year, the National Society for Performance and Instruction (NSPI) honored the book with its Communication of the Year award over stiff competition. These awards confirm the judgment of the many individual instructors who chose this book to introduce their students to the world of instructional technology.

We wish to thank the many instructors who contributed to *Instructional Media*'s success. Through their reviews, formal responses to market research and informal advice, they have helped shape the book to meet the needs of students and teachers in the field of instructional media. With their input, we believe that this expanded and updated second edition will continue its standard of excellence.

From the Authors

In the preface to the first edition, we related how the decision to write this book grew out of a survey of instructors of basic media utilization courses. The results of that survey and a subsequent one in 1980 helped in determining the scope of the book. Reviews of the draft manuscript by knowledgeable people in the field helped us fine tune the manuscript. The success of this process convinced us to maintain close contact with users of the text as the best way to prepare for the new edition.

About a year after publication, a number of adopters were asked to critique the book chapter by chapter. Thanks to all those who responded to that questionnaire, we found out a lot about what was working well and what needed revision.

At the time the first edition was published, we realized that the annual convention of AECT did not provide a forum for teachers of media courses to exchange ideas and techniques. We decided to create such a forum by offering a preconvention workshop on methods of teaching a basic media course. We have conducted workshops at each AECT convention since 1982. These exchanges have been helpful both to the participants and to us. We have become better acquainted with the problems of teachers of media courses in a wide variety of institutions. The participants benefited not only from the activities of the workshops but also from the sharing of course outlines and materials through the network created by the workshop. We believe that their courses are better as a result of this experience, and we know that our efforts have improved significantly.

Many of our readers have given us their reactions on aspects of the book. We take such comments very seriously. We are particularly pleased to hear that students enjoy reading the book.

A number of instructors have taken advantage of the offer we made in the *Instructors Guide* to engage in a telelecture with their students. This has been an invaluable way for us to maintain contact with readers in a wide variety of settings. The most distant telelecture was to Guam.

When we were preparing the first edition, we class tested each chapter with our own classes at Indiana University and Purdue University. We continue to solicit feedback from our own students as we develop new material. We are determined to maintain the reputation of the text as one that is classroom tested.

Basic Assumptions

For readers not familiar with the first edition, we repeat our original convictions: (1) a rapprochement can be reached between the so-called "humanist" and "technological" traditions in the field of education; (2) a proper introduction to this field must involve not only technical skills but also understanding of the pedagogical rationales underlying the use of media/technology; and (3) to be comprehensive a textbook such as this must encompass not only the traditional audiovisual media and the newer electronic media but also the nonhardware psychological technologies.

Special Features

This new edition maintains the special features introduced in the first edition and adds two new features. Our survey of adopting instructors in 1983 indicated that these features aroused interest and contributed to better retention of media knowledge and skills among their students. The retained features are:

- **Outlines.** Each chapter begins with a broad outline of the contents, thus providing a quick advance organizer.
- **Objectives.** A detailed list of performance objectives precedes the text of each chapter.
- **Closeups.** These serve as miniature case studies of media applications; many of the vignettes in this edition are drawn from business/industry settings.

- **Media Files.** Actual materials in different media formats are highlighted. The materials shown have been selected as *typical* of a given class, not as *exemplary.* No endorsement—nor even commercial availability—is implied.
- **How To . . .** Various media production and operation procedures are spelled out with clear, illustrated, step-by-step instructions. Each is boxed for easy reference.
- **Appraisal Checklists.** Separate checklists have been developed for appraising each media format. Users have permission to photocopy these lists for personal use. This makes it easy to preview materials systematically and to preserve the previews for later reference.
- **AV Showmanship.** This feature gives specific tips on delivering media presentations with flair and dramatic effect.
- **Flashbacks.** These are brief vignettes that lend a sense of perspective and often provide fascinating behind-the-scenes glimpses of historic developments.

What's New

Because so many college course instructors have mentioned that many of their students come from or are preparing to enter the field of training, both in the public and private sector, there is significantly greater attention paid to adult instruction in terms of content and examples.

To say that ours is a rapidly changing field is no mere cliché; it is a basic fact of life for us. Recent advances in computer and video technology have prompted thorough revamping of our treatment of computers (Chapter 13), television (Chapter 9), and interactive video (Chapter 7).

In Chapter 3 we reworked the treatment of visual design principles with both more conceptual rigor and many more visual examples.

Through the telelectures we have found that students are fascinated with the potential implications of

"mind expanding" techniques and instrumentation. Therefore, in Chapter 14 we added extensive discussion of trends in biotechnology and video games as they may affect instruction.

We have also felt it important, particularly for those readers choosing instructional technology as a profession, to discuss more fully some of the institutional characteristics and constraints of education. By doing this, we can help new professionals understand better the innovation process and organizational impediments to innovation. This material is also covered in Chapter 14.

The highly favorable response by students to the "How To . . ." sections prompted us to increase and improve the "How To . . ." items throughout the book. A couple of Flashbacks and many new Media Files and Closeups have been added, particularly in reference to business/industry applications of media.

To help readers tune in on and to sift through the abundance of software for the new electronic technology flooding the marketplace these days, Appendix A has been expanded with extensive additional sources of commercial materials and reviewing services, especially for computers and video.

A new feature added in this edition is **Lexicon**, a short list of new or specialized vocabulary terms introduced at the beginning of each chapter. This alerts readers to watch for these terms in the chapter, where they are discussed in context. The **Lexicon** terms and many other specialized terms are gathered into a new **Glossary**, given at the end of the book as **Appendix D**.

Appendix A suggests sources for the various types of materials discussed in the chapters. It has been thoroughly updated and revised for this edition. **Appendix B** lists sources of free and inexpensive materials. **Appendix C** deals with the emerging issues of copyright law as they pertain to users of instructional media. Recent legal interpretations are discussed. Our point of view is that an informed approach to the spirit as well as the letter of the law can result in giving the instructor more "elbow room" than generally has been considered possible.

Instructors who adopt this book for a course or a workshop can obtain an *Instructor's Guide*, published separately. It contains suggested course syllabi, detailed outlines of chapters, transparency masters, and sample test items.

We continue to welcome comments about the book. Please send suggestions to us so that we can keep future editions responsive to the demands of the times.*

Robert Heinich
Michael Molenda
James D. Russell

---

*Send the comments to Dr. Robert Heinich, Department of Instructional Systems Technology, School of Education, Indiana University, Bloomington, IN 47405.

ACKNOWLEDGMENTS

Early drafts of the first edition were reviewed by Ted Cobun, East Tennessee State University; Arni Dunathan, University of Missouri; Terry Holcomb, North Texas State University; Robert Hunyard, Northern Illinois University; Bruce Petty, Oklahoma State University; William Winn, University of Calgary.

The editorial, design, graphic, photographic, and production staffs at Wiley faced the formidable task of making an award-winning book even better. The high standard set by the first edition made the complex job of collaboration even more difficult. The team at Wiley was obviously up to the challenge.

Kristine Brancolini of Indiana University assisted us in compiling the bibliographies for each chapter and shaped up the Glossary with her keen eye and deep understanding of the subject matter. Carl Stafford of Purdue University lent his considerable expertise to an expanded chapter 10. John Soudah contributed his excellent photographic skills under considerable pressure of deadlines. The good work of Michael Neff, Deane Dayton, Danny Callison, Jim Owens, William Orisich, and Doris Brodeur evidenced in the first edition has been carried into the second. We thank the media publishers and manufacturers who supplied photographs and gave us permission to use them.

Carole Bagley of Mankato State University worked closely with us on revising Chapter 13, Computers, and made innumerable contributions to the content of the chapter and to the source lists appearing in Appendix A.

Colleagues from other universities mentioned here provided valuable suggestions at various points in the development process:

Earl E. Adreani
Boston University

Larry Albertson
University of Nebraska

Philip J. Brody
University of Kansas

J. Gordon Coleman
Baylor University

Keith Collins
Northern Illinois University

Wallace Draper
Ball State University

Lester Elsie
University of Toledo

Gary Ferrington
University of Oregon

Jack Garber
University of Wisconsin—Eau Claire

Robert A. Gray
Baylor University

David Gueulette
Northern Illinois University

Kathryn Holland
Kutztown University

Charles E. Jaquith
Central Michigan University

Doreen Keable
St. Cloud State University

Robert B. Krueger
University of Wisconsin—River Falls

David Redmond
West Chester State College

Russell Reis
West Chester State College

Rhonda S. Robinson
Northern Illinois University

Clair Rood
University of Wisconsin—La Crosse

Charles F. Roth, Jr.
University of Michigan—Flint

Tony Schulzetenberg
St. Cloud State University

James A. Shuff
Henderson State University

Don C. Smellie
Utah State University

Ross C. Snyder
Missouri Southern State College

Charles Vance
Ithaca College

Nancy H. Vick
Longwood College

Robert Ward
Bridgewater State College

John Wedman
University of Northern Iowa

E. J. Zeimet
University of Wisconsin—La Crosse

We are grateful to our colleagues from our own university for their many and valued forms of support.

Finally, we thank our families whose continued support made this new edition possible.

R.H.
M.M.
J.D.R.

C O N T E N T S

S P E C I A L   F E A T U R E S

Close Up

Appraisal Checklist

Instructional Media

*M*edia and Instruction

C H A P T E R 1

Outline

Objectives

After studying this chapter, you should be able to:

1. Identify the range of information vehicles available for both education and mass communication.
2. Distinguish between "differentiation" and "integration."
3. Explain the "concrete-to-abstract continuum" as presented in the text, indicating how it can be used to aid in the selection of media.
4. Relate differentiation and integration to the concrete-to-abstract continuum.
5. Diagram and explain a communication model (Shannon, Shannon-Schramm, or one of your own design).
6. Analyze a given instructional situation in terms of one of the communication models.
7. Describe the transactional nature of communication.
8. Define or describe "technologies of instruction" and cite an example.
9. Describe and distinguish between CMI and CAI.
10. Discuss five roles or purposes of media in the instructional process. Your discussion should include an example of media in each of these roles.
11. Indicate the relationship between "structure" and "flexibility" in instructional situations.
12. Demonstrate by examples the relationship between instructional media and flexibility in instructional design.
13. Describe the role of instructional media in the "out-of-school" setting, indicating their function and types of uses.
14. Discuss the relationship between humanism and instructional technology in the classroom.

Lexicon

medium/media

format

technology

concrete-abstract continuum

iconic

differentiation

integration

communication model

The technical terms listed in this section are discussed in the book and are defined in the Appendix D Glossary.

THE PERVASIVENESS OF MASS MEDIA

Living as we do in a society in which instantaneous, worldwide communication of information is commonplace, we can easily forget that several decades ago such a phenomenon would have seemed preposterous, at best the stuff of dreams and poetry. Philosopher Ralph Waldo Emerson, for example, could stir the imagination toward poetic contemplation of such a notion as he memorialized the battle of Concord Bridge, which signaled the start of the American Revolution: "Here once the embattled farmers stood, And fired the shot heard round the world." But never could our poet have imagined that the day would come when momentous gunfire could literally be "heard round the world."

In truth, of course, it took many months for this opening volley of war to be "heard" throughout the American colonies, and years for it to be "heard" around the world. Imagine, if you will, what would have happened had modern communications technology and mass media been available in 1775. The whole world would have heard the shots and witnessed the scene at Concord Bridge via communications satellite. A few hours later, newspapers would have reported the incident in greater detail. Almost simultaneously, television and radio would have begun to present in-depth coverage of the event, complete with background information about relations between Britain and its American colonies, interviews with eyewitnesses to the battle, and statements by politicians and pundits concerned with its national and international implications. Newspapers and periodicals would have continued to

▲ **Figure 1.1**

Hotels, motels, and even private homes now use satellite receiving dishes to bring television programs directly into the building from satellites overhead.

present the public with even more information and details. Within a few weeks, speculative and informative paperback books about the battle would have been ready for mass consumption, and a few months later more scholarly works exploring the deeper political, social, and military implications of the affair would have been in print.

The notion of television cameras mounted on Concord Bridge in 1775, of Barbara Walters securing an exclusive interview with Sam Adams, of Mike Wallace interrogating that "rabble-rousing dirty little atheist Tom Paine" (as his Tory enemies called him) on *60 Minutes,* or of Tom Bro-

kaw interviewing the patrician George Washington and the possibly mad King George III on world television may make us smile, as may the notion of mass-market paperback accounts of the battle of Concord Bridge appearing on the shelves of colonial village stores and apothecaries. But the smile should be a thoughtful one, especially for those of us concerned with education. There is no doubt that modern communications technology has vastly increased our ability to witness events as they happen and thereby has vastly increased our exposure to information

▲ **Figure 1.2**
Music and information, broadcast or recorded on cassette, go with us everywhere.

▲ **Figure 1.3**
Sesame Street is viewed by millions of children at home, in schools, and in day care centers in North America and abroad.

and experience. The very pervasiveness of this technology in our everyday lives, however, tends to obscure the fact that it is a relatively new phenomenon, with implications for education that are only now beginning to be fully understood and appreciated.

Just as they do for adults, mass media today provide more and more varied sources of information for children. There are more magazines, newspapers, and books, not to mention textbooks and other printed instructional materials, designed specifically for children than ever before. Children today are rarely out of earshot of radio (witness, for example, the phenomenon of young ears

seemingly glued to hand-carried transistor radios and tape players); and, of course, there is television.

There are children's television programs specifically designed to instruct as well as entertain—*Sesame Street* and *Mister Rogers' Neighborhood,* for example. There are numerous programs primarily designed to attract young viewers for commercial reasons, but that nevertheless do provide information and experiences to which previous generations of children are unlikely to have been exposed. And there are the programs intended primarily for adults but watched by countless children.

With all these communications sources, learners today have absorbed more information and vicariously experienced many more phenomena than people of previous generations. They have witnessed the undersea world of Jacques Cousteau and have followed the adventures of man into space. The hidden

world of our natural environment has been revealed to them through modern photographic techniques and devices such as strobe-light photography that stops action at a thousandth of a second and microscopic and time-lapse photography that can reveal the wondrous formation of crystals or the blossoming and decay of a flower.

They also learn to handle and process data at a far more sophisticated level than other generations. The computer is taken for granted in the same way that television is. As the comic strip *Bloom County* suggests, children may be involved in experiences their parents do not comprehend. The intrusion of adolescents into data banks by way of personal computers is well known. A paradox of today is that youngsters now enter the adult world much earlier than their parents did—but that it is not necessarily the world of their parents.

All of which is to say that learners of all ages are to some extent "different" today from learners of previous generations simply by virtue of their exposure to mass media and information technology. There is no question of whether or not modern communications technology should be brought into the learning situation. It is already there, as it is in other facets of society, in the experiential and environmental background of teacher and student alike. The real question is, How can we best use this pervasive technology for effective education? This book will help answer that question.

In the remainder of the first chapter, we will present an introduction to and overview of the major premises and themes of the book. We begin with a brief review of certain key learning concepts, particularly as they relate to effective use of media for instructional purposes. From there we move on to a discussion of communication, for without appropriate communication there cannot be effective teaching. We then discuss the general concept of technology of instruction, with some emphasis on the germinal instructional technology that has emerged from applications of reinforcement theory. We present

▼ **Figure 1.4**

▼ **Figure 1.5**

a preview of some general educational strategies to which instructional media are particularly applicable, followed by a discussion of the growing use of instructional media outside the formal educational setting. We close with an affirmation of the theme that pervades this entire text: properly and creatively used instructional technology and instructional media can provide us with hitherto unattainable opportunities to individualize and humanize the teaching/learning environment.

Some Basic Definitions

Medium; media (plural): In this book used in the general sense of a means of communication. Derived from the Latin *medium,* "between," the term refers to anything that carries information *between* a source and a receiver.

Film, television, radio, audio recordings, photographs, projected visuals, printed materials, and the like are media of communication. They are considered *instructional media* when they are used to carry messages with an instructional in-

tent. The middle chapters of this text are concerned with instructional applications of media such as these.

Format: The physical form in which a medium is incorporated and displayed. For example, motion pictures are available in 35-mm, 16-mm, and 8-mm formats. Cassette tape is an audio format. Print is a verbal format.

Material: An item of a medium format; in the plural, a collection of items of a medium format or of several media formats, often used

◀ **Figure 1.6**
Personal computers bring the information revolution into the home.

▶ **Figure 1.7**
The clarity and simplicity of language in most news magazines makes them accessible to young and old alike.

▼ **Figure 1.8**
The original mass medium—the newspaper—delves into the events of the day more deeply than radio or television.

in a general sense. For example, *Instructional materials are available from many sources.*

Technology: This term has three meanings in this book; the meaning in each instance can be identified by the context.

1. Technology as a process— "the systematic application of scientific or other organized knowledge to practical tasks;" * the process of devising reliable and repeatable solutions to tasks.
2. Technology as product—the hardware and software that result from the application of technological processes. We must remember that a film is as much a product of technology as the projector that displays it. The book is as much a product of technology as the press that prints it.
3. Technology as a mix of process and product—uses in instances where: (a) the context refers to the combination of technological processes and resultant products. For example, *Technology is constantly expanding our information delivery systems* implies both the process of invention and the devices that result; (b) process is inseparable from product. For example, the technology of computers is inherently an interaction between hardware and software (the program).

Learning: A general term for a relatively lasting change in performance caused directly by experience; also the process or processes whereby such change is brought about. Learning is *inferred* from performance.

Instruction: Deliberate arrangement

of experience(s) to help a learner achieve a desirable change in performance; the management of

learning, which in education and training is primarily the function of the instructor.

John Kenneth Galbraith. The New Industrial State. Boston: Houghton Mifflin, 1967, p. 12.

Epigrams

It was the funeral of President Kennedy that most strongly proved the power of television to invest an occasion with the character of corporate participation. It involved an entire population in a ritual process.

Marshall McLuhan

In an electric information environment, minority groups can no longer be contained—ignored. Too many people know too much about each other. Our new environment compels commitment and participation. We have become irrevocably involved with, and responsible for, each other.

Marshall McLuhan

It turns out that TV is a powerful educational medium even when it isn't trying to be, even when it's only trying to entertain. There must be millions of people who have learned, simply by watching crime dramas in the past few years, that they have the right to remain silent when arrested.

Herb Schlosser

The book is one of the first, and very possibly the most important, mass-produced product, and its impact demonstrates the falsity of the common notion that mass production per se brings about the massification of men.

David Riesman

Just as the printing press democratized learning, so the television set has democratized experience.

Daniel J. Boorstin

Television is the first mass-produced, organically composed symbolic environment into which our children are born and in which they will live from cradle to grave. . . . Television is a total cultural system (as was tribal religion) with its own art, science, statecraft, legendry, geography, demography, character types, and action structure.

George Gerbner

Today we immerse ourselves in sound. We've all become acoustic skin-divers. Music is no longer for listening to, but for merging with.

Edmund Carpenter

Do you in fact think that television stops anybody from reading? Yes, I believe that middle-class children are less well-read than they were, although probably far better informed about public affairs.

Kenneth Clark

Electronic media have made all the arts environmental. Everyone can avail himself of cultural riches beyond what any millionaire has ever known.

Edmund Carpenter

THE "WHY" OF USING INSTRUCTIONAL MEDIA

Too frequently instructors use media without any reference to guiding principles of how the experiences contained in those media will be used by learners. *Without a good theoretical rationale, use of specific materials may become simply mechanical, with the fond hope that what is presented to learners will eventually become meaningful to them.* We will help you develop conceptual and theoretical bases on which to choose specific materials and methods by discussing the relationships between media, learning, and instruction in the following three contexts:

1. The developmental learning process of differentiation and integration.
2. The attributes of media in reference to developmental learning.
3. Communication models that can help you analyze and deal with human communication problems.

Differentiation and Integration in Learning

Very young children tend to react to situations as a whole. For example, when a baby tastes something objectionable, the whole body tends to respond, not just the taste organs (Figure 1.9). Through experience children start differentiating their responses to the environment. They start distinguishing between mother and father and the other people they come in contact with, including siblings. They soon separate dogs from cats and then become aware of varieties of dogs and varieties of cats. These differentiations based on experience lead to the development of concepts, that is, the development of the ability to classify objects by characteristics they have learned to identify. At this

▲ **Figure 1.9**
Babies respond to sensory stimuli with their whole bodies.

point, verbal labels have some meaning. Prior to the acquisition of experience, verbal labels may lead to a diffuse and confused response.

The next step in the children's process of mental growth is to integrate those differentiations into generalizations and abstractions. Once again responding to the total environment but from an entirely different point of view, they now start organizing their differentiations into series of constructs—new wholes or classes. The skill of integration helps students to achieve working generalizations. The children who have gone through the process of differentiating first dogs from cats and then certain dogs from other dogs are now in a position to deal with the class, dog, in a much more meaningful and useful way.

Thus far we have talked primarily about the development of a child's ability to differentiate. However, the same principles apply to *any* learner of *any* age who happens to be naïve in a particular subject area. For many years, the theme of a visitor from another planet having to make new differentiations and integrating them into appropriate constructs has provided playwrights (*Visit to a Small

Planet*), novelists (*Stranger in a Strange Land*), and TV writers (*My Favorite Martian* and *Mork and Mindy*) opportunities to make humorous and perceptive comments on our own culture. Adult learners can usually make new differentiations more quickly than children but instructors need to remember that adults do still have to make them.

People handicapped by sensory impairment have a particularly hard time making accurate and consistent differentiations. The hearing impaired, for example, have difficulty in mastering the spatial meanings of prepositions such as *above, below, by, behind, at.* Instructors need to be prepared for learning problems of handicapped students whose experiences have been distorted by inadequate sensory abilities.

The Concrete-Abstract Continuum

Thus far we have discussed differentiation/integration in reference to learning. But learning is guided by instruction, and instruction is the job of the teacher. Hoban once pointed out that the business of education is not learning, but the management of learning, that is, instruction. The teacher organizes the experiences of learners in a way that helps them change their performance in a meaningful way.

The psychologist Jerome Bruner, in developing a "theory of instruction," proposes that the instruction provided to a learner should proceed from direct experience, through iconic representations of experience (as in pictures, films, etc.), through symbolic representation (as in words).* He further states that "the sequence in which a learner encounters materials" has a direct effect on achievement of mastery of the task.† The development of instruction should parallel the differentiation-integration learning process. Bruner points out that this applies to *all* learners, not just children. When a learning task is presented to adults who

*Jerome S. Bruner. *Toward a Theory of Instruction.* Cambridge: Harvard University Press, 1966, p. 49.

†Ibid.

Flashback: DALE'S CONE OF EXPERIENCE

In one of the first textbooks written about the use of audiovisual materials in schools, Hoban, Hoban, and Zissman stated that the value of audiovisual materials is a function of their degree of realism. In developing this concept, the authors arranged various teaching methods in a hierarchy of greater and greater abstraction, beginning with what they referred to as "the total situation" and culminating with "words" at the top of the hierarchy.[a]

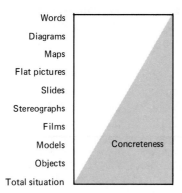

In 1946, Edgar Dale took the same construct and developed what he referred to as the "Cone of Experience."[b]

In the Cone of Experience, we start with the learner as participant in the actual experience, then move to the learner as observer of the actual event, to the learner as observer of a mediated event (an event presented through some medium), and finally to the learner observing symbols that represent an event. Dale contended that learners could make

Dale's Cone of Experience. From *Audio-Visual Methods in Teaching*, Third Edition, by Edgar Dale. Copyright 1946, 1954, © 1969 by Holt, Rinehart and Winston. Reprinted by permission of Holt, Rinehart and Winston, p. 108.

profitable use of more abstract instructional activities to the extent that they had built up a stock of more concrete experiences to give meaning to the more abstract representations of reality.

It is interesting that psychologist Jerome Bruner, working from a different direction, devised a descriptive scheme for labelling instructional activities that parallels Dale's. As shown here, Bruner's concepts of enactive, iconic, and abstract learning may be superimposed on Dale's Cone. Bruner, though, intended to emphasize the nature of the mental operations of the learner rather than the nature of the stimuli presented to the learner.[c]

[a]Charles F. Hoban, Sr., Charles F. Hoban, Jr., and Samuel B. Zissman. *Visualizing the Curriculum.* New York: Dryden, 1937, p. 39.
[b]Edgar Dale. *Audio-Visual Methods in Teaching.* New York: Holt, Rinehart and Winston, 1969, p. 108. From *Audio-Visual Methods in Teaching*, Third Edition, by Edgar Dale. Copyright 1946, 1954 © 1969 by Holt, Rinehart and Winston. Reprinted by permission of Holt, Rinehart and Winston CBS College Publishing.
[c]Bruner, loc. cit.

have no relevant experiences on which to draw, learning is facilitated for them when instruction follows a sequence from actual experience through iconic, to symbolic representations.‡ As we will discuss later, an important first step in instruction is to determine the nature of any learner's current level of experience. The principles that Fleming and Levie derive from research underscore Bruner's position.* Concrete experiences facilitate learning *and* the acquisition, retention, and usability of abstract symbols.

Instructional media not only provide the necessary concrete experiences, but also help students integrate prior experiences. Many students have watched various aspects of the construction of a high-

way or a street. They have seen the machine that lays the asphalt down; they have seen graders at work; and they have seen a number of other stages of road building. However, they need to have all these experiences integrated into a generalized notion of what it means to build a highway. A film that can show all of these processes in relation to each other is an ideal way to integrate their various experiences into a meaningful abstraction.

In the beginning of this chapter, we mentioned that children today, because of television and movies, acquire many mediated experiences at a much earlier age than children of previous generations. These experiences are extremely helpful to them in making the kinds of differentiations referred to above. However, we cannot assume that those differentiations have been achieved, or that they are accurate. The teacher

should check to make sure those differentiations have been made on a sound basis, and should help students integrate the experiences that they have acquired into meaningful constructs.

Historically, improving the balance between concrete and abstract learning experiences was a key reason for using instructional media. However, current research questions the nature of the distinctions between media made by earlier authors. The relative concreteness and abstractness of various media and methods and their comparative effectiveness in learning is not as clearcut as we once believed. Most instructional materials use a combination of presentation forms that vary in their degree of realism; for example, films (motion pictures) or filmstrips (still pictures) may be captioned or narrated (verbal symbols). In certain circumstances, line drawings (visual symbols) have been shown to be more effective

‡See Flashback, page 8.

*Malcolm Fleming and W. Howard Levie. *Instructional Message Design.* Englewood Cliffs, N. J.: Educational Technology Publications, 1978, pp. 107–111.

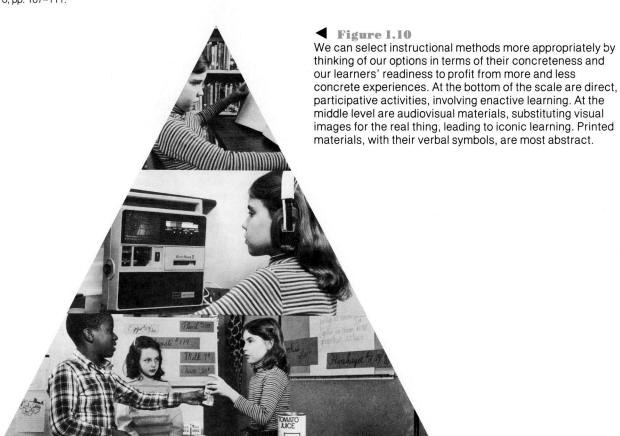

◄ **Figure 1.10**
We can select instructional methods more appropriately by thinking of our options in terms of their concreteness and our learners' readiness to profit from more and less concrete experiences. At the bottom of the scale are direct, participative activities, involving enactive learning. At the middle level are audiovisual materials, substituting visual images for the real thing, leading to iconic learning. Printed materials, with their verbal symbols, are most abstract.

than realistic photographs (still pictures). It now seems clear that a second key to effectiveness is learner response—what mental processing or overt practice is conducted in response to the audiovisual stimuli. Regardless of the appeal of a mode of presentation, the ultimate test is learner response and performance.

Decisions regarding trade-offs between concreteness of a learning experience and time constraints have to be continually made by the instructor. In general, as you move up Dale's Cone (see Flashback, p. 23) toward the more abstract media, more information can be compressed into a shorter period of time. It takes more time for students to engage in a direct purposeful experience, a contrived experience, or a dramatized experience than it does to present the same information in a motion picture, a recording, a series of visual symbols, or a series of verbal symbols. For example, a field trip can provide a learning experience relatively high in concreteness, but it also takes up a good deal of instructional time. A motion picture depicting the same experiences as the field trip could be presented to the students in a much shorter period of time and with much less effort. Similarly, a simulation (a contrived experience) such as the game "Ghetto" can help students relate to new situations and solve new problems, but such a simulation game does take more time than a more abstract learning experience such as watching a brief television documentary about ghetto life. In such cases, the instructor must decide whether the particular nature of the experience is worth the extra time it may take. If you look at Table 1.1, you will see that training directors consider contrived experiences (role playing, simulations) well worth the time they take. They often use filmed or videotaped simulations to take advantage of both "reality" and time compression.

The instructor must also decide whether or not the learning experi-

▲ **Figures 1.11 and 1.12**
Are high school students likely to develop greater interest in and appreciation for social problems by participating in a simulation than by watching a television documentary? What other differences might there be in learning outcomes? Are these differences sufficient to justify the greater time expenditure of the simulation game?

ence is appropriate to the experiential background of the student. The greatest amount of information can be presented in the least amount of time through printed or spoken words (the top of the concrete-to-abstract continuum and cone). But if the student does not have the requisite experiential background and knowledge to handle these verbal symbols, time saved in presentation will be time lost in learning. As mentioned before, the

instructor finds out if the right match has been made by relying on what is perhaps *the* basic principle of instruction: learning means appropriate change in response, or performance. Because of this, emphasis in contemporary instructional research is placed on analysis of learner response as the key to choosing appropriate instructional experiences.

As Dale has pointed out, a model such as his Cone of Experience, while not an accurate representation

TABLE 1.1   MEDIA/METHOD PREFERENCES OF TRAINERS IN BUSINESS AND INDUSTRY

Instructional Format	% of Respondents	
	Currently Using	Not Currently Using, but Will Be Using in 12 Months
Lectures	89.4%	3.2%
Overhead transparencies	83.7%	3.7%
Videocassettes	78.3%	6.7%
Role playing	77.0%	4.8%
Slides	74.7%	3.9%
Case studies	71.3%	5.4%
16-mm films	70.6%	3.5%
One-to-one instruction	68.3%	4.1%
Audiocassettes	61.4%	3.2%
Self-tests	56.8%	5.4%
Games and simulations	54.2%	5.6%
Programmed instruction	39.5%	7.4%
Sound filmstrips	38.4%	2.0%
Computer-assisted instruction	19.1%	12.2%
Interactive video	9.1%	7.4%
Videodiscs	4.6%	2.0%

Source: Survey reported in *Training* (October 1983), p. 50.

▲ **Figure 1.13**
Management trainees often participate in role-playing exercises to gain concrete experience in dealing with people.

of complex relationships, is, nonetheless, a practical guide to analyzing the characteristics of instructional media and methods and how these media may be useful.

Applying Research to Practice

Different media formats present different advantages and limitations regarding any given teaching/learning problem. Too often in the past, media advocates have acted as though all audiovisual formats were inherently superior to printed or spoken words as channels for learning. Each new mechanical marvel that came along was regarded as a possible panacea, the one best solution to all instructional problems. Audiovisual researchers typically set up studies that were, essentially, efforts to demonstrate the superiority of the "latest and greatest" media tool over conventional lecture methods or over

some less sophisticated media form. The findings of these "media comparison" studies, however, cast doubt on the assumptions that audiovisual tools are always preferable to verbal ones and that we may someday develop an ideal delivery system for all purposes—"the best medium."

The Flashback "What Has Research Taught Us?" critiques this research in some detail. For the practitioner, a major question arises: if a majority of studies conclude that there is "no statistically significant difference" in learning between the media treatment and conventional instruction, does this mean that audiovisual presentations are approximately equivalent to lectures in terms of instructional usefulness? Not really. At most, it means that when certain audiovisual materials are used in the same way as a lecture is used, for the same purposes as a lecture (e.g., verbal recall), with a random sample of learners, and *all other conditions are held constant,* outcomes measured by specific tests will be similar. But the qualifications listed here are assumptions that good instructors specifically reject in actual practice. They do not use audiovisual materials in the same way as print or lecture materials. They select media that suit particular *objectives;* audiovisual presentations can be powerful, for example, in conveying a historical period's feel, in building empathy with others, in showing a role model in action. Good instructors select media for those learners who can profit from them. And they *evaluate* effectiveness not just on the basis of immediate verbal recall but also on the basis of what impact the experience had on the imagination, feelings, and long-term comprehension of the viewer.

The ASSURE Model described in Chapter Two was developed as a planning aid to help assure that media are used to their maximum advantage, not just as interchangeable substitutes for printed or oral messages. Contrary to the requirements

People who are just beginning study in the field of instructional media typically hold the misconception that this is a very young field, one in which formal research probably began around the 1950s or perhaps the 1960s. In fact, well-conceived psychological studies of learning from films were being conducted as early as 1919, when Lashley and Watson investigated the adaptation of World War I training films to civilian use.

A large-scale study of the instructional uses of films in the Chicago public schools was reported by Freeman in 1924.[a] The Lashley-Watson studies[b] and the Chicago school studies yielded considerable insight into the instructional potentials of film and arrived at surprisingly sophisticated conclusions about the role of media in the classroom. Many of their findings seem to have been rediscovered by researchers studying the "new medium" of each succeeding generation. In the following quotations from the Chicago school studies, try substituting the term "television," "computer-assisted instruction," or "videodisc" whenever "film" or "visual media" are mentioned:

> *The relative effectiveness of verbal instruction as contrasted with the various forms of concrete or realistic material in visual media depends on the nature of the instruction to be given and the character of the learner's previous experience with objective materials.*
>
> *The peculiar value of a film lies not in its generally stimulating effect, but in its ability to furnish a particular type of experience.*
>
> *Films should be so designed as to furnish to the teacher otherwise inaccessible raw material for instruction but should leave the organization of the complete teaching unit largely to the teacher.*
>
> *The teacher has been found superior to all visual media in gaining and sustaining attention.*
>
> *Each of the so-called conventional forms of instruction that employ visual media has some advantage and some disadvantage, and there*

are circumstances under which each is the best form to use.[c]

Media Comparison Studies

However, these promising beginnings were largely abandoned in favor of experimental designs in which one group of learners (the experimental group) is exposed to an audiovisual presentation of some sort while a similar group (the control group) receives "conventional instruction"—often a lecture. All are given the same final test, the results of which are used to indicate the effectiveness of the experimental version. Sometimes two media forms are compared, for instance, film versus slide/tape. This type of study is known as a media comparison study.

Reviews of media comparison studies regularly point out that a majority of the studies find that there is "no statistically significant difference" in learning between the experimental treatment and the control treatment. Does this mean that audiovisual presentations are equivalent to lectures or that films are equivalent to slide/tapes in their impact on the audience?

Critics have pointed out a number of major faults in the very conception of media comparison studies that cast doubt on their utility as guides for making real life decisions. First, what was compared with what? In some cases the "media" treatment was nothing more than a filmed or videotaped lecture, to ensure that the two treatments had the same content and method, differing only in delivery system. The film or videotape chosen in the study may or may not have made use of color, motion, or other special visual possibilities of the medium. Furthermore, the test items used to measure achievement often were drawn largely from the verbal information in the soundtrack, not from the visual content. On the other side of the coin, the "conventional instruction" treatment varied greatly from study to study, consisting of whatever was considered to be the traditional method in that setting: e.g., a lecture, a lecture plus discussion, textbook reading, or any combination of these or other methods.

It is no wonder that the cumulative results of these media comparison studies are difficult to interpret. As one critic has put it, it is like trying to compare "can-of-worms A" with "can-of-worms B."

[a]Frank N. Freeman. *Visual Education*. Chicago: University of Chicago Press, 1924, p. 79.

[b]K. S. Lashley and J. B. Watson. *A Psychological Study of Motion Pictures in Relation to Venereal Disease Campaigns*. Washington, D.C.: U.S. Interdepartmental Social Hygiene Board, 1922, p. 3.

[c]Paul Saettler. "Design and Selection Factors." *Review of Educational Research* 38, no. 2 (April 1968), p. 116.

Unfortunately, the more successful the researchers were in controlling the conditions of the "media" treatment, the less it resembled what would be normal good practice in media utilization. For example, in order to control as many extraneous variables as possible, the "media" treatment ordinarily excluded such normal practices as introductory and follow-up discussion of the media presentation. What was needed to meet laboratory standards of purity bore little resemblance to what creative instructors do with either media *or* conventional instruction.

Analysis of the *content* treated in these studies reveals another bias—a bias toward cognitive subject matter, as opposed to attitudinal, interpersonal, or motor skill objectives. Further, attainment of the objectives was usually measured by ordinary paper-and-pencil verbal tests. Thus, the experiments typically revolved around highly verbal content being measured by highly verbal instruments (often using college students as subjects—an unusually verbally adept sector of the general population). This may help explain why lecture and textbook treatments—being highly verbal—yielded comparable results to the "media" treatments.

Implications for Practice

Select Materials Based on Their Attributes. An insight derived from the errors made in media comparison research is that one cannot generalize findings about one film to all films, or one video lesson to all video lessons. Each material has its own set of attributes. One videotape may make full use of the potentials of the medium—graphics, animation,

drama, etc.—while another may be no more than a recording of a "talking head." Each would have an entirely different impact on the imagination, feelings, and long-term comprehension of the viewer (despite the fact that each might yield the same score on an immediate posttest of verbal recall).

Materials must be examined in light of the specific objectives of the lesson and the specific needs and interests of learners. Does *this* filmstrip supply the needed realistic pictures of everyday life in ancient Roman times? Does *this* computer-assisted instruction module provide practice in making the kinds of decisions that loan officers make? Does *this* videocassette show a close-up view of a proper weld? In short, what attributes are needed for proper communication of the idea involved, and does this specific material have those attributes?

Utilize Material for Maximum Impact. If nothing else, research and practical experience have shown that much of the effectiveness of media depends on *how* they are integrated into the larger scheme. Wilbur Schramm, one of the most respected contemporary communication researchers, summarized it well:

> *Motivated students learn from any medium if it is competently used and adapted to their needs. Within its physical limits, any medium can perform any educational task. Whether a student learns more from one medium than from another is at least as likely to depend on* how *the medium is used as on* what *medium is used.*[d]

The user of the material can help increase the impact of any audiovisual material by applying sound utilization techniques: having selected material with appropriate attributes, introduce it to learners by relating it to prior learning and indicating how it relates to today's objectives, present it under the best possible environmental conditions, elicit a response from viewers, review the content, and evaluate its impact.

For a detailed, readable review of the research on educational media and school media centers see: Gene L. Wilkinson. *Media in Instruction: 60 Years of Research.* Washington, D.C.: Association for Educational Communications and Technology, 1980.

[d]Wilbur Schramm. *Big Media, Little Media.* Beverly Hills, Calif.: Sage Publications, 1977, p. iv.

▲ **Figure 1.14**
Instructor use of audiovisual media includes not only *presentation* of information but also learner *response* to the presentation.

of research, the requirements of practice demand that the conditions surrounding the materials *not* be held constant. Indeed, one of the most important roles of media is to serve as a catalyst for change in the whole instructional environment. The effective use of media demands that instructors be better organized in advance, that they think through their objectives, that they alter the everyday classroom routine, and that they evaluate broadly to determine impacts on mental abilities, feelings, values, interpersonal skills, and motor skills. The "no significant difference" shibboleth can be dispelled by careful selection of materials to fit particular learners' needs and objectives and by adept integration of the materials into the overall lesson.

Communication Models

Instruction is the arrangement of information to produce learning. The *transfer* of information from a source to a destination is called communication. Because new learning usually depends on taking in new information, effective instruction cannot take place unless communication takes place. It is, therefore, helpful to know something about the communication process if we are to use instructional media effectively.

How do we communicate with one another? More importantly, how do we communicate so that the message we wish to communicate is correctly received by the person for whom it is intended? A number of attempts have been made to analyze communications by use of mathematical or verbal models as means of representing key elements in the communication process.* We will use one of the most seminal of these, the Shannon model, to help you analyze and solve instructional problems.

The model was developed by Claude E. Shannon of the Bell Telephone Laboratories. Warren Weaver, as coauthor of a book with Shannon, is the popularizer of the model.** When Shannon developed his communication model, he was interested solely in the technical aspects of communication—a fact that is clear from his definitions (Figure 1.15). He was interested in what happens to messages when they go through mechanical or electronic information transmission systems, not in the *meaning* of the message. Whether the radio station in our example in Figure 1.15 selected Beethoven's Fifth Symphony or one of the Top 40 pop tunes makes no difference.

For instructional purposes, however, the meaning of the message and how the message is interpreted are of paramount importance. The Schramm† adaptation of the Shannon model incorporates Shannon's concern with the technical aspects of communication, but its central concern is with communication, reception, and interpretation of meaningful symbols. This is at the heart of instruction (Figure 1.16).

Let us examine the Shannon-Schramm model, first as it applies to communication per se in a television newscast, and then as it applies to communication in instructional situations.

---

*For a discussion of communication models, see John Ball and Francis C. Byrnes, eds. *Research, Principles and Practices in Visual Communication.* Washington, D.C.: Association for Educational Communications and Technology, 1960.

**Claude E. Shannon and Warren Weaver. *The Mathematical Theory of Communication.* Champaign, Ill.: University of Illinois Press, 1949, p. 7.

†Wilbur Schramm. "Procedures and Effects of Mass Communication." In Nelson B. Henry, ed., *Mass Media and Education.* Fifty-Third Yearbook of the National Society for the Study of Education, Part II. Chicago: University of Chicago Press, 1954, p. 116.

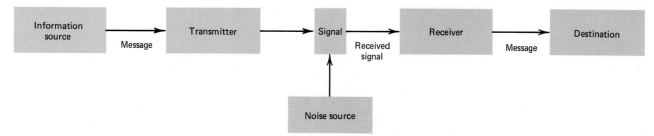

▲ **Figure 1.15**

A message is selected by an *Information Source*; for example, a recording of a top 40 tune by a radio station. That message is then incorporated by the *Transmitter* into a carrier wave. The signal is then received by an individual's radio set (*Receiver*) and transformed into the message reaching your ear (*the Destination*). Acting on the signal as it is being transmitted are various distorting factors that Shannon called "*Noise Source*." In the case of AM radio transmission, for example, the signal is subject to distortion caused by electronic disturbance in the atmosphere. To use another example, if you were showing a film in your class, the reception of both image and sound by your students would be affected by a number of external "noise sources," such as excessive light in the room interfering with the image on the screen, noisy heating units, loud conversation in the hallway, and the trumpet lesson in the room next door. Noise is any distortion of the signal *after* it has been transmitted and *before* it is received.

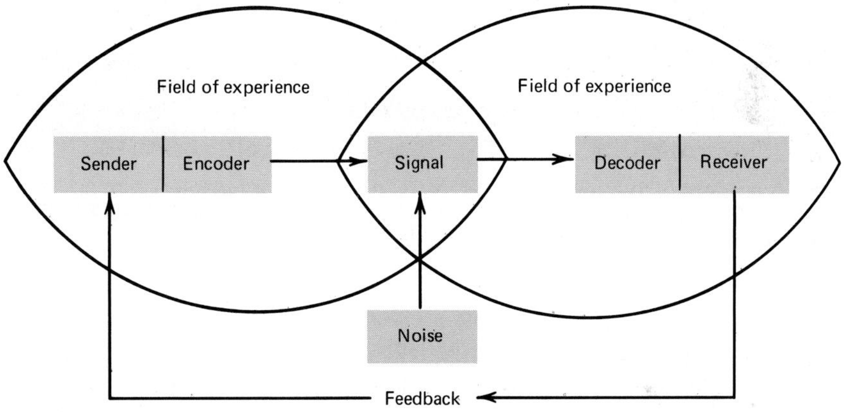

Newscast Communication. Television stations receive much of their newscast content from news services such as Associated Press and United Press International. The stories that will be broadcast are selected and edited by station personnel, transmitted by the television station, received by television sets, and emitted as image and sound to the receiver.

On the technical level, the Federal Communications Commission with its technical regulations and standards, the individual television stations, and the manufacturers of television sets and equipment do their utmost to make sure that the signal is transmitted and received accurately.

We must remember, however, that technical limitations can affect the visual and audio quality of transmitted and received signal and hence the quality of its interpretation. For example, antenna requirements for good reception vary considerably, depending on distance from source,

▲ **Figure 1.16**

Schramm's adaptation of the Shannon model emphasizes that only where the sender's and the receiver's fields of experience overlap is there communication; for example, a spoken word—the signal—may be understood by both but will communicate only part of the richness of meaning that both people have for that word.

land contour, and other interference factors. We should keep in mind that Shannon's "noise" factors affect technical quality; for example, an ambient light level suitable for the average viewer might prevent a vision-impaired viewer from seeing a screen image clearly. Or a low sound level suitable for most listeners might cause message deterioration for a listener with hearing problems.

On the meaning level, the communication process starts with the station news staff's selection of stories they think will be important and interesting to the viewers. Now the decision has to be made as to the form the newscast will take. Should a particular story be delivered exactly as received from the wire service or should it be rewritten with a local flavor? Should video clips or graphics be used to help give the story more meaning? These are decisions of the *sender,* who then *encodes* the message according to those decisions.

▲ **Figure 1.17**
Like the journalist selecting from among various stories, the film editor selects from among various shots to construct a movie sequence, *encoding* the message to communicate most effectively to the viewer.

How members of the news staff perform this function depends on their knowledge and skill—that is, their *field of experience.* The transmitted signal is then decoded by those viewers (*receivers*) tuned to the station. How the receiver interprets the message depends upon his or her knowledge—that is, *field of experience.*

Encoding and decoding can function effectively only in reference to the nature of the accumulated experiences of sender and receiver. Obviously, a receiver who has a poor grasp of standard English or a very low level vocabulary will have difficulty in correctly interpreting (decoding) the newscast message. Or let us say the signal (the encoded message) is about politics in Great Britain. To correctly interpret the message, the receiver must have some knowledge (experience) of international politics and of Great Britain itself—that is, the signal must be within the receiver's field of experience.

It is important to keep in mind that "meaning" per se cannot be transmitted. What are actually transmitted are *symbols* of meaning, such as words and pictures. As authors of this book, for example, we cannot directly transfer to you the personal "meanings" we have built up in our own minds about instructional media. (We even have trouble doing so among ourselves!) The most we can do is to transmit verbal and graphic symbols from which you can evoke your own "meanings." The most we can hope for is that our skills and knowledge will enable us to encode our messages in such a manner that your skills and knowledge can be used to decode and interpret them correctly.

Instructional Communication. The principles of communication that help us analyze a television newscast can also be applied to instructional situations. If you are using television for instructional purposes, either as an individual or as a member of an instructional television team, you will likely be called upon to help select and encode curricular content into meaningful symbols to achieve learning objectives. How successful the instruction will be depends upon the same factors that influence the success of a television newscast. For example, success will depend on your skill in encoding symbols that are meaningful to the students (the receivers) and on their skill in decoding them. Obviously, if the signal (the message) is within the field of experience of both you and your students, the opportunity for successful communication is at its optimum.

Unlike the newscast, however, instructional television is intended to *instruct* and not merely to communicate information. *Instructional communication is communication specifically designed to broaden and extend the field of experience of a learner.* As a classroom teacher, for example, you would prepare your students for the instructional telecast (with a preliminary discussion of the topic, an overview of content, etc.), and you would design follow-up activities to reinforce and extend the range of what has been learned through the telecast.

Ideally, material presented to a student should be sufficiently within his or her field of experience so that he or she can learn what is needed to be learned, but enough outside the field of experience to challenge and extend that field. How far the instruction can extend beyond the student's field of experience before confusion sets in depends on many factors. Perhaps the most important of these is the ability of the student. Able students can assume more of the responsibility for extending their own fields of experience than less able students. Slower students will need instructional content closer to their field of experience in order to be successful. Most retarded learners will require instruction that is almost entirely within their relatively limited field of experience. In Chapter 2, we will discuss the determination of "specific entry competencies" with particular attention to identifying to student's field of experience as he enters a lesson.

There will be times when the learning task (message) may not be within the field of experience of the *instructor*. When this occurs, both instructor and student seek to extend their respective fields of experience, and the instructor should not feel peculiar about being in this position. Some of the most effective learning takes place when instructor and student must seek the answers together.

Another very important distinction between television (or any other medium) as a communication medium and as an instructional medium involves feedback from the receiver (see Figure 1.18). We usually think of feedback as some form of test, but many other techniques are available to indicate to the teacher how students are receiving instruction. Facial expressions, body language, discussion responses, student conferences, homework, responses on short daily quizzes, etc., are all forms of feedback. Not only does feedback help us to ascertain whether instruction has been successful or unsuccessful, but it also tends to take the burden off the student and place it where it more appropriately belongs—on the sender of the message (the instructor). Instructors are frequently tempted to blame the student when instruction is not successful. The real problem may be that the instruction has not been designed or delivered appropriately.

If feedback (evaluation) indicates that instruction has been less than successful, the Shannon-Schramm model and Dale's Cone of Experience (concrete-to-abstract continuum) can help us identify the source or sources of the problem and can suggest remedies. If "noise" unduly interfered with your signal, instruction can be repeated under more favorable conditions. If you made an error in appraising your students' field of experience, the concrete-to-abstract

▲ **Figure 1.18**
In the classroom, *feedback* from the receivers consists of all the messages, verbal and nonverbal, that tell the instructor whether or not the point is getting across.

continuum may suggest a more appropriate entry level for your particular group. If the message was not encoded properly, the continuum can help you identify more suitable materials, or you can adjust your utilization of the materials to produce more effective instruction.

Transactional Nature of Communication

We emphasize that communication is an interpretive transaction between or among individuals. As noted above, the sender of a message encodes it according to his or her skill and knowledge (field of experience) and the receiver decodes it according to his or her field of experience. In the feedback process, however, the receiver (student) does more than decode the message. He or she must also encode his or her interpretation of the signal for relay back to the sender (teacher), who, in turn, must decode it. In effect, receiver becomes sender and sender becomes receiver. And both interpret the message according to their fields of experience (Figure 1.19).*

---

*Schramm, "Procedures and Effects," p. 119.

▼ **Figure 1.19**
A transactional model of the communication process shows that during human communication when the receiver responds to the message he or she becomes the sender and vice versa. And both sender and receiver *interpret* the other's signals based on their past experience.

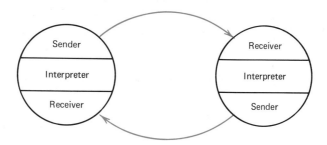

This is an extremely important point to keep in mind. You must decode your students' feedback signals according to *their* interpretation of instructional content, which may or may not be the same as yours, and which will very likely differ, at least in detail, from student to student. For example, instructional information about the labor movement in the United States may be interpreted one way by the child of a business executive and another way by the child of a union member. Black students and white students may interpret a film on slavery quite differently. The limited sensory abilities of some handicapped students may lead them to interpret instructional content differently from nonhandicapped children.

Students raised in other countries will bring their cultural assumptions with them. For example, in the United States, the owl is often used as a symbol of wisdom, but in one region of Nigeria, it is an omen of evil. As an instructor, you must always be sensitive to the fact that student response to a communication signal is a product of student experience.

▲ **Figures 1.20 and 1.21**
The picture on the left shows one of the classic demonstrations of the transactional nature of visual perception. The right-hand head appears to be larger than the left-hand one. However, the second picture shows that the heads are actually the same size but that the shape of the room and size of the windows have been manipulated. Our past experiences with right-angle walls and equal sized windows leads us to interpret the image incorrectly.

◄ **Figure 1.22**
Listeners with different cultural backgrounds may derive different meanings from the same message.

TECHNOLOGIES OF INSTRUCTION

Up to this point we have been discussing ways in which audiovisual media and materials can help improve communication and thereby improve instruction. The emphasis has been on the "things" of instruction—the *products* of technology. But instruction is more than communication alone, and technology *as a process* is a powerful tool for analyzing and solving instructional problems.

The principal definition of *technology* used in this book refers to "the systematic application of scientific or other organized knowledge to practical tasks."* Adapting this definition to instruction, we may define *instructional technology* as the application of our scientific knowledge about human learning to the practical tasks of teaching and learning. A technology of instruction, thus, is a particular, systematic arrangement of teaching/learning events designed to put our knowledge of learning into practice in a predictable, effective manner to attain specific learning objectives.

Over the years, many such arrangements have been devised, including programmed instruction, computer-based instruction, Audio-Tutorial systems, modular instruction, and simulation/gaming. Some technologies of instruction incorporate audiovisual media, others do not. Some employ electronic or mechanical devices, but others, such as programmed books and simulation games, may involve no such devices. (Specific technologies of instruction are discussed in detail in Chapter 11.) However, they all have one thing in common: they focus on the learner and on scientific principles of human learning.

Programmed instruction, for example, is based upon principles of human learning developed by behavioral psychologist B. F. Skinner and others in the 1950s. The teaching/learning arrangement worked out by

*Galbraith, loc. cit.

▲ **Figure 1.23**
The "teaching machine" was one of the first outgrowths of the programmed instruction movement. The learner makes an overt response and checks the correctness of that response before proceeding to the next item.

these early instructional technologists consists essentially of printed informational material interspersed with blank spaces. The student fills in these spaces as he or she reads along, the correct response being based in each case on information previously supplied. Filling in the blanks requires the learner to "process" the information rather than merely receive it passively. Most important, provision is made within the programmed material for immediate feedback to the student as to the correctness of response. Immediate

awareness of correct response was looked upon by behavior psychologists as a kind of reward that would "reinforce" what had been learned and would encourage further learning. (Reinforcement theory will be discussed more fully in Chapter 11.) Programmed instruction emphasizes the principle that human learning is an active process, not just reception of information. Communication is only the first step in learning.

Other technologies of instruction developed more recently have also emphasized learning as a process requiring active participation by the student. But in the conventional classroom, it is not always easy to carry out these functions. How can each student be kept actively participating in the learning process? How can the busy instructor monitor each student's responses and administer appropriate rewards and corrections? Technologies of instruction aim to provide workable procedures for doing these things. A well-designed instructional simulation game, for example, employs rules that ensure that individual players spend time practicing some newly learned skill (response). A referee, other player, or some such device monitors the performance and points (reinforcers) are given on the basis of the performance.

It should not be inferred, however, that all current technologies of instruction are exclusively derived from reinforcement theory. Reinforcement theory sparked the movement and continues to provide new principles and techniques, but other organized areas of knowledge, such as group dynamics, cognitive psychology, information theory, and developmental psychology, have provided bases for other and newer technologies of instruction.

COMPUTER TECHNOLOGY AND INSTRUCTION

For many years computers have been used widely by educational agencies for administrative purposes such as maintaining student records and scheduling classes. More recently, with the advent of the microcomputer, applications to direct instruction have been increasing rapidly. The computer, especially when combined with electronic transmission systems, can be used in an almost unlimited variety of ways in an almost unlimited variety of instructional situations and settings. The general concept of computer-based education, however, is commonly considered to encompass two major categories: computer-assisted instruction (CAI) and computer-managed instruction (CMI).

CAI uses the computer directly as a medium of instruction and an information delivery system. The computer's ability to engage in instructional "dialogue" with the student while delivering information makes it adaptable to any number of instructional situations. CMI is basically a management technique for keeping track of instruction and supplying support services, such as materials appropriate to specific learning objectives, at specific stages of learner progress.

Given the growing sophistication of computer technology and its increasing applicability to information delivery and instruction, we can be sure that the use of computers for instructional purposes at home, in school, and in other instructional settings, will continue to grow (see Chapter 13). More avant-garde facets of computer technology, such as video games and microprocessors made from organic molecules, are explored in Chapter 14.

▲ **Figure 1.24**
With a television screen for displaying verbal and visual material, a keyboard for student responses, and a microprocessor to branch learners down different paths, the microcomputer brings new possibilities for individualizing instruction.

▲ **Figure 1.25**
Educators are exploring ways to use computers to manage the data teachers need for sound decision making.

INSTRUCTIONAL MEDIA IN OUT-OF-SCHOOL SETTINGS

The development of sophisticated instructional media and our growing knowledge of how to use these media for effective learning have opened up instructional options not only for students in formal educational institutions but also for learners outside such institutions. Today, virtually any institutional setting can become a classroom with the aid of, and sometimes even near-total dependence upon, instructional technology.

Growth of Training Programs

Business, industrial, and financial institutions have today become major settings for instruction. No one knows exactly how much money U.S. corporations spend annually on "in-house" education and training of their employees (estimates range upward from $10 billion), but it is certain that the sum is tremendous and that it has begun to approach that spent on public school education. The Motorola Corporation offers a good example of commitment to continuing training of personnel. In 1984, Motorola set aside 1.5 percent of each employee's salary for training. In 1985, the figure rose to 2 percent and in 1986 it will level out at 3 percent.

As the economy becomes even more service-oriented, the amount of money spent on training will increase correspondingly. According to *Training* magazine, 44 percent of training budgets is devoted to managerial and supervisory personnel, and 18 percent to personnel involved in sales.* These percentages are most likely to increase in the future. Hardware and software expenditures for training purposes are currently around $1.5

Training (October 1983), p. 41.

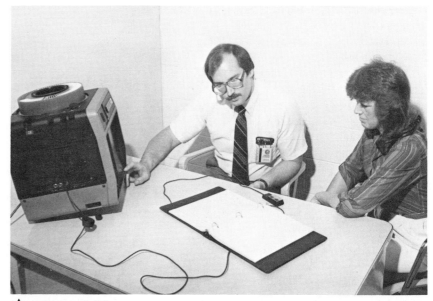

▲ **Figure 1.26**
Business/industry training is becoming increasingly committed to the notion that mediated, self-paced instruction is a key factor in training productivity.

▲ **Figure 1.27**
An audiovisual learning station provides in-service training in nursing skills.

billion. The costs of custom-designed training by outside agencies and use of outside consultants and services are also around $1.5 billion. At $3 billion, the training market is more attractive than the education market to producers of instructional products.*

The federal government began supporting training programs directly

*Ibid.

with the Jobs Training Partnership Act of 1983. The act stipulates that 70 percent of the 3.6 billion allocated must be spent on training. Private Industry Councils decide where the money will be spent, and most of it is expected to be allocated to on-the-job training. Significantly, the Department of Labor, not the Department of Education, administers the act. Congress may have been indicating that it had lost faith in education and was willing to shift federal money to training.

Many of the nation's labor unions operate extensive training programs for their members, and some even include funding for membership education in their contract negotiations. Hospitals and other social welfare institutions have developed educational facilities to help keep their personnel abreast of current techniques and professional practices. Libraries, museums, and community centers of all types are likely to be organized centers of out-of-school education; and, of course, both national and local government agencies have contributed greatly to the trend toward instruction outside the formal educational setting.

The implications of this growing phenomenon are clear. In view of the increasing diffusion of instruction in our society, formal educational institutions now must be viewed as just one among many settings for education. As more and more instruction moves outside the school setting, more and more reliance will be placed on instructional media to meet diverse learning objectives.

Preferred Media and Methods in Training Programs

As one might expect, the media and methods preferred by training directors are often different from those used by educators. One of the major reasons for this is that the curricula of the schools are fairly uniform, while training programs are often industry-specific. Formats of media that lend themselves to local production are preferred by training directors. For example, slides are used more frequently than filmstrips; in schools the reverse is true. Videotape is employed more often than films in training, while in the schools many more films than videotaped programs are circulated.

▲ **Figure 1.28**
Because institutional training often requires materials custom-made for specific settings, video recording is a primary source of materials in this sector.

Another difference arises from the fact that training directors are dealing with adults rather than children and adolescents. Role-playing, games, and simulations are used much more frequently in training programs, particularly with management, supervisory, and sales personnel. These are jobs that require a great deal of interaction with people, and the types of training methods that develop relevant skills are given high priority. The trainees will have to call on those skills immediately after the training session and are more likely to become impatient with methods more abstract than the situation demands.

Refer back to Table 1.1 (page 11) and think about your education. In your experience, where are training and education similar and where are they different in regard to methods and media?

MEDIA / TECHNOLOGY AND INSTRUCTIONAL STRATEGIES

Although instructional media may be used effectively in a wide variety of teaching/learning situations, they lend themselves particularly well to certain generalized educational purposes. Let us at this point briefly preview these purposes and suggest some basic strategies for their attainment, before fully discussing them in connection with specific media.

Support for Teacher-Based Instruction

The most common use of media in the instructional situation is for supplemental support of the instructor. Certainly there can be no doubt that properly designed instructional media can enhance and promote learning and support teacher-based instruction. But their effectiveness depends on the instructor (as will be

Flashback: MEDIA AND EDUCATIONAL INNOVATION

In the last thirty years the introduction of a wide variety of new instructional methods, techniques, and curricula into North American education has contributed to the growing use of instructional media in the classroom. One could say it all started in 1954 with the School Mathematics Study Group (SMSG) at the University of Illinois, a group dedicated to revising elementary and secondary mathematics. Soon after, in 1957 Gerald Zakarias initiated the Physical Science Study Committee (PSSC), dedicated to wholesale revision of the teaching of physics in American high schools. Although both SMSG and PSSC had already been initiated before the dramatic launching of Sputnik by the Soviet Union in 1957, there is no doubt that Sputnik accelerated the interest of Congress and educators in revising and making more rigorous the curricula of the public schools.

After the success of the Physical Science Study Committee, a rapid succession of science curriculum projects were funded and brought to fruition. Notable among these was the Biological Science Curriculum Study (BSCS), responsible for making drastic changes in high school biology. According to a study made by the Educational Testing Service, BSCS was the curricular innovation that penetrated American high schools most quickly.

Along with curricular revisions came an emphasis on new instructional methods—or perhaps we should say reemphasis, since Dewey and other progressive educators had attempted to initiate many of the same innovations in the 1920s and 1930s. In the 1960s, Jerome Bruner emphasized the importance of "discovery" in instruction, insisting that children should experience the thrill of intellectual discovery in their school careers. Bruner was responsible for a widely respected innovation in the elementary curriculum, a program he entitled *Man: A Course of Study*. Discovery was a basic part of the program and discovery elements were designed into the media accompanying the program. Bruner postulated three major modes of learning: the enactive or direct experience, the iconic or pictorial experience, and the symbolic, highly abstract experience. He suggested that, ideally, students should proceed from direct experience to iconic experience to symbolic experience, and that students could not handle abstract experiences unless they had a rich background in the other two modes of

learning. All the curricular innovation projects sponsored by the academic disciplines relied heavily on the use of instructional media to achieve their objectives.

Concomitant with these innovations were changes in the organizational structures of the schools. For example, modular scheduling in secondary schools made a drastic change in the school day. Team teaching was introduced, an approach that frequently used television as an integrating factor. The notion of grouping students according to factors other than simply grade level was brought to the fore. In the elementary schools, new organizational arrangements were introduced. For example, the Individually Guided Education (IGE) program, developed at the University of Wisconsin, organized instructional teams within the elementary school to focus on the most effective instructional arrangement for the individual child. The Individually Prescribed Instruction (IPI) program developed at the University of Pittsburgh successfully adapted programmed instruction for use at the elementary school level. In IPI, students progress through a series of short modules individually and are evaluated by the teacher after completion of each module.

Instructional media have played a vital role in most of our recent educational innovations.[a] Without modern-day instructional technology, many, if not most, of them might have been impossible.

---

[a]Catherine Cornbleth. "Curriculum Materials and Learning." *Practical Applications of Research* (A Newsletter of Phi Delta Kappa, September 1979), p. 2.

made clear in the chapters that follow).

Research has long indicated the importance of the instructor's role in effective use of instructional media. For example, early studies showed that when teachers introduced films, relating them to learning objectives, the amount of information students gained from films increased.* Later research confirmed and expanded upon these original findings. Ausubel, for example, developed the concept of "advance organizers" as aids to effective instructon.† An advance organizer may take the form of an overview of or an introduction to lesson content, a statement of principles contained in the information to be presented, a statement of learning objectives, etc. Whatever the form, it is intended to create a "mind set" for reception of instruction.

Advance organizers can be effective instruments for ensuring that media play their proper role as supplemental supporters of instruction. Many commercially produced instructional materials today have built-in advance organizers, which may be used as is or adapted by the instructor for specific educational purposes.

Student Drill and Practice

Certain media formats and delivery systems lend themselves particularly well to student drill-and-practice exercises. For example, learning laboratory instruction and programmed instruction are well suited to these purposes (Figure 1.30). Audio tapes can be used effectively for drill and practice in spelling, arithmetic, and language instruction.

*Walter A. Wittich and J. G. Fowlkes. *Audio-visual Paths to Learning.* New York: Harper & Bros., 1946.

†David Ausubel. *Educational Psychology.* New York: Holt, Rinehart and Winston, 1968.

▲ **Figure 1.29**
The instructor's skill in weaving audiovisual materials into the lesson is the single most important determinant of successful learning from media.

▲ **Figure 1.30**
The listen-and-respond capabilities of the language laboratory support drill and practice in foreign languages and other similar subjects.

Discovery Learning

Instructional media can help promote the "discovery" or "inquiry" approach to learning and teaching. For example, films may be used for discovery teaching in the physical sciences. Students study the films to perceive the relationships represented in the visuals and then go on to "discover" the principles that explain those relationships. This could be as simple as seeing a balloon being weighed before and after being filled with air.

In the social sciences, various media formats can be used to present learners with visual and auditory experiences that provoke lesson-related inquiry. Media formats can also be used to confront professional and business trainees with "real-life" situations requiring inquiry into problems and discovery of their solutions. Films, simulations, and simulation games are often used to effect such "learning laboratory" situations.

▲ **Figure 1.31**
Visual imagery seen on recorded video programs can stimulate creative writing activities.

▲ **Figure 1.32**
By putting task directions on audio cassette, instructors can use media to *manage* instruction more efficiently.

▶ **Figure 1.33**
Synchronized sound/slide presentations can be coupled with programmed instruction techniques for effective individualized instruction.

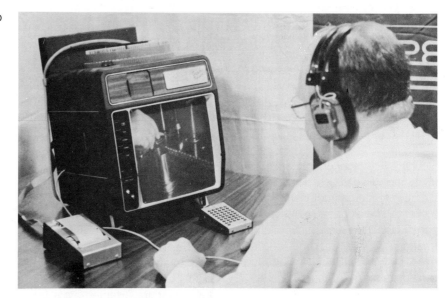

Management of Instruction

Instructional media can permit a more productive relationship between instructor and student by allowing the teacher to become a manager of instruction rather than merely a dispenser of information. Media utilization allows teachers to spend more of their time diagnosing and correcting student problems, consulting with individual students, and teaching on a one-to-one and small-group basis (Figure 1.32).

How much time the teacher can spend on such activities will depend on the extent of the instructional role assigned to the media. Indeed, under certain circumstances, the entire instructional task may be left to the media. Experimental programs have demonstrated, for example, that an entire course in high school physics can be successfully taught through use of films and workbooks without direct classroom intervention by the teacher. Successful programmed courses in calculus have been developed for use by able students whose high schools have no such course.

This is not to say, of course, that instructional technology can or should replace the teacher, but rather, that media can help teachers become creative managers of the learning experience rather than merely monitors of instructional situations.

Individualized Instruction

Individualized instruction, wherein students use learning materials specifically designed or chosen to suit their individual interests, abilities, and experience, is now almost universally accepted as an important and productive instructional strategy. Interestingly, this comparatively recent educational innovation has developed more or less apace with instructional media, with media contributing to the increasing growth (and, indeed, to the effectiveness) of individualized instruction and individualized instruction contributing to the increasing use of media in instruction.

Almost any instructional medium or media combination can be adapted for use in individualized instruction. Programmed instruction, for example, is specifically designed for individualized learning, as is the Audio-Tutorial system of instruction, which relies on audio recordings to individually guide student learning activities.

We will return to this point—the contribution of instructional media to the concept of individualized instruction—many times throughout this text.

Special Education

By now you may have inferred that instruction could be more individualized than it currently is. By *individualized* we do not necessarily mean that each student receives a separate instructional treatment, but that, at least, groups of students who exhibit certain common characteristics can be treated differently from groups of students with other characteristics. In this way we can best adjust instruction to the characteristics of the students. Handicapped children in particular need special instructional treatment. Mentally retarded children need highly structured learning situations because (referring back to our

▼ **Figure 1.34a**
For the benefit of the hearing impaired, the Public Broadcasting Service (PBS) transmits many of its programs with captions. Shown here is ABC's "Barney Miller," broadcast with "closed" captions, visible only on television sets with special decoders.

communication diagram) they lack the necessary field of experience and the ability to incorporate messages within their constructs. They need much more of the message placed within the context of their field of experience in order to expand that field of experience at all. Students who have impaired hearing or impaired vision require different kinds of learning materials; more emphasis should be placed on audio for visually impaired students than for normally sighted individuals. Talking books, for example, are available for visually impaired students to use in the institutional special education setting and in the home. Adjusting instruction to all of these groups requires a heavy reliance on media and materials and the appropriate selection of these materials to fit specific purposes.

Although severely handicapped students need to be helped through special education classes and courses, the trend today is to "mainstream" students whose disabilities do not preclude them from profiting from exposure to regular classroom activities. Instructional media specifically designed for such students and/or classroom adaptation of media to compensate for physical and mental disabilities can contribute enormously to effective instruction of handicapped students and can help prevent their unwarranted (albeit unintentional) neglect by the busy regular-classroom teacher.

▼ **Figure 1.34b**
The Kurzweil Reading Machine allows those with impaired sight to "read" books. The device scans a printed page, analyzes letter combinations via computer, and reads back the words by means of a voice synthesizer.

STRUCTURE AND FLEXIBILITY

Recent research lends considerable support to the principle that the amount of time students spend on the instructional task is directly and positively related to achievement.* Media-directed instruction concentrates student time on task. For example, television teachers have frequently commented that their televised instruction is more concentrated and has fewer diversions than their classroom instruction. The learning laboratory has the effect of increasing the time spent directly on task.

Students achieve more when instruction has some degree of structure, when they know what is expected of them, and when the instructional environment is arranged to facilitate achievement of instructional objectives.† For example, if inquiry skills are the goal of instruction, then the obligation of the teacher is to be sure the environment is arranged to facilitate the necessary gathering of data from which inferences can be made by the student. Both the *kind* and *degree* of structure vary with instructional objectives.

Structure gives students confidence because it reduces ambiguity about objectives and purposes of learning. This is as true of adults in training programs as it is of students in schools and colleges. Acquisition of the skills necessary to do the job contributes more to a feeling of confidence than do motivational or inspirational sessions, concluded researchers at DCW Research Associates from a study of sales managers.

*N. L. Gage. *The Scientific Basis of the Art of Teaching.* New York: Teachers College Press, 1978, pp. 34–40.

†David L. Clark, Linda S. Lotto, and Martha M. McCarthy. "Factors Associated with Success in Urban Elementary Schools." *Phi Delta Kappan* (March 1980), pp. 467–470. Also Gage, op. cit., pp. 31–33.

Their findings "suggest that trainers concerned with motivational programs to enhance self-confidence in job performance might do well to look at task-oriented programs designed to assist individuals to get greater control of the elements of their jobs that tend to affect job performance."*

Structure, however, does not rule out flexibility. Even in a structured situation, accommodation should be made to individual needs and interests. Structured instruction need not be *excessively* task-oriented. Nor does it rule out exploration, creativity, and self-direction.†

The correct blend of structure and flexibility to best meet your instructional objectives will depend on a variety of factors, including the subject matter under study and the learning characteristics of your students— that is, their age and general level of intelligence and their specific knowledge about and attitude toward the topic at hand.

Drill and practice exercises are likely to be more structured than, say, a discovery lesson in geography. We would also expect a mathematics lesson on fractions to be more structured than a social science lesson on contemporary urban problems.

In general, younger children respond well to, and indeed need, a high degree of lesson structure. The Montessori method for teaching very young children, for example, is highly structured, and its success depends on a carefully worked out sequence of instruction and materials utilization. Yet the uninformed visitor to a Montessori type classroom might think the children are simply playing and having fun (Figure 1.35).

In general, lower-ability students prefer fairly well structured lessons

In Montessori schools, carefully structured activities stimulate and channel children's curiosity.

▼ **Figure 1.36**
Audiovisual materials provide a springboard for small-group discussion—an alternative to the lecture and textbook.

primarily because they do not have a high degree of confidence in their ability to work independently, nor in their ability to pull together what are to them unrelated strands of subject matter. Higher-ability students respond well to a more flexible approach, since they have more confidence in their abilities (provided, of course, they are not students with high anxiety levels, or who prefer structured situations).

Motivation influences the tolerance students have toward a structured or flexible learning situation. Students who are highly motivated will be able to tolerate a very wide range of degree of structure. Students with little

motivation will prefer learning situations that guide them to specific instructional ends. If given too much flexibility or too much independence in a learning situation, students with relatively low motivation will tend to lose direction along the way and not arrive at the specific goals that were set in the learning situation or to abandon the pursuit of those goals completely during the course of instruction.

Training (October 1983), p. 16.

†Gage, op. cit., p. 40.

Keep in mind that by *structure* we mean the extent to which the materials in the learning situation lead the student step-by-step to the specific objectives set by the program. Structure has nothing to do with difficulty. In the case of students with low motivation, we are not suggesting that the material be difficult or present difficult problems, but that a structured learning situation can gently lead students toward instructional goals and instill a degree of confidence they would not pick up in a situation that was extremely flexible or that placed a great deal of the responsibility to learn on their shoulders.

The role of media in allowing flexibility in learning is clear: materials—print and audiovisual—are attractive alternatives to the routine of the lecture. Materials that are relatively open-ended can be adapted to a variety of teaching/learning styles and situations. Self-instructional materials make possible such flexible arrangements as independent study and small-group work. Flexibility is enhanced when alternatives to teacher-talk are available.

Whatever blend of structure and flexibility you choose, instructional media can help you achieve your goals. Media and media systems can be structured toward specific learning objectives or they can easily be made open-ended and adapted to creative independent study and instructional flexibility.

TECHNOLOGY AND "DEHUMANIZATION"

More than a few observers of the educational scene have argued that the widespread use of instructional technology in the classroom must lead to treating students as if they too are machines rather than human beings—that is, that technology dehumanizes the teaching/learning process. It is, on the contrary, a major theme of this book that, properly used, modern instructional media can individualize and thus humanize the teaching/learning process to a degree hitherto undreamed of. The danger of dehumanization lies not in the use of instructional media but in the way in which teachers perceive their students. If teachers perceive learners as machines, they will treat them as such with or without the use of instructional media. If teachers perceive their students as human beings with rights, privileges, and motivations of their own, they will treat them as such with or without instructional media. In other words, it is not technology that tends to mechanize people but the uses to which people put technology.

One of our most thoughtful observers of life in the classroom is Philip Jackson of the University of Chicago. He has been concerned about the quality of life in American classrooms and has found them somewhat impoverished. Perhaps it will be easier to visualize a humanistic classroom by looking at the traits of a mechanistic classroom. In the book, *The Teacher and the Machine,* Jackson states that "the greatest intellectual challenge of our time is not how to design machines that behave more and more like humans, but rather, how to protect humans from being treated more and more like machines."* He goes on to clarify what

he means by human mechanization: "the process by which people are treated mechanically; that is without giving thought to what is going on inside them." It is interesting that his illustrations of human mechanization in schools show how student attention, assignments, learning tasks, and discussion are mechanized with means as simple as the human voice and the teacher's right to turn students on and off. Six ways that human beings (students) are treated mechanically, as paraphrased by Lange, are:

1. We turn them on and off whenever it suits our fancy.
2. It is unnecessary to offer an explanation of why they are working.
3. They are owned (no plans and future of their own; or unwillingly they relinquish their own plans and energies).
4. They are all work; idleness is waste (no play except as the owner may work them as part of his play).
5. A machine/human's worth is judged by the quality of its products.
6. There is absence of human empathy (no need to feel sorry for a machine that functions improperly).*

Jackson is disturbed that teachers in classrooms are treating many of their students mechanistically.

So we have seen that the question is not so much what is used in the classroom as how students are treated. A corollary of this statement is that it is not so much *what* a teacher teaches but *how* a teacher teaches. For example, many teachers, particularly in English and social studies, consider themselves "humanists" but may be anything but humanistic to their students. They may treat those students in the way in which Jackson said people can be treated mechanistically (Figure 1.37).

---

*Philip W. Jackson. *The Teacher and the Machine.* Pittsburgh: University of Pittsburgh, 1968, p. 66.

---

*Phil C. Lange. "Review of *The Teacher and the Machine.*" *AV Communication Review* (Spring 1969), p. 102.

To reinforce this point, consider a case in which the introduction of machinery can make the instructional situation more humanistic. As research has indicated, students who have a high level of anxiety are prone to make mistakes and to learn less efficiently when under considerable pressure. Many teachers exert too much pressure on high-anxiety students, thereby making the instructional situation not only disagreeable, but prone to error. Given the same sequence of instruction mediated through a machine that will continue only at the command of the student, the student can reduce the pressure simply by not responding. In other words, the machine patiently awaits the command of the student to begin, whereas an overbearing teacher waits for no such command.

Contrary to what some educators believe, technology and humanism can work together or go their separate ways. Figure 1.39 suggests four basic mixes of technology and humanism.

Let's look at four examples of a mix of technology and humanism to see where each falls in Figure 1.39:

A. A college lecture with little or no interaction between professor and student.
B. A course consisting of a required series of modules, each composed of performance objectives, materials to be used to complete objectives, and a self-evaluation test.
C. The same as B, except that students choose modules based on counseling sessions with an instructor and meet periodically to discuss the content of the modules.
D. A group that meets on a regular basis to discuss common reading assignments.

These examples are overly simplified and only illustrative, but they serve as a basis for analyzing the relationship between humanism and technology. They illustrate that training/instruction can be low in both humanism

▲ **Figure 1.37**
Lecture-style instruction may or may not lead to humanistic ends. Are individual differences being cared for? Are students actively "processing" the information?

▲ **Figure 1.38**
Technology, in the form of audiovisual or print materials, can help free the teacher for one-to-one interaction—doing what humans do best.

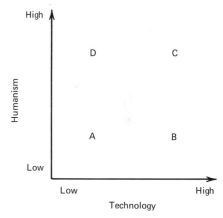

▲ **Figure 1.39**
Technology and humanism are not opposite ends of a single scale, but rather two different variables, either of which can be high or low.

and technology just as it can be high in both.

To reiterate, instructional technology does not preclude a humane teaching/ learning environment. On the contrary, instructional media can

help provide a learning atmosphere in which students actively participate, as individual human beings, in the learning process. When instructional media are used properly and creatively in the classroom, it is the machines that are turned on and off at will—not the students.

References

Print References

Arnstine, Donald. "Learning, Communication, and the School Use of Media." *British Journal of Educational Technology* (May 1979), pp. 135–142.

Asimov, Isaac. "His Own Particular Drummer." *Phi Delta Kappan* (September 1976), pp. 99–103.

Barnouw, Eric. *Tube of Plenty.* (New York: Oxford University Press, 1975).

Culkin, John. "A Schoolman's Guide to Marshall McLuhan." *Saturday Review* (March 18, 1967), pp. 51–53, 70–72.

Fiske, John. *Introduction to Communication Studies.* (New York: Methuen, 1982).

Fleming, Malcolm L., and Hutton, Deane W., eds. *Mental Imagery and Learning.* (Englewood Cliffs, N.J.: Educational Technology Publications, 1983).

Fox, G. T., and DeVault, M. V. "Technology and Humanism in the Classroom: Frontiers of Educational Practice." *Educational Technology* (October 1974), pp. 7–13.

Haney, John B., and Ullmer, Eldon J. *Educational Communications and Technology.* 3d ed. (Dubuque, Ia.: Wm. C. Brown Company, 1980).

Heinich, Robert, ed. *Educating All Handicapped Children.* (Englewood Cliffs, N.J.: Educational Technology Publications, 1979).

Hoban, Charles F. "Educational Technology and Human Values." *AV Communication Review* (Fall 1977), pp. 221–242.

Hooten, David E. "Educational Technology and the Adult Learner." *Educational Technology* (October 1976), pp. 20–25.

Kaye, Anthony, and Keith, Harry, eds. *Using the Media for Adult Basic Education.* (Totowa, N.J.: Biblio Distribution Center, 1982).

Kolesnik, W. B. *Humanism and/or Behaviorism in Education.* (Boston: Allyn & Bacon, 1975).

Locatis, Craig N., and Atkinson, Francis D. *Media and Technology for Education and Training.* (Columbus: Merrill, 1984).

Marlow, Eugene. *Managing the Corporate Media Center.* (White Plains, N.Y.: Knowledge Industry, 1981).

Marsh, Patrick. *Messages That Work: A Guide to Communication.* (Englewood Cliffs, N.J.: Educational Technology Publications, 1983).

"Media in Health Care Education." *Instructional Innovator* (January 1982), pp. 20–35.

Petrie, Joyce. *Mainstreaming in the Media Center.* (Phoenix, Az.: Oryx Press, 1982).

Pillon, Nancy Bach, ed. *Reaching Young People Through Media.* (Littleton, Colo.: Libraries Unlimited, 1983).

Programming to Help Children Use Media Creatively. (Chicago: American Library Association, 1983).

Proulx, R. "The Dialectics of Andragogy and Instructional Technology." *NSPI Journal* (July 1980), pp. 3–4.

Rice, Ronald E. *The New Media: Communication, Research, and Technology.* Beverly Hills, Calif.: Sage, 1984.

Salomon, Gavriel. *Communication and Education: Social and Psychological Interactions.* (Beverly Hills, Calif.: Sage, 1981).

Severin, Werner, and Tankard, James W., Jr. *Communication Theories: Origins, Methods, Uses.* (New York: Hastings House, 1979).

Sigda, Robert B. "Using Media to Teach Science." *Instructional Innovator,* (September 1983), pp. 27–29.

Stakenas, Robert G., and Kaufman, Roger. *Technology in Education: Its Human Potential.* Fastback #163. (Bloomington, In.: Phi Delta Kappa Educational Foundation, 1981).

Taylor, Kenneth I. "Media in the Context of Instruction." *School Media Quarterly,* (Spring 1976), pp. 223–224, 237–241.

Thomas, James L., ed. *Nonprint in the Elementary Curriculum: Readings for Reference.* (Littleton, Colo.: Libraries Unlimited, 1982).

———. *Nonprint in the Secondary Curriculum: Readings for Reference.* (Littleton, Colo.: Libraries Unlimited, 1982).

Wiley, Ann L. *Sources of Information for Instructional Technology.* (Syracuse, N.Y.: ERIC Clearinghouse on Information Resources, 1981).

Wilkinson, Gene L. *Media in Instruction: 60 Years of Research.* (Washington, D.C.: AECT, 1980).

Audiovisual References

Case Studies in Communication. Salenger Educational Media, 1982. 16-mm film. 18 minutes.

The Child of the Future: How He Might Learn. Montreal: National Film Board of Canada, 1965. 16-mm film. 60 minutes.

Communication Feedback. Rockville, Md.: BNA Film, 1965. 16-mm film. 21 minutes.

A Communication Model. Bloomington, Ind.: Indiana University Audio-Visual Center, 1967. 16-mm film. 30 minutes, color.

Communication: The Name of the Game. Roundtable Film and Video, n.d. One videocassette. 28 minutes.

Communications and Media. Learning Corporation of America, 1982. 16-mm film or videocassette. 20 minutes.

Communications Primer. Classroom Film Distributor, 1954. 16-mm film. 22 minutes, color.

Media for Presentations. Bloomington, Ind.: Indiana University, 1978. 16-mm film. 20 minutes, color.

Perception and Communication. Columbus: Ohio State University, 1967. 16-mm film. 32 minutes.

This Is Marshall McLuhan: The Medium Is the Massage. New York: McGraw-Hill, 1968. 16-mm film. 53 minutes.

To Help Them Learn. Washington, D.C.: Association for Educational Communications and Technology, 1978. 16-mm film. 21 minutes, color.

Understanding Educational Technology. Washington, D.C.: Association for Educational Communications and Technology, 1977. Sound filmstrip with cassette.

Possible Projects

1-A. Read one of the books cited in the chapter or a book relating to a topic in the chapter and write or record on audio tape a report. The report should be approximately two-and-one-half double-spaced, typed pages or five minutes in length.

1-B. React to any of the topics or ideas presented in the chapter. Your reaction and comments may be written or recorded (approximately five double-spaced, typed pages or ten minutes in length).

1-C. Analyze an instructional situation (either real or hypothetical) and identify the elements of the communication process and their interrelationship.

1-D. Prepare a "position paper" (approximately five double-spaced typed pages) on a topic such as the role of humanism versus technology in education, or structure versus flexibility in teaching.

1-E. Describe an actual use of instructional media in an out-of-school setting based upon your experiences or readings.

Systematic Planning for the Use of Media

Outline

Objectives

After studying this chapter, you should be able to:

1. Describe six procedures (steps) in the systematic planning for the use of media (the ASSURE model).
2. List two general and two specific learner characteristics that could affect media selection.
3. Discuss the rationale for stating objectives for instruction. Your discussion should include three purposes or uses of objectives.
4. Write objectives that include performance terms, conditions (if necessary), and appropriate criteria.
5. Classify given objectives into cognitive, affective, motor skill, and interpersonal skills domains; rate them as "higher" or "lower" within each domain.
6. Describe the basic procedures for selecting, modifying, and designing materials, and indicate when each procedure is appropriate.
7. Explain how learner characteristics affect the selection of media.
8. State two examples of situational constraints on the selection of mediated materials.
9. Describe two ways of modifying materials without actually altering the original materials.
10. List and describe the five basic steps in utilizing instructional materials.
11. Identify general showmanship techniques in reference to strong and weak sectors of the classroom "stage," body positions, and movements.
12. Describe several methods for eliciting student response during and after using media.
13. Justify the need for requiring learner response when using media.
14. Compare and contrast the techniques for evaluating student achievement and the techniques for evaluating media and methods.

Lexicon

performance objective

criterion

cognitive domain

comprehension

affective domain

internalization

characterization

motor skill domain

articulation

interpersonal skills domain

covert/overt response

showmanship

THE ASSURE MODEL

All effective instruction requires careful planning. Teaching with instructional media is certainly no exception to this educational truism. This chapter examines how you can systematically plan for the effective use of instructional media. We have constructed a procedural model to which we have given the acronym ASSURE, because it is intended to *ASSURE effective use of media in instruction.*

The ASSURE model, a procedural guide for planning and delivering instruction that incorporates media, implies several assumptions. It assumes that a particular audience has been identified (e.g., the class that you teach), that training or instruction really is required (e.g., students don't

A Model to Help ASSURE Learning

A S S

Analyze Learner Characteristics

The first step in planning is to identify the learners. Your learners may be students, trainees, or members of an organization such as a Sunday school, civic club, youth group, or fraternal organization. You must know your students to select the "best" medium to meet the objectives. The audience can be analyzed in terms of two types of traits: (1) general characteristics, and (2) specific entry competencies— knowledge, skills, and attitudes about the topic.

State Objectives

The next step is to state the objectives as specifically as possible. The objectives may be derived from a needs assessment, course syllabus, stated in a textbook, taken from a curriculum guide, or developed by the instructor. Wherever they come from, they should be stated in terms of what the learner will be able to do as a result of instruction. The conditions under which the student or trainee is going to perform and a statement of acceptable performance level should be included.

Select, Modify, or Design Materials

Once you have identified your audience and stated your objectives, you have established the beginning (audience's present knowledge, skills, and attitudes) and the ending points (objectives) of instruction. Your task now is to build a "bridge" between these two points. There are three options: (1) select available materials, (2) modify existing materials, or (3) design new materials.

know how to use the new laboratory microscopes), and that the content of the instruction has been competently analyzed in terms of its scope, sequence, and accuracy (e.g., you decide to follow the curriculum guide of the state department of education).

If any of these assumptions are not met, additional steps beyond the scope of the ASSURE model and this text are needed. These additional steps fall into the realm of *instructional development*—the entire process of analyzing needs, determining what content must be mastered, es-

tablishing educational goals, designing materials to help reach the objectives, and trying out and revising the materials in terms of learner achievement.

U R E

Utilize Materials

Having either selected, modified, or designed your materials, you then must plan how the materials will be used and how much time will be spent using them. Next, prepare the class and ready the necessary equipment and facilities. Then present the material using the "showmanship" techniques and suggestions described in the chapters of this text. Finally, follow up with class discussion, small group activities, or individual projects and reports.

Require Learner Response

Learners must practice what they are expected to learn and should be reinforced for the correct response. The first time they are expected to perform the behavior called for in the objectives should *not* be on the examination. Instead there should be activities within the lesson that allow learners to respond and to receive feedback on the appropriateness of their performances or responses.

Evaluate

After instruction, it is necessary to evaluate its impact and effectiveness. To get the total picture, you must evaluate the entire instructional process. Did the learners meet the objectives? Did the media assist the trainees in reaching the objectives? Could all students use the materials properly? Was the environment comfortable (room temperature suitable, comfortable seating, no distracting noises)? Did the instructor facilitate learning by providing the necessary assistance for individual students?

The assumption that instruction is really necessary is particularly crucial. It is now widely recognized in business/industry training that spending money and effort on unnecessary training is a major source of waste. It occurs, however, because training is the most obvious solution to performance problems. For example, the sales force of Amalgamated Houseware Industries is falling short of its target in sales of dustpans. So the marketing vice-president suggests that the training department develop a self-instructional motivational video cassette on "Dynamic Dustpan Sales Techniques." In reality, it may be that the salespeople already *know* how to sell dustpans, but that Amalgamated dustpans are notoriously poorly engineered, or that the whole market for dustpans is depressed, or that higher commissions can be earned on other products in the Amalgamated line. If the cause of the problem is not a lack of knowledge, training will not solve the problem. Techniques for properly diagnosing learning needs or the sources of performance problems include needs assessment and front-end analysis (i.e., analysis prior to a commitment to design instruction).

The techniques of instructional development in its broad sense—including needs assessment, front-end analysis, task analysis, performance appraisal, instructional product design, prototype testing, and the like—go beyond the scope of the ASSURE model. They are well treated, however, in other textbooks; some suggested titles are found under "Instructional Development" in the Print References listed at the end of this chapter.

ANALYZE LEARNER CHARACTERISTICS

If instructional media are to be used effectively, there must be a match between the characteristics of the learner and the content of the learning material and its presentation. The first step in the ASSURE model, therefore, should be analysis of your audience. Are your learners ready for the learning experience you wish to offer them? Is there a match between the learners' characteristics and your materials and methods?

It is not always feasible to analyze every psychological or educational trait of your audience. There are, however, several factors about your learners that are critical for making good media and method decisions. First, in the category of *general characteristics* are broad identifying descriptors such as age, grade level, job/position, intellectual aptitude, and cultural or socioeconomic factors. General characteristics are factors that are not related to the content of the lesson. These factors help you to determine the level of the lesson and to select examples that will be meaningful to the given audience.

Under the heading of *specific entry competencies* you should think about content-related qualities that will more directly affect your decisions about media and methods: prerequisite skills (do learners have the knowledge base required to enter the lesson, such as the technical vocabulary?), target skills (have learners already mastered some of the skills you are planning to teach?), and attitudes (are there biases or misconceptions about the subject?).

Even a superficial analysis of learner characteristics can provide helpful leads in selecting instructional methods and media. For example, if your learners tend to be on the lower end of intellectual aptitude, they are more likely to need the special assists inherent in audiovisual presentations. By the same token, students with substandard reading skills may be reached more effectively with nonprint media. If you have a group widely diverging in aptitudes, consider self-instructional materials to allow self-pacing and other aspects of individualization.

If you are dealing with a particular ethnic or cultural subgroup, you might want to give high priority to considerations of ethnic/cultural identity in selecting particular materials.

If learner apathy toward the subject matter is a particular problem, consider using a highly stimulating instructional approach, such as a dramatic videotape or a simulation game.

Use Concrete Experiences for New Concepts

Learners entering a new conceptual area for the first time will need more direct, concrete kinds of experiences (e.g., field trips, role playing). The more advanced have a base for using audiovisual or even verbal materials. Heterogeneous groups, including learners varying widely in their conceptual sophistication or in their first-hand experience with the topic being discussed, can profit especially from an audiovisual experience like a videotape presentation. The videotape provides a common experience, one that is relatively concrete and shared by everyone in the same way. This common experiential base can serve as an important point of reference for subsequent group discussions and individual studies.

For instructors dealing with a familiar audience, analysis of general characteristics will be something of a given. Determining specific entry competencies, though, may require some data gathering through means such as informal questioning or testing with standardized or teacher-made tests.

At times, however, audience analysis may be more difficult. Perhaps your students are new to you and you have had little time to observe and record their characteristics. Perhaps your learners are a more heterogeneous group than is ordinarily found in the classroom—business trainees, for example, or a civic club, a youth group, or fraternal organization—thus making it more difficult to ascertain if all or even a majority of your learners are ready for the media and method of instruction you are considering. In such cases, academic and other records may be helpful, as may direct questioning of and conversation with learners and group leaders.

Test Learner Characteristics

Entry testing and/or pretesting may be necessary to verify your assumptions. *Entry testing* is commonly used to refer to assessments, both formal and informal, that determine whether or not the student possesses the necessary prerequisites (entry skills). *Prerequisites* are those competencies that the learner must possess in order to benefit from the instruction, but that you or the media are not going to teach. For example, you may

▼ **Figure 2.1**
Any instructional planning makes assumptions about the learners; these assumptions ought to be verified by testing.

be teaching an apprentice lathe operator to read blueprints and assume—and hence not teach—that he or she can make metric conversions. The necessary conversions are properly referred to as prerequisites and should be assessed before instruction by an entry test.

Pretests are also given before instruction, but measure the content to be taught. If the learners have already mastered what you plan to teach, you are wasting your time and their time by "teaching" it. For example, you might be presenting a seminar on the use of parables for church school religious educators. If the ability to "define the term *parable*" is one of your objectives, you might pretest to see if any or a majority of your participants can already define the term.

In any case, you should make every effort to assess the characteristics and capabilities of your audience and to match your media and instructional methods to these characteristics and capabilities. Although you would not use ordinary audio media with a student handicapped by deafness or a filmstrip with a totally blind learner, you could fall into less obvious traps.

Suppose, for example, you intend your learners to observe cell division under a common laboratory microscope. Learner analysis leads you to believe, correctly, that your learners are able to identify visual representations of the parts of a cell—membrane, nucleus, mitochondrion, etc. Fine. They should, then, be able to identify these parts under a microscope. You proceed with your lesson, and then find to your chagrin that some of your learners do not know how to operate a laboratory microscope! Your lesson plan has failed, or at best enjoyed limited success, because of improper and incomplete assessment of learner characteristics.

STATE OBJECTIVES

The second step in the ASSURE model for using instructional media is to state the objectives of instruction. What learning goal is each learner expected to reach? More precisely, what new *capability* should the learner possess at the completion of instruction? Thus, an objective is a statement not of what the instructor plans to *put into* the lesson, but of what the learner ought to *get out of* the lesson.

Your statement of objectives should be as specific as possible. For example, "my students will improve their mathematical skills" is far too general to qualify as a specific lesson objective. It does, however, qualify as a "goal"—that is, a broad statement of purpose. A properly stated specific objective might be: "The second-grade students will be able to solve any single-digit addition problem within five seconds."

Why should you state instructional objectives? In the first place, you must know your objectives in order to make the correct selection of media and methods. Your objectives will, in a sense, dictate your choice of media and your sequence of learning activities. Knowing your objectives will also force you to create a learning environment in which the objectives *can* be reached. For example, if the objective of a unit of a drivers training course is "to be able to change a flat tire within fifteen minutes," the learning environment must include a car with a flat tire. If, on the other hand, the unit objective is to be able "to name and describe the tools necessary to change a flat tire," a driver's manual or textbook would probably suffice.

Another basic reason for stating your instructional objectives is to help assure proper evaluation. You won't know if your learners have achieved an objective unless you are absolutely sure what that objective is. For information on deriving test items from objectives, see pages 55–58.

To be sure of
hitting the target,

shoot first

and whatever you hit,
call it the target.

▲ **Figure 2.2**
Some archers may use this approach, but is it appropriate for designing instruction?

Particularly note the box titled "Test Items: General."

Without explicit objectives your students won't know what is expected of them.

If objectives are clearly and specifically stated, learning and teaching become objective-oriented. Indeed, a statement of objectives may be viewed as a type of contract between teacher and learner: "Here is the objective. My responsibility as the instructor is to provide learning activities suitable for attaining the objective. Your responsibility as the learner is to participate conscientiously in those learning activities."

Elements of Well-Stated Objectives
A well-stated objective starts by naming the audience for whom it is intended (e.g., "newly hired sales representatives," "ninth-grade algebra students," and the like) and then specifying (1) the *performance* or capability to be learned, (2) the *conditions* under which the performance is to be observed, and (3) the *criterion* or standard of acceptable performance.

Performance. An objective should always include what the learner is expected to be able to do upon completion of instruction. Performance must be *observable*. Subjective terms such as "know," "understand," or "appreciate," should not be the operative verbs in statements of objectives. Use verbs such as "measure," "discuss," or "construct," which denote observable behavior (see the list of suggested performance verbs below).

Performance should be stated in terms of what the *learner* is expected to be able to do, not what the *teacher* is going to do. "The teacher will describe five harmful consequences of excessive use of alcohol" is not an objective. It is merely an instructional activity. The objective would be: "You (the learner) will be able to describe five harmful consequences of excessive use of alcohol."

One useful format for stating multiple objectives for a given unit of instruction is to list each individual objective with its appropriate per-

The Helpful Hundred:
Suggested Performance Verbs

Add	Defend	Kick	Reduce
Alphabetize	Define	Label	Remove
Analyze	Demonstrate	Locate	Revise
Apply	Derive	Make	Select
Arrange	Describe	Manipulate	Sketch
Assemble	Design	Match	Ski
Attend	Designate	Measure	Solve
Bisect	Diagram	Modify	Sort
Build	Distinguish	Multiply	Specify
Carve	Drill	Name	Square
Categorize	Estimate	Operate	State
Choose	Evaluate	Order	Subtract
Classify	Explain	Organize	Suggest
Color	Extrapolate	Outline	Swing
Compare	Fit	Pack	Tabulate
Complete	Generate	Paint	Throw
Compose	Graph	Plot	Time
Compute	Grasp (hold)	Position	Translate
Conduct	Grind	Predict	Type
Construct	Hit	Prepare	Underline
Contrast	Hold	Present	Verbalize
Convert	Identify	Produce	Verify
Correct	Illustrate	Pronounce	Weave
Cut	Indicate	Read	Weigh
Deduce	Install	Reconstruct	Write

formance verb. For example, "On completion of this unit, the college sophomore will be able to:

1. Define *sociology*.
2. Describe three significant events in the development of sociology as an academic discipline.
3. Identify six misconceptions about sociology from a list of eight statements.
4. Analyze the results of a sociological study and state one appropriate conclusion from the study.
5. State and justify his or her position on the biological basis of socialization."

The exact form of your statement of objectives is not critical. The important thing is that the statement be precise and tailored to your audience. Using the informal "you" rather than the more formal "the student" is preferable if the objective is meant primarily to be read by the students. Using "you" helps to personalize the statement.

Conditions. A statement of objectives should include the conditions under which performance is to be observed, if such conditions are relevant. For example, may the student use notes in describing the consequences of excessive use of alcohol? If the objective of a particular lesson is to be able to identify birds, will identification be made from color representations or black/white photographs? What tools or equipment will the student be allowed to use in demonstrating mastery of the objective? What resources will the student *not* be allowed to use? Thus, for example, "Given a political map of Europe, you will be able to mark the major coal producing areas."; "Without notes, textbook, or any library materials, you will be able to write an essay on the relationship of nutrition to learning."

Check Yourself

Are the following statements written in *behavioral (performance) terms*? (Complete and then check your answers below.)

YES	NO	
____	____	1. The Labor Negotiations trainee will grasp the true significance of the Taft-Hartley Law.
____	____	2. The carpentry vocational trainees will learn the common tools in the woodworking shop.
____	____	3. The first-year medical student will be able to name all the bones in the hand.
____	____	4. The high school debate club member will include ten supporting facts in a written paragraph on "The Value of National Health Insurance."
____	____	5. The junior high school student will list on the chalkboard three major causes of the American Civil War.
____	____	6. The kindergarten student will sit straight and quietly in his or her seat while the teacher is talking.
____	____	7. The high school sophomore will show a favorable regard for volleyball by joining an intramural volleyball team.
____	____	8. The Anthropology 101 student will develop a sense of the cultural unity of humankind.
____	____	9. By the end of their orientation, new employees will appreciate the importance of productivity within the corporation.
____	____	10. The elementary school student will demonstrate a desire for a clean environment by voluntarily picking up litter in the classroom and on the playground.

Answers

1. No 2. No 3. Yes 4. Yes 5. Yes 6. Yes 7. Yes 8. No 9. No 10. Yes

---

Criteria. A well-stated objective should include the criteria (or standards) by which acceptable performance will be judged. The criteria may describe quantity or quality or both. Ideally, the standards should be based on some real-world requirement. What level of skill is needed on the job? What degree of mastery is required to enter the next unit of study?

Time and accuracy are meaningful dimensions for many objectives. How quickly must the observable behavior be performed—for example, to solve five quadratic equations in five minutes, or to run a mile in less than eight minutes? How accurate must the results be—to the nearest whole number or within one-sixteenth of an inch or plus or minus 1 mm? If the

learning activity is archery, criteria for performance acceptability might be stated, as follows: "The student will shoot ten arrows from fifty yards within five minutes and hit a three-foot-diameter target with at least seven of the arrows."

Quantitative criteria for judging acceptable performance may sometimes be difficult to define. How, for example, can an industrial arts teacher specify how smoothly a piece of wood must be sanded? How can an English instructor state quantitative criteria for an essay or short story? Here performance is qualitative. Your task is more difficult in such cases, but not impossible. The industrial arts teacher, for example, might stipulate that the wood be comparable to a given example, or judged satisfactory by the teacher or a peer. The English instructor might stipulate that the student's work will be scored for development of theme, characterization, originality, or the like. Again, a model story might be used as an exemplar. A quantitative criterion for the English instructor might be that more than five spelling and punctuation errors will be unacceptable. Whether quantitative or qualitative criteria are used, they should be as appropriate and as specific as you can make them (see Appraisal Checklist, p. 42).

The important consideration in appraising your objectives is whether the intent of the objectives, regardless of their format, is communicated to the user. If your objectives meet all the criteria in the Appraisal Checklist but still do not communicate accurately your intentions to your colleagues and students, they are inadequate. The final judgment on any objectives must be determined by their usefulness to you and your learners.

Classification of Objectives

Objectives may be classified according to the primary type of learning outcome they are intended to bring about. The more commonly used classifications of human learning set out four major categories, referred to as the "domains" of learning: (1) cognitive learning, (2) affective learning, (3) motor skill learning, and (4) interpersonal skills learning.

Cognitive learning involves intellectual assimilation of information and knowledge. It ranges from simple recall, or memorization, to creation of new relationships.

Affective learning involves attitudes, feelings, and emotions. Affective learning skills range from simple awareness of a particular value to the internalization of clusters of feelings and values to form a well-integrated pattern of behavior ("character").

Check Yourself

Do the following statements include an acceptable statement of *condition*? (Complete and then check your answers below.)

YES   NO

1. Given a political outline map of South America, the sixth-grade student will be able to name eleven of the thirteen countries.
2. After completing the beginner's course, the young stamp collector will be able to distinguish a "plate block" from a "first day cover."
3. Without the aid of a calculator or any reference materials, the student of statistics will be able to calculater the chi-square value of a given set of data.
4. The management trainee in the labor negotiations course will be able to categorize correctly examples of different types of strikes (e.g., wildcat strike, sit-down strike, sympathy strike, etc.).
5. The naval officer candidate will be able to determine if an actual submarine is in "diving trim" when provided with data on its weight and volume.
6. A Nigerian primary school student will be able to construct a sundial using the illustrated instructions in the science workbook.
7. The Red Cross Lifesaving badge trainee will be able to rescue swimmers who show signs of distress in the water.
8. A college student enrolled in music appreciation will recognize the pattern typical of the romantic symphony in Beethoven recordings played in class.
9. Given two water-filled goblets and a spoon, the science education teacher-trainee will be able to demonstrate the principle of sympathetic vibration.
10. The speech therapist will be able to classify speech defects into one of the five main types of speech problems (e.g., aphasia).

Answers

1. Yes 2. No 3. Yes 4. No 5. Yes 6. Yes 7. No 8. Yes 9. Yes 10. No

◀ **Figure 2.3**

Motor skill learning involves athletic, manual, or other physical action skills. It ranges from simple imitative movements to physical skills requiring complex neuromuscular coordination.

Interpersonal skills learning involves interaction among people. These are people-centered skills that involve the ability to relate effectively with others. Examples include teamwork, counseling techniques, administrative skills, salesmanship, discussion activities, and customer relations.

Most learned capabilities contain elements of three or four of the domains since we are urging the use of performance objectives that involve some observable behavior. Nevertheless, the primary emphasis can usually be classified as cognitive, affective, motor skill, or interpersonal. For example, to achieve the objective of performing a somersault on a trampoline, the learner must have cognitive knowledge of the sequence of steps involved in the procedure. But the objective is primarily mastery of certain physical skills; hence it would be classified as a motor skill objective.

Or let us say the objective of an elementary school lesson is to get the children to pick up classroom litter voluntarily. A certain amount of cognitive learning might be involved: understanding, for example, how litter can contribute to accidents or why a clean classroom is easier to learn in than a cluttered one. The primary objective, however, is to change the children's behavior by changing their attitude toward littering and is, hence, an affective objective.

Most interpersonal skills tend to have some elements of attitude and require some basic knowledge to be applied. For example, if you are training someone to become a salesperson, he or she must be taught general sales skills (interpersonal); in addition, he or she must demonstrate the proper attitude toward the customer and have the necessary knowledge about the product or service to be sold.

Check Yourself

Do the following statements include a properly stated *criterion of acceptable performance*? (Complete and then check your answers below.)

YES NO

1. On a questionnaire at the end of the course, each management trainee will write at least two favorable comments about the course.
2. The machine shop trainee will be able to operate properly the Model 63-9 metal lathe.
3. In a controlled situation without access to any references, the college student of romantic poetry will be able to write an essay on the three themes in Shelley's poetry.
4. During a nature hike, the youth camper will be able to identify correctly at least three different geological formations.
5. The basketball squad member will be able to sink 75 percent of her free throws in a single practice session.
6. The vocational education student in basic electricity will operate a potentiometer to determine the resistance of resistors.
7. In a ballet practice session, each new dance company member will display proper form.
8. While being observed without his or her knowledge, the high school chemistry student will demonstrate all the safety precautions listed on the chart in the laboratory.
9. The football team member will be able to name correctly the formations illustrated by each of twelve diagrams.
10. Given a list of authors, the junior high school student will match the names of each with titles of their works.

Answers
1. Yes 2. No 3. No 4. Yes 5. Yes 6. No 7. No 8. Yes 9. Yes 10. Yes

Levels of the Domains of Learning

A knowledge of the levels of the domains of learning is useful as a guide to determine whether your objectives cover an appropriate range of skills and to decide the *sequence* of teaching those skills. It is very easy to fall into the habit of teaching only low-level skills within a particular domain and to slight more advanced levels, since objectives that include high-level skills are likely to be more difficult to state and test.

Appraisal Checklist: Objectives Statements

	High		Medium		Low

Audience

Specifies the learner(s) for whom the objective is intended
☐ ☐ ☐ ☐ ☐

Performance

Describes the *capability* expected of the learner following instruction
—stated as a *learner* performance
—stated as *observable* behavior
—describes a real-world *skill* (versus mere test performance)
☐ ☐ ☐ ☐ ☐

Conditions

Describes the *conditions* under which the performance is to be demonstrated
—equipment, tools, aids, or references the learner may or may not use
—special environmental conditions in which the learner has to perform
☐ ☐ ☐ ☐ ☐

Criterion

States, where applicable, the *standard* for acceptable performance
—time limit
—accuracy tolerances
—proportion of correct responses required
—qualitative standards
☐ ☐ ☐ ☐ ☐

Levels of Cognitive Learning.*

The cognitive domain is based on a progression from *simple* to *complex* mental performance:

1. *Knowledge:* recalling specifics, remembering, defining, recognizing, repeating (e.g., You will recite from memory *Paul Revere's Ride* by Longfellow.).
2. *Comprehension:* translating, interpreting, paraphrasing, summarizing, extrapolating (e.g., You will describe in your own words the story of *Paul Revere's Ride*.).

3. *Application:* using ideas and information (e.g., You will relate *Paul Revere's Ride* to modern communication techniques during a time of war.).
4. *Creation:* breaking down an example or system into its components; combining components to form results new to the student (e.g., You will compose an original poem following the rhyme scheme and imagery of *Paul Revere's Ride*.).

Levels of Affective Learning.*

The affective domain is organized according to the degree of internalization—the degree

to which the attitude or value has become part of the individual:

1. *Receiving:* being aware of and willing to pay attention to a stimulus (listen or look) (e.g., The student will sit quietly while the teacher reads Longfellow's *Paul Revere's Ride*.).
2. *Responding:* actively participating, reacting in some way (e.g., The student will ask questions relating to *Paul Revere's Ride*.).
3. *Valuing:* voluntarily displaying an attitude, showing an interest (e.g., The student will ask to read another story or poem about Paul Revere.).
4. *Characterization:* demonstrating an internally consistent value system, developing a characteristic lifestyle based upon a value or value system (e.g., The student

*Adapted from Benjamin S. Bloom, ed. *Taxonomy of Educational Objectives, Handbook I: Cognitive Domain.* New York: David McKay Company, 1956.

*Adapted from David R. Krathwohl et. al. *Taxonomy of Educational Objectives, Handbook II: Affective Domain.* New York: David McKay Company, 1964.

will devote a percentage of his or her free time to studying American history.).

Levels of Psychomotor Learning.*

The psychomotor domain may be seen as a progression in the degree of *coordination* required:

1. *Imitation:* repeating the action shown (e.g., After viewing the film on the backhand tennis swing, you will demonstrate the swing with reasonable accuracy.).
2. *Manipulation:* performing independently (e.g., Following a practice period, you will demonstrate the backhand tennis swing scoring seven of the ten points on the performance checklist.).
3. *Precision:* performing with accuracy (e.g., You will demonstrate an acceptable backhand tennis swing, returning successfully at least 75 percent of practice serves to the backhand.).
4. *Articulation:* performing unconsciously, efficiently, and harmoniously, incorporating coordination of skills (e.g., During a tennis match, you will execute the backhand stroke effectively against your opponent returning nine out of ten of all types of shots hit to the backhand side.).

Types of Interpersonal Skills Learning.†

The types of interpersonal skills can be classified into six categories:

1. *Seeking/giving information:* asking for/offering facts, opinions, or clarification from/to another individual or individuals. (e.g., You will ask your supervisor about the meaning of a new work rule.)

2. *Proposing:* putting forward a new concept, suggestion, or course of action. (e.g., You will make a job enrichment suggestion to your supervisor.)
3. *Building and supporting:* extending, developing, enhancing another person, his/her proposal, or concepts. (e.g., In a departmental meeting you will suggest an amendment to someone's motion.)
4. *Shutting out/bringing in:* excluding/involving another group member from/into a conversation or discussion. (e.g., In a departmental meeting you will ask a quiet member to give his or her ideas.)
5. *Disagreeing:* providing a conscious, direct declaration of difference of opinion, or criticism of another person's concepts. (e.g., During a lunchroom discussion you will defend a new work rule against a colleague's attack.)
6. *Summarizing:* restating in a compact form the content of previous discussions or considerations. (e.g., Before giving your comments in a departmental meeting you will summarize the arguments that have been presented.)

Objectives and Individual Differences

Objectives, whether in the cognitive, affective, motor skill, or interpersonal skills domain, may, of course, be tailored to individual learners. There is no rule that all students in a learning situation must reach objectives at the same time. In fact, if there were a rule on this matter, it would be that all students are *not* required or expected to do so. Nor is there a rule that the particulars of an objective be the same for all students. Again, if there were a rule it would state that they *not* be the same.

For example, the physical education teacher knows that not all the students in class will be physically able to run 200 yards in less than one minute after one week of practice and training. The specifics of the objective must be adapted to particular individuals. Similarly, the teacher of math or English or any subject may alter specifics of an objective to accommodate slower-than-average learners. Or, on the other hand, the teacher may add "enrichment" tasks and objectives to accommodate gifted learners. Criteria will, of course, also be altered to accommodate changes in expected levels of achievement.

▼ **Figure 2.4**
In a group of handicapped learners there may be as many different standards for each objective as there are individuals.

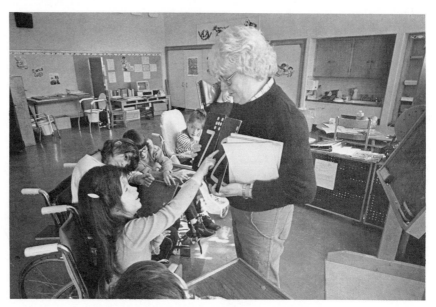

---

*Adaptation based upon published works of E. Simpson (University of Illinois) and R.H. Dave (National Institute of Education, New Delhi, India).

†Adapted from Neil Rackham and Terry Morgan. *Behaviour Analysis in Training*. London: McGraw-Hill, 1977.

Flashback: ORIGINS OF BEHAVIORAL OBJECTIVES

Ralph Tyler, a professor at Ohio State University, is generally considered to be the father of behavioral objectives as we know them today. Tyler's original interest was in test-item construction. His main contribution was to point out the importance of constructing test items based on behaviorally stated objectives that could be determined by analyzing the curriculum content.[a]

However, it was those in the programmed instruction movement, and particularly Robert Mager, who popularized the use of objectives by educators. Mager was a research scientist at Fort Bliss, Texas, working on a study to compare an experimental version of a course with an ongoing Army course. He drafted the objectives for the course and insisted that they be signed by the proper authorities before instruction began. Later, while employed by Varian Associates in Palo Alto, California, he was involved in designing a one-day session on programmed instruction for school administrators. In order to teach them to discriminate between properly written and poorly written programmed instruction, Mager decided to write a branching program with a variety of instructional errors:

Robert F. Mager

> *But what topic to write on? I couldn't think of one. I stared at the typewriter, counted the leaves on the tree outside the window, and checked my fingernails. Nothing. Finally, while thinking about the nature of the target population (audience), I had a flash! I'll fix you, I said to myself. I'll write about a topic that will get you so emotionally aroused that you won't be able to see programming from the subject matter. And I began to type out a dogmatic (error-filled) branching program called "How to Write Objectives." In addition to such pedagogical niceties as branching the reader to pages that didn't exist, I berated them on the wrong answer pages with comments such as "How can you sit there and SAY a thing like that. You're lying and you know it." And "Now look here! I don't want to have any trouble with you. So read the little gem: 'How do YOU know? Have you ever tried seriously to specify exact objectives for an academic course? Or are you upset simply because what is being suggested sounds like work?'"[b]*

Mager's initial program on writing objectives was duplicated and generated a great deal of discussion and provided practice in spotting good and bad characteristics in an instructional program. In Mager's words, "The day was a huge success."[c]

Later Mager learned that at least two professors at local colleges were using his error-laden practice program as a text in their education courses, so he modified the original program and published *Preparing Objectives for Programmed Instruction*[d] in 1961. He and others quickly realized that his objectives could be applied to much more than just programmed learning, so the following year the book was re-released with the title *Preparing Instructional Objectives*.[e] The book is a classic in the field of education; now in its revised second edition, it has sold over one-and-a-half million copies. As Mager says, "If you're not sure where you're going, you're liable to end up someplace else—and not even know it."

[a]Ralph Tyler. "The Construction of Examinations in Botany and Zoology." *Service Studies in High Education*. Bureau of Educational Research Monograph, no. 15. Columbus: Ohio State University, 1932.
[b]Robert F. Mager, "Why I Wrote . . ." *NSPI Journal* (October 1976), p. 4
[c]Ibid.
[d]Robert F. Mager. *Preparing Objectives for Programmed Instruction*. Palo Alto, Calif.: Fearon Publishers, 1961.
[e]See References at end of this chapter.

Objectives are not intended to *limit* what a student learns. They are intended only to provide a minimum level of expected achievement. Serendipitous or incidental learning should be expected to occur (and encouraged) as students progress toward an objective. Each learner has a different field of experience (as discussed in Chapter 1), and each has different learning characteristics (as discussed earlier in this chapter). Because of such individual differences, incidental learning takes different forms with different students. Class discussions and other kinds of student involvement in the instructional situation, therefore, should rarely be rigidly limited to a specific objective. Student involvement should allow for incidental learning to be shared and reinforced. Indeed, in order to foster incidental learning and provide for individual differences, it is sometimes advisable to have the students specify some of their own objectives.

SELECT, MODIFY, OR DESIGN MATERIALS

The pedagogical significance of choosing appropriate materials is magnified by the pervasive presence of instructional media in the classroom setting. Research has shown that, on the average, 90 to 95 percent of instructional class time is spent on activities based on the use of instructional materials.*

Obtaining appropriate materials will generally involve one of three alternatives: (1) selecting available materials, (2) modifying existing materials, or (3) designing new materials. Obviously, if materials are already available that will allow your students to meet your objectives, these materials should be used to save both time and money. When the media and materials available do not match your objectives or are not suitable for your audience, an alternate approach is to modify the materials. If this is not feasible, the final alternative is to design your own materials. Even though this is a more expensive and time-consuming process, it does allow you to prepare materials to precisely serve your audience and meet your objectives.

Selecting Available Materials and Methods

The majority of instructional materials used by teachers and trainers are "off the shelf"—that is, ready-made and available from school, district, company collections or other easily accessible sources. How do you go about making an appropriate choice from available materials?

*P. Kenneth Komoski, "How Can the Evaluation of Instructional Materials Help Improve Classroom Instruction Received by Handicapped Learners?" In R. Heinich, ed., *Educating All Handicapped Children*. Englewood Cliffs, N.J.: Educational Technology Publications, 1979, pp. 189–191.

▲ **Figure 2.5**
The NICEM indexes list commercially produced materials available in various media formats.

Survey of Sources. Your first step might be to survey some of the published media reference guides to get a general idea of what is available. Unfortunately, no single comprehensive guide exists to all audiovisual materials available in all media formats in all subjects; you may have to consult several sources for a given problem.

One of the more comprehensive sources is the set of indexes published by NICEM (National Information Center for Educational Media). The NICEM indexes are arranged according to media format—e.g., slides, filmstrips, overhead transparencies, 16-mm films, etc. In addition, there are several indexes devoted to specific topics, cutting across multiple media formats—e.g., environmental studies, health and safety, psychology, and vocational/technical education. These indexes do not include evaluations.

There also is a separate data bank for information and materials on special education: NICSEM (National Information Center for Special Education Materials). NICSEM publications provide information on the content of materials and their applicability to specific handicapping conditions.

This information is intended to help in preparing individualized education plans for handicapped learners. (See Appendix A for details about NICEM and NICSEM.)

If you are working in elementary or secondary education, there are several additional sources that cover a broad range of media formats; for example, *Core Media Collection for Elementary Schools* and *Core Media Collection for Secondary Schools*. These books recommend specific audiovisual titles as core materials for elementary and secondary school library collections.

For general and adult audiences, a major reference source is the *Reference List of Audiovisual Materials Produced by the United States Government*. It describes all the training and educational materials produced by the Armed Forces and other government agencies that are available for general purchase. (See Appendix A for further details on all the reference sources discussed here.)

Beyond the sources described above, you will have to turn to the more specialized guides and indexes that are limited to specific media formats or specific subjects. While these are too many and too diverse to list here, they are mentioned in the individual chapters dealing with different media formats and they are gathered under the heading of "Specialized Information Sources" in Appendix A. Also, see Appendix B for sources of free and inexpensive materials.

Selection Criteria.
Your actual selection of specific materials will largely depend on the following factors:

1. The characteristics of the learners.
2. The nature of the objectives.
3. The instructional approach.
4. The constraints of the instructional situation.

Just as there must be a match between learner and objectives, there also must be a match between learner and materials. Is the vocabulary level of the material appropriate? Is the reading or listening level appropriate? Does the level of illustrative detail match the experience level of the learners? If the material must be manipulated, do the learners possess the skills necessary to so so?

The selected materials must, of course, be relevant to your objectives. Does the material contain the information and activities necessary to achieve them? No matter how good it might be on other counts, of what benefit is it if it doesn't help you and your students attain your objectives?

Your choice of media may be influenced by the instructional approach involved in the lesson. Different media lend themselves to different instructional approaches and purposes. For example, filmstrips are more useful for individualized instruction than are multiscreen slide/tape presentations. One media form may fit an instructional situation stressing inquiry learning (e.g., silent loop film); another may be best suited for a lesson stressing open-ended discussion (e.g., videocassette). A format such as film may be ideal for increasing motivation, but a simulation exercise might be better for introducing a new topic.

Your selection of instructional materials will also be influenced by the constraints of the instructional situation. Can sufficient classroom time be scheduled for proper use of the materials? Will all the necessary equipment be available (projectors, tape recorders, etc.)? If the materials require assistance of aides, are the necessary personnel available? Does the learning environment lend itself to use of your materials? For example, opaque projectors require a completely darkened room. Will your budget cover the cost of your materials? Some films and equipment, for example, have high rental fees.

Media Appraisal Checklist.
We have now analyzed a number of media selection criteria related to learner characteristics, objectives, instructional approach, and situational constraints. If these criteria are to be *applied* to your own day-to-day selection decisions, they must be summarized into a usable checklist. In later chapters we provide suggested checklists for each of the specific classes of media. The form shown on page 48, "Appraisal Checklist: Generalized," suggests the general criteria you would look for regardless of the media format.

The Instructor's Personal File.
Every instructor should develop a file of media references and appraisals for personal use. This personal file card need not be as detailed as the appraisal form. What you are primarily interested in recording are instructional strengths and weaknesses. Figure 2.6 illustrates a suggested personal file form that is relatively simple and will fit on a 4-by-6-inch card. Under "synopsis," you can note the overall content of the item. Under "utilization pointers and problems," you might note information about vocabulary used in the material, lack or inclusion of opportunities for student response, timeliness of the content, inclusion of sensitive topics, etc.

Modifying Available Materials
If you cannot locate entirely suitable materials and media off the shelf, you might be able to modify what is available. This can be both challenging and creative. In terms of time and cost, it is a more efficient procedure than designing your own materials, although type and extent of necessary modification will, of course, vary.

Perhaps the only visual available showing a piece of equipment being used in a junior high woodworking

Title: _____   Format: _____

Length: _____   Source: _____   Technical data: _____

Synopsis:

Utilization pointers and problems (e.g., new vocabulary):

▲ **Figure 2.6**
Your personal file cards will provide an informal record of your own personal experiences with particular materials.

class is from a repair manual and contains too much detail and complex terminology. A possible solution to the problem would be to use the picture but modify the caption and simplify or omit some of the names of the labelled parts.

In a business or industry new employee orientation program, you may be using a slide set developed by corporate headquarters. Where possible and appropriate, you can replace existing slides with slides showing local facilities and local personnel.

Or perhaps there is just one film available that shows a needed visual sequence, but the audio portion of the film is inappropriate because it is at too high or too low a conceptual level or discusses inappropriate points. In such a case, a simple solution would be to show the film with the sound turned off and provide the narration yourself. Another modification technique, which many instructors overlook, is to show just a portion of a film, stop the projector, discuss what has been presented, then continue with another short segment followed by additional discussion. A similar approach may be used for sound filmstrips with audio tape. You can rerecord the narration and use the appropriate vocabulary level for your audience—and even change

the emphasis of the visual material. If a transcript of the original narration is available, you probably will want to refer to it as you compose your own narration.

Modification also can be made in the audio portion of foreign language materials (or English language materials used in a bilingual classroom). Narrations can be changed from one language to another or from a more advanced rendition of a foreign language to a simpler one.

Videocassette recorders now provide teachers with the opportunity to modify television programs that previously were available only as shown on the air. With video playback units available in most schools, many producers now distribute programs having educational potential in videotape format. Programs may also be recorded off the air for replay on playback units.* Procedures and practices for modification of videotape are much the same as for film (as noted above). Videocassette recorders also, of course, give the teacher much more flexibility in using television programs for instructional purposes. Programs can be shown at whatever time best suits the instructional situation and to whatever student group or groups that can best profit from viewing them.

One frequently modified media format is a set of slides with an audiotape. If the visuals are appropriate but the language is not, it is possible to change the language. It also is possible to change the *emphasis* of

---

*Broadcast materials vary in their recording restrictions. See Appendix C for general guidelines; consult a media specialist regarding specific programs.

▼ **Figure 2.7**
The most basic way of modifying material such as a film is to show only a part of the material or to show segments interspersed with group discussion.

Appraisal Checklist: Generalized

Title_____

Producer/distributor_____

Length_____minutes   Production date_____

Audience/grade level_____

Cost_____   Subject area_____

Format:
☐ audio tape/cassette
☐ slides
☐ filmstrip
☐ film
☐ videotape-cassette
☐ other_____

Objectives:

Brief description:

Entry capabilities required:
prior knowledge
reading ability
math ability
other

Rating	High		Medium		Low
Likely to arouse student interest	☐	☐	☐	☐	☐
Accuracy of information	☐	☐	☐	☐	☐
Technical quality	☐	☐	☐	☐	☐
Provides meaningful student participation	☐	☐	☐	☐	☐
Evidence of effectiveness (e.g., field-test results)	☐	☐	☐	☐	☐
Provides guidance for discussion/follow-up	☐	☐	☐	☐	☐

Requirements:
equipment
facilities
personnel

Strong points:

Weak points:

Reviewer_____

Position_____

Recommended action_____   Date_____

the narration. For example, an original audiotape might emphasize oceans as part of an ecosystem, whereas the teacher may want to use the slides to show various types of fish found in oceans. Rewriting the narration could adapt the material to the teacher's purpose while using the same slides. Redoing the tape can also change the *level* of the presentation. A slide-tape presentation produced to introduce a new product could have three different audio tapes. One tape could be directed toward the customer, another could be prepared for the sales staff, and the third for the service personnel.

Instructional games can be readily modified to meet particular instructional needs. It is possible to use a given game format and change the rules of play in order to increase or decrease the level of sophistication. Many instructional games require the players to answer questions. It is relatively easy for the teacher to prepare a new set of questions at a different level of difficulty or even on a new topic.

If you try out modified materials while they are still in more or less rough form you can then make further modifications in response to student reaction until your materials meet your exact needs.

A word of caution about modifying commercially produced materials (and, indeed, about use of commercial products in general): be sure your handling and use of such materials does not violate copyright laws and restrictions. If in doubt, check with your school administrator or legal advisor. (Copyright laws and guidelines are discussed in Appendix C.)

Designing New Materials

It is easier and less costly to use available materials, with or without modification, than to start from scratch. There is seldom justification for reinventing the wheel. However, there may be times when your only recourse is to design your own materials. As is the case with selecting from available materials, certain basic considerations must be taken into account when designing new materials. For example:

Objectives— what do you want your students to learn?

Audience— what are the characteristics of your learners? Do they have the prerequisite knowledge and skills to use and/or learn from the materials?

Cost— is sufficient money available in your budget to meet the cost of supplies (film, audio tapes, etc.) you will need to prepare the materials?

Technical expertise— do you have the necessary expertise to design and produce the kind of materials you wish to use? If not, will the necessary technical assistance be available to you? (Try to keep your design within the range of your own capabilities. Don't waste time and money trying to produce slick professional materials when simple inexpensive products will get the job done.)

Equipment— do you have available the necessary equipment to produce and/or use the materials you intend to design?

Facilities— if your design calls for use of special facilities for preparation and/or use of your materials, are such facilities available?

Time— can you afford to spend whatever time may be necessary to design and produce the kind of materials you have in mind?

UTILIZE MATERIALS

The next step in the ASSURE model is the one that all the other steps lead up to and away from: the presentation itself. To get maximum learning impact from your presentation, formal research stretching back to U.S. military training in World War II and the practical experience of several generations of teachers indicate that certain utilization procedures must be followed: in short, preview the materials, practice the presentation, prepare the environment, prepare the audience, and present.

Preview the Materials

No instructional materials should be used blind. During the selection process you should have determined that the materials are appropriate for your audience and objectives. Published reviews, reports of field tests, distributors' blurbs, and colleagues' appraisals all add evidence. However, the prudent instructor will insist on previewing the materials. Only such detailed familiarity with the contents can enable you to properly wrap the lesson around the audiovisual material.

For example, an industrial trainer ordered a videotape on fraction-to-decimal conversions. The information describing the videotape indicated that the content was exactly what many of the company employees needed. The videotape arrived ten days before the presentation, but the trainer did not take time to preview it. When the videotape was shown it met with giggles and laughs; although the content was appropriate, the videotape was addressed to an elementary school audience. The adults were understandably distracted by the level of the narration and the examples used.

In addition, sensitive content may need to be eliminated or at least discussed prior to showing to prevent student embarrassment and/or impediment of learning. In one case, an elementary teacher and her young students were horrified to find that an unpreviewed and ostensibly unobjectionable film on Canada's fur seals contained a sequence showing baby seals being cold-bloodedly clubbed to death by hunters.

Practice the Presentation

After previewing the materials, you should practice your portion of the presentation. It is advisable to go through the presentation at least once well in advance and then to review your notes immediately before the presentation. However, do not overpractice, or the presentation will sound "canned."

▼ **Figure 2.8**
Preview.

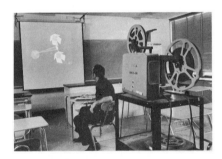

▼ **Figure 2.9**
Practice.

Some presenters prefer to practice before a mirror; others like to have a colleague or friend present to provide feedback. Media can be used to provide a "replay" of your practice. An audiotape recording will let you hear how you sounded—what you said and how you said it. If you are concerned about how you look, how you handle manipulable objects, or whether or not you have any distracting mannerisms, you should use a video recording. The camera and recorder can be set up in the rear of the room, turned on, and allowed to operate while you go through the presentation.

The newness of the material, the importance of the presentation, and the amount of time available will determine how many times you practice and the type of "mirror" you use—a real mirror, a friend, an audiotape recorder, or a videotape recorder. The importance of practice cannot be overstated. Don't just "walk through it" in your mind, actually stand up and perform as you will in front of your group.

▼ **Figure 2.10**
Prepare environment.

Prepare the Environment

Wherever the presentation is to take place—classroom, auditorium, meeting room, or whatever—the facilities will have to be put in order. Certain factors are taken for granted for any instructional situation—comfortable seating, adequate ventilation, climate control, suitable lighting, and the like. Utilization of many media requires room darkening, convenient power supply, and access to light switches. At the least the instructor should check that the equipment is in working order and should arrange the facilities so that all the audience can see and hear properly. More specific details on audiovisual setups are found in Chapter 10.

Prepare the Audience

Research on learning tells us very clearly that what is learned from a presentation depends highly on how the learners are *prepared* for the presentation. In everyday life we notice that entertainers are obsessed with having the audience properly warmed up. Nobody wants to come after "a hard act to follow" or to come on "cold." The same applies to media.

▼ **Figure 2.11**
Prepare audience.

Proper *warm-up* from an instructional point of view will generally consist of an introduction including: a broad overview of the content of the presentation, a rationale of how it relates to the topic being studied, a motivation (creating a "need to know"—how the learner will profit from paying attention), and cues directing attention to specific aspects of the presentation.

Several of these functions—directing attention, arousing motivation, providing a rationale—may be served simply by informing the viewers of the specific objectives.

In certain cases, other steps will be called for. For example, unfamiliar vocabulary may need to be introduced, or special visual effects, such as time-lapse photography, may need explanation. Other preparation steps relevant to particular media will be discussed in later chapters.

Present the Material

This is what you've been preparing for, so you will want to make the most of it. Our term for this is "showmanship." Just as an actor or actress must control the attention of an audience, so must an instructor be able to direct attention in the classroom. The later chapters on individual media point out "showmanship" techniques relevant to each specific media format. General showmanship tips for all types of presentations are given in this chapter.

AV SHOWMANSHIP—GENERAL TIPS

- **You are a medium.**

Most audiovisual presentations include some sort of live performance by the instructor, perhaps as narrator or actor, perhaps as both. As a performer, you become an important component of the medium. Indeed, in a sense, you yourself become a medium, one that must perform effectively if your presentation is to be successful.

Be natural. Your audience will quickly sense affectation. Do not try to be someone or something you are not. But, by all means be enthusiastic! Successful actors know that their "energy level" directly affects audience response.

Avoid distracting mannerisms. Do you have an annoying habitual mannerism—smoothing your hair, twisting your watch, clicking a ballpoint pen— or a "verbal tic" such as inserting "um" or "you know" at every pause? Such mannerisms can become very annoying to an audience. The listener stops hearing the message and begins concentrating on the mannerism. The first step toward controlling such distractors is to become aware of them. Videotaping yourself in action can be an effective aid to discovering and correcting them.

- **Your classroom is a stage.**

When you are making a presentation from the front of a classroom you are functioning like an actor on the stage. Your impact on the audience can be strengthened by observing a few of the basic principles of stagecraft.

Strong Areas. The front of the classroom, the "stage," can be divided into six sections, as shown

in Figure 2.12. Note that the front (near the audience) is generally stronger than the back, and that the center is stronger than either side. Of the two

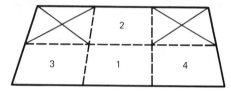

▲ **Figure 2.12**
The sectors of the "stage" vary in strength, with front center strongest and the rear corners weakest.

sides, the left (as seen by the audience) is stronger than the right.

The audiovisual presenter can use these strengths and weaknesses to good psychological advantage by using position to feature the dominant points of a presentation. See, for example, Figures 2.13, 2.14, and 2.15.

▲ **Figure 2.13**
The screen, because of its placement in the center, has clear dominance over the presenter.

AV SHOWMANSHIP—GENERAL TIPS

▲   **Figure 2.14**
The presenter, situated in the front center, here has a more dominant placement.

▲   **Figure 2.15**
Here the presenter is in a moderate position, but the display table, being at the front center, takes precedence.

Body Position.   Facing the audience full-front is the strongest position. Three-quarters full-front is weaker; profile is weaker yet. Weakest is the one-quarter view, with the back nearly turned toward the audience. The use of chalkboards or charts will push you toward the weak position unless you consciously avoid it. (See Figures 2.16, 2.17, 2.18 and 2.19.)

Movement.   Given a static scene, any movement attracts the eye. This is one reason that nervous gestures are objectionable; they may distract attention from a point to be made. But movement can also be used positively to underscore important points. Experienced speakers often signal the beginning of a new topic by pausing and shifting their

position, possibly walking to a different part of the room. But some movements are definitely stronger than others. As illustrated in Figure 2.20, the strongest movement is toward the front center of the "stage" from one of the weaker areas. Conversely, the weakest movement is away from the front center, especially toward a corner.

In Figure 2.15, if the speaker leaves the lectern to approach the display table, he or she will be executing a very strong movement that will add dramatic emphasis to the presentation.

• **Keep it light.**
A relaxed environment has been shown to increase suggestibility, a state conducive to rapid, effective

▼   **Figure 2.16**
The full-front body position is the strongest one.

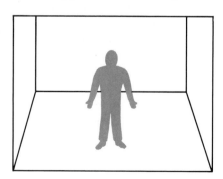

▼   **Figure 2.17**
Three-quarters full front is the second strongest body position.

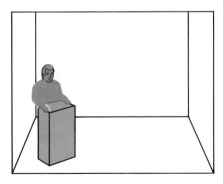

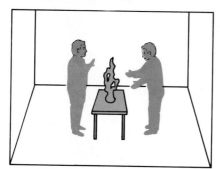

▲ **Figure 2.18**
Standing in profile, these figures are in a rather weak body position.

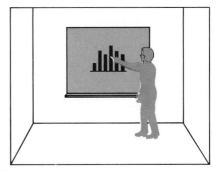

▲ **Figure 2.19**
A one-quarter view body position is the very weakest.

learning. Humor can be very effective in establishing a relaxed environment, no matter what the age of the audience or the seriousness of the study. A joke, a humorous aside, poking fun at yourself, can help build receptiveness. Obviously, humor should flow naturally from the instructional situation and should never be forced. Negative humor, such as sarcasm or ethnic jokes, has a high likelihood of offending your audience and should not be used.

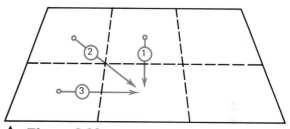

▲ **Figure 2.20**
The three stage movements shown here give the greatest emphasis to the presenter, in the order indicated by the numbers.

• **Keep a surprise in store.**
Don't be afraid to surprise your audience. Unexpected conclusions and surprising visuals can add dramatic emphasis to your presentation.

• **Control attention.**
Eye contact with your audience is extremely helpful in controlling attention. One of the great advantages of the overhead projector is that it allows you to maintain eye contact with your audience during presentation, since you are at the front of the room and the room is lighted. Eye contact is more difficult with slides and filmstrips.

Keep in mind that attention naturally gravitates toward the brightest light in a given area. If you want your viewers to shift their attention from a lighted screen back to you, turn off the projector. Users of overhead projectors sometimes forget this simple rule. They leave a visual on the screen after they are finished with it or leave the projector on after the

lesson segment is completed. When they then move on to a new topic, audience attention remains focused on the lighted screen rather than on the instructor.

• **Keep sight and sound synchronized.**
One sure way to confuse (and madden) your audience is to fail to synchronize sound and visuals. Careful scripting will help you avoid this serious pitfall. If a projectionist is advancing your visuals, provide a copy of the script containing clearly marked directions. If no such script is available, arrange ahead of time for signals which will alert the projectionist when to advance visuals. A nod of the head or an unobtrusive wave of the hand will suffice. A trumpeted "Next slide please!" is distracting and not at all necessary.

REQUIRE LEARNER RESPONSE

The fifth step in the ASSURE model is encouraging student response to the instructional stimuli. Educators have long realized that participation in the learning process *by the learner* enhances learning. In the early 1900s, John Dewey urged reorganization of the nation's curriculum and instruction to make student participation a central part of the process. Later, behavioral psychologists such as B. F. Skinner demonstrated that instruction providing for constant reinforcement of desired behaviors is more effective than instruction in which responses are not reinforced. The implications for the teacher are very clear. The most effective learning situations are those that provide for student response and for reinforcement of correct response.

The learner involvement may entail several senses. The learners can *see* the desired action. They can *hear* a smooth running engine. They can *touch* the different fabrics. They can *smell* the odor of gas from a chemical reaction. They can *taste* the different seasonings.

Student response to an instructional situation may range from simple recitation of facts to completion of a product (a dress, a term paper). The responses might even consist of designing and producing instructional media suitable to a specific segment of classroom instruction. Building learner participation and opportunity for response into the instructional situation is highly desirable since it has been firmly established as an effective teaching technique.

▲ **Figure 2.21**
Videotapes can be stopped to allow live interaction during a presentation.

Some media lend themselves to student participation more than others—at least on the surface. For example, student response to projected still pictures is easier to manage than response to a motion picture. Students can read or elaborate on captions in filmstrips, discuss what is on the screen, or refer to other materials while the image is held on the screen. (Substitution of sound filmstrips for silent tends to weaken this advantage.) However, students can also participate in and respond to the showing of a film. For example, May and Lumsdaine demonstrated that overt responses (vocalized verbal responses) during a film improved learning. The same authors cited research demonstrating that psychomotor skills are learned better if practiced while the skills are being performed in a film.* Overt written responses during the showing of a film (or any other fixed-pace medium) have been shown to facilitate learning, unless the responses are so involved that students are prevented from watching the film.

Materials may be designed to include covert or overt responses. A covert response might be silent repetition of key vocabulary at specified points in the lesson. An overt response might consist of vocalizing or writing out the key words. Manipulation of materials would also be an overt response. In general, covert responses are just as effective as overt responses for short learning sequences. Sequences of longer duration are learned better when students respond overtly.

Although delayed confirmation or correction of response may be effective in certain situations, immediate feedback is generally better. Immediate confirmation of *correct* response is particularly important when working with students of lower-than-average abilities. For such students, evidence of immediate success can be a strong motivating force for further learning.

Discussions, short quizzes, and application exercises can provide opportunities for response and reinforcement during instruction.

*Mark A. May and A. A. Lumsdaine. *Learning from Films.* New Haven: Yale University Press, 1958.

▲ **Figure 2.22**
Self-instructional modules incorporate the active response originated by programmed instruction.

Follow-up activities can provide further opportunities. Teacher guides and manuals written to accompany instructional materials often contain suggested techniques and activities for eliciting and reinforcing student response.

Programmed instruction is a technology of instruction based on the premise that student response and reinforcement are essential to effective learning. One of the major contributions of the programmed instruction movement is that educators have been encouraged to design learner participation, response, and reinforcement into a wide variety of instructional situations and media combinations. Learning activities packages, Audio-Tutorial techniques, and computer-based instruction are just a few examples of incorporation of the programming principles of response and reinforcement into various media and technologies of instruction.

Since computers lend themselves well to learner response and reinforcement, they may be used to provide instruction on any topic (including computers themselves). For example, if you were training someone to operate a computer system for billing purposes, a computer could be used to simulate the "real world" environment. The computer could provide the instruction on proper billing entry procedures and then require the learner to actually enter some simulated billing data into the computer. Because of the computer's response capability, it could immediately tell the learner if he or she had done the procedures correctly. If correct, the learner could be reinforced by the computer. If incorrect, the computer could indicate what the learner had done improperly, demonstrate the correct procedure, and give the learner another set of data to enter. In this case the computer provides the instruction, calls for learner response, and provides immediate feedback as to the correctness of the response. As you study the chapters that follow, you will note how reinforcement principles can be incorporated into the design and utilization of specific instructional media.

EVALUATE

The final component of our ASSURE model for effective learning is evaluation. The most frequently thought of type of evaluation is the paper-and-pencil test; the most frequently thought of purpose, to measure student achievement. There are, however, many purposes of evaluation. Three that we will discuss here are evaluation of learner achievement, evaluation of media and methods, and evaluation of the instructional process.

Evaluation of Learner Achievement

The ultimate question in the instructional process is whether or not the students have learned what they were supposed to learn. Can they display the capabilities specified in the original statement of objectives? The first step in answering this question was taken back near the beginning of the ASSURE process, when you formulated your objectives, including in that statement of objectives a *criterion* of acceptable performance. You now want to assess whether the learner's new skill meets that criterion.

The method of evaluating achievement depends on the nature of the objective. Some objectives call for relatively simple cognititve skills; for example, recalling Ohm's law, distinguishing adjectives from adverbs, describing a company's absence policy, or summarizing the purposes of the European Common Market. Objectives such as these lend themselves to conventional written tests or oral examinations. Other objectives may call for process type behaviors (for example, conducting an orchestra, performing a forward roll on a balance beam, operating a metal lathe, or solving quadratic equations), the creation of products (a sculpture, a written composition, a window display, or an account ledger), or the holding of attitudes (tolerating divergent political opinions,

Test Items: General

Assume the objective is "Given a diagram of the human trachea, the student nurse will explain a bronchocele, describing cause and treatment." A possible test item would be: "What is a bronchocele? Describe the cause and treatment in your answer."

In broadcaster training the objective might be "Given the pertinent information, facts, and figures, the student shall write a twenty-second and a thirty-second broadcast news story using correct broadcast style." The evaluation could be: "Using the information provided, compose a twenty-second radio news story using correct broadcast style."

For military training an objective could be: "With the aid of a topographic map, the officer shall call for field artillery fire using the four essential items of information in prescribed military sequence." The written test could call for: "How would you call for artillery fire upon point X on the accompanying topographic map?"

Performance Checklist: Driving Skills

Name_____ Class_____

Directions: Check yes or no with an X in the proper space.

Did the student:	Yes	No
1. Fasten seat belt before starting car?		
2. Use the nine o'clock and three o'clock hand position on steering wheel?		
3. Drive with the flow of traffic yet stay within the speed limit?		
4. Come to full and complete stops at stop signs?		
5. Keep at least a two-second interval behind the vehicle ahead?		
6. Stay in the proper driving lane—not cross center line?		
7. Obey all traffic signs and signals?		
8. Negotiate all turns properly (according to driving manual)?		
9. Avoid excessive conversation with passengers?		
10. Display courtesy to other drivers?		

Instructor's name_____ Date_____

appreciating expressionist painting, observing safety procedures while on the assembly line, or contributing money to community charities).

The evaluation procedures should be directly correlated with the objectives stated earlier in the ASSURE model. See the box titled "Test Items: General" for examples.

Capabilities of the process, product, or attitude type could be assessed to some extent by means of written or oral tests. But test results would be indirect and weak evidence of how well the learner has mastered the objective. More direct and stronger evidence would be provided by observing the behavior *in action*. This implies setting up a situation in which the learner can demonstrate the new skill and the instructor can observe and judge it.

In the case of process skills, a performance checklist can be an effective, objective way of recording your observations. An example is shown below. Other types of activities that can be properly evaluated through performance checklist are sales techniques, telephone answering

▼ **Figure 2.23**
A process- or performance-type skill should be judged according to observation of the performance itself.

skills, and face-to-face customer relations. During the instructional process these types of activities may need to be evaluated in a simulated situation, with other learners, or the instructor role playing the customer/client.

For product skills, a product rating checklist can guide your evaluation of critical subskills and make qualitative judgments more objective. An example is shown below. Other types of products that lend themselves to evaluation by a rating scale include pastry from a bakery, compositions in an English course, and computer programs.

▶ **Figure 2.24**
The ability to create a product should be judged according to the quality of the product itself; a rating checklist is helpful for calling attention to the most critical qualities of the product.

Product Rating Checklist: Welding

Name_____ Date_____

Directions: Rate the welded product by checking the appropriate boxes. Add comments if you wish.

Base metal(s)_____   Filler metal(s)_____

Profile:	Excellent	Very Good	Good	Fair	Poor
Convexity (1/32-inch maximum)	☐	☐	☐	☐	☐
Fusion on toe	☐	☐	☐	☐	☐
Overlap	☐	☐	☐	☐	☐
Amount of fill	☐	☐	☐	☐	☐

Workmanship:	Excellent	Very Good	Good	Fair	Poor
uniform appearance	☐	☐	☐	☐	☐
arc strikes	☐	☐	☐	☐	☐
bead width	☐	☐	☐	☐	☐
bead start	☐	☐	☐	☐	☐
bead tie-in	☐	☐	☐	☐	☐
bead termination	☐	☐	☐	☐	☐
penetration	☐	☐	☐	☐	☐
amount of spatter	☐	☐	☐	☐	☐

Overall evaluation:

Evaluator comments:

Attitudes are admittedly difficult to evaluate. For some attitudinal objectives, long-term observation may be required to determine if the goal has really been attained. In day-to-day instruction we usually have to rely on what we can observe here and now, however limited that may be. A commonly used technique for making attitudes more visible is the attitude scale, an example of which is shown below. A number of other suggestions for attitude measurement can be found in Robert Mager's *Developing Attitude Toward Learning*.*

Evaluation of Media and Methods

Evaluation, as noted above, also includes assessment of instructional media and methods. Were your instructional materials effective? Could they be improved? Were they cost effective in terms of student achievement? Did your presentation take more time than it was really worth? Particularly after first use, instructional materials need to be evaluated to determine if future use, with or without modification, is warranted. The results of your evaluation should be entered on your personal file form. As part of evaluation of your media, you may want to follow-up on the Appraisal Checklist used to select the media. (See page 48.) Did the media assist the students in meeting the objectives? Were they effective in arousing student interest? Did they provide meaningful student participation?

Class discussions, individual interviews, and observation of student behavior should be used to sound out evaluation of instructional media and methods. Failure to attain objectives is, of course, a clear indication that something is wrong with the instruction. But student reaction to your instructional unit can be helpful in more subtle ways. Student-teacher discussion may indicate that your audience would have preferred independent

Attitude Scale: Biology

Each of the statements below expresses a feeling toward biology. Please rate each statement on the extent to which you agree. For each, you may: (A) strongly agree, (B) agree, (C) be undecided, (D) disagree, or (E) strongly disagree.

A	B	C	D	E
strongly agree	agree	undecided	disagree	strongly disagree

_____ 1. Biology is very interesting to me.
_____ 2. I *don't* like biology, and it scares me to have to take it.
_____ 3. I am always under a terrible strain in a biology class.
_____ 4. Biology is fascinating and fun.
_____ 5. Biology makes me feel secure, and at the same time it is stimulating.
_____ 6. Biology makes me feel uncomfortable, restless, irritable, and impatient.
_____ 7. In general, I have a good feeling toward biology.
_____ 8. When I hear the word *biology*, I have a feeling of dislike.
_____ 9. I approach biology with a feeling of hesitation.
_____ 10. I really like biology.
_____ 11. I have always enjoyed studying biology in school.
_____ 12. It makes me nervous to even think about doing a biology experiment.
_____ 13. I feel at ease in biology and like it very much.
_____ 14. I feel a definite positive reaction to biology; it's enjoyable.

study to your choice of group presentation. Or perhaps viewers didn't like your selection of overhead transparencies and feel they would have learned more if a film had been shown. Your students may let you know, subtly or not so subtly, that your own performance left something to be desired.

You may solicit learner input on the effectiveness of specific media such as a film or videotape. You may design your own form or use one similar to the "Module Appraisal Form".

Evaluation of the Instructional Process

Although ultimate evaluation must await completion of the instructional unit, evaluation is an ongoing process. Evaluations are made before, during, and after instruction; for example, before instruction, learner characteristics are measured to ensure that there is a fit between student skills and the methods and materials you intend to use. In addition, materials should be appraised prior to use, as noted earlier in this chapter. During instruction, evaluation may take the form of student practice

---

*See References at end of this chapter.

Module Appraisal Form

User_____

Date_____

Comments

1. The objectives of this module were:

   Clear   Unclear
   7   6   5   4   3   2   1

2. The learning activities were:

   Very Interesting   Dull
   7   6   5   4   3   2   1

3. The scope (coverage) was:

   Adequate   Inadequate
   7   6   5   4   3   2   1

4. The module was:

   Difficult   Easy
   7   6   5   4   3   2   1

5. Overall, I consider this module:

   Excellent   Poor
   7   6   5   4   3   2   1

6. Working as I did (alone/or in a group) was:

   Very Useful   Useless
   7   6   5   4   3   2   1

of a desired skill, or it may consist of a short quiz or self-evaluation. Evaluation during instruction usually has a diagnostic purpose—that is, it is designed to detect and correct learning/ teaching problems and difficulties in the instructional process which may threaten attainment of objectives.

Evaluation is not the end of instruction. It is the starting point of the next and continuing cycle of our systematic ASSURE model for effective use of instructional media.

Close-Up:
Consumer Testing of Educational Products

As the Consumers Union provides objective evaluative information about household products to general consumers, the EPIE (Educational Products Information Exchange) Institute provides educational hardware and software evaluations to the education and training communities.

The EPIE Institute is a nonprofit agency in operation since 1967. Its purpose is to "gather and disseminate descriptive and analytical information—along with empirical information on performance and effects on learners—about instructional materials, equipment, and systems." P. Kenneth Komoski has been executive Director of EPIE since it's founding.

Two quarterly periodicals are published by the EPIE Institute: *EPIE Materials Report* and *EPIE Equipment Report*, in addition to a pair of monthly newsletters: *EPIEgram: Materials* and *EPIEgram: Equipment*. EPIE accepts no advertising or commercial sponsorship of any kind. All income is derived from memberships, subscriptions, workshops, and nonrestrictive grants. Examples of some of the reports issued in recent years are: "Selector's Guide for Elementary School Social Studies Programs," "Selector's Guide for Secondary Language Arts Programs," and "Videocassette Recorders/Players—Laboratory Test Findings."

EPIE involvement in computing increased dramatically in 1982 when it formed a consortium with Consumers Union and several school districts and universities for the purpose of evaluating microcomputer software and hardware. Evaluations are published in a series of booklets, called *Pro/Files*, and a monthly *EPIE MICROgram Newsletter*.

In addition to these publications, the EPIE Institute offers in-service workshops on selection criteria and consultation with individual user agencies. To learn more about the Institute and its services, contact: EPIE Institute, P.O. Box 839, Water Mill, NY 11976.

References

Print References

Allen, Sylvia. *A Manager's Guide to Audiovisuals*. (New York: McGraw-Hill, 1979).

Anderson, R. H. *Selecting and Developing Media for Instruction*. 2d ed. (New York: Van Nostrand Reinhold, 1983).

Bloom, Benjamin S., et al. *Taxonomy of Educational Objectives: Handbook 1: Cognitive Domain*. (New York: David McKay Company, 1956).

Brockhoff, Marna. "Behaviorial Objectives and the English Profession." *English Journal* (September 1979), pp. 55–59.

Brown, James W.; Lewis, Richard B.; and Harcleroad, Fred F. *AV Instruction: Technology, Media, and Methods*. 6th ed. (New York: McGraw-Hill, 1983).

Clark, F. E., and Angert, J. F. "Teacher Commitment to Instructional Design: The Problem of Media Selection and Use." *Educational Technology* (May 1981), pp. 9–15.

Clark, Ruth Colvin, et al. "Training Content Experts to Design Instruction." *Performance and Instruction* (September 1983), pp. 10–15.

Davies, Ivor K. *Objectives in Curriculum Design*. (Maidenhead, England: McGraw-Hill, 1976).

Dewey, John. *Democracy and Education*. (New York: Macmillan, 1916).

Fortune, Jim C., and Hutson, Barbara A. "Does Your Program Work? Strategies for Measuring Change." *Educational Technology* (April 1983), pp. 38–41.

Gerlach, Vernon S., and Ely, Donald P. *Teaching and Media: A Systematic Approach*, 2d ed. (Englewood Cliffs, N.J.: Prentice-Hall, 1980).

Gronlund, Norman E. *Stating Behavioral Objective for Classroom Instruction*. (New York: Macmillan, 1970).

Haladyna, Thomas M., and Roid, Gale H. "Reviewing Criterion-Referenced Test Items." *Educational Technology* (August 1983), pp. 35–38.

Kenny, Michael. *Presenting Yourself: A Kodak How-to Book*. (New York: Wiley, 1982).

Koroluk, Lorne E. "Using Instructional Resource Cards." *Educational Technology* (March 1983), pp. 24–25.

Krathwohl, D. R., et al. *Taxonomy of Educational Objectives: Affective Domain*. (New York: David McKay, 1964).

Kurfiss, J. "Linking Psychological Theory and Instructional Technology." *International Journal of Instructional Media* 9, no. 1 (1981–82), pp. 3–10.

Lanese, Lorena D. "Applying Principles of Learning to Adult Training Programs." *Educational Technology* (March 1983), pp. 15–17.

Mager, Robert F. *Developing Attitude Toward Learning*. 2d ed. (Belmont, Calif.: Fearon-Pitman, 1984).

_____. *Preparing Instructional Objectives*. Revised 2d ed. (Belmont, Calif.: Fearon-Pitman, 1984).

_____, and Pipe, P. *Analyzing Performance Problems*. 2d ed. (Belmont, Calif.: Fearon-Pitman, 1984).

Nadler, Leonard. *Designing Training Programs: The Critical Events Model*. (Reading, Mass.: Addison-Wesley, 1982).

Pett, Dennis, "Effective Presentations." *NSPI Journal* (April 1980), pp. 11–14.

Ragan, Tillman J. "The Oldest Medium." *Educational Technology* (May 1982), pp. 28–29.

Renner, P. *The Instructor's Survival Kit: A Handbook for Teachers of Adults*. (Vancouver, B.C.: Training Associates, Ltd., 1983).

Romiszowski, A. J. *The Selection and Use of Instructional Media*. (London: Kogan Page, 1974).

Timpson, W. M., and Tobin, D. N. *Teaching as Performing: A Guide to Energizing Your Public Presentation*. (Englewood Cliffs, N.J.: Prentice-Hall, 1982).

Tyler, Ralph. "The Construction of Examinations in Botany and Zoology." *Service Studies in Higher Education*. Bureau of Educational Research Monographs, no. 15. (Columbus: Ohio State University, 1932).

Wittich, Walter, and Schuller, Charles F. *Instructional Technology: Its Nature and Use*. 6th ed. (New York: Harper & Row, 1979).

Instructional Development

Briggs, Leslie J., ed. *Instructional Design: Principles and Practices*. (Englewood Cliffs, N.J.: Educational Technology Publications, 1977).

Dick, Walter, and Carey, Lou. *Systematic Design of Instruction*. (New York: Scott Foresman, 1977).

Gagne, Robet M., and Briggs, Leslie J. *Principles of Instructional Design*. (New York: Holt, Rinehart, and Winston, 1979).

Kemp, Jerrold. *Instructional Design: A Plan for Unit and Course Development*. 2d ed. (Belmont, Calif.: Fearon Publishers, 1977).

Romiszowski, A. J. *Designing Instructional Systems*. (New York: Nichols, 1981).

Audiovisual References

Audiovisual Spectrum of the 80's. National Audiovisual Association, 1982. Sound filmstrip.

Instructional Technology: An Introductory Series. Norwood, Mass.: Beacon Films, 1979. Videotapes. Titles: "Principles of Learning," "Media Utilization," and "Designing Instruction."

Non-Verbal Communication. Salenger Educational Media, 1982. 16mm film. 17 minutes.

Novel Techniques for Evaluating Media. Audio Tapes, University of Colorado, 1982. Audiotape.

Patterns for Instruction. Roundtable Films, 1981. One videocassette, 1 leader's guide. 21 minutes.

Possible Projects

2-A. Plan a presentation using the procedures described in this chapter. Your description must include:
1. Description of learners:
    a. General characteristics.
    b. Specific knowledge, skills, and attitudes.
2. Objectives for the presentation.
3. Description of how you selected, modified, or designed instructional materials.
4. Procedures for the use of the materials.
5. Plans for learner involvement and reinforcement.
6. Evaluation procedures.

2-B. Classify a set of objectives into the cognitive, affective, motor skill, or interpersonal skills domains.

2-C. Write at least five performance objectives for a lesson you might actually teach; cover as many domains and levels as possible.

2-D. Select a chapter from a textbook of interest to you and derive a set of performance objectives that you feel are intended by the author.

2-E. Select a lesson you might teach, such as a chapter from a textbook, and develop a set of evaluation instruments (not necessarily all paper-and-pencil test items).

2-F. Use the "Appraisal Checklist: Generalized" to appraise sample audiovisual materials. Submit the materials and your completed checklist to your instructor.

Visual Literacy

Outline

The Concept of Visual Literacy
Visuals as Referents to Meaning
Realism in Visuals
Picture Preferences of Students
Teaching and Learning the Skills of Visual
    Literacy
  Decoding and Learning from Visuals
  Learner Variables in Decoding
  Encoding: Learning from the Making of
    Visuals
Photography for Instruction
  Which Type of 35-mm Camera?
Researching How People Look at Visuals
Designing Literate Visuals
  Arrangement
  Balance
  Color
  Lettering

Objectives

After studying this chapter, you should be able to:

1. Define or describe "visual literacy."
2. State a rationale justifying visual literacy training for all people.
3. Describe the function of a visual in the communication process.
4. Discuss the relationship between the degree of realism in a visual and the amount of learning from it.
5. Describe the relationship between people's preferences in visuals and the amount of learning from these preferred visuals.
6. List and describe *five* levels of decoding a visual.
7. State briefly the effect of developmental age and cultural background on visual literacy.
8. Identify three techniques for teaching visual literacy.
9. Explain the significance of eye-movement research for instruction.
10. Distinguish among 35-mm, Type 126, Type 110, and disc cameras in terms of the advantages and limitations of each.
11. Apply effective composition rules when taking photographs.
12. Prepare a layout for a visual in which the arrangement exhibits dynamism, emphasis, and graphic harmony (unity).
13. Prepare a layout for a visual in which informal balance is employed for greater dynamism.
14. Select a psychologically effective color scheme for an instructional display.
15. Apply guidelines for legibility and color contrast in adding lettering to a visual.

Lexicon

visual literacy
referent
iconic
differentiation
integration
sequencing
f/stop
composition
depth of field
"rule of thirds"

THE CONCEPT OF VISUAL LITERACY

Until recently, the concept of literacy was applied almost exclusively to the ability to read and write. In the mid-1960s, however, we began to hear of a different kind of literacy, "visual literacy." This new concept of literacy came in response to the realization that specific skills are needed to "read" and "write" visual messages, just as they are needed to read and write printed ones.

Visual literacy is the learned ability to *interpret* visual messages accurately and to *create* such messages. Thus interpretation and creation in visual literacy may be said to parallel reading and writing in print literacy.

Visual literacy has also become a "movement" within the field of education. The movement now has its own professional association—the International Visual Literacy Association—with its own periodicals. And educators see a growing number of courses and workshops devoted to visual literacy.

The upsurge of concern for visual literacy has accompanied the almost quantum leap in the production and distribution of visual messages in recent years. The ubiquitous television set comes immediately to mind, but the television set does not stand alone. New technologies of printing and reproduction have also contributed to this flood of visual messages. Illustrations (including graphics) now abound in books, periodicals, and newspapers as never before. We are surrounded by visual messages on billboards and posters. Advertising of all kinds has become increasingly visual. Even T-shirts have gotten into the act!

Obviously, this wealth of visual messages calls for a concerted effort to help people interpret accurately the flood of visual messages. They supply us with information (and misinformation). They influence our attitudes, our opinions, our lives. As recipients of communications, we need to become adept at "reading" visual messages. As managers of learning, we need to teach our students the skills of visual literacy so that they too can "read" visual messages correctly and use them to their educational advantage.

◀ **Figure 3.1**
Visual literacy—the ability to interpret and create visual messages—parallels traditional print literacy—the ability to interpret and create verbal messages in print form.

VISUALS AS REFERENTS TO MEANING

The essence of any communication activity is the transmission of signals intended to evoke meanings in the mind of the recipient. Effective verbal communication depends on the assumption that both sender and receiver have enough of a field of experience in common to ensure that the message is understood as intended. We all know, however, that effective verbal communication is a hit-and-miss proposition. The process all too often fails due to language differences, variations in age and experience, cultural and social differences, etc.

The primary function of a visual as a communication device is to serve as a more concrete *referent* to meaning than the spoken or written word. Words are arbitrary symbols. They don't look or sound (usually) like the thing they represent. Visuals, however, are *iconic*. They normally resemble the thing they represent. As such, they serve as concrete clues to meaning. The more iconic, or pictorial, they are—that is, the closer they come to representing the thing or concept being referred to (the referent)—the more likely they are to prevent breakdown in communication. It is a general principle of human communication that the likelihood of successful communication is increased when a concrete referent is present. Lacking the actual presence of the thing being discussed, the next best referent is a visual representation of it.

▶ **Figure 3.3**
The graphic symbol, cartoon, line drawing, and photograph represent a continuum of realism in visuals.

REALISM IN VISUALS

The various kinds of projected and nonprojected visuals discussed in the chapters that follow differ in many ways: size, composition, color, etc. One fundamental difference among them is their degree of realism. No media form, of course, is totally realistic. The real object or event will always have aspects that cannot be captured pictorially, even in a three-dimensional color motion picture. The various visual media can, however, be arranged from highly abstract to relatively realistic as indicated in Figure 3.3

One might naturally conclude that effective communication is always

▼ **Figure 3.2**

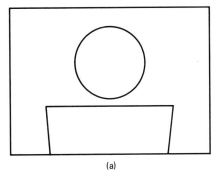
(a)

(b)

(c)

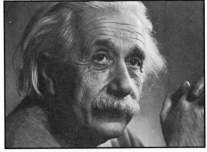
(d)

best served by the use of the most realistic visual available. After all, the more realistic a visual is, the closer it is to the original. This, however, is not necessarily so. There is ample research evidence that under certain circumstances realism can actually interfere with the communication and learning process. For example, the ability to sort out the relevant from the irrelevant in a pictorial representation grows with age and experience. So, for younger children, and for older learners who are encountering an idea for the first time, the wealth of detail found in a realistic visual may increase the likelihood of the learner's being distracted by irrelevant elements of the visual.

As Dwyer notes in his review of visual research. "The arbitrary addition of stimuli in visuals makes it difficult for learners to identify the essential learning cues from among the more realistic background stimuli."* Dwyer concludes that rather than being a simple yes-or-no issue, the amount of realism desired has a curvilinear relationship to learning. That is, either too much or too little realism may affect achievement adversely (Figure 3.4).

---

*Francis M. Dwyer. *Strategies for Improving Visual Learning.* State College, PA.: Learning Services, 1978, p. 33.

▼ Figure 3.4
Visuals tend to become less useful for instruction as they approach the extremes of very abstract or very realistic.

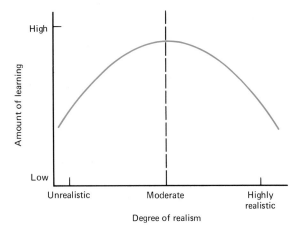

PICTURE PREFERENCES OF STUDENTS

We need to make a distinction between the pictures people *prefer* to look at and those from which they learn the most. People do not necessarily learn best from the kinds of pictures they prefer. For example, research on picture preferences indicates that children in upper elementary school tend to:

1. prefer color to black and white.
2. choose photographs over drawings.
3. choose realism in form and color.
4. (younger children) prefer simple over complex illustrations.
5. (older children) prefer complex over simple illustrations.*

Teachers have to make appropriate choices between *effective* illustrations and *preferred* illustrations.

---

*Barbara Myatt and Juliet Mason Carter. "Picture Preferences of Children and Young Adults." *Educational Communication and Technology* (Spring 1979), p. 47.

TEACHING AND LEARNING THE SKILLS OF VISUAL LITERACY

As with verbal literacy, there is by no means unanimous agreement about what exactly are the skills and subskills of visual literacy, nor about how they can be taught and acquired most effectively. We can, however, safely assume that visual skills mean abilities to decode and encode visuals.

Decoding includes "reading" visuals accurately, understanding and relating the elements of a visual, being able to translate from visual to verbal and vice versa, and appreciating the aesthetics of visuals.

Encoding includes using the tools of visual media to communicate effectively with others and to express one's self through visuals.

Decoding and Learning from Visuals

Decoding of visual stimuli and learning from them require practice. Seeing a visual does not automatically ensure learning from it. The student must be guided toward correct decoding of the visual. One effective technique is to guide your students to see and "read" the visual on various levels. Learning begins with differentiation: students identifying the individual elements of a picture and classifying them into various categories. It then proceeds through integration: students putting the pieces together, relating the whole to their own experiences, drawing inferences, and creating new conceptualizations from what they have learned.

See how this approach might be used with Figure 3.5.

Learner Variables in Decoding

How a learner decodes a visual may be affected by many variables. We have already discussed individual differences and learner variables in

Level of Learning	Sample Questions

A. Differentiation
  1. Observe the basic elements depicted.
  2. Analyze the relevant details of the basic elements and how they are related.
	1. Identify the objects and people in the picture.
	2. How old is each person? What are they wearing? What are they doing? Etc.

B. Integration
  3. Relate to your experience.
 	
  4. Draw inferences.
 	
  5. Create new constructs.
	3. Is this how you bathe? Are the appliances like the ones in your home? Etc.
	4. Is this probably an American home? Is the bath water hot or cold? How did it get into the tub? What will probably happen next? Etc.
	5. Write a story about living in a household like this with people such as these.

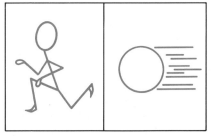

▲ **Figure 3.6**
An active posture, as in the figure on the left, communicates movement more reliably than arbitrary graphic conventions such as speed lines, as in the figure on the right.

▲ **Figure 3.5**
A domestic scene from another culture, in this case from France, can provide practice in "reading" a picture on different levels.

Chapter 2. Two of these variables, however, are particularly germane to education for visual literacy: developmental age and cultural background.

Age.   The findings of developmental psychology suggest that visual literacy is influenced by maturity. Prior to the age of twelve, children tend to interpret visuals section-by-section rather than as a whole. In reporting what they "see" in a picture, they are likely to single out specific elements within the scene. Students who are older, however, tend to summarize the whole scene and report a conclusion about the "meaning" of the picture. Hence, abstract symbols or a series of still pictures whose relationship is not clearly spelled out may fail to communicate as intended with younger viewers.

We have already noted that realistic visuals may distract younger children. However, Dwyer notes, "As a child gets older, he becomes more capable of attending selectively to those features of an instructional presentation that have the greatest potential for enhancing his learning of desired information."*

Developmental age may also influence the interpretation of artistic conventions employed in line drawings: speed lines, foreshortening, size differences to connote distance, etc. For example, research indicates that motion cues are more likely to convey the idea of motion to children who have developed beyond the "preoperational" stage as defined by Piaget (around age seven) than to younger children. It has also been found that an active posture, such as that of a running figure, communicates well with all ages, whereas arbitrary conventions, such as speed lines, do not (Figure 3.6).†

Cultural Background.
In teaching visual literacy, we must keep in mind that decoding visuals may be affected by the viewer's cultural background. Different cultural groups may perceive visual materials in different ways. In a sense, this variable might be subsumed under prior learning experience, as discussed in Chapter 2. But these differences are

*Dwyer, op cit., p. 229.

†Ronald A. Saiet. "Children's Understanding of Implied Motion Cues." (Ph.D. diss., Indiana University, 1978).

more difficult to appraise. Cultural background has a strong influence on learning experience. For example, let us say your visual literacy instruction includes use of visuals depicting scenes typical of the home life and street life of inner-city children. It is almost certain that students who live in such an area will decode these visuals differently than will students whose cultural (and socioeconomic) backgrounds do not include firsthand knowledge of inner-city lifestyles. Similarly, scenes depicting life in the Old West might be interpreted quite differently by an American Indian child than they would be by, say, a black, white, or a Mexican-American child (Figure 3.7).

Cultural differences as a factor in visual literacy may be even more pronounced if the decoder's cultural background is primarily foreign. In one research experiment, for example, a photograph of a bullfighter was seen through one lens of a stereoscopic viewer and a photograph of an American baseball player through the other. A Mexican looking quickly through the viewer reported seeing only a bullfighter. A native of the United States saw only the baseball player. Only after guidance by the researcher did each come to realize that the stereoscopic viewer contained two pictures.*

The iconic connotations of a visual may be affected by cultural differences. For example, a group of U.S. students and students from other countries were shown the two drawings (the Liberty Bell and Justice) illustrated in Figure 3.8. Each student was asked to state in one word what each drawing symbolized. U.S. students invariably responded "liberty" and "justice." Most foreign students, whose cultural backgrounds did not include the historical associations Americans attach to a particular

cracked bell, saw no abstract connotation at all in the drawing at the left. To them it was merely "bell." Many foreign students also failed to find any symbolism in the drawing of the robed woman on the right. Their response was merely "statue." Some, however, interpreted it as symbolizing "equality," a response that indicates a sharing, to some extent, of a common symbolic meaning. Others felt the drawing symbolized a religious concept, "angel," "God," or, in

the case of some Islamic students, "pilgrimage" (to Mecca).

The symbolic connotations of color and color preference may also be culturally biased. Cultures vary widely as to how the color spectrum is perceived. Westerners see red, orange, yellow, green, blue, and violet as more or less distinct and equidistant points along a spectrum. But this kind of color perception is by no means universal. Even less universal are the symbolic values given to vari-

▼ **Figure 3.7**
The cultural biases of a communicator, though unspoken, may be perceived vividly by viewers having a different cultural background.

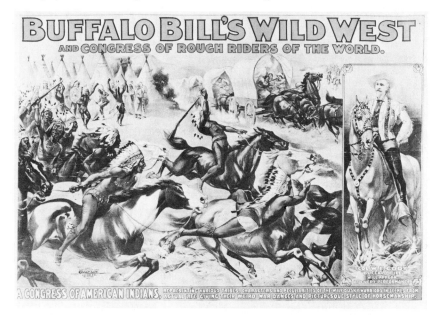

▼ **Figure 3.8**
Symbolic images may be interpreted differently depending on cultural background.

*James W. Bagby. "A Cross-Cultural Study of Perceptual Predominance in Binocular Rivalry." *Journal of Abnormal and Social Psychology,* 54 (1957), pp. 331–334.

ous colors. Black, for example, is generally accepted in Western countries as the color of mourning. In some Eastern countries, however, the color of mourning is white.

Some years ago the federal government, in an attempt to ensure that all the Navahos of the Southwest who wished to vote in a tribal election could do so, color-coded the names of the two candidates on the ballot. This, they felt, would ensure participation in the election by those Navahos who were nonliterate in English. Navahos who could not read the names of the candidates could be instructed beforehand which candidate was represented by which color. Unfortunately, the colors chosen by the government determined the outcome of the election. The loser happened to be assigned a color that to the Navahos symbolized bad luck!

Although you cannot eliminate all misconceptions in decoding arising out of differences in cultural background, you should always be cautious about using visuals that may without prior explanation cause confusion in some of your students.*

---

*A discussion of cultural differences in interpreting visuals and how to deal with them, is found in James Mangan. "Cultural Conventions of Pictorial Representations." *Educational Communication and Technology* (Fall 1978), pp. 245–267.

Encoding: Learning from the Making of Visuals

Visual literacy, as we have noted, includes skill in "writing" as well as in "reading" visuals. Visual literacy programs employ a wide variety of techniques and activities to teach skills in encoding visuals. Some hint of this variety is illustrated in the accompanying "Close-up."

One skill nearly always included in visual education curricula is that of *sequencing*. Reading specialists have long known that the ability to sequence—that is, to arrange ideas in logical order—is an extremely important factor in verbal literacy, especially in the ability to communicate in writing.

Close-Up:
Visual Literacy Education

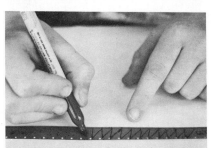

An exemplary visual literacy education program was developed at an elementary school in a Midwestern state. By producing visual materials themselves, the children manipulate colors, shapes, symbols, and spatial relationships. They develop perceptual skills and expressive abilities. Practice in drawing inferences from pictorial sequences leads to better critical viewing skills: distinguishing fantasy, persuasion, and propaganda from facts.

Student visual production projects are integrated into the basic curriculum. For example, experimentation with simple animation by drawing directly onto 16-mm film is a good chance to put math skills to work by calculating the number of frames needed to produce the desired action.

The visual literacy program spans the entire kindergarten through sixth-grade curriculum. More complex projects entail storyboarding and production planning. This contributes to growth of problem-solving ability.

In-service teacher training and parent involvement are integral elements of this program. A major role of parents is to participate in their children's home TV viewing—to encourage wholesome viewing habits and critical viewing skills.

Excessive television viewing has often been cited as contributing to the decline of verbal literacy in today's children. Obviously, television takes away from time that might otherwise be spent in such activities as social play or reading. Specialists, however, are inclined to think the problem goes deeper. Television presents a predigested, orderly stream of imagery. Visual referents to meaning are prominent and are presented in logical order. The message (meaning) is easily grasped even by the passive viewer. In writing, the child practices sequencing skills in order to communicate effectively with others. Television viewing provides for no such incentive or practice.

Youngsters fed a steady diet of television must be made aware that visual sequencing is not always provided. It is a learned skill, just as it is in reading and writing. For this reason, many visual literacy education programs, especially for primary school children, emphasize creative activities in arranging and making visuals. A popular set of instructional materials for this purpose is the *Photo-Story Discovery Kit* series developed in the 1960s by Eastman Kodak Company and now distributed by the Association for Educational Communications and Technology (AECT). Some sample cards from a more recent commercially developed set are shown in the accompanying "Media File."

One of the best ways to develop "encoding" skills is to encourage students to present their message through a pictorial medium. Most older students have access to a camera that takes slides. They should be encouraged to present reports to the class by means of well-thought-through sets of slides. The 35-mm slide is also a medium for students to use to develop their aesthetic talents (Figure 3.9). Portable videotape equipment can be used even by elementary children and is an excellent way of giving students the opportunity to present ideas and events pictorially.

The importance of visual literacy in today's society can scarcely be overstressed. Teachers of young children have a special responsibility to see to it that students do not leave their classrooms visually illiterate. Visual literacy may even be seen as an essential survival skill. As one observer puts it:

There is no easy way to develop visual literacy, but it is as vital to our teaching of the modern media as reading and writing was to print. It may, indeed, be the crucial component of all channels of communication now and in the future. *

———
*Donis A. Dondis. *A Primer of Visual Literacy.* Cambridge, Mass.: MIT Press, 1973.

▲ **Figure 3.9**
The preparation of a slide presentation is an inexpensive and feasible way to demonstrate visual creativity.

PHOTOGRAPHY FOR INSTRUCTION

We assume that if you are concerned with visual education you will have access to a camera and sufficient skill in using it to make your own photographs and slides as aids to teaching visual literacy. However, you should be aware of some of the more recent innovations in camera technology brought about by advancements in electronics and optics. For example, the 35-mm camera has long been associated with professional photography and sophisticated equipment. However, since the late 1970s there are 35-mm cameras readily available that are as small and compact as the "Instamatics" of a few years ago. The model shown in Figure 3.10 is little bigger than the roll of 35-mm film and take-up spool it uses.

In addition, recent advances in miniaturization of microprocessors (computers) have made possible the development of a camera that not only contains apparatus that sets the light controls automatically, but also includes a pair of sensors that measure the distance from your subject, analyze the information, and automatically set the focus (Figure 3.11).

Media File:
Story Sequencing Card Sets

Beginning or remedial readers can improve comprehension and logic skills by arranging story cards in proper sequence. Each set of cards tells a story in comic strip form. Clues to proper sequence are given in the pictures and text on each card. Shape and size of card give additional hints. Five different sets are available, each emphasizing a particular comprehension skill: sequencing, cause and effect, main ideas, drawing conclusions, and predicting outcomes.

Source: Educational Insights

▲ **Figure 3.10**
Miniature 35-mm cameras are available that are little larger than the roll of film and its take-up spool.

▲ **Figure 3.11**
Automatic *focus*, as well as automatic exposure, is available on some 35-mm cameras. On this model the distance sensors are located on either side of the brand name.

▲ **Figure 3.12**
Disc cameras feature an extremely compact film format.

▲ **Figure 3.13**
A 35-mm rangefinder camera.

▲ **Figure 3.14**
A 35-mm single-lens reflex camera.

▲ **Figure 3.15**
Automatic features allow the amateur photographer to concentrate on composing the desired picture.

For strictly amateur picture taking, the 110 and disc format cameras have become widely accepted. Both are very simple to use and their compactness makes them easy to carry around. Some of the features of better 35-mm cameras have been built into the 110 cameras, considerably improving flexibility and image quality. But both formats have limitations that make them less than ideal for instructional purposes. According to tests by Consumers Union, prints made from 110 negatives were judged by a panel of viewers to be significantly poorer in quality than ones made from 35-mm, and prints from disc negatives were poorer than 110 prints.* If your picture taking is limited to snapshots of class activities, the 110 and disc formats are adequate. For instructional purposes, the 126 Instamatic and, preferably, 35-mm are the formats of choice.

Consumer Reports (November 1982), pp. 554–555.

Which Type of 35-mm Camera?

The type of camera you choose depends on the kinds of pictures you find useful for instruction. If you do not take extreme close-ups and do not have use for telephoto and other special lenses, then you may prefer a rangefinder camera for portability, reliability, and simplicity (Figure 3.13). The quality of the image taken by a moderately priced rangefinder camera is very good.

If, however, you need to take extreme close-ups, have a use for a variety of lenses (wide angle, telephoto), and do a lot of copying, then a single lens reflex (SLR) camera is what you want. While it is bulkier and more awkward to use, the SLR is more flexible than a rangefinder type camera (Figure 3.14).

Both types of cameras are available in models with automatic and semiautomatic exposure controls. Before the incorporation of photocells and microprocessors into cameras, even amateur photographers

had to know the relationships between film speed, lens opening (f/stop), and shutter speed. Today's picture taker need learn only a few simple steps from the instruction manual to achieve a proper exposure on the film. Sometimes unusual lighting situations call for modifications of camera-determined settings. A little experience with the camera will guide such modifications. Relieved of the necessity to determine exposure, the photographer can concentrate on composing the picture. (See Figure 3.15.)

Most instructors in education and training use slides far more often than they do prints. Unless you can afford the luxury of two cameras, and the bother of carrying them around, you will probably be better off keeping slide film in your camera. If you find later that you need prints, very satisfactory ones can be made from slides. If very large photographs are required (8″ × 10″ or larger), laser technology can make prints of remarkable quality from slides. On the other hand, while making slides from prints is possible, the results are nowhere near as satisfactory.

Having chosen a camera and type of film, you will find guidelines for taking instructionally useful photos in "How To . . . Compose Better Pictures."

For hints on planning a slide or slide-tape presentation, see "How to . . . Develop a Sound-Slide Presentation" in Chapter 7. Further technical information on photography and suggestions for working with student photography will be found in the items listed in the Audiovisual References at the end of this chapter.

Relationship between Film Speed, Lens Opening, and Shutter Speed When Light on Scene Held Constant		
Film Speed	f/Stop	Shutter Speed
100	f/8	1/250
100	f/11	1/125
200	f/8	1/500
200	f/11	1/250
400	f/8	1/1000
400	f/11	1/500

▲ **Figure 3.16**
All the above exposures are identical if the amount of light on a scene is held constant. If film speed stays the same and the lens opening (and consequently the amount of light) is reduced 50 percent (f/8 to f/11), the shutter speed must be cut in half (and consequently the amount of light increased 100 percent) to maintain the same exposure. If the film speed is increased 100 percent (from 100 to 200) and the exposure is to remain the same, either the lens opening must be reduced 50 percent (f/8 to f/11) or the shutter speed must be increased 100 percent (1/250 to 1/500) to compensate.

RESEARCHING HOW PEOPLE LOOK AT VISUALS

All instructors ought to be concerned about *how* people look at pictorial and graphic materials and what they see in them because these factors determine considerably what people get out of the materials. There are basically two ways to determine what people notice: (1) make inferences based on what individuals have learned from pictorial material, and (2) determine the pattern of eye movements as they look at the same pictorial material. The first is relied on most heavily by the behaviorists, who assume that, regardless of how people look at something, what they can recall is all that matters. Other psychologists, however, while not disputing the importance of response, maintain that if perception is not efficient or effective, communication is not efficient or effective. Furthermore, if the ways in which people view and interpret pictures and graphics can be guided, then people will learn more because attention will be directed to relevant content and not misdirected by irrelevant cues.

As a corollary, we can also say that the more we know about perceptual "sets" of students, the better we will be able to design visuals to take advantage of those sets, or to overcome perceptual obstacles. For example, research on eye movement of people looking at still photographs indicates that viewers tend to look first at the upper left-hand portion of a picture. The picture area in Figure 3.17 has been divided into thirds. The percentage at each intersection represents the frequency with which people first look at that part of the picture area. If upper and lower figures are combined, we see that observers tend to look first at the left-hand side of a picture two out of three times. It has been said that this is a culturally

determined perceptual set because people from Western cultures learn to read and write from left to right. If so, then those people who learn to read from right to left, such as readers of Arabic and Hebrew, might be expected to look first at the upper right area.

This information is relevant not only to your decision about where you should place important content in a picture area, but also to how people will interpret certain graphic representations. How you interpret Figure 3.18 may depend on your cultural background. Do you see the graphic as many branches coming together to form a mainstream, or do you interpret the drawing as a mainstream being separated into many tributaries?

When designing visuals we can take advantage of this research by placing at least the start of our main message where the eye first strikes the area. The research does not mean that *all* important information should be located in the upper left

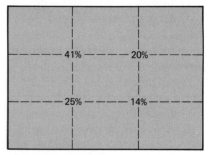

▲ **Figure 3.17**
Research in the United States indicates a tendency for viewers to begin reading a picture beginning in the upper left portion and to focus attention at the intersections suggested by the "rule of thirds."

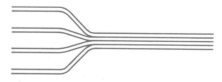

▲ **Figure 3.18**
How does it look to you? Are the branches converging into one trunk or is a main stream diverging into smaller streams?

HOW TO... COMPOSE BETTER PICTURES

Taking better pictures means making the *subject* most prominent and *composing* the elements of the picture.

Subject. How you place your subject in the frame is critical in taking effective pictures.

- Zero in on your real subject. Cut out the unnecessary elements in a picture, even if it's yourself.
- Scale indications are important, particularly if the object being photographed is not common.
- Eliminate distracting backgrounds that may also cause poor exposure; e.g., make sure blinds or draperies are closed if you are shooting toward them.
- If you are photographing a moving object, put more space in front of the object than back of it.
- Be cautious about possible distortion when taking dramatic angle shots. When taking pictures of a building, get as high as you can to reduce the angle of a shot. This is where a telephoto lens comes in handy.
- If a feeling of depth is important place an object in the foreground—but not so that it is distracting.

Composition. In addition to the comments above, the following will help you frame your pictures for a more pleasing appearance and instructional clarity.

- Use the "rule of thirds." Divide a picture area in thirds both vertically and horizontally. The center of interest should be near one of the intersections of the lines.

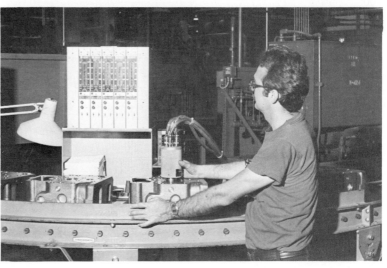

- Avoid splitting a picture exactly in half with a horizontal line. It is tempting to do so in photos that include beach and sea or the horizon.

- When taking a scenery shot or one of a building, framing the scene with something in the foreground often improves the picture in terms of interest and perspective.

- Learn to control depth of field—the region of sharp focus in front of and behind your subject. Shallow depth can often make a subject more dramatic. On the other hand, extreme depth can make scenery more striking. Depth of field can be controlled by varying the distance between you and your subject, the lens used, and the f/stop selected.

You will notice your photographs steadily improving as you master the arrangement of your subject.

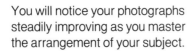

area or even in the left half of a picture. But it does indicate that if the message is required (by the nature of the content) to be in the lower right, the eye of the observer will have to be *led* there. This can be achieved by use of such pictorial elements as color, composition, texture, etc. The important point is that the tendency of people *not* to look first in the lower right must be compensated for if the message is located there.

How people look at moving as well as still images has been the subject of several research studies. Expensive and delicate apparatus is required to track the eye movements of film or television viewers. The apparatus used in a series of studies on eye movement is shown in Figure 3.19.

One of the most important of several findings of such studies concerns eye fixation on relevant cues.* For example, during a science telecast, the eyes of many of the students frequently strayed to an irrelevant microscope visible over a

---

*Egon Guba et al. "Eye Movements and TV-Viewing in Children." *AV Communication Review* 12, no. 4, pp. 386–401.

shoulder of the instructor. In another sequence, the eyes of the viewers watched the lips of the instructor rather than what he was demonstrating. When only his hands and the object were shown on the screen, the viewers fixated on the demonstration. The lesson to be learned here is that distractors must be kept out of the frame of the image.

Another important finding demonstrates the importance of movement. When the picture on the screen is static, viewers "tune out" after a while. When the image is changed by introducing motion or changing the picture, the viewers "tune in" again. Changes in the image help keep students' attention on the visual.

DESIGNING LITERATE VISUALS

Locally produced visuals should contribute to, not detract from, the development of visual literacy. Well-designed visuals—charts, posters, graphics for slides or television, bulletin board displays, and the like—not only promote learning of the subject matter but also provide aesthetic models for students' own creative growth.

When one is creating visuals, important design considerations are best faced by starting with a preliminary sketch of the intended visual. In commercial art this "blueprint" of the finished work is referred to as a rough layout. At the rough layout stage little attention is paid to rendering the artistic details, but careful consideration is given to choosing the right words and images, arranging them for best effect, selecting a lettering style, and choosing colors.

The basic design considerations to keep in mind in planning your rough layout are summarized in the following mnemonic device:

Use	**A**rrangement,
	Balance, and
	Color
to maximize	**D**ynamism
	Emphasis,
	Fidelity, and
	Graphic **H**armony.

Arrangement

The visual and verbal elements of the layout should be arranged in a pattern that captures the viewer's attention and directs it toward the relevant details. The manipulation of line, space, and mass are the designer's primary tools. The arrangement should be clear enough to attract and focus attention quickly. A regular geometric shape (e.g., oval, rectangle, triangle) provides a convenient framework to build on because its

▲ **Figure 3.19**
Current eye movement research is facilitated by automatic monitoring devices that record the movements of the pupils as they scan a picture.

Flashback: THAT INCOMPARABLE MORAVIAN

One day in the late 1640s, Massachusetts's Cotton Mather, ever zealous to make Puritan New England the cultural center of the New World, noted in his journal his disappointment that a certain "incomparable Moravian" was not, after all, to become an American by accepting the presidency of Harvard College:

That brave old man, Johannes Amos Comenius, the fame of whose worth has been trumpeted as far as more than three languages could carry it, was indeed agreed . . . to come over to New England, and illuminate their Colledge and Country, in the quality of a President, which was now become vacant. But the solicitation of the Swedish Ambassador diverting him another way, that incomparable Moravian became not an American.

Who was this Johannes (John) Amos Comenius? Why had his fame as an educator spread all the way from Europe to Mather's Massachusetts Bay Colony?

Comenius was born in 1592 in Moravia (now part of Czechoslovakia). He was a clergyman of the United Brethren, an evangelical Protestant reform sect known popularly today as the Moravian Church. At the time of his consideration for the presidency of Harvard, he was living in exile in Sweden. Indeed, the religious persecutions of the Thirty Years War and its aftermath had forced Comenius to live most of his life away from his native Moravia.

Despite this and the deprivations of war, however, Comenius achieved fame throughout Europe as an educational reformer and writer of innovative textbooks and other educational works. His *Janua Linguarum Reserata* (*The Gate of Language Unlocked*) was a Latin language textbook that taught a basic vocabulary of 8000 carefully selected words and the principal points of Latin grammar. The instructional strategy of the *Janua* consisted of Latin sentences about a variety of topics, forming a kind of encyclopedia of basic human knowledge of that time. Comenius also argued that the teaching of languages should be divided into stages parallel to four human developmental stages. For this insight, Piaget acknowledged Comenius as a forerunner of genetic psychology.[a] The *Janua* became one of the great pedagogical best-sellers of all time and it influenced—wittingly or

IOHAN~AMOS COMENIVS,
MORAVVS. Aº ÆTAT 50: 1642
Croli sculpsit

unwittingly—virtually all later scholars of language instruction.

Comenius was, in addition, one of the earliest and certainly the most renowned champions of what we call visual literacy and visual education. The last fourteen years of his life were spent in Amsterdam. It was from his haven there that Comenius oversaw the publication in 1657 in Nuremberg of the work for which he is today best known and on which he had been working for years: *Orbis Sensualium Pictus* (*The Visible World Pictured*).

Orbis Sensualium Pictus was the first illustrated textbook specifically designed for use by children in an instructional setting. (It was not the first children's picture book. The English printer Caxton, for example, had produced an illustrated edition of Aesop's *Fables* as early as 1484.) The design and illustrations of Comenius's text were expressly intended to enhance learning. The 150 woodcut drawings were learning and teaching devices, not mere decoration. The text embodied application of educational theories espoused by the author over a period of forty years. It is interesting to note, for example, that Comenius chose Aristotle's observa-

---

[a]Jean Piaget. *J. A. Comenius, Pages Choisies.* Paris: UNESCO, 1957.

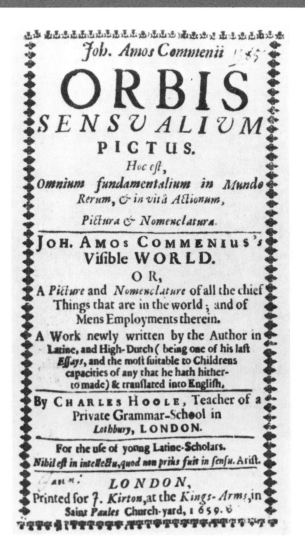

rently considered to be well supported by empirical research:

1. Use of the concept name in contiguity with each presented example facilitates concept learning.
2. An effective combination of iconic and digital signs appears to be a pictorial stimulus and a verbal response, e.g., label or description.
3. The better organized or patterned a message is perceived to be, the more information we can receive (and process) at one time.
4. We can perceive at a glance and hold in immediate memory up to about seven items.
5. The more familiar the message to its audience, the more readily it is perceived.
6. The more mature and/or the more motivated the learner, the greater can be the size of an instructional unit.
7. Simplified examples such as line drawings, cartoons, charts, and diagrams have been found more effective than realistic pictures.
8. Side-by-side arrangement . . . facilitates perception of differences.
9. The sizes of unfamiliar objects are perceived as relative to that of familiar objects.
10. Abstract concepts can be learned from a variety of verbal structures; e.g., . . . sentence contexts, described examples, . . .
11. The active form of sentence structure is easier to learn and use in solving problems than is the passive form.[b]

Examine the sample pages from *Orbis Sensualium Pictus* carefully. Can you find Comenius's application of the above principles in the unit illustrated there?

Even beyond these message design innovations we find that other aspects of *Orbis Sensualium Pictus* foreshadowed techniques that today are closely identified with a "technology of instruction":

1. Instruction is broken down into small units, with attention paid to their proper sequencing. (In fact, the book was intended to be part of a series of texts, increasingly complex in language and treatment of topics.) Although contemporary developers of programmed instruction were probably not consciously aware of Comenius's

tion *Nihil est in intellectu, quod non prius fuit in sensu* (there is nothing in the mind which was not first in the senses), to adorn his title page. The primacy of this principle has been supported increasingly by modern psychological research.

Orbis Sensualium Pictus is truly remarkable for having incorporated, more than three hundred years ago, so many educational concepts that seem thoroughly modern. Underlying Comenius's use of visuals was a theory of perception based on the idea that we learn through our senses and that this learning "imprints" a mental image which leads to understanding. A real object is preferable for this process, but visuals may be used in the learning environment as substitutes for the real thing.

Many principles of modern-day "message design" and "visual literacy" are embodied in Comenius's text, including the following, which are cur-

[b]Malcolm Fleming and W. Howard Levie, *Instructional Message Design.* Englewood Cliffs, N.J.: Educational Technology Publications, 1978, *passim.*

pioneering work, their techniques were fore-shadowed by his.

2. Vocabulary and conceptual level are purposely scaled down to be comprehensible at the primary-school age.

3. Each element in an illustration is numbered and keyed to a description in the text to maintain maximum order and clarity.

4. The typography is designed to provide visual emphasis to key words. The Latin text is set in roman type, with key words in italics. The English text (as with the German in the first edition) is set in black-letter type with roman type for key words. Such a use of multiple type faces was highly innovative at the time.

Although Comenius's work was based on scientific principles far in advance of his time, his philosophy of education was basically humanistic. His greatest hope was to make education a pleasure rather than a burdensome chore. For him, "instructional technology" had but one purpose: to develop the full human potential.

The design and illustrations of *Orbis Sensualium Pictus*, he tells us in his preface, were intended "to entice witty children to it, that they may not conceit a torment to be in the school, but dainty fare. For it is apparent, that children (even from their infancy almost) are delighted with Pictures, and willingly please their eyes with these sights." His pedagogical aim, he tells us, was that children "may be furnished with the knowledge of the prime things that are in the world, by sport and merry pastime."

The idea that learning should be a "merry pastime" rather than a burdensome chore is startlingly modern. Indeed, centuries were to pass before this basic educational philosophy became what it is today—the common wisdom. Aptly called "that incomparable Moravian" in his own time, Johannes Amos Comenius may still be called so in ours.

(104)

LI.

Piscatio.

Fiſhing.

(105)

The Fiſher-man 1. catcheth fiſh,
    either on the ſhoar,
with an Hook, 2.
which hangeth by a line
from the angling-rod,
and on which
the bait ſticketh ;
    or with a
Cleek-Net, 3.
which hanging
on a Pole, 4.
is put into the water ;
    or in a Boat, 5.
with a Trammel-Net 6.
    or with a Weel, 7.
which is laid in
the water by Night.

Piſcator 1.
captat piſces,
    five, in littore,
Hamo, 2.
qui ab *arundine*
filo pendet,
& cui inhæret
Eſca ;
    five
Fundâ, 3.
quæ pendens
Perticâ, 4.
aquæ immittitur ;
    five, in *Cymba,* 5.
Reti, 6.
five *Naſſâ,* 7.
quæ per Noctem
demergitur.

pattern is predictable to most viewers, guiding the eye along. Arrangements that approximate certain letters of the alphabet have the same virtue. The letters C, O, S, Z, L, and T are frequently used as underlying patterns in display layouts. Of course, the words used in the layout, as well as the pictures, form part of the arrangement.

Besides this basic underlying shape, one other principle should guide your arrangement. The "rule of thirds," mentioned earlier in regard to photographic composition, also applies to graphic layout. Elements arranged along any of the one-third dividing lines take on a liveliness, a possibility of movement. The most dominant and dynamic position is at any of the intersections of the one-third dividing lines (especially the upper left intersection). The most stable and least interesting point on the grid is dead center. Obviously, items placed in the corners or around the edges tend to create an unbalanced, uncomfortable feeling.

Having established an overall pattern, you will want to make sure that the important points of your message receive emphasis. The primary rule for this is to restrict the display to a *single idea.* In advertising this is called the "unique selling proposition"—deciding on the one main point you want to emphasize or "sell" with the display. Corollary to this is *eliminating irrelevant cues* from the visual field. Again, as in photographic composition, your goal is to filter out details that might distract the viewer from your message.

Emphasis is also achieved by devices that direct attention one way or another. *Line* is a major contributor to eye movement:

- Horizontal lines give a feeling of stability and rest.
- Vertical lines imply strength; they draw the eye upward; they can be barriers in a visual field since the normal "reading" pattern is horizontal.

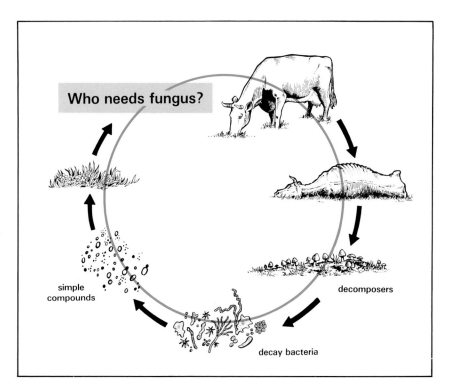

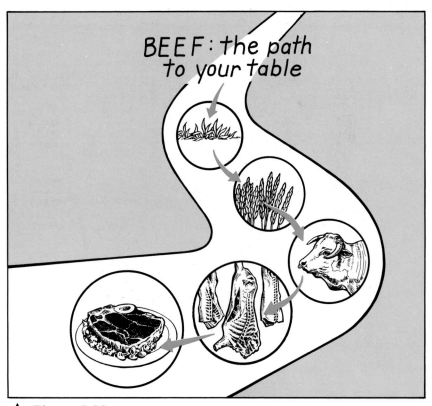

▲ **Figure 3.20**
Arrangement should follow an overall pattern, for example, that of a letter of the alphabet. Figure continues on page 80.

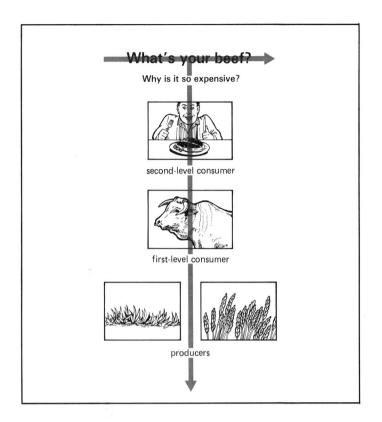

What's your beef?

Why is it so expensive?

second-level consumer

first-level consumer

producers

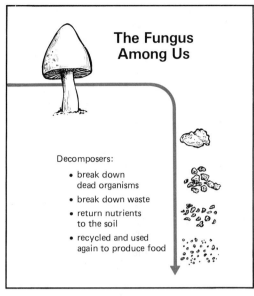

The Fungus Among Us

Decomposers:

- break down dead organisms
- break down waste
- return nutrients to the soil
- recycled and used again to produce food

◄ ▲ **Figure 3.20**
continued

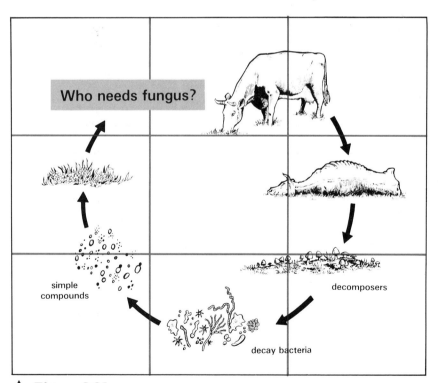

Who needs fungus?

decomposers

simple compounds

decay bacteria

▲ **Figure 3.21**
The "rule of thirds" suggests that the most important elements of your display should be placed near the one-thirds intersections.

▲ **Figure 3.22**
Horizontals suggest tranquility.

▲ **Figure 3.23**
Vertical lines grab our attention against a commonly horizontal background.

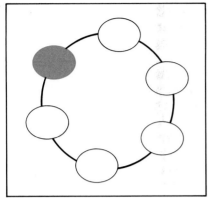

▲ **Figure 3.24**
Contrast in *shape* and in *color* attract attention.

• Diagonal lines strongly imply movement, action, and dynamism. Crossed diagonals give a sense of conflict. Curved lines also give a feeling of motion. These factors help explain the popularity of rounded patterns and S and Z patterns as basic arrangements for visuals.

Contrast, too, lends emphasis. Any element that is different from those surrounding it will tend to stand out. The contrast or variation may be in terms of size, shape, color, or orientation (e.g., one character in a picture is standing on his head). Of course, a device as blatant as an arrow can be used as a pointer to direct the viewer's attention.

Balance
A psychological sense of equilibrium or *balance* is achieved when the "weight" of the elements in a display is equally distributed on each side of the axis—either horizontally, vertically, or both. When the design is repeated on both sides, the balance is symmetrical or *formal.* In most cases, though, for displays that aim to catch the eye and serve an informational purpose the designer aims to achieve an asymmetrical or *informal* balance. Here, there is rough equivalence of weight, but with different elements used on each side; e.g., one large open square on one side,

Balance

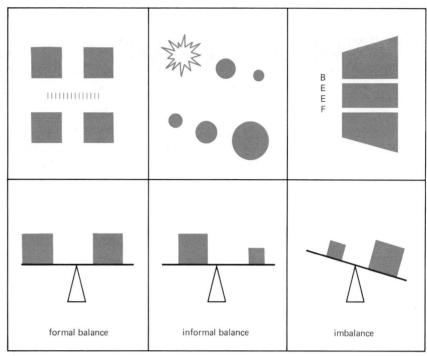

▲ **Figure 3.25**

three small dark circles on the other. Informal balance is preferred because it is more dynamic and more interesting. Arrangements such as the C, S, Z, "lazy T," and the like are frequently used as frameworks because they supply precast molds for asymmetrical layouts. Imbalance—having distinctly disproportionate weight distribution—ordinarily should be avoided as psychologically jarring.

Color
Several functions may be served by the colors selected for use in a visual: (1) to heighten the realism (fidelity) of the image by depicting its actual colors, (2) to point out similarities and differences and to highlight important cues (emphasis), and (3) to create a particular emotional response. The first two functions are self-explanatory, but the third one requires some elaboration.

Artists have long appreciated that blue, green, and violet are perceived as "cool" while red and orange are "hot." It is now understood that there is a physiological basis to this perception in the manner in which colors are focused in the human eye. The warmer colors appear to be approaching the viewer; the cooler colors seem to be receding from us. The designer can capitalize on this tendency by highlighting important cues in red and orange, helping them leap toward the viewer.

Contemporary research in the psychology of motivation reveals that different colors stimulate more than the visual senses. They have "taste": blue is sweet, orange is edible. They have "smell": pink, lavender, yellow, and green smell best. They have other psychological connotations: dark red and brown evoke masculine images of earth, wood, and leather; gold, silver, and black suggest the prestige and status associated with wealth.

So the designer needs to decide whether some emotional connotation will help advance the intended message. Are there some affective objectives consciously being aimed at? What mood should be associated with the idea? How can the sensory appeal of the message be improved with a judicious choice of color?

The key to achieving the desired emotional response is the term *judicious*. Graphic harmony is lost if too many colors are used in the same display; so is emphasis. One way to reduce the busyness of a color scheme is to choose analogous colors—colors that are next to each other on the color wheel, such as violet, red, and red-orange.

Lettering

As mentioned earlier, any words that are incorporated into your visual should be integrated into the arrangement so as to create a unified whole, contributing to graphic harmony. The style of the lettering should be consisten throughout and should harmonize with the "feel" of the display as a whole. If your visual has primarily an aesthetic or motivational objective, one of the more ornate lettering styles might be appropriate; but for straight forward informational or instructional purposes a simple lettering style is recommended. The gothic or roman sans-serif (without serifs) style is most readable. Equally important, these alphabets are easily reproducible by hand lettering.

For best legibility, use lowercase letters, adding capitals only where normally required. Short headlines may be written in all capitals, but phrases of more than a half dozen words and full sentences should follow the rule of lowercase lettering.

The color of the lettering should contrast with the background color both for the sake of simple legibility and for the sake of emphasis, in cases where you want to call particular attention to the verbal message. Legibility depends mainly on difference in darkness between the lettering color and the background color. The chart in Figure 3.27 provides a handy guide to the color combinations that yield suitable background/lettering contrast for nonprojected visuals, such as bulletin board displays.

In the case of projected visuals, legibility often becomes an overriding consideration. For slides or overhead transparencies that contain verbal material, the color combination of lettering and background is critical. Figure 3.28 indicates that the most legible combination is black lettering on a yellow background, followed by green, red, or blue on white ("white" means clear film).

Size of lettering. Displays such as bulletin boards and posters are often meant to be viewed by people situated thrity, forty, or more feet away. In these cases the size of the lettering is crucial in legibility. A common rule of thumb suggests that the lettering be ¼-inch high for each eight feet of viewer distance. This means, for example, that to be legible to a student seated in the last seat of a 35-foot-long classroom the lettering would have to be at least one inch in height. Figure 3.29 illustrates these minimum specifications for lettering height.

Spacing of lettering. The distance between the letters of the individual words must be judged by experience rather than on a mechanical basis. This is because some

▼ **Figure 3.26**

Lettering

Gothic sans-serif

Aa Bb Cc Dd Ee Ff Gg Hh Ii Jj Kk Ll Mm Nn Oo Pp etc.

Roman sans-serif

Aa Bb Cc Dd Ee Ff Gg Hh Ii Jj Kk Ll Mm Nn

▼ **Figure 3.27**
Suggested lettering colors for nonprojected visuals.

Background Color	Lettering Color
White	Red, green, blue, black, brown, purple
Yellow	Red, blue, black, brown, green
Light blue	Yellow, brown, purple, black, dark blue, red
Dark blue	Red, green, yellow, white
Light green	Brown, red, black
Dark green	Black, white, yellow
Light red	Green, black, blue
Dark red	Green, white, yellow
Dark brown	Black, white, yellow, light green
Light brown	Green, dark blue, dark red, black
Light gray	Dark blue, red, black
Black	White, red, light blue, green

(a)
Black on yellow

(b)
Green, red, or blue on white (clear film)

(c)
White (clear film) on blue

(d)
Black on white (clear film)

(e)
Yellow on black

◀ **Figure 3.28**
Suggested lettering colors for projected visuals. Most legible is black on yellow (example a), and so on in descending order of legibility.

letters (e.g., capital A, K, W, and X) are quite irregular in shape compared to the rectangular letters (e.g., capital H, M, N, and S) and circular letters (e.g., capital C, G, O, and Q). When the rectangular letters or circular letters are combined with each other there are rather regular patterns of white space between letters. But when irregular letters are combined with others, the patterns of white space can be very uneven. The only way to even out this potentially distracting unevenness is to space all your letters by "optical spacing." What appears "even" to the eye is spacing in which the total square inches of white space between each letter is equal.

The vertical spacing between lines of printed material is also important for legibility. If the lines are too close together they will tend to blur together at a distance; if they are too far apart they will seem disjointed, not part of the same unit. For a happy medium, the distance between the lines should be slightly less than the average height of the letters. To achieve this, use a ruler to draw lines lightly on your rough layout; separate the lines by about one-and-one-half times the height of your average lowercase letters.

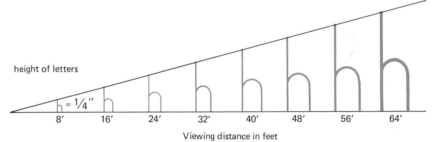
height of letters
h = 1/4"
8' 16' 24' 32' 40' 48' 56' 64'
Viewing distance in feet

▲ **Figure 3.29**
Minimum height of letters for visibility at increasing distances.

GOOD
MINE
LABWORK
"optical spacing"

▲ **Figure 3.30**
Optical spacing: Estimating the spacing between letters is easy when only regular letters are involved (e.g., all round or all rectangular); irregular combinations of letters require estimating spaces that allow equal square inches of white space between each pair of letters.

Text is difficult to read when lines are too close together.

Text seems disconnected when lines are too separated.

Text is most legible when separation is 1½ times average letter height.

▲ **Figure 3.31**

The Literate Litany:
Summary of Visual Design Guidelines

Arrangement
- geometric shapes or letters as frameworks
- "rule of thirds"
- limit to a single main idea
- call attention to key ideas by contrasts

Balance
- use informal balance
- consider lettering as part of the balance equation

Color
- consider psychological overtones
- keep color simple; use analogous colors

Lettering
- harmonize with visual "feel"
- simple style letters
- color contrast with background
- size: ¼ inch per eight feet of viewer distance
- optical spacing

References

Print References

Berwald, Jean-Pierre. "Teaching Foreign Language by Means of Subtitled Visuals." *Foreign Language Annals* (October 1979), pp. 375–378.

Bloomer, Carolyn M. *Principles of Visual Perception.* (New York: Van Nostrand Reinhold, 1976).

Braden, Roberts, and Hortin, John A. "Identifying the Theoretical Foundations of Visual Literacy." *Journal of Visual Verbal Languaging* 2, no. 2 (1983), pp. 37–42, 58–66.

Cassidy, Michael, and Knowlton, James Q. "Visual Literacy: A Failed Metaphor?" *Educational Communications and Technology* (Summer 1983), pp. 68–90.

Debes, John. "Some Foundations for Visual Literacy." *Audiovisual Instruction* (November 1968), pp. 961–964.

Do You See What I Mean? Learning through Charts, Graphs, Maps, and Diagrams. (Dickson, Australia: Curriculum Development Centre, 1980).

Doelker, Christian. "Audio-Video Language—Verbal and Visual Codes." *Educational Media International* (March 1980), pp. 3–4.

Dondis, Donis A. *A Primer of Visual Literacy.* (Cambridge, Mass.: MIT Press, 1973).

Eckhardt, Ned. "The Learning Potential of Picture Taking." *Media and Methods* (January 1977), pp. 48–50, 53.

Feldman, Edmund B. "Visual Literacy." *Journal of Aesthetic Education* (October 1976), pp. 195–200.

Fleming, Malcolm. "Characteristics of Effective Instructional Presentation: What We Know and What We Need to Know." *Educational Technology* (July 1981), pp. 33–38.

Fransecky, Roger B. "Visual Literacy and Teaching the Disadvantaged." *Audiovisual Instruction* (October 1969), pp. 28–31.

Hortin, John A. "A Need for a Theory of Visual Literacy." *Reading Improvement* (in press).

_____. "Visual Literacy and Visual Thinking." In L. J. Ausburn, ed., *Australian Society of Educational Technology National Yearbook, 1981.* (Hawthorn, Australia: ASET, 1982).

_____. "Visual Thinking for Adult Learning." *Adult Education Research Conference Proceedings.* (Lincoln, Nebr.: AERC, in press).

Kemp, Jerrold E. *Planning and Producing Audiovisual Materials.* 4th ed. (New York: Harper & Row, 1980).

Lesser, Michael L. "A Humanist Looks at Visual Literacy." *Audiovisual Instruction* (September 1975), pp. 31–32.

Midgley, Thomas K. "Graphics: Inexpensive, Creative Visuals." *Educational and Industrial Television* (April 1976), pp. 50–51.

Pictures of Ideas: Learning through Visual Comparison and Analogy. (Dickson, Australia: Curriculum Development Centre, 1980).

Simonson, Michael R., and Volker, Roger P. *Media Planning and Production.* (Columbus: Charles E. Merrill, 1984).

Sless, David. *Learning and Visual Communication.* (New York: Wiley, 1981).

Thomas, James L. *Nonprint Production for Students, Teachers, and Media Specialists: A Step-by-Step Guide.* (Littleton, Colo.: Libraries Unlimited, 1982).

Walker, David A. *Understanding Pictures: A Study in the Design of Appropriate Visual Materials for Education in Developing Countries.* (David A. Walker, 1979).

What a Picture! Learning from Photographs. (Dickson, Australia: Curriculum Development Centre, 1981).

Williams, Catherine. *Learning from Pictures.* 2d ed. (Washington, D.C.: AECT, 1968).

Audiovisual References

Audiovisual Production Techniques. Indiana University Audio-Visual Center, 1982. Sound slide series (6 series). Series titles: "Designing Visuals That Communicate" (4 sets); "Fundamentals of Photography" (3 sets); "Lettering for Instructional Materials" (5 sets); "Visuals for Projection" (3 sets); "Audio Principles" (3 sets); "Duplication" (2 sets); and "Electricity and the Media Specialist" (1 set).

Bring Your Message into Focus. Eastman Kodak Co., 1982. Kit (dissolve slide program). 20 minutes.

Experiencing Design. Burbank, Calif.: Encore Visual Education, 1975. Four sound filmstrips, 58 frames, color.

How Does a Picture Mean? Washington, D.C.: Association for Educational Communications and Technology, 1967. Filmstrip, 76 frames, color.

How to Take Better Pictures. Media Tree, 1982. Slide set with audiocassette.

Making Sense Visually. Washington, D.C.: Association for Educational Communications and Technology, 1969. Sound filmstrip, 76 frames, color.

Oh, C. Y. *Introduction to the Preparation of Instructional Materials.* 32 slide-tape sets, textbook, and student manual. Edmonton, Canada: Avent Media, 1980.

The Simple Camera. Washington, D.C.: Association for Educational Communications and Technology. 12 filmstrips, color.

A Visual Fable. Washington, D.C.: Association for Educational Communications and Technology, 1973. Sound filmstrip, with record or cassette. 18 minutes, color.

Possible Projects

3-A. Select a photograph and analyze it using the five levels of learning given in this chapter (page 67).

3-B. Design some instructional activities to improve visual literacy skills of learners you now work with or might in the future. Your description of the lesson should include the materials (or a description of the materials), the role/activities of the students, and the role of the teacher.

3-C. Select a series of photographs from your own collection and criticize them in terms of composition.

3-D. Select a visual or a display and appraise it in terms of intended audience, objectives, arrangement, balance, and color.

3-E. Design a rough layout of a display related to your interests. Appraise it in terms of arrangement, balance, and color.

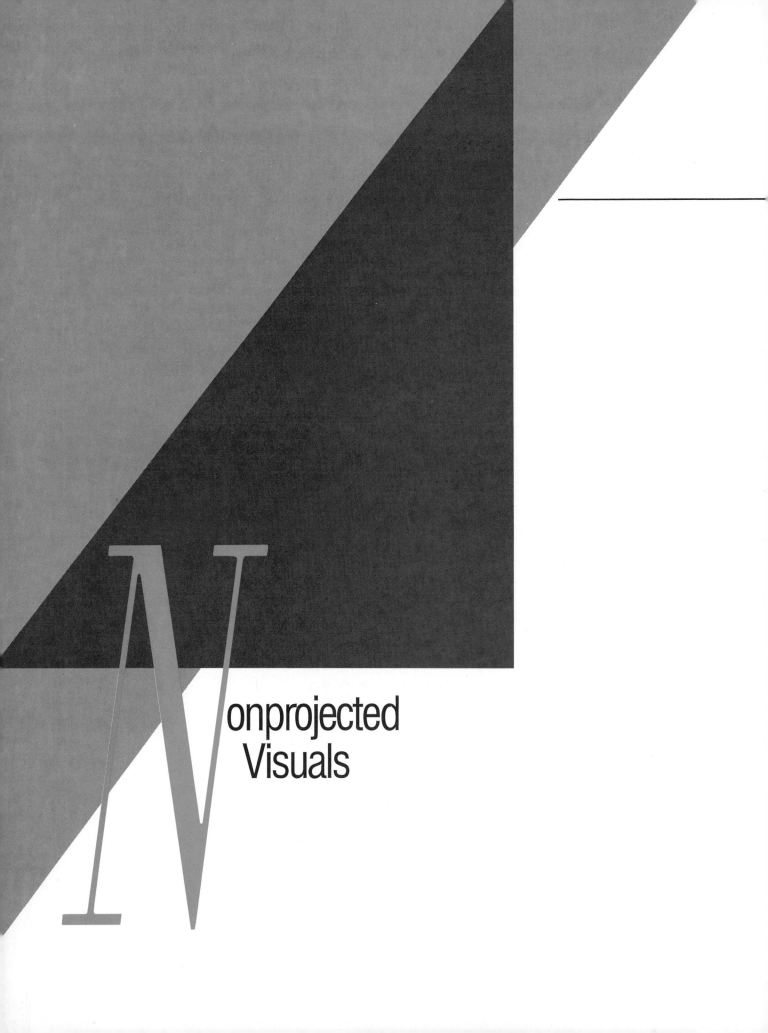

Nonprojected Visuals

Outline

Still Pictures
    Advantages
    Limitations
    Classroom Applications of Still Pictures
Graphic Materials
    Drawings
    Charts
    Graphs
    Posters
    Cartoons
Realia
Models
Preserving Nonprojected Visuals
    Mounting Nonprojected Visuals
    Laminating Nonprojected Visuals
    Filing and Storing Nonprojected
      Visuals
Display Formats
    Chalkboards
    Multipurpose Boards
    Pegboards
    Bulletin Board Displays
    Cloth Boards
    Magnetic Boards
    Flip Charts
    Exhibits
Selection of Nonprojected Visuals,
      Utilization and Learner Response

Objectives

After studying this chapter, you should be able to:

1. List five attributes (advantages and/or limitations) of nonprojected still pictures.
2. Describe at least three classroom applications of still pictures.
3. Identify five criteria for selecting still pictures and apply the "Appraisal Checklist: Still Pictures" to actual materials.
4. Demonstrate at least three techniques (showmanship tips) to enhance the use of still pictures with a group.
5. Define graphic material and describe three types of graphics.
6. Describe five applications for graphic materials in your teaching.
7. Apply the "Appraisal Checklist: Graphic Materials" to actual materials.
8. Define *realia*.
9. Discuss the special advantages of models and/or realia for instruction.
10. Identify two methods of preserving nonprojected visuals and state three reasons for doing so.
11. Compare the advantages/limitations of rubber cement mounting with the advantages/limitations of dry mounting.
12. Describe five formats or devices for displaying visuals.
13. Demonstrate at least three techniques (showmanship tips) for improving your utilization of chalkboards.
14. State a major advantage that cloth boards and magnetic boards have over chalkboards.
15. Demonstrate five techniques (showmanship tips) to enhance the use of flip charts.

Lexicon

study print
graphics
bar graph
line graph
circle graph
pictorial graph
realia
dry mounting
lamination
multipurpose board
flip chart

Nonprojected visuals are, simply, visuals that do not require projection viewing. Because they are so abundant and easily obtainable, they are likely to be used more extensively in the classroom than any other visual medium of instruction. Indeed, nonprojected visuals are so common in our environment that educators are sometimes inclined to underestimate their importance in learning. But in some situations (e.g., due to lack of electricity, isolation, low budget, very small group size), they may be the *sole* source of audiovisual stimuli.

For the purpose of discussion, let us divide nonprojected visuals into four broad categories: (1) still pictures, (2) graphics, (3) realia, and (4) models. After we have discussed still pictures, graphics, and models we will turn our attention to various ways of displaying them in the instructional setting.

▲ **Figure 4.1**
Varied types of nonprojected visuals.

STILL PICTURES

Still pictures are *photographic (or photograph-like) representations of people, places, and things.* The still pictures most commonly used in instruction are photographs, illustrations from books, periodicals, catalogs, etc., and *study prints (oversized illustrations* commercially prepared to accompany specific instructional units).

Advantages
Nonprojected still pictures can translate abstract ideas into a more realistic format. They allow instruction to move from the level of verbal symbols in Dale's Cone of Experience to the more concrete level of still pictures.

They are readily available in books (including textbooks), magazines, newspapers, catalogs, and calendars. In addition, you may purchase large study prints for use with groups of students from educational supply

▼ **Figure 4.2**
A study print with flash cards showing details of the larger picture.

▲ **Figure 4.3**
A series of still pictures can approximate the impression of a motion picture sequence.

companies or you may obtain them from your media center or library.

Still pictures are easy to use since they do not require any equipment. They are relatively inexpensive. Many can be obtained at little or no cost. Still pictures can be used in many ways at all levels of instruction and in all disciplines.

Limitations

Some photographs are simply too small for use before a group. It is possible to enlarge any picture, but that can be an expensive process; however, the opaque projector (described in Chapter 5) can be used to project an enlarged image before a group.

Still pictures are two-dimensional. The lack of three-dimensionality in a picture can be compensated for by providing a series of pictures of the same object or scene from several different angles or positions.

They do not show motion. However, a series of sequential still pictures can suggest motion (Figure 4.3).

Classroom Applications of Still Pictures

There are numerous applications of nonprojected still pictures. Photographs may be used in a variety of ways. Teacher-made and/or student-made photographs may be used to illustrate and to help teach specific lesson topics. Photographs of local architecture, for example, can illustrate a unit on architectural styles. (In this case, the students' skill in "reading" a visual could be reinforced by the instructor's pointing out that merely looking at the buildings in our environment is not the same as really "seeing" them.) Photographs taken on field trips can be excellent sources of information for classroom follow-up activities.

Students can and should understand that textbook pictures are not decorations, but are intended to be study aids and should be used as such. Students should be encouraged to "read" them as aids to learning. Skill in decoding textbook pictures may also be included in instructional objectives to motivate the learners to use them for study purposes. The quality and quantity of illustrations are, of course, important

factors in textbook choice. See "Appraisal Checklist: Still Pictures," p. 90. Pictures from newspapers and periodicals may be used in similar ways.

Study prints—photographic enlargements printed in a durable form for individual use—also have many applications in the instructional setting. They are especially helpful in the study of processes—the production of iron or paper, for example, or the operation of the internal combustion engine. They are also very useful in teaching the social sciences. In geography they may help illustrate relationships between peoples and their environments that, because of space limitations, could not easily be depicted in textbook pictures.

All types of nonprojected still pictures may be used in testing and evaluation. They are particularly helpful with objectives requiring identification of people, places, or things.

Nonprojected still pictures may also be used to stimulate creative expression such as the telling or writing of stories or the composing of poetry.

Appraisal Checklist: Still Pictures

Title or content of picture(s)_____

Producer/distributor (if known)_____

Series (if applicable)_____

Date (if known)_____

Objectives (stated or implied):

Brief description:

Entry capabilities required:
—Prior subject matter knowledge
—Visual skills
—Other

Rating	High		Medium		Low
Relevance to your objectives	☐	☐	☐	☐	☐
Authenticity and accuracy of the picture	☐	☐	☐	☐	☐
Simplicity (uncluttered by irrelevant or distracting material)	☐	☐	☐	☐	☐
Timeliness (out-of-date elements)	☐	☐	☐	☐	☐
Scale (a familiar object can provide scale for unfamiliar objects)	☐	☐	☐	☐	☐
Technical quality (exposure, contrast, focus, detail, colors)	☐	☐	☐	☐	☐
Size (adequate visibility for your intended audience)	☐	☐	☐	☐	☐

Strong points:

Weak points:

Reviewer_____

Position_____

Recommended action_____ Date_____

GRAPHIC MATERIALS

Our second major category of non-projected visuals is graphic materials, often referred to simply as "graphics." *Graphics are nonphotographic, two-dimensional materials designed specifically to communicate a message* to the viewer. They often include verbal as well as symbolic visual cues.

As a group, graphics demand special caution in use by instructors. Because the images are visually symbolic rather than fully representational, they leave more room for viewers to misinterpret the intended meaning. This phenomenon was discussed in Chapter 3. As one example, research on newspaper readers' interpretations of editorial cartoons indicates that a large proportion of viewers may draw conclusions that are the *opposite* of what the artist intended. Psychologists find that people tend to "project" their own

Close-Up: Using Still Pictures

In a psychology course, for the unit on experimental methods, the students use the photographs in their textbook as study aids, since they are excellent illustrations of the mazes and other experimental apparatuses described in the text. During the class, the teacher draws attention to the photographs in the text and later asks various students to relate the pictures to the corresponding printed material. The teacher has also written the objectives for the course in a way that requires students to use the illustrations during their study.

Study prints are used by a fifth-grade teacher to show techniques for vegetable gardening. The teacher works with the children in small groups. While some of the students are working on other activities in the classroom and in the media center, the teacher gathers ten to twelve students around her to discuss the study prints. Her objective is for the students to be able to "describe the proper method of spacing tomato plants." The students are shown the study prints and then describe what they see in terms of recommended procedures for measuring, planting, etc.

AV SHOWMANSHIP—STILL PICTURES

Use large pictures that everyone can see simultaneously. To hold pictures steady when showing them to a group, rest them against a desk or table or put them on an easel. (If the pictures are not large enough for all to see, use one of the projection techniques described in Chapter 5.)

Limit the number of pictures used in a given period of time. It is better to use a few visuals well than to overwhelm your audience with an overabundance of underexplained pictures.

Except for purposes of comparison and contrast, use just one picture at a time. Lay one picture flat down on your desk or table before going on to the next. Don't keep them in view on the chalk tray, for example. If you do, your students' attention may be on Picture 1, 2, or 3 while you are trying to get them to attend to your discussion of Picture 4.

Keep your audience's attention and help them learn from the picture by asking direct questions about it: "Why did the architect use brick in this part of the building?" "Why are the workers in this factory wearing protective clothing?"

When still pictures are displayed for nonsupervised perusal by the students, try to provide written cues to help highlight important information contained in the pictures. Another technique is to display questions and answers pertaining to the pictures alongside each. Cover the answers with flaps of paper. Have each student immediately check his or her own response for accuracy.

▲ **Figure 4.4**
Viewers tend to project subconsciously their own meanings into ambiguous images.

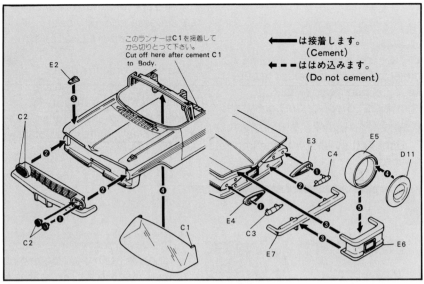

▲ **Figure 4.5**
A diagram for assembling a scale-model plastic automobile. The use of visual symbols reduces dramatically the need for words.

hopes, fears, and preconceptions into images or verbal messages that are ambiguous. This is the basis of the Rorschach or "inkblot" diagnostic test (Figure 4.4). The younger or less visually literate the audience, the more guidance the instructor will have to provide to ensure that the intended message is conveyed.

Let us explore five types of graphics commonly found in the classroom situation: drawings (including sketches and diagrams), charts, graphs, posters, and cartoons.

Drawings

Drawings, sketches, and diagrams *employ graphic arrangement of lines to represent persons, places, things, and concepts.* Drawings are, in general, more finished and representational than sketches, which are likely to lack detail. Stick figures, for example, may be said to be sketches. Diagrams are usually intended to show relationships or to help explain processes, such as how something works or how it is constructed (Figure 4.5).

Use of drawings may be similar to use of photographic still pictures. Drawings are readily found in textbooks and other classroom materials. They can be used in all phases of instruction, from introduction of the topic through evaluation. Because they are likely to be less detailed and more to the instructional point than photographic materials, they are easily understood by students of all ages.

Teacher-made drawings can be very effective teaching and learning devices. They can be drawn on the chalkboard (or some other appropriate surface) to coincide with specific aspects of the instructional unit. They can also be used as substitutes for or adjuncts to still pictures. For example, stick figures can be quickly and easily drawn to show motion in an otherwise static representation.

Charts

Charts are *graphic representations of abstract relationships such as chronologies, quantities, and hierarchies.* They appear frequently in textbooks and training manuals as tables and flowcharts. They also are published as wall charts for group viewing in

the form of organization charts, classification charts (e.g., periodic table), and time lines.

A chart should have a clear, well-defined instructional purpose. In general (especially for younger students), it should express only one major concept or configuration of concepts. If you are developing your own charts, be sure they contain the minimum of visual and verbal information needed for understanding. A cluttered chart is a confusing chart. If you have a lot of information to convey, develop a series of simple charts rather than a single complex one. The most important thing to keep in mind is "keep it simple."

Types of Charts

Organization charts show the relationship or "chain of command" in an organization such as a company, corporation, civic group, or government department. Usually they deal with the interrelationship of personnel or departments.

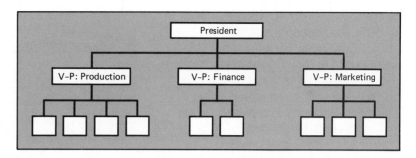

Classification charts are similar to organization charts, but are used chiefly to classify or categorize objects, events, or species. A common type of classification chart is one showing the taxonomy of animals and plants according to natural characteristics.

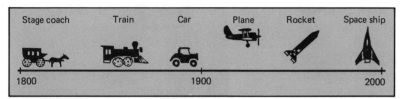

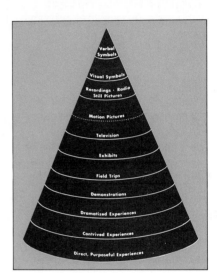

Time lines illustrate chronological relationships between events. They are most often used to show time relationships of historical events or the relationship of famous people and these events. Pictures or drawings can be added to the time line to illustrate important concepts. Time lines are very helpful for summarizing the time sequence of a series of events.

Flowcharts (or process charts) show a sequence, a procedure, or, as the name implies, the "flow" of a process. Flowcharts are usually drawn horizontally and show how different activities, ingredients, or procedures merge into a whole.

Tabular charts (or tables) contain numerical information or data. They are also convenient for showing time information when the data are presented in columns, as in timetables for railroads and airlines.

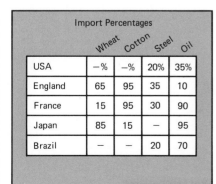

Import Percentages				
	Wheat	Cotton	Steel	Oil
USA	—%	—%	20%	35%
England	65	95	35	10
France	15	95	30	90
Japan	85	15	—	95
Brazil	—	—	20	70

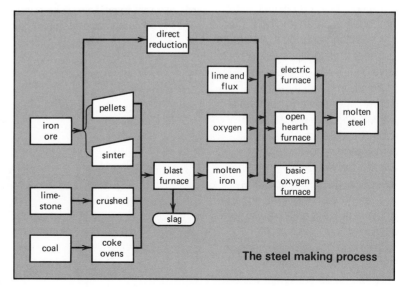

The steel making process

A well-designed chart should communicate its message primarily through the visual channel. The verbal material should supplement the visual, not the reverse. For an example see Figure 4.6. This chart was developed for use by elementary school teachers in Arabic-language-speaking countries. Although you probably cannot translate the verbal descriptions you might want to imagine yourself trying to teach with this chart. How much do the visuals alone communicate?

Graphs

Graphs provide a *visual representation of numerical data*. They also illustrate *relationships between units of the data and trends in the data.* Many tabular charts can be converted into graphs, as shown in Figure 4.7. Data can generally be interpreted more quickly in graph form than in tabular form. Graphs are also more visually interesting. There are four major types of graphs: bar, pictorial, circle, and line. The type you choose to use will largely depend on the complexity of the information you wish to present and the graph interpretation skills of your audience.

Posters

Posters incorporate *visual combination of lines, color, and words*, and are intended to catch and hold attention at least long enough to *communicate a brief message*, usually a persuasive one. To be effective, posters must be colorful and dynamic. They must grab attention and communicate their message quickly. One drawback in using posters is that their message is quickly blunted by familiarity. Consequently, they should not be left on display for too long a time. Commercial billboards are an example of posters on a very large scale.

Posters can be used effectively in numerous learning situations. They can stimulate interest in a new topic, a special class, or a school event.

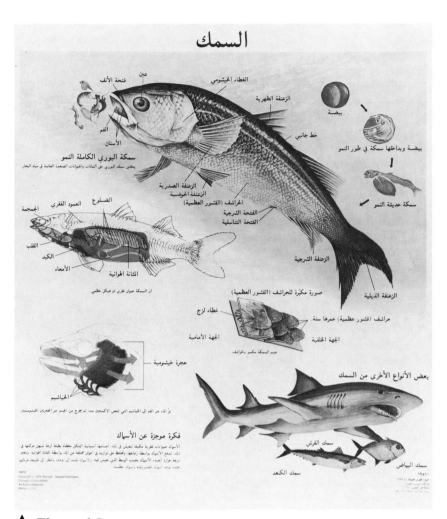

▲ **Figure 4.6**
A chart designed for use in Arabic-speaking countries.

▼ **Figure 4.7**
A line graph can make a table of data easier to interpret.

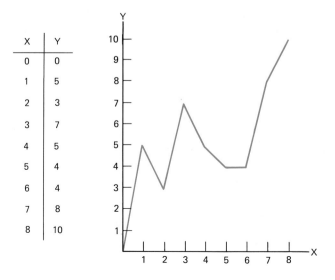

X	Y
0	0
1	5
2	3
3	7
4	5
5	4
6	4
7	8
8	10

They may be employed for motivation—luring students to a school meeting, for example, or to the media center, or encouraging them to read more. In industrial education courses, science laboratories, and other situations where danger may be involved, posters can be used to remind students of safety factors ("Always wear your safety glasses"). Posters can be used to promote good health practices ("Don't Smoke!"). A very effective teaching and learning technique is to have students design posters as part of a class project—during fire prevention week or dental health month, etc.

Posters may be obtained from a variety of sources. Commercial poster companies publish catalogs containing pictures of their wares. Other companies and advertising organizations have posters available without cost to teachers for use in their classrooms. Two of the most

Types of Graphs

Bar graphs are easy to read and can be used with elementary-age students. The height of the bar is the measure of the quantity being represented. The width of all bars should be the same to avoid confusion. A single bar can be divided to show parts of a whole. It is best to limit the quantities being compared to eight or less; otherwise the graph becomes cluttered and confusing. The bar graph, a one-scale graph, is particularly appropriate for comparing similar items at different times or different items at the same time; for example, the height of one plant over time or the heights of several students at any given time. The bar graph shows variation in only one dimension.

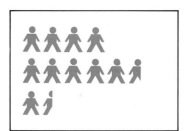

Pictorial graphs are an alternate form of the bar graph, in which a series of simple drawings is used to represent the value. Pictorial graphs are visually interesting and appeal to a wide audience, especially young students. However, they are slightly more difficult to read than bar graphs. Since pictorial symbols are used to represent a specific quantity, partial symbols are used to depict fractional quantities. To help avoid confusion in such cases, print values below or to the right of each line of figures.

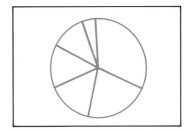

Circle (or pie) graphs are relatively easy to interpret. In this type of graph, a circle or "pie" is divided into segments, each representing a part or percentage of the whole. One typical use of the circle graph is to depict tax-dollar allocations. The combined segments of a circle graph should, of course, equal 100 percent. Areas of special interest may be shown separately from the others, just as a piece of pie can be illustrated separately from a whole pie.

Line graphs are the most precise and complex of all graphs. Line graphs are based on two scales at right angles. Each point has a value on the vertical scale and a value on the horizontal scale. Lines (or curves) are drawn to connect the points. Line graphs show variations in *two* dimensions—how two or more groups of quantities changed over time. For example, a graph can show the relation between pressure and temperature when the volume of a gas is held constant. Since line graphs are precise, they are very useful in plotting trends. They can also help simplify a mass of complex information.

◀ **Figure 4.8**
Posters can be a medium for students to express their own messages.

common sources of posters are airlines and travel agencies. Movie posters and political posters are also available. Stores and supermarkets are often willing to give posters (and other display materials) to teachers when they are no longer needed. And, of course, you can make your own posters.

Appendix B gives further guidance on obtaining free and inexpensive materials.

Cartoons

Cartoons, line drawings that are rough caricatures of real people and events, are perhaps the most popular and familiar graphic format. They appear in a wide variety of print media—newspapers, periodicals, textbooks, etc.—and range from comic strips intended primarily to entertain to drawings intended to make important social or political comments. Humor and satire are mainstays of the cartoonist's skill.

Cartoons are easily and quickly read and appeal to children and adults alike. The best of them contain wisdom as well as wit. As such, they can often be used by the teacher to make or reinforce a point of instruction. As discussed earlier, appreciation and interpretation may depend on the experience and sophistication of the viewer. Research studies consistently have found that people tend to project their own feelings and prejudices into editorial cartoons. For example, a politician shown slinging mud at his opponent may be seen by supporters as a hero punishing the "wicked". Further, since they usually refer to contemporary characters dealing with current issues and events, editorial cartoons quickly become dated. Today's immediately recognized caricature becomes tomorrow's nonentity. Be sure that the cartoons you use for instructional purposes are within the experiential and intellectual range of your students.

Appraisal Checklist: Graphic Materials

Title or Content of Graphic:_____

Producer/distributor (if known)_____

Series (if applicable)_____

Date (if known)_____

Objectives (stated or implied):

Format

- [ ] Drawing
- [ ] Chart
- [ ] Graph
- [ ] Poster
- [ ] Cartoon

Brief description:

Entry capabilities required:
—Prior subject matter knowledge
—Visual skills
—Other

Rating	High		Medium		Low
Simplicity (few elements or ideas to catch and hold the attention of the viewer)	☐	☐	☐	☐	☐
One main idea (to provide unity)	☐	☐	☐	☐	☐
Relevance to curricular objectives	☐	☐	☐	☐	☐
Color (attracts and holds attention)	☐	☐	☐	☐	☐
Verbal information (reinforces the ideas presented in the visual)	☐	☐	☐	☐	☐
Learner comprehension	☐	☐	☐	☐	☐
Legibility for classroom use	☐	☐	☐	☐	☐

Strong points:

Weak points:

Reviewer_____

Position_____

Recommended action_____   Date_____

Close-Up:
Getting Them Involved with Graphics

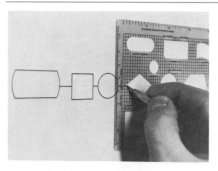

Use of Charts.   As part of a training program for production supervisors, charts are used to illustrate graphically the various steps in the production process. The students develop charting skills as the program progresses. Each trainee creates a flowchart to represent production within a company. Charts are developed to represent raw material and labor inputs and to compare them with plant outputs. Production outputs over time are graphed on line graphs. The data on individually prepared graphs are then compared with national averages over the same time period.

Use of Cartoons.   A high school social studies class has its learning reinforced by political cartoons. The teacher has collected hundreds of such cartoons from various sources over the years and uses relevant cartoons to illustrate key points in the lessons. To get the students even more involved, the teacher has them draw their own cartoons relating to historical and political events being studied. The best of these student-drawn cartoons are saved for use with future classes.

REALIA

Realia—real things: objects such as coins, tools, artifacts, plants, animals, etc.—are not always thought of as visuals, since the term *visual* implies representation of an object rather than the object itself. Nevertheless, this category includes some of the most accessible, intriguing, and involving materials in educational use. The gerbils that draw a crowd in the kindergarten, the terrarium that introduces middle schoolers to the concept of ecology, the collection of Revolutionary era coins, the frogs dissected in the college biology laboratory, the real baby being bathed in the parenting class . . . just a few examples of the potentials of realia for elucidating the obscure and stimulating the imagination.

▼ **Figure 4.9**
There is no substitute for the real thing for learning some complex tasks.

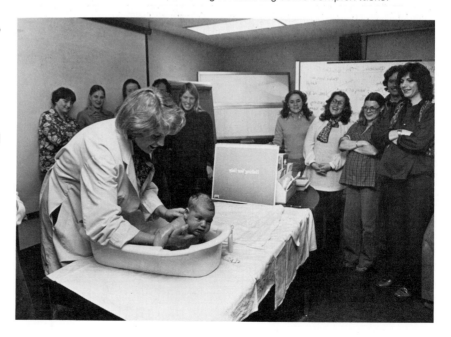

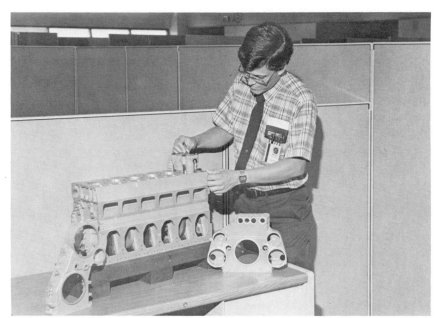

◄ Figure 4.10
A cutaway of a machine reveals the hidden mechanisms.

▼ Figure 4.11
Cultural artifacts come to life when presented in a well designed exhibit.

Being, by definition, concrete objects, realia are the instructional aids most closely associated with the bottom of Dale's Cone of Experience: direct purposeful experience (see Chapter 1). As such, they are ideal media for introducing learners to a new subject. Used as part of concept learning, they supply flesh-and-blood mental images, giving meaning to otherwise merely abstract words.

Realia may be used as is or modified to enhance instructional utility. Examples of modification include:

- Cutaways—devices such as machines with one wall cut away to allow close observation of the inner workings.
- Specimens—actual plants, animals, or parts thereof preserved for convenient inspection.
- Realia exhibits—collections of artifacts, often of a scientific or historical nature, brought together with printed information to illustrate a point.

Besides their obvious virtues as means of presenting information, raising questions, and giving hands-on learning experiences, realia also can play a valuable role in the evaluation phase of instruction. Real objects can be displayed in a central location with learners directed to identify them, classify them, describe their functioning, discuss their utility, or compare and contrast them. Such a testing situation emphasizes the real-world application of the topic of study, aids transfer-of-training, and helps transcend the merely verbal level of learning.

MODELS

Models are *three-dimensional representations of a real thing*. A model may be larger, smaller, or the same size as the object it represents. It may be complete in detail or simplified for instructional purposes. Indeed, models may provide learning experiences real things cannot provide. Important details can, for example, be accented by color. Some models can be disassembled to provide interior views not possible with the real thing.

▶ **Figure 4.12**
An anatomical model, being three-dimensional, is a more concrete referent than a photograph, drawing, or even a motion picture.

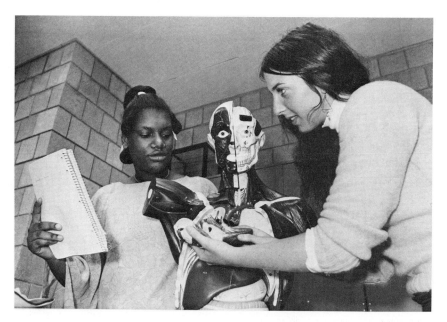

Models of almost anything, from insects to airplanes, can be purchased for classroom use. A wide variety of plastic model kits are also available for assembly by you and/or your students. Assembly itself can be instructional. Classroom construction of plastic model kits appeals to children of all ages (and, indeed, to adults) and can stimulate inquiry and discovery. Assembly activites help sharpen both cognitive and psychomotor skills.

Familiarize yourself with your model before using it in classroom instruction. Practice your presentation. If your model is a working one, be sure you know just how it works. Be sure your audience does not get the wrong impression of the size, shape, or color of the real object if the model differs from it in these respects. Whenever feasible, encourage your students to handle and manipulate the model. It is a good idea to store models out of sight when not being used for instruction. Left standing around, they are likely to take students' attention from other classroom activities.

Mock-ups—simplified representations of complex devices or processes—are widely prevalent in industrial training. By highlighting essential elements and eliminating distracting details, mock-ups clarify the complex. They are sometimes constructed as working models to illustrate the basic operations of a real device. This allows individuals or small groups to manipulate the mock-up at their own convenience, working with the concept until they comprehend it. The most sophisticated type of mock-up, the simulator, is discussed in Chapter 12.

▼ **Figure 4.13**
This mock-up of an engine provides the trainee with a full-scale working model with only distracting details deleted.

PRESERVING NONPROJECTED VISUALS

One drawback in using nonprojected visuals in the classroom is that they are easily soiled or otherwise damaged as they are passed from student to student. Repeated display, storage, and retrieval can also add to wear and tear. Mounting and laminating are the two most effective preservation techniques and they can contribute to the instructional effectiveness of nonprojected visuals.

Mounting Nonprojected Visuals

Mount nonprojected visuals on construction paper, cardboard, or other such materials of sufficient durability.

The color of the mounting material should not draw attention away from the visual. It is generally a good idea to use pastel or neutral tones rather than brilliant or primary colors. Using one of the minor colors in the visual as the color for the mounting can provide harmony. The total effect of your mounting should be neat and pleasing to the eye. Borders, for example, should be evenly cut, with side borders of equal width and the bottom border slightly wider than the top.

A variety of glues, cements, and pastes are available for mounting purposes. When used according to directions, almost all of them are effective. Some white glues, however, are likely to cause wrinkles in the picture when the adhesive dries, especially if used full strength. If you run into this problem, dilute the glue; for example, use four parts Elmer's Glue to one part of water. Cover the entire back of the visual evenly with the adhesive before placing it on the mounting board. If excess adhesive seeps out around the edges, wipe it off with a damp cloth or sponge.

Glue sticks, marketed under names such as Stix-A-Lot and Pritt, may be used in place of liquid glues. They have the advantage of not running out around the edges of the ma-

▲ **Figure 4.14**
Glue sticks are convenient and effective for doing paste-ups and mounting pictures.

terial. Rubber cement can eventually damage and discolor photographs. Glue sticks are less likely to do so (Figure 4.14).

Rubber Cement Mounting.
One of the most commonly used adhesives for mounting purposes is rubber cement. It is designed specifically for use with

paper products. It is easy to use and less messy than many other liquid glues. Excess cement can easily be wiped away, and it is inexpensive. Rubber cement does, however, have two disadvantages. When the container is left uncovered for any length of time, the adhesive tends to dry out and thicken. Periodic doses of thinner (available commercially) may be necessary to keep the cement serviceable. A second disadvantage is

HOW TO...MOUNT PICTURES USING RUBBER CEMENT

- Cut picture to size. Edges should be straight and corners square.

- Mark location of picture on mounting board with pencil to assist putting picture in correct position

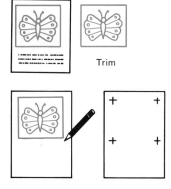

Trim

(Continued)

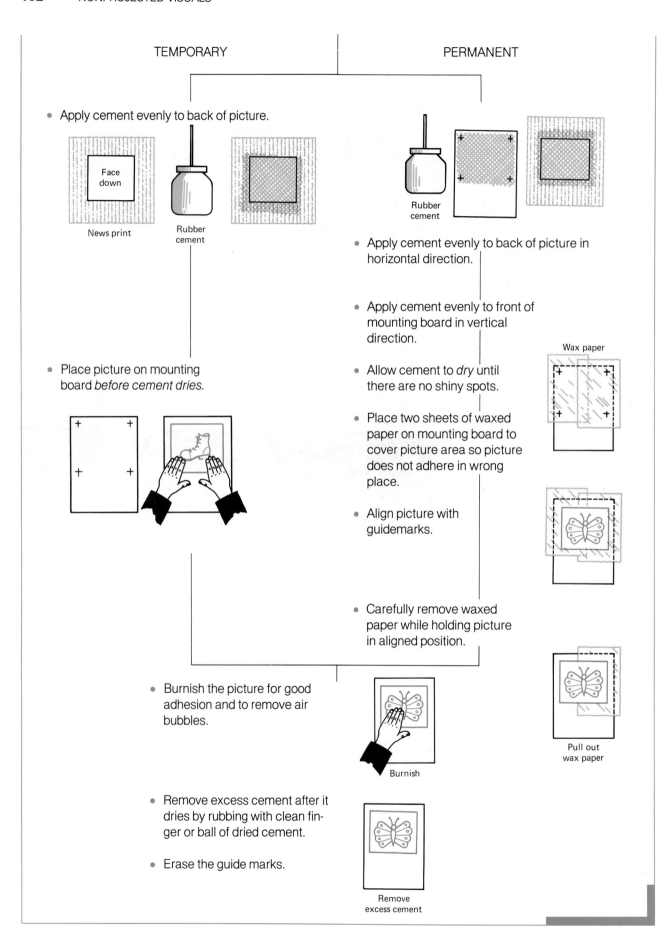

TEMPORARY

- Apply cement evenly to back of picture.

News print · Rubber cement

- Place picture on mounting board *before cement dries.*

- Burnish the picture for good adhesion and to remove air bubbles.

- Remove excess cement after it dries by rubbing with clean finger or ball of dried cement.

- Erase the guide marks.

PERMANENT

Rubber cement

- Apply cement evenly to back of picture in horizontal direction.

- Apply cement evenly to front of mounting board in vertical direction.

- Allow cement to *dry* until there are no shiny spots.

- Place two sheets of waxed paper on mounting board to cover picture area so picture does not adhere in wrong place.

- Align picture with guidemarks.

- Carefully remove waxed paper while holding picture in aligned position.

Wax paper

Burnish

Pull out wax paper

Remove excess cement

that the adhesive quality of rubber cement tends to diminish over a period of time. Constant exposure to dry air may eventually cause it to lose its grip. This disadvantage may be compensated for with special precautions as noted for permanent rubber cement mountings. However, even these will not last indefinitely.

Dry Mounting. Dry mounting employs a specially prepared paper impregnated with heat-sensitive adhesive. The paper is available in sheets and in rolls and is marketed under such names as Fusion-4000 and MT-5. The drymounting tissue bonds the backing material to the back of the visual. A dry mount press is used to supply the heat and pressure necessary to activate the tissue's adhesive. The process is rapid and clean and results in permanent high quality mounting.

One disadvantage of dry mounting is that it is relatively expensive. However it is possible to dry mount visuals without a dry mount press by using an ordinary household iron. Set the iron on "silk" or "rayon." Do *not* use steam. Follow the procedure described in "How to . . . Dry Mount Pictures." The tip of the household iron can be used in place of a tacking iron. Tack the tissue to the picture and the tissue to the mounting board as described. Place a sheet of clean paper over the top of the picture, dry-mounting tissue, and mounting board combination. Holding the materials in position, carefully and slowly move the iron over them while applying pressure (Figure 4.15). Remove the paper and allow the mounting to cool. If the picture is not completely adhered to the mounting board, cover again and apply more heat and pressure.

Laminating Nonprojected Visuals

Lamination provides visuals with protection from wear and tear by covering them with clear plastic or plastic-like surfaces. Lamination helps to

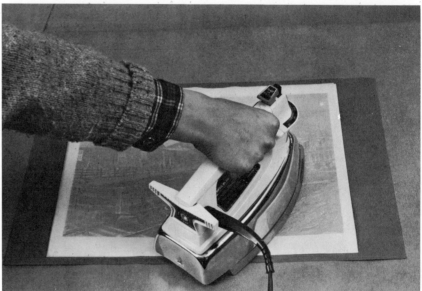

▲ **Figure 4.15**
A picture can be attached to a mounting board by means of dry mounting tissue and an ordinary household iron.

protect visuals against tears, scratches, and sticky fingers. Soiled surfaces can be wiped clean with a damp cloth.

Lamination also allows you to write on your visuals with a grease pencil or water-soluble ink for instructional purposes. The writing can be easily erased later with a damp cloth or sponge. A teacher of mathematics, for example, might write percentage

figures on a laminated illustration of a pizza or a pie in order to help teach the concept of fractions. You can also have students write on laminated materials to facilitate learner responses. When the lesson is completed, the markings can be erased and the material made ready for further teaching. Classroom materials other than nonprojected visuals may also be laminated for extra durability and to allow for erasable writing by teacher and students—workbook pages, for example.

HOW TO... DRY MOUNT PICTURES

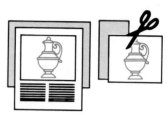

Dry the mounting board and picture before trimming picture by placing in dry mount press for about one minute at 225° F. Close press, but do *not* lock.

Place a sheet (either side up) of dry-mounting tissue over the *back* of the *untrimmed* picture, with sheet overlapping edges.

Attach the tissue to the back center of the picture with tip of a tacking iron set on "medium."

Turn picture and tissue over and trim both simultaneously to desired size. (A paper cutter works best, but razor knife with metal straight edge or scissors may be used.)

Place the picture and dry-mounting tissue on the mounting board and align in proper position.

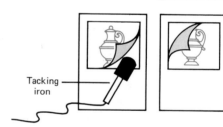

Tack the tissue to the mounting board at two *opposite* corners.

Tacking iron

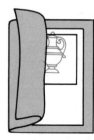

Cover mounting board and picture with clean paper on both sides.

Place in dry mount press preheated to 225° F for about one minute.

Remove from dry mount press and allow the materials to cool. (Placing the cooling materials under a metal weight will help prevent curling.)

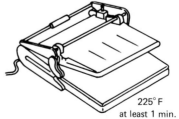

225° F
at least 1 min.

HOW TO... LAMINATE PICTURES WITH A DRY MOUNT PRESS

The dry mount press should be heated to 225° F. If you live in an area with high humidity, you may get better results if you pre-heat the visual (to remove excess moisture) in the press for about 45 seconds. Close the press but do not lock it.

Cover the picture to be laminated with a piece of laminating film slightly larger than the picture. The inside of the roll (dull side) contains the heat sensitive adhesive and should be toward the visual. Press the film onto the picture with your hands. Static electricity should cause the film to stay in place.

Put the picture and laminating film in a cover of clean paper to protect the visual and to prevent the adhesive from getting onto the surfaces of the dry mount press.

Insert the material in press for one minute. Remove it; if the adhesion is not complete, put it back into the press for another minute. It may be helpful to put a magazine or a ¼-inch stack of paper on top of the picture to increase the pressure and improve adhesion between the picture and the laminating film.

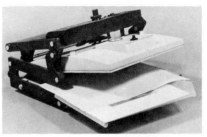

The simplest but also least effective technique for laminating visuals is to spray them with plastic from a can. More effective and durable procedures involve using sheets of clear plastic cut to size. Rubber cement may be used for adhesion. Apply the rubber cement to the face of the visual and to one side of the plastic sheet. Allow the adhesives to dry and then carefully press the plastic over the surface of the visual.

Plastic sheets with adhesive backing (such as Con-Tact shelf paper) are also available for laminating purposes. Remove the backing cover to expose the adhesive and carefully press the clear plastic sheet on the visual. Any portions of the plastic sheet which extend beyond the edges of the visual can be cut off, or doubled back for additional protection.

Rolls of laminating film for use with a dry mount press are available from commercial sources.

Filing and Storing Nonprojected Visuals

You will find it handy to have a system for filing, storing, and retrieving your nonprojected visuals. The nature of the filing system which you use will depend upon the number of nonprojected visuals in your collection and how you intend to use them. The simplest filing system usually involves grouping them according to the teaching units in which they are used. Elementary teachers often categorize them by subject or curriculum area (e.g., math, science, language arts, social studies, etc.) and then subdivide them (e.g., seasons, foreign countries, jobs, addition, subtraction, place value, telling time,

etc.). Some instructors, especially those who teach just one subject, set up their filing system according to the chapters in their textbook, the topics they cover, or by objectives. Teachers who use just a few visuals sometimes file them with their other teaching materials for each lesson.

Noting the size of the visuals will help you determine the most appropriate storage container. Many teachers store their pictures in file folders or large mailing envelopes. If the pictures are slightly larger than the mailing envelopes, you can open the envelopes on two adjacent sides, and the envelope will serve as a useful pocket. If the pictures are considerably larger than the 9-by-11-inch file folders or the envelopes you have available, you can use artist's portfolios, which are available in various sizes up to 36 by 48 inches.

In addition to a workable filing system and proper size storage containers, you should have a clean, out-of-the-way place to store your visuals when they are not in use. The storage

▲ **Figure 4.16**
Large format mounted pictures can be stored conveniently in an artist's portfolio.

location can range from elaborate built-in drawers or filing cabinets to simple cardboard storage cartons. There is no problem in using cardboard cartons to store files of pictures and other visuals if you have a clean and dry location to place the cartons. Of course, the cartons should be readily accessible when you need them. Some teachers use the tops of closets in their classrooms or a corner of a supply room as storage spaces.

DISPLAY FORMATS

If you are going to use nonprojected visuals, such as photographs, drawings, charts, graphs, or posters, you need a way to display them. Nonprojected visuals may be displayed in the classroom in a wide variety of ways, ranging from simply holding up a single visual in your hand to constructing elaborate exhibits for permanent display. Classroom items commonly used for display of nonprojected visuals include chalkboards, multipurpose boards, pegboards, bulletin boards, cloth boards, and magnetic boards. Flip charts may also be used for display of visuals. Exhibits, a display format incorporating a variety of materials such as realia and models along with visuals, are also common. How you display your visuals will depend upon a number of factors, including the nature of your audience, the nature of your visuals, the instructional setting, your lesson objectives, and, of course, the availability of the various display formats.

Chalkboards

The most common display surface in the classroom is, of course, the chalkboard. Once called "blackboards," they, like chalk, now come in a variety of colors. Although the chalkboard is most commonly used as a medium of verbal communication, it can be used as a surface upon which to draw visuals (or pictures can be fastened to the molding above the chalkboard or placed in the chalk tray) to help illustrate instructional units and serve as adjuncts to verbal communication. Graphics, such as sketches and diagrams, charts and graphs, may be drawn on the chalkboard for display to the class.

A chalkboard is such a commonplace classroom item that instructors often neglect to give it the attention and respect it deserves as an instructional device. Using a chalkboard effectively requires conscious effort.

Multipurpose Boards

Some newer classrooms are equipped with multipurpose boards instead of chalkboards. As the name implies, they can be used for more than one purpose. They have a smooth white plastic surface and use special marking pens rather than chalk. They are cleaned with a damp cloth or special felt eraser. Sometimes called "visual aid panels," they usually have a steel backing and can

▶ **Figure 4.17**
The chalkboard is universally recognized as a flexible and economical display format; however, *effective* use requires some conscious effort.

AV SHOWMANSHIP—CHALKBOARD

Put extensive drawing or writing on the chalkboard before class. Taking too much time to write or draw creates restlessness and may lead to discipline problems.

Cover material such as a test or extensive lesson materials with wrapping paper, newspaper, or a pull-down map until you are ready to use it.

Eye contact with students is important! Face the class when you are talking. Do not talk to the board. Do not turn your back to the class any more than absolutely necessary.

Vary your presentation techniques. Do not over-use or rely entirely on the chalkboard. Use hand-outs, the overhead projector, flipcharts, and other media during instruction when appropriate.

Print neatly rather than using script. For a 32-foot-long classroom, the letters should be 2- to 2½-inches high and the lines forming the letters should be ¼-inch thick.

Check visibility of chalkboard from several positions around the room to be sure there is no glare on the board. In case of glare, move the board (if portable), or pull window shades.

If your printing normally runs uphill or downhill, use water soluble felt-tip pen markings as temporary guidelines for straighter printing. The guidelines will not be wiped off by a chalk eraser but may be washed off when no longer needed.

Hold the chalk so that it does not make scratching noises.

Use colored chalk for emphasis, but don't over-use it.

Move around so you do not block what you have written on the chalkboard. Do not stand in front of what you have written.

Use chalkboard drawing aids such as rulers, chalkboard stencils, and templates (patterns) to save time and improve the quality of your drawings.

For frequently drawn shapes, use a template cut from wood or heavy cardboard. A dresser drawer knob or empty thread spool mounted on the template makes it easier to hold in position while tracing around it.

Outline your drawings with barely visible lines before class and then fill them in with bold lines in front of the class. Your audience will think you are an artist!

HOW TO... DEVELOP A BULLETIN BOARD DISPLAY

1. *Decide upon an objective.* Limit the display to one topic or objective. More than one idea usually results in confusion on the part of the viewers.
2. *Generate a theme and incorporate it into a headline.* It is a challenge to work out a catchy theme that will entice the viewer into further examination. Wording should be simple, couched in the viewer's language, and visually integrated into the arrangement of the display (as discussed in Chapter 3).
3. *Work out a rough layout.* Guidelines for literate visuals are discussed in Chapter 3. The blueprint you develop here should reflect those guidelines.
4. *Gather the materials.* Obtain or make the illustra-tions, photographs, or other visual materials. Select a background material; e.g., cloth, wrapping paper, aluminum foil, colored construction paper, shelf paper, or the like. Lines on the display can be made from ribbon, yarn, string, wire, or paper strips. Lettering may be freehand, drawn using a lettering guide, pressed on with dry transfer type, cut from construction paper; preformed plastic and ceramic letters are also available.
5. *Put up the display.* Setting up the display should be easy if all the preceding steps have been carried out. Step back and appraise it from a technical standpoint, and observe student reactions to evaluate its instructional effectiveness.

▲ **Figure 4.18**
Newer multipurpose boards can be written on with liquid markers; they can also be used as a projection screen and magnetic board.

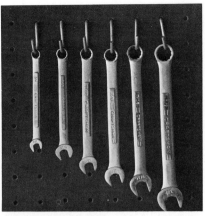

▲ **Figure 4.19**
Pegboards are especially useful for displaying heavy objects.

▲ **Figure 4.20**
A bulletin board display with a seasonal theme may be the basis for a motivational display of student work.

be used as a magnetic board for display of visuals (Figure 4.18). The white nonglare surface is also suitable for projection of films, slides, and overhead transparencies. Materials (figures, letters, etc.) cut from thin plastic will adhere to the surface when rubbed in place.

Pegboards

Another popular display surface is the pegboard. It is particularly useful for displaying heavy objects, three-dimensional materials, and visuals.

Pegboards are made of tempered masonite with ⅛-inch holes drilled 1 inch apart. Pegboard material is usually ⅛-inch thick and comes in 4-by-8-foot sheets which can be cut to any size. Special metal hooks and holders can be inserted into the pegboard to hold books, papers, and other objects. A variety of these special hooks are available in most hardware stores. Golf tees can also be inserted into the holes for holding lightweight materials such as posters and visuals mounted on cardboard. For a background effect, the entire pegboard

surface can be covered with cloth or colored paper. Golf tees or the special hooks can then be inserted through the cloth or paper.

Bulletin Board Displays

The name *bulletin board* implies an area in which bulletins—brief news announcements of urgent interest—are posted for public notice. This may have been the original purpose and it may still be true of some cases, but it does not describe the most general use of these display spaces. Physically, a bulletin board is a *surface of variable size and shape made of a material that holds pins, thumbtacks, and other sharp fasteners without damage to the board.* In practice, bulletin board displays tend to serve three broad purposes: (1) decorative, (2) motivational, or (3) instructional.

The decorative bulletin board is probably the most common, certainly in schools. Its function would seem to be to lend visual stimulation to an environment that otherwise would be rather sterile. As such, it could contribute to youngsters' aesthetic development. More often, though, it offers a tired, predictable cliché,

typically based on a seasonal motif: September—autumn leaves; October—witches and pumpkins; November—pilgrims and Indians; December—Santa Claus, reindeer, and Christmas trees; January—snowflakes; February—Valentine hearts and presidential silhouettes; March—kites and shamrocks; April—showers; May—flowers. Do students tire of the predictability of

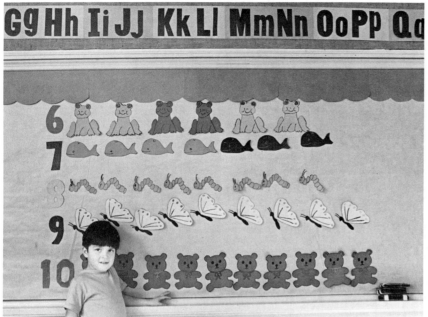

▲ **Figure 4.21**
The greatest student learning may derive from participating in the construction of a bulletin board display rather than from looking at it.

▲ **Figure 4.22**
The location of a display depends on its intended use. A high-traffic location (such as A and B) is suitable for a motivational message or an announcement meant to capture attention at a glance. A quiet corner (such as C) or an individual learning center (such as D) would be more appropriate for an instructional display designed to be studied at some length.

such displays? No one seems to have asked. Perhaps the best justification for such seasonal flourishes is the preservation of deeply ingrained cultural traditions.

Displaying student work exemplifies the motivational use of the bulletin board. The public recognition offered by such displays seems to play an important role in the life of the classroom. It fosters pride in achievement, reinforcing students' efforts to do a good job. It is also a relatively effortless display for the teacher to put together. The display of student work lends itself to combination with the decorative motif.

The third broad purpose is instructional, complementing the educational or training objectives being pursued within the formal curriculum. Rather than merely presenting static informational messages, many creative instructors design displays that actively invite participation. Such displays ask questions and give viewers some means of manipulating parts of the display to verify their answers—flaps, pockets, dials, movable parts, and the like.

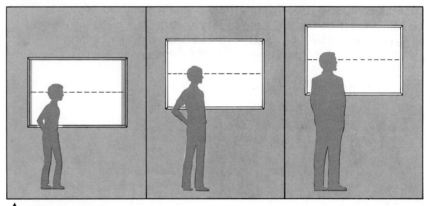

▲ **Figure 4.23**
The placement of a display should vary according to the average height of the intended viewers. A useful rule-of-thumb is to match the middle of the display with the viewer's eye level.

Another form of learner participation is to take part in the actual construction of the display. There are many fervent testimonials from teachers affirming the value of such activities to their students. For example, one language arts teacher approached a unit on the family by requiring each student to cut out or draw a picture concerning the family (but it could not be an actual picture of a family). These pictures were combined into a montage that served as the centerpiece for a lively discus-

sion of the symbolic significance of the images depicted. Posting news photographs is a way of stimulating discussion of current events.

Bulletin boards need not always be attached permanently to the wall. Portable boards may be set on an easel for temporary display purposes or integrated into a learning center. The possible proliferation of such boards leads to a cautionary note: beware of clutter—too many competing visual messages will tend to drown them all out.

▲ **Figure 4.24**
Cloth boards are often used to involve students in story telling.

Cloth Boards

Cloth boards are constructed of *cloth stretched over a sturdy backing material such as plywood, Masonite, or heavy cardboard.* The cloth used for the board may be of various types, including flannel, felt, or hook-and-loop material.

Flannel is inexpensive and readily available. Pieces of flannel stick together when gentle pressure is applied. Visuals cut from flannel can be drawn on with felt-tip markers and put on the flannel board. You can also back still pictures and graphics with flannel. Coarse sandpaper sticks to flannel and can also be used to back visuals for attachment to the board. Pipe cleaners, available in a variety of colors, and fuzzy yarns stick to the flannel and can be used for drawing lines and letters. Felt,

slightly more expensive than flannel, has the same properties. Durability of adhesion is less than could be desired with flannel and felt, so slant the board slightly to help prevent materials from slipping or falling off.

The best cloth board, and the most expensive, is made from "hook-and-loop" materials (Velcro and Teazlegraph). The hook-and-loop board has a fine but fuzzy surface composed of tiny, strong nylon loops. The material used for backing visuals and other items to be attached to the board has a coarse, hooklike texture. When pressed together, the two surfaces stick firmly. The hooklike material

can be purchased in rolls or strips. One great advantage of the hook-and-loop board is that it can support large and heavy visuals, even entire books and three-dimensional objects. One square inch of the cloth can support up to ten pounds of properly backed visual material.

Cloth boards are particularly useful for instruction requiring that visuals be easily moved around to illustrate a process or sequence. They can also be easily removed from the board.

Teachers of reading and other creative activities often use the cloth board to illustrate stories, poems, and other reading materials. Visuals depicting characters and scenes in a story, for example, can be placed on the board and moved around as the story unfolds. Creativity may be further encouraged by allowing the children to manipulate cloth board materials. Shy children may particularly profit from this kind of activity. It encourages them to speak through the visual representations of story characters as they manipulate illustrations on the board.

Be sure you have proper storage space for your cloth board and cloth board visuals when not in use. Proper storage will help keep them clean and prevent them from being bent or torn. If possible, store your materials on a flat surface rather than stacking them up against a wall. If you use sandpaper backing on your visuals, put paper between them during storage. Sandpaper can scratch the surface of visuals.

Magnetic Boards

Magnetic boards serve much the same purpose as cloth boards, but their adhesion is due to magnetism. Visuals are backed with magnets and then placed on the metal surface of the board. Magnetic boards, magnets, and flexible strips of magnetic material for use in backing are available commercially. Plastic lettering with magnetic backing is available from supply stores and can be used for captioning visuals.

HOW TO... MAKE A CLOTH BOARD

The base of the cloth board can be a piece of plywood, particle board, or heavy cardboard of whatever size you desire. Tan or gray materials make a good background. Cut the cloth material several inches larger than the board. Stretch the cloth tightly over the edges of the board and fasten it with small nails, thumbtacks, staples, or tape. Covering the face of the board with white glue (Elmer's glue) before covering it will help the cloth to adhere to the board. Do not put the glue on too heavily or it will soak through the cloth and appear unsightly even though it dries clear.

A two-sided cloth board can be made by sewing two pieces of cloth together in the form of a bag. Two different colors of cloth can be used and give you a choice of backgrounds. The wood base or heavy cardboard is then inserted into the bag and the open end sewn or pinned in place. Pinning it in place allows you to remove the cloth in order to clean it.

Make a bag by sewing three sides of the cloth.

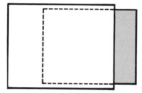

Turn it inside out and insert a stiff backing

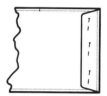

Pin the open end in place.

Any metal surface in the classroom that a magnet is attracted to can serve as a magnetic board. For example, some chalkboards are backed with steel and will thus attract magnet-backed visuals. Chalk can be used on such chalkboards for captioning or to depict lines of association between visuals. Steel cabinets and metal walls and doors can be used as magnetic boards.

You can make your own magnetic board from a thin sheet of galvanized iron, a cookie sheet, a lap tray, or any similar thin sheet of metal. Paint the sheets in the color of your choice with paint designed for use on metal surfaces or cover with Con-Tact paper. Unpainted surfaces are likely to be unattractive and to cause glare. Another alternative is to fasten steel screening to a nonmetal surface (plywood, perhaps) and cover it with a piece of cloth.

The major advantage of magnetic boards is that they provide for easier and quicker maneuverability of visuals than even cloth boards do. For example, magnetic boards are often used by physical education instructors to demonstrate rapid changes in player positions. Magnetic boards also provide greater adhesive quality. Visuals displayed on a magnetic board are not likely to slip or fall. They move only when you *want* to move them.

Flip Charts

A *flip chart* usually refers to a *pad of large-sized paper fastened together at the top and mounted on a wooden or metal easel*. The individual sheets

▼ **Figure 4.25**
A portable magnetic board allows quick manipulation of items for arithmetic drill.

▼ **Figure 4.26**
The flip chart—a flexible, "user-friendly" display format.

each hold a limited verbal/visual message and are arranged for sequential presentation to a small group. The messages can be written extemporaneously while the presenter is talking or can be prepared ahead of time and revealed one at a time. Commercially produced materials are also available in this format; they are especially prevalent in reading and science instruction and military training. Pre-prepared visual sequences are especially useful for instruction involving sequential steps in a process.

Each sheet can be displayed and discussed before flipping it over and moving on to the next one. The diagrams or words can serve as cues, reminding the presenter of the next point in the presentation.

The most common use of flip charts, though, is for the extemporaneous drawing of key illustrations and key words to supplement a stand-up presentation. As such it is an extremely versatile, convenient, and inexpensive media format. The flip chart requires no electrical power, has no moving parts to wear out, can be used in a wide range of lighting conditions, is portable, and requires only a marking pen as peripheral equipment. Next to the chalkboard it is the most "user-friendly" audiovisual tool.

Audience members, too, seem to regard the flip chart in friendly terms. It seems casual and comfortable, a pleasing change of pace in an increasingly high technology world. It is an exceptionally valuable aid to any group discussion process. Ideas contributed by group members can be

HOW TO...MAKE A PORTABLE FLIP CHART

Determine the number of pages you wish to use and stack them evenly.

Fasten them together with staples or by some other means to assure they will remain in position. If there is a likelihood you will want to change the sequence of the pages for instructional purposes use removable fastening pins.

Fasten a cover of heavy paper or light cardboard to the sheets. Two thicknesses of covering may be used for extra durability.

Hinge the cover and sheets together at the top.

For even more rigidity, the assembled flip chart may be mounted on light wood or heavy cardboard. The sheets can be held in place by placing a strip of cardboard or light wood on the face of the chart through which bolts can be inserted to make contact with the backing. Use wing nuts to fasten the bolts. If the backing is cardboard, heavy tape, such as duct tape or bookbinding tape, can be used to secure the sheets to the backing.

The inside covers of the flip chart may be treated with special "blackboard paint," thus giving you a small portable chalkboard to work with in your presentation. You can also convert the inside covers into miniature display boards by lining them with cloth or metal.

Front view

Back view

◀ **Figure 4.27**
Flip charts are standard equipment in the sales and marketing classrooms at AT&T Communications.

recorded in a way visible to all participants. Comments and corrections can be made and the results can be preserved. Finished sheets can be torn off the pad and taped to walls or windows for later reference.

The humble flip chart has been around for a long time and its future appears secure.

Exhibits

Exhibits are displays of various types of nonprojected visuals designed to form an integrated whole for instructional purposes. (Projected visuals may also be included in the exhibit.) Any of the visuals discussed in this chapter, including models and realia, may be included in an exhibit. Any of the display methods discussed may be used to contribute to it. Exhibits may be used for much the same instructional purposes and in much the same ways as their individual compo-

nents are used. Techniques for using them in the instructional situation are also similar.

Exhibit locations are readily available in most classrooms. Simple exhibits can be set up on a table, shelf, or desk. More complex exhibits may require considerable floor space and special constructions (a booth, for example).

AV SHOWMANSHIP—FLIP CHARTS

Keep the lettering and visuals simple, but large enough for everyone to see.

Use marking pens that provide sharp contrast but will not bleed through to the next sheet.

Talk to the audience, not to the flip chart.

Avoid blocking students' view of the flip chart.

Be sure your materials are in proper sequence.

Reveal sheets only when you are ready to discuss them, not before.

Print rather than using cursive lettering.

Be sure the flip chart is securely fastened so it will not fall apart during your presentation. (The sudden collapse of your flip chart may get a laugh, but not the kind of laugh you may want.)

Put summary points on a separate sheet rather than paging back as you make your summary.

◄ **Figure 4.28**
A complex exhibit such as this one at the Lowell, Massachusetts National Historic Park may bring together realia, still pictures and other visuals, and verbal information.

▼ **Figure 4.29**
A simple teacher-made exhibit may consist of a few artifacts and a brief verbal explanation or question.

Student assembly of an exhibit can be an excellent learning experience and can foster both retention of subject matter and sharpening of visual skills. For a lesson in transportation, one sixth-grade teacher had each student bring in a replica of a vehicle. Some students made their own vehicles from construction paper. Others brought in toys from home or contributed vehicles assembled from hobby kits (boats, cars, trucks, trains, space ships, etc.). The teacher placed tables and other classroom furniture along a wall to provide the children with a shelf on which to arrange and display their three-dimensional visuals. On the wall above this make-shift exhibit surface, the teacher

placed a long sheet of paper containing a time line. The time line illustrated vehicles of transportation from early time (humans and beasts), through the present (trains, cars, planes, etc.), and on into the future (space vehicles from *Star Wars* and *Star Trek*). The exhibit was a great success with the children and with the teacher.

SELECTION OF NONPROJECTED VISUALS, UTILIZATION, AND LEARNER RESPONSE

The ASSURE model discussed in Chapter 2 applies to nonprojected visuals as well as to all other media. However, because of the diversity of formats and countless uses of nonprojected visuals, it is difficult to provide a concise set of principles and procedures for them.

First, you must analyze your audience and determine its nature and characteristics. Find out what its members already know about the topic. Then state your objectives in terms of what you want your audience to be able to do after viewing the presentation of visuals.

When selecting, modifying, or designing visuals, you should decide upon visuals that will best communicate your instructional message under the conditions in which you will be using them. Keep them simple! Be certain that all titles, lettering, figures, and the visuals themselves are large enough to be seen from the intended viewing distance.

Many utilization techniques are included in the showmanship tips presented in this chapter. Plan your presentation or display carefully. Start where the audience is (as determined from your audience analysis). Organize the presentation in a logical sequence. Practice your presentation before a mirror or colleague.

Build learner activity and response into the use of the visuals. Involve the viewers as much as possible. Repetition and emphasis will help your audience remember key points. Watch them to see if they are following the presentation. Use questions and dialogue to keep them interested and to provide opportunities for learner response.

Finally, as recommended in the ASSURE model, evaluate your visuals and associated presentation. Through formal and informal evaluation, determine if most of your audience was able to meet your objectives. Determine which parts of the presentation were received best, and worst. Solicit feedback from your audience, then make the necessary revisions.

References

Print References

Nonprojected Visuals

Alesandrini, K.L. "Pictures and Adult Learning." *Instructional Science* (May 1984), pp. 63–77.

Bullough, Robert. *Creating Instructional Materials*. (Columbus: Charles E. Merrill, 1974).

The Center for Vocational Education. *Prepare Teacher-Made Instructional Materials*. (Athens, Ga.: American Association for Vocational Instructional Materials, 1977).

_____. *Present Information with Models, Real Objects, and Flannel Boards*. (Athens, Ga.: American Association for Vocational Instructional Materials, 1977).

Coplan, Kate. *Poster Ideas and Bulletin Board Techniques for Libraries and Schools*. 2d ed. (New York: Oceana Publications, 1980).

Do You See What I Mean? Learning through Charts, Graphs, Maps, and Diagrams. (Dickson, Australia: Curriculum Development Centre, 1980).

Hill, Donna. *The Picture File: A Manual and a Curriculum-Related Subject Heading List*. (Hamden, Conn.: Linnet Books, 1978).

Hollister, Bernard C. "Using Picture Books in the Classroom." *Media and Methods* (January 1977), pp. 22–25.

Jones, Colin. "Cartoons in the Classroom." *Visual Education* (November 1976), pp. 21–22.

Kemp, Jerrold E. and Dayton, Deane K., *Planning and Producing Instructional Media*. 5th ed. (New York: Harper & Row, 1985).

Kohn, Rita, *Experiencing Displays*. (Metuchen, N.J.: Scarecrow Press, 1982).

Krulek, Stephen, and Welderman, Ann M. "The Chalkboard—More Than Just for Chalk." *Audiovisual Instruction* (September 1976), p. 41.

Marino, George. "A Do-It-Yourself 3-D Graph." *Mathematics Teacher* (May 1977), pp. 428–429.

Minor, Ed. *Handbook for Preparing Visual Media*. 2d ed. (New York: McGraw-Hill, 1978).

_____ and Frye, Harvey R. *Techniques for Producing Visual Instructional Media*. 2d ed. (New York: McGraw-Hill, 1977).

Moore, Randall P. " Photographs as Instructional Tools." *American Biology Teacher* (October 1975), pp. 432–434.

Satterthwait, Les. *Graphics: Skills, Media and Materials*. 3d ed. (Dubuque, Ia.: Kendall-Hunt, 1977).

Smith, Judson. "Choosing and Using Easels, Display Boards, and Visual Control Systems." *Training* (May 1979), pp. 51, 53–56.

Sumey, Violet, and Wade, Saundra. *Library Displays*. (Minneapolis: T. S. Denison, 1982).

Trimblay, Roger. "Using Magazine Pictures in the Second-Language Classroom." *Canadian Modern Language Review* (October 1978), pp. 82–86.

Wagner, Betty Jane, and Stunard, E. Arthur. *Making and Using Inexpensive Classroom Media*. (Belmont, Calif.: Pitman Learning, 1976).

Waller, Robert H. W. "Four Aspects of Graphic Communication: An Introduction to This Issue." *Instructional Science* (September 1979), pp. 213–222.

Bulletin Boards

Alsin, Mary Lou. "Bulletin Board Standouts." *Early Years* (September 1977), pp. 66–69.

Carney, Loretta J. "No Comment: Eloquent Dissent." *Social Education* (November 1976), pp. 586–587.

Center for Vocational Education. *Prepare Bulletin Boards and Exhibits.* (Athens, Ga.: American Association for Vocational Instructional Materials, 1977).

"Hands-on Bulletin Boards." *Instructor* (January 1984), pp. 34–37.

Kelley, Marjorie. *Classroom-Tested Bulletin Boards.* (Belmont, Calif.: Fearon Publishers, 1961).

Kincheloe, Joe L. "No More Turkey-Lurkeys!" *Instructional Innovator* (September 1982), pp. 24–25.

Koskey, Thomas. *Baited Bulletin Boards.* (Belmont, Calif.: Fearon Publishers, 1954).

Prizzi, Elaine, and Hoffman, Jeanne. *Teaching off the Wall: Interactive Bulletin Boards That Teach with You.* (Belmont, Calif.: Pitman Learning, 1981).

Ruby, Doris. *4-D Bulletin Boards That Teach.* (Belmont, Calif.: Pitman Learning, 1960).

———, and Ruby, Grant. *Bulletin Boards for the Middle Grades.* (Belmont, Calif.: Pitman Learning, 1964).

Audiovisual References

Display and Presentation Boards. Chicago: International Film Bureau, 1971. 16-mm film or videocassette. 15 minutes, color.

Dry Mounting with Heat Press. Salt Lake City, Utah: Media Systems, Inc., 1975. Filmstrip or slides, 40 frames, color.

Heat Laminating. Salt Lake City, Utah: Media Systems, Inc., 1975. Filmstrip or slides, 40 frames, color.

Lettering: A Creative Approach to Basics. Stamford, Conn.: Educational Dimensions Group, 1978. 2 sound filmstrips with audiocassettes.

Production Techniques for Instructional Graphic Materials. Columbus: Charles E. Merrill, 1977. 27 filmstrips in basic series, 12 filmstrips in advanced series, 18 audiocassettes.

Tables and Graphs. Weekly Reader Filmstrips. Guidance Associates, 1981. 4 filmstrips with audiocassettes. Grades 3–6.

Three-Dimensional Displays. Burbank, Calif.: Encore Visual Education, 1975. 4 sound filmstrips with audiocassettes.

Suppliers of Materials and Equipment

Graphics, Mounting, Laminating, Lettering

Dick Blick
Box 1267
Galesburg, Illinois 61401

Demco Educational Corp.
P.O. Box 1488
Madison, Wisconsin 53701

Chartpak
One River Road
Leeds, Massachusetts 01053

Seal, Inc.
251 Roosevelt Drive
Derby, Connecticut 06418

Cloth Boards

Ohio Flock-Cote Co.
14500 Industrial Avenue N.
Maple Heights, Ohio 44137

Instructo Corporation
1635 North 55th Street
Paoli, Pennsylvania 19301

Charles Mayer Studios
168 East Market Street
Akron, Ohio 44308

Maharam Fabric Co.
420 New Orleans Street
Chicago, Illinois 60610

Bulletin Boards and Magnetic Boards

Bangor Cork Co.
William and D Streets
Pen Argyl, Pennsylvania 18072

Bulletin Boards and Directory Products
724 Broadway
New York, New York 10003

Charles Mayer Studios
168 East Market Street
Akron, Ohio 44308

Eberhard Faber, Inc.
Crestwood
Wilkes-Barre, Pennsylvania 18701

Magna Magnetics
777 Sunset Boulevard
Los Angeles, California 90046

Methods Research Corporation
Farmingdale, New Jersey 07727

Weber-Costello Company
1900 Narragansett Avenue
Chicago, Illinois 60639

Possible Projects

4-A. Select three pictures and mount one with temporary rubber cement, one with permanent rubber cement, and a third with dry mount tissue.

4-B. Select several pictures that are approximately 8-½-by-11 inches and laminate them utilizing the cold or heat process.

4-C. Select a set of still pictures you might use in your teaching. Then appraise them using the "Appraisal Checklist: Still Pictures." Turn in the pictures and appraisal forms.

4-D. Plan a lesson in which you use a set of still pictures. Within this lesson show evidence that you have followed the utilization principles suggested. Submit pictures with lesson.

4-E. Devise for your subject field one graph (line, bar, circle, pictorial) and one chart (organization, classification, time line, tabular chart, flowchart). Each of these should be prepared on a separate sheet. Evaluation will be based on the "Appraisal Checklist: Graphic Materials."

4-F. Make a list of ten possible posters students could make to depict aspects of your teaching area. Prepare *one* yourself to serve as a motivational device. The poster should be at least 12-by-14 inches.

4-G. Review Chapter 3 or examine books on bulletin board displays. Prepare rough layouts for two displays pertinent to your subject area. Construct one of these.

4-H. Obtain an example of a real object or model that you could use for instruction. Submit the object or model and a description of how you would use it, including an objective.

4-I. Prepare a cloth board, magnetic board, flip chart or exhibit. Submit the material, a description of the intended audience, the objectives, how it will be used, and how it will be evaluated.

Projected Visuals

C H A P T E R 5

Outline

Objectives

After studying this chapter, you should be able to:

1. Define projected visuals.
2. Describe the characteristics and operation of overhead transparency projection systems including three advantages and three limitations.
3. Discuss two applications of the overhead in your teaching field.
4. Describe three utilization techniques to enhance your use of the overhead projector.
5. Describe the following techniques for overhead transparency production: write-on, thermal film method, electrostatic method, and spirit duplication.
6. Describe three utilization techniques to enhance the effectiveness of overhead transparencies in instructional situations.
7. Describe the characteristics of slides including three advantages and three limitations.
8. Synthesize an instructional situation in which you might use a series of locally produced slides.
9. Describe the basic operation of a Kodak Visualmaker.
10. Describe the characteristics of filmstrips including three advantages and three limitations.
11. Synthesize an instructional situation in which you might use a commercially produced filmstrip.
12. Describe two utilization techniques to enhance your use of filmstrips.
13. Describe the characteristics and operation of opaque projection systems including two advantages and three limitations.
14. Discuss two applications of opaque projection in your teaching field.
15. Describe three utilization techniques to enhance the effectiveness of opaque projection in instructional situations.

Lexicon

projected visual
fresnel lens
transparency
slide
filmstrip
opaque projection
overhead projection
thermal film
electrostatic copying (xerography)
spirit duplication

Because an illuminated screen in a darkened room tends to rivet the attention of viewers, projected visuals have long been popular as a medium of instruction as well as of entertainment. The lighted screen is a silent shout—a shout likely to be heard and heeded even by the most reluctant learners.

It is not too fanciful to conjecture that some of this attraction is due to the aura of "magic" that seems to surround such presentations. The room lights are dimmed; the viewers grow quiet in expectation; a switch is thrown and (presto!) a large, bright image appears on the screen. You have their attention. They are ready to receive your message. Exploit this readiness by selecting materials that will maintain the viewers' attention and by using them in a way that *involves* viewers actively in the learning process.

Projected visuals refer to *media formats in which still images are projected onto a screen.* Such projection is usually achieved by passing a strong light through transparent film (overhead transparencies, slides, and filmstrips), magnifying the image through a series of lenses, and casting this image onto a reflective surface. Opaque projection is also included in this category. In opaque projection, light is cast onto an opaque image (one that does not allow light to pass through), such as a magazine picture or printed page. The light is reflected from the material onto mirrors which transmit the reflection through a series of lenses onto a screen.

This chapter will focus on the characteristics and applications of overhead projection, slides, filmstrips, and opaque projection—the most widely accepted means of providing projected visuals in education and training settings.

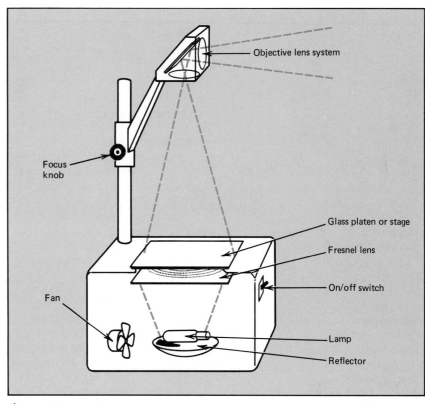

▲ **Figure 5.1**
Overhead projector, cutaway view.

OVERHEAD PROJECTION

Because of its many virtues, the overhead projection system has advanced rapidly in the past three decades to become the most widely used audiovisual device in North American classrooms.

The typical overhead projector is a very simple device (Figure 5.1). Basically, it is a box with a large aperture or "stage" at the top. Light from a powerful lamp inside the box is condensed by a special type of lens, known as a fresnel lens, and passes through a transparency (approxi-

mately 8 by 10 inches) placed on the stage. A lens and mirror system mounted on a bracket above the box turns the light beam 90 degrees and projects the image back over the shoulder of the presenter.

Because of the widespread familiarity of overhead projection, the general term *transparency* has taken on, in the instructional setting, the specific meaning of the large format 8-by-10 inch film used with the overhead projector. Transparencies may be composed of photographic type film, clear acetate, or any of a number of other transparent materials capable of being imprinted with an image by means of chemical or heat processes.

Transparencies may be used individually or may be made into a series

▲ Figure 5.2
The overhead projector has been adapted to many uses outside the classroom; here finalists in a national crossword puzzle contest perform before an audience.

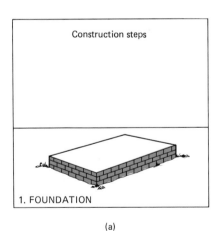

(a)

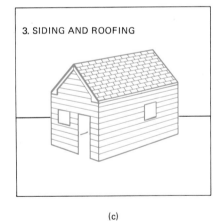

(c)

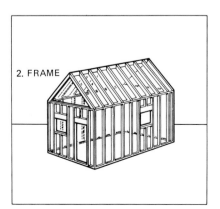

(b)

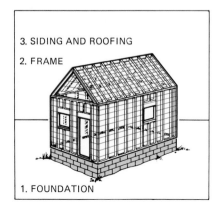

(d)

of images consisting of a base visual with one or more "overlays" attached to the base with hinges. Complex topics can be explained step-by-step by flipping on a series of overlays one at a time that add additional features to a diagram (Figure 5.3).

Advantages

The overhead projection system has a number of unique features that give it the tremendous versatility for which it is acclaimed by so many instructors.

Its bright lamp and efficient optical system generate so much light on the screen that the overhead can be used in *normal room lighting*.

The projector is operated from the front of the room with the presenter *facing the audience*, allowing direct eye contact to be maintained.

Most overhead projectors are light in weight and easily portable. All are *simple to operate*.

A *variety of materials* can be projected, including cutout silhouettes, small opaque objects, and many types of transparencies.

Projected materials can be *manipulated* by the presenter. You can point to important items, highlight them with colored pens, add details during the lesson (notes, diagrams, etc.) by marking on the transparency with a marking pen, cover part of the message and progressively reveal information in a step-by-step procedure. As noted above, complex visuals can be presented in a series of overlays.

Commercially produced transparencies are available covering a broad

◄ Figure 5.3
By means of overlays, complex visuals can be built up step by step.

121

▲ **Figure 5.4**
With the overhead projector the presenter maintains eye contact with viewers.

▲ **Figure 5.5**
Some overhead projectors can be collapsed into a compact carrying case for true portability.

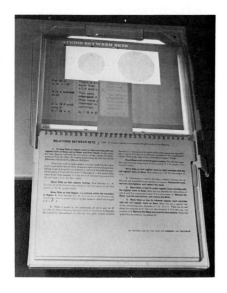

Media File:
"Ancient Egypt" Overhead Transparencies

A book containing a dozen full-color, tear-out transparencies showing aspects of life in Ancient Egypt, mythological characters, and the like. Each transparency is accompanied by a teacher's guide providing a script to follow. Duplicating masters for quizzes included.

Source: Milliken Publishing Co.

range of curricular areas. A major directory of commercially available overhead transparencies is published by the National Information Center for Educational Media (NICEM)—*Index to Educational Overhead Transparencies.* See Appendix A for details and other sources.

Instructors can easily prepare their own transparencies (several common methods of production are explained later in this section).

Information that might otherwise have to be placed on a chalkboard during class session (lesson outlines, for example) may be prepared ahead for presentation at the proper time. Research indicates that retention of main points improves significantly when visual outlines are presented.

A recent study indicates that the use of overhead transparencies also has positive attitudinal effects in business meetings. In a study by the

Wharton Applied Research Center, candidates for master's degrees in business administration participated in a business simulation that included group meetings to decide whether or not to introduce a new product. The findings showed that:

- More individuals decided to act on the recommendations of presenters who used overheads than on the recommendations of presenters who did not.
- Presenters who used overheads were perceived as better prepared, more professional, more persuasive, more credible, and more interesting.
- Groups in which presenters used overheads were more likely to reach consensus on their decisions than groups where no overheads were employed.*

◄ **Figure 5.6**
Commercially produced overhead transparency sets may provide highly structured guides for the instructor, including sequential overlays and detailed lecture notes.

*A Study of the Effects of the Use of Overhead Transparencies on Business Meetings. Philadelphia: Wharton Applied Research Center, The Wharton School, University of Pennsylvania, 1981.

◀ **Figure 5.7**
In business meetings, projected images help focus attention, channel discussion, facilitate reaching a consensus.

Limitations

The effectiveness of overhead projection presentations is heavily dependent on the presenter. The overhead projector cannot be programmed to display visual sequences by itself, nor is an audio accompaniment provided.

The overhead system does not lend itself to independent study. The projection system is designed for large-group presentation. Of course, an individual student could look at a transparency by holding it up to the light or laying it on a light table, but since captions or audio tracks are not a part of this format the material would ordinarily not be self-instructional.

Printed materials and other non-transparent items, such as magazine illustrations, cannot be projected immediately, as is possible with the opaque projector. To use the overhead system such materials have to be made into transparencies by means of some production process.

Distortion of images is more prevalent with the overhead than with other projection systems. The projector is commonly placed at desktop level to facilitate the instructor's writing on

Media File:
"Map Reading" Overhead Transparencies

A series of twenty-seven full-color transparencies for use on the overhead projector designed for teaching basic geographic understanding. Divided into thirteen lessons, packaged in a self-contained viewing stage book. Includes correlated notes next to every transparency. Topics include: location, scale, contour, projections, and map symbols.

Source: Denoyer-Geppert.

transparencies. The screen, on the other hand, needs to be placed on a higher level for clear audience sight lines. This discrepancy in levels causes a distortion referred to as the "keystone effect." (This problem and its solution are discussed in Chapter 10.)

Applications

As indicated by its ubiquitous presence in the classroom, the overhead system has a myriad of group instruction applications, too numerous to list here.

One indication of the breadth of applications is the fact that commercial distributors of transparencies have made available materials for virtually all curricular areas, from kindergarten through college levels and in business and industry. These materials

AV SHOWMANSHIP—OVERHEAD

In addition to the general utilization practices, here are some hints specifically related to overhead projection:

Start by projecting an *outline* to show learners what will be presented.

Avoid diminishing the possible impact of overhead projection by using the projector as a doodle pad. For *random notes* or *verbal* cues, use the chalkboard.

Shift the audience attention back to you by *switching off* the projector during changes of transparencies and, especially, when you have finished referring to a particular transparency.

Plan ways to *add meaningful details* to the transparency during projection; this infuses an element of spontaneity. If the basic transparency is a valuable one which will be reused, cover it with a blank acetate before drawing.

Place your *notes* (key words) on the frame of the transparency. Do not try to read from a prepared script.

Use *dual projectors* to retain the outline while covering secondary issues on second projector. Dual projection is also helpful in multilanguage presentations.

Direct viewer attention to parts of the transparency by the following techniques:

Point to specific portions, using a pencil as a pointer. Lay the pencil directly on the transparency, because any elevation will put the pencil out of focus and any slight hand movement will be greatly exaggerated on the screen. Avoid pointing to the screen.

Reveal information one line at a time to control pace and audience attention by placing a sheet of paper under the transparency.

Mask unwanted portions by covering them with a sheet of paper or using cardboard "windows" to reveal one section at a time.

Overlay new information one step at a time. Build up a complex idea by superimposing transparencies one at a time. Up to four overlays can be used successfully.

---

range from single simple transparencies to elaborate sets replete with multiple overlays, masking devices, and other teaching aids. Transparent plastic devices such as clocks, engines, slide rules, and the like are available. These can be manipulated by the instructor to demonstrate how the parts interact as they are displayed on the screen.

Creating Overhead Transparencies

As previously noted, one of the major advantages of the overhead system is that instructors—and students—can easily prepare their own transparencies. Beginning with simple hand drawing on clear acetate sheets, numerous other methods of preparing transparencies have evolved over the years. We will look closely at only the processes most commonly used at the classroom production level—direct drawing, thermal film process, and electrostatic film process (xerography).

Direct Drawing Method.

The most obvious way of quickly preparing a transparency is simply to draw directly on a transparent sheet with some sort of marking pen. Clear acetate of five to ten mils (.005–.010 inches) thickness is recommended. Other types of plastic can be used, even household food wrap and dry cleaning bags. Although some of these alternatives may be a great deal cheaper than the thicker acetate, some of them also impose limitations in terms of durability, ease of handling, and ability to accept different inks (i.e., disintegrating completely under alcohol-based inks). If

▼ **Figure 5.8**
Most overhead projector users like to draw directly on the transparency, in this case to add significant details to a previously prepared visual.

available, blue-tinted acetate is preferred because it reduces the glare of the projected image.

Although the glass platen or stage of the overhead projector generally measures about 10 by 10 inches, your drawing and lettering should be restricted to a rectangular "message area" of about 7½ by 9½ inches. This fits the dimensions of acetate sheets, which are commonly cut into rectangles of 8 by 10 inches or 8½ by 11 inches.

Some overhead projectors come equipped with a pair of roll attachments made to carry long rolls of plastic which can be advanced or reversed by a small hand crank. This assures a steady supply of transparency material for extemporaneous use. It also allows a series of images to be prepared in advance in proper sequence. Such rolls can be saved for later reuse.

In addition to the transparency, you will need a writing instrument. Felt-tipped marking pens are the handiest for this purpose. They come in two general types—*water-soluble* and *permanent ink*. Within these two types a wide variety of pens are available. Not all are suitable for overhead transparencies. Here are some important cautions to keep in mind:

- Markers with *water-soluble* ink generally will not adhere well to acetate; the ink tends to bead up and disappear as the water evaporates. A label stating "for overhead marking" means it *will adhere* to acetate and project in color. Such special pens can be erased readily with a damp cloth. This allows you to reuse the acetate sheet—a considerable advantage in view of the escalating cost of acetate, which is a petroleum product.
- Virtually all the permanent-ink felt-tipped pens will adhere to acetate, but only those labelled "for overhead marking" are sure to project *in color*. Otherwise the ink itself may be opaque and project only in black.
- Permanent inks really are permanent. They can be removed only with special plastic erasers.

Less frequently used but very serviceable are *wax-based* pencils, often referred to as "grease pencils." Unless otherwise marked, they will project black. The great advantage of wax-based pencils is that they can be erased from acetate with any soft, dry cloth.

Finally, there are some specially treated ("frosted") acetate sheets made to be typed on directly by a typewriter or written on with a pencil. This option should be used with some caution, however. It may encourage the unwarranted use of a visual medium for purely verbal instruction. In addition, most typewritten letters are too small to be legible when projected in a classroom. However, if a legible type is available (such as "Primary" typeface or IBM's "Orator" type) and the subject matter is necessarily verbal, typing on "frosted" sheets may be a useful alternative.

Thermal Film Process.

In the thermal film process infrared light passes through a specially treated acetate film onto a prepared master underneath. The art work and lettering on the master are done with a heat-absorbing material such as India ink, ordinary lead pencil, or other substance containing carbon. An image is "burned into" the film wherever it contacts such carbonaceous marking.

Depending on the film used, a number of different color patterns are possible. The most common pattern is color or black print on a clear or pastel background, analogous to positive film. Clear or colored lines can also be put on a black background, analogous to negative film.

Another option is the use of printed, commercially prepared transparency masters. Thermal film producers and other audiovisual publishers offer a broad range of printed masters—many thousands of individual titles covering virtually all curricular areas. Some publishers offer sets of masters specifically correlated with the leading textbooks in language arts, reading, math, social studies, and science.

To use commercially prepared thermal masters, simply remove one from the book or folder in which it is packaged, lay the thermal film on it with the notch in the upper right corner, and run both through the copier. Commercial masters may, of course, be altered by the instructor to better suit the needs of a particular audience.

Electrostatic Film Process (Xerography).

The rapidly evolving technology of xerography provides the newest

◀ **Figure 5.9**
Plastic erasers will remove permanent ink, at least that of the same manufacturer.

HOW TO...MAKE THERMAL TRANSPARENCIES

First prepare the master. Any ordinary white paper may be used. Draw the artwork by hand or paste illustrations from other sources (magazine illustrations, photocopies, etc.) onto the master. Lettering, added by hand, by mechanical lettering guide, or by paste-up of existing lettering, must consist of a carbonaceous substance. An alternative is to create the visual using any types of materials and then electrostatically copy it and use the copy as the master. (Note that some electrostatic copies work better than others. Experiment with what is available to you.)

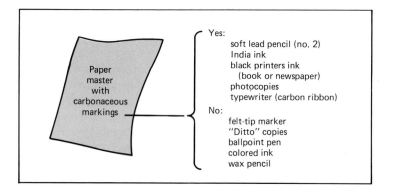

Paper master with carbonaceous markings

Yes:
soft lead pencil (no. 2)
India ink
black printers ink
(book or newspaper)
photocopies
typewriter (carbon ribbon)

No:
felt-tip marker
"Ditto" copies
ballpoint pen
colored ink
wax pencil

Second, place a sheet of thermal acetate over the master. Most brands of acetate have a notch in one corner of the film to ensure that it is put on correctly. The notch should always be placed at the upper right-hand corner of the master.

Thermal film

THERMAL COPIER

Third, feed the two sheets into a thermal copy machine, using the dial setting recommended by the manufacturer. Transfer of the image to the acetate requires only a few seconds. Then separate the two sheets. The film is ready for projection! The master is not affected in the production process and may be reused to make additional copies of the transparency.

method of producing transparencies. Xerox brand copy machines and other office copiers that operate by the electrostatic process can now be used to prepare black-and-white transparencies. Some models, such as the Xerox 6500, can produce high-quality full-color transparencies from originals on paper or from slides, but these costly machines are not widely available.

Similar to the thermal process, this process requires a paper master and specially treated film. In this case the film is electrically charged and light sensitive (rather than heat sensitive). The steps outlined above for thermal film are essentially the same as those needed to produce an electrostatic film transparency. However, since the xerographic process responds to darkness of the image rather than carbon content, it is not necessary to confine the art work to carbonaceous images. Any substance that yields a good opaque mark can be used.

Spirit-Duplication Process.
If you are already planning to make a spirit-duplicator master (often referred to by the brand name, Ditto), it is just one simple extra step to make a transparency from that master.

After you have prepared a regular spirit-duplicator master and mounted it on the duplicating machine, feed in a sheet of frosted acetate with the etched side up. If greater permanence is desired, the resulting transparency can be sprayed with a clear plastic spray, such as Krylon, which will remove the matte effect and protect the ink image from smearing.

An advantage of this process is that it allows you to use a master you may have prepared for another purpose to produce a transparency. Your students may then refer to their own copies of the visual while you project an image of it. A disadvantage is that the process requires some special materials—the frosted acetate and plastic spray.

Flashback: TRANSPARENCIES FROM THE PRINTED PAGE

Harvey Frye, the developer of many visual production techniques, accidentally discovered a process for "lifting" colored photographs from magazines and projecting them with the overhead. He recalled,

One evening, I was teaching rubber cement mounting in my basic production course. As is usually the case, students spilled rubber cement on the table top. This particular evening a student forgot and applied rubber cement to the face of the picture instead of the back side. Realizing what he had done, he threw the picture face down on the table where some rubber cement had been spilled. When the two surfaces of rubber cement touched, there was instant adhesion. It was left there until the end of class.

As always, I washed the tables with water to clean the surfaces for the next morning's class. As I washed the table, water ran over the picture. When I reached the end of the table where the picture was stuck, I pulled the wet page from the table surface. To my amazement and joy, I found a beautiful ink image on the table. There was a white chalky residue floating on the wet table surface which I later learned was the clay coating on the paper. The clay coating was the important element in making the transfer process possible.

This accident gave me a clue to a possible approach to transfer printed ink images from paper to acetate. Rubber cement is not water-soluble so it will remain stable while the clay coating, solvent in water, will break down, permitting the ink image to remain on the rubber cement surface. Thus, the first picture lift was made by applying rubber cement to an acetate surface and to the front of a picture printed on clay-surfaced paper such as Life *and* Time *magazines.*

During the mid-50s Harvey Frye and his assistants at Indiana University experimented and tried to find variations in the process. For simplicity's sake, they found that Frisket film used by airbrush artists as a mask was transparent and had a rubber cement type adhesive on one side. By pressing this down tightly on the picture surface, it would lift an image quite successfully. For a short time, this process was referred to as the "Fryeon" process in honor of its discoverer.

Harvey Frye continued to experiment with additional processes for making transparencies. His experimentation led him to use a piece of acetate that would withstand heat, spraying it with several coats of acrylic spray. After it dried, he placed a picture on the sprayed side and placed the combination in a mounting press. The process worked. The idea was introduced to Seal, Incorporated, who manufacture dry mount presses. After additional research they developed Transpara-Film. This product permitted the production of good, heavy-weight colored transparencies using heat.

Since Harvey Frye's experimentation in the 50s, a variety of methods for "lifting" have appeared using both hot and cold techniques. The hot processes include the use of clear laminating film with a dry mount press. The cold processes can use a variety of products such as clear Con-Tact paper. Unfortunately, in recent years publishers have modified their printing processes for "slick" clay-coated magazines and now spray them with a clear plastic film, so the "lifting" processes do not work on as many magazines as they did when accidentally discovered by Frye in the early 1950s.

HOW TO... DESIGN OVERHEAD TRANSPARENCIES

Whatever production process you choose for preparing your transparencies, keep in mind these design guidelines based on research and practical experience:

- *Horizontal* format covers projected viewing area best.

- *Visual* ideas should be used for overheads. Diagrams, graphs, and charts should be incorporated. If not, consider using chalkboard or print to convey verbal information.

- *A single concept* should be expressed in simple, uncluttered visuals. In general, not more than three or four images per transparency.

- *Minimum verbiage* should be included, with not more than six words per line and six or fewer lines per transparency.

- *Key words* help the audience remember each point. These are usually most effective as "headlines" at the top of the visual.

- *Legibility* is important. One quick way to check it is to lay the transparency on the floor over a white piece of paper. If you can read it from a standing position, your audience should be able to read it when projected. Use letters at least 3/16-inch high.

- *Overlays* can explain complex ideas by adding information sequentially to the base transparency.

SLIDES

The term *slide* refers to a *small-format photographic transparency individually mounted for one-at-a-time projection.*

The size of slide most frequently encountered in educational use is 2-by-2 inches. (metric equivalency either 50 by 50 millimeters or 5 by 5 centimeters), measured by the outer dimensions of the slide mount. When 35-mm and other popular types of slide film are sent out to be processed they are usually returned mounted in 2-by-2 inch mounts. The actual dimensions of the *image* itself will vary with the type of film (Figure 5.10).

Another standard format still found in occasional use is the 3¼-by-4-inch slide, used with the projector known popularly as the lantern slide projector. It represents one of the oldest formats of image projection, being descended from the old "magic lantern" slides which were a popular entertainment medium back before the days of motion pictures.

The chief reason to use the lantern slide is that it is larger than 2-by-2-inch slides. Maps charts, tables, and other detailed subjects can be presented more effectively since the larger film affords greater detail in the image. When the image is projected it can fill a larger screen with less loss of definition and less room darkening required.

A second advantage of the larger size of the slide is that it allows slides to be hand-drawn. Various pencils and inks can be drawn directly onto frosted glass; silhouettes or thin specimens can be mounted between clear glass mounts; and photos, including the Polaroid instant type, can be shot on slide film in this format. The recent addition of the Polaroid option plus newer projectors featuring automatic advance and remote control have helped bring this older format more up-to-date.

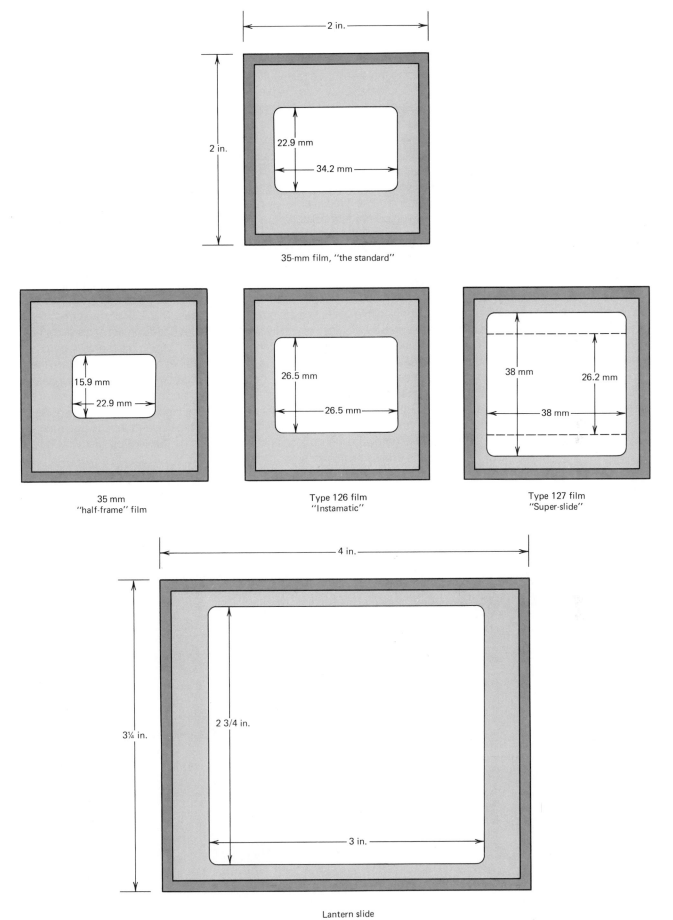

▲ **Figure 5.10**
Common 2-by-2 inch slide formats compared with the lantern slide format.

Advantages

Since slides can be arranged and re-arranged into an infinite variety of sequences they are more flexible than filmstrips or other fixed-sequence materials.

As photographic equipment is continually refined and simplified, more and more amateurs are able to produce their own slides. Automatic exposure controls, easy focusing, and high-speed color films have contributed to this trend. High-quality color pictures can be taken by any amateur photographer.

The assembly of slide programs is facilitated by today's automatic projectors, which hold sets of slides in trays and feed them into place in sequence. Most automatic projectors also offer the convenience of remote control advancing of slides, allowing the presenter to remain at the front of the room or off to a side while advancing the slides via a pushbutton unit connected by wire to the projector. Certain models can be preset to advance automatically. This feature allows continuous showing in exhibits, display cases, and other automated situations.

General availability and ease of handling make it relatively easy to build up permanent collections of slides for specific instructional purposes. Instructors may collect and store their own collections, or the slides may be compiled and kept in a learning resource center. Such collections enable users to assemble presentations partially or wholly from existing pictures, thus reducing the expense required for new production.

Slides can be integrated into individualized instruction programs. Although slides have been developed primarily as a large-group medium, recent hardware innovations have made slides feasible for small-group and independent study as well. However, the complex nature of these new mechanisms makes them relatively expensive. Thus slide-tape viewers for individual use are more likely to be found in learning resource centers than in classrooms (Figure 5.13).

Limitations

Since slides, unlike filmstrips, come as individual units, they can easily become disorganized. Even when they are stored in trays, if the locking ring is loosened the slides can come spilling out.

Slide mounts come in cardboard, plastic, and glass of varying thicknesses. This lack of standardization can lead to jamming of slides in the slide-changing mechanism: cardboard becomes dog-eared with the frayed edges getting caught in the mechanism; plastic mounts swell or warp in the heat of the lamp; glass mounts thicker than the aperture chamber fail to drop into showing position.

Slides which are not enclosed in glass covers are susceptible to accu-

▼ **Figure 5.11**
Originally, slides were fed into the projector one at a time, and manual feed projectors are still in use.

▼ **Figure 5.12**
The Ektagraphic III is Kodak's latest updating of the Carousel line of slide projectors.

▼ **Figure 5.13**
The slide-tape format has been adapted for individual viewers.

AV SHOWMANSHIP—SLIDES

In addition to the general guidelines for audiovisual utilization discussed in Chapter 2, here are several specific practices that can add professionalism to your slide presentations:

Use a remote control advance device; this will allow you to stand at the side of the room. From this position you can keep an eye on the slides while maintaining some eye contact with the audience.

Make *very* certain your slides are in sequential order and right-side up. Disarrangement can be an embarrassment to you and an annoyance to your audience. Refer to the section below, "How to…Thumb Spot Slides," to find a foolproof method of avoiding this embarrassment.

Employ visual variety. Mix the types of slides, using verbal title slides to help break the presentation into segments.

Prepare a way to light up your script after the room lights are dimmed; a penlight or flashlight will serve this purpose.

Limit your discussion of each slide—even a min-ute of narration can seem long to your audience unless there is a complex visual to be examined at the same time.

Plan and rehearse your narration to accompany the slides if it is not already recorded on tape.

If there is a "talky" section in the middle of your presentation, put a gray or black slide on rather than holding an irrelevant slide on the screen. (Gray slides can be produced locally or purchased from commercial sources. They let through enough light to allow the presenter to be seen, avoiding total darkening of the room during the "blackout.")

Consider adding a musical accompaniment to your live or recorded narration. This can help to establish the desired mood and keep your audience attentive. But do not have music playing in the background when providing narration.

Begin and end with a black slide. A white flash on the screen at the beginning and end is irritating to the eye and appears amateurish.

---

mulation of dust and fingerprints. Careless storage or handling can easily lead to permanent damage.

A final limitation of slides is their cost in comparison to filmstrips. The cost *per frame* of a commercially produced slide set may be two to three times the cost per frame of a filmstrip of equal length.

The examples below give some idea of the types of slide materials available through commercial channels. A major directory of commercially available slides is published by the National Information Center for Educational Media (NICEM)—*Index to Educational Slides*. See Appendix A for details and other sources.

Local Production of Slides.

As noted earlier, a major advantage of slides as an instructional device is the ease with which they can be produced by instructors—and students. Modern cameras are so simple to operate that even the most amateur of photographers can expect usable results. As

Applications

Like other forms of projected visuals, slides may be used at all grade levels and for instruction in all curricular areas. A good many high-quality slides are available commercially, individually, and in sets. In general, the fine arts, geography, and the sciences are especially well represented with commercially distributed slides.

Media File:
Harbrace "Science 700" Slides

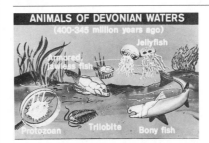

ANIMALS OF DEVONIAN WATERS
(400-345 million years ago)

"Science 700" consists of three sets of slide programs: Life Science, Earth Science, and Physical Science. All the slides are developed with dark backgrounds to allow projection on chalkboards in normal room lighting.

Source: Harcourt, Brace, Jovanovich.

HOW TO... "THUMB SPOT" SLIDES

There are eight possible ways a slide can be placed in a projector. *Seven of them are wrong* (e.g., upside-down, backwards, sideways, etc.). To avoid all seven mistakes a standardized procedure is recommended for placing a reminder spot on the slide.

First, your slides should be arranged and numbered in the order in which they are to be shown.

Then take each slide and hold it the way it is supposed to be seen on the screen, that is, right-side up with any lettering running left to right—just as it would be read. (If the slide lacks lettering or other orienting information, hold it so that the *emulsion* side is toward the screen.)

IL 5-20 (W81)

Then simply place a spot on the bottom lefthand corner.

This spot is referred to as a "thumb spot" because when the slide is turned upside-down to be placed in the projector your thumb will grip the slide at the point of the thumb spot, as shown below.

Before all the slides are put in the tray in proper order, some users like to run a felt-tip pen across the tops of the slide mounts in a diagonal line. This way if some slides later get out of order they can be replaced just by following the line.

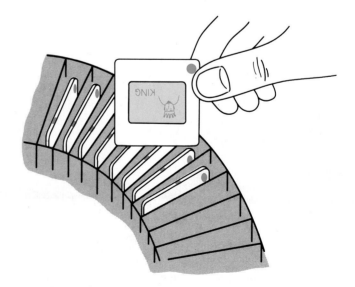

Media File:
"Contemporary Painting and Sculpture" Slides

A set of 480 slides illustrates contemporary works of painting and sculpture, including landscapes, figurative, still life, new realism, pop art, and surrealism.

Source: Art Now, Inc.

with all locally produced materials, instructor- and student-made slides are likely to have an immediacy and a specificity lacking in commercially produced instructional materials. Further, such locally produced efforts gain credibility by depicting local people and conditions.

Among the myriad possibilities, here are some ideas of typical subjects for slide presentations:

- Providing a local "plant tour" for new employees without walking through the plant.
- Making a visual history of your community, school, or organization.
- Demonstrating local operating and sales procedures for real estate agents.
- Documenting student activities, products of student work, community problems (e.g., crime and pollution).
- Presenting preoperative explanation about a surgical procedure personalized for a specific surgeon's patients.
- Showing people at work in various jobs, for career awareness.
- Illustrating the uses of a company's products throughout the world.
- Teaching a step-by-step process with close-ups of each operation.
- Simulating a field trip.
- Promoting public understanding of your school or organization.

Using the Kodak Visualmaker. Along with modern camera technology, a further boon to teacher/student production of slides has been a device called the Kodak Ektagraphic Visualmaker. This device permits reproduction of flat visual materials—such as magazine illustrations, maps, charts, photographs, business forms, and the like—without the need for specialized photography skills. The secret is in the Visualmaker hardware itself: a copy stand containing a built-in supplementary lens that is positioned and focused to allow easy picture taking with a Kodak Instamatic camera. This preset mechanism eliminates the need for extra lenses and specialized skills in proper framing of the picture (See "How To . . . Make Slides with the Visualmaker").

◀ **Figure 5.14**
Teacher-made slides can be used to provoke discussion before or after a field trip.

HOW TO...MAKE SLIDES WITH THE VISUALMAKER

The basic steps for making slides from visuals are simple and foolproof:

1. *Select a suitable visual.* Keep in mind that the flash unit will flood a lot of light onto the picture. If the picture is shiny, that light will reflect back in the form of glare. So avoid glossy photos and glass, acetate, and such surfaces. White backgrounds, too, should be avoided. Photographs, drawings, and tables from books, magazines, and other printed materials generally reproduce well.[a]
2. *Attach the Instamatic camera to one of the two copy stands included in the Visualmaker kit.* The Visualmaker kit is equipped with a copy stand with an 8-by-8-inch frame and a smaller one with a 3-by-3-inch frame. Choose the one that frames your visual best.
3. *Compose the shot.* If your visual is equal to or larger than the frame, keep in mind that its outer edges will be lost. Make sure that important visual information is no more than 7½ inches square (for the large copystand) or 2¾ inches square (for the small copystand). Keep critical information out of the "bleed" area around the border.

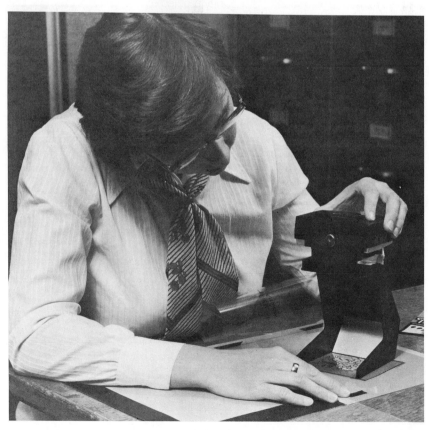

4. *Add lettering, if appropriate.* Lettering can be added to your visual with a typewriter if you are using the small copystand. Size and specifications are shown. However, if you are using the large copystand, you will need to use dry-transfer letters, cutouts, a "primary" or "bulletin board" typewriter, or some other special lettering method. The letters should be at least ⅜-inch high in order to be legible when projected on the screen.

```
TYPED LETTERING
FOR SLIDES SHOULD
BE ALL CAPITALS,
DOUBLE-SPACED,
AND NO MORE THAN
SEVEN LINES LONG.
```

5. *Mask the visual, if necessary.* If your visual is smaller than the frame, mask the extra space with dark construction paper or other such matte material as shown. Textured fabrics also make attractive backgrounds. Again, avoid white or shiny materials, to reduce possible glare.

6. *Snap the shutter and it's done!* The Visualmaker system is designed to provide adequate, even lighting by means of the flash unit supplied with the kit. The type of flash unit is determined by what vintage Visualmaker you are using. Two models are in common use: the Kodak Ektagraphic Visualmaker and the Kodak Ektagraphic EF Visualmaker. The former is the older model, distributed prior to 1979; it uses Magicubes as a lighting source. The EF model comes equipped with a special electronic flash unit (thereby doing away with the need to keep a stock of Magicubes on hand). Hold the camera down firmly with one hand while squeezing the shutter release with the other hand.

NOTE: Three-dimensional objects will photograph well if they are not too thick. With the large Visualmaker copystand, the sharp-focus area extends up to about 1½ inches above the table top. With smaller copystand, ½-inch is approximately the thickness limit.

For more complete information, see the Kodak publication *Simple Copying Techniques with a Kodak Ektagraphic Visualmaker* (publication #S-40), available from audiovisual dealers or the Eastman Kodak Company, Rochester, NY 14650.

[a]Remember that published materials including illustrations are protected by the copyright laws. For an extensive discussion of educator's rights and responsibilities refer to Appendix C.

FILMSTRIPS

A *filmstrip* is a *roll of 35-mm transparent film containing a series of related still pictures intended for showing one at a time.*

Various filmstrip formats have evolved since the advent of the filmstrip over a half century ago. Formats most widely seen today are the single frame and the double frame filmstrip. The difference between the two types is illustrated below. Note that in the single frame format the images are printed *perpendicular* to the length of the film, whereas in the double frame format the images are *parallel* to the length of the film. A second major distinction is that the double frame image has twice the area of the single frame image. It is, in fact, the same size and configuration as the 35-mm slide before the slide is cut apart and mounted. (In North America the single frame format is standard; in Europe the double frame is more common.)

Commercially produced filmstrips typically contain about twenty to sixty images or "frames" and are stored rolled up in small plastic canisters.

Until the 1960s most filmstrips were silent; that is, there was no audio accompaniment. Narrative information was printed at the bottom of each frame. Since that time there has been a growing trend toward having recorded sound tracks accompany the filmstrip. Initially the narration, music, sound effects, and so on were recorded on phonograph records and were played on record players either separate from the projector or built into it. Currently audiocassette tapes are becoming the standard means for giving *sound filmstrips* their "voice." It should be noted that the sound track is not recorded on the filmstrip itself; rather, it comes on a separate cassette tape which is played back on a regular cassette recorder or on one built into the filmstrip projector unit.

For most sound filmstrips, the record or tape contains, besides the sound track, a second track carrying inaudible signals that automatically trigger the projector to advance to the next frame. Depending upon the capability of the projector, users generally have a choice of manually advancing the filmstrip according to audible beeps or setting the projector to run automatically according to the inaudible synchronization pulses.

Advantages

The filmstrip has gained considerable popularity because of its compactness, ease of handling, and relatively low cost. A filmstrip of sixty frames will fit comfortably in the palm of your hand and weighs only a few ounces. It is inserted easily into a simple projector. A commercially distributed filmstrip costs substantially less *per frame* than a set of slides or overhead transparencies purchased from commercial sources.

The sequential order of the frames can often be a teaching and learning advantage. A chronological or step-by-step process can be presented *exactly in order* without any fear of hav-

▼ **Figure 5.17**
Newer model silent filmstrip projectors feature easy threading and remote-control advance.

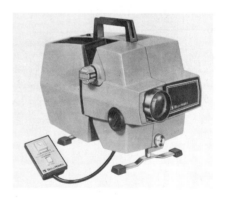

▼ **Figure 5.15**
The filmstrip and its canister make a small, light package.

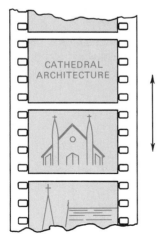

Single frame filmstrip
. . . standard in the U.S.

◀▼ **Figure 5.16**
Comparison of the single-frame filmstrip and 35-mm slide formats.

movement through projector

Double frame
filmstrip

ing any of the pictures out of sequence or upside-down, as can sometimes happen with slides.

In contrast with audio and motion media, the pace of viewing filmstrips can be controlled by the user. This capability is especially relevant for independent study, but is also important for teacher-controlled group showings. A slow, deliberate examination of each frame might be suitable for the body of a lesson, while a quick runthrough might suffice for purposes of advance overview and review. Not only the pace, but also the level of instruction can be controlled. Particularly with silent filmstrips, the vocabulary and/or level of

narration supplied by the presenter can be adapted to audience abilities.

Filmstrips lend themselves well to independent study. Many types of tabletop viewers are made especially for individual or small-group use. Young children have no difficulty loading light, compact filmstrips into these viewers. The fixed sequence of the frames structures the learner's progress through the material; the captions or recorded narration add a verbal component to the visuals, creating a convenient self-contained learning "package." And because the user controls the rate of presentation, the filmstrip allows self-pacing when used for independent study.

Limitations

Having the frames permanently fixed in a certain sequence has disadvantages as well as advantages. The main drawback is that it is not possible to alter the sequence of pictures without destroying the filmstrip. Backtracking to an earlier picture or skipping over frames is cumbersome.

Since the filmstrip is pulled through its projector by means of toothed sprocket wheels, there is the constant possibility of tearing the sprocket holes and/or damaging the film. Improper threading or rough use

can cause tears which are very difficult for you to repair, although, if you have a 35-mm splicing block, not impossible. (In cases where damage to the sprocket holes is extensive, the frames can be cut apart and mounted individually to be used as slides.)

Applications

Because they are simply packaged and easy to handle, filmstrips are well suited to independent study use. They are popular items in study carrels and media centers. Students enjoy using filmstrips on their own to help prepare research reports to their classmates.

The major difference in application between slides and filmstrips is that slides lend themselves to teacher-made presentations while filmstrips are better suited to mass production and distribution. Further, slide sets tend to be used in a more open-ended fashion than filmstrips. Nowadays filmstrips are usually packaged as self-contained kits. That is, the narration to accompany the pictures is provided either in the form of captions on the filmstrip, or a recorded sound track on record or cassette. Other teacher support materials may be integrated into the kit.

As with the other sorts of projected visuals discussed in this chapter, filmstrips find appropriate applications in a wide variety of subjects and grade levels. Their broad appeal is attested to by the constantly growing volume of commercial materials available. Tens of thousands of titles are already in distribution. Indeed, it would be difficult to identify an audiovisual medium offering a larger number of different titles in commercial distribution.

A small sample of the broad range of filmstrips on the market is illustrated by the examples below. A major directory of commercially available filmstrips is published by the

▼ **Figure 5.18**
Sound filmstrip projectors combine cassette and filmstrip functions in one machine.

▼ **Figure 5.19**
A compact tabletop viewer for silent filmstrips.

▼ **Figure 5.20**
The tabletop sound filmstrip viewer can serve an individual or a small group and it can be viewed in a fully lighted room.

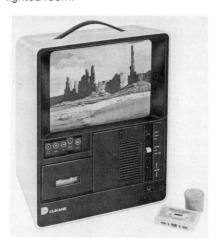

National Information Center for Educational Media (NICEM) *Index to 35mm Filmstrips.* See Appendix A for details and other sources.

An innovation introduced in 1984 may foreshadow a future role for the filmstrip as an element in interactive video programs. The Society for Visual Education (SVE), a major commercial distributor of filmstrips, produced a single videodisc incorporating more than 30,000 still pictures. The videodisc player is connected to a microcomputer containing a computer-assisted instruction program. The computer program presents verbal instruction *and* controls the videodisc player, calling up particular pictures onto the display screen as needed. The entire videodisc—all 30,000 images—can be scanned in less than five seconds and the desired frame inserted in the lesson. As

is discussed in detail in Chapter 7, interactive video is usually thought of as combining moving images (television) with computer interaction, but in many learning situations only still pictures are needed. The SVE system could suit those purposes, eliminating television production costs and recycling vast libraries of existing pictures.

▼ **Figure 5.21**
A filmstrip library of 30,000 frames can be stored on a single videodisc.

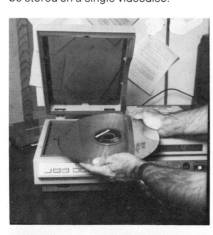

Media File:
"Myths of Greece and Rome" Filmstrip

Dramatic filmstrip stories introduce some of the great myths and dominant themes in mythology. Carefully detailed and researched artwork with captions illustrates how these ancient characters still play a role in our language, culture, science, and symbolism.

Source: Society for Visual Education, Inc.

Media File:
"The American Revolution: Who Was Right?" Filmstrip

The American Revolution would never have occurred if there had not been disagreement between England and her colonies. Both sides of the issues are revealed through visuals and spoken dialogue. One recording discusses the topic from the English point of view and the other recording gives the American interpretation using the same visuals. The categories have been carefully selected in order to present material that was not only relevant in 1776, but is still discussed and pertinent today.

Source: Denoyer-Geppert.

AV SHOWMANSHIP—FILMSTRIP

The general utilization guidelines discussed in Chapter 2 apply comprehensively to filmstrip use. There are several additional points, though, that pertain especially to filmstrips:

Do not feel compelled to run the filmstrip all the way through without stopping. You can do this as a kind of *overview* and then go back and reshow it, pausing for discussion at key frames.

Encourage *participation* by asking relevant questions during the presentation.

Use filmstrips to *test* visually the mastery of visual concepts. This can be done, for instance, by projecting individual frames without the caption or sound track and asking students to make an identification or discrimination.

OPAQUE PROJECTION

Opaque projection, as noted above, is a method for *projecting opaque visuals by reflecting light off the material rather than transmitting light through it*. The opaque projector was among the first audiovisual devices to come into widespread use and is still used because of its unique ability to project a magnified image of two-dimensional materials and some three-dimensional objects.

The opaque projector works by directing a very strong incandescent light (typically about 1000 watts) down onto the material. This light is reflected upward to strike a mirror which aims the light beam through a series of lenses onto a screen (Figure 5.22).

The process of reflected, or indirect, projection is optically less efficient than the direct projection process used for showing slides, filmstrips, and overhead transparencies. Consequently, the image on the screen is dimmer and much more complete room darkening is required. Still, opaque projection makes such a wide range of visual materials available for group viewing that it should not be overlooked as a valuable tool.

Advantages

Opaque projection allows on-the-spot projection of readily available classroom materials, such as maps, newspapers, and illustrations from books and magazines (Figure 5.23).

It permits group viewing and discussion of student work, such as drawings, student compositions, solutions to math problems, and the like.

Three-dimensional objects, especially relatively flat ones such as coins, plant leaves, and insect specimens, can be magnified for close-up inspection.

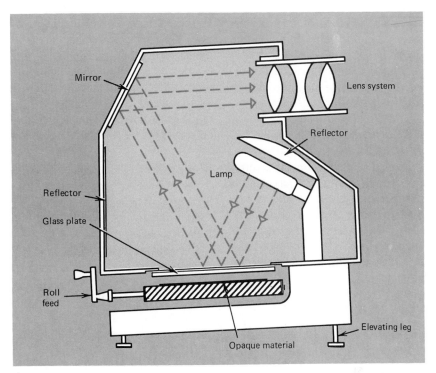

▲ **Figure 5.22**
Opaque projector, cutaway view.

▼ **Figure 5.23**
The opaque projector can be used to magnify small objects, such as coins, as well as print materials and pictures.

Limitations

The relative dimness of the reflected image demands rather complete room darkening if the visual is to be clear enough for instructional purposes. Areas that cannot be sufficiently darkened are unsuitable for opaque projection.

The opaque projector is bulky, heavy, and cumbersome to move.

The high-wattage lamp generates a lot of heat, raising the room temperature and possibly even making parts of the projector unsafe to touch. The heat may also damage the materials being projected if they are exposed too long to the projector's light. If metal objects are being projected they may rapidly become too hot to handle.

Applications

The opaque projector is useful for many small groups or classroom size groups (up to about twenty) that need to view some printed or visual material together. Applications may be found in all curricular areas at all grade levels. Here are just a few typical examples:

All subjects—group critique of student work and review of test items.

Art—group discussion of reproductions of paintings and architectural details; close-up views of fabrics and weaving styles; study of advertising layouts.

Business—group work on business and accounting forms, organization charts, sales territory maps, parts of a product, and the like.

Home economics—group viewing of sewing patterns, textiles, recipes, etc.

Industry—projection of blueprints for group study; description of assembly line flow with production diagrams.

Language arts—group critique of student compositions, picture books, or reference books.

Medical—group study of anatomical drawings; discussion of diabetic diets and food exchange charts.

Military—review of maps and official documents; illustration of flight plans.

Music—group reading of musical scores.

Religious education—Bible story illustrations; group examination of religious documents.

Science—magnification of specimens; group study of geologic maps, tables of random numbers, and the like.

Social studies—map study; viewing of artifacts from other cultures, post cards, and atlas illustrations.

AV SHOWMANSHIP—OPAQUE PROJECTION

In addition to the general principles of audiovisual utilization discussed in Chapter 2, there are several special techniques that apply particularly to opaque projection.

Since the opaque projector requires near-total room darkening, be prepared to operate in the dark. A student should be stationed at the light switch to help you avoid tripping over students, cords, and other obstacles in getting to and from the projector in the dark. Although the projector does spill quite a bit of light around its sides, you may need to use a *flashlight* to follow any prepared notes or script.

Most opaque projectors are equipped with a built-in optical *pointer*—a bright arrow that can be aimed at any point on the screen. Experiment ahead of time so that you will be able to aim the pointer effectively during the presentation. It can be used to focus viewers' attention to particular words on a printed page, details of an art work, and so on.

For some purposes (especially in teaching elementary-school language arts) it is useful to arrange pictures on a long strip or roll of paper. In this way you can put a series of illustrations into a fixed sequence to tell a story or show steps in a process. This simulates the action of a filmstrip.

The opaque projector will accept a wide range of picture sizes. When you are setting up the projector, be sure to use the *largest* of your illustrations to center the image on the screen. If you center with a smaller picture, the bigger one will extend beyond the edges of the screen when you get to it. This will force you to stop in the middle of the presentation (and thus distract your audience) to adjust for the big picture.

Appraisal Checklist: Projected Visuals

Series title (if applicable)_____

Individual title_____

Producer/distributor_____   Date_____

Length_____frames   _____minutes (sound track)

Intended audience/grade level_____   Subject area_____

FORMAT:

☐ Overhead

Objectives (stated or implied):

☐ Slides

☐ Filmstrip

Brief description:

Entry capabilities required:
— prior subject matter knowledge
— reading ability
— math ability (or other)

Rating	High		Medium		Low
Likely to arouse student interest	☐	☐	☐	☐	☐
Technical quality	☐	☐	☐	☐	☐
Provides relevant viewer practice/participation	☐	☐	☐	☐	☐
Relevant to curricular needs	☐	☐	☐	☐	☐
Focuses clearly on its objectives	☐	☐	☐	☐	☐
Evidence of effectiveness (e.g., field test results)	☐	☐	☐	☐	☐
Provides guide for follow-up, discussion	☐	☐	☐	☐	☐
Free from race, gender, other bias	☐	☐	☐	☐	☐

Strong points:

Weak points:

Reviewer_____

Position_____

Recommended action_____   Date_____

▲ **Figure 5.24**
Copying visuals for classroom display is easy with the opaque projector.

One especially handy application of the opaque projector is to use it to copy or adapt illustrations for classroom display. You can make your own enlargement of any original picture that you might want to display on the chalkboard or as part of a bulletin board. The procedure is easy. Place the material to be copied in the projector and dim the room lights. Adjust the projector to enlarge (or reduce) the image to the size you want, and direct the projected image onto the surface on which you are working. Then trace over the projected image in whatever detail you wish. Every line of the original can be reproduced, or just the outlines for a more stylized effect. Your students will be impressed with your "artistic ability," and maybe you will be too.

SELECTION CRITERIA FOR PROJECTED VISUALS

This chapter has attempted to survey broadly the many similarities and differences among several major formats of projected visuals—overhead projection, slides, filmstrips and opaque projection. You might have noticed that the differences are mainly logistical ones—small technical differences that lead to trade-offs in cost, portability, flexibility, and so on. Basically, projected visuals look very much alike on the screen. For the viewer/learner there is, in most cases, "no significant difference" among these formats in terms of learning impact. So it is appropriate that the chapter close by emphasizing the commonalities among the various types of projected visuals. The "Appraisal Checklist: Projected Visuals" is designed to apply equally to the various formats.

References

Print References

Barman, C. "Some Ways to Improve Your Overhead Projection Transparencies." *American Biology Teacher* (March 1982), pp. 191–192.

Beatty, LaMond F. *Filmstrips.* (Englewood Cliffs, N.J.: Educational Technology Publications, 1981).

Bohning, G. "Storytelling Using Overhead Visuals." *Reading Teacher* (March 1984), pp. 677–678.

Brainard, Alan J. "Preparing Effective Slides for Classroom Use." *Engineering Education* (February 1976), pp. 412–414.

Burton, D. "Slide Art." *School Arts* (February 1984), pp. 23–26.

Center for Vocational Education. *Present Information with Overhead and Opaque Materials.* (Athens, Ga.: American Association for Vocational Instructional Materials, 1977).

————. *Present Information with Filmstrips and Slides.* (Athens, Ga.: American Association for Vocational Instructional Materials, 1977).

Dayton, Deane K. "How to Make Title Slides with High Contrast Film, Part 1." *Audiovisual Instruction* (April 1977), pp. 33–36.

DeChenne, J. "Effective Utilization of Overhead Projectors." *Media and Methods* (January 1982), pp. 6–7.

Effective Visual Presentations. (Rochester, N. Y.: Eastman Kodak, 1979).

Elliot, Floyd. *The Filmstrip—A Useful Teaching Aid.* (Montreal, Canada: National Film Board of Canada, 1963).

Gibson, Stephanie S. "Teaching Basic Concepts with Slides." *Arithmetic Teacher* (October 1977), pp. 47–48.

Green, Lee. *501 Ways to Use the Overhead Projector.* (Littleton, Colo.: Libraries Unlimited, 1982).

Johnson, Roger. "Overhead Projectors: Basic Media for a Community College." *Audiovisual Instruction* (March 1978), pp. 21–22.

Jones, J. Rhodri. "Getting the Most out of an Overhead Projector." *English Language Teaching Journal* (April 1978), pp. 194–201.

Kueter, Roger A., and Miller, Janeen. *Slides*. (Englewood Cliffs, N. J.: Educational Technology Publications, 1981).

McBride, Dennis. *How to make Visual Presentations*. (New York: Art Direction Book Company, 1982).

May, Jill P. *Films and Filmstrips for Language Arts: An Annotated Bibliography*. (Urbana, Ill.: National Council of Teachers of English, 1981).

Perez, Fred. "Using Slides to Promote Intramurals." *Journal of Physical Education and Recreation* (May 1978), p.63ff.

Radcliffe, Beverly. "Using the Overhead Projector for Homework Correction." *Foreign Language Annals* (April 1984), pp. 119–121.

Rees, Alan L. "Cartoon Slides for the Language Class." *English Language Teaching Journal* (July 1978), pp. 274–281.

Ring, Arthur. *Planning and Producing Handmade Slides and Filmstrips for the Classroom*. (Belmont, Calif.: Pitman Learning, 1974).

Runte, Roseann. "Focusing in on the Slide—Its Practical Applications." *Canadian Modern Language Review* (March 1977), pp. 547–551.

Sheard, B. V. "They Love to Read Aloud from Filmstrips." *Teacher* (May 1973), p. 66ff.

Walther, R. E. "Mind-Bending Visuals." *Training* (April 1978), pp. 34–35.

White, Gene. "From Magic Lanterns to Microcomputers: The Evolution of the Visual Aid in the English Classroom. *English Journal* (March 1984), pp. 59–62.

Winters, Harold A. "Some Unconventional Uses of the Overhead Projector in Teaching Geography." *Journal of Geography* (November 1976), pp. 467–469.

Audiovisual References

"Color Lift" Transparencies. Salt Lake City, Utah: Media Systems, 1975. Filmstrip or slides, 40 frames, captioned.

Effective Projection, Photography for Audiovisual Production, and *The Impact of Visuals in the Speechmaking Process*. Eastman Kodak, 1982. 3 filmstrips with audiocassettes.

"I Like the Overhead Projector Because . . ." Washington, D.C.: National Audiovisual Center, 1977. Filmstrip with audiocassette, 12 minutes, color.

Use of the Overhead Projector and How to Make Do-It-Yourself Transparencies. Swan Pencil Co., n.d. 80 slides with cassette. 18 minutes.

Possible Projects

5-A. Take a series of slides for use in your teaching. Describe your objectives, the intended audience, and how the slides will be used.

5-B. Design a lesson around a commercially available filmstrip. Describe your objectives, the intended audience, how the filmstrip will be used, and how the lesson will be evaluated. (If possible, submit the filmstrip with the project.)

5-C. Prepare transparencies using both the write-on and thermal method.

5-D. Prepare a set of visuals for use with an opaque projector.

5-E. Preview a set of slides or a filmstrip. Complete an appraisal sheet (from the text or one of your own design) on the materials.

5-F. Examine *two* of the selection sources for slides, filmstrips, or overheads and report on the kinds of materials you believe would be appropriate for your teaching situation.

Audio Media

Outline

Objectives

After studying this chapter, you should be able to:

1.   Distinguish between "hearing" and "listening."

2.   Identify four areas of breakdown in audio communication and specify the causes of such breakdowns.

3.   Describe four techniques for improving listening skills.

4.   Discuss ten attributes of audio media including five advantages and five limitations.

5.   Describe the four types of audio media most often used for instruction. Include in your description the distinguishing characteristics and limitations.

6.   Describe one possible use of audio media in your teaching field. Include the subject area, the audience, objective(s), role of the student, and the evaluation techniques to be used.

7.   Identify five criteria for appraising/selecting audio materials.

8.   Discuss the techniques for making your own audio tapes including guidelines for the recorder controls, the acoustics, microphone placement, tape content, and audio presentation.

9.   Distinguish among the common types of microphones.

10.   Describe two procedures for duplicating audio tapes.

11.   Describe two procedures for editing audio tapes.

12.   Identify the advantages of "rate-controlled audio playback."

13.   Describe a situation in which a telelecture would enhance an instructional activity.

14.   Describe a situation in which a teleconference would be more cost effective than conventional methods.

15.   Select the best audio format for a given instructional situation and justify the selection of that format stating advantages and/or disadvantages.

Lexicon

hearing
listening
open reel tape
cassette
audio card
oral history
acoustics
rate controlled playback
telelecture
teleconference

If you were asked which learning activities consume the major portion of a student's classroom time, would you say reading instructional materials, answering questions, reciting what one has learned, or taking tests? Actually, typical elementary and secondary students spend about 50 percent of their school time just listening (or at least "hearing," which, as we shall see, is not the same as "listening"). College students are likely to spend nearly 90 percent of their time in class listening to lectures and seminar discussions. The importance, then, of audio media in the classroom should not be underestimated. By *audio media* we mean the various means of recording and transmitting the human voice and other sounds for instructional purposes. The audio devices most commonly found in the classroom are the phonograph or record player, the open reel tape recorder, the cassette tape recorder, and the audio card reader.

Before going on to discuss these audio formats in particular and audio media in general, let us examine the hearing/listening process itself, as it pertains to the communication of ideas and information and to the development of listening skills.

THE HEARING / LISTENING PROCESS

Hearing and listening are not the same thing, although they are, of course, interrelated. At the risk of some oversimplification, we might say that hearing is a *physiological* process, whereas listening is a *psychological* process.

Physiologically, *hearing* is a process in which sound waves entering the outer ear are transmitted to the eardrum, converted into mechanical vibrations in the middle ear, and changed in the inner ear into nerve impulses that travel to the brain (Figure 6.2).

The psychological process of *listening* begins with someone's awareness of and attention to sounds or speech patterns, proceeds through identification and recognition of specific auditory signals, and ends in comprehension.

The hearing/listening process is also a communication/learning process. As with visual communication and learning, a message is encoded by a sender and decoded by a receiver. The quality of the encoded message is affected by the ability of the sender to express the message clearly and logically. The quality of the decoded message is affected by the ability of the receiver to comprehend the message.

The efficiency of communication is also affected by the hearing/listening process as the message passes from sender to receiver. The message can be affected by physical problems such as impaired hearing mechanisms. It also can be affected by auditory fatigue. The brain has a remarkable capacity for filtering out sounds it doesn't want or need to hear. We have all had the experience of "tuning out" a boring conversationalist, or gradually losing cognizance of noises (the ticking of a clock, traffic outside a window, etc.) that seemed obtrusive when we first encountered them. Nevertheless, in the classroom extraneous noise can

▲ **Figure 6.1**
Elementary/secondary students spend about half of their in-school time listening to others; at the college level closer to 90 percent of class time is spent listening.

cause auditory fatigue and make communication difficult. A monotonous tone or a droning voice can also reduce communication efficiency by contributing to auditory fatigue.

The message can also be affected by the receiver's listening skills or lack of them. The receiver must be able to direct and sustain concentration on a given series of sounds (the message). He or she must have the skill to "think ahead" as the message is being received (we think faster than we hear, just as we think faster than we read or write) and use this time differential to organize and internalize the information so that it can be comprehended.

Breakdowns in audio communications, then, can occur at any point in the process: encoding, hearing, listening, or decoding, as illustrated in Figure 6.3. Proper encoding of the message depends upon the sender's skill in organizing and presenting it. For example, the vocabulary level of the message must be within the vocabulary range of the receiver. And, of course, the message itself must be presented in such a way that it is within the receiver's experiential range. The transmission process can be affected if the sender speaks too loudly or too softly or if the receiver has hearing difficulties or auditory fatigue. Communications can be reduced by the listener's lack of attentiveness or lack of skill in auditory analysis. Finally, communication can break down because the receiver lacks the experiential background to internalize, and thus comprehend, the message.

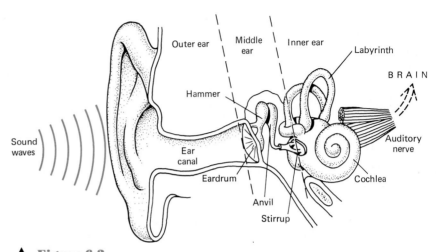

▲ **Figure 6.2**
The physiological process of human hearing.

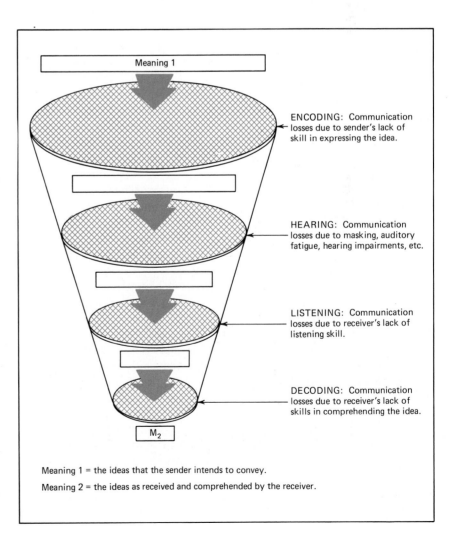

ENCODING: Communication losses due to sender's lack of skill in expressing the idea.

HEARING: Communication losses due to masking, auditory fatigue, hearing impairments, etc.

LISTENING: Communication losses due to receiver's lack of listening skill.

DECODING: Communication losses due to receiver's lack of skills in comprehending the idea.

Meaning 1 = the ideas that the sender intends to convey.

Meaning 2 = the ideas as received and comprehended by the receiver.

▶ **Figure 6.3**
The hearing/listening process: impediments at each step act like filters, reducing the perceived meaning to a small fraction of the original intended meaning.

DEVELOPING LISTENING SKILLS

In formal education, much attention is given to reading, a little to speaking, and essentially none to listening. Listening is a skill, and like all skills, it can be improved with practice. You should first determine that all of your students can hear normally. Most school systems regularly request the services of speech and hearing therapists who administer audiometric hearing tests that provide the data you need. There are also standardized tests that measure students' listening abilities. These tests are often administered by the school district, so you should check to see if listening test scores are available.

There are a number of techniques the teacher can use to improve student listening abilities:

▲ **Figure 6.4**
Listening skills are being taught at all levels. It is a major component of many management development programs.

1. *Directed listening.* Before orally presenting a story or lesson, give the students some objectives or questions to guide their listening. Start with short passages and one or two objectives, then gradually increase the length of the passage and the number and complexity level of the objectives or questions.

2. *Following directions.* Give the students directions individually or as a group on audio tape and ask them to follow these instructions. You can evaluate the students' abilities to follow the audio instructions by examining worksheets or products of the activity. When giving directions orally, the "say it only once" rule should be observed so that a value is placed on both the teacher's and student's time and the incentive to listen is reinforced.

3. *Listening for main ideas, details, or inferences.* Keeping the age level of the students in mind, you can present an oral passage and ask the students to listen for the main idea and then write it down. A similar technique can be used with details of and inferences to

be drawn from the passage.

4. *Using context in listening.* Younger students can learn to distinguish meanings in an auditory context by listening to sentences with words missing and then supplying the appropriate words.

5. *Analyzing the structure of a presentation.* The students can be asked to outline (analyze and organize) an oral presentation. The teacher can then determine how well they were able to discern the main ideas and to identify the subtopics.

6. *Distinguishing between relevant and irrelevant information.* After listening to an oral presentation of information, the student can be asked to identify the main idea and then rate (from most to least relevant) all other ideas that are presented. A simpler technique for elementary students is to have them identify irrelevant words in sentences or irrelevant sentences in paragraphs.

CHARACTERISTICS OF AUDIO MEDIA

Advantages

Audio media have many desirable attributes. First and foremost, they tend to be inexpensive forms of instruction. In the case of audio tape, once the tapes and equipment have been purchased there is no additional cost, since the tape can be erased after use and a new message recorded.

Audio materials are readily available and very simple to use. They can be adapted easily to any vocabulary level and can be used for group or individual instruction.

Students who cannot read can learn from audio media. For young nonreading students, audio can provide early language experiences.

Audio can present stimulating verbal messages more dramatically than can print. With a little imagination on the part of the teacher, audio can be very versatile.

Audio cassette recorders are very

portable and can even be used "in the field" with battery power. Cassette recorders are ideal for home study. Many students already have their own cassette machines. Audio tapes are easily duplicated in whatever quantities are needed.

Limitations

As with all media, audio instructional devices have limitations. Audio tends to fix the sequence of a presentation even though it is possible to rewind the tape and hear a recorded segment again or advance the tape to an upcoming portion.

Without someone standing over them or speaking with them face-to-face, some students do not pay attention to the presentation. They may "hear" the presentation but not "listen" to and comprehend it.

The initial expense of playback and recording equipment may be a problem. Development of audio materials by the instructor is time-consuming. Determining the appropriate pace for presenting information can be difficult if your listeners have a wide range of listening skills and experiential backgrounds.

Storage and retrieval of audio tapes and phonograph records can also cause problems.

AUDIO FORMATS

Let's examine the comparative strengths and weaknesses of the audio formats most often used for instructional purposes—phonograph records (disc recordings), the open reel tape, the cassette tape, and the audio card, plus two formats more suited to home and office use, microcassettes and cartridges.

Phonograph Records

The phonograph record (disc recording) has a number of attributes that make it an excellent instructional medium. Its frequency response is such that it can reproduce the audio spectrum even beyond the limits of human hearing. All types of communication, from the spoken word, through the sounds of a hurricane or the mating call of the yellow-billed

Media File:
"Law: You, the Police, and Justice" Record

The impact of the spoken word is frequently greater than print, particularly when emotional atmosphere is of more importance than the literal meaning of conversations or arguments between people or the impassioned statements by participants in a real-life drama. This record is alive with the feelings of real people talking about the law in natural and unrehearsed settings. Included are youths, police officers, lawyers, a judge, and a boy and a girl in serious trouble with the law. The recordings were made in a bowling alley, on a city street, in a police station, in a jail for juvenile girls, and at an actual courtroom trial. The situations portrayed will raise many questions about relationships between youth and the apparatus of civil control and law.

Source: Scholastic Records.

Media File:
"Singing Games and Folk Dances" Record Series

Undoubtedly, the most frequently used piece of mediaware in the primary classroom is the phonograph. At this age level, learning experiences are frequently tied to physical activity. One of the favored ways of managing this type of instructional effort in a classroom of energetic youngsters is a carefully planned sequence of activities on a phonograph record. The teacher is free to lead the group in the action called for on the disc. A typical collection of such activities is included in this series.

Source: Bowmar Records.

▲ **Figure 6.5**
A vast diversity of audio material is easily accessible on phonograph record. At the elementary school level, records have long been among the most used audiovisual materials.

Media File:
"I Can Hear It Now" Record Series

Edward R. Murrow brings the voices of people who made history into the social studies classroom. The three-record set is a compendium of sounds from thirty years of American history (1919–1949). A portion of the recording traces the career of President Harding and includes excerpts from speeches before he came into office and six months, twelve months, eighteen months, and twenty-six months after he was inaugurated. Statements by Senator Fall and others connected with the famous Teapot Dome oil scandal are presented. The story of the Second World War is told through the sounds of the war and the voices of people involved in it. The record includes the announcement of the invasion of Poland by the Germans and excerpts from several speeches by Winston Churchill. Franklin D. Roosevelt's speech asking Congress to declare a state of war after the attack on Pearl Harbor, General Eisenhower's message on D-Day, and General MacArthur's acceptance of the Japanese surrender also are heard.

Source: Columbia Records.

cuckoo, to Beethoven's Ninth Symphony, are recorded on phonograph records. A major directory of commercially available records is published by the National Information Center for Educational Media (NICEM)—*Index to Educational Records*. See Appendix A for details and other sources.

Selections are separated by "bands" thereby making cuing of segments easier. The location or band of each segment of the recording is usually indicated on the label of the record and on its sleeve or dustcover. Because phonograph records are stamped from a master in a fairly high-speed process, they are relatively inexpensive.

Despite all the advantages of phonograph records, they are not without serious limitations from an instructional point of view. The most limiting is that you cannot economically prepare your own records. A record is easily damaged if someone drops the stylus (needle) on the disc or otherwise scratches the surface. Excess heat and improper storage may cause the disc to warp and make it difficult, if not impossible, to play. Storage can pose another problem in that records take up more space than either open reel or cassette tapes with the same amount of information recorded on them.

Audio Tapes
The major advantage of magnetic audio tape over discs is that you can record your own tapes easily and economically, and when the material becomes outdated or no longer useful you can erase the magnetic signal on the tape and reuse it. Tapes are not as easily damaged as discs and they are easily stored. Unlike discs, broken tapes can be repaired.

Of course, there are some limitations to magnetic tape recordings. In the recording process certain undesirable sounds are sometimes recorded along with the intended material. Even a relatively low level noise can ruin an otherwise good recording. The fact that audio tapes can be erased easily can pose a problem as well. Just as you can quickly and easily erase tapes you no longer need, you can accidentally and just as quickly erase tapes you want to save. It is difficult to locate a specific segment on an audio tape. Counters on the recorder assist retrieval, but they

are not very accurate. Audio tapes also tend to deteriorate in quality when stored for a long period of time.

Open Reel Tapes.
Open reel (or reel-to-reel) tapes are, as their name implies, tapes that wind from one exposed reel to another exposed reel. This accessibility of the tape makes it easier to alter its message, either by "dubbing" (described later in this chapter) or by splicing (described later in this chapter).

Open reel tapes have the disadvantage of having to be threaded manually. For example, let's say you wish to use only part of one open reel tape and continue your lesson with part or all of another. When you come to the end of the wanted portion of the first tape, you must wind the tape back on the supply reel before removing it from the recorder.

AUDIO FORMATS

		Speeds	Advantages	Limitations	Uses
Phonograph record (disc recording)	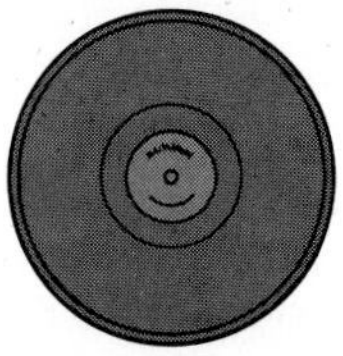 Diameters: 7, 10, 12 in.	78 rpm[a] 45 rpm 33⅓ rpm 16⅔ rpm	• Excellent frequency response • Compatibility of records and phonographs • Selection easily cued • Wide variety of selections • Inexpensive	• Impractical to prepare locally • Easily scratched • Can warp • Requires much storage space	• Music • Long narrations • Classroom listening • Historical speeches • Drama, poetry
Open Reel audio tape (reel-to-reel)	Reel sizes: 3, 5, 7 in. 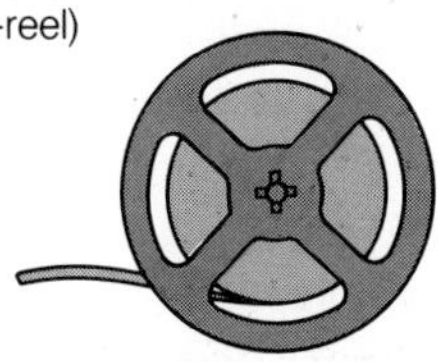 Tape ¼ in. wide	7½ ips[b] 3¾ ips 1⅞ ips	• Can be prepared locally • Can be erased and used again • Not easily damaged • Easily stored • Broken tapes easily repaired • Excellent frequency response • Easily edited	• Accidental erasure • Difficult to use (threading) • Unlabelled or mislabelled tapes • Selection difficult to locate and cue	• Teacher-made recordings • Group listening • Self-evaluation
Cassette audio tape	Size: 2½ by 4 by ½ in. 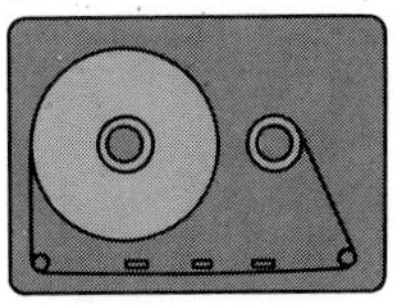 Tape ⅛ in. wide	1⅞ ips	• Very portable (small and light) • Durable • Easy to use (no threading) • Can prevent accidental erasing • Requires little storage space	• Tape sometimes sticks or tangles • Noise and hiss • Poor fidelity (inexpensive models) • Broken tapes *not* easy to repair • Difficult to edit	• Listening "in the field" using battery power • Student-made recordings • Extended discussions • Individual listening
Microcassette	Size: 1⁵/₁₆ by 1³/₃₂ by ²¹/₆₄ in. 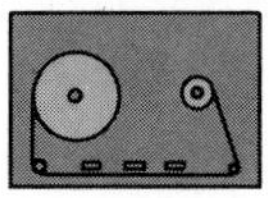 Tape ⅛ in. wide	¹⁵/₁₆ ips	• Very compact • Portable • Fits in pocket	• Not compatible with other cassettes • Poor fidelity	• Dictation by business executives • Amateur recording • LIMITED EDUCATIONAL USE
Audio cartridge (eight-track tape)	Size: 5½ by 3⅞ by ⅞ in. 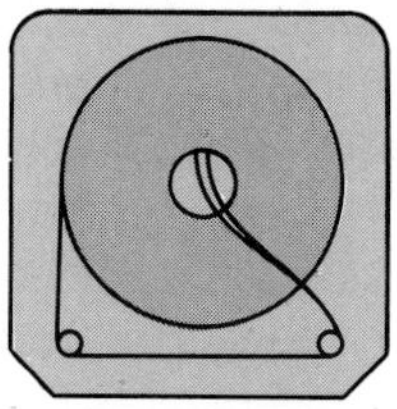 Tape ¼ in. wide	3¾ ips	• Continuous loop on one reel • Minimum tape breakage • Automatically switches from one track to another • Easy loading	• Cannot rewind • Cannot record economically • Difficult to cue a specific portion • Hardware not built for classroom use	• Continuous play • Playback only • Entertainment (music) with home and auto systems • Radio station use • LIMITED EDUCATIONAL USE
Audio card	3½ by 9 in. or 5½ by 11 in.  ¼ in. magnetic stripe	2¼ ips 1⅛ ips	• Sound with visual • Student can record response and compare with original • Designed for individual use • Participation; involvement	• Most cards less than 8 seconds • Time-consuming to prepare	• Vocabulary building • Concept learning • Associating sounds with visuals • Technical vocabulary

[a] rpm = revolutions per minute.

[b] ips = inches per second.

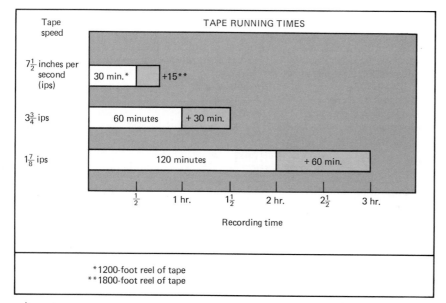

Tape speed	TAPE RUNNING TIMES					
$7\frac{1}{2}$ inches per second (ips)	30 min.*	+15**				
$3\frac{3}{4}$ ips	60 minutes	+ 30 min.				
$1\frac{7}{8}$ ips	120 minutes		+ 60 min.			

Recording time: $\frac{1}{2}$ 1 hr. $1\frac{1}{2}$ 2 hr. $2\frac{1}{2}$ 3 hr.

*1200-foot reel of tape
**1800-foot reel of tape

▲ **Figure 6.6**
The running time of a reel of audio tape can be estimated easily with this chart. The common 1200-foot reel of tape will run for one hour at the common speed of $3\frac{3}{4}$ inches per second; doubling the speed of the tape will halve running time to 30 minutes; halving the speed of the tape will double the running time to 2 hours.

Cassette Tapes.

The cassette tape is in essence a self-contained reel-to-reel system with the two reels permanently installed in a rugged plastic case (Figure 6.7). The ⅛-inch-wide tape is permanently fastened to each of the reels. Cassette tapes are identified according to the amount of recording time they contain. For example, a C-60 cassette can record sixty minutes of sound using both sides (that is, thirty minutes on each side). A C-90 can record forty-five minutes on each side. Cassettes are available in C-15, C-30, C-60, C-90, and C-120 lengths, and other lengths can be specially ordered. The size of the plastic cassette containing the tape is the same in all cases and all can be placed on any cassette machine.

The cassette is durable—virtually immune to shock and abrasion. It is the easiest of the tape formats to use since it requires no manual threading. It can be snapped into and out of a recorder in seconds. It is *not* necessary to rewind the tape before removing it from the machine. Accidental erasures can be avoided by breaking out the small plastic tabs on the edge

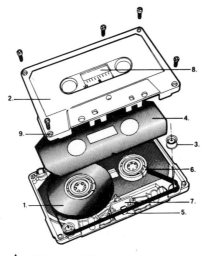

▲ **Figure 6.7**
"Exploded" view of an audio cassette: (1) the ⅛-inch tape, (2) styrene housing, (3) idler rollers, (4) lubricated liner, (5) pressure pad, (6) hub and clip, (7) metal shield, (8) clear index window, (9) screw (or other closure method).

of the cassette.

Storage is also convenient. A cassette collection can be stored in about one-third the space required for open reel tapes with the same amount of program material on them.

With all of these attributes you might wonder if there are any drawbacks. Unfortunately, longer cassette tapes, particularly C-120s, sometimes become stuck or tangled in the recorder due to the thinness of the tape. If this happens, and unless the content on the tape is one of a kind and of considerable value to you, you are best advised to throw the tape away. If it sticks or gets tangled in the machine once, it is likely to do so again. If a cassette tape breaks, its smaller size and difficult access make it much more difficult to splice than the open reel tape. However, there are special cassette splicers that make the job easier. The frequency response and overall quality (fidelity) of cassette playback units are not as good as those of reel-to-reel machines or record players because of the small speakers in most portable cassette playback units. However, for most instructional uses the quality is more than adequate.

A major directory of commercially available audio tapes is published by the National Information Center for Educational Media (NICEM)—*Index to Educational Audio Tapes*. See Appendix A for details and other sources.

Audio Cards

Another widely used audio instructional format is the audio card (Figure 6.8). An audio card is similar in appearance to a computer card. It contains a strip of magnetic recording tape near the bottom edge. The audio card is essentially a flashcard with sound. The card is inserted into a slot on a machine, such as the Bell and Howell Language Master or the Audiotronics Tutorette (Figure 6.9), and a transport mechanism moves the card through the slot. Up to fifteen seconds of sound can be played through the speaker (or headset for individual use). The audio card is used in a dual-track system that allows the student to record his or her own response on the card and then

▲ **Figure 6.8**
The audio card reader allows individual or small-group practice of skills that can be broken into small steps. At 2¼ ips about a dozen words can be recorded on a 10-inch card.

▶ **Figure 6.9**
Audiotronics "Tutorette" audio card reader.

▲ **Figure 6.10**
VOXCOM's "Card Reader Adapter" fits onto a regular cassette recorder; its adhesive-backed magnetic tape can be attached to any paper materials to add teacher-made narrations to existing visuals.

APPLICATIONS OF AUDIO MEDIA

play it back for comparison with the prerecorded response. If the student's response is incorrect, it can be erased and rerecorded correctly by simply running the audio card through the machine again while depressing the record lever. Both the student's and the prerecorded response can be replayed as often as desired by just flipping a lever. The prerecorded message is protected from erasure by a switch on the back of the machine. The teacher can use the switch to change the prerecorded message.

A similar device that can be attached to a standard cassette recorder is the VOXCOM Audible

Graphics System (Figure 6.10). The device "makes paper talk and teach." The VOXCOM system uses adhesive-backed audio magnetic tape that allows the teacher to add sound to any piece of paper, thin cardboard, or plastic. The sound tape can be affixed to the back of workbook pages or photographs. Transparent plastic sleeves are available to accommodate newspaper clippings and materials up to 3½-by-5 inches in size. VOXCOM is a slow-speed card reader (.4 ips*), so the 3½-by-5-inch plastic sleeve will provide up to 12½ seconds of sound. A standard 8½-by-11 inch sheet of paper with an 11-inch strip of magnetic tape on the back will provide nearly 30 seconds of recording time. Some prepared materials are available in this format, but the system is such that the teacher can easily create a wide variety of "talking" materials to fit specific instructional purposes.

The uses of audio media are limited only by the imagination of teachers and students. They can be used in all phases of instruction from introduction of a topic to evaluation of student learning. Perhaps the most rapidly growing general use of audio media today is in the area of self-paced instruction and in "mastery learning." The slow student can go back and repeat segments of instruction as often as necessary since the recorder/playback machine can serve as a *very* patient tutor. The accelerated student can skip ahead or increase the pace of his or her instruction.

Prerecorded audio materials are available in a wide variety of subjects. For music classes, records and tapes can be used to introduce new material or to provide musical accompaniment. The sounds of various musical instruments can be presented individually or in combinations. In preschool and primary grades, tapes and records can be

---

*Inches per second.

used for rhythm development, storytelling, playing games, and acting out stories, songs, etc. In social studies, the tape recorder can bring the voices of persons who have made history into the classroom. The sounds of current events can also be presented.

One special application of prerecorded audio media is "talking books" for blind or visually impaired students. A "Talking Books Program" has been set up by the American Printing House for the Blind to make as much material as possible available to the visually impaired. At present over 11,000 book titles are available, along with recordings of several current periodicals. The service is a cooperative effort of the Library of Congress and fifty-six regional libraries in the United States. The materials are provided on 8⅓-rpm records which require special players.

Audio tapes can easily be prepared by teachers for specific instructional purposes. For example, in industrial arts, audio tapes can describe the steps in operating a machine or making a product. Recordings of class presentations by the teacher can be used for student make-up and review. One of the most common uses of audio materials is for drill work. For example, the student can practice spelling vocabulary

words recorded by the teacher on tape, multiplication tables, taking dictation or typing from a prerecorded tape, or pronunciation of foreign language vocabulary.

History can come alive when students get involved in an *oral history* project. This entails the recording of interviews with living witnesses of the recent or more distant past.

Tape recorders can be used to record information gleaned from a field trip. Upon return to the classroom, the students can play back the tape for discussion and review. Many museums, observatories, and other public exhibit areas now supply visitors with prerecorded messages about various items on display, which may (with permission) be rerecorded for playback in the classroom.

Students can also record themselves reciting, presenting a speech, performing music, etc. They can then listen to the tape in private or have the performance critiqued by the teacher and/or other students. Initial efforts can be kept for comparison with later performances and for reinforcement of learning. Many small-group projects can include recorded reports that can be presented to the rest of the class. Individual students

can prepare oral book reports and term papers on tape for presentation to the class as a whole or one student at a time. One high school literature teacher maintains a file of taped book reports that students listen to before selecting books for their own reading. It is also possible for the students and teacher to bring interviews with local people or recordings of discussion of local events and concerns into the classroom.

An often overlooked use of audio materials is evaluation of student attainment of lesson objectives. For example, test questions may be prerecorded for members of the class to use individually. Students may be asked to identify sounds in a recording (to name the solo instrument being played in a particular musical movement, or to identify the composer of a particular piece of music). Students in social studies classes could be asked to identify the historical person most likely to have made excerpted passages from famous speeches, or they could be asked to identify the time period of excerpted passages from their content. Testing and evaluating in the audio mode is especially appropriate when teaching and learning has also been in that particular mode.

▼ **Figure 6.12**
In the language laboratory, audio tapes allow modeling of proper speech, student response, corrective feedback, and evaluation of mastery.

▼ **Figure 6.11**
A "Talking Books" record player and disc recording.

Cassette: The Constant Companion

A few years ago, the American Psychological Association surveyed a sample of its membership to determine their preferred medium for continuing professional development. The cassette won handily, beating out traditional standbys such as newsletters, workshops, and conferences. Like print, the cassette can go wherever the individual goes, and players are as common as telephones. More so when one considers that there are more cassette players than phones in cars!

American corporations are using cassettes most often as extensions of sales training and for personnel development. An executive of the Gillette Corporation estimates that the company's sales representatives in rural areas spend the equivalent of eighteen to twenty-five weeks a year in their cars. During that time, they can be receiving product information, sales leads, and customer information.

Many companies, and individuals have found cassette tapes extremely useful for personnel development. Usually the tapes are closely integrated with workbooks for two reasons: (1) requiring the user to go constantly back and forth from tape to workbook means attention is more certain to be constant; and (2) overt response reinforces what is learned (R in the ASSURE model). Perhaps the most commonly used cassette programs are the ones that develop basic skills: reading improvement, writing skills development, listening skills. Motivation programs are also popular.

Some companies have exploited the dramatic capabilities of the audio medium in management training programs dealing with conflict resolution and stress management. The low price of cassettes compared to video or a series of seminars plays an important part in the decision to use audio tape.

Media File:
"The Professional Guide to Career Success" Cassette Tape/Workbook

Whether you're entering the job market for the first time or seeking to move up from where you are, help in making your job search more effective is always welcome. This new cassette/workbook program enables the job seeker to: identify and avail himself or herself of the unadvertised job market, where 80 to 85 percent of all job openings exist; ensure that the new job is economically and professionally rewarding; enhance job security in today's uncertain market. The package, consisting of six audio cassette tapes integrated with a workbook, lays out a step-by-step search strategy.

Source: Information Management Institute.

Media File:
"Bankruptcy in the Third World" Cassette Tape

Emanuel Frenkle of the Bank of America, Joe Collins of the Institute for Food and Development Policy, and moderator Philip Mandari of the Pacifica Foundation discuss the conditions and consequences of private bank loans to foreign nations. According to Collins, loans intended to foster development, modernization, and trade end up benefitting the elite, at the expense, usually, of the poor. Frenkle maintains that in the long run such loans lead to a healthy economy for the good of the whole society. Admittedly a compressed treatment of a complex problem, this tape will raise issues for discussion among college students and concerned personnel in the area of international commerce.

Source: Pacifica Tape Library.

The 1984 ASTD Buyer's Guide and Consultant Directory lists more than 30 companies that offer audio cassettes as at least part of their product line. One company that buys tapes from speakers and organizations and rents them to companies is the Tape Rental Library in Covesville, Virginia. In Pasadena, California, Gerald McKee publishes the *Audio-Cassette Newsletter* and *Audio-Cassette Directory*. In 1979, the directory listed 550 producers of cassette program-

ming. By 1983, that number had increased to 685. McKee is certain the figure is much higher but identifying all producers is difficult. What can be said with certainty is that the market for cassettes as an information medium is still growing.*

---

*Stephen Beitler. "The Case for Cassettes." *American Way* (October 1983), pp. 166–169.

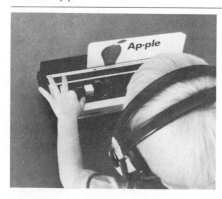

Prerecorded Audio Cards (Vocabulary Practice). In an elementary classroom, the teacher uses a set of audio cards for vocabulary building. They are used on an individual basis with children who are having difficulty grasping the meaning of words because they cannot attach the appropriate spoken word to the printed form of the word or to the object it represents. The audio cards provide simultaneous visual and auditory stimuli designed to increase a child's spoken vocabulary. The teacher shows the student how to use the machine and the cards, then lets the child work alone. Later, the teacher uses the same cards without the machine, holding them up one at a time and asking the child to say the word.

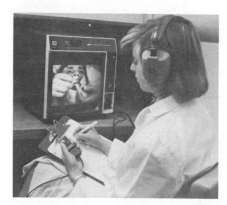

Teacher-Prepared Audio Tapes (Direct Instruction). In a vocational-technical school, dental laboratory technology students are instructed on the procedures for constructing prosthetic devices such as partial plates and bridges by listening to an audio tape prepared by their instructor. To be efficient and effective in their work, these students must have both hands free and their eyes must be on their work, not on a textbook or manual. Audio tapes allow the students to move at their own pace, and the instructor is free to circulate around the laboratory and discuss each student's work individually.

Teacher-Prepared Audio Tapes (Shorthand Practice). In a high school business education class, the students practice taking dictation by listening to audio tapes prepared by the teacher and other individuals in the school, such as the principal, guidance counselor, or shop instructor. The variety of voices on the tapes allows the students to practice dealing with different voices, different accents, and a variety of dictation speeds. The business teacher categorizes the tapes according to difficulty of transcription and word speed. The students begin with the easy tapes and then move to more difficult ones. The teacher is also experimenting with a variable-speed tape recorder, which will allow her to present the same tape to the students at a variety of speeds. Individually, the students use the variable-speed recorder to determine how fast they can take dictation and still maintain accuracy.

Prerecorded Audio Cassette (Sales Information). The sales representative of a manufacturing company pops a cassette into the sound system of the car and, after a few seconds, a popular tune fills the air. The song fades away and the voice of the marketing manager comes in: ''What's new at Marflap Manufacturing is a vastly improved system for . . .'' Another song follows the information about the new system and, after that, more news about Marflap products. The cassette makes the automobile a learning environment, thereby making use of otherwise wasted time.

Teacher-Prepared Audio Tapes (Listening Skills). A teacher of ninth-grade students with learning difficulties (but average intelligence) provides instruction on how to listen to lectures, speeches, and other oral presentations. The students practice their listening skills with tapes of recorded stories, poetry, and instructions. Commercially available tapes of speeches and narration are also used. After the students have practiced their listening skills under teacher direction, they are evaluated using a tape they have not heard before. The students listen to the five-minute tape without taking notes and then are given a series of questions dealing with important content of the passage.

Student-Prepared Audio Tape (Gathering Oral History). One of the most exciting projects in a twelfth-grade social studies class is the oral history project. The students interview local senior citizens regarding the history of their community. Only one student interviews each senior citizen, but the interviewing task is rotated among the students, and the entire class assists in determining which questions should be asked. In preparation for this project, the students study both national and local history. All the tapes prepared during the interviews are kept in the school media center. Excerpts are duplicated and edited into programs for use with other social studies classes and for broadcast by the local radio station. This audio tape project serves the dual purpose of informing students and local residents about local history and collecting and preserving information that might otherwise be lost.

Student-Prepared Audio Tapes (Oral Book Report). The tape recorder can be used for presenting book reports. Students may record their book reports during study time in the media center, or at home. The reports are evaluated by the teacher and the best ones are kept on file in the media center. Other students are encouraged to listen to them before selecting books for leisure reading. Since the reports are limited to three minutes, the students are required to extract the main ideas from the book and to organize their thoughts carefully. During the taping, they practice their speaking skills. They are encouraged to make the report as exciting as possible in order to get other students to read the book.

Student-Prepared Audio Tapes (Self-Evaluation). As part of a sales training program in a large insurance company, trainees learn sales presentation principles through taped examples and associated programmed booklets. They are then asked to prepare a series of their own sales presentations for different types of clients and for selling different types of insurance. The trainees outline their presentation, practice, and then record them on audio tape. For example, they role play making a presentation on group health insurance to the board of directors of a large corporation. After the simulated presentation they listen to the recording and evaluate their performance using a checklist provided in the teaching materials. If they are not satisfied with their performance, they can redo the tape. Since no instructor is present, the inexperienced salesperson is not embarrassed by mistakes made during a training period. Later the instructor will listen to and critique the tape for the individual trainee. The final step in the training program is a "live" presentation, with the other trainees role playing the clients.

Appraisal Checklist: Audio Materials

Title_____

Producer/distributor_____

Series (if applicable)_____

Date (if known)_____   Price_____

Format	Speed	Time
__Record	__rpm	__min.
__Reel-to-reel	__ips	
__Cassette		

Objectives (stated or implied):

Brief description:

Entry capabilities required:
— Prior subject matter knowledge
— Audio skills
— Other

Rating

	High		Medium		Low
Accuracy	☐	☐	☐	☐	☐
Sound quality	☐	☐	☐	☐	☐
Student involvement	☐	☐	☐	☐	☐
Interest level	☐	☐	☐	☐	☐
Vocabulary level	☐	☐	☐	☐	☐
Overall value	☐	☐	☐	☐	☐

Strong points:

Weak points:

Reviewer_____

Position_____

Recommended action_____   Date_____

SELECT AUDIO MATERIALS

In selecting audio materials to use in your instruction, first determine what materials are available locally. If appropriate materials are not available, refer to the various directories of audio materials (see Appendix A). Materials both commercially and locally produced which seem appropriate should be previewed before introducing them to your students. The appraisal checklist can serve as a model for the sort of form you can use to guide your selection decisions.

MAKING YOUR OWN AUDIO TAPES

As previously noted, a major advantage of audio tapes as instructional media is the ease with which they can be prepared by teacher and students. All that is needed is a blank audio tape, a tape recorder, and bit of know-how.

The first order of business in making an audio tape is to familiarize yourself with the operation of the particular tape recorder you intend to use.

Recorder Controls

Most recorders have clearly marked knobs, dials, or levers for control of the recorder's mechanism: on/off, playback, tone, volume, etc. Experiment a bit. For volume control, try a moderate setting. A high setting expands the pickup range of the recorder's microphone, increasing its ability to pick up extraneous sounds and unwanted noises. A high setting also tends to distort the sounds you do wish the microphone to pick up. Many newer recorders have *automatic volume control*, thus making it unnecessary for you to adjust volume while recording. While playing back the tape, experiment with the tone control until you find the tone level that will give you the most lifelike quality. A high treble setting generally records the human voice more faithfully.

Acoustics and Microphone Placement

Wherever you record—in the classroom, at home, on a field trip—you need to consider the area's acoustics. Sparsely furnished rooms with plaster walls and ceilings and bare cement or tile floors are likely to be excessively "live," with distracting sound reverberations interfering with the fidelity of the recording. Such areas can, of course, be improved by installation of acoustic tiles and carpeting. However, you will probably have to make do with more makeshift improvements—throw rugs, for example, or even heavy blankets or sheets of cardboard on the floor. Cardboard and blankets may also be used to cut down on bare wall reverberations. Fabric-covered movable screens and drawn window shades and draperies may help. (The latter will also help eliminate unwanted noise from outside.)

Many recording problems can be traced to the microphone's inability to ignore sounds. Unlike the brain, which can concentrate on only meaningful sounds (your quiet conversation with a friend in a restaurant, for example) and ignore extraneous ones (the clink of dishes, doors opening and closing, the air conditioner, other conversations), the microphone picks up every sound within its range and transmits them all faithfully to the recording device. Thus microphone placement becomes an artful compromise between maximum pickup of desired

▶ **Figure 6.13**
The absence of nearby walls and the separation between microphone and recorder help reduce extraneous sounds.

sounds and minimal pickup of extraneous ones.

Avoid placing the microphone close to any hard surface that might act as a sounding board. In a classroom, for instance, the recording setup should be at least six feet from the chalkboard, windows, or hard walls. Since many tape recorders themselves generate unwanted clicking, whirring, and humming noises, keep the microphone as far as possible from the recorder. Correct positioning will often require a bit of trial-and-error testing. As a rule of thumb, your mouth should remain about a foot away from the microphone. If you are much closer, ''popping'' of p's and b's and other ''breathy'' sounds may become annoying. Do not speak directly into the microphone, but rather, talk over it. Placing the microphone on a cloth or some other sound-absorbing material or on a stand will decrease the possibility of noise being transferred to the microphone from the desk or table. Avoid handling sheets of paper near the microphone. If possible, use index cards or some such materials and handle them quietly. For recording multiple sound-source performances (such as musical shows), other variables must also be taken into consideration. For instance, a

greater sound-to-microphone distance might be needed in order to pick up the entire range and scope of sounds emanating from a musical ensemble.

Microphones

A wide variety of microphones are available; they vary in the type of generating element used in their construction, their sensitivity, their directionality, and in other technical features.

The basic function of any microphone is to convert sound waves into electrical energy. The major components of all microphones are similar.

Sound waves enter the microphone to strike the diaphragm, which vibrates from the pressure of the sound waves. Connected to the diaphragm is a generating element that converts these vibrations into electrical impulses (Figure 6.15).

As noted, microphones differ with regard to their directionality, that is, the pattern of the area from which they can efficiently pick up the signal or ''pickup pattern.'' The microphones most commonly found in educational use these days are the two basic directional types—*unidirectional* and *omnidirectional*. The differences in their pickup patterns are illustrated in Figure 6.16.

▼ **Figure 6.15**
The main components of a microphone, cutaway view.

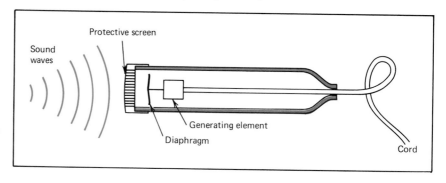

▼ **Figure 6.14**
A good setup for at-home or in-school recording.

Microphone Types	Attributes
Crystal	• Simplest construction • Least expensive • Fragile • Sensitive to temperature and humidity • Can be used for speech
Ceramic	• Simple construction • Moderately expensive • Produces weak signal • More rugged than crystal • Not sensitive to temperature and humidity
Dynamic (moving coil)	• High quality • Good fidelity • Very rugged • Very reliable • Expensive
Condenser or electret	• Good frequency response • Sensitive to physical shock • Sensitive sound pickup • Not sensitive to mechanical vibration

AUDIO LESSON RECORDING

Tape Content and Audio Presentation Techniques

Introduce the subject of the audio tape and other appropriate material ("This is Biology 101, Lesson 2, on plant function . . .") at the outset of your recording. Identifying the tape is particularly important if it is to be used for individual instruction.

Try to use conversational rather than pedantic or "textbook" diction. Of course, the normal rules of grammar and clarity of expression must be followed. Talk to the tape recorder as you would normally talk to a friend.

Explore your subject with your listener. Do not lecture on it. In general, your presentation will come across as more natural if you work from informal notes. If you do feel you must work with a more formal script, remember that a good script requires special writing skills and skill in script reading.

Keep the tape short even if it is to be used only by adult students—twenty to twenty-five minutes for adults and even less for younger students.

Whenever appropriate for your learning objectives, involve your listener(s) in meaningful learning activities. You might, for example, supply a study guide or worksheet for use along with the tape. Such materials may contain lesson objectives, key information, diagrams or other visuals, questions to be answered, or practice exercises. Try, also, to provide ample space for students to take notes while listening to the tape. These ancillary materials can also be used for review purposes after the lesson has been completed (Figure 6.17).

▼ **Figure 6.16**
Pickup patterns of two common types of microphones: (a) the unidirectional or "cardioid" microphone; (b) the omnidirectional microphone.

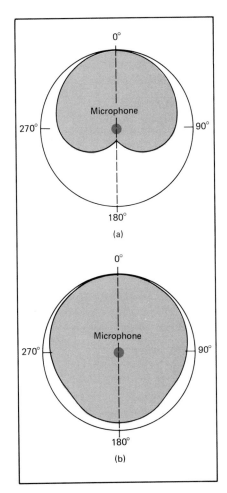

▼ **Figure 6.17**
Sample page from a study guide to accompany an audio lesson.

OBJECTIVE 3: Compute depreciation using the "straight-line method."

"Straight-Line" Method Summarized

Formula $\dfrac{\text{Cost of the Asset - Estimated Salvage Value}}{\text{Number of Accounting Periods in Productive Life}}$

Application $\dfrac{\$1250 \text{ Cost} - \$250 \text{ Salvage}}{5 \text{ Years of Productive Life}}$ = $200 to be DEPRECIATED Each Year

. . . .
TURN OFF TAPE AND COMPLETE ACTIVITY NO. 4.
. . . .

Activity #4

A machine costs $2600 and was estimated to have a four-year service life and a $200 salvage value. Calculate the yearly depreciation using the straight-line method.

ANSWER_____

. . . .
TURN ON TAPE AND COMPLETE ACTIVITY NO. 5 WHILE LISTENING.
. . . .

Activity #5

Advantages of the "units-of-production" method are:
1. _____
2. _____
3. _____
4. _____

Disadvantages of the "units-of-production" method are:
1. _____
2. _____

Note, however, that if you include student activities you may have to allow time on the tape for the listener to complete an activity. In addition, different students will take varying amounts of time to complete these activities. Rather than trying to guess how much quiet time to leave on the tape, you can provide a brief musical interlude (approximately ten seconds) as a signal for the student to turn off the tape and perform the activity or exercise. The student can then return to the tape, hear the music again, and know that nothing has been missed.

If your listeners are to use slides with your audio presentation, a non-vocal signal should be used to indicate when to advance the slides rather than continually repeating "Change to the next slide." There are electronic tone devices available for this purpose, or a door chime can be used. A simple technique for producing your own signal is to tap a spoon on a glass partially filled with water.

When you are finished with the recording, give it a critical evaluation. As a guide, you might use a checklist such as the one shown below. It may also be helpful to have a colleague and/or students listen to the tape and give you their reactions to it.

DUPLICATING AUDIO TAPES

It is a relatively simple procedure to duplicate (or "dub") an audio tape. You can duplicate your tapes by one of three methods: the acoustic method, the electronic method, and the high-speed duplicator method.

The *acoustic* method does not require any special equipment, just two recorders (cassette, reel-to-reel, or one of each). One recorder plays the original tape, the sound of which is transferred via a microphone to blank tape on the other recorder. The drawback to this method is that fidelity is lessened as the sound travels

through the air to the microphone, and the open microphone may pick up unwanted noise from the environment (Figure 6.18).

The *electronic* method avoids this problem. The signal travels from the original tape to the dubbing recorder via an inexpensive patch cord. The cord is attached to the output of the first machine and the "line" or auxiliary input of the second. It picks up the signals of the original tape and transfers them electronically to the duplicating tape (Figure 6.19).

If you use reel-to-reel recorders for both playing and recording, you can save half the normal duplicating time

▼ **Figure 6.18**
Configuration for duplicating by means of the *acoustic* method.

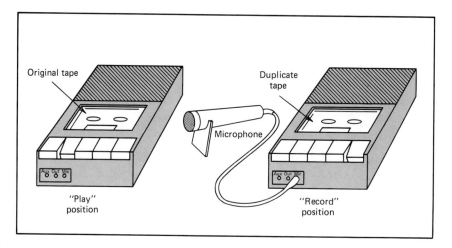

▼ **Figure 6.19**
Configuration for duplicating by means of the *electronic* method.

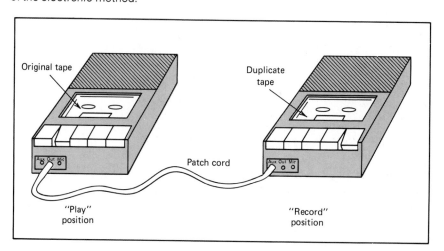

Checklist for Teacher-Prepared Audio Tapes

- ☐ minimum extraneous background noise
- ☐ constant volume level
- ☐ voice quality and clarity
- ☐ clarity of expression
- ☐ conversational tone
- ☐ listener involvement
- ☐ coordination with worksheet or study guide, if used
- ☐ content clear
- ☐ duration not too long or too short

by playing 3¾-ips tapes at 7½ ips. The speed of the machine doing the recording must also be set at 7½ ips. The duplicated tape can then be played back at the 3¾-ips rate of original tape.

The *high-speed duplicator* method requires a special machine. Master playback machines have a series of up to ten "slave units," each of which can record a copy of the original tape at sixteen times its normal speed.

Multiple copies of a thirty-minute cassette tape can be duplicated in about one minute (Figure 6.20). Since the master and slave units are connected by a patch cord, fidelity is likely to be very good, and there is no danger of picking up background noise.

▼ **Figure 6.20**
A high speed tape duplicating system. This sophisticated Telex® model handles both open reel and cassette tapes; it can duplicate up to eleven cassettes at one time.

HOW TO... PREVENT ACCIDENTAL ERASURE OF CASSETTE TAPES

Cassette tapes provide protection against accidental erasure. At the rear corners of each cassette are small tabs which can be broken out. The tab on the left controls the top side of the tape. The tab on the right controls the bottom side. No machine will record a new sound on a side of a tape for which the appropriate tab has been broken out.

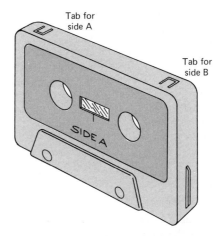

Tab for side A

Tab for side B

SIDE A

If you want to reuse the tape, carefully place some cellophane tape over the hole where the tab was removed. The tape can then be used for a new recording. Most prerecorded tapes come with both tabs already removed to prevent accidental erasure.

EDITING AUDIO TAPES

You may wish to edit your audio tapes, either to remove errors and imperfections or to adapt a tape to a specific learning situation. There are two general methods for editing tapes: mechanical editing and electronic editing.

Mechanical editing (splicing) involves physically removing unwanted portions of the tape or changing the sequence of materials by reordering sections of the tape. If you plan to do mechanical editing, record your original tape on only one side and at the fastest speed possible. Open reel tapes can be mechanically edited more easily than cassette tapes because they are wider and more accessible. Splicing tape and splicing blocks are available for both open reel and cassette tape. Follow the specific instructions given for the equipment you are using. The general procedures for splicing are shown in the "How To" below.

For *electronic editing*, set up two recorders as described for tape duplication and then record just the portion of the original tape that you want on the second tape. You can accomplish the same effects (deleting and resequencing) as with mechanical editing, but the results may not be as precise.

HOW TO...SPLICE AUDIO TAPE

First method: Overlap ends of broken tape (shiny sides up), lining up the tapes as precisely as you can, and cut diagonally with a pair of sharp scissors.

Butt the cut ends against each other and press splicing tape (*not* cellophane tape) over the butted ends. Trim off the excess splicing tape, cutting very slightly into the audio tape.

Second method (using a splicing block): The splicing block has a diagonal groove in it to guide the razor blade when cutting the tape. Press right-hand tape into the channel of the block, extended slightly past diagonal guide. Cut the tape with a razor blade. Repeat with left-hand tape.

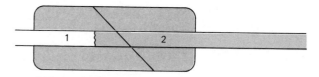

Move both ends of tape to the left to avoid cutting guide. Cut off about 3/4-inch of tape from a roll of 7/32-inch-wide splicing tape. Lay splicing tape across butted ends of audio tape and press to adhere. If this is done carefully, no trimming is necessary.

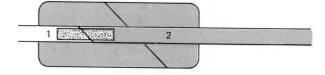

Plastic splicing blocks can be found in audio supply stores. A durable metal block is made by EDITALL Corporation.

RATE-CONTROLLED AUDIO PLAYBACK

A relatively recent and promising innovation in audio instructional technology has been the introduction of equipment that can play back recorded speech either at a faster or slower rate than the rate at which it was recorded—without loss of intelligibility. Before this technological breakthrough, playing a tape back at a higher speed resulted in high-pitched distortion, as if the speaker were a chattering chipmunk. Slowing down the playback resulted in a low-pitched, unintelligible garble.

The pedagogical significance of this innovation lies in the fact that although the average person speaks at 100 to 150 words per minute, most of us can comprehend spoken information at the rate of 250 to 300 words per minute. Research has shown that most students learn as quickly and retain as much when spoken instruction is speeded up. On the other hand, slowing down recorded instruction also has instructional advantages, especially in working with slow learners or in special education situations and in foreign language instruction. It is also useful in ordinary circumstances for emphasizing a specific instructional point or for explaining a particularly difficult one.

Early speech compressors (technically, speeding up recorded speech is called "compressing") were costly and their technology not very refined. The machines could only be set at certain fixed speeds, such as 200 words per minute. The entire recording had to be made and played back at this rate.

▲ **Figure 6.21**
This Variable Speech Control compact recorder allows playback at up to twice the normal rate when the "speed control" and "pitch control" are moved together.

Newer compressors provide for variable speed rates. Recorders can now be equipped with rate-control devices that, using a tape recorded at normal speaking speed, are capable of providing variable rates of speech at the discretion of the listener, from half the normal speed to 2½ times normal speed. Changing the rate during playback allows the listener to listen at his or her own pace, skimming over familiar material at a high rate, slowing down for material that may require more time for comprehension.

Research has shown that learning time can be cut (as much as 50 percent and an average of 32 percent) and comprehension increased (as much as 9.3 percent and an average of 4.2 percent) through use of compressed and variable-speed audio tapes.* One reason that comprehension increases with accelerated listening rate may be that the listener is forced to increase his or her concentration on the material and is also freed from the distractions that often

accompany normal speech, such as pauses, throat clearing, and other extraneous sounds. A slow, monotonous speaking rate also allows listeners' minds to wander.

Research also indicates that variable-speed audio tapes can be very effective in increasing reading speed. One junior high school teacher prepared variable-speed tapes of printed material for his students to listen to as they read the material. The students' reading rate gradually increased with increase in their listening rate. The ear, it seems, helps train the eye.

---

*See the listings under Olsen, Hughes, and Short in the References.

TELELECTURE AND TELECONFERENCE SYSTEMS

The telephone has only recently come into its own as an instrument of educational and training technology. Through the addition of microphones and special amplifiers to the regular telephone system, "telelecture" and "teleconference" systems can be created that allow students or meeting participants to engage in conversation with individuals or groups at other locations. These systems can bring people in different geographic areas together at a fraction of the cost of a face-to-face meeting. The special equipment involved can be rented from most local phone companies; it can also be purchased if frequency of use warrants owning the equipment.

Telelecture

In a *telelecture*, an individual, typically a content specialist or well-known authority, addresses a group listening by means of a telephone amplifier; the listeners may ask questions of the resource person, with the entire group able to hear the response. Groups can, for example, discuss politics or current issues with

their elected representatives or candidates for public office. They can talk with great writers about literature. They can discuss topics from their textbook with the author of the text. In the business setting, experts on a given product or service can pass along up-to-date information to middle managers, successful sales representatives can share their techniques with others, new policies can be explained to employees, and so forth.

Planning is very important for a successful telelecture. Arrangements may have to be made with the telephone company to have the telelecture equipment available. The resource person must be arranged for in advance and a mutually convenient time must be settled upon for the telelecture. The speaker should be briefed by the teacher as to the purposes and objectives of the telelecture call and the types of questions that the students are likely to ask. The students should prepare for the call by deciding what kinds of questions to ask, or perhaps even who will ask which questions.

When the call has been put through, the teacher should briefly introduce the speaker (a more lengthy description of the speaker's background and the objectives of the telelecture will have been presented during preparation of the class for the telelecture). Usually the speaker will make some introductory statement and then call for a question-and-answer period. A predetermined time limit should be set for the length of the call. After the telelecture, the students can discuss it, write reports, make evaluations, and suggest future activities. As a courtesy, a personal thank you note from the class might be sent to the resource person.

If the telelecture presentation requires visuals to supplement the audio, the speaker can send slides or overhead transparencies in advance. He or she can direct the instructor as to when to project a transparency or to advance the slides during the call. A more sophisticated technique is to use a "telewriting" device. With this device, the speaker can write on a special electronic pad and the message will be transmitted via tele-

▼ **Figure 6.23**
AT&T Communication employs sophisticated teleconference systems in its sales and marketing education, including the Gemini® Electronic Blackboard as a means of transmitting chalkboard displays to remote sites.

▼ **Figure 6.22**
The portable telelecture set allows group listening to and student participation in telephone conversations.

Flashback: THE BEE WHO CAME IN FROM THE COLD

The time was summer 1915. World War I had already begun and America was poised for her own entry into the conflict. Talk of Allied and German espionage activities in America was in the air—and so was a persistent and peculiar noise which could be heard nightly on the radio airwaves up and down the East Coast.

The strange noise perplexed radio ham operators, not to mention the U.S. Secret Service. It began promptly each night at eleven o'clock and continued into the wee hours of the morning. One ham operator described it as "a musical note, like the buzzing of a titanic bumblebee" speeding through space. Was it a secret signal being sent to one of the warring parties? Very likely. But what kind of code was it being sent in? How could anyone decode a bumblebee's buzz?

The sinister noise and the question of how an intelligible message could be encoded in it so disturbed one New Jersey ham operator that he recorded excerpts from it on his own homemade wax cylinder recorder. He did so faithfully for two weeks but was still unable to solve the mystery.

Then one night he forgot to fully wind his recording machine. As the machine slowed down it began to play back the buzzing more slowly. The operator found that the buzzing did indeed contain an encoded message, a message encoded not in some fiendishly clever code, but in the simple, universally known Morse code of dots and dashes!

The station transmitting the messages was later found by U.S. authorities and shut down. The messages had been recorded in simple Morse code at standard speed. The recording was then compressed (played at high speed) and transmitted in this form to Germany. There it was rerecorded and played back at its original speed. There was no code to be broken at all. It was merely a matter of ingenuity in using the then-current technology of "rate-controlled audio playback." Incidentally, the ingenuity may have been German but the technology was American. The recorders used in the operation had been developed and manufactured by the American Telegraphone Company. Six machines had been sold unknowingly to the German Navy on an order from Denmark.

Source: Adapted from Robert Angus. "75 Years of Magnetic Recording." *High Fidelity Magazine* (March 1973), pp. 42–50.

phone lines and can be projected on a screen at the listeners' location. The speaker can thus add diagrams, drawings, equations, or any hand-drawn figures to the audio portion of the telelecture.

Teleconference

It is not surprising that telephone companies promotes use of their telephone lines by buying television commercials and magazine ads for teleconferencing. But their message is well taken. Many organizations have found that teleconferencing can reduce training and information exchange expenses. In a *teleconference*, groups at separate geographic locations use microphones and special amplifiers that are linked together to allow everyone to actively participate in one large meeting. Holding a conference by telephone can save a great deal of travel time and expense. For training ("teletraining") or information exchange, illustrative material can be sent in advance and displayed on cue at the appropriate time, or "telewriting" equipment may be used.

Recently, the members of the International Association of Business Communicators were surveyed on their attitudes toward, and experiences with, teleconferencing. They regarded training and development activities as most appropriate for teleconferencing. They offered the following tips for successfull teleconferences:

1. Keep transmission time under two hours.
2. Punctuate the presentation with discussion and questions at each viewing location.
3. Choose speakers who are comfortable with and skilled at audio—and TV—presentations.
4. Focus speaker time on just a few topics—favor intensity over diversity.
5. Provide supporting materials.
6. Design a format that encourages interaction—limit the number of sites, provide a local resource/discussion leader, and encourage discussion among presenters and participants.*

*As reported in *Training and Development Journal* (February 1983), p. 8.

References

Print References

Alley, Douglas. "Radio Tapes: A Resource for English Teachers." *English Journal* (October 1979), pp. 40–41.

Banerjee, Sumanta. *Audio Cassettes: The User Medium.* (Paris: UNESCO, 1977).

Bradtmueller, Weldon G. "Auditory Perception as an Aid to Learning in the Content Areas." *Journal of the Association for the Study of Perception* (Spring 1979), pp. 27–29.

Center for Vocational Education. *Present Information with Audio Recordings.* (Athens, Ga.: American Association for Vocational Instructional Materials, 1977).

Chilcoat, George W. "Commercial Radio Broadcasts of Propaganda: An Activity for Teaching About World War II." *Social Studies* (November/December 1983), pp. 247–250.

Clifford, Martin. *Microphones: How They Work and How to Use Them.* (Blue Ridge Summit, Pa.: TAB Books, 1977).

Cuker, S. *Time Compressed Speech: An Anthology and Bibliography.* (Metuchen, N.J.: Scarecrow Press, 1974).

DeMuth, James E. "Audio Cassettes as a Means of Professional Continuing Education for Pharmacists." *Adult Education* (Summer 1979), pp. 242–251.

Gates, Ward M. "Recording Tips for Teachers." *Clearing House* (January 1976), pp. 229–230.

Hafernik, Johnnie Johnson, and Surguine, Harold. "Using Radio Commercials as Supplementary Materials in ESL Listening Classes." *TESOL Quarterly* (September 1979), pp. 341–345.

Harnishfeger, L. *Basic Practice in Listening.* (Denver, Colo.: Love Publishing, 1977).

Hughes, Lawson H. "Developments in Rate-Controlled Speech." *NSPI Journal* (September 1976), pp. 10–11.

James, Charles J. "Are You Listening? The Practical Components of Listening Comprehension." *Foreign Language Annals* (April 1984), pp. 129–133.

Jones, Barry. "Le Jeu des Colis—An Exercise in Foreign Language Communication." *Audio-Visual Language Journal* (Winter 1979). pp. 159–167.

Kelly, Patrick, and Ryan, Steve. "Using Tutor Tapes to Support the Distance Learner." *International Council for Distance Education Bulletin* (September 1983), pp. 19–23.

Lowenthal, Jeff, and Jankowski, Pat. "A Checklist for Selecting The Right Teleconferencing Mode." *Training and Development Journal* (December 1983), pp. 47–49.

Monson, Mavis. *Bridging the Distance: An Instructional Guide to Teleconferencing.* (Madison, Wis.: University of Wisconsin, Extension Division, 1978).

Olsen, Linda. "Technology Humanized—the Rate Controlled Tape Recorder." *Media and Methods* (January 1979), p. 67.

Postlethwait, S. N. "Audio Technology: Audio Tape for Programming Instruction." *Educational Broadcasting* (July-August 1976), pp. 17–19.

Short, Sarah H. "A Comparison of Variable Time-Compressed Speech and Normal Rate Speech Based on Time Spent and Performance in a Course Taught by Self-Instructional Methods." *British Journal of Educational Technology* (May 1977), pp. 146–156.

———. "The Use of Rate Controlled Speech to Save Time and Increase Learning in Self-Paced Instruction." *NSPI Journal*, May 1978, pp. 13–14.

Smith, Judson. "How to Buy Headsets and Listening Centers." *Training* (September 1977), pp. 92–95.

Stevenson, J. "Educational Broadcasting and the New Technologies." *Educational Media International* (No. 4, 1983), pp. 30–31.

Ullom-Morse, Ann, et al. "The Use and Acceptance of Compressed Speech by Nursing Students." *NALLD Journal* (Winter 1979), pp. 20–27.

Vazquez-Abad, Jesus, and Mitchell, P. David. "A System Approach to Planning a Tele-Education System." *Programmed Learning and Educational Technology* (August 1983), pp. 202–209.

Wieder, Alan. "Oral History in the Classroom: An Exploratory Essay." *Social Studies* (March/April 1984), pp. 71–74.

Wipf, J.A. "Shortwave Radio and the Second Language Class." *Modern Language Journal* (Spring 1984), pp. 7–12.

Zimmerman, William. *How to Tape Instant Oral Biographies.* (New York: Guarionex Press Ltd., 1982).

Audiovisual References

Basic Audio. Alexandria, Va.: Smith-Mattingly Productions, 1979. Videocassette. 30 minutes, color.

Learning about Sound. Chicago: Encyclopedia Brittannica Educational Corporation 1975. 16-mm film. 17 minutes, color.

Sound Recording and Reproduction. Salt Lake City, Utah: Media Systems, Inc. 1978. 6 filmstrips with audiocassettes, color.

Tape Recorders. Salt Lake City, Utah: Media Systems, Inc., 1978. Filmstrip with audiocassette, color.

Tips on Tapes for Teachers. Boulder, Colo.: National Center for Audio Tapes, 1972. Audiocassette.

Utilizing the Tape Recorder in Teaching. Salt Lake City, Utah: Media Systems, Inc., 1975. 2 filmstrips with audiocassette, color.

Possible Projects

6-A. Prepare an audio tape including your voice and some music. It will be evaluated using the criteria in the ''Checklist for Teacher-Prepared Audio Tapes.'' Include a description of how the tape will be used, along with its objective(s).

6-B. Obtain any commercially prepared audio materials and appraise them using a given set of criteria, such as ''Appraisal Checklist: Audio Materials,'' or using your own criteria.

6-C. Do a short oral history of your school or organization by interviewing people associated with it for a long time. Edit your interviews into a five-minute presentation.

6-D. Prepare an outline for a short oral presentation. Deliver your presentation as if you were addressing the intended audience and record it. Critique your presentation for style as well as content. Revise and try again.

6-E. Practice editing by deliberately recording a paragraph from a news report or a literary work with the sentences out of order. Put the paragraph back in proper sequence by editing the recorded tape.

6-F. Develop a brief audio-tutorial lesson. Choose a basic skill, such as spelling or arithmetic, or a performance aid—e.g., how to make out a bank check or how to fill out an application form. Design the lesson with paper and pencil first, then record the tape. Try the lesson out on your fellow students.

Multimedia Systems

Outline

Objectives

After studying this chapter, you should be able to:

1. Define *multimedia* systems and state a rationale for the use of multimedia systems.
2. Identify three advantages of sound-slide programs.
3. Describe four combinations of projected visuals and audio materials including three procedures for synchronizing them.
4. Describe an instructional situation in which you could use an audio plus projected visual presentation. Your description should include the topic, the audience, the objectives, and a rationale for using this media format.
5. Describe and/or apply the basic steps involved in the planning of a slide-tape presentation.
6. Discuss instructional applications of dissolve units and automatic programmers.
7. Describe an instructional situation in which you could use a multi-image presentation. Your description should include the topic, the audience, the objectives, and a rationale for using this media format.
8. Describe the characteristics and applications of variable motion programming devices.
9. Diagram the components of a typical interactive video system.
10. Match the characteristics of interactive video systems with appropriate instructional applications.
11. List five considerations when preparing, purchasing, and/or selecting multimedia kits.
12. Describe a multimedia kit that you could use in your teaching field. Your description should identify the topic, the audience, the overall objectives, and the contents of the kit.
13. Describe the characteristics, advantages, limitations, and applications of classroom learning centers.
14. Discuss the teacher's role in learning-center management.
15. Identify three methods of providing learner feedback in a classroom learning center.
16. Design a learning center for your discipline. Your description should include the audience, objective(s), how materials will be obtained and used, the types of learner response, and how it will be evaluated.

Lexicon

multimedia systems
storyboard
multi-image
multi-screen
dissolve unit
automatic programmer
variable motion programming
interactive video
learning center
carrel

We have previously considered various basic models of audio and visual instructional media. We will now explore various combinations of these media and how these combinations can be used for instructional purposes. Media combinations are generally referred to as *multimedia systems.*

The multimedia concept involves more than using multiple media for a given instructional purpose. It involves integrating each medium and medium format into a structured, systematic presentation. Each instructional medium in a multimedia system is designed to complement the others so that, ideally, the whole multimedia system becomes greater than the sum of its parts.

The use of multimedia systems in the classroom and training center has received considerable impetus from the general trends toward individualization of learning and encouragement of active student participation in the learning process. Multimedia systems are especially adaptable to these current educational and training concepts.

Multimedia systems are also multisensory and thus simulate learning as it takes place in the world outside the classroom. Learning in the real world is indeed multimedia and multisensory learning. We are constantly learning via all our senses and via a multitude of stimuli—newspapers, books, radio, television, pictures, etc.

In this chapter we will discuss the major multimedia systems commonly used in the classroom: sound-slide combinations, multi-image systems, variable motion programming, interactive video, multimedia kits, and learning centers.

▲ **Figure 7.1**
A multimedia kit for basic reading skills.

▶ **Figure 7.2**
Like any other instructional approach, multimedia presentations can be overdone.

SOUND-SLIDE COMBINATIONS

Combining 2-by-2-inch slides with audio tape is the easiest multimedia system to produce locally, which is one reason for the increasing popularity of its use in the instructional setting. The system is also versatile, easy to use, and effective both for group instruction and independent study. A well-done sound-slide pre-

▼ **Figure 7.3**
The sound-slide set is a familiar example of a multimedia system.

▼ **Figure 7.4**
Sound-slide sets may consist of various combinations of audio and visual formats. The slide-tape combination is one that can be locally produced by ordinary users.

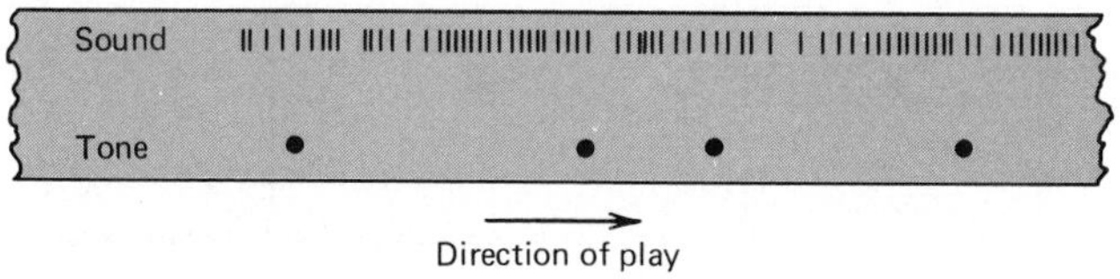

| Sound | ⅡⅠⅠⅠⅠⅢⅢ ⅢⅡ Ⅰ ⅠⅢⅢⅢⅢⅢⅢⅢ ⅢⅢ ⅢⅢⅢⅢⅢⅢⅢⅠⅠ Ⅰ Ⅰ ⅠⅠⅠⅢⅢⅢⅢⅢⅢ ⅢⅠ ⅢⅢⅢⅢⅢ |
| Tone | ● ● ● ● |

Direction of play ⟶

▼ **Figure 7.5**
Synchronized sound-slide programs are controlled by inaudible tones put on one track of the tape.

<table>
<tr><td colspan="2" rowspan="2"></td><td colspan="2">VISUALS</td></tr>
<tr><td>Slides</td><td>Filmstrip</td></tr>
<tr><td rowspan="2">SOUND</td><td>Audio Tape</td><td>Local production</td><td>Commercial</td></tr>
<tr><td>Phonograph record</td><td>Commercial</td><td>Commercial</td></tr>
</table>

sentation can have significant dramatic impact, thus further enhancing the learning process. Filmstrips may also be combined with audio tape, to the same general educational purposes as sound-slide presentations.

Sound-slide programs can be developed locally by teachers or students. In terms of emotional impact and instructional effectiveness they may rival film or television productions, yet they can be produced for a fraction of the cost and effort. Indeed, sound-slide sets are produced frequently as prototypes of more elaborate film or video projects, since they allow the presentation to be tried out and revised in its formative stages.

Sound-slide sets are available from commercial sources. However, mass distribution programs of this sort usually are converted to a filmstrip/audio tape format, since filmstrips require less storage space than slides and are less expensive. Some commercial programs are available with phonograph records instead of audio tapes. Major guides to identifying the many thousands of sound-slide and

filmstrip sets available commercially are two National Information Center for Educational Media (NICEM) publications—*Index to Educational Slides* and *Index to 35mm Filmstrips*. See Appendix A for details and other sources.

The visuals in sound-slide programs may be advanced manually or automatically. In manual operation, the visual and audio components are usually on two separate machines. You begin by projecting the title slide or frame on the screen and then starting the sound track. An audible beep on the sound track signals you to advance the slides or filmstrip to the next visual. In manual operation, it is important that you test out at least the beginning of the program to make certain that you have sound and visuals in proper synchronization. Note also that some soundtracks do not contain a beep signal, in which case a script containing instructions for advancing visuals must be used.

In automatic advancing of visuals with an audio tape, two sound tracks are used, one for the audible narration and one with inaudible tones that activate the advance mechanism on the slide or filmstrip projector, as shown in Figure 7.5.

Applications

Sound-slide presentations may be used in almost any instructional setting and for instructional objectives involving the presentation of visual images to inform or to evoke an emotional response. They may be used to excellent effect in group instruction, and they can be adapted to independent study in the classroom and in the media or learning center. This comparatively simple multimedia system is especially versatile as a learning/teaching tool in that more

HOW TO... DEVELOP A SOUND-SLIDE PRESENTATION

Here is a simple approach to developing your own sound-slide presentation:

Step 1. Analyze your audience both in terms of general characteristics and specific entry characteristics (as described in Chapter 2).
- Why are they viewing the presentation?
- What is their motivation toward your topic?
- How much do they already know about the subject?

Step 2. Specify your objectives (as described in Chapter 2).
- What do you want to accomplish with the presentation?
  —learning to be achieved
  —attitudes to be formed or changed
  —skills to be developed
- What should the viewers be able to *do* after the presentation?
  —activity or performance?
  —under what conditions?
  —with what degree of skill?

Step 3. Having completed your audience analysis and stated your objectives, you now have a much clearer idea of how your presentation will fit into your overall lesson plan, including what might precede it and follow it. Perhaps you will decide at this point that a sound-tape presentation is *not* really what you need to do after all.

If it is what you need to do, get a pack of planning cards (use index cards or cut some sheets of paper into 4-by-6-inch rectangles). Draw a large box in the upper left-hand corner of each card.

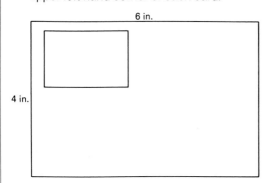

Step 4. Take a planning card. In the box draw a rough sketch of whatever image comes to your mind when you think about one of your major points.[a] You don't have to start with the *first* point, just whatever comes into your mind first. Your sketch may be a symbol, a diagram, a graph, a cartoon, or a photo of a person, place or thing, for example.

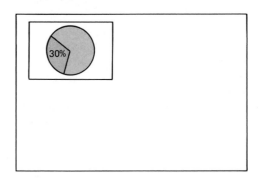

Step 5. Below your sketch, write a brief statement that captures the essence of the point you are trying to make. State it in as few words as needed to cue yourself to the thought. Some developers prefer to start with the visuals and then write the narration. Others prefer to do the narration first. Actually developing a sound-slide presentation is likely to be a dynamic process, with visual and narration evolving one from the other, separately and simultaneously. In some cases, of course, your narration will be already at hand—printed information, for example, or a story or poem—and all that remains is to develop the proper visuals to fit it. Or, the visuals may already be in hand—slides from a field trip, for example—and all you have to do is organize them and develop your script to accompany the visuals.

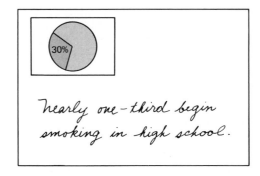

Step 6. Make a card for the thought that *leads into* the point you have just sketched. Then do another one about the thought that *follows* your first one. Continue like this, building a chain of ideas as you go along.

Step 7. When you run out of ideas in the chain, switch to one of the other major points that hasn't fallen into sequence yet.

Step 8. Arrange the cards in sequential and logical order. (This technique is called "storyboarding" and is described in more detail elsewhere in this chapter.)

Would some other arrangement liven up the beginning and the end of your presentation? Keep in mind the "psychology" of the situation as you thought it through in your audience analysis. The *beginning* and the *end* are generally the best places to make major points. Have you grabbed the viewer's attention right from the beginning?

How about pacing? Are any complicated ideas skimmed over too lightly? Do sections get bogged down in unnecessary detail? Add or subtract cards as needed.

You should have at least one slide on the screen for every point you make. Each slide should be on the screen long enough to support the point, but not so long that it gets tiresome to look at.

As a rule of thumb, you can estimate the number of slides you need by timing your presentation and multiplying the number of minutes by five or six. This means one slide change about every ten or twelve seconds. You may find that you need more slides in some instances, fewer in others. Don't be afraid to use "filler" slides to hold visual interest. They're perfectly acceptable as long as they relate to the topic.

Step 9. Edit your planning cards in terms of practicality. Be sure you have ready access to the artistic talent and/or photographic equipment needed to turn your sketches into slides.

Step 10. Use your notes to prepare an audio script.

Consider using two different voices for the narration, perhaps one male and one female for variety.

Would sound effects add impact to your presentation? How about actual sounds from the place where you will be shooting the pictures? You can take along a recorder and pick up background sounds and personal interviews while doing the photography.

Consider, too, adding music, especially as a finishing touch to the beginning and end. Be careful to keep it unobtrusive. Avoid highly recognizable tunes, trendy songs that will date your presentation, and music aimed at very specialized tastes.

Step 11. Rehearse your presentation, imagining that your cards are slides on the screen. Time your presentation and see if you need to shorten or lengthen it. To keep your audience's attention, limit your show to fifteen minutes. If you need more time than that, break it into two or more parts interspersed with audience activity.

Now you are ready to turn your sketches into slides! (To record your tape, see Chapter 6.)

---

[a]The visual organization hints given here are adapted from *How to Give a Better than Offhand Talk.* . . . Rochester, N.Y.: Eastman Kodak.

▲ **Figure 7.6**
Sound-slide programs are readily adapted to individual use.

◀ **Figure 7.7**
The storyboard helps in visualizing the total presentation and rearranging parts within it.

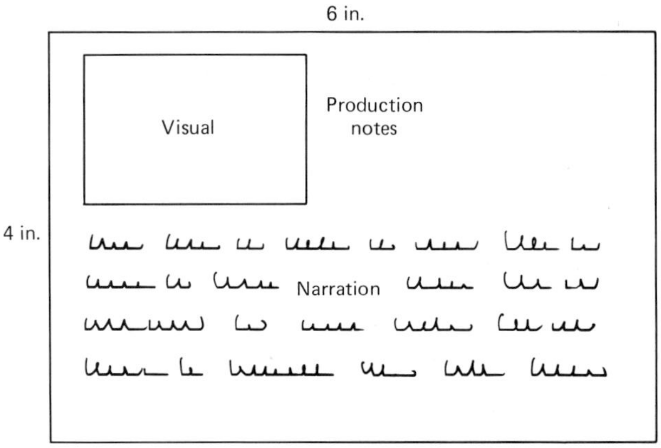

◀ **Figure 7.8**
A sample storyboard card.

than one narration can be prepared for a given set of visuals. For example, a simple set of visuals might have one audio narrative suitable for introduction of and preliminary instruction in a study unit and another narrative for more detailed study. The narration could be on two or more vocabulary levels—one for regular students and another for educationally handicapped students. For foreign language instruction, one audio tape might be narrated in the student's native language and a matching narration recorded on another tape in the foreign language being taught. This technique can also be used in bilingual situations.

Storyboarding

As previously noted, storyboarding is an important step in the development of audiovisual presentations. Storyboarding, an idea borrowed from film and television production, is a technique for helping you generate and organize your audiovisual materials. A sketch or some other simple representation of the visual you plan to use is put on a card or piece of paper along with production notes pertaining to production of the visual and verbal cues to its accompanying narration. After a series of such cards have been developed, they are placed in rough sequence on a flat

surface or on a storyboard holder designed to keep them in place.

Index cards are commonly used for storyboarding because they are durable, inexpensive, and available in a variety of colors and sizes. Small pieces of paper can also be used.

The individual storyboard cards can be divided into areas to accommodate the visual, the narration, and the production notes (Figure 7.8). The exact format of the storyboard card should fit your needs and purposes. Design a card that facilitates your working rather than constraining yourself to an existing or recommended format.

You can make a simple sketch or write a short description of the desired visual on the card. Polaroid pictures or visuals cut from magazines can also be used.

Some people like to use different colored cards for different topics within the program, or various colors for objectives, content, and types of media (visuals, audio, films, etc.).

Each component (slide, overhead, film sequence) should be on a separate card.

When a series of cards has been developed, the cards can be laid out on a table or placed on a storyboard holder. The cards are sequenced in tentative order, thus giving you an overview of the production. The storyboarding technique facilitates addition, deletion, replacement, revision, and refinement of the sequence, since the cards can easily be discarded, added to, or rearranged. The display of cards also allows others (teachers, students, production assistants) to look at the presentation in its planning stage. Number the cards in pencil; you may wish to change numbers as your planning progresses.

HOW TO... MAKE A STORYBOARD HOLDER

You can construct an inexpensive storyboard holder from cardboard and strips of clear plastic. Obtain one or two pieces of cardboard about the size that you need to accommodate the number of cards which you will be using. About 18-by-24 inches is a convenient size if you plan to carry the storyboard holder with you.

If you use two pieces, they can be hinged in the middle (as shown above) with bookbinding tape or wide masking tape, giving you a usable surface measuring 36-by-24 inches when unfolded. If you do not plan to move the storyboard frequently, you could use a larger piece of cardboard (perhaps from a large appliance box such as a refrigerator carton) which could give you up to 6-by-4 feet of usable surface.

Staple or tape 1-inch-wide strips of clear plastic on the cardboard to hold the cards. If you are planning to use 3-by-5-inch index cards, the strips should be attached about 4 inches apart. One-inch strips of paper or light cardboard can be used to keep the card in place instead of the clear plastic, but this has the disadvantage of not allowing you to read the portion of the card that is behind the strip.

Several cards in sequence on a page can be photocopied for use with the final script, thus avoiding duplication of effort and providing a convenient assemblage of visuals, narration, and production notes.

Your narration can be written from the notes on your storyboard cards. It is a good idea to triple space the typing of the final script for easy reading and last-minute changes. Marking pauses on the script with a slash (/) and underlining key words will help you record your narration effectively.

MULTI-IMAGE SYSTEMS

The multi-image presentation is another very popular multimedia system. Whether you call the system "multi-image" or "multi-screen" depends primarily upon the way you design it. *Multi-image* refers to the use of two or more separate *images*, usually projected simultaneously in a presentation. (It does not usually refer to two images from a single source.) *Multi-screen* refers to the use of more than one screen in a single presentation. The two concepts usually go hand in hand, since the multiple images are often projected on adjacent multiple screens. Most often the images are projected from slides, but overhead transparencies, filmstrips, or motion pictures may also be used.

Planning a Multi-Image Presentation

Having learned how to develop a single-screen presentation, you could choose as your next project a two-screen or even a three-screen presentation—although it should be pointed out that multiple-image presentations require even more planning and attention to detail. A two-screen presentation may require more than twice the time and effort needed to produce a single-screen one, and a three-screen display may require more than four times as much time.

A "development chart" can help ease your extra burden. After you have storyboarded the sequence of your material, use the development chart for your production notes on the images to appear on each screen and for your notes on accompanying narration (see Figure 7.10.).

Multi-image presentations must be carefully planned to fit your audience (multiple images may confuse younger students) and to meet your objectives. You should do a complete practice run-through prior to classroom presentation to be sure that the sequencing is correct and that equipment is operating the way you want it to operate.

Multi-image productions can incorporate film clips, overhead transparencies, slides, or a series of slides to simulate movement. They can also incorporate dissolve units.

▲ **Figure 7.9**
Showing a broad panorama is a typical application of multi-image systems.

Left screen	Right screen	Narration

Left screen	Middle screen	Right screen	Narration

▲ **Figure 7.10**
Sample development charts for multi-image or multi-screen presentations.

▲ **Figure 7.11**
Adding a dissolve unit allows you to make smooth transitions between images.

Dissolve Units

You can achieve dramatic effects in your slide/tape presentations by using a dissolve unit and two slide projectors. A dissolve unit has a mechanism for slowly turning one projector bulb off, causing one picture to fade out, while the other picture slowly appears on the same screen. The screen does not go black between pictures, but rather, one picture fades into the next. With a dissolve system you can gradually overlap images, blend or change directly from one visual to another, or blend one image into the other while the level of screen illumination remains constant. This provides a smooth visual presentation without any intervals of darkness on the screen between slides.

All dissolve units require at least two projectors focused to a single point on the screen so that the images will overlap. The projectors may be placed alongside each other or stacked one above the other (as shown in Figure 7.12).

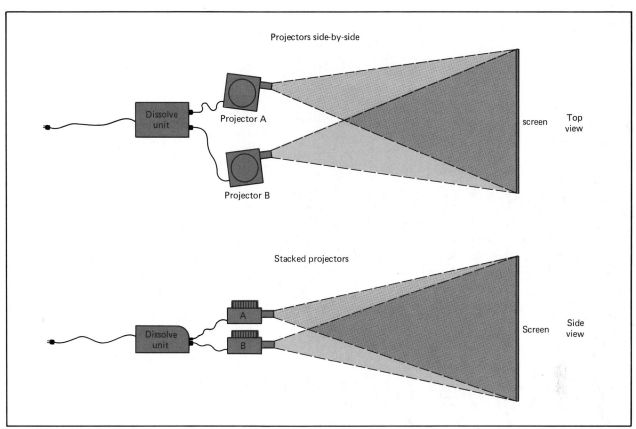

▲ **Figure 7.12**
When using a dissolve unit, the projectors may be aligned side-by-side or stacked one above the other.

You can achieve some very interesting effects by superimposing images from the two projectors. You can add elements to a particular visual or eliminate unneeded ones. You can make an object appear to rotate, or make a head turn or a facial expression change in apparent response to a comment on the audio tape.

With the push of a button, you can control the speed and type of dissolve. A fast dissolve provides an instantaneous change from one visual to the next. A medium dissolve, lasting a couple of seconds, provides a visual blend between the slides. A slow dissolve allows one image to change more gradually into the next. The modes of changes available on most fade/dissolve units include:

Cut mode—the slide presentation switches from one projector to the other with instantaneous image change.

Dissolve mode—the first slide gradually fades in intensity as another slide from the second projector increases in intensity, creating a fading and overlapping effect as slides are changed.

Fade-out/fade-in mode—the slide gradually fades as light is reduced until there is total darkness on the screen; then a new image appears as light is gradually increased.

Automatic Programmers

There is a limit to the number of pieces of equipment you (with or without helpers) can operate and control directly. Fortunately, *automatic programmers* are available that can control a number of projec-

tors. They can also be programmed to stop during your presentation for discussion or questions from the audience and then resume at the touch of a button.

There are two common types of programmers: magnetic tape and microcomputers. Magnetic-tape programmers are increasing in popularity and use and at the same time decreasing in cost. The newer microcomputers can also be used to control multi-image presentations. Microcomputers are very versatile and relatively easy to program for this function.

Automatic programmers enable you to operate motion pictures, filmstrips, and slide projectors together, separately, or in any combination with synchronized sound from an audio tape. A typical three-screen setup with dissolve control for each projector is shown in Figure 7.14.

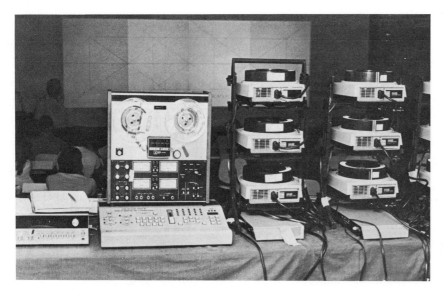

▲ **Figure 7.13**
A multi-image presentation controlled by an automatic programmer using magnetic tape.

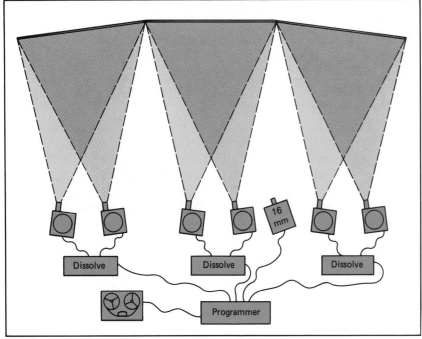

▲ **Figure 7.14**
Setup for a three-screen presentation using dissolve units and an automatic programmer.

APPLICATIONS OF MULTI-IMAGE SYSTEMS

Multi-image presentations can be used creatively in a variety of instructional situations. For example, one screen could be used to present an overview or long-range view of a visual while another presents a close-up view or a detail of it. This technique might be used to show the relationship of a component of a system or process to its entirety, or to show a detail of a work of art in relationship to the complete piece. Two or more images could be projected side-by-side for students to compare and contrast different art forms, or art and architectural forms in different periods of history.

"Before and after" shots could be used in industrial arts classes, for example, to show the final results of a furniture refinishing project; or they could be used in a social studies class to show the inroads of industrialization on an ecological system. In electronics instruction, schematic codes of circuit components could be shown next to visuals of the actual components. Similarly, line drawings of an object can be exhibited adjacent to its photograph, or a photograph can be displayed on one screen and data or questions about the picture presented on another. A map of an area might be shown on one screen, and a photograph or aerial view of the area presented in another.

Two or more screens may also be used to present wide-angle or panoramic views of a visual that might be impossible to present on a single screen. Multiple-screen images can also be used to show physical activities in more detailed sequence, such as swimming, diving, swinging a tennis racquet, or hitting a golf ball. They can also be used to present several views of the same object to achieve a three-dimensional effect or to allow viewers to see an object from different distances and angles.

Multi-image presentations can also be used very effectively for learning in the affective domain and for establishment of mood. For example, one could provide a visually dramatic background for listening to musical and choral works, plays, and readings.

▲ **Figure 7.15**
A typical *instructional* application of multiple images is to show a significant detail alongside a larger view of a scene.

VARIABLE MOTION PROGRAMMING

One of the most versatile multimedia systems utilizes an 8-mm film and an audio cassette. In contrast to standard motion picture presentations, the sound and the picture in the 8-mm film–audio cassette system are separated into two individual packages. The audio tape moves at a constant speed, but the film can be programmed to move at variable speeds from still (stop action) up to 24 frames per second. The film cartridge contains 50 feet of Super-8-mm film and includes 3600 frames (visuals) that can be shown individually or in rapid succession to simulate motion. The film and sound are synchronized by inaudible pulses recorded on the audio cassette. The systems provide "variable motion sound filmstrips" with the impact of motion pictures and the teaching effectiveness of still pictures.

The most commonly available of these systems is Beseler's Cue/See. This system can intermix the equivalent of slides, filmstrips, and motion

▲ **Figure 7.16**
A variable motion system such as Beseler's Cue/See® combines cartridged Super-8-mm film and an audio cassette programmed to show a mixture of still and motion pictures.

pictures along with narration or sound effects. Separate audio cassettes allow the user to choose which narration to use with a given film. The projection mechanism is essentially a variable speed projector with a built-in tape player and synchronization device. The machinery is light, weighing about twenty pounds, and is thus readily portable.

The speed at which the image changes on the screen can be determined by the nature of the material being presented. Separation of "sound track" from the film permits the film to be moved at variable speeds while the tape is moving at a constant speed. Just as pulses advance the frames of a filmstrip, pulses in this system advance the

frames of the film slowly, to illustrate specific lesson points, or very rapidly, to create motion.

The machine has a built-in rear projection screen as well as a mirror and lens system for projecting the image on a screen, so it is suitable for individual or small-group use. It can show slow motion, time lapse, or stop action. The machines also incorporate a "skipped" frame mechanism that allows two, three, or even five frames at a time to be advanced at high speed without detection by the viewer, since each new frame is advanced in less than a hundredth of a second. This feature is particularly valuable when the same film is used with separate audio tapes for two different types of audiences.

The major disadvantages of the system are initial cost of the equipment, the lack of commercially available materials, and the time and expense required for local production. The cost of production goes up very rapidly as you move beyond simple presentations. Also, in order to produce your own materials, you must have a device called a "skip-frame pulse generator" to put the sound frequency pulses on the audio cassette.

Close-Up:
Teaching Welding with Variable Motion Programming

In Troy, Ohio, at the Hobart School of Welding Technology, variable motion programs for the Beseler CUE/SEE are used in fifteen welding courses. The programs include "live action" motion sequences required to effectively teach welding skills, slow motion for better understanding of the techniques, and still pictures when these visual media are more beneficial.

Each program is followed by "job practices" in which the trainee is expected to duplicate the procedures demonstrated with actual welds. The trainee can view a portion of the filmed demonstration, practice that skill through hands-on experience with metal and welding rods, check his or her progress, then view the next portion of the demonstration and practice it. Each trainee uses workbooks during instruction and at the practice location as a reference when the instructor is with other students.

These materials are being used by the Hobart School for classroom training and laboratory practice. The system is sold to high schools and vocational-technical schools as well as to industries that employ welders. Industrial applications include on-the-job training and refresher courses. Because of the individualized nature of the variable motion programming, a "class" of trainees is not necessary. The instructor can be a master welder who answers questions and checks the trainee's work.

One teacher says, "My high school and adult learners believe they learn more rapidly using the Hobart audiovisual program." Another user reports, "This system will greatly reduce our welding training costs and provide welder skill, in a shorter time period to pass various qualification tests."

Applications

Variable motion programming is especially useful in learning situations that lend themselves to integration of still visuals and moving pictures. As noted above, since the audio cassette is separate from the film cassette, you can use different sound tracks with the visual component of the system. For example, in a foreign language class, the audio could be in English on one cassette tape and in a foreign language on the other. A demonstration in an industrial arts class or in a home economics class could use one film cassette with separate audio tapes geared to beginning, intermediate, and advanced students. Tapes can also be geared to different ability levels.

When the same instruction is needed for a large number of students in widely scattered locations, the variable motion system becomes cost effective. For example, the U.S. Army uses the Beseler Cue/See to provide individual or small-group instruction on standard military procedures and the use of common pieces of equipment. Businesses sometimes use one film with separate narrations for training of personnel and for product promotion.

INTERACTIVE VIDEO

Interactive video has all the features of variable motion programming and more. Interactive video creates a multi-media learning environment that capitalizes on the features of both instructional television and computer-assisted instruction. It is an instructional delivery system in which recorded video material is presented under computer control to viewers who not only see and hear the pictures and sounds, but also make active responses, with those responses affecting the pace and sequence of the presentation.

▲ **Figure 7.17**
An interactive video setup using videocassette as the picture source (see upper left shelf).

The video portion of interactive video is provided through videotape or videodisc. Videodiscs (see Chapter 9 for more detail) can provide color, motion, and sound. The images can be presented in slow motion, fast motion, frame-by-frame, or single frame—equivalent to a slide or film-strip display. The audio portion of a videodisc may occupy two channels, making possible two different narrations with any specific motion sequence. Many of the features of videodiscs can be obtained with currently available videotape systems at a lower cost.

The "interactive" feature of interactive video is provided through a computer, usually a micro. Computers have very powerful decision-making abilities, which video players lack. Combining these technologies means the strengths of each can compensate for the limitations of the other to provide a rich educational environment for the learner. Interactive video is a powerful, practical method for individualizing and personalizing instruction.

System Components

The heart of an interactive video system is a computer, usually a microcomputer. (See Figure 7.18.) The computer provides the "intelligence" and interactivity required for interactive video. The computer can command the video player to present audio and/or video information from the videotape or videodisc, wait for the learner's response, and branch to the appropriate point in the instructional program from that response.

The learner communicates with the instructional program by responding to audio, visual, or verbal stimuli displayed through the video monitor. Input devices provide the means for these responses. They may include a keyboard, a touch sensitive panel, a light pen, voice activation, or a three-dimensional simulator. (See "Close-up: CPR Computer/Videodisc Learning System," p. 186.)

The computer storage system consists, usually, of a floppy diskette. The diskette holds the instructional program and may also store information such as student responses, response time, and accuracy of responses throughout the lesson.

The video player offers a sophisticated means of storing visual and audio information. The videotape or videodisc can provide color, sound

▼ **Figure 7.18**
The components of an interactive video system.

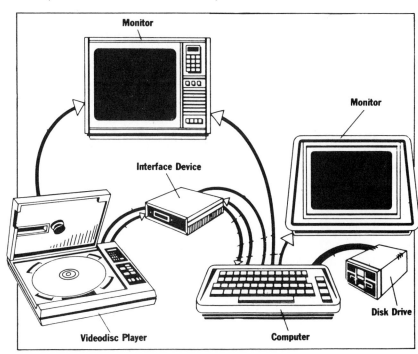

(two different audio tracks on videodisc), still visuals, or motion pictures.

The video monitor is used to display the video signal and sound from the video player. The monitor can be either black/white or color, but color is usually preferred.

The computer display provides the output from the computer program, usually in the form of printed verbal information, but graphics or sound are also possible. Some interactive video systems combine the video monitor and the computer display, making it possible to overlay computer lettering or graphics on a video image from the tape or disc. Some commercially available videodisc players have the computer, the memory, and input devices built into them.

Advantages

One of the major advantages of interactive video is that it requires learner response (the R of the ASSURE model). Learners respond through typing on a keyboard, touching the screen, or manipulating objects connected to the system. By requiring frequent response, interactive video captures learners' attention and holds their interest to a greater extent than does videotape alone. The system allows the learner to actively participate in an educational video presentation that is thereby adapted to the learner's ability and knowledge level.

Another important feature of interactive video is its branching (nonlinear) capability. Depending upon the response of the learner, the computer can branch to another section of the video program to provide remedial instruction rather than simply repeating the original information. Or the system may branch to a new section of the video to provide enrichment material for the learner. When the learner has mastered the objective or already has knowledge of the subject matter or skill, the program can be branched to a new topic or

▲ **Figure 7.19**
An interactive video setup using videodisc as the picture source.

more advanced treatment of the same topic. In some cases the student may choose what to study from a "menu."

As a result of its learner response and branching capabilities, interactive video can serve as an individualized, self-paced system capable of presenting information in an order determined by and appropriate to a learner's responses and needs.

Two additional advantages of interactive video are its convenience and variety. A variety of media formats are included in one system. Text, audio, graphics, still pictures, motion pictures, and manipulation of objects can all be combined in one instructional system without requiring numerous projectors, tape recorders, and synchronization equipment. From the student's perspective the operation of the system is very simple, in many cases requiring only the use of a keyboard. A large amount of content and a variety of information are made available to the learner in a matter of seconds.

From the instructor's point of view, a further advantage is the record-keeping ability of the system. The computer can be programmed to keep track of learner responses, for tracking the learner's progress, for determining where the learner will be directed next, and for assisting the instructor in revising the program. The system lends itself to the collection of

research data on factors affecting student learning and the measurement of the effectiveness of various instructional techniques.

Limitations

The most significant limitation of interactive video is its cost. Expensive equipment—including a computer, video playback unit, and monitor—is required for each student. It is expensive to produce and update videotape and even more costly and difficult to produce and update a videodisc. Videodiscs can only be mastered by a limited number of companies at the present time.

The complexity and high cost of developing and mass-producing videodiscs limits their use primarily to high-volume informational or training applications in business and industry. They currently are not in widespead use in formal education, beyond demonstration projects.

Videotape is less expensive than videodisc as a format for producing small numbers of copies, but it has the drawbacks of being slower in search time (to get from one frame to another) and less efficient in showing a particular single frame. Most videocassette machines lack slow motion and fast motion. Consequently, the user must trade off the more expensive costs of producing videodiscs for fewer capabilities and increased time required to access material on a videotape.

Applications

Interactive video systems are currently being used in a variety of instructional applications. Formal education demonstration projects cover a wide range, from physics instruction to teaching special education students to tell time. The programs can challenge a small group of gifted

Close-Up:
Safety Training via Interactive Video

The Clark Equipment Company, manufacturer of fork lift trucks in Battle Creek, Michigan, has developed an operator safety refresher course using interactive video. The course was designed in response to supervisors who expressed concern that they didn't have time to do the refresher training. In addition, the supervisors were concerned about the time they wasted in retraining operators. The operators themselves didn't see the need to be retrained in order to learn about something they did every day. An interactive videotape system was selected for the safety training.

Training via interactive video was compared with training using conventional videotape. Studies involved Clark employees and operators in other companies that had purchased Clark fork lifts. The results indicated higher initial learning and retention of the content after twenty-four days that was almost 20 percent higher for the operators using the interactive video system. Training time for the operators was reduced, as well as time required by the supervisors to provide the training. Consequently, there was a significant reduction in the wages and overhead devoted to training.

Furthermore, the training system motivated operators to request other opportunities to learn using interactive video. In addition, there was no evidence in the interactive video group to indicate any effects of age or experience on an operator's score as there was in the group of operators learning from ordinary videotape.

Source: D. Wooldridge and Thomas Dargan. "Linear vs. Interactive Videotape Training." *International Television.* (August 1983), pp. 56–60.

---

students or provide remedial instruction for slow learners. The materials can be used by individuals or an entire class. Most teachers feel that their greater effectiveness is with individuals.

One of the first interactive educational videodiscs was "The Development of Living Things" released by McGraw-Hill in 1978. The program teaches the fundamentals of developmental biology for high school and college students.

Data generated by school and university projects indicate that those students working with interactive video systems achieve mastery level with greater facility, transfer learned concepts more effectively to the performance environment, and retain a greater portion of information and skills over time than do other students.

In business and industry, these systems are being used, for example, to train automobile mechanics to troubleshoot electronic ignition systems, to improve communication skills for bank tellers, and to teach relaxation and stress management techniques to executives. One company reports reducing the training time of lift truck operators from three hours to one hour by replacing classroom training with interactive video training. (See "Close-up: Safety Training via Interactive Video.")

Technical repair skills also can be taught with interactive video. A program can teach the trainee to locate a faulty component and can visually demonstrate how to adjust or replace the component while oral instructions are provided through one of the two audio channels on the videodisc. Data collected regarding such a system indicate that mechanics using it did demonstrate mastery of the maintenance skills. Moreover, both training time and training costs for the interactive video group were less than half of those of the traditional on-the-job training group.

Interactive video programs are also being used to teach and reinforce interpersonal skills through intensive simulation. For example,

Close-Up:
CPR Computer/Videodisc Learning System

Cardiopulmonary resuscitation, or CPR, is currently being taught using interactive video. Developed by David Hon of the American Heart Association, the system incorporates a variety of media including an optical videodisc player, a monitor, a microcomputer, and a random access audio player. At the "heart" of the system is a mannequin wired with an array of sensors placed at key points in its lung system that monitor the depth and placement of CPR compressions.

As the trainee practices these compressions, he or she receives several different types of feedback: audiovisual "coaching" from the doctor on the screen, a visual readout on the computer monitor (indicating, for instance, that hand placement is too high or depth is too shallow), audio tones to indicate proper timing of each compression, and a graphic pattern on the computer detailing overall performance.

At various points during the program, the computer asks evaluative questions in "fill-in" or multiple-choice format. Using a light pen or typing in a response, the trainee actively participates in learning CPR. The computer monitors and displays learner progress throughout the course. Video segments can be accessed for review and for detailed explanations when necessary.

After the instructional segment of the program is completed, the student is ready for evaluation. The same computer/videodisc system with mannequin monitors the student's final "hands-on" performance for certification and "asks" questions about CPR.

Source: Biomedical Communications (September 1981).

welfare caseworkers and sales personnel can benefit through such programs. One of the "Big-Three" automakers uses videodiscs to train its sales personnel within the dealerships as well as to sell automobiles to customers. The same video sequences are used for both. One of the audio channels is directed to the customer, pointing out the important sales features of the various makes and models. The other audio channel is used by the sales staff to learn critical information concerning how their cars compare to the competition. Sales pointers are included as well.

In the lobbies of a Denver bank's branches an interactive video designed to be used by customers provides a dramatization of how the automatic teller machine works and, upon request from the customer, describes various bank services. At the push of a button, the customer can learn about the various savings programs available, the types of loans offered by the bank, and investment opportunities.

Interactive video systems are also used for remote shopping by presenting features of various items and responding to customer questions selected from a menu. Sales increases between 50 percent and 350 percent have been reported for products presented in stores and airports by an "intelligent" videodisc point-of-purchase system.

In the medical field interactive video systems are being used for patient education; e.g., on weight control and on diabetes. Doctors are receiving in-service education through a library of medical simulations on patient management, differential diagnosis of stomach pain, and various diagnostic techniques. This last series has been accredited by the American Medical Association. One of the most widespread applications of interactive video is the teaching of cardiopulmonary resuscitation (CPR). (See "Close-up: CPR Computer/Videodisc Learning System.")

The military is a big user of interactive video, for tasks such as Jeep mechanical maintenance, visual simulation of life inside a military tank, and simulation of the task of calling for artillery fire. In 1980 a course was developed around an interactive video system for troubleshooting the new HAWK missile system. Evaluation of this training simulation provided impressive evidence of the power of interactive video. The videodisc simulation replaced equipment costing up to $4000 per student hour and provided more opportunities for practice than could be possible with the actual equipment. All trainees attained 100 percent mastery after interactive video training and did so in less than half the time of trainees taught by conventional means. In the latter group, only 30 percent reached mastery.

Army recruiters now provide significant decision-making information to potential recruits through a videodisc-based interactive system. The videodisc materials are used to strengthen positive attitudes through modeling and aggressive public relations. The Army's various job types and training opportunities are explained and visually demonstrated by the system in response to a potential recruit's questions. Recruiting offices using the videodisc system currently realize almost double the number of recruits compared to matched samples from offices without the system.

MULTIMEDIA KITS

A multimedia kit is a collection of teaching/learning materials involving more than one type of medium and organized around a single topic. The kits may include filmstrips, slides, audio tapes, records, still pictures, study prints, overhead transparencies, single-concept films, maps, worksheets, charts, graphs, booklets, real objects, and models.

Some multimedia kits are designed for use by the teacher in classroom presentations. Others are designed for use by individual students or by small groups. The variety and wide range of instructional purposes to which such kits may be put is indicated below in the discussion of commercially available and teacher-made multimedia kits.

Commercial Multimedia Kits

Commercial multimedia kits are available for a variety of educational subjects. For example, the Society for Visual Education markets a series of multimedia kits ("learning modules") with titles such as *Beginning Math Concepts, Metric System, Communi-*

ties in Nature (an ecology unit), *Planning the Human Community, Initial Consonant, Vowel Sounds,* and *Threshold to Reading.*

These learning modules include sound filmstrips, cassette tapes, floor games, board games, posters, full-color photographs, activity cards, lotto cards, murals, wall charts, geometric shapes, flash cards, student workbooks, and a teacher's manual. They stimulate active participation; encourage individualized, multi-sensory learning; and help make learning exciting and enjoyable. Clearly defined objectives are stated and supported with suggested teaching strategies for using the materials in the kit. The kits are versatile in that they may be used in traditional or open classrooms. In short, they provide a systematic approach to the use of multimedia materials for instructional purposes.

Many other multimedia kits on a wide variety of topics are available from commercial sources, some of which contain, among other materials, transparencies, laboratory materials for science experiments, and even puppets to act out story concepts.

Media File:
"Creative Leadership for Teacher Growth" Multimedia Kit

Training Sunday School teachers is an ongoing task in religious education because of the rather high turnover rate from year to year. This multimedia kit is designed to be used by the teacher trainer and contains materials for four 1½- to 2-hour sessions. Included in the kit are two audio cassettes, forty overhead transparencies, twenty-eight duplicating masters, a leader handbook, and three different teacher guidebooks.

Each of the four sessions is built around a lesson plan in the leader's handbook and includes objectives and activities correlated with the various media included in the kit. Initial topics in this series are: "Creative Leadership Communication," "Nurturing My Students," and "Discipline—A Topic for All Seasons."

Source: David C. Cook Publishing Co.

▲ **Figure 7.20**
Multimedia kits provide varied sensory experiences; they give the concrete referents needed to build a strong foundation for more abstract mental abilities.

Teacher-made Multimedia Kits

Multimedia kits can also be prepared by teachers. First of all, you must decide if the kit is to be used by the students. Obviously, this decision will affect your choice of materials. Obviously, too, you will have to decide if you are going to prepare only one kit for student use or if you are going to duplicate the kit so that more than one student can have access to it at any given time. Another alternative might be to make a variety of kits and have the students take turns using them.

Availability and cost of materials will also affect your choice of materials to be included in the kit. Cost is particularly important if duplicate kits are to be provided and if materials are not reusable. Remember too that if the kits are to be taken home for unsupervised individual use, allowance should probably be made for loss or damage to some items. Nevertheless, cost is not an insurmountable problem. Many simple but satisfactory resource materials are free. Multimedia kits need not be expensive to be effective.

It is important that the components of the kit be integrated—that is, that each component contribute to attainment of your lesson objective. Multimedia activities should also be correlated with other relevant learning activities in the classroom.

The availability of equipment will also affect your selection of materials. If filmstrips or other projected visuals are included, for example, you will need a projector for group use. A hand-held viewer, however, might suffice for individual use. Audio materials will require playback machines.

Multimedia kits should be designed to teach specific knowledge and skills. They should involve the student in the learning process as he or she handles and manipulates the resource materials.

Your multimedia kit should include some sort of introduction to its topic and instructions on or suggestions about how the various components of the kit are to be used. If the kit is to be used only under your direct supervision, oral introduction and instructions may suffice. In most cases, however, a printed study guide should be included with your kit. The guide should introduce the topic of the kit and relate its components to the learning objective. It should give instructions for using the materials included in the kit and include directions for the learning activities involved. Questions and space for responses may also be contained in the guide. The study guide should be as simple as possible, containing just the essential directions and relevant information.

Some teachers prefer to put their study guide materials on audio tape. This procedure can be helpful for slow readers and may be essential for very poor readers and nonreaders.

It is important for the teacher to monitor each student's progress in order to reward successes and to alleviate frustrations. At the conclusion of each kit's use, the student should discuss the activity with the teacher individually or in a small group. The teacher and the student(s) can go over the nature of the problem presented in the kit, compare answers (if appropriate), and discuss the concepts learned from the multimedia kit. The follow-up discussion can be used as an evaluative device in addition to or instead of a written quiz.

Shoe boxes make handy containers for teacher-made multimedia kits. Each box should have a label indicating its topic and perhaps its learning objective. A list of materials included in the kit can be pasted on the inside of the box lid as an aid to use and as a check to make certain that all the materials are returned.

Applications

The instructional uses of teacher-made multimedia kits are limited only by teacher ingenuity. Following are a few examples.

Because such kits typically center on realia and other such concrete materials, they lend themselves especially well to *discovery* learning. Questions are used to guide students' exploration of the material and arrival at conclusions.

A multimedia kit on magnetic fields might include (among other materials) several types of magnets, such as permanent and electromagnets, and an assortment of metal objects that may or may not be attracted to them. For older students, iron filings might also be provided. A kit on aerodynamics might include paper or balsa along with patterns and instructions for constructing various types of aircraft. If proper safety precautions are taken, you might allow the stu-

dents to fly their models and award prizes for the longest or highest flight.

Mathematical topics are especially suitable for multimedia kits. Such a kit could include a statement of the problem(s) the student must solve, suggestions for procedures to use,

and materials needed. A kit on metric measurement, for example, could include a metric ruler or meter stick, various objects to be measured, and suggestions for taking metric measurements of various objects in the classroom.

▲ **Figure 7.21**
Multimedia kits frequently include raw materials for student inquiry into the phenomena of nature.

Close-Up:
Teacher-made Multimedia Kit

An elementary teacher developed a series of separate multimedia kits on science topics for use with her third-grade class. She incorporated real objects, such as magnets, small motors, rocks, harmless chemicals, and insect specimens in the kits. She also gathered pictures from magazines and old textbooks associated with each topic. A study guide, prepared for each unit, required the student to inquire into the topic, make hypotheses, and conduct investigations. Audio tapes were prepared for use at school and at home for those students who had access to cassette players.

The students enjoyed taking the kits home to work on the experiments. The response from parents was very positive. Several parents reported that they too learned by working through the activities with their children. Students often preferred to stay in at recess and work on the multimedia kits in the science corner.

Flashback: THE MATCH PROGRAM

Multimedia kits were an integral part of the Materials and Activities for Teachers and Children (MATCH) program[a] developed by the Children's Museum in Boston during the late 1960s. The program incorporated learning materials and activities in the form of a series of multimedia kits designed to be used by elementary-school students and teachers. The focus was on nonverbal learning and the acquisition of skills not unique to any one subject matter area. The program emphasized the development of thinking, feeling, and learning skills through direct experience with authentic materials.

The long-range goal of the MATCH project was to

explore the ways of communicating nonverbally through the use of a variety of media. The developers combined various materials with classroom activities in the form of kits designed to teach specific objectives. Sixteen such kits were developed. The kits, designed to be used for two or three weeks, supplemented regular classroom instruction. Each MATCH multimedia kit was independent of the other kits and could be used in any order or combination. The 16 titles were:

Grouping Birds	Musical Shapes and
The City	Sounds
The Algonquins	Rocks
Seeds	Japanese Family
A House of Ancient	Medieval People
Greece	Waterplay
Houses	Imagination Unlimited
Animal Camouflage	"Paddle-to-the-Sea"
Netsilik Eskimos	The MATCH Box Press

For example, the kit on the Netsilik Eskimos was designed especially for third and fourth graders. Its purpose was to put children in touch with the traditions of the Netsilik Eskimos by focusing on their lives during the seal-hunting season. The kit materials illustrated Netsilik hunting technology, spiritual beliefs, social relations, and leisure activities as they related to seal hunting. The media in the kit

LEARNING CENTERS

The development of multimedia instructional technology and the growing interest in small-group and individualized instruction have led to the establishment of special learning environments generally called *classroom learning centers*. A learning center is an individualized environment designed to encourage the student to use a variety of instructional media, to engage in diversified learning activities, and to assume major responsibility for his or her own learning.

Learning centers may be set up in any suitable and available classroom space. Or they may be set up outside the classroom, in a laboratory, for example, or even in a school corridor.

Learning center materials may include practically any or all of the media and multimedia formats mentioned in this text. Center materials may be purchased from commercial producers or may be teacher-made.

Carrels

Although simple learning center activities might be carried out at a student's desk or some other open space, it is advisable that learning centers be confined to a clearly identifiable area and that they be at least partially enclosed to aid concentration and avoid distraction. Learning

carrels (booths), which may be purchased from commercial sources or made locally, will provide a clearly identifiable enclosure.

Carrels may be made by placing simple cardboard dividers on classroom tables, or free-standing commercially constructed carrels complete with electrical connections and rear projection screens may be purchased.

Carrels are often referred to as being either "wet" or "dry." A dry carrel provides private space for study or other learning activities but contains no electrical equipment. The typical library carrel is a dry carrel. A wet carrel, on the other hand, is equipped with or has outlets for audiovisual mechanisms such as cas-

included authentic Eskimo artifacts and materials, such as seal-hunting tools, boots, a seal skin, a drum, an Eskimo amulet, three films showing seal hunting and Eskimos setting up camp, a model igloo, figures, a book, and a record. Kit activities included simulating a seal hunt, recreating everyday activities of Netsilik life, hearing the story of the sea spirit Nuliajuk, and performing the Netsilik drum dance.

Learning activities throughout the entire series were designed to be relevant to the children's interests while keeping the objectives of the unit in mind. Most of the activities were designed for small-group participation, with four to six children taking part in the activity. The most important characteristic of these activities was that they were intended to place responsibility for learning in the hands of the child and thus to make the child the agent of his or her own learning.

The teacher's manual for each kit stressed reliance on real objects and other visual media, concentration on limited objectives, and integration of learning activities. Provision for motivating student participation and learning was built into each unit, as were opportunities for providing feedback to the learners. All units were designed to be used for 1 or 1 1/2 hours a day over a period of two to three weeks.

Each kit was tried out in some 15 to 22 classrooms involving a total of 330 teachers and over 10,000 children. The director of the MATCH project summarized the results of the field test as follows:

Teachers and children were overwhelmingly enthusiastic about the units and this form of teaching. Teachers judged class interest, attention, participation, and learning to be greater than usual. They delighted in having such rich material to work with. Children who were previously unresponsive participated, often for the first time. Many children surprised their teachers with what they could do. The units altered the relationship between teacher and children, making it more collaborative rather than teacher-directed. Teachers said they could see what the children were learning and therefore didn't need special tests.[b]

---

[a]B. A. Sanderson, and D. W. Kratochvel. *Materials and Activities for Teachers and Children—The MATCH Program*. Palo Alto, Calif.: American Institutes of Research, 1972.
[b]F. H. Kresse. *Materials and Activities for Teachers and Children: A Project to Develop and Evaluate Multi-Media Kits for Elementary Schools. Final Report, vol. 1*. Boston: The Children's Museum, 1968, p. 7.

sette recorders, projection screens, television monitors, or computer terminals.

▼ **Figure 7.22**
A "wet" carrel provides facilities for audiovisual media.

Applications

Learning centers can be used for a number of basic instructional purposes and are often categorized according to their primary purpose.

As *teaching centers* they can be used to introduce new content or skills and to provide an environment for individual or small-group instruction in lieu of whole-class instruction. Teaching the basics of the "three R's" lends itself quite well to the learning center instructional approach.

As *skill centers* they can provide the student with an opportunity to do additional practice or can reinforce a lesson that has previously been taught through other media or teaching techniques. For example, a skill center might be designed to reinforce

skill in using prefixes for students who are learning to read.

As *interest centers* they can promote present interests or stimulate new interests and encourage creativity. For example, a get-acquainted center on insect life might be set up

▼ **Figure 7.23**
As a *skill center*, this learning center provides motivating practice in language skills.

in the classroom before actually beginning a unit on specific insects.

As *remedial centers* they can be used to help students who need additional assistance with a particular concept or skill. A student who has difficulty determining the least common denominator of a group of fractions, for example, could be given the needed help in a remedial learning center.

As *enrichment centers* they can provide stimulating additional learning experiences for those students who have completed other center or classroom activities. Students who have completed their assigned math activities, for example, may be allowed to go to the center on "How Computers Work."

Advantages and Limitations of Learning Centers

Aside from exposing students to a variety of multimedia learning experiences, the advantages of learning centers are chiefly those that generally apply to individualized learning and teaching. Learning centers allow the teacher to move around the classroom and provide individual help to students when they need it.

Centers encourage students to take responsibility for their own learning and allow them to learn at their own pace (thus minimizing the possibility of failure and maximizing the likelihood of success). They provide for student participation in the learning experience, for student response, and for immediate feedback to student response. Students tend to spend more time on the task of learning.

On the other hand, learning centers do have some drawbacks. They can be costly. A great deal of time must be spent in planning and setting up centers and in collecting and arranging for center materials. The teacher who manages the learning center must be a very good classroom manager and organizer—and must avoid the temptation to let the learning center replace him or her.

Learning Center Management

There are a variety of learning center management strategies. A block of time can be set aside for use of each center and students can be assigned to it for certain periods. The length of the time block should be determined

by the age of the students and the content of the center. The alternative of having the students move from center to center on their own is acceptable as long as they are held accountable for getting the "job" done. (See the film "Classroom Learning Centers," cited in Audiovisual References.)

In using learning centers, your role is not to teach one subject or to control the students from the front of the room. Instead, it is to move around and deal with students on an individual or small-group basis. While circulating about the classroom, you can

▼ **Figure 7.24**
A program based on learning centers requires careful planning and organization to assure access by each student as needed.

Close-Up:
"Indy 500" Learning Center

A fifth-grade teacher in Indianapolis capitalizes on local enthusiasm for the Indianapolis 500 car race by designing a math learning center based upon car numbers and speeds. Center material includes a variety of questions. "What is the difference in speed between Car 20 and Car 14?" "How many cars have even numbers?" "If an Indianapolis race car gets 1.8 miles per gallon, how many miles can it go on one tank of fuel (40 gallons)?" The center has colorful pictures and souvenir postcards of the cars and drivers. Each student draws, colors, and numbers his or her own race car, which goes in the "Victory Circle" when the lesson is completed. The students complete worksheets, for which they are awarded "completed laps" rather than numerical points. When they have completed their "500 miles," they have "finished the race" and receive a miniature checkered flag. The center is designed so that all students can eventually master its content and be rewarded by receiving a flag.

assist students who are having difficulty, while becoming actively involved in the learning process with the students and assessing the progress of each student.

With an hour class period, it is helpful to have ten or fifteen minutes at the end of the period for group discussion and wrap-up. Of course, follow-up activities may be available for the students when learning center projects are completed.

Designing Your Own Learning Center Materials (ASSURE Model)

As noted above, elaborate learning centers may be purchased from commercial sources. You may, however, wish to design your own somewhat less elaborate center. The ASSURE model lends itself to the structuring of any learning environment. Let us consider how you might go about planning and designing your own center according to the ASSURE model discussed in Chapter 2.

Analyze Learner Characteristics.
Diagnosis of student characteristics is the key to placing your students in the learning center that best suits their abilities, needs, and interests.

State Objectives.
Determine the learning objective(s) you wish your students to attain in the center. State these objectives in terms of student behavior. Be sure the center includes a statement of objectives for user reference. A statement of objectives might be included in the center's printed material, or it might be recorded on tape.

Select, Modify, or Design Materials.
Your selection of materials, of course, should be dictated by the abilities and instructional needs of your students and by the availability of slides, filmstrips, audio tapes, realia, multimedia kits, printed materials (worksheets and instruction

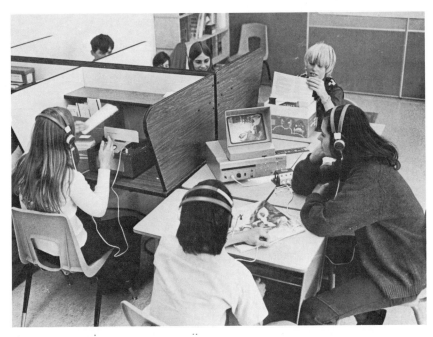

▲ **Figure 7.25**
Learning centers offer opportunities for informal teacher-student interaction.

sheets), etc. Ideas for materials to include in your center, either as is or adapted for your own specific purposes, may be gleaned from descriptions of commercially produced learning centers and from audio-visual periodicals and reference books. A list of the materials contained in your center should be included in the center for user reference.

Utilize Materials.
Learning centers are designed for use by individual students or small groups. Grouping has the advantage of allowing the students to interact as they utilize center materials, thus learning from one another's efforts and mistakes and reinforcing correct responses. In either case, instructions for using center materials should be included in your center. They should be concise and as clear as possible, in print format or on audio tape.

The exact nature and order of learning activities within the center may be strictly controlled by the teacher or may be left in whole or in part up to the student. In most cases

it is advisable to control activities at the outset and gradually increase students' freedom to choose activities as they demonstrate ability to assume responsibility for self-direction. Similarly, assignment to specific centers may be strictly controlled or left in whole or in part up to the students.

Be available to your students when they are using center materials. Many students, particularly younger children, need or can profit by frequent teacher contact as they use the materials and carry out the activities of the learning center. Circumstances may also warrant scheduling short one-to-one conferences with center users at periodic intervals.

Require Learner Response.
Learning centers should be designed to include opportunities for learners to respond to center materials and receive feedback to their reponses. There are various ways of providing such opportunities. You might, for example, provide an answer key to printed or audio-taped questions. The key might be included within the center or placed outside it, perhaps on a bulletin board. The latter option allows the

student to get up and move around a bit, thus alleviating the sense of confinement some children may feel with prolonged center use. Answers might also be put on the back of an activity card. Puzzle pieces may also be used to provide for student responses and feedback. This device entails putting questions and answers on a piece of paper or cardboard and then separating questions from answers by zigzag cuts. Only the correct answer portion of the paper will fit a given question, as shown in Figure 7.25. It is advisable to use a variety of techniques for providing feedback to learner response. In all cases, feedback to learner response should be as immediate as possible. Instant feedback has the distinct advantage of reinforcing correct responses and correcting wrong ones while material is fresh in the student's mind.

Evaluate. Attention to student response and the provision of feedback will have given you some opportunity to evaluate student progress toward attainment of your center's learning objectives. Further evaluations can be made through periodic testing while work is in progress and through individual conferences. When the learning center project is completed, student mastery of the center's objectives can be tested by traditional end-of-lesson written tests, performance tests, or other appropriate techniques.

Now is the time, also, to evaluate the learning center itself. Did most of its users attain its learning objectives? If not, why not? Were your materials well chosen? Were they too difficult for your students to work with or manipulate, or too easy? Did your center provide the right learning environment? Was it too dark? Too bright? Too noisy? Were your objectives clearly understood? Were your instructions clear? Your own careful observations and solicitations of student comments and suggestions will help you evaluate your center.

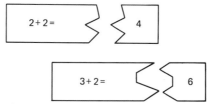

▲ **Figure 7.26**
Examples of self-checking puzzles for math drills.

References

Print References

Multimedia Systems

Benedict, Joel A., and Crane, Douglas A. *Producing Multi-Image Presentations.* (Tempe, Ariz. Arizona State University, 1976).

Bretz, Rudy, with Schmidbauer, Michael. *Media for Interactive Communication.* (Beverly Hills, Calif.: Sage Publications, 1983).

Bullough, Robert V. *Multi-Image Media.* (Englewood Cliffs, N.J.: Educational Technology Publications, 1981).

Dunn, Rita, and Dunn, Kenneth. "Seeing, Hearing, Moving, Touching, Learning Packages." *Teacher* (May/June 1977), pp. 48–51.

Effective Visual Presentations. (Rochester, N.Y.: Eastman Kodak, 1979).

"A Few More Images Can Mean a Lot More Learning." *Training* (March 1976), pp. 28–31.

Goldstein, E. Bruce. "The Perception of Multiple Images." *AV Communication Review* (Spring 1975), pp. 34–68.

A Guide to Effective Presentations for Teaching, Training and Selling Multi-Image Productions. (St. Paul, Minn.: Wollensak/3M, 1977).

Hershberger, Linda. "How Interactive Training Affects Corporations." *Educational/Industrial Television* (January 1984), pp. 64–65.

Hitchens, Howard B. "The Production of Multimedia Kits." *Educational Media International* (March 1977), pp. 6–13.

Jonassen, David H. "The Generic Disc: Realizing the Potential of Adaptive, Interactive Videodiscs." *Educational Technology* (January 1984), pp. 21–24.

Kenny, Michael F., and Schmitt, Raymond F. *Images, Images, Images: The Book of Programmed Multi-Image Production.* (Rochester, N.Y.: Kodak Motion Picture & Audiovisual Division, 1981).

McMeen, George R. "Toward the Development of Rhetoric and Content in the Communication of Meaningful Verbal Information in Multimedia Instructional Materials." *Educational Technology* (September 1983), pp. 22–25.

Perrin, Donald G. "A Theory of Multi-image Communication." *AV Communication Review* (Winter 1969), pp. 368–382.

Planning and Producing Slide Programs. (Rochester, N.Y.: Eastman Kodak, 1975).

Learning Centers

Beach, Don M. *Reaching Teenagers: Learning Centers for the Secondary Classroom.* (Santa Monica, Calif. Goodyear Publishing, 1977).

Blake, Howard E. *Creating a Learning-Centered Classroom.* (New York: A & W Visual Library, 1977).

"Book Nooks and Classroom Crannies: How to Make a Classroom Anything but Ordinary." *Instructor* (August 1982), pp. 22–25.

Christman-Rothlein, Liz, and Meinbach, Anita M. "Tornadoes: A Center Approach." *Science Activities* (November-December 1981), pp. 27–30.

Cooper, Arlene. "Learning Centers: What They Are and Aren't." *Academic Therapy* (May 1981), pp. 527–531.

Evans, Richard M. "Troubleshooting Individualized Learning Centers." *Educational Technology* (April 1984) pp. 38–40.

Feldhusen, Hazel. "Teaching Gifted, Creative, and Talented Students in an Individualized Classroom." *Gifted Child Quarterly* (Summer 1981), pp. 108–111.

Godfrey, Lorraine L. *Individualizing through Learning Stations.* (Menlo Park, Calif.: Individualized Books Publishing Co., 1972).

Gruendike, Janis L. "Centering on Sea Life in the Classroom." *Science and Child* (October 1982), pp. 26–27.

Kerr, Janice H., and Darling, Carol A. "A 'Family Fair' Approach to Family Life Education." *Childhood Education* (September-October 1983), pp. 12–16.

Lutz, Charlene Howells, and Brills, Patricia. "Ten-Minute Super Centers." *Instructor* (September 1983), pp. 158–175.

Marshall, Kim. *Opening Your Class with Learning Stations.* (Palo Alto, Calif.: Learning Handbooks, 1975).

Maxim, George W. *Learning Centers for Young Children.* (New York: Hart Publishing Co., 1977).

Nations, Jimmy E. ed. *Learning Centers in the Classroom.* (Washington, D.C.: National Education Association, 1976).

Orlich, Donald C., et al. "Science Learning Centers—An Aid to Instruction." *Science and Children* (September 1982), pp. 18–20.

Schirmer, Terry A., and George, Michael P. "Practical Help for the Long-Term Learning Disabled Adolescent." *Teaching Exceptional Children* (Winter 1983), pp. 97–101.

Strauber, Sandra K. "Language Learning Stations." *Foreign Language Annals* (February 1981), pp. 31–36.

"Walk-in, Talk-in, Learn-in Labs." *Instructor* (August 1983), pp. 48–52.

Warner, Laverne. "A Rationale for Effective Teaching in Classroom Centers." *Capstone Journal of Education* (Summer 1981), pp. 18–21.

Audiovisual References

Classroom Learning Centers. Birmingham, Ala.: Promethean Films, 1976. 16-mm film, color.

Creating Slide-Tape Programs. Washington, D.C.: Association for Educational Communications and Technology, 1980. Filmstrip with audiocassette, color.

Development of a Slide-Tape Instructional Presentation. National Audio-Visual Center, 1979. Slides with cassette. 16 minutes.

Effective Visual Presentations. Rochester, N.Y.: Eastman Kodak, 1978. Slide set with audiocassette and 16-mm film, color.

How to Produce Better Sound/Slide Shows. Slide Images, 1980. Slides with cassette.

Planning a Presentation. Bloomington, Ind.: Agency for Instructional Television, 1980. 16-mm film or videocassette.

Series Ten. Viscom, 1979. 10 slide sets, 10 audiocassettes, and 10 guides.
  Module 1: How to Write and Storyboard A.V. Programs
  Module 2: Cures for the Ten Most Common Design Problems
  Module 3: Producing Artwork for Slide Shows.
  Module 4: Photography for A.V. Shows
  Module 5: Basic Special Effects
  Module 6: Advanced Special Effects
  Module 7: Animation and Movement
  Module 8: Assembling and Programming A.V. Programs
  Module 9: Producing Soundtracks for A.V. Programs
  Module 10: Designing A.V. Facilities

Synchronizing a Slide/Tape Program. Rochester, N.Y.: Eastman Kodak, 1976. Slide set with audiocassette. 12 minutes, color.

Writing Learning Activity Packages. Educational Filmstrips, n.d. 2 filmstrips with cassettes.

Possible Projects

7-A. Plan a lesson in which you use a sound-slide set or sound filmstrip. With this lesson show evidence that you have followed the utilization principles suggested in Chapter 2 as well as other pertinent suggestions from this chapter. Include a brief description of the audience and your objectives.

7-B. Develop a set of storyboard cards for an instructional sound-slide presentation.

7-C. Locate and examine a multimedia kit in your field of interest. Prepare a written or oral report on the possible applications and relative merits of the kit.

7-D. Locate and examine a variable motion or interactive video system. Prepare a written or oral report on the possible applications and relative merits of the system for your instructional needs.

7-E. Design a classroom learning center. Describe the audience, the objectives, and the materials/media to be incorporated. Explain the roles of the students and the teacher in using the center. Evaluate its actual effectiveness if used or potential effectiveness if not used.

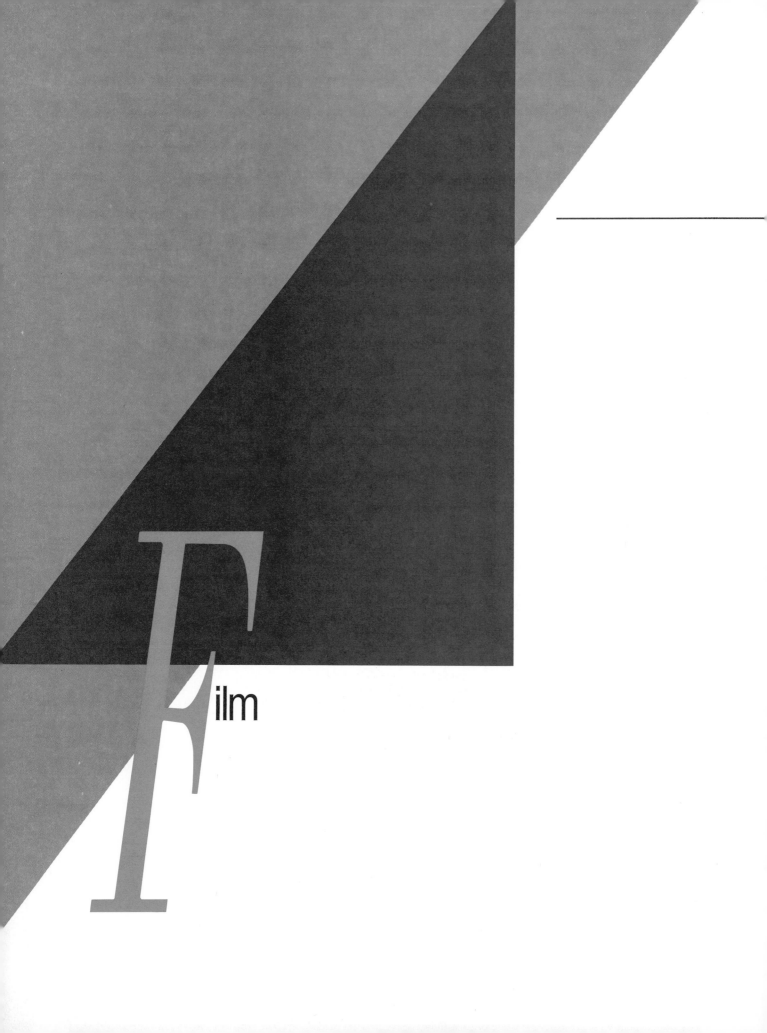

Film

Outline

Objectives

After studying this chapter, you should be able to:

1. Describe how a movie presents motion.
2. Describe two techniques by which sound can be added to motion picture film.
3. Identify three different film formats.
4. Describe five attributes of film.
5. Identify two film conventions that must be learned.
6. List seven instructional values (advantages) of film.
7. List three limitations of films.
8. Identify five criteria useful in appraising films.
9. Discuss why caution must be used in the use of sponsored films.
10. Define documentary film and explain why a particular film selected from this chapter fits the definition.
11. Relate the ASSURE model to effective film presentation, including specific examples.
12. Explain the use of film as an ''aesthetic experience'' and include three examples with your explanation.
13. Describe a situation in your teaching field in which students might produce their own film or videotape.
14. Discuss the possible future of film as an instructional medium.
15. Identify two specific sources where you can get information about films.

Lexicon

persistence of vision

time-lapse

slow motion

freeze frame

animation

sponsored film

documentary

cinéma vérité

In a previous chapter we spoke of the aura of "magic" surrounding the projection of visuals, of how the brilliant illumination of a screened image in a darkened room tends to grab the attention of viewers, and of how this attribute can contribute to effective learning. We come now to an instructional medium in which the power to hold attention greatly contributes to a mind-set conducive to learning—the film, which adds the magic of motion to the projected visual image.

WHY A MOVIE MOVES

Essentially, movie movement is an illusion. A movie moves because our sensory apparatus tricks us into thinking it moves. At the bottom of the next page is the first of a series of still pictures that end on page 221. If you flip these pages at a fast enough rate of speed, you will create the illusion of movement. Your eye retains an image for a brief moment after it has been viewed. If the next image is exposed to view before this trace of the previous image fades, the images blend together, creating the impression of actual movement. The basic function of all the "hardware" connected with the recorded moving image—camera, projector, etc.—is to take advantage of this "persistence of vision" sensory phenomenon.

Because the camera photographs a scene as a series of separate, discrete images, motion picture film consists of a sequence of slightly different still pictures called *frames*. When these frames are projected on a screen at a certain speed (at least 12 frames per second), the images appear to be in continuous motion.

Each still picture (frame) is held stationary at the film aperture (1), as seen on the left side of Figure 8.1. While it is stationary, the shutter (2) is open, permitting the light from the projection lamp to pass through the image, go through a focusing lens system (3), and display the picture on the screen. Then the shutter closes and a device like a claw (4) engages the sprocket holes and pulls the film down so that the next frame is in position, as shown in detail on the right side of Figure 8.1. (Ironically, the film "moves" only when the audience doesn't see the image). The claw withdraws, the shutter opens, and the next picture is projected on the screen.

Although the film moves past the aperture intermittently, the top sprocket wheel (5) pulls the film into the projector at a steady 24 frames per second (sound speed), and the bottom sprocket wheel (6) pulls the film out of the projector at the same steady rate of speed. If no slack were

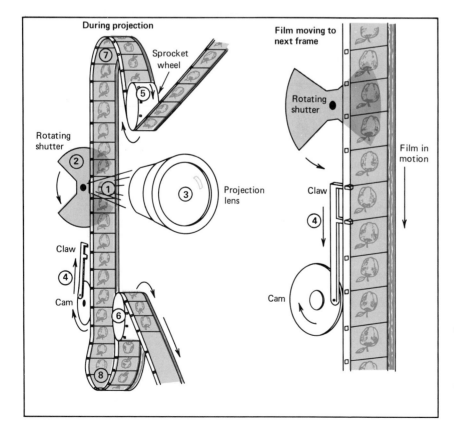

◄ **Figure 8.1**
The basic mechanics of motion picture film projection. (From Wyman, Raymond, *Mediaware: Selection, Operation, and Maintenance*, 2nd ed., Copyright © 1969, 1976. Wm. C. Brown, Dubuque, Iowa. Reprinted by permission.)

put into the film at upper and lower loops (7) and (8), the film would be torn apart. These two loops compensate for the two different motions the film must have. Because sound cannot be accurately recorded or reproduced on a film that is not moving smoothly, the intermittent movement of the film must be smoothed out by the bottom sprocket and an idler system before the film reaches the sound drum.

SOUND ON MOTION PICTURE FILM

The sound that accompanies a film is contained in a *sound track* that runs down one side of the film (Figure 8.2). The track may be *optical* or *magnetic*. An optical sound track is actually a photographic image of sound recorded at one edge of the film in variable shades of dark and light. A magnetic sound track is one in which sound is recorded on magnetic tape bonded to one edge of the film.

Projectors that will handle either only one or both types of sound tracks are available. However, in projectors built to handle both types, the separate mechanisms required to pick up the sound in each format must be positioned one behind the other. Consequently, the sound that accompanies a specific image (or frame) is recorded at a slightly different distance from that frame for each of the formats, as shown in Figure 8.3.

▼ **Figure 8.2**
Comparison of optical and magnetic sound tracks. In the 16-mm optical sound track system, the sound accompanying a specific image (frame) is recorded on the film 26 frames ahead of that frame. Note that the displacement (separation between image and sound) differs for each of the other film formats. The proper setting of the lower loop on all film projectors is critical for keeping the picture and sound synchronized.

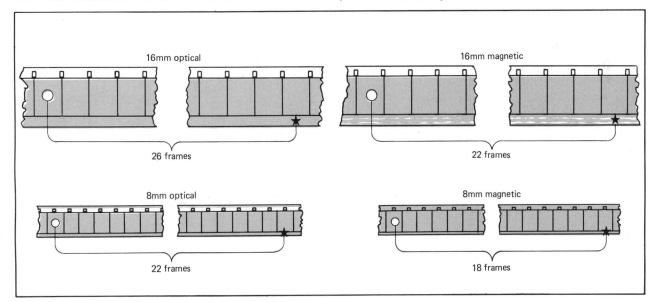

16mm optical · 26 frames
16mm magnetic · 22 frames
8mm optical · 22 frames
8mm magnetic · 18 frames

▶
Flip the pages of the text from here to page 211. If you flip them fast enough, the stills will appear to move, approximating ½ second of screen action.

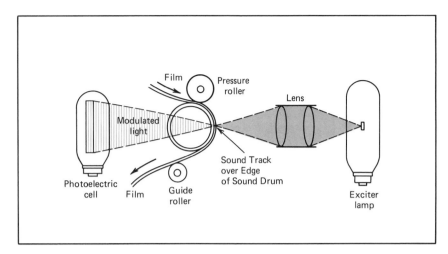

◀ **Figure 8.3**
Playback of optical sound tracks. The steady light from the exciter lamp passes through the sound track, picking up the image of the recorded sound. This image is then focused on a photoelectric cell. The varying light pattern of the optical sound track is converted into correspondingly varying electrical impulses by the photoelectric cell. These very weak signals are amplified and then converted back into sound waves by the speaker. (From Wyman, Raymond, *Mediaware: Selection, Operation and Maintenance*, 2nd. ed., Copyright © 1969, 1976. Wm. C. Brown, Dubuque, Iowa. Reprinted by permission.)

FILM FORMATS

Motion picture film comes in various widths and image sizes. For theatrical films 35-mm film is most commonly used. The size most commonly used for instructional films and entertainment films shown in schools is 16-mm film.

The most common formats of motion picture film are illustrated in Figure 8.4. Note how the physical characteristics of the film changed with the addition of sound, and how the sprocket hole size and image area of 8-mm film changed in the evolution from the original 8-mm to Super-8-mm size.

ATTRIBUTES OF FILM

Because most of us are inclined to think of the film as a medium designed primarily to produce a "realistic" image of the world around us, we tend to forget that a basic attribute of the moving image (whether recorded photographically on film or electronically on videotape) is its ability to *manipulate* temporal and spatial perspectives. Filmic manipulation of time and space not only serves dramatic and creative ends, it also has important implications for instruction.

▼ **Figure 8.4**
Common motion picture film formats.

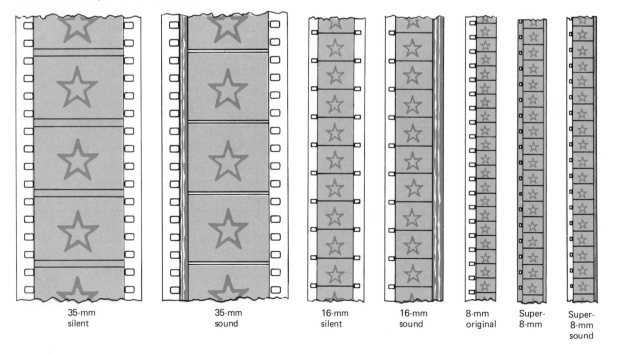

35-mm silent   35-mm sound   16-mm silent   16-mm sound   8-mm original   Super-8-mm   Super-8-mm sound

Flashback: MR. EDISON'S DREAM

Thomas A. Edison, whose work in developing the kinetograph (a camera that used film rolls) and the kinetoscope (a peep-show device) contributed greatly to the development of motion pictures, had high hopes for the instructional value of this popular medium. As depicted in the cartoon from *The Chicago Tribune* of 1923, he fully expected the motion picture to revolutionize education, give new life to curricular content, and provide students with new motivation for learning.

We all know that the history of the motion picture took a turn quite different from that anticipated by Edison. "Movies" were quickly and eagerly adopted as an entertainment medium, but in education the acceptance of film as a useful medium has been

Thomas A. Edison.

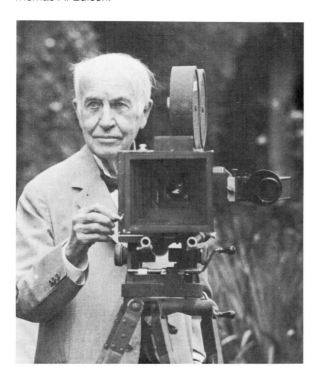

glacially slow. Part of the problem was technical. The standard size for film quickly became set at 35-mm, which meant that equipment for projection was bulky and expensive. Also, the film base that was used for many years, cellulose nitrate, was extremely flammable and many state regulations required a film to be projected only from an enclosed booth and by a licensed projectionist. Thus, films were too expensive for schools to use for other than special occasions. There was also resistance on the part of the educational establishment to acknowledge the educational value of this "frivolous" new invention. Its very success as an entertainment medium automatically made it suspect as an educational tool.

The first extensive use of film as an educational

Manipulation of Space

Film permits us to view phenomena in microcosm and macrocosm—that is, at extremely close range or from a vast distance. Charles and Ray Eames made a film called *Powers of Ten* that within a few minutes takes us from a close-in observation of a man lying on a beach to views of the man as observed from distances expressed as increasing powers of ten until he disappears from sight. Perspective then changes quickly in the reverse direction and the film ends with a microscopic view of the man's skin. A similar effect can be seen in a National Film Board of Canada film titled *Cosmic Zoom*. This film starts with a microscopic examination of the skin of a man in a rowboat and then moves farther and farther away

medium occurred during World War I, outside the classroom, when psychologists working with the U.S. Army produced a series of training films on venereal disease. The research techniques used to determine the effectiveness of those films set the pattern for research in film evaluation for several decades.

After World War I, several prestigious organizations combined forces to produce a series of American history films that became known as the *Yale Chronicles of America Photoplays*. This series of films was also the subject of extensive research and documented for the first time the effectiveness of films in direct instruction, even though the films were considerably handicapped because they were made in the "silent" era.

When sound on film finally did become a reality, many educators resisted its use in educational films. They felt that by putting a sound track on a film the producer was imposing external standards on every class in the country. They insisted that teachers should be free to narrate films according to principles and practices prescribed locally. Teacher narration of films, however, was favored by theorists and administrators but not by practitioners. (Anyone who has ever attempted to narrate a film knows what a difficult task it can be.) Some administrators also resisted the use of sound films in the classroom because this newer technology made existing inventories of silent film projectors and silent films obsolete. Eventually, of course, films incorporating sound became commonplace in the instructional setting.

World War II gave an even greater impetus to the educational use of films. In a crash program to train Americans in the skills necessary to produce weapons of war, the Office of Education engaged in an extensive program of film production under the leadership of Floyde Brooker. Most of the films produced by the Office of Education were technical. Although educational quality was uppermost in the

minds of the production teams under Brooker, there was no opportunity to do any extensive formative evaluation. The armed forces also produced films during this period for training purposes and their research indicated that films (and other audiovisual media) contributed significantly to the success of their training programs.

The success of instructional technology, including film, in achieving war-related instructional objectives created sentiment among educators and laypeople alike for more widespread use of this technology in the nation's schools.

While the publishing industry in general was reluctant to get into the unfamiliar territory of motion pictures, Albert Rosenberg, who had worked with Floyde Brooker in the Office of Education, convinced the McGraw-Hill Book Company that it should create what was to become known as its Text–Film Division. McGraw-Hill quickly developed an impressive catalog of instructional films for col-

Floyde Brooker directing one of the wartime training films of the U.S. Office of Education.

until we lose track of him entirely and, from some vantage point far from earth, see only the world of which he is a part. Both films are extremely effective examples of how film can manipulate spatial perspective.

Multi-image presentations are often manipulations of space. For example, the film *A Place to Stand* persuades the viewer that Ontario, Canada, is a great place to live by showing exciting scenes from different parts of the province in split-image format. As many as six different images are on the screen at one time. The viewer gets the impression of being instantly transported around the province.

▲ **Figure 8.5**
Cosmic Zoom

leges and universities as well as for public schools. Slowly other companies joined McGraw-Hill and Encyclopaedia Britannica Films (which had been formed in 1938 through the purchase of ERPI[a], the first company to produce educational films in quantity) in producing films for the school and college market. Coronet Films became one of the largest producers of educational films, along with Young America Films, later purchased by McGraw-Hill.

The movement to study film as an art form (see page 216) prompted the establishment of companies specializing in the distribution of films that explore the aesthetic qualities of the medium. Contemporary Films (later bought by McGraw-Hill) led the way. Other companies followed suit and, as short films were shown less and less in movie theaters, the 16-mm market became the prime distribution vehicle for films of artistic and experimental merit. Since it was founded in 1939 by John Grierson, the National Film Board of Canada has been a major producer of films in this genre.

The late 1950s witnessed the introduction of 8-mm film into education. Cartridged, looped 8-mm films quickly acquired the label "single concept films" because they concentrated on presenting a single event or process for study. Because 8-mm cartridges were easily inserted in their projectors and the projectors were small, portable, and simple to use, they lent themselves particularly well to individual and small-group study and to incorporation into programs of individualized instruction. However, mechanical problems with the projectors and the vulnerability of the film itself discouraged use. This format has been all but abandoned. (See the discussion of 8-mm *video* in Chapter 9.)

The introduction of 8-mm film also gave considerable impetus to the movement toward student-produced films. Although some school districts—Denver, for example—had previously been active in film production, 16-mm film was not, by and large, a very satisfactory medium for school production.

With 8-mm, however, film, camera, and projector were easier to handle and less expensive. Once 8-mm film was introduced into the schools, school-produced motion pictures became much more common. Soon student film festivals were being held on a regular basis at local, state, and national levels.

In the meantime, as sales of 16-mm educational films increased, commercial publishers were encouraged to produce film "packages"—series of films to be incorporated as major components of various courses. This trend led in the late 1950s to the introduction of complete courses on film. Encyclopaedia Britannica Films, for example, produced a complete course in high-school physics, consisting of 162 half-hour films in color.

Educational television soon became the primary source of most filmed courses used in the instructional setting, and, with the rise of videotape technology, television itself, both educational and commercial, became a major force in the growing use of recorded moving images for instructional purposes.

Mr. Edison's dream of the immediate and overwhelming impact of the film on education may have been a little fuzzy around the edges—as dreams sometimes are—but it was not, after all, so far off the mark. It took a quarter century longer than the Wizard of Menlo Park had anticipated for the film to become an important factor in education and another quarter century for it to reach its present state of instructional prominence. His dream did come true, in its own time and in its more realistic way—as dreams sometimes do.

---

[a]Education Research Products, Inc. Maurice Mitchell, when president of EBF, was fond of commenting that he was not sure if ERPI was a company or a condition.

Alteration of Time

Film permits us to move through space in what might be called altered time. The *Cosmic Zoom* film shows movement through space in continuous time and far faster than we could possibly move in reality. But we can also take out pieces of time, so to speak, as we move through space.

For example, we are all familiar with the type of film sequence in which two automobiles approach each other at high speed and the film suddenly cuts to a scene showing the wreckage of both cars. Time has been taken out of that sequence but we all accept the fact that the two cars did come together in real continuous time. In other words, film convinces us that we have witnessed an event even when we have not seen it in its entirety. This is an important convention for educational as well as entertainment films. For example, it

would take an impossibly long time for students actually to witness a highway being constructed, but a carefully edited film of the different activities that go into building a highway can recreate the essentials of such an event in a few minutes.

Compression of Time: Time-Lapse

Film can compress the time that it takes for an event to occur. We have all seen films of flowers slowly opening right before our eyes. Simple arithmetic indicates that if a process normally takes four hours and we want to be able to see that process in one minute on the screen, then a single picture must be taken of that process every 10 seconds. When projected at normal sound speed, the process will be shown in one minute. This technique has important instructional uses. For example, the process of a chrysalis turning into a butterfly is too slow for classroom observation. However, through time-lapse cinematography, the butterfly can emerge from the chrysalis in a matter of minutes on the screen. (Renowned British composer Sir Michael Tippett attributes the inspiration for his fourth symphony to seeing a time-lapse film of the growth of a single cell into a baby—an interesting instance of one medium triggering creativity in another.)

▼ **Figure 8.6**
Time-lapse cinemaphotography allows us to watched the slow process of metamorphosis in condensed time.

▲ **Figure 8.7**
Slow motion: a moment is expanded by exposing more than 24 frames (up to several thousand) of film per second.

Expansion of Time: Slow Motion

Time also can be expanded by film. Some events occur too fast to be seen by the naked eye. By photographing such events at extremely high speeds and then projecting the film at normal speed we can observe what is happening. A chameleon catches an insect too rapidly for the naked eye to observe. High-speed cinematography can slow down the motion so that the process can be observed.

Motor skill tasks are often better analyzed if photographed at higher than normal speeds and studied at normal speed. Many training programs can be improved by this type of task analysis.

Revealing the Unseen World

Films can help us observe operation of objects we normally cannot see. For example, X-ray cinematography can show how human bones move or how the valves of the heart work.

Arrested Motion: Freeze Framing

Films permit us to isolate components of an event for detailed study. For example, the film maker can select any image in a motion sequence and print that image over and over again so that one moment is held frozen on the screen. We are all familiar with this technique in television and in feature films. It is also useful in instructional films; for example, freezing a pole vaulter to allow study of the athlete's technique at various stages of the vault.

Moving the Motionless: Animation

Time and space can also be manipulated in animated films. Animation is a technique whereby the film maker gives motion to otherwise inanimate objects. If such an object is photographed, then moved a very short distance and photographed on one frame of film, then moved and photographed again, and so on, when the film is projected the object will look as though it has been continuously moving through space. There are various and sophisticated techniques for achieving animation, but basically animation is made up of a series of photographs of small displacements in space of objects or images. The film *Frame by Frame* illustrates various animation techniques. Animation, however, can even be achieved without the use of a camera. With a technique popularized by Canadian film maker Norman McLaren, in films such as *Begone Dull Care*, images may be drawn directly on film, which, when projected sequentially, will give the illusion of movement.

▼ **Figure 8.8**
Frame by Frame.

▲ **Figure 8.9**
Begone Dull Care.

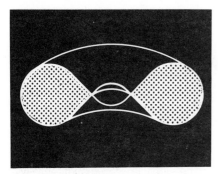

▲ **Figure 8.10**
Turning a Sphere Inside Out.

Computer-Generated Animation

Animation can also be achieved by the use of computers. The animated images generated by the computer can be displayed on a cathode-ray tube and then photographed by a motion picture camera, or they can be electronically imprinted directly on videotape. While computer-generated images have generally been of interest primarily for aesthetic reasons, a number of instructional films have used computer animation techniques. One such effort is a fascinating film in the mathematics of topology titled *Turning a Sphere Inside Out.*

UNDERSTANDING FILM CONVENTIONS

The devices and techniques used in film making to manipulate time and space are for most of us readily accepted conventions. We understand that the athlete whose jump is stopped in mid-air is not actually frozen in space, that the flashback is not an actual reversal of our normal time continuum, that the light bulb does not really disintegrate slowly enough for us to see that it implodes rather than explodes. Teachers of young children, however, must keep in mind that the ability to make sense out of film conventions is an acquired skill. When do children learn to handle flashbacks, dissolves, jump cuts, etc? Unfortunately, we know very little about when and how children learn to make sense of filmic manipulation of reality, and much research on the matter remains to be done.

Some insight into the kind of difficulties that may be encountered in the instructional situation because of student inability to handle film conventions can be gleaned from the experiences of film makers involved with adults unfamiliar with standard film conventions.

After World War II, film crews from the United States were send to various parts of the world to make instructional films designed to help the people better their skills in farming, housing, sanitation, etc. One crew member working in rural Iran noted that in the United States film makers could have a man walk out a door in lower Manhattan and immediately pick him up in another shot at Times Square. In Iran this technique was not possible. Viewers there would insist that the man be shown making the journey to Times Square. In other words, rural Iranians, because they were at that time unfamiliar with the conventions of time-space manipulations, could not accept this filmic view of reality.

John Wilson, another American film producer of the period, commented:

We found that the film is, as produced in the West, a very highly conventionalized piece of symbolism, although it looks very real. For instance, we found that if you were telling a story about two men to an African audience and one had finished his business and he went off the edge of the screen, they wanted to know what happened to him; they didn't accept that this was just the end of him and that he was of no more interest to the story. . . . We had to follow him along a street until he took a natural turn. . . . It was quite understandable that he could disappear around the turn. The action had to follow a natural course of events. . . .*

The film is not, of course, alone among media in its reliance upon accepted conventions for interpretation and appreciation. Flashback techniques are regularly used in literature and usually accepted by readers. The theatrical convention of the "aside" is readily accepted by playgoers. The following anecdote about Picasso illustrates how a new artistic convention may seem to the uninitiated to be merely a distortion of reality rather than, as intended, a particular and valid view of reality. It also illustrates how a convention (in this case a convention of photography) can become

---

*Joan Rosengren Forsdale and Louis Forsdale. "Film Literacy." *The Teachers College Record.* (May 1966), p. 612.

so readily accepted and commonplace that we are amusingly surprised at being reminded it exists:

Picasso showed an American soldier through his villa one day, and on completion of the tour the young man felt compelled to confess that he didn't dig Picasso's weird way of painting, because nothing on the canvas looked the way it really is. Picasso turned the conversation to more acceptable matters by asking the soldier if he had a girl back in the States. The boy proudly pulled out a wallet photograph. As Picasso handed it back, he said "She's an attractive girl, but isn't she awfully small?"*

A word should also be said here about the bearing of experiential and cultural background on interpretation of films and film conventions. As with all other media, what the viewer brings to the film determines what he or she takes from it. In *American Time Capsule*, a Charles Braverman film about the history of the United States, for example, even if the student were able to handle the film convention of rapid projection of briefly glimpsed images on a screen, the film would be virtually meaningless if the viewer had no experiential background in American history.

As to the importance of cultural determination of filmic interpretation, perhaps it will suffice to note that in Thailand, each episode of television's *Laverne and Shirley* begins with the following announcement: "These women are from an insane asylum." Apparently, this is the only context in which the Thai culture can accept the antics of these two U.S. cultural heroines.

---

*Ibid., p. 609.

ADVANTAGES OF FILM

The film's ability to manipulate time and space has, as noted earlier, important instructional implications. Let us now consider several other related characteristics of film and look at just a few of the ways they can be turned to instructional advantage.

1. The most obvious instructional attribute of film is its ability to show *motion*. This characteristic gives the film a distinct advantage over all other media for use in instructional situations in which the depiction of motion can contribute understanding.

2. Film can present a *process* more effectively than other media. For example, industrial operations (manufacturing processes, assembly-line operations, etc.) can be observed and studied through use of film, with the camera offering manipulated views of such processes unobtainable with other media. Difficult-to-observe scientific experiments, such as measuring the speed of light, can be shown easily by means of film.

3. Film permits *safe observation* of phenomena that might be hazardous to view directly—for example, total eclipse of the sun or dangerous scientific experiments and demonstrations. Violent or disruptive events can also be safely viewed on film—natural disasters, such as a volcanic eruption, or man-made violence.

◀ **Figure 8.11**
Tasks involving a sequence of step-by-step operations lend themselves well to film presentation.

▼ **Figure 8.12**
The eruption of Mt. St. Helens: destructive in real life, instructive on film.

4. Research has shown that films are particularly useful in teaching *skills*. Learning a skill is likely to require repeated observation and effort before the skill is mastered. Film can present the skill over and over again for observation and emulation.
5. The ability of film to *dramatize* events makes it particularly suitable for instruction in the social sciences and humanities. Dramatizations can bring historical personages and events to life. They can deepen the student's appreciation of the creative merit of literary works. Students can learn to deal with human relations problems by observing problem situations (particularly helpful in business/industry programs designed to train personnel to handle difficult *human relationship* situations smoothly).
6. Because of their great *emotional impact*, films are very useful for teaching and learning within the affective domain. Personal and social attitudes can be changed by films designed to do so. A film on oral hygiene, for example, can help lead a child to develop better dental care habits. Documentaries and commercial "message films," such as *The Day After* can influence social, cultural, and political attitudes, for adults as well as children. The Payne Fund Studies in the

▲ **Figure 8.13**
With film you can observe a complex skill being repeated over and over.

▶ **Figure 8.14**
The Pilgrims.

▲ **Figure 8.15**
Through dramatization, film can simplify the complexity of management problems, as in *Performance Appraisal*.

◀ **Figure 8.16**
The Day After.

▲ **Figure 8.17**
Face to Face dramatizes a human relations problem, which is left for viewers to solve through discussion.

▶ **Figure 8.18**
Although not a true ethnographic film in itself, *Nanook of the North*, made in 1922, vividly portrayed the impact of modernization on traditional life-styles.

early 1930s demonstrated that children's attitudes toward minority groups can be influenced by films.

7. Open-ended filmic episodes can be used effectively in *problem-solving* instruction. For example, an interpersonal problem can be dramatized on film and its resolution left to the class to discover through group discussion or through individual written assignments.

8. The subtleties of *unfamiliar cultures* and their relation to our own can be captured on film for observation. A film on Eskimo life, for example, will help students understand the influence of physical environment on lifestyle. A film depicting life in a developing nation will help students appreciate the impact of modernization on traditional cultures. A film on the marriage rites of an exotic people will lead to better understanding of the relationship between culture and sexual mores. In recent years, ethnog-

raphers have become prolific producers of films, an effective way to document indigenous life-styles, particularly those of primitive cultures. Some exemplary feature-length ethnographic films* are: *The Hunters, The Tribe That Hides from Man,* and *The Nuer, River of Sand*. Examples of shorter ethnographic films are: *Gravel Springs Fife and Drum, Mosori Monika,* and the series of films by Julien Bryan on the *Indians of South America*.

9. Films *command attention* in the instructional situation. Eye movement studies, for example, show that when viewers have lost interest in an image on the screen, their attention can be immediately regained by altering the rhythm of the projected images.

---

*Producer and distributor sources of all films in this chapter can be found in the NICEM *Index to 16mm Films*, and rental sources are listed in *The Educational Film Locator of the Consortium of University Film Centers*. See Appendix A for details.

10. The *cuing power* of the film in instruction is likely to be greater than that of other media. Techniques such as close-ups and image-freezing can direct the attention of the student to specific concepts and isolate key components of the situation to be understood or the problem to be solved, thereby minimizing irrelevant cues. Irrelevant cues may also be minimized by filming only the essential elements of a process or situation. Training films often use this technique, especially for novices in the program.

11. Film, of course, is an ideal format for instruction of *heterogeneous groups with common interests* and/or learning objectives. They can be shown to large or small audiences, with a minimum of instructor intervention, within the formal educational setting (a film on how a bill becomes law shown to students of government, for example) or outside such a setting (a film on company operations shown to management trainees).

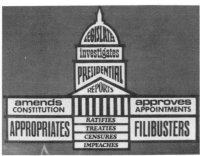

▲ **Figure 8.19**
Through a film such as *U.S. Congress* a group of people with varied backgrounds can be taught a common message.

▲ **Figure 8.20**
Clarissa (holding the megaphone) is dared to do something potentially dangerous in order to be accepted as a member of a neighborhood gang in *I Dare You*.

LIMITATIONS OF FILM

As with all other instructional media there are, of course, limitations to the instructional effectiveness and value of film. The film is not the best medium for all instructional purposes and in all instructional situations. For example, although a film may be stopped and one frame held on the screen for detailed study or discussion, a filmstrip or set of slides would be better for study of a sequence of still phenomena, such as a series of maps.

Films run at a fixed pace (24 frames per second) but not every viewer's mind runs at exactly that pace; some are likely to be falling behind while others are waiting impatiently for the next point.

Film is exceedingly expensive, and rapidly becoming more so because of the increasing cost of raw film stock (the price of silver has made black-and-white film nearly as costly as color film).

Partly because of the high cost, most instructional films are purchased through district, regional, or state agencies and kept in more or less centrally located collections rather than in individual schools. This means that films must usually be ordered well in advance of their scheduled use. Careful planning is required; without such planning, an expensive, albeit valuable, instructional medium could well be wasted.

This list of instructional values shows that films are useful in many ways in all areas of the curriculum. Social studies benefits especially from the ability of film to recreate the past and to document how people live. The film's dramatic and expressive powers are of particular value to the language arts and literature. Science makes extensive use of film's ability to make processes and relationships clear. Better mathematics films use the graphic ability of film to represent mathematical functions and relationships. The capability of films to present real life situations is an invaluable aid in training supervisory personnel.

Because of the power of films, teachers need to be very careful about the possibility of creating misinterpretations or of reinforcing socially undesirable attitudes. For example, students who have not yet mastered understanding of film conventions may not interpret a film the way in which the film maker intended. The film *Phoebe* uses a stream-of-consciousness approach as the protagonist fantasizes about what the reactions of parents and boyfriend, Paul, to her announcement of her pregnancy will be, and as she recalls details of her relationship with Paul. A number of students (and parents) have misinterpreted the speculations and memories of a tortured mind as being the attitude of the film maker toward all involved in the story.

Teachers have used the film *Toys* with upper elementary students, partly because that age group is featured in the film. However, fourth and fifth graders are so absorbed with the virtuoso animation of toys engaged in hectic battle that they never get past the surface excitement to see the antiwar message that impresses the adult viewer. Many guidance films use dramatized situations to provoke discussion of the problems explored. Some of the role models portrayed, however, may be very appealing to students. For example, in *I Dare You* from the *Inside/Out* series, the characters are very likable and the pranks they play are appealingly daring. Improperly handled, the film could easily be a lesson in imitation—the last thing the producer or teacher wants! A teacher must continually check not only to be sure that the desired outcomes from film showings are being achieved, but also to ensure that undesirable side effects are not being produced.

▶ **Figure 8.21**
Obtaining a film from a central library entails many steps.

Appraisal Checklist: Film

Title_____   Format ___16-mm

Producer/distributor_____   ___8-mm

Date (if known)_____   Length_____   ___other

Audience/grade level_____   _____

Subject area(s)_____   ___color
    ___black/white

Objectives (stated or implied):

Brief description (include presentation style: animated, dramatic, etc.):

Entry capabilities required:

    ___language ability
    ___prior subject matter knowledge

Rating	High		Medium		Low
Likely to arouse student interest	☐	☐	☐	☐	☐
Technical quality	☐	☐	☐	☐	☐
Opportunity for viewer participation	☐	☐	☐	☐	☐
Relevance to curriculum (or learning task)	☐	☐	☐	☐	☐
Accuracy of information	☐	☐	☐	☐	☐
Scope of content	☐	☐	☐	☐	☐
Organization of content	☐	☐	☐	☐	☐
Student comprehension	☐	☐	☐	☐	☐

Strong points:

Weak points:

Reviewer_____

Position_____

Recommended action_____   Date_____

LOCATING AND APPRAISING FILMS

As mentioned above, because of the high cost of 16-mm films as well as the impracticality of local production, an individual school or small organization is unlikely to have its own film collection. So most instructors must acquire films on loan from an outside agency—the school district, state library, or rental library, for instance. A basic resource for you, then, is a collection of catalogs of those rental agencies you are most likely to turn to for films. To be more thorough in your search you will want *The Educational Film Locator*, a comprehensive listing of the films that are available in various college and university rental collections. If you are just beginning your search you should consult the *Index to 16mm Educational Films*, published by the National Information Center for Educational Media (NICEM), as a means of finding out just what films are currently available overall; it provides listings according to subject. Details on these and other directories are found in Appendix A.

After a film has been identified, located, and acquired, you will want to preview and appraise it carefully.

Official appraisal forms for films used in schools vary considerably among school districts and regional agencies. Some are meticulously drawn up to cover almost all conceivable criteria for rating a film as to its usefulness in a given teaching/learning situation. Others rate films in a much more perfunctory manner. A good appraisal form should not only help agencies choose films that will be most useful in future instructional situations, but also provide a public record that can be used to justify the purchase of specific titles. Comparative cost effectiveness of instructional methods is always on the minds of training directors and school and college administrators. Purchase of expensive materials such as films must be justified by

carefully planned selection procedures. (See the accountability section in Chapter 14.) The appraisal form on page 210 is one that has proved useful for selecting films that will contribute to the instructional program.

As mentioned in Chapter 2, you should also construct and keep a card file of film notes for your personal use. Your specific instructional purposes may be quite different from the general instructional needs catered to on an official form. Included in the accompanying box is an example of a card form that can help you make best use of the films available to you. Fill out the card form after using the film and add or modify entries after each use of the film.

Personal Film Record

Title_____Format [16-mm, 8-mm, video?][a]_____

Length_____Source [where you got it]___B/W___Color___Sound___

Synopsis:_____

_____

_____

_____

_____

Style of production [documentary, animation, narration, open-ended]_____

Utilization pointers and problems: [vocabulary, controversial topic or treatment, introduction needed, supplementary materials needed, etc.]

_____

_____

Follow-up activities:_____

_____

[a]Notations in brackets would not appear on form. They indicate the kind and character of the information to be entered on form.

SPONSORED FILMS

Private companies, associations, and government agencies sponsor films for a variety of reasons. Private companies may make films to promote their products or to enhance their public image. Associations and government agencies sponsor films to promote causes: better health habits, conservation of natural resources, proper use of park and recreation areas. Many of these sponsored films make worthwhile instructional materials. They also have the considerable advantage of being free.

A certain amount of caution, however, is called for in using sponsored films for instructional purposes.

Some private-company films may be too flagrantly self-serving. Or they may deal with products not very suitable for certain instructional settings: the making of alcoholic beverages, the production of cigarettes. Some association and government films may contain a sizable dose of propaganda or special pleading for pet causes along with their content. Ralph Nader's Center for the Study of Responsive Law has issued a report highly critical of instructional materials distributed free by industry.* It claims that many sponsored materials subtly influence the curriculum in socially undesirable ways. Certainly you must preview sponsored films.

Properly selected, many sponsored films can be valuable additions to classroom instruction. Modern Talking Picture Service is one of the major distributors of sponsored films. The best single source of information on sponsored films is the *Educator's Guide to Free Films*. Details on this and similar free and inexpensive sources are given in Appendix B.

---

*Sheila Harty. *Hucksters in the Classroom: A Review of Industry Propaganda in the Schools.* Washington, D.C.: Center for Study of Responsive Law, 1980.

DOCUMENTARIES: FROM NEWSREEL AND TRAVELOGUE TO *CINÉMA VÉRITÉ* AND DOCUDRAMA

Broadly speaking, the *documentary* deals with fact, not fiction or fictionalized versions of fact. As such, it has long held a special place in the use of films for instructional purposes. Through the work of film makers such as Robert Flaherty in the United States and John Grierson in England, the documentary has also acquired a reputation for artistic merit.

Grierson defined the documentary as "a creative treatment of actuality." He believed that the documentary should have a point of view, that it should be a vehicle for presenting and interpreting "human problems and their solutions in the spheres of economics, culture, and human relations." Thus, Grierson, Flaherty, and other like-minded film makers inaugurated the concept of the documentary as a socially significant film form rather than merely a vehicle for presentation of newsreel footage and "travelogue" material. Flaherty's film on the Eskimos of Hudson Bay, *Nanook of the North*, is generally cred-

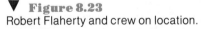

▼ **Figure 8.23**
Robert Flaherty and crew on location.

▲ **Figure 8.24**
The making of *Nanook of the North.*

ited with generating worldwide recognition of the documentary as a distinct film genre. (Figure 8.27).

The advent of sound on film gave further impetus to the growth and development of the documentary. By the late 1930s many countries had inaugurated documentary film units or were commissioning documentaries from independent producers. In the United States important and classic documentaries were produced both by government film units (e.g., *The River, Power and the Land*) and by independent film units (e.g., *The City, Valleytown, And So They Live*). In Great Britain, government units produced documentary classics such as *Night Mail* and *Song of Ceylon*. In Spain renowned feature film director Luis Buñuel made the striking film *Las Hurdes* (released in the United States as *Land without Bread*). In Belgium Henri Storck directed what is regarded by many as the classic film on slums and slum clearance, *Les Maisons de la Misére* (1937). In the

Soviet Union the work of Dziga Vertov culminated in the technical and conceptual tour de force *Man with a Movie Camera* (1929). In Germany, the two controversial but classic films by Leni Riefenstahl, *Triumph of the Will* (a film of the Nazi Party Congress of 1934) and *Olympia* (the 1936 Olympic games in Berlin), were prominent among a number of powerful documentaries.

Newsreels were a standard part of commercial movie programs in the 1930s and 1940s. Presented before the showing of the feature film, newsreels were little more than illustrated headlines depicting current news in segmented and superficial form. *The March of Time* (1934) took a different approach—a documentary approach. For an average length of 18 minutes, *The March of Time* examined one topic in reasonable depth and often with a point of view. Today, many of *The March of Times* films are still valuable as historical perspectives of critical events and issues. For example, the *March of Time* film *Palestine*, made before the state of Israel was formed, gives students an opportunity to examine a current issue from a unique historical point of view.

During World War II, the documentary was widely used by all combatants in training programs and for propaganda purposes. More than a few "propaganda" documentaries, however, also had lasting artistic and historical merit and many still serve instructional purposes—John Huston's *Let There Be Light*, for example,

and Humphrey Jennings's *The Silent Village* and *Diary for Timothy*.

The documentary has always been an important training ground for directors and cinematographers, and the post–World War II period saw a number of documentaries made by people who later became well known for their work in feature films: Alain Resnais's *Night and Fog*, Tony Richardson's *Momma Don't Allow*, Lindsay Anderson's *Every Day but Christmas*, among others.

Today television has become the prime influence on the continuing development of documentary films. The commercial networks, primarily through their news departments, and the Public Broadcasting System regularly produce and broadcast significant documentaries that are later released in 16-mm-film form. Programs such as *Vietnam: A Television History*, *The Selling of the Pentagon*, *Yo Soy Chicano*, and the Jacques Cousteau and National Geographic specials are examples of outstanding TV

▼ **Figure 8.27**
Le Duc Tho and Henry Kissinger, chief negotiators at the Paris Peace Talks, are shown in *Vietnam: A Television History.*

▼ **Figure 8.25**
The City.

▼ **Figure 8.26**
Man with a Movie Camera.

documentaries that have wide use in education as 16-mm films.

The term *cinéma vérité* is the French translation of the Russian term *kino pravda* (film truth), coined by Russian director Dziga Vertov. In recent years, the term has come to be identified with a film-making technique in which the camera becomes either an *intimate observer* of or a *direct participant* in the events being documented.

The advocates of *cinéma vérité* as a "participant observer" thrust their cameras and sound equipment into the action, following it wherever it may lead. Films such as *Lonely Boy* (on the early career of pop singer Paul Anka), *Primary* (about the 1960 primary contest between John Kennedy and Hubert Humphrey in Wisconsin), and *Warrendale* (about a home for disturbed children) are examples of this type of *cinéma vérité*.

Camera and microphone may also become part of the action in *cinéma vérité*—that is, a "provocateur" of events or theme development. The penetrating but unobtrusive interview in which participants often seem to

▲ **Figure 8.29**
Frederick Wiseman's *High School.*

be interviewing themselves is a hallmark of this technique. Outstanding examples of this approach are the films of Marcel Ophuls such as *The Sorrow and the Pity* (about French resistance to and collaboration with the Nazi conquerors of France in World War II).

Documentaries such as those noted above, as well as films such as Frederick Wiseman's *High School, Hospital,* and *Law and Order*, which combine the *cinéma vérité* techniques of camera and microphone as intimate observer *and* participant, are provocative discussion and learning materials, especially for students in-

▲ **Figure 8.30**
Foxfire.

volved in or being trained to become involved in the institutions portrayed in the documentaries and for students with special interest in sociopolitical themes.

Documentaries have also become an important historical record and source of information about cultural lifestyles fast disappearing from the American scene. The Foxfire program, for example, which began in Rabun Gap–Nacoochee School in Georgia with student publication of *Foxfire,* a magazine devoted to documenting disappearing local skills such as how to make soap or how to make an ox cart, also resulted in several films, including *Foxfire* and *Aunt Arie.* Films such as *Tinker, The Last Pony Mine, Gravel Springs Fife and Drum,* and *The Bakery* (Canada) document disappearing trades and sociocultural mores.

Almost all present-day documentaries contain a social or political message, stated or implied, and evaluation of this message is, of course, part of the teaching/learning process.

▼ **Figure 8.28**
Lonely Boy.

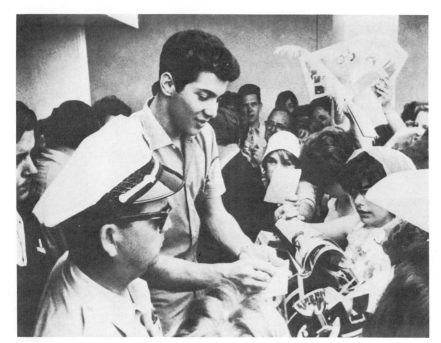

▼ **Figure 8.31**
The Bakery.

▲ **Figure 8.33**
Select material.

▲ **Figure 8.32**
Death of a Princess.

Normally, the documentary's point of view is not too difficult to ascertain. A relatively new development, however, the "docudrama," has complicated the process. In general, the docudrama is a dramatization (with actors) of current newsworthy events and trends, rather than creative reportage. Although the makers of docudramas insist their films are dramatizations of fact, not fiction, the line between "docu" and "drama" may sometimes be difficult for the viewer to draw. Evaluation of point of view may, hence, also be comparatively difficult.

The film *Death of a Princess*, a dramatization of the search of an English journalist for the truth behind published reports that a young Saudi Arabian princess and her lover had recently been publicly executed for adultery at the instigation of her royal father, is a prime example of the docudrama genre. Shown on PBS, the film generated considerable controversy. Did it document Saudi-Arabian ruling-class mores and Islamic legal principles? Or did it dramatize them in such a way that fiction prevailed over fact?

EFFECTIVE FILM USE: THE *ASSURE* MODEL

As pointed out in Chapter 2, effective use of media depends on consideration of all the steps of the ASSURE model, regardless of the media format being contemplated. In using film you would analyze the learners and state the objectives in the same way as you would for any other medium. However, the subsequent planning steps would have a different flavor because of the special characteristics of the film medium.

Select Materials
Ideally you should preview your film selection before showing it to the class to be sure it meets your teaching/learning criteria. Unfortunately, preview is not always possible. You may have to rely on official appraisal forms and/or teacher-guide materials that accompany the film, or, if you have used the film before, on your personal appraisal form. Once you have selected your film, you may wish to tailor its use to meet your instructional needs. To use only part of the film you will have to cue parts of

the film separately for showing. You may wish to stop the film at various points for discussion. Perhaps you will decide you need to use supplementary materials in order to reach your objectives. For example, the film you have chosen for a geography lesson may not contain a map of the area under discussion. You will, then, want to make sure that such a map is available in the viewing area for student reference.

Utilize Materials
Do not present the film cold. Effective utilization of the film as an instructional medium requires that it be effectively introduced. Students should be given some idea of the content of the film you are about to present and informed as to how the content relates to the learning objectives involved. You may wish to alert them to

▲ **Figure 8.34**
Utilize material.

▲ **Figure 8.35**
Require learner response.

particular features of the film that relate to these objectives. Include special instructions in your introductory "advance organizer." Perhaps new vocabulary words contained in the film need to be explained prior to its showing. Discuss any concepts not likely to have been previously encountered by the students.

Require Learner Response

Follow-up activities for reinforcement of learning should include class discussion of the film's content, particularly points of the film that directly relate to your learning objectives. They may also include individual and small-group discussion of the film, library work, writing assignments, or other such activities. Films are powerful motivators. Be prepared to take advantage of this attribute with diverse follow-up activities to encourage new or increased interests.

Evaluate

Your evaluation of the film as an effective or ineffective instructional instrument will be at least partly based

▲ **Figure 8.36**
Evaluate.

on class discussion of the film and your observation of student reaction to its content. Tests based on learning objectives will contribute further, and perhaps more reliable, data on which to base your evaluation. When your evaluation is completed, enter the results on your personal appraisal form.

THE FILM AS AN ART FORM

Although we are primarily concerned with the film as an instructional medium, we should keep in mind that the film is also an art form and can be studied and appreciated as an aesthetic experience in much the same manner as literature and the fine arts. Marshall McLuhan once commented

AV SHOWMANSHIP—FILM PROJECTION

General guides to projection practice are in Chapter 10. Some additional advice is necessary for film projection.

Many classrooms have a wall-mounted screen in the front of the room. In some classrooms, unfortunately, the door is near the front of the room and often has a large window in it or a window area beside it. If light from the hall interferes with the brightness of the projected image, you may have to cover part or all of the window area with poster board or butcher paper. If this is not possible, move the projector closer to the screen to get a brighter picture. Remember that a smaller, brighter image is better than a larger, dimmer one.

You should always set the focus and note the correct sound level before the class assembles; then turn the volume knob back down to zero and run the film back to the beginning. Some films have focus and sound level adjustment footage before the start of the film. If so, you can properly set focus and sound before you reach the beginning of the film.

It is *not* good showmanship to project the academy leader (the strip of film with the number sequence on it). The first image the audience should see is the title or opening scene of the film.

When ready, start the projector, turn on the lamp, and turn the volume knob to the predetermined level (this is particularly important when the film has no introductory music). Fine adjust the focus and sound after you start the projector.

Most projectors must run a few seconds before the sound system stabilizes. Therefore, if you stop the film to discuss a particular sequence, the viewers may miss a few seconds of narration or dialogue when you start the projector. If this is so, turn the volume knob down, back up the film a few feet, start the projector, turn on the lamp, and then turn up the sound.

When the film is over, turn off the lamp, turn down the sound, and stop the projector. Run the rest of the film footage through after class. Rewind the film if you are going to show it again. If you are not showing it again, and if you used the same size reel the film came on, you need not rewind the film. The agency you got it from will rewind the film during routine inspection. Before putting the film back in the container, fasten down the end of the film with a piece of tape. The film normally arrives with the film held down with tape. Peel it off and stick it on the projection cart so that you can use it later to hold the end down. The film is better protected when this is done.

---

that introduction of a new technology tends to make an art form out of the preceding one, and, indeed, it was only after the introduction of television that film achieved general and widespread acknowledgement as an art form.

Today, schools have come to accept the film (and film making) as an aesthetic experience worthy of study as such. In elementary schools, film as an aesthetic experience is widely regarded as a logical extension of language arts. In many high schools, film study is now incorporated as a unit in literature courses. Most colleges and universities have courses devoted to the study of film and many offer at least a minor in film study. The University of Southern California, which, incidentally, established the first cinema department in an American university, offers a freshman

Media File:
"The Red Balloon"

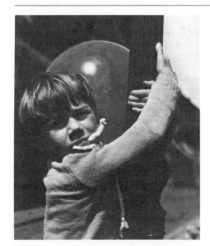

Perhaps the most popular children's film ever made, this Academy Award winner was voted the best of all films awarded Blue Ribbons during the first ten years of the American Film Festival (1958–68). A fantasy, the nonnarrated film tells the story of a boy whose faithful balloon follows him to school and church and through the streets of Paris. A street gang chases the boy and his balloon in order to destroy it. At the end, all the balloons of Paris converge to carry the boy off to a fantasy land of peace.
Source: Janus Classic Collection/Films Inc.

Media File:
"Gulf Stream"

This film effectively combines information with aesthetic presentation. The viewer is taken on a 2000-mile, 15-day journey from the equatorial origins of the Gulf Stream up the Atlantic coast to Newfoundland. Animated drawings and satellite photographs are intercut with live footage to show how the stream is affected by winds, other currents, the sun, and the earth's rotation. Marine life in the stream is explored, making the film a stimulating mixture of ecological and meteorological information. Creative writing and film making classes as well as those in the sciences would find this film useful.

Source: Bullfrog Films.

Media File:
"The Loon's Necklace"

A classic film, *The Loon's Necklace* uses the telling of a folk legend to reveal the social and cultural life of the Indians of the Pacific Northwest. The unique masks made by the Indians and shown to us on film tell us much about how they perceived themselves in relation to the forces of nature and to the supernatural.

Source: Encyclopædia Britannica Education Corporation.

STUDENT-MADE FILMS

The introduction of 8-mm film as a replacement for the less easily handled and more expensive 16-mm film gave considerable impetus to the now relatively widespread production of student-made films in schools and colleges.

Considerable versatility was added to this format with the introduction of a method to record sound directly on the film while it is being exposed. The use of videotape and portable videotape equipment has also contributed to simplification of production of student-made films and has thus further stimulated this growing activity.

Many student-made films are produced in connection with secondary school English programs, a natural extension of the English program's normal concern with literary communication and self-expression. A 16-mm film called *The Moving Image—8-mm* demonstrates vividly how one secondary school teacher, inexperienced in film production, organized and conducted her English class to produce films. Many very fine films have come out of such classes, and a few student-made films have even been accepted for commercial distribution.

course in film as an option in its required humanities sequence.

Both in high schools and in colleges, belonging to a film club and going to film showings as extracurricular activities have grown rapidly in recent years. Outside the educational setting, film societies dedicated to the aesthetic appreciation of films have sprung up in many communities. The availability of fine commercial films in 16-mm format and the establishment of collections of noteworthy films, foreign and domestic, in many pubic libraries have given considerable impetus to such activities.

The Media Files included here present some exemplary films representative of scores of films available for study and appreciation of the film as an art form (as well as for instruction, given the proper instructional situation). For lists of other films of this kind see Gaffney, *Films Kids Like*, Parlato, *Superfilms*, and Jones and Dratfield in the References at the end of this chapter.

▼ **Figure 8.37**
Even elementary school-age students have produced their own 8-mm film successfully.

Media File:
"The Hunter"

*T*he Hunter portrays the excitement of a pre-teenage boy upon receiving a BB gun as a birthday present. After imagining himself as a soldier and then as a defender of an encircled wagon train, he sees a cardinal and kills it. As he reaches down to pick it up, the enormity of his act dawns upon him. The film ends with the boy slowly walking away from the dead bird. The low-key style of the film is very effective in riveting attention on the main point of the film—that guns are not toys.

Source: Aims Media, Inc.

Media File:
"A Case of Working Smarter, Not Harder"

*T*raining films can be competitive at film festivals as well as effective instructionally. This award-winning film demonstrates that good managers have the ability to focus on long-range goals as well as on immediate objectives. A case study, the subject of the film is a manager who changes from an overworked, compulsive problem solver to an effective, productive innovator. The system he develops draws attention from the public as well as the business community. Research has established that a film is more effective when the target audience can project itself into the roles portrayed on the screen. This film is an excellent example of that quality.

Source: CRM/McGraw Hill.

THE FUTURE OF FILM

Recorded moving images will always have a firm place in instruction. Motion pictures and videotape have proved their usefulness in just about every kind of instructional situation. The main question is in what format the moving image will be displayed in the classroom of tomorrow. As of now, videotapes have not made a significant impact on the use of commercially produced films. Surveys conducted at Indiana University* indicate that videotape is used primarily to distribute locally produced or recorded program material. However, the cost of videotape in comparison with film is making it more attractive as a substitute for film. If manufacturers of video equipment can perfect video projection to the point where large screen images are sharp and faithful in color rendition, the last technical obstacle to overtaking film as the medium for moving images will have been overcome.

By the time that has happened, however, videodisc may have replaced videotape as the most popular format. Because they can be mass produced like phonograph records, videodiscs should be considerably cheaper than videotape. Videodiscs are also a more versatile format for instructional purposes, as Chapter 9 points out. It could well be that in the future, film will be a "Flashback" in the chapter on video!

---

*Report of Second Annual Survey of the Circulation of Educational Media in the Public Schools. Bloomington, Ind.: Audio-Visual Center, Indiana University, 1978.

◀ **Figure 8.38**
Ready to screen the final product of a student 8-mm film project.

References

Print References

Arwady, Joseph W. "The Oral Introduction to the Instructional Film: A Closer Look." *Educational Technology* (July 1980), pp. 18–22.

Beatty, LaMond F. *Motion Pictures*. (Englewood Cliffs, N.J.: Educational Technology Publications, 1981).

Blackaby, Linda; Georgakas, Don; and Margolis, Barbara. *In Focus: A Guide to Using Films*. (New York: New York Zoetrope, 1981).

Burmester, D. "Short Films Revisited." *English Journal* (January 1984), pp. 66–72.

Cassidy, J.M. "Lights, Camera, Animation!" *School Arts* (February 1984), pp. 36–38.

Center for Vocational Education. *Present Information with Films*. (Athens, Ga.: American Association for Vocational Instructional Materials, 1977).

Cox, Carole. "Films Children Like—and Dislike." *Language Arts* (March 1978), pp. 334–338.

Gaffney, Maureen, ed. *Films Kids Like*. (Chicago: American Library Association, 1973).

_____, *More Films Kids Like*. (Chicago: American Library Association, 1977).

_____, and Laybourne, Gerry Bond. *What To Do When the Lights Go On: A Comprehensive Guide to 16 mm Films and Related Activities for Children*. (Phoenix, Ariz.: Oryx Press, 1981).

Guide to Classroom Use of Film/Video. Compiled by Shirley A. Fitzgibbons. Edited by Deborah Davidson Boutchard. 2d ed. (Washington, D.C.: National Education Services, American Film Institute, 1981).

Jacobs, Lewis. *Documentary Tradition*. (New York: W.W. Norton, 1980).

Johnson, Stephen C. "Films for the Social Studies: Pedagogical Tools and Works of Art." *Social Education* (May 1976), pp. 264, 270–272.

Jones, Emily S., and Dratfield, Leo. "40 Years of Memorable Films." *Sightlines* (Fall/Winter 1983/84), pp. 15–17.

Langer, J. "What Is a Documentary?" *Cinema Papers* (October 1982), pp. 442–445, 487, 489.

Limbacher, J. L. "Feature Films to Teach Literature." *English Journal* (January 1981), pp. 86–88.

McDonald, Bruce, and Orsini, Leslie. *Basic Language Skills through Films: An Instructional Program for Secondary Students*. (Littleton, Colo.: Libraries Unlimited, 1983).

Marcus, Fred N. *Short Story/Short Film*. (Englewood Cliffs, N.J.: Prentice-Hall, 1977).

Mast, Gerald. *A Short History of the Movies*. (Chicago: University of Chicago Press, 1981).

Meierhenry, W. C. "Some Historical and Current Developments in Motion Pictures." In *Educational Media Yearbook 1982*, edited by James W. Brown and Shirley N. Brown. (Littleton, Colo.: Libraries Unlimited, 1982).

Mercer, John. *The Information Film*. (Champaign, Ill.: Stipes Publishing, 1981).

Parlato, Salvatore J., Jr. *Films Too Good for Words: A Directory of Non-Narrated 16-mm Films*. (New York: Bowker, 1973).

_____. *Superfilms: An International Guide to Award-Winning Films*. (Metuchen, N.J.: Scarecrow Press, 1976).

Shemin, J. B. "Experimenting with Film as Art for Kids." *Film Library Quarterly*, no. 1 (1982), pp. 15–19.

Street, Douglas, ed. *Children's Novels and the Movies*. (New York: Ungar, 1984).

Vick, Nancy H. "Freedom to View: Coping with Censorship, A Summary Report." *Sightlines* (Spring 1981), pp. 5–6.

Audiovisual References

And Yet It Moves. New York: Phoenix Films, 1981. 16-mm or videocassette. 8 minutes.

Animation (set). Fountain Valley, Calif.: Warner Educational Productions, 1981. 2 filmstrips with cassettes. 59 frames and 65 frames. 14 minutes each.

Basic Film Terms: A Visual Dictionary. Santa Monica, Calif.: Pyramid Films, 1970. 16-mm film or videocassette. 15 minutes.

Basic Movie Making. Rochester, N.Y.: Eastman Kodak Co., 1973. 16-mm film. 14 minutes.

Claymation. Santa Monica, Calif.: Pyramid Films, 1980. 16-mm film. 8 minutes.

The Eye Hears and the Ear Sees. Montreal, Canada: National Film Board of Canada, 1970. 16-mm film. 59 minutes.

Facts about Film. 2d ed. Chicago, Ill.: International Film Bureau, 1975. 16-mm film or videocassette. 10 minutes.

Frame by Frame: The Art of Animation. Santa Monica, Calif.: Pyramid Films, 1973. 16-mm film or videocassette. 13 minutes.

The Moving Image—8mm. Bloomington: Indiana University, 1976. 16-mm film. 27 minutes. Color.

Odette's Ordeal. Wilmette, Ill.: Films Incorporated, 1976. 16-mm film. 38 minutes. Color.

Project the Right Image. Lincoln, Nebr.: Great Plains ITV Library, 1976. 16-mm film or videocassette. 14 minutes.

So You Wanna Make a Film. Lawrence, Kans.: Centron Films, 1980. 16-mm or videocassette. 9 minutes.

Teaching Basic Skills with Film. Mississauga, Ontario, Canada: Marlin Motion Pictures Ltd., 1981. Videocassette.

Teaching Basic Skills with Film. New York: Learning Corporation of America, 1980. 16-mm film. 90 minutes.

Organizations

American Film Institute
John F. Kennedy Center for the Perform-
ing Arts
Washington, D.C. 20566

American Library Association
50 E. Huron Street
Chicago, Illinois 60611

Association for Educational Communications and Technology
1126 Sixteenth Street, N.W.
Washington, D.C. 20036

Educational Film Library Association, Inc.
43 W. 61st Street
New York, New York 10023

Media Center for Children
3 West 29th Street
New York, New York 10001

University Film Association
School of Communications
University of Houston
Houston, Texas 77004

Periodicals

American Cinematographer
American Society of Cinematographers
Corp.
1782 N. Orange Drive
Los Angles, California 90028

American Film Magazine
American Film Institute
John F. Kennedy Center for the Perform-
ing Arts
Washington, D.C. 20566

Booklist
American Library Association
50 E. Huron Street
Chicago, Illinois 60611

Film News
250 West 57th Street
Suite 1527
New York, New York 10019

Instructional Innovator
Association for Educational Communications and Technology
1126 16th Street, N.W.
Washington, D.C. 20036

Instructor
Instructor Publications, Inc.
P.O. Box 6099
Duluth, Minnesota 55806

Landers Film Reviews
Landers Associates
Box 69760
Los Angeles, California 90069

Learning
P.O. Box 2580
Boulder, Colorado 80322

Media & Methods
American Society of Educators
1511 Walnut Street
Philadelphia, Pennsylvania 19102

Media Index
343 Manville Road
Pleasantville, New York 10570

Sight and Sound
111 Eighth Avenue
New York, New York 10011

Sightlines
Educational Film Library Association, Inc.
43 W. 61st Street
New York, New York 10023

Super-8 Filmmaker
Sheptow Publishing
3161 Fillmore Street
San Francisco, California 94123

Teacher
Macmillan Professional Magazines, Inc.
262 Mason Street
Greenwich, Connecticut 06830

Possible Projects

8-A. Preview a film and critique it with a film appraisal form such as the "Appraisal Checklist: Film" in this chapter.

8-B. Observe a teacher using a film in a classroom situation and evaluate the teacher's use of the film, pointing out good and bad techniques.

8-C. Examine one or more of the film lo-cators included in Appendix A, and submit a report on the sorts of films available in the field(s) of interest to you.

8-D. Plan a lesson in your subject field in which you will use a specific film. Secure and preview this film from an appropriate source. Then make a specific lesson plan showing how you would implement the principles of utilization suggested for this medium.

8-E. Review a documentary (or *cinéma vérité*) film. Your review may be written (approximately 700 words) or recorded on tape (approximately five minutes). Briefly summarize the content of the film and de-scribe your reactions to it.

 From *Movement in Classical Dance*, Indiana University Audio-Visual Center.

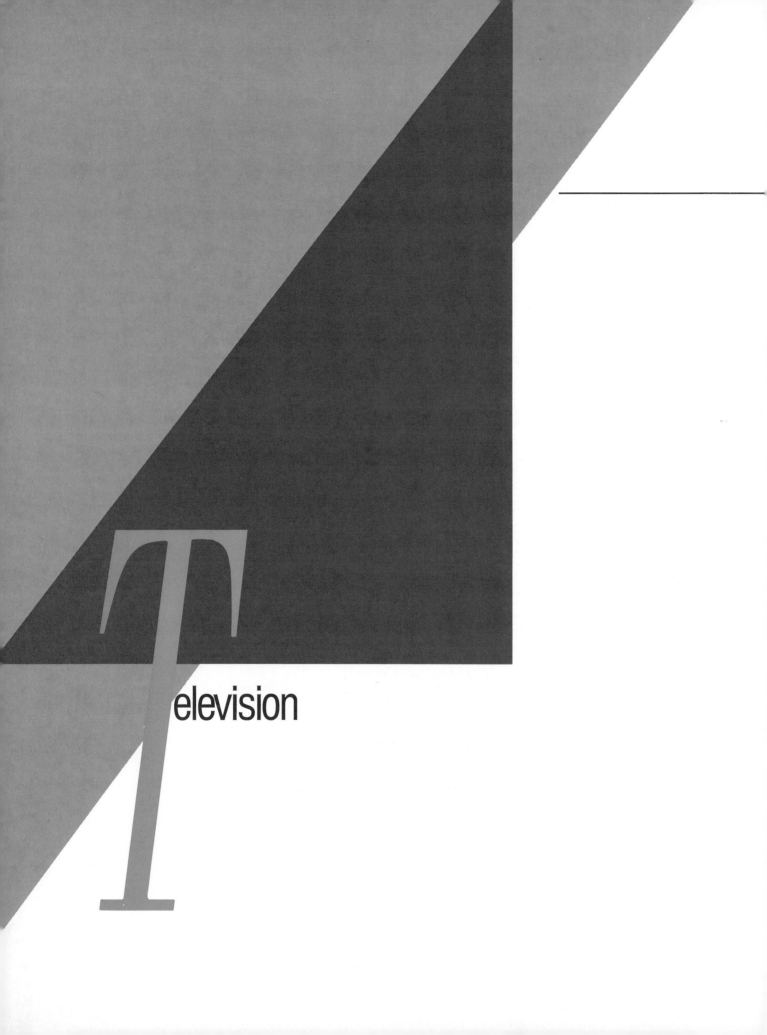

Television

Outline

Objectives

After studying this chapter, you should be able to:

1. Identify advantages and limitations of television as an instructional medium.
2. Characterize the uses of ITV in (a) elementary and secondary schools, (b) higher education, and (c) business/industry. Indicate the number of teachers, students, and organizations using it; types of programs and applications; typical usage patterns; and growth rate.
3. Describe the following instructional television delivery systems: (a) broadcast via commercial station, (b) broadcast via noncommercial station, (c) closed-circuit system, (d) cable TV system, (e) microwave, and (f) portable video.
4. Identify an educational application of *each* of the delivery systems included in Objective 3.
5. Differentiate between the role of public television in home and in-school viewing.
6. Discuss educational potentials of CATV not available with standard broadcast television delivery systems.
7. Describe ITFS and characterize its current role in American education.
8. Identify four different storage/playback formats for portable video.
9. List six important selection criteria that apply to instructional television programs.
10. Describe three educational situations in which instructional television (ITV) programs might be locally produced.
11. Describe the necessary components for a single-camera video recording system, indicating not only the components but how they should be arranged for good recording quality.
12. Apply the basic steps of media utilization specifically to instructional television.

Lexicon

instructional television
closed-circuit television
cable television (community antenna television)
    head-end
    public access channel
microwave transmission
portable video
videocassette
videodisc

ATTRIBUTES OF TELEVISION

In the mid-1980s, as television entered its fourth decade as a mass medium, it had blossomed from a remote, expensive, restricted business to what some referred to as the "television of abundance." Television is now easily accessible for use in education not only via over-the-air broadcasts but also by means of closed-circuit and cable TV systems, all of which may be linked by satellite relays. Vast libraries of programs are now available on videocassette and videodisc, making TV materials nearly as available as audio tapes and records. Further, portable video recorders enable instructors—and their students—to create their own materials.

Clearly TV now represents many things and is a rich resource for instruction and training.

Advantages

Like film, TV can present color moving pictures with sound. As such it shares many of the instructional advantages of film. But a major difference is that, being an electronic rather than a mechanical process, television can be transmitted long distances and its signals recorded and played back instantly.

By means of broadcasting, large audiences can be reached at a low cost per person. Viewers dispersed over vast geographic areas can experience a live event simultaneously. Learners can be reached at home, making "open learning" a reality.

▲ **Figure 9.1**
Broadcasting educational programs for at-home viewing brings the concept of open learning to life.

At the same time, this mass medium is becoming an individual medium. The development of small, inexpensive home video recorders makes it feasible for students to view video materials on an individually prescribed basis.

Limitations

The complex electronic technology that affords television so many of its advantages is also, in a sense, its Achilles' heel. The complexity of the technology allows many possibilities for disruption of the communication flow. Programs may be poorly produced, even in sophisticated studio surroundings. Atmospheric conditions may disturb broadcast signals or satellite reception. Classroom receivers may malfunction. There is, in short, always the possibility that technical difficulties over which the instructor has little or no control will intervene between the lesson and the learner.

Cost may be another limiting factor. Even basic equipment (color TV receivers, for example) can be expensive. Sophisticated equipment (cable distribution systems, satellite reception setups) can cost a great deal of money. Hardware costs are only the most visible expenses. In the long run, the human labor involved in production, distribution, maintenance, and utilization usually overshadow the original equipment costs. So, unless large numbers of learners are being served or unless TV is performing a vital teaching function that cannot be performed efficiently and effectively by less expensive means, these costs may be difficult to justify.

In typical use the TV image is displayed on a rather small surface. This means that for ordinary classroom purposes one TV receiver is needed for approximately every thirty viewers, a cumbersome arrangement for large-group situations. This limitation can be overcome by using the newer large-screen TV projection systems but their cost is still prohibitive for many educational applications.

Perhaps television's most serious limitation as an instructional tool is that under typical conditions it is a one-way channel of communication. A feedback loop can be provided by means of push-button student response systems or even "talk-back" arrangements. Such systems have been in use since the earliest days of instructional television experimentation and are employed in numerous special cases. But in normal practice one-way communication is still the rule.

TELEVISION IN TODAY'S INSTRUCTIONAL SETTINGS

We all know how television has permeated North American popular culture since it first leaped into visibility a scant 30 years ago. How has it fared as an instructional tool in this relatively short period of time—in the schools, in higher education, in nonformal education, in training?

We will use the term *instructional TV* or *ITV* to refer to any planned use of video programs to meet specific instructional goals regardless of the source of the programs (including commercial broadcasts) or setting in which they are used (including business/industry training).

Instructional TV in the Schools

In the United States, television has become widely available as a resource to supplement and enrich the curricula of elementary and secondary schools. However, it is still not used in a systematic manner by a large proportion of teachers. The availability and use of ITV has been documented by a series of mail questionnaire surveys conducted by the

Corporation for Public Broadcasting (CPB) since 1977. According to the most recent data:

- 70 percent of all school districts can receive broadcast ITV off-air from a public TV station.
- 97 percent of all teachers have access to television sets (three-quarters of which are color sets); the degree of access is one set per five elementary teachers and one per ten teachers at higher levels.
- 81 percent of all teachers have access to video recording and playback equipment.
- 29 percent of all teachers actually use at least one ITV series regularly (viewing at least three-quarters of the programs in one series). Average viewing time per week by their students is one hour and 45 minutes.*

Comparing the 1984 data with the 1977 findings, a number of interesting trends appear:

- Overall, the number of school districts reporting *availability* of ITV

---

*John A. Riccobono. *Availability, Use, and Support of Instructional Media, 1982–83. Summary Final Report of the School Utilization Study.* Washington, D.C.: Corporation for Public Broadcasting, 1984.

▲ **Figure 9.2**
Between public television station broadcasts and prerecorded video tapes, almost all schools in the United States have access to instructional television.

programming increased sharply, from 73 percent to 91 percent; however, at the classroom level, the percentage of teachers who claim ITV is available to them has remained quite constant, around 70 percent.
- The percentage of all teachers who actually *use* ITV regularly declined slightly—from 33 percent to 29 percent.

Close-Up:
Instructional Television in Broward County, Florida.

This county-wide school district provides ITV to its classrooms in a number of forms, including a four-channel microwave system reaching all 147 schools and a telephone hookup allowing teachers to call in requests for transmissions. Furthermore, programs can be duplicated for later playback on the school's own videocassette recorder, and tapes can be borrowed from the loan library for up to five days. A monthly program guide describes dozens of programs available each month.

- Video recordings now surpass broadcast programs as the leading source of ITV availability.
- Regular use of ITV remains higher among elementary teachers than among middle/junior high and senior high teachers.
- Teachers are spending more time integrating ITV programs into ongoing lessons; for example, average follow-up discussion time rose from 13 minutes to 22 minutes. Discussion time is longer at higher grade levels.

Concerning the content of ITV programming, Table 9.1 shows the 20 most used ITV series, according to teachers who used ITV regularly or occasionally in 1982–83. The most used series tended to be those intended for the primary and intermediate grade levels, although two of the three most popular series are aimed at high school and adult audiences and deal with science themes. In general, science, social studies, and language arts—in that order—are the most popular content areas for ITV.

An innovative new series for grades 4–6, "The Voyage of the Mimi," began in 1984. Aimed at mathematics and science skills, the series integrates broadcast TV programs about a whaling expedition with microcomputer software on topics such as maps, navigation, and ecosystems. Simulation programs on the computer enable students to face problems just like those shown on the video programs.

Instructional TV in Higher Education

In higher education the use of television for instruction appears to be widespread but quite conservative. According to a Corporation for Public Broadcasting survey,* 71 percent of all colleges and universities in the United States were making some use

*Peter J. Dirr and Ronald J. Pedone. "Television Use in Higher Education." *Educational and Instructional Television*, (December 1979), pp. 39–47.

TABLE 9.1 MOST WIDELY USED ITV SERIES IN 1982–83.

Rank	Series	Intended Grade Level	Total Teachers Using
1	Electric Company	Primary, intermediate	104,000
2	Nova	High school	94,400
3	National Geographic Specials	High school	77,500
4	Inside Out	Intermediate	74,600
5	All About You	Primary	72,500
6	Goodbody	Primary	69,000
7	Read All About It	Intermediate	55,300
8	Gather-Round	Primary	55,000
9	Mulligan Stew	Intermediate	46,400
10	ThinkAbout	Intermediate	46,000
11	It Figures	Intermediate	44,600
12	Stories of America	Primary	42,200
13	Sesame Street	Pre-school, primary	34,400
14	Book Bird	Primary, intermediate	33,900
15	Life on Earth	High School	32,900
16	Shakespeare	High School	27,500
17	Cover to Cover	Intermediate	25,300
18	Storybound	Primary	25,000
19	Zoo Zoo Zoo	Primary	24,700
20	After School Specials	Intermediate	24,200

Source: John A. Riccobono. *Availability, Use, and Support of Instructional Media, 1982–83. Summary Final Report of the School Utilization Study.* Washington, D.C.: Corporation for Public Broadcasting, 1984.

Media File:
"ThinkAbout" Television Series

Designed to strengthen the reasoning skills of fifth and sixth graders and to reinforce their language, mathematics, and study skills, this series unifies the basics by focusing on their common denominator—thinking. The sixty 15-minute programs have won a number of awards, including the Achievement in Children's Television award given by Action for Children's Television.

Source: Agency for Instructional Television.

Media File:
"Arts Alive" Television Series

Junior high school students often have opportunities for artistic expression—to *do* the arts. The "Arts Alive" series encourages them to participate and to *know about* the arts: how they function in society and how artists create. The thirteen programs cover visual arts, dance, music, drama, the role of the arts in life, and the societal value of arts. The host is Lynn Swann, well-known professional football player and dancer.

Source: Agency for Instructional Television.

Media File:
"Reading Rainbow" Television Series

This fifteen-program series was developed for summer viewing to highlight good books and encourage summer reading by children aged five to nine. Each episode enters into the world of one book through location photography, animation, and original music and dance. Actor LeVar Burton hosts the series. Surveys following the first season indicated that library and bookstore demand for books featured on "Reading Rainbow" increased substantially. An estimated six million viewers watched at least one episode.

Public Broadcasting Service. Funded by the Corporation for Public Broadcasting & Kellogg Company.

of television; 61 percent reported specifically instructional use. The proportions varied considerably with the type of institution; only 50 percent of private four-year colleges made instructional applications, whereas 64 percent of the community colleges and 86 percent of the public four-year universities did.

Although some institutions served sizable enrollments of students in many different courses, the typical pattern was very limited. In the most common case only a few courses were offered via television, enrolling a total of only about a hundred students. Further, despite television's potential for extending the university's reach beyond the campus, only about 14 percent of the total college TV effort was devoted to off-campus course work.

Since the time of the CPB survey, however, some new television-based approaches to off-campus education have evolved. Often referred to under the label "distance education," some of these efforts have taken root and are expanding the opportunities for adults to receive continuing education conveniently and economically.

Resource sharing—achieving economies of scale—is the key to economic viability of most distance education projects. The TAGER network in the Dallas, Texas region, for example, shares the resources of nine local colleges in telecasting courses and transmits graduate engineering classes to employees at

nearby industrial plants. IHETS in Indiana is basically a telecommunications network among the state's universities, but it too offers continuing education to engineers, physicians, and others at the workplace.

The consortium approach—pooling resources of many institutions—to financing telecourse production was pioneered by the Agency for Instructional Technology (formerly Agency for Instructional Television) at the elementary/secondary school level. A similar organization at the college/university level has taken shape as the International University Consortium for Telecommunications in Learning (IUC), described in the accompanying Close-Up.

According to the most recently available reports by public television stations, there were a number of series broadcast for formal educational purposes by more than a handful of public television stations. The fifteen most frequently distributed postsecondary television series are shown in Table 9.2.

The shortage of high-quality instructional video programs worthy of mass distribution has traditionally hindered the success of large-scale adult continuing education efforts. A

TABLE 9.2 MOST FREQUENTLY BROADCAST FORMAL POSTSECONDARY SERIES

Rank	Series	Number of Stations Carrying	Percent of Stations
1	Understanding Human Behavior	70	53
2	Focus on Society	60	46
3	Personal Finance and Money Management	48	37
4	It's Everybody's Business	47	36
5	Making It Count	36	27
6	Contemporary Health Issues	36	27
7	American Government Survey	33	25
8	America: The Second Century	32	24
9	Art of Being Human	31	24
10	Oceanus	30	23
11	Growing Years	27	21
12	American Story	26	20
13	Business of Management	23	18
14	Writer's Workshop	18	14
15	Voyage	17	13

Source: Public Television Licensees' Educational Services, 1982–83. Washington, D.C.: Corporation for Public Broadcasting, 1984.

Close-Up:
Off-Campus Continuing Education via Television

During the 1970s and 1980s a shrinking college-age population led many four-year and two-year colleges to think seriously about ways of attracting new audiences. Television seemed to be an ideal mechanism for bringing the college to the student, particularly to the potential student who was unable to reside on a campus as a full-time student. This arrangement would be mutually beneficial, offering higher education opportunities to the student and new audiences to the college.

The success of the British Open University provided a model that was emulated by quite a number of experimental projects in North America, one of the most ambitious being the University of Mid-America. Most of these efforts faltered, however, lacking one or more of the critical elements for viability.

An organizational model that appears more promising is the consortium. One of these, the International University Consortium for Telecommunications in Learning (IUC), headquartered in Maryland, has grown steadily, encompassing over twenty colleges and a like number of public television stations by 1984. The membership includes two Canadian distance education institutions—Athabasca University in Edmonton and the Open Learning Institute in Vancouver. Thanks to the cooperative sharing of telecourse materials, institutions such as these are able to offer broad enough arrays of courses to enable an adult to obtain a bachelor's degree at home by television. A typical student for such at-home television participation is female, the mother of children who are in school or just beyond school age, and anticipating reentry into the job market.

---

significant breakthrough on this problem occurred in 1981 when publisher/philanthropist Walter H. Annenberg announced his intention to donate $150 million over a fifteen-year period toward the improvement of such programs. In collaboration with the Corporation for Public Broadcasting (CPB), the Annenberg/CPB Project invites proposals for innovative program ideas or other telecommunications applications. The most worthy are funded for implementation. In 1984 the first wave of Annenberg-funded programs began to be distributed in North America. Some of these are described in the accompanying Media Files.

Media File:
"The Write Course" Telecourse

This thirty-lesson telecourse consists of video lessons closely integrated with textbook readings, study guides, and writing assignments comprising a one-semester college level course in composition. The course covers basic writing skills, such as pre-writing, planning a composition, and composing effective sentences and paragraphs. Funded by the Annenberg/CPB Project.

Source: Dallas County Community College District, The Annenberg/CPB Collection.

Media File:
"Congress: We The People" Television Series

Veteran TV journalist Edwin Newman hosts this new public television series, an inside look at how Congress works. Taped at the U.S. Capitol and in congressional home districts, the documentary-style series mixes videotape footage with commentary by leading members of Congress and political scientists as it considers such topics as elections, lobbying, party leadership, ethics, and congressional committees and staffs. Series editor Norman Ornstein, a prominent congressional scholar, also appears in the programs. This twenty-six-program series was funded by the Annenberg/CPB Project to be offered as a college credit telecourse.

Source: WETA/26, The Annenberg/CPB Collection.

Media File:
"Faces of Culture" Telecourse

A post-secondary anthropology telecourse with twenty-six half-hour video programs, "Faces of Culture" features film footage from around the world focusing on how every society is based on an integrated culture that satisfies the needs of its members. Cultures as diverse as the Aymara of Bolivia, the Pygmies of Zaire, the Yanomamo of Venezuela, and others are examined as well as the more familiar cultures of the industrialized Western world. Produced by Coast District Community College (California).

Source: Coast Telecourses.

Business / Industry Applications

The extent to which business and industrial organizations rely on television for job training and basic skill instruction is revealed by a 1980 survey* indicating that over 700 such organizations were using instructional television programs. Indeed, the vast majority of user organizations operate television "networks," sending their programs to seven or more viewing locations. Hundreds of corporations, among them IBM, Ford Motor Company, Coca-Cola, John Deere, Equitable Life Assurance, Norwich Laboratories, and Burlington Industries, operate "corporate video networks" with more than fifty outlets. Most organizations produce their own programs, about eighteen a year on the average. The total annual program output of corporate video is far greater than the combined output of the major commerical television networks, and total usage has increased each year that this survey has been conducted.

Government agencies and some of the nation's larger private institutions (labor unions, public interest groups, foundations, etc.) produce instructional television programs for distribution within their organizations.

Smaller organizations and businesses have generally been inhibited in their use of ITV because of the high costs involved. The advent of videocassettes and portable field production equipment, however, has spurred use of instructional television in these sectors.

---

*Judith M. and Douglas Brush. *Private Television Communications: 1980 and Beyond.* Berkeley Heights, N.J.: International Television Association, 1980.

INSTRUCTIONAL TV DELIVERY SYSTEMS

There are literally thousands of institutions and agencies, public and private, using video communications for instruction within formal and nonformal education settings. The overall impression is one of tremendous diversity. One way to organize a closer look at this panorama is to consider one-by-one each of the major ITV "delivery systems," that is, the physical methods used to package and transmit programs to users: commercial and noncommercial broadcasting, closed-circuit TV, cable systems, microwave transmission, and portable video.

Broadcasting by Commercial Stations

Both entertainment and instructional TV trace their roots to the commercially licensed stations that began to make their impact as instruments of mass communication in the early 1950s. Early attempts to reach mass audiences with educational programming were made using commercial channels, including such pioneering efforts as NBC's *Continental Classroom* (described in the accompanying Flashback).

Although the commercial networks soon dropped the idea of becoming major vehicles for instructional television, commercial broadcasting still plays a major role in ITV in the United States. In fact, about one-quarter of the television programs used today in schools originate with *commercial* stations. Most of these programs are not designed with educational intents (although in some areas educational programs such as *Sesame Street* and *The Electric Company* are carried by commercial stations). They are, instead, programs intended to

entertain and/or inform the general public, but which can be adapted to instructional purposes by classroom teachers. Such programs might include classic and contemporary dramas, dance and musical performances, science programs, dramas based on historical situations (such as *The Jesse Owens Story* and *The Day After*), documentaries, and in-depth coverage of current news events.

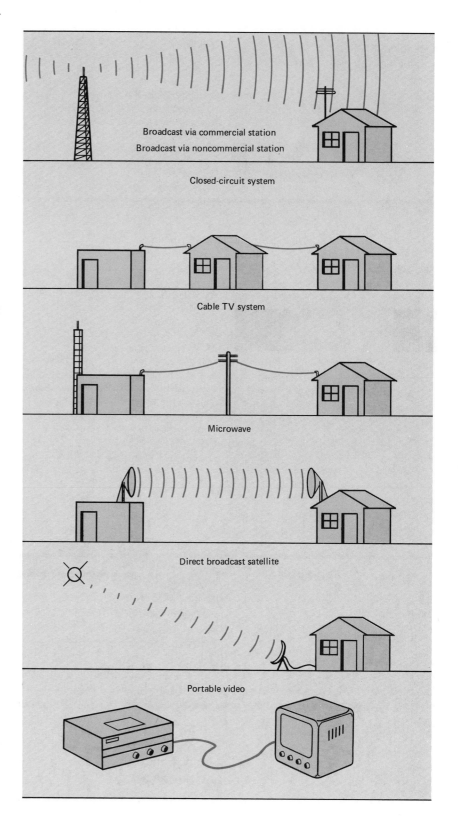

▶ **Figure 9.3**
The major delivery systems by which ITV programs reach viewers.

In addition to such programs, commercial television may also provide what might be called incidental instructional opportunities. Popular programs regularly viewed by students at home may provide experiential background upon which the creative teacher can build learning experiences.

Television, as we know, has considerable potential in the area of attitude formation. Popular dramatic series (even situation comedies) often revolve around moral dilemmas: Should the doctor inform the parents of the unwed pregnant teenager about her condition, or should the girl's condition be considered a private and confidential matter between doctor and patient? Is the policeman who knows that a brutal murderer will go unpunished justified in taking the law into his own hands by, say, planting false evidence against the murderer? More and more teachers are finding popular commercial programs a prime resource for discussion of moral and ethical issues.

Commercial broadcast programs are made more accessible and adaptable to classroom use through the publication of teacher's guides by organizations such as Prime Time School Television (PTST). These guides suggest ways that teachers can use commercial programs in various curricular areas, e.g., science, mathematics, literature, history, and agriculture. PTST guides are sent directly to teachers who subscribe to this service; they are also placed as inserts in journals that reach classroom teachers, e.g., *Learning* and teacher's editions of Scholastic magazines.

Figure 9.4
''Big Bird,'' a main character on *Seasame Street*, after more than 15 years still the most recognized series from Children's Television Workshop.

▼ **Figure 9.5**
The Electric Company, designed to improve reading skills for 6- to 9-year-olds, has been the most heavily viewed program in American schools since its inception in the early 1970s.

Broadcasting by Noncommercial Stations

The 290-plus TV stations in the United States that hold noncommercial licenses are referred to collectively as *public television stations*, a term designating their common commitment to operate not for private gain but for the public benefit. Although these stations have various patterns of ownership, they tend to operate along roughly similar lines. Just as most commercial stations act as outlets for commercial network programming, most public television stations serve as outlets for the network programming of the Public Broadcasting Service (PBS). Their evening schedules feature PBS offerings and other programs aimed at home viewers in general, while during the day time hours these stations typically carry instructional programs designed for specific school or college audiences.

Home Audience Programming.   Public television attempts to offer an alternative type of programming for viewers that are not well served by the mass audience programs of commercial broadcasting. In reaching out to selected

subgroups, public TV programming does not usually attract viewers on a scale comparable to the commercial networks. However, well-produced series such as *Wall Street Week, Masterpiece Theatre*, and *Nova* have won critical acclaim and loyal audiences that in recent years have grown to a size comparable to those of their commercial rivals. On a more general plane, public opinion polls indicate that over 60 percent of American adults can name their local public TV channel and do watch such programs at least occasionally.

As mentioned above in regard to commercial programs, the types of programs carried on public TV—documentaries, dramas, public affairs features, musical performances, science programs, and the like—are often useful as adjuncts to instruction in schools and colleges.

In-School Instructional Programming.

Programs for direct classroom use are a mainstay of most public TV stations' daytime schedules. The average station transmits about 40 elementary and

---

Flashback: CONTINENTAL CLASSROOM

All things considered, Sputnik I has to get the credit for breathing life into this project, the NBC-TV series which had a five-year run from 1958 to 1963. Sometime after Sputnik spurted aloft on October 4, 1957, NBC's Director of Public Affairs and Education, Edward Stanley, was coming back from Europe. He read that New York State's Commissioner of Education, the late James Allen, was planning a refresher course for science teachers in the state. Probable cost: $600,000. Stanley thought that ''for not a great deal more than that you could reach every science teacher in the country.'' And, he thought further, ''we could do the whole damn thing.''

While Splutnik may have catalyzed *Continental Classroom*, two people, more than any others, made it work. Ed Stanley had the institutional punch and the moxie to argue and lead, at a level essential for a venture of this scope. Then, Dorothy Culbertson, executive producer in the public affairs department, brought intelligence and important persuasiveness to both the critical fund raising and direct management of the project.

Assembling the series actually amounted to a kind of benevolent brokerage by Stanley and Culbertson. At his suggestion, she talked to the Fund for the Advancement of Education about using the NBC-TV network for college credit courses. They were ''excited.'' At almost the same time, the American Association of Colleges for Teacher Education (AACTE) approached NBC tentatively. Would it put up $25,000 to study how TV could be used to improve teacher training? ''I thought it was a helluva good idea,'' recalls Stanley. But his vision was broader: Would they be interested in something considerably bigger? Indeed they would, they said. This became vital in the funding arrangements that were to follow.

It seemed apparent that NBC alone could not float the concept. And so, after appeals to the Ford Foundation, it finally agreed to put in $500,000, a major share of the first year's expected cost. Then, following beguiling calls from Culbertson, added increments of $100,000 apiece came in from a number of large corporations. As a practical matter, the funds all went to AACTE, which thereupon paid NBC for its facilities, at cost.

By then, the apt series title had been locked up, as an outgrowth of a conversation between Stanley and noted educator Dr. James Killian, then Science Advisor to President Eisenhower. ''What you'd have here,'' Stanley explained, ''would be a continental classroom.'' Dr. Killian liked the idea, and the coinage stuck.

On October 6, 1958, the daily broadcasts began on the NBC network. That first year, the topic was ''Atomic Age Physics,'' a college-level course 165 lessons long. Says Stanley: ''Physics was the subject that was in trouble then. Many people teaching

20 secondary series. There is also a rapidly growing trend toward distribution of programs by videocassette in addition to broadcast distribution by stations.

ITV programs tend to be about 15 minutes (at the earlier grade levels) to 30 minutes long, and a single program is often repeated at different hours throughout the week to allow for flexibility in classroom scheduling. Contrary to the popular image, broadcast ITV programs usually do not present core instruction in basic subject areas. One leading researcher described ITV's contemporary role thusly:

1. To assist the classroom teachers in those subjects in which they often have the most difficulty (for example, art, music, "new" mathematics, science, and health);

2. To supplement the classroom instruction in subject areas in which limited classroom resources may prevent full examination of historical or international events; and

---

it had received their degrees before atomic energy was invented." And the man to teach these teachers was Dr. Harvey White, professor of physics at the University of California at Berkeley. Moving in to the NBC project, he lined up a veritable "Who's Who" of American scientists as guest lecturers. There's probably never been another national refresher course quite like it.

White and the other *Continental Classroom* teachers who were to follow had to do 130 lectures of their own in a year's time, five a week. They were under fantastic pressure. They would work from outlines, rather than from prepared scripts. NBC tried to let their talent go into the studio when they wanted. Largely, this meant afternoon sessions. A four-hour stretch of studio time allowed for camera-blocking, a dress rehearsal, and the tape-recording.

NBC's audience-research specialists estimated that 400,000 viewed "Physics," while 600,000 tuned in to "Chemistry," in the second year. But at no time over the five-year span of *Continental Classroom* did more than 5,000 sign up for actual credit in a course. Even so, to Lawrence McKune of Michigan State, that first series on physics was unique:

For the first time in the history of education, 4,905 students . . . in all parts of the United States, studied precisely the same course with the same teacher at the same hour, using the same outlines and the same texts.

In the second year, NBC repeated physics at 6 A.M., then ran its new chemistry course at 6:30. Physicists began watching chemistry, and the chemists brushed up on their physics, a neat refresher switch.

By 1960, the mathematicians were asking for a course. This time, a new approach was tried. The first half of the year was devoted to algebra; John Kelley of Berkeley taught three days a week, and Julius Hlavaty took the Tuesday–Thursday pair. Then, in the second "term," Frederick Mosteller, chairman of statistics at Harvard, carried the main load on Probability and Statistics, while Paul Clifford of Montclair State College did the "applications" on Tuesday–Thursday. By that particular term, as many as 320 colleges and universities were granting credit for the course. Stanley notes that "few of them were giving probability in those days."

At that point, the Ford Foundation decided to cut off its financial support. And even though a number of corporate sponsors stuck with the project, Stanley began to feel a budget squeeze (a cutback to two TV cameras, instead of the normal three). Regardless, Stanley still managed to come up with a star performer for that fourth year, the late Peter Odegard, then chairman of the political science department at Berkeley and former president of Reed College.

Successful? Stanley says that Odegard's "American Government: Structure and Function" had an audience of 1.5 million. The League of Women Voters, he recalls, "were convinced we did this especially for them!"

But then *Continental Classroom* folded. Why? "Money," says Stanley. "The company did lose a little, and wasn't willing to take a chance on raising some money the next year." The series budget—it ran between $1.2 million and $1.5 million annually—was "not a helluva lot for a network, not really." But NBC must have thought so. "American Government" was rebroadcast in the fifth year, and *Continental Classroom* ended officially on May 17, 1963.

ªExcerpted from Robert D. B. Carlisle. *College Credit through TV: Old Idea, New Dimensions.* Lincoln, Neb.: Great Plains National Instructional Television Library, 1974.

▲ **Figure 9.6**
Because *Inside/Out* and other such affectively oriented programs are aimed at helping viewers cope with personal problems, post-viewing discussions are an integral component of the total lesson.

3. To bring outside stimulation in subject areas, such as literature, where teachers have difficulty exciting and motivating the students.*

The licensees of the public television stations report that they have formal, ongoing liaisons with over half of the post-secondary institutions in their viewing areas.* Of these, about half of the colleges actually offer telecourses on their local station. Extrapolating from these figures to all the colleges and universities in the United States, it would appear that about 20 percent offer telecourses via public television stations.

*Saul Rockman; "Instructional Television is Alive and Well." In Cater and Nyhan, eds., *The Future of Public Broadcasting*. New York: Praeger, 1976, p. 79.

†*Public Television Licensees' Educational Services, 1982–83*. Washington, D.C.: Corporation for Public Braodcasting, 1984.

Closed-Circuit Television

The term *closed-circuit television* refers to a TV distribution system in which the sender and receiver are physically linked by wire. At its simplest, a connection between a single camera and a receiver within the same room (e.g., for image magnification in a science lab) constitutes closed-circuit TV (CCTV). Or several classrooms could be linked to a studio to form a building-wide CCTV system. Campus-wide and school-district-wide interconnections are also possible. In some areas, South Carolina and Indiana for example, one finds campus and district centers connected by statewide CCTV linkages forming networks of impressive scope. For special purposes, transcontinental telephone lines can be leased to set up CCTV hookups of national scope. A common example is the showing of championship boxing matches in theaters projected on a large screen.

Another application in business is the *videoconference*, a teleconference business meeting (see Chapter 6) in which the participants can see each other as they converse. This special closed-circuit application requires elaborate technical arrangements to work well. A manned control center is needed to coordinate the cameras and microphones. Videoconferences are frequently set up and run by a conference service under contract with the users.

One of the principal advantages of CCTV is that such systems, since they do not operate through the airwaves controlled by government agencies, can be set up freely by anyone who has the money to do so. Although the cost tends to increase with the size of the coverage area (unlike through-the-air delivery systems), the freedom, privacy, and multichannel capability of CCTV makes it an attractive option for some educational purposes.

Because cost increases as geographic coverage increases, CCTV is not widely used in large school districts. It has, however, become the leading delivery system for ITV on college and university campuses.

Cable Television

The cable concept of television program delivery was first applied commercially in the 1950s in isolated towns where, due to interference from a mountain overshadowing the town, people were unable to receive a viewable signal from the nearest TV station. Local businessmen developed the idea of building a master antenna atop the mountain. There the weak signals were amplified and fed into a coaxial cable that ran down the mountain into the town. By paying an installation charge and a monthly subscription fee, a customer could have his or her home connected to the cable. This idea of having a single tall antenna to serve a whole community gave the process the name *community antenna television*, or CATV, now more commonly known as cable television.

Most CATV systems in operation today still basically resemble the original master antenna model, in which broadcast television signals are captured by a favorably situated high-mast antenna (see Figure 9.7). The signals are amplified and delivered to the head-end of the system where they are processed, fed into a trunk line, and further amplified. The sig-

nals then proceed along feeder lines and eventually to smaller drop lines that enter individual homes and other buildings. The signal-carrying cables are installed underground in some systems (especially in congested urban areas), but ordinarily they are strung out along telephone poles, with a fee paid to the telephone company for this use of its property.

By 1984, well over half the households in the United States could avail themselves of cable television if they wished, and about 38 percent of all homes had opted to do so. The cable subscriber, besides getting a strong, clear video image on the screen, has access to more channels than are readily available over the air. Some of these channels are "public access" outlets for use by community and

▲ **Figure 9.8**
The QUBE experiment in Columbus, Ohio allowed home viewers to interact with programs by means of a five-button responder. Introduced in 1977, it was not a commercial success and has been discontinued.

special interest groups. Others are used for sporting events, special movie showings, programs imported from distant independent stations, etc.

Innovative Educational Applications of CATV.

Thousands of educational institutions are now plugged into CATV systems, often without charge from the local cable operator. In many cases, schools and colleges are operating public access channels for their own institutional and/or instructional purposes.

The availability of multiple channels facilitates a number of special services: (1) transmission of several programs simultaneously and repetition of programs at different hours for more flexible matching with classroom schedules; (2) the aiming of specialized programs at small sub-groups, for example, those speaking foreign languages or having sight or hearing impairment; (3) retrieval of remotely stored libraries of video materials, allowing teachers—or individual students—access to materials on demand without the logistic struggle often associated with instructional media use.

The Future.
Actually, the number of channels available on many cable systems is still small—the average system supplying less

▼ **Figure 9.7**
Typical cable television distribution system.

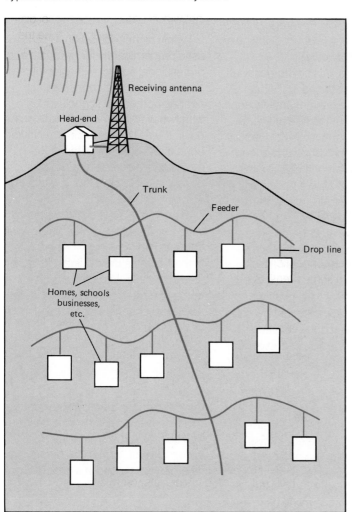

Receiving antenna

Head-end

Trunk

Feeder

Drop line

Homes, schools businesses, etc.

than a dozen channels. Recent developments, however (such as fiber optics as a replacement for coaxial cable and improvements in the system's other hardware components), foreshadow the development of CATV systems capable of supporting scores, even hundreds, of transmission channels.

But what has caused futurists among educators really to sit up and take notice is the characteristic of CATV which most distinguishes it from other television delivery systems: its ability to transmit signals not only from sender to receiver but also from the receiver back to sender. Although most cable systems today send signals only "down-stream" to the home or school, the technology is available to permit return communications "upstream" back to the sender. These return signals can take the form of simple yes/no digital communications, audio signals alone, or full television images with accompanying sound. Each of these feedback possibilities evokes exciting prospects for converting ITV into a two-way, interactive medium of instructional communication. A major ongoing demonstration of cable television's potential for two-way communication, was begun in late 1980 by the Canadian government and Bell Canada for subscribers in Toronto and Quebec.

Microwave Transmission (ITFS)

The only television delivery system in the United States set up exclusively for educational purposes is also the least well known.

In 1963, eleven years after the Federal Communications Commission reserved certain VHF (Very High Frequency) and UHF (Ultra High Frequency) channels for noncommercial use, it established the Instructional Television Fixed Service (ITFS), setting aside channels in the microwave band of 2500–2690 MHz for instructional use by educational institutions

▲ **Figure 9.9**
State-wide networks have been constructed using microwave and cable links. Through Indiana's system, Purdue University offers continuing education to engineers at their places of employment.

Later rules allowed the ITFS to expand into the areas of audio and hard-copy transmission and into two-way television systems.

The ITFS system has one major technical limitation. Signals broadcast at these high microwave frequencies travel in a line-of-sight pattern. Consequently, coverage of ITFS is limited to areas in direct sightline of the transmission tower.

Nevertheless, this coverage is sufficient in many educational situations. Coverage can generally extend over areas about the size of a large school district, and, unlike closed-circuit television, no wiring is required for connection among classrooms. Like cable, ITFS allows transmission on multiple channels; the average licensee operates about six channels. This greatly expands the broadcasting possibilities in a given locale beyond what would exist merely with VHF and UHF outlets. Because the system operates on frequencies above those that can be received on ordinary sets without a converter, it offers a higher degree of audience selectivity and programming privacy than regular broadcasts. Also, cost of equipment and operation is lower than for regular broadcast television.

At the present time ITFS delivers less of the total ITV used in classrooms than any of the other delivery systems discussed here, but it has been growing slowly over the years. There are now over 100 licensees op-

erating some 600 microwave channels, but geographic distribution is uneven. Twenty-three states and the metropolitan area of Washington, D.C. have no ITFS systems at all. On the other hand, in Milwaukee and Los Angeles, most of the available ITFS channels are already being used by educational institutions. Most of the area channels in the New York and San Francisco area are also in use—not, however, by the city public school districts, but by suburban and parochial schools.

Catholic school systems, having largely missed out on the earlier allocation of VHF and UHF channels for educational purposes, have become prominent users of ITFS. The Catholic schools in New York City and Brooklyn operate some twenty-three channels; a newer system in Chicago has ten channels. Other sizable Catholic operations are centered in Milwaukee, San Francisco, Boston, and Miami.

Within higher education, ITFS is used predominantly for graduate and professional school extension purposes. Typical use connects engineering or medical schools (often with two-way links) with professionals out in the field who require continuing education updating. Some of the most sophisticated technical systems in all of ITV are found within this sector.

In short, ITFS is a delivery system with considerble potential. It may well come to play a more prominent role in the future as the available frequencies in the VHF and UHF bands become saturated and educators seek additional channels for distributing video materials.

Satellites: Direct Home Reception

Communication satellites now carry most international telephone calls as well as most broadcast television transmissions. Virtually all of today's satellites are placed in a geosynchronous orgit—an orbit synchronized with the speed of the earth's own rotation. By keepig pace with the spin of the earth, they appear to remain motionless above the same spot on the ground. Geosynchronous satellites operate as transmitting stations on top of an imaginary tower so tall (22,300) miles high) that they can "see" nearly half of the earth's surface at one time. Theoretically, three properly placed geosynchronous satellites could cover the entire globe. However, because of the immense and growing amount of communications traffic, over 80 satellites are actually in use at this time.

The trend in recent years has been to design larger, more complicated satellites and to put more transmission power up in the satellites. The greta advantage of doing so is that reception equipment on the ground can be smaller and less complicated. For example, Telstar, launched in 1962, required an earth receiver with an 85-foot dish. In 1974, the ATS-6 satellite, weighing a ton-and-a-half itself, needed a dish only nine feet in diameter on the ground. Today's satellites permit transmission direct to home dish receivers only three feet across.

Private individuals and organizations have already begun setting up their own backyard dish antennas, sometimes referred to as TVROs (pronounced teev-row), for "Television Reception Only." By aiming a TVRO at one of the dozen satellites hovering over North America you can tap directly into the nonstop stream of television programming that is constantly being relayed by American and Canadian broadcasters and cable operators. The legal issues of ownership of these signals is yet to be settled, but the richness of the resource is indisputable: commercial

▲ **Figure 9.10**
The technology for satellite television reception has become simplified to the point that an apartment complex can operate its own dish to bring satellite signals directly to its residents.

and educational programs, sports, movies, special ethnic programming, and more.

A satellite receiver is still an expensive proposition; nevertheless, tens of thousands of such systems are being sold annually. Direct satellite reception at the home, school, and workplace is an increasingly realistic alternative delivery system.

Portable Video

The final delivery system involves neither wires nor over-the-air broadcasting. We are using the term *portable video* to refer to the several methods of playing back ITV programs right in the classroom by means of video recorders. The distribution system itself—the record/playback machine—is portable and can be set up wherever needed.

Newer recording formats, such as the videocassette and videodisc, now give instructors greater flexibility in choosing what programs they want to use and when and where they want to use them. They even make feasible the use of video materials by learners on an individualized basis.

Videocassette.
The conventional recording medium for video programs is magnetic tape similar to that used in audio recording. The tape may be used either in an open-reel format or enclosed in a cassette.

▼ **Figure 9.11**
"Portable video" allows playback of programs in the classroom without broadcasting or closed-circuit facilities.

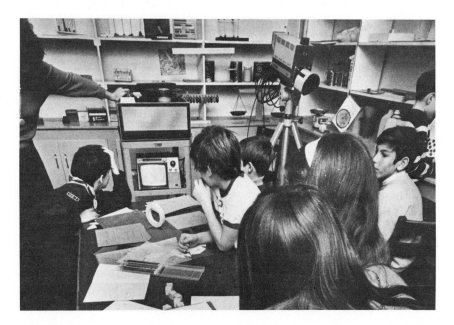

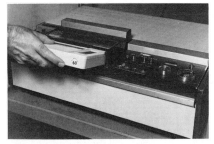

▲ **Figure 9.12**
The ¾-inch videocassette format.

▲ **Figure 9.13**
The ½-inch videocassette format.

▲ **Figure 9.14**
The 8-mm videocassette camera-recorder is the newest video recording format.

Currently, the most favored videocassette format for educational/industrial recording is that using 3/4 inch tape, a format pioneered by Sony's U-Matic system in the early 1970s.

The success of the 3/4-inch videocassette helped stimulate demand for a less expensive home version. The result is the 1/2-inch videocassette which is rapidly gaining in popularity both for home and for institutional use. There are two 1/2-inch videocassette formats on the market, Sony's Betamax and the VHS (Video Home System) offered by a number of competing Japanese manufacturers. Unfortunately, the two systems are incompatible, using different tape speeds and transport mechanisms. So recordings made for one system can not be used with the other. However, the VHS system has gradually taken over a larger share of the market year by year, suggesting that it may become the standard.

The most recent addition to the videocassette family is the 8-mm videotape camera-recorder system introduced by Kodak in 1984. This miniature format features a single-unit camera and recorder weighing

only five pounds. In addition to its superior portability, the 8-mm videocassette format has the considerable advantage of having an already agreed technical standard accepted by 126 companies. This guarantees international compatibility among the Kodak model and each of its competitors. None of the previous videotape formats offered this consumer benefit when they first reached the marketplace.

Videodisc. A more recent addition to video recording and storage systems is the videodisc. As the name implies, audiovisual signals are recorded on plastic discs, rather than on magnetic tape, for playback on television screens. The great promise of videodiscs lies in their ability to store massive amounts of audiovisual information in a compact package. Since videodiscs can have a slow-motion and stop-frame capability, still pictures and even print can be stored as readily as TV presentations. With a storage capacity of some 54,000 frames on each side, one twelve-inch videodisc can hold one hour of color TV programming, about a thousand filmstrips, or several thousand pages of print. In addition, some videodisc players contain a microprocessor with memory storage capability, al-

lowing them to be programmed to present branching sequences of programmed instruction. (Interactive video is discussed in detail in Chapter 7.)

Given these attributes, plus the very significant fact that discs can be mass-produced at low cost, it seems reasonable to suppose that videodiscs are destined to play an increasingly important role in the storage and presentation of instructional materials. However, there are some qualifications you should be aware of. When videodisc players began to be mass marketed in 1980 it became evident that several technically different and *incompatible* systems would compete for consumer acceptance and institutional use. Two different playback systems exist: the optical type, using laser beams either reflected from or passed through the

Figure 9.15
The laser type videodisc player.

disc, and the capacitive type, using a pickup arm in a way similar to a phonograph. Each has advantages—the optical system having more durable software and the capacitive system being simpler and less expensive. The latter system, however, has not met with notable success in the marketplace and may be headed for obsolescence.

Regardless of which technical system is considered, educational users have to decide beween interactive and noninteractive (straight playback) systems. The latter offers just straight-ahead playback of conventional video programs without random access or variable speed. This is the system marketed principally to home consumers; it offers educators widespread access to inexpensive off-the-shelf programs for low-cost playback machines. Interactive systems with computer capabilities built in allow rapid access to individual frames, automatic stops in the program for questioning, and branched responses dependent on the learner's answer. The hardware and software costs for interactive systems are considerably higher than for single videodisc players.

The recent introduction of a laser disc system for *local recording* lowers one barrier to wider acceptance of the video disc by individual schools and small organizations.

Summary. Obviously, accessibility of comparatively inexpensive and highly portable video recording equipment has important logistic implications. Flexibility of scheduling ITV is enhanced even further by ready access to video recorders than it is by access to multichannel delivery systems such as cable television. ITV programs can be taped and put away for use at just the right time to suit specific learning objectives and particular instructional situations. Libraries of recorded material can be built up and stored in centralized banks for retrieval by hand or if usage justifies, for remote electronic retrieval.

STEPS TO ASSURE EFFECTIVE LEARNING

As with other audiovisual media, the effectiveness of learning from video materials depends heavily on the instructor's planning and utilization practices. The ASSURE model provides a useful outline to carry you through these planning steps. We will assume that you have analyzed your students' characteristics and instructional needs and that your chosen educational goals have been converted into usable performance objective statements. Our discussion here will begin with the third element of the ASSURE model.

Select: Instructional TV Program Selection

In some cases the instructor has no real control over the selection of ITV materials. A program or series may be administratively mandated as an integral part of the curriculum. In most cases, however, instructors do have some discretionary control over selection of ITV materials, either as individual teachers or as members of a selection committee.

The development of sophisticated delivery systems and easy-to-use video tape recorders has stimulated an increase in the number and variety of available televised instructional materials. Program guides and directories can help keep you abreast of available materials in your areas of interest and guide you toward selection of materials best suited to your particular teaching needs. The most comprehensive listing of current educational video recordings is the *Index to Educational Video Tapes* published by the National Information Center for Educational Media (NICEM). For the postsecondary level, over a thousand recorded courses are described in *Televised Higher Education: Catalog of Resources.* In addition, *Videolog, Video Source Book,* and *Chicorel Index to Video*

Tapes and Cassettes are annual directories of programs encompassing both entertainment and educational topics. All are described in greater detail in Appendix A.

As with all other instructional media, you should also develop and maintain your own personal ITV program appraisal file. Only you can really know how well the materials work (or don't work) for you and your students. Included here is a suggested ITV program appraisal form. You may wish to use it as is or to adapt it to your particular needs.

Modify / Design: Local Production of Instructional TV

A feature that separates television from many of the other audiovisual media is that the instructor is not limited to off-the-shelf materials but can with reasonable ease prepare custom materials to fit local needs. "Do-it-yourself" television has become commonplace since the popularization of the battery-operated portable video recording systems—the

▼ **Figure 9.16**
The porta-pak camera/videocassette recorder system is easily carried and operated by one person.

HOW TO...SET UP A SINGLE-CAMERA VIDEO PRODUCTION

Components of the Single-Camera System.   A typical single-camera system setup is shown below. Its basic components are a camera, a microphone, a recorder, and a monitor/receiver.

Camera.   The heart of the portable video camera is the pick-up tube, which is basically a vacuum tube that converts light rays into electronic signals that are transmitted through a cable to the video recorder. The camera may be a viewfinder type. The viewfinder camera is so named because it has built into it a small TV set that allows the operator to monitor the image being received by the pick-up tube. Even small hand-held cameras typically contain built-in viewfinders with 1-inch screens. The nonviewfinder camera costs several hundred dollars less since it lacks the built-in monitor. It may be used for fixed-camera purposes, however, and it can be used for other local production purposes if it is hooked up to a separate monitor, allowing the operator to aim and focus the camera according to the image shown in the monitor.

Microphone.   Hand-held cameras usually come with a microphone built into the front of the camera. This microphone has "automatic level control," a feature that automatically adjusts the volume to keep the sound at an audible level. The camera, so to speak, "hears" as well as "sees." The problem is that these microphones amplify *all* sounds within their range, including shuffling feet, coughs, street

A compact color television camera complete with viewfinder, zoom lens, and microphone.

A typical hand-held color camera; note the pistol grip with on/off trigger, zoom lens, built-in microphone, and eyepiece at the back (to magnify the small viewfinder).

A miniature lavalier microphone clipped to a necktie.

Unidirectional microphone with windscreen, meant to be hand-held.

Omnidirectional microphone with windscreen in desk stand.

noises, and equipment noise, along with sounds that are wanted. You may, therefore, want to bypass the built-in microphone by plugging in a separate microphone better suited to your particular purpose.

In selecting a microphone, remember that television is more than pictures. Indeed, the audio track usually carries more critical information than the visual. (If you doubt this, try watching your favorite TV show with the sound turned off.) So the selection and handling of the microphone are of vital importance. The best advice is to think of your portable video system as an audio recorder plus a video recorder, and to make the same careful preparations as you would for an audio recording session.

The lavalier, or "neck mike," is a good choice when a single speaker is being recorded. It can be clipped to a tie or dress, hung around the neck, or even hidden under light clothing. A desk stand may be used to hold a microphone for a speaker or several discussants seated at a table. The microphone might be unidirectional or omnidirectional, depending on the number and seating arrangements of the speakers. For situations in which there is unwanted background noise or the speaker is moving, a highly directional microphone should be used, usually held by hand and pointed toward the sound source.

Recorder.   You have a variety of recorder formats to choose from, including the 3/4-inch and 1/2-inch videocas-

A field recording unit with camera and recorder combined in a single unit.

A generalized setup for single-camera recording.

settes described earlier. The recorder is either a table-top deck or in the lighter, more compact form of the porta-pak, intended to be carried over the shoulder or in a backpack position.

Whatever the type of recorder chosen, the recording principle is the same. In fact, it is analogous to audio recording, with both sound and pictures being converted into magnetic impulses that are stored in the metallic oxide molecules in the tape.

Monitor/Receiver. The final major component of the single-camera VTR system is the monitor/receiver, the device on which the recording is played back. The name is derived from the dual capabilities these units usually possess. Television signals may be sent through cables in the form of a "video signal," as in a closed-circuit TV studio. A "monitor" is a TV set built to pick up video signals; a "receiver" is a TV set built to pick up radio frequencies. A "monitor/receiver" is a unit especially adapted to receive both. The flick of a switch allows it to go from off-air pickup to playback of a VTR connected to it by cable.

Recording Setup for the Single-Camera System. Here are some tips for an effective arrangement for single-camera VTR recording:

1. The monitor/receiver and recorder are set on a sturdy mobile cart. This allows easy movement of the equipment around the room. The cart can be swiveled around so that the monitor/receiver faces the camera operator (to allow monitoring when a nonviewfinder camera is being used). In most cases it is advisable to turn the monitor/receiver away from on-camera performers to avoid distracting them during recording. It can easily be swiveled back for later "instant replay" viewing.

2. The camera is mounted on a sturdy, wheeled tripod,

maximizing mobility and stable support.

3. The camera is outfitted with a zoom lens, an expensive option, but one that adds great flexibility to the system. The zoom lens, having a variable focal length, can be adjusted to provide a wide-angle view, a medium view, or a close-up view with just a twist of the wrist. You should, however, resist the impulse to zoom in and out during a shot unless there is very good reason for doing so.

4. The camera and mobile cart are placed close to the wall. This arrangement helps reduce the likelihood of passersby tripping over the profusion of cables that connect all the components to each other and to the power source.

5. The camera is aimed away from the window (or other

bright light source). Cameras used in this system usually are equipped with automatic light-level control enabling them to adjust automatically to the brightest light striking the lens. If there is a window in back of your subject, the camera will adjust to that light, thus throwing your subject into shadowy darkness. An important caution when recording outdoors: one of the greatest hazards to the pick-up tube in your camera is exposure to direct sunlight. Aiming at the sun can cause its image to be burned into the pick-up tube, possibly causing irreparable damage.

6. The subjects are well lighted. If natural light is insufficient, you may supplement it with incandescent or fluorescent lighting in the room. Today's pick-up tubes operate well with a normal level of artificial light.

7. The camera is positioned so that the faces of all subjects can be seen. A common mistake in taping a classroom scene is to place the camera at the back of the room. This provides a nice full-face view of the teacher, but makes reaction shots of the students nearly impossible to see. Placement of the camera at the side of the classroom is a reasonable compromise when recording classroom interaction.

8. A desk-stand microphone is used. This allows pickup of the voices of all subjects, while reducing the pickup of unwanted background noises.

"porta-pak." This technological advance has liberated ITV production from the confines of the engineer-dominated studio. It allows ITV production to be taken "into the field," wherever that might be: the science laboratory, the classroom, the counseling office, the athletic field, the factory assembly line, the hospital, the neighborhood, even the home. Equally important, the simplicity of the system has made it feasible for nonprofessionals, instructors and students alike, to create their own video materials.

Applications. Locally produced video could be used for virtually any of the purposes described earlier in relation to still pictures, audio, and film; but its unique capability is to capture sight and sound for immediate playback. So this medium would fit best with activities that are enhanced by immediate feedback: group dynamics sessions, athletic practice, skills training, and interpersonal techniques (e.g., "microcounseling" and "microteaching").

Other applications that emphasize the *local* aspect of local video production are:

- Dramatization of student stories, songs, and poems.
- Student documentaries of school or neighborhood issues.
- Preservation of local folklore.
- Demonstrations, for example, of science experiments, eliminating delays and unanticipated foul-ups.
- Replays of field trips for in-class follow-up.
- Career information on local businesses via field recordings.

Of course, many organizations have more elaborate facilities than the simple single-camera field units that we are describing here. But closed-circuit TV studios and the like are the domain of the media special-

ist or engineer. Our focus is on the typical sort of system that instructors might expect to be using by themselves.

Utilize Materials

The next step after selecting or producing your video materials is to put them into actual use in the classroom.

Preview. It is not always possible to view a TV program prior to use, but you can usually read about the program in a teacher's guide. In the case of broadcast programs, utilization guides are often published in advance in education journals, as discussed earlier.

Prepare the Environment. Before students can learn from any instructional TV presentation, they first have to be able to see it and hear it! Provide proper lighting, seating, and volume control. These elements are described in detail in Chapter 10.

Prepare the Audience. Research in educational psychology as well as the practical experiences of thousands of teachers in all sorts of settings demonstrate that learning is greatly enhanced when learners are *prepared* for the coming activity. No competent instructor would advocate approaching a TV lesson by suddenly stopping the regular lecture, switching on the TV set, and abandoning the classroom for a coffee break. Yet we know that many instructors do just that.

To start the "warm-up" before the TV lesson, create a mind-set by reviewing previous related study. Help students see how today's lesson fits into the total picture. Create a "need to know." Stimulate curiosity by asking questions, and evoke questions the *students would like answered* about this subject.

Clarify the objectives of the lesson. Mention cues—specific things to look for—in the TV presentation. It

Appraisal Checklist: Television

Series title_____

Program title (or number)_____

Producer/distributor_____

Production date_____   Program length_____min.

Intended audience/grade level_____Subject area_____

Objectives (stated or implied):

Brief description:

Entry capabilities required:

    —prior knowledge
    —reading ability/vocabulary
    —math ability

Rating	High		Medium		Low
Likely to arouse student interest	☐	☐	☐	☐	☐
Technical quality	☐	☐	☐	☐	☐
Provides meaningful viewer participation	☐	☐	☐	☐	☐
Objectives relevant to curricular needs	☐	☐	☐	☐	☐
Focuses clearly on objectives	☐	☐	☐	☐	☐
Evidence of effectiveness (e.g., field-test results)	☐	☐	☐	☐	☐
Teacher's role clearly indicated	☐	☐	☐	☐	☐
Provides guide for discussion/follow-up	☐	☐	☐	☐	☐

Strong points:

Weak points:

Reviewer_____

Position_____

Recommended action_____   Date_____

Single-camera field recording video systems open up new possibilities for applications such as: practice with visual feedback for motor skill development, teacher self-improvement through micro-teaching practice and critique, and student documentation of community activities.

helps to list such cues on the chalkboard or on a handout so that students can refer to them as the lesson proceeds (and during the follow-up activities). If large amounts of new information are to be retained, give students some "advance organizers"—memory hooks on which they can hang the new ideas. Be sure to preview any new vocabulary needed.

Present the Material. A well-designed ITV presentation will call for frequent student participation. By responding yourself, you provide an example the students will follow. Learners are quick to detect and act according to your attitude toward the material. Many studies have indicated that the instructor's attitude—often conveyed nonverbally—significantly affects students' learning from TV.

Situate yourself so that you can observe learner reactions. Watch for

▼ **Figure 9.17**
The instructor's attitude toward and handling of video materials has a major impact on student receptivity toward the material.

AV SHOWMANSHIP—TELEVISION

Let's summarize key points in using television presentations to the best instructional advantage:

Check lighting, seating, and volume control to be sure that everyone can see and hear the TV set.

Get students mentally prepared by briefly reviewing previous related study and evoking questions about today's topic.

List on chalkboard the main points to be covered in the TV presentation.

Preview any new vocabulary.

Most important, get involved in the program yourself. Watch attentively and respond when the presenter asks for a response. Be a good role model. Highlight major points by adding them to the chalkboard during the lesson.

Support the presentation with meaningful follow-up activities.

---

clues indicating difficulties or boredom. Note individual reactions for possible use in the follow-up discussion. Deal with individual discipline problems as quickly and unobtrusively as possible.

Require Learner Response

If active participation was not explicitly built into the TV lesson it is all the more important to stimulate response after the presentation. The ability to generalize new knowledge and transfer it to real-life applications depends on learner practice under a variety of conditions. The possibilities for follow-up activities are virtually limitless. A few of the common techniques are:

- Discussion—question and answer sessions, buzz groups, panel discussions, debates.
- Dramatization—role playing, skits, oral presentations.
- Projects—experiments, reports, exhibits, models, demonstrations, drawings, story-writing, bulletin boards, media productions.

Evaluate

Assessment of student learning can be carried out informally by observing performance during the follow-up activities. Individual projects can be good indicators of successful learning. In many cases, though, more formal testing serves a valuable purpose. First, tests that are followed by feedback concerning correct answers can provide an efficient review and summary of the main points of the lesson. Second, objective tests can help pinpoint gaps that need to be followed up in the classroom and they can identify individuals who need remedial help. In this way, the instructor can complement the media component by catering to individual differences in ways the media cannot.

References

Print References

General

Atienza, Loretta J. *VTR Workshop: Small Format Video*. (Paris: UNESCO, 1977).

Bensinger, Charles. *Video Guide*. (Santa Fe, N.M.: Video-Info Publications, 1981).

Bunyan, John A. *More Practical Video*. (White Plains, N.Y.: Knowledge Industry, 1984).

Center for Vocational Education. *Present Information with Televised and Videotaped Materials*. (Athens, Ga.: American Association for Vocational Instructional Materials, 1977).

Combes, Peter, and Tiffin, John. *Television Production for Education*. (New York: Focal Press, 1978).

Eilber, Carol B. *Cable Television: What Educators Need to Know*. (Kettering, Ohio: National Federation of Local Cable Programmers, 1981).

Gothberg, Helen M. *Television and Video in Libraries and Schools*. (Hamden, Ct.: Shoe String Press, 1984).

Gross, Lynne S. *The New Television Technologies*. (Dubuque, Iowa: W.C. Brown, 1983).

Jones, Maxine H. *See, Hear, Interact: Beginning Developments in Two-Way Television*. (Metuchen, N.J.: Scarecrow Press, 1984).

Organizing Educational Broadcasting. (Paris: UNESCO, 1982).

Schultz, Jill M. with Tobe Berkovitz. *A Teacher's Guide to Television Evaluation for Children*. (Springfield, Ill.: Charles C. Thomas, 1981).

Senour, Robert A., and Campbell, Lloyd. "How to Use Both Audio Tracks on Your VCR." *Instructional Innovator* (January 1981), pp. 42–43.

The SITE (Satellite Instructional Television Experiment) Experience. (Paris: UNESCO, 1983).

Smith, Welby A. *Video Fundamentals.* (Englewood Cliffs, N.J.: Prentice-Hall, 1983).

Utz, Peter, ed. *Video User's Handbook.* 2d ed. (White Plains, N.Y.: Knowledge Industry, 1982).

Wiegand, Ingrid. *Professional Guide to Video Production.* (White Plains, N.Y.: Knowledge Industry, 1984).

Wood, Donald N., and Wylie, Donald G. *Educational Telecommunications.* (Belmont, Calif.: Wadsworth, 1977).

School Television

Abelman, R. "Children and TV: The ABCs of TV Literacy." *Childhood Education* (January/February 1984), pp. 200–205.

Doerken, Maurine. *Classroom Combat: Teaching and Television.* (Englewood Cliffs, N.J.: Educational Technology Publications, 1983).

Du Bey, Kenneth. "How to Videotape Through a Microscope." *Audiovisual Instruction,* (January 1978), p. 33.

Eanet, Alan S., and Toth, Sandra M. "Using TV in a Science Course." *Audiovisual Instruction* (March 1976), pp. 38–40.

Emmens, Carol A. "The Fourth Basic: Courses in Viewing Television Critically." *School Library Journal* (February 1982), p. 45.

Far West Laboratory for Educational Development. *Inside Television: A Guide to Critical Viewing.* (Palo Alto, Calif.: Science & Behavior Books, 1980).

Gibbons, J. F. "Tutored Videotape Instructions: A New Use of Electronics Media in Education." *Science* (March 1977), pp. 1139–1146.

Gould, Edwin, and Southerland, Vincent. "TV Typing: Learning the Keyboard through Instructional Telelvision." *Business Education World* (September/October 1976), pp. 14–15.

Hilliard, Robert L., and Field, Hyman H. *Television and the Teacher: A Handbook for Classroom Use.* (New York: Hastings House, 1976).

Holt, David. "Very Special Students, Very Special Video." *Media and Methods,* (January 1978), pp. 46–48.

Kaplan, Don. *Video in the Classroom: A Guide to Creative Television.* (White Plains, N.Y.: Knowledge Industry, 1980).

Lewis, Richard F. "Using Canadian *Sesame Street* Segments in Elementary Classrooms to Teach French." *Programmed Learning and Educational Technology* (August 1983), pp. 190–196.

Minow, Newton N., and Mills, Lynn M. "Prime Time School Television: Doing Something About TV." *Phi Delta Kappan* (June 1978), pp. 665–667.

Penman, Brian, et al. *Making Television Educational.* (Toronto, Canada: Ontario Secondary School Teacher's Federation, 1976).

Potter, Rosemary L. "How the Schools Are Using TV: A Sampling of Approaches and Materials." *Media and Methods* (October 1980), pp. 31–33.

Quisenberry, Nancy, and Klasek, Charles. "TV as a Teacher's Ally." *Instructor* (March 1978), pp. 82–85.

Sokoloff, Michele, and Muskat, Linda. "Cable in the Classroom." *Media and Methods* (April 1983), pp. 10–15.

Thompson, Margery. "Television May Be Just What's Needed to Teach the Basics." *American School Board Journal* (January 1978), pp. 41–42.

Williams, P. A.; Haertel, E.; Haertel, G.; and Walberg, H. "Impact of Leisure-Time Television on School Learning: A Research Synthesis." *American Educational Research Journal* (Spring 1982), pp. 19–50.

Withey, Stephen B., and Abeles, Ronald P., eds. *Television and Social Behavior: Beyond Violence and Children.* (Hillsdale, N.Y.: Lawrence Erlbaum, 1980).

Television in Adult and Higher Education

Abel, John D., and Creswell, Kent W. "A Study of Student Attitudes Concerning Instructional TV." *E&ITV* (October 1983), pp. 72–79.

Blythe, Hal, and Sweet, Charlie. "Using Media to Teach English." *Instructional Innovator,* (September 1983), pp. 22–24.

Brush, Judith M., and Brush, Douglas. *Private Television Communications: 1980 and Beyond.* (Berkeley Heights, N.J.: International Television Association, 1980).

Dranov, Paula; Moore, Louise; and Hickey, Adrienne. *Video in the 80s: Emerging Uses for Television in Business, Education, Medicine, and Government.* (White Plains, N.Y.: Knowledge Industry, 1980).

Eyster, George W. "ETV Utilization in Adult Education." *Adult Leadership* (December 1976), pp. 109–111.

Gueulette, David G. "Television: The Hidden Curriculum of Lifelong Learning." *Lifelong Learning: The Adult Years*, No. 5 (1980), pp. 4–7, 35.

Helmantoler, Michael C. "The Non-Traditional College Student and Public TV." *Community and Junior College Journal* (March 1978), pp. 13–15.

McInnes, James. *Video in Education and Training.* (New York: Focal Press, 1980).

McKinney, Fred, and Miller, David J. "Fifteen Years of Teaching General Psychology by Television." *Teaching of Psychology* (October 1977), pp. 120–123.

Tate, Pamela J. and Kressel, Marilyn, ed's. *The Expanding Role of Telecommunications in Higher Education.* (San Francisco: Jossey-Bass, 1983).

Zuber-Skerrit, Ortrun. *Video in Higher Education.* (New York: Nichols, 1984).

Videodiscs

Bennion, Junious L., and Schneider, Edward W. *Videodiscs.* (Englewood Cliffs, N.J.: Educational Technology Publications, 1981).

Bon, A. "The Educational Uses of the Videodisc Coupled with the Microcomputer." *Educational Media International* (No. 4, 1983), pp. 18–20.

Gayeski, Diane M., and William, David. "Interactive Video—Accessible and Intelligent." *E&ITV* (June 1984), pp. 31–32.

Kozen, Nancy. "Videodisc Bibliography." *Performance and Instructional Journal* (November 1983), pp. 34–35.

Nugent, Gwen, and Stepp, Robert. "The Potential of Videodisc Technology for the Hearing Impaired." *Exceptional Education Quarterly* (Winter 1984), pp. 104–113.

Sigel, Efrem, ed. *Video Discs.* 2d ed. (White Plains, N.Y.: Knowledge Industry, 1984).

Tiedemann, D. "A Brief History of Videodisc." *Educational Computing Magazine* (January 1984), pp. 38–39.

Winslow, Ken. "Videodisc Systems—A Retrospective." *Educational and Industrial Television* (March 1981), pp. 38–39.

_____. "Programmable Videodiscs and Videogames—What They Can Mean to Instruction and Training." *Educational and Industrial Television* (April 1977), pp. 23–24.

"What's Happening in Videodiscs?" *E&ITV* (June 1984), pp. 48–55.

Audiovisual References

Basic Television Terms: A Video Dictionary. Santa Monica, Calif.: Pyramid Films, 1977. 16-mm film or videocassette. 17 minutes.

Cost Effective Creative Video. Alexandria, Va.: Smith-Mattingly Productions, 1979. Videocassette. 30 minutes.

Educational Communications via Satellite. Washington, D.C.: National Aeronautics and Space Administration, 1980. 16-mm film series.

How to Watch TV. Columbus, Ohio: Xerox Educational Publications, 1980. 4 filmstrips with cassettes. 12 minutes each.

Introducing the Single Camera VTR/VCR System. Alexandria, Va.: Smith-Mattingly Productions, 1979. Videocassette. 30 minutes.

Learn Video via Video. (Series) Imero Fiorentino Association, 1981. 3 videocassettes.

TV: An Inside View. Salt Lake City, Utah: Media Systems, 1976. 3 filmstrips with cassettes.

Television Viewing Skills. Austin, Tex.: Southwest Educational Development Laboratory, 1980. Multimedia kit.

Utilizing Instructional Television. Salt Lake City, Utah: Media Systems, 1976. 2 filmstrips with cassettes.

Video—A Practical Guide—And More. (Series). Video International Publishers, 1981. 12 videocassettes. 30 mins. each.

Videodisc in Education. Logan, Utah: Department of Instructional Media; Center for Instructional Product Development, Utah State University, 1981. Videocassette. 23 mins.

What Is Microteaching? London: British Council, 1980. 16-mm film. 20 minutes.

Organizations

Agency for Instructional Technology (AIT)
[formerly Agency for Instructional Television]
P.O. Box A
Bloomington, Indiana 47402-0120

AIT produces television programs and computer courseware as the coordinating agency of a consortium that includes most of the United States and the Canadian provinces. It serves as a national distribution center also. It publishes a newsletter and an annual catalog listing dozens of series incorporating several hundred separate programs. Emphasis is on the elementary/secondary levels.

Association for Educational Communications and Technology (AECT)
1126 Sixteenth Street, N.W.,
Washington, DC 20036

AECT holds conferences, publishes journals and books related to instructional uses of media including TV, and represents the educational communication/technology profession. Its Division of Telecommunications provides a home for members who work in instructional TV and radio.

Corporation for Public Broadcasting (CPB)
1111 Sixteenth Street, N.W.
Washington, DC 20036

CPB is a nonprofit, private corporation established and funded in part by the federal government. It performs a broad coordinating function for the nation's public radio and television stations and supports the interests of public broadcasting in general. CPB carries out research on educational applications of television and coordinates the Annenberg Project, aimed at providing programming for higher education.

International Consortium for Telecommunications in Learning (IUC)
Center of Adult Education
Adelphi Road at University Blvd.
College Park, Maryland 20742

A cooperative organization consisting of some twenty colleges and universities and a corresponding number of public television stations in the United States and Canada. It aims to provide bachelor's level course work to adults unable to enroll in full-time on-campus programs. IUC develops its own courses and adapts British Open University courses. Each member institution grants its own degrees.

International Television Association (ITVA)
6311 North O'Connor Road, Suite 110
Irving, Texas 75039

ITVA is an organization of nonbroadcast television professionals in eight countries, primarily North America. It supports the use of television in the private sector—training, communications, and public relations—and sponsors regional and national conferences and an awards program.

Action for Children's Television
46 Austin Street
Newtonville, Massachusetts 02160

Annenberg/CPB Project
1111 Sixteenth Street, N.W.
Washington, DC 20036

Association for Media and Technology in Education in Canada (AMTEC)
c/o W.R. Hanson, Calgary Board of Education
Instructional Services Department
3610 Ninth Street S.E.
Calgary, Alberta T2G 3C5

Bicultural Children's Television (BCTV)
Suite B, 155 Callan Avenue
San Leandro, California 94577

Cable Television Information Center
1800 Kent Street, Suite 1007
Arlington, Virginia 22209

Children's Television Workshop
1 Lincoln Plaza
New York, New York 10023

Federal Communications Commission (FCC)
1919 M Street, N.W.
Washington, DC 20554

Prime Time School Television (PTST)
212 W. Superior St.
Chicago, Illinois 60610

Public Service Satellite Consortium (PSSC)
1660 L Street, N.W., Suite 907
Washington, DC 20036

Western Educational Society for Telecommunication (WEST)
c/o Station KAET
Arizona State University
Tempe, Arizona 85281

Periodicals

Audio-Visual Communications
United Business Publications
475 Park Avenue South
New York, New York 10016

E & I TV (Educational and Industrial Television)
C.S. Tepfer Publishing Co.
51 Sugar Hollow Road
Danbury, Conn. 06810

Instructional Innovator
AECT
1126 Sixteenth Street, N.W.
Washington, DC 20036

Media in Education and Development
IEEE Service Center
445 Hoes Lane
Piscataway, New Jersey 08854

Teachers Guide to Television
699 Madison Avenue
New York, New York 10021

Possible Projects

9A. Investigate three to five research studies that have been done on the effects of television. Include in your report a description of these studies and the conclusions reached.

9B. Interview a teacher who uses television regularly in the classroom and report on this in terms of purposes, advantages, utilization techniques, and problems the individual has with the use of the medium.

9C. Select any three hour time block of commercial programs children and youth are apt to view and report what you observed:
1. Programs seen and your reaction to their potential educational value.
2. Amount and kind of commercial ads during this period.
3. Evidence of sex stereotyping and the number of presentations of a multi-cultural/multiracial nature.
4. Your overall reaction to what students would have gained from this period of viewing.

9D. Appraise two different television programs for possible use in the classroom using the "Appraisal Checklist: Television." Your critique should include the purpose of the program and how you would plan to utilize this program in your classroom.

9E. Examine two of the TV software directories listed in the chapter or in Appendix A and report on areas in which you found materials you might use.

9F. If you are a classroom instructor and have access to a video recorder, you might plan and produce at least a ten minute program on a topic of your choice.

9G. Using the references given in this chapter, read four articles that deal with various ways teachers are utilizing television in the classroom. Report on these readings and give your personal reactions to these attempts.

M ediaware and Media Setups

Outline

Objectives

After studying this chapter, you should be able to:

1. Operate each of the following pieces of equipment: tape recorder (reel-to-reel and cassette), record player, overhead projector, slide projector, filmstrip projector, opaque projector, 16-mm film projector, and video tape recorder.

2. Indicate the basic care and maintenance procedures which ought to be observed with the pieces of equipment listed in Objective 1.

3. Identify a possible remedy when given a potential problem with any of the pieces of equipment listed in Objective 1.

4. Describe the consequences of using an improper stylus with a phonograph record.

5. Describe four general factors that should be taken into consideration when using audio equipment for group instruction. Your description should include volume and tone setting, speaker placement, type and size of speaker, and echo/feedback.

6. Relate speaker size to audience size.

7. Describe how to overcome the problem of audio feedback.

8. Identify and discuss the five variables that affect visual projection and describe how they would be applied in an example situation.

9. State and apply a general rule (the "2-by-6 rule") for matching screen dimensions and audience seating.

10. List the distinguishing characteristics of the four major types of screen surface and apply these variables to specific projection situations.

11. State and apply a general rule for determining the height of screen placement.

12. Name three types of projection lamps and discuss advantages and/or limitations of each.

13. Describe the procedures for replacement of lamps, including types of lamp and handling procedures.

14. Relate lens focal length to image size.

15. Discuss four general features of projection carts and describe examples of each.

16. Describe the "keystone effect" and state two ways to correct it.

17. Relate projector location to image size and shape.

18. Distinguish between the 1000 Hertz system for slide synchronization and the 50 Hertz system for filmstrip synchronization in terms of audio tape format and type of equipment needed.

19. Describe the "ideal" physical arrangements for class viewing of television. Your description must include the factors of seating, monitor placement, lighting, and volume with the minimum and maximum distances and angles.

Lexicon

stylus
feedback
2-by-6 rule
focal length
keystone effect
Hertz (HZ)
automatic programmer

Most media users are not—and do not expect to become—electronic wizards, but they do want to be able to use audiovisual media effectively. The most fundamental element of effective media use is simply keeping the equipment—the mediaware—running and being ready to cope with the snags that always seem to occur at the most inopportune times.

This chapter gives guidelines for the setup of projection equipment, screens, and speakers and then provides step-by-step operating procedures for the major types of mediaware. Included with each item are hints for the proper care of your mediaware and a troubleshooting checklist to help you cope with the most commonly occurring malfunctions.

Be aware that the equipment operation guides are not intended to be read straight through. They are meant to be *referred to* while you practice with actual AV equipment.

Also, the operating instructions in the guides are necessarily somewhat general since they must cover a range of equipment models. If your own mediaware differs markedly from the descriptions given here, refer to the operating instructions provided by the manufacturer.

If you have the responsibility for recommending or actually purchasing mediaware you should become familiar with *The Equipment Directory of Audio-Visual, Computer and Video Products* issued annually by NAVA, the International Communications Industries Association, and with the equipment evaluations published by the EPIE (Educational Products Information Exchange) Institute. These resources are described in the References section at the end of this chapter.

TAPE RECORDERS

The part of a tape recorder needing most frequent attention is the record/playback head. To get good-quality recording or playback, the tape must make full contact with the record/playback head. Each time the tape passes across the head, small bits of debris are deposited on it. Eventually, this debris will interfere with proper contact between the tape and the head. Therefore, the record/playback head should be cleaned regularly. Most manufacturers recommend cleaning after five to ten hours of use. Of course, it should be done more frequently when the machine is used in dusty areas, such as in a machine shop, close to a woodworking area, or near a chalkboard.

For cleaning tape recorder heads, you should use special head cleaning fluid (available at most stores selling tape recorders or from audiovisual suppliers). Apply with a cotton swab.

Tape Recorder Troubleshooting

Problem	Possible Remedy
Recorded voice or music is too low-pitched—sounds like a drawn-out drone	You are playing back at a slower speed than was originally recorded; raise the speed.
Recorded voice or music is too high-pitched—the "chipmunk" effect	You are playing back at a faster speed than was originally recorded; lower the speed.
Sound is faint and indistinct	Record/playback head needs cleaning; use a tape recorder head cleaner.
Hissing in background	Excess noise may be caused by head having become magnetized by long use of recording mode. Have a qualified specialist demagnetize ("degauss") the head(s). Or you may have a bad tape, try another.
Two different sound sources are heard simultaneously—one normal, the other backwards	Your playback machine has a different head configuration than the original recorder (e.g., yours is single-track, original is dual-track). Or the heads of the recorder may be out of alignment and may need to be adjusted by a qualified technician.

Do not use carbon tetrachloride, which can damage the heads, or alcohol, which can leave a residue of its own on the head. Alcohol can also damage tapes if they are played immediately after cleaning. In addition, over a period of time, carbon tetrachloride and alcohol can cause rubber parts of the pressure rollers to deteriorate.

The entire tape path should be inspected for dirt or damage that might interfere with proper tape operation. Most importantly, follow the recommended maintenance procedures in

HOW TO... OPERATE A REEL-TO-REEL TAPE RECORDER

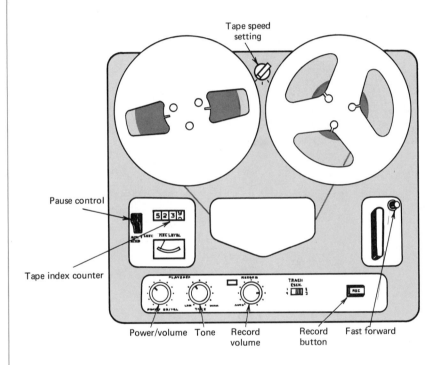

Tape speed setting

Pause control

Tape index counter

Power/volume   Tone   Record volume   Record button   Fast forward

Set up
- Open case and connect power cord to AC outlet.
- Position the feed reel (the full one) on the left spindle and the take-up reel on the right one.
- Turn power switch "on."
- Thread tape.
- Press button to set tape index counter at zero.
- Set tape speed.

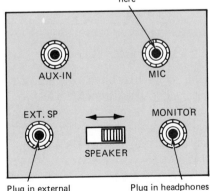

Plug in microphone here

AUX-IN   MIC

EXT. SP   MONITOR

SPEAKER

Plug in external speaker here

Plug in headphones here to monitor recording while in progress

Operate
- Plug in microphone.
- Turn record control to "auto" (if your recorder has an automatic record level setting).
- Press "record" button and *hold* while you move lever to "forward" position.
- Record your voice on tape.
- Rewind tape to starting point by moving lever to "rewind."
- Play back your recording.

Disassemble
- Rewind tape.
- Turn power control "off."
- Return to storage conformation.

HOW TO... OPERATE A CASSETTE RECORDER

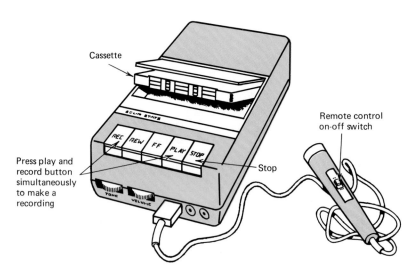

Cassette

Press play and record button simultaneously to make a recording

REC   REW   F.F   PLAY   STOP

TONE   VOLUME

Remote control on-off switch

Stop

Set up
- Connect power cord to AC outlet.
- Press "stop" key.
- Insert cassette (full reel on left side).

Operate
- Press "play" key.
- Press "stop" key.

Record
- Connect microphone to recorder.
- Press "play" and "record" keys simultaneously.
- Record your voice.
- Rewind tape to starting point by pressing "rewind" key.
- Play tape.

Disassemble
- Rewind tape.
- Remove cassette.
- Restore to storage conformation.

Cassette Recorder Troubleshooting

Problem	Possible Remedy
Tape comes out of cassette and snarls around the capstan of recorder	1. Very thin tape, as found in longer length cassettes (e.g., C-120) is especially prone to do this. Convert to shorter length (thicker) tapes. 2. The plastic hub of the take-up reel may be rubbing against the cassette. Try rotating the hub with a pencil to see if you can free it. 3. Mechanical problem: Take-up spindle is not pulling hard enough because of faulty clutch or belt. Have cassette repaired by qualified specialist.
"Record" button on cassette will not stay down	The "accidental erasure" tab on the back of the cassette has been broken out. Place tape over the gap left by the missing tab if you want to record something new on the cassette.

the manual that accompanies the recorder. Do not oil any tape recorder unless the manufacturer specifically recommends doing so. Most tape recorders are designed so that they do not need lubrication.

Audio equipment in general is subject to buildup of carbon or other contaminants on the contacts inside the volume and tone controls. This buildup causes an annoying scratching sound whenever the control knob is turned. Usually the problem can be resolved quickly and easily by spraying "tuner cleaner" (available at hi-fi and electronics supply stores) directly onto the shaft of the control. More stubborn fouling of the contacts might require some disassembly of equipment to get the spray closer to the source of the trouble.

RECORD PLAYERS

The component of a record player (phonograph) that is most likely to cause problems for the user is the stylus ("needle") assembly. Fortunately, most of these problems can be recognized and remedied by even the most "nonexpert" of people.

Phonograph records come in three basic types, classified according to the speed at which they revolve on the turntable (RPM = revolutions per minute). Each type has a different groove width:

78 RPM the original standard type, no longer being produced; it has the widest grooves.

45 RPM grooves are about one-half the width of those on 78 RPM re-

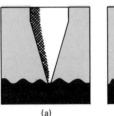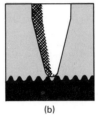

(a)   (b)

cords, allowing more recording time per inch.

33⅓ RPM often referred to as "microgroove" because its grooves are narrower than those of 78 and 45 RPM records.

Each of these basic record types requires a stylus whose tip diameter exactly matches the width of the record's grooves. If the tip of the stylus is too narrow for the record, it will ride on the bottom of the groove instead of along its sides (where the signal is encoded), thereby picking up the signal poorly and possibly damaging the groove itself. If the stylus tip is too wide, it will ride too high in the groove, thereby failing to pick up recorded sounds properly, possibly skipping out of the grooves entirely, and causing excessive wear on the grooves. (See Figure 10.1.) It is essential, therefore, that your stylus be one that fits the type of record you

◀ **Figure 10.1**
Mismatches between stylus size and type of record.

HOW TO... OPERATE A RECORD PLAYER

Controls

Tone arm lock

Set up
- Open case and connect power cord to AC outlet.

Operate
- Turn amplifier and turntable power "on."
- Set turntable speed control.
- Place record on turntable.
- Release tone arm from the locking screw or locking clip.
- Position tone arm on record.
- Adjust volume control.
- Adjust tone control.
- Turn amplifier and turntable power "off."

Disassemble
- Place turntable speed control in "neutral" (if possible).
- Lock the tone arm into place.
- Return to storage conformation.

Record Player Troubleshooting

Problem	Possible Remedy
Tone arm skates across record	1. Stylus may not be the proper one for the record. If the stylus does match the record speed, the tone arm may not be exerting sufficient pressure; if the machine has an adjustment to correct this, increase the pressure slightly, but only within the limits recommended for your phonograph—usually 2 to 7 g. In many cases the tracking pressure may already be too great, thus guaranteeing even faster wear on records and the stylus. 2. Check the stylus for excessive wear; replace if worn.
Sound is tinny, murky, distorted	1. Replace stylus if worn. 2. Cartridge may be cracked; if so, replace it.
No sound	1. Check to see if the volume is turned on. Sometimes it is a separate control from the on/off switch for the turntable. 2. Determine if wires to cartridge are broken.
Turntable revolves jerkily ("wow" sound) or too slowly	The idler wheel may have become flattened on one side or may have oil on it, causing it to make poor contact with the turntable rim. Consult an audiovisual specialist or repairperson to check the idler wheel.

wish to play. Most styli today, however, are compatible with both 33⅓ RPM and 45 RPM records.

Most modern styli have tips of diamond or sapphire and are thus extremely durable. They are not, however, damage proof. One frequent cause of damage to the stylus is allowing it to strike down hard upon a record or empty turntable. Do not move or carry the player around without first securely fastening the tone arm (which contains the stylus assembly). Continual playing of cracked or warped records can also damage the stylus, as can using it on a wrong RPM recording.

Keep the stylus clean of any dust it may pick up as it glides over records.

If your phonograph does not have a cleaning brush attached to the tone arm, clean your stylus periodically with a quick flick of a soft brush from back to front (to avoid dislodging the stylus from its cartridge). Do not use your fingertip for this purpose. You may damage the stylus by too heavy a touch. Further, your finger may leave a deposit of oil that will attract additional dust.

Even if your stylus is well cared for, it will gradually wear out and need to be replaced. If you think that a stylus might need changing, inspect it closely with a strong magnifying glass, or a stylus microscope, available at hi-fi shops. A worn stylus will show one or more flattened surfaces instead of a smoothly rounded tip. Removal of the stylus usually involves nothing more complex than unplugging its cartridge from the tone arm. If in doubt, consult an audiovisual or hi-fi specialist about the selection of a proper stylus and its proper installation.

▲ **Figure 10.2**
Styli and cartridges come in many configurations; this one is a typical plug-in stylus/cartridge combination.

AUDIO SETUPS

Built-in Speaker Systems

Most audiovisual equipment intended for use in educational settings comes equipped with a built-in speaker system. The built-in speaker is usually a single-unit "piston" speaker. This kind of unit is suitable for many but not all instructional purposes. Small speakers built into the chassis of table-model recorders, phonographs, filmstrip projectors, and so on, often lack the fidelity necessary for audio clarity throughout a large audience area. Because built-in single-speaker units have a limited frequency response, sounds falling outside this range may become distorted—bass sounds, for example, may cause the speaker to vibrate.

Portable cassette recorders are particularly troublesome when used for playback in an average-size classroom. Even under the best conditions, the sound quality of portable cassettes is severely limited by their undersized speakers. If such a unit is used to play back material in which audio fidelity is essential (a musical composition, for example), an auxiliary speaker should be used. A high efficiency speaker for instance, one having a 6- or 8-inch diameter—may be plugged into the earphone or external-speaker jack of the cassette player to provide better fidelity.

Size alone, however, does not guarantee high quality in a speaker. If high fidelty audio is needed, two-way speakers (bass and treble speaker in one cabinet) or three-way speakers (bass plus mid-range tweeter plus regular tweeter) are highly desirable. Such speakers may require an auxiliary amplifier when used in conjunction with AV equipment, but they are capable of reproducing the complete frequency range audible to human beings.

▲ **Figure 10.3 and 10.4**
You have to be aware of the built-in speaker when using audio equipment. A setup that is comfortable for the operator may aim the speaker away from the audience; such a setup should be corrected by turning the speaker to face the audience.

Another problem with built-in speakers is that they are often built into the side of the machine containing the controls. This is fine when the operator of the tape recorder or the phonograph is also the listener. But if the apparatus is placed on a table or desk and operated by an instructor for the benefit of an audience, the speaker will be aimed *away from* the audience (see Figures 10.3 and 10.4). A simple way to remedy this situation is to turn the machine around so that the speaker faces the audience and operate the controls from beside rather than in front of the machine.

In the case of film projectors with a built-in speaker facing out of the side, the problem is compounded by the fact that film projectors are usually set up near the back of the room. Thus, the speaker may face away from the majority of the audience. The problem may be even further aggravated by noise from the projector itself. About all you can do to alleviate such a situation is to move the projector or, if feasible, rearrange your seating pattern so that the built-in speaker will be facing at least the majority of your audience.

If you are operating in a lecture hall or auditorium that has a built-in public address system you will want to plug your projector or player into that system. This might require an adapter to match up the output plug and input jack.

Detached Speaker Systems

The detachable speakers that accompany some film projectors and stereo tape recorders are generally large and sensitive enough to provide adequate quality sound throughout the instructional area if, as with other separate speaker systems, you give consideration to their individual placement.

Whenever possible, speakers should face toward the center of your audience. If reverberation is a problem, however, especially in long narrow rooms, the speaker may be aimed diagonally across the audience to help alleviate this situation (see Figure 10.5).

In the case of film projection, it is also important that the speaker be placed as close as possible to the screen. Psychologically, we are conditioned to expect sound to come directly from its source. We are, consequently, most comfortable with film sound when it appears to be coming directly from the screen image that constitutes its source.

Be sure nothing obstructs the sound waves as they travel from the speaker toward your audience. Certainly you would not place the

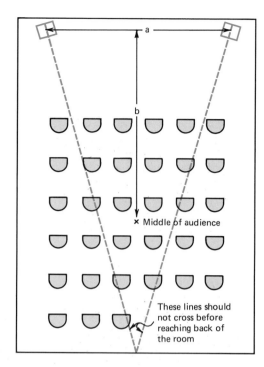

◀ **Figure 10.5**
A suggested speaker placement: the detachable speaker is placed near the screen, raised to head level, aimed toward the audience with no obstructions in the way.

▶ **Figure 10.6**
An appropriate stereo speaker placement for a typical size classroom: the distance between the speakers equals the distance to the middle of the audience.

speaker behind an actual sound barrier, but even classroom furniture (desks, chairs) and the audience itself may present physical obstructions to sound. To avoid such interference, place the speaker on a table or some other kind of stand so that it is at or above the head level of your seated audience, as in Figure 10.5.

If you are using a stereophonic system, the speakers should be far enough apart so that the sound is appropriately balanced between the two. As a rule of thumb, the distance between the speakers should equal the distance from the speakers to the middle of the audience. Thus, in the typical 22-by-30 foot classroom, stereo speakers would be placed 15 to 18 feet apart—nearly in the corners of the room. (See Figure 10.6.)

Feedback

Feedback is the name given to that annoying squeal that so often intrudes in public address systems or tape recorders being used as voice reinforcers. The usual cause is simple: The signal coming out of the speaker is fed back into the microphone. The most direct remedy is to make sure that the speakers are set up *in front* of the microphone. If the speakers cannot be moved, you may be able to stop the feedback by adjusting the tone and volume controls or even by moving the microphone. (Omnidirectional microphones are more likely to cause feedback problems than unidirectional microphones.)

Volume and Tone Setting

Because sound wave intensity decreases rapidly over distance, achieving a comfortable sound volume for all listeners can be quite a challenge. This is particularly true in larger rooms, for it is difficult to reach the back of the room without generating a very loud sound at the front. This, of course, can cause considerable discomfort to those seated near the speaker. An ideal solution would be to use several low-power sources rather than a single high-power one. But since this is usually not feasible, you can only strive to achieve a reasonable compromise through proper

setting of the volume control. By moving around the room during the presentation (unobtrusively), you can get a feel for the best volume setting to suit your situation. The problem may be further alleviated by not seating students at the extreme front or back.

The tone control can be used to correct certain other acoustical problems. For instance, low frequency (bass) sounds will reverberate annoyingly under certain conditions ("boominess"). This can be compensated for somewhat by turning the tone control of the film projector or tape recorder toward "treble." This also tends to improve the audibility of male speakers' low-pitched voices. Conversely, high-pitched sounds can be dampened with the tone control.

OVERHEAD PROJECTORS

In terms of its mechanics and electronic components, the overhead projector is a very simple apparatus, with few components requiring special maintenance procedures. Reliable as it is, however, it should not be taken for granted. Take a few basic precautions to ensure that the projector keeps putting on a bright performance.

Keep the overhead projector as clean as possible. The horizontal stage tends to gather dust, fingerprint smudges, and marking-pen traces. It should be cleaned regularly with window spray or a mild solution of soap and water. The lens in the head assembly should also be kept free of dust and smudges. Clean it periodically with lens tissue and a proper lens-cleansing solution. The fresnel lens under the stage may also need cleaning eventually, but this procedure is better left to the specialist. The lens is a precision optical element requiring special care. In addition, some disassembly of the unit may be required to get at the lens.

The best way to prolong the life of the expensive lamp in the overhead projector is to *allow it to cool before moving* the projector. Move the projector with care. Keep the projector on a cart that can be rolled from one location to another. When hand carrying the apparatus, hold on to the body of the projector, not the thin arm of the head assembly. The head assembly arm is not intended to be a carrying handle. Used as such, it can easily be twisted out of alignment, thus distorting the projector's image.

HOW TO... OPERATE AN OVERHEAD PROJECTOR

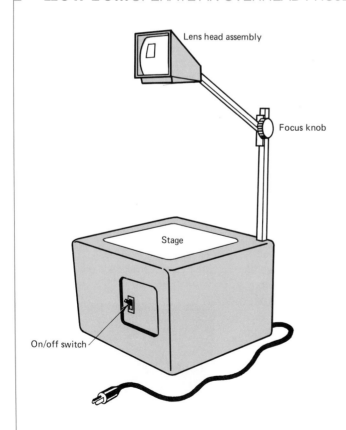

Lens head assembly

Focus knob

Stage

On/off switch

Set up
- Connect power cord to AC outlet.

Operate
- Turn projector "on." (With some projectors you have to click through two positions to reach the "on" position.)
- Position transparency on stage.
- Adjust projector to eliminate keystoning. (See page 271.)

(Not this ⬡ or this ⬡ But this ▢)

- Focus image.
- Practice writing on the transparency and erasing.

Disassemble
- Restore to storage conformation.

Overhead Projector Troubleshooting

Problem	Possible Remedy
No light after flipping switch	1. Be sure projector is plugged into an electrical outlet. 2. Turn the switch all the way on. Many overheads have a three-position switch: off, fan, and on. 3. If lamp is burned out, switch to spare lamp within projector if it has this feature. Otherwise, you will need to replace the lamp. Be sure to use a lamp of the same wattage (too high a wattage can cause overheating). Do not handle the lamp while it is hot. Avoid touching the new lamp with bare fingers; this could shorten its life. 4. Switch may be defective. If so, replace it.
Dark edge with light in center of image	The fresnel lens is upside-down. Turn it over if you know how; if not, have a qualified specialist do it.
Dark spot on area of screen	The lamp socket within the projector needs adjustment. The task is best done by a trained audiovisual technician.
Dark spot on screen or failure of lens to focus despite all adjustment of focus	After determining that it is not simply a matter of dirt on the lens or improper use of the focus control, check for a warped fresnel lens. This lens is plastic and can become warped from excessive heat, usually caused by the fan not running properly. Have a qualified specialist repair the fan or thermostat and replace the fresnel lens.

SLIDE PROJECTORS

In normal use, slide projectors require little special attention to keep working smoothly. The only regular maintenance required of the user is to clean the front element of the projection lens if it shows finger marks. More likely to cause difficulties are the slides themselves, which should always be stored away from heat and handled only by their mounts. The most frequent cause of foul-ups in slide presentations is a slide that jams because it is warped or frayed ("dog-eared"). Remount slides that could cause jams.

The Kodak Ektagraphic III projector has a number of desirable features not found on earlier models. For example, the projection lamp can be changed from the rear of the projector without having to turn the projector over. There is a quick release on the elevation stand so the projected image can be raised without having to turn the adjustment knob many times by hand. In addition, the "select" function allows the carousel tray to be turned when the power is off. Finally, the controls are on the side of the projector where the operator usually stands.

Even though some new projectors, such as the Ektagraphic III, do not project a distracting white "image" when there is not a slide in position, it is still recommended that you include a dark slide at the beginning and end of your presentation. Solid plastic slides work best.

The purchase and use of a carrying case for your slide projector is highly recommended if the projector is to be moved from location to location, especially from building to building. Slide projectors should only be moved on a projector cart or within a carrying case. The case provides a place to store the projector, tray, remote control unit, a spare lamp, and

▼ **Figure 10.7**
The newer Kodak slide projectors feature more convenient controls.

HOW TO... OPERATE A SLIDE PROJECTOR

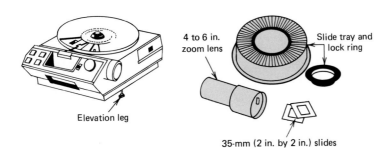

Elevation leg

4 to 6 in. zoom lens

Slide tray and lock ring

35-mm (2 in. by 2 in.) slides

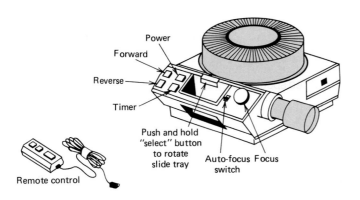

Power
Forward
Reverse
Timer
Push and hold "select" button to rotate slide tray
Auto-focus switch
Focus
Remote control

Set up

- Connect power cord to AC outlet (power cord is stored in a compartment on the bottom of the projector.)
- Plug in remote control cord with white dot on top.
- Insert lens.
- Check to see that bottom ring is locked on slide tray. If not, lock it or slides will drop out.
- Load slides into tray and tighten the locking ring on the tray.
- Seat slide tray on projector. *Note* the notch at "0."

Operate

- Set automatic timer at "m" (manual operation).
- Move on/off switch to "low" or "high" lamp setting.
- Position image on screen, making it smaller or larger by means of the lens barrel.
- Focus image with focus knob.
- Project slides using remote control or buttons on the forward side of the projector.

Disassemble

- Press and hold "select" button while turning the tray to "0." The "select" function will not operate when projector is off, except on the Ektagraphic III model.
- Remove slide tray.
- Allow lamp to cool before switching off.
- Remove slides from slide tray.
- Restore to storage conformation.

remote extension cords. The carrying case helps to keep all the accessories together, decreasing the chances for loss, as well as providing protection from damage and dust.

More serious damage can occur if the slide projector falls because it has been propped up precariously on top of a stack of books or on some other unstable base. This happens all too often because the projector's elevation leg seems never to be quite

long enough to raise the image up to the top of the screen. Better solutions are to use a higher projection table, to raise the whole projection table, or to raise the whole projector by placing it on a sturdy box or similar platform.

Slide Projector Troubleshooting

Problem	Possible Remedy
Can't find power cord	Look for a built-in storage compartment. On the Kodak Carousel, the power cord is stored in a latched compartment underneath the projector.
No power after plugging in	If you are sure the outlet is "live" (a fuse or circuit breaker may have killed all electrical power in the room), check the circuit breaker on the slide projector. On some models a button on the bottom of the projector must be pressed after changing lamps.
Fan runs but lamp does not light	Some projectors have separate switches for "Lamp" and "Fan" or a two-stage switch for these two functions. Make sure all switches are properly set. Then check for burned-out lamp. If neither of these is the problem, have technician check the projector.
Image not level	Most slide projectors have an adjustment knob on one of the rear feet. Use the knob to raise or lower that side.
Without slides, the blank image is distorted	1. The lenses may be out of alignment or broken. This is especially likely with the Kodak Carousel, in which several lenses are loosely held in place on the underside of the projector. Often they can be adjusted easily by aligning them correctly in their slots.
	2. If an image of the lamp filament is seen on the screen, the lamp has been incorrectly installed and should be seated properly.
Projector gets very hot; slides begin to burn	Stop immediately! The Kodak Carousel has a heat-absorbing glass between the lenses next to the lamp. If this flat glass is broken or missing the heat builds up quickly and can cause damage.
Slide mounts begin to warp	For plastic black and white mounts, check to see that *white side* of mount is *facing* the lamp. If the dark side of mount is facing lamp, a build-up of heat can cause the mount to warp (or even melt, in the case of plastic mounts).
Slide image upside-down or backwards	Remove the slide and reverse it. (Improper loading can be avoided by "thumb-spotting" slides. See Chapter 5.)
Slide jams in gate	1. Manually remove the slide. On the Kodak Carousel, press the "select" button (power must be on). If the slide does not pop up, the tray will have to be removed. Turn off the power and use a coin to turn the screw in the center of the tray; this unlocks the tray, allowing it to be lifted off and giving access to the gate for manual removal of the slide.
	2. Jamming can be avoided by not placing bent slides in the tray. Plastic mounts have a tendency to warp; cardboard mounts fray; glass mounts may be too thick for the slide compartment of the tray. For this reason, jamming is more likely with *narrow* slide compartments, as are found in the 140-slide Carousel trays. Use the 80-slide universal tray whenever possible.

▲ **Figure 10.8**
A proper carrying case prolongs the life of slide projectors that are moved frequently.

FILMSTRIP PROJECTORS

A filmstrip projector requires the same sort of care and handling as a slide projector. With the filmstrip projector, however, an additional concern is keeping the film gate clean. Lint and dirt in the gate may be seen around the edges of the projected image and are an annoyance to the viewer. The film gate can be cleaned with a special aperture brush (also used with motion picture projectors) or with some other nonmetal, soft-bristle brush.

Filmstrip projectors that come in enclosed cases carry a warning to remove the projector from the case before operating it. This is to ensure that air can circulate freely to the cooling fan located on the underside of the projector. Any interference with the fan, such as a sheet of paper sucked up against the fan grid or an accumulation of dust adhering to the fan grid, can lead to overheating and damage to filmstrips.

HOW TO... OPERATE A FILMSTRIP PROJECTOR

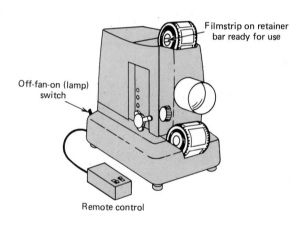

Filmstrip on retainer bar ready for use

Off-fan-on (lamp) switch

Remote control

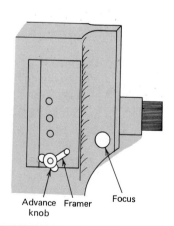

Advance knob   Framer   Focus

Set up
- Connect power cord to AC outlet.

Operate
- Turn projector "on."
- Place filmstrip on retainer bar.
- Thread filmstrip down into film slot. Be sure that "START" or "FOCUS" appears at head of filmstrip.
- Turn advance knob until "FOCUS" frame appears.
- Adjust framer so the full frame is projected when you click the advance knob.
- Turn projector "off."

Disassemble
- Return filmstrip to container. Do not pull the end of the filmstrip to tighten the roll. Start with a tight roll at the center and continue, holding the film by the edges.
- Restore to storage conformation.

Filmstrip Projector Troubleshooting

Problem	Possible Remedy
Dark areas or smudges projected on the screen	Clean the lens.
Dirt/lint visible at edges of projected image	Foreign matter in the film gate. Clean with an aperture brush or other brush with no metal components.
	Filmstrip is not properly framed. Correct with framer knob.
	If this is the first frame you see, the filmstrip has been inserted tail-first. Withdraw it and insert the head end. (If the lettering appears backwards, you have threaded it with the wrong side facing the screen; reverse it. The ends of the strip should curl toward the screen.)

HOW TO... OPERATE AN OPAQUE PROJECTOR

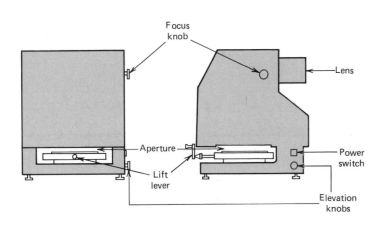

Set up
- Connect power cord to AC outlet.

Operate
- Turn projector "on."
- Use lift lever to open platen.
- Insert material.
- Close platen.
- Focus picture.
- Elevate projector.

Disassemble
- Remove material.
- Turn lens back into projector.
- Lower elevation.

OPAQUE PROJECTORS

The opaque projector presents a few unique operating problems. Because of the aperture size and the focal length of the lens, the opaque projector will be placed 10 to 12 feet from the screen. This, then, usually puts a very bulky piece of equipment in the middle of the audience. Consequently, the projector must be positioned below eye level so students can see over it, and the front elevated causing keystoning. The noisy fan sound and the light that spills from the projector also create distractions from the presentation.

One last point—a WARNING! Some of the older opaque projectors can transfer heat to paper. There have been instances of the paper becoming hot enough to burn. If you are using an opaque projector, keep an eye on the material, especially if the paper is old and dry. Should the paper begin to darken, remove it immediately!

PROJECTION SETUPS

Arranging a proper environment for viewing projected visuals involves several variables, including audience seating pattern, screen size, type of screen surface, screen placement, type of lens, and projector placement.

In most cases, the instructor only has to deal with a couple of these variables, probably seating pattern and projector placement. For everyday teaching situations the classroom often will be equipped with a

▼ **Figure 10.9**
With proper attention to projection variables, even makeshift facilities can become learning environments.

Opaque Projector Troubleshooting

Problem	Possible Remedy
No light after flipping switch	1. Be sure projector is securely plugged into an electrical outlet. 2. Check lamp. If burned out, replace it. Since you must push down very hard on the lamp while twisting it, be sure to use a cloth. 3. Switch may be defective. If so, have a media technician replace it.
Line through picture	The piece of glass between the material and the lamp may be broken. Be sure to replace it with the manufacturer's glass since this glass has special properties for resisting heat and pressure.
Glass is broken	Someone applied too much pressure when loading the material. The material should be snug in the projector—not tight.
Brown spot appears within projected image	The material is beginning to burn. GET IT OUT!

screen of a certain type attached in a fixed position, and the projector will already have its own lens.

There may be times, however, when you will have to make decisions about any or all of these variables—for instance, setting up an in-service workshop in the school cafeteria or running a film showing at a youth group meeting in a church hall. Let us examine some guidelines for handling each of these variables by looking at a specific hypothetical case.

Seating Arrangement

Let us assume that the room you are to use for projecting visuals is 22 feet wide and 30 feet long, a fairly typical size both for formal and nonformal instructional settings. Let us further assume that you must arrange seating for between thirty and forty viewers, a fairly typical audience size. Figure 10.10 illustrates a conventional seating pattern for a group of this size (in this case, thirty-six viewers). Note that the seats are arranged across the narrower room dimension. If the

seats were turned to face the left or right side of the room and arranged across its 30-foot length, viewers along either end of the rows would have a distorted view of the screen. Note too, that the first row of seats is set back somewhat from the desk area, where the screen is to be set up, so that front-row students will not be too close to the screen for comfortable viewing.

If the room is closer to a square in shape you might want to consider placing the screen in the corner and seating the audience in diagonal rows. This possibility will be examined later in terms of screen placement.

Screen Size

A general rule of thumb (the "2-by-6" rule) accepted by most audiovisualists dictates that no viewer should be seated closer to the screen than two screen widths or farther away than six screen widths. This means that in our hypothetical case, in which the farthest viewer could be 30 feet from the front of the room, a screen about 5 feet wide (60 inches)

would be required to ensure that this farthest-away viewer is within six screen widths of the screen $(30 \div 6 = 5)$. A square screen is generally preferable, since it can be used to show rectangular images (film, slides, filmstrips, etc.) as well as square images (overhead and opaque projections). Thus, in this case a screen measuring 60-by-60 inches is recommended, as illustrated in Figure 10.11.

With a zoom lens on a carousel slide projector or a 16-mm projector, you can put the projector at the rear of any normal-size classroom and "fill" a 70-inch screen.

Screen Surfaces

Projection screens vary in their surface treatments. Various surfaces have different reflectance qualities and offer different viewing-angle widths.

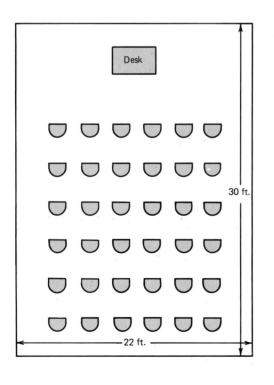

◀ **Figure 10.10** Typical size classroom arranged to seat 36.

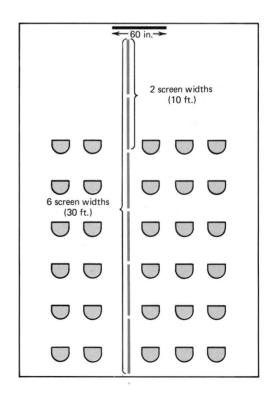

▶ **Figure 10.11** Appropriate screen size for typical size classroom, according to the "two-by-six" rule.

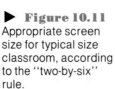

Matte White Surface. The matte screen has a smooth, non-shiny surface that has the lowest reflectance but provides a constant level of brightness over the widest viewing angle (more than 45 degrees on either side of the center axis). It is durable and inexpensive. Matte white screens can be rolled up for storage or carrying. Because of these qualities the matte white screen is the one most commonly used in instructional settings. In addition, a matte white screen can be cleaned with an extra-strength household cleaner such as Mr. Clean. None of the other surfaces can be cleaned.

Beaded Surface. The beaded screen is a white surface covered with small glass beads. Approximately two to four times more light is reflected from this surface than from the matte white surface. However, the beads tend to reflect light straight back toward the light source, narrowing the optimal viewing area. In fact, beyond 25 degrees on either side of the center axis the brightness is less than that of a matte white screen. Beaded screens are primarily recommended for long, narrow halls.

Lenticular Surface. The lenticular screen is made from a plastic material that has a pattern molded into the surface, usually a series of very narrow ridges running vertically up the screen. It represents a compromise between the beaded and the matte white surfaces, being nearly as reflective as the former and offering

▼ **Figure 10.12**
Comparison of reflectance and recommended viewing angles for four different screen surfaces.

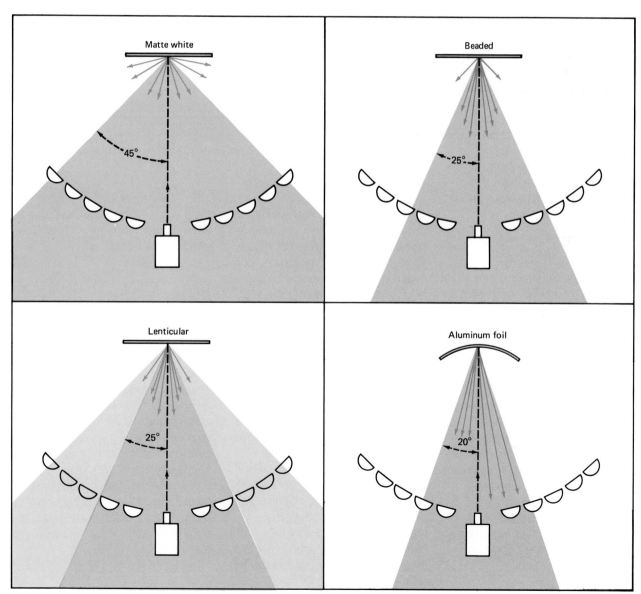

nearly the breadth of viewing angle of the latter. Like the beaded screen, the lenticular screen provides the brightest image within 25 degrees of the center axis and a dimmer image out to about 45 degrees. It must be stretched tight to be effective. It is more expensive than the matte or beaded screen and is seldom used in schools.

Aluminum Foil Surface.

Developed by Kodak under the trade name Ektalite, this is the brightest surface available, about twenty times brighter than the matte white surface. However, it has a very narrow viewing angle, with visibility limited to about 20 degrees from the center axis. Screen size is also limited, 40-by-40 inches being the largest standard size. It is rigid and cannot be rolled up. Its greatest advantage is visibility in full room-light. It is particularly recommended for small group use in conditions of high ambient light.

The major features of these screen types are shown in comparison in Figure 10.12. Given the room dimensions and audience size in our hypothetical case, a matte white screen would be most suitable.

Screen Placement

In most cases, placement of the screen at the center of the front of the room will be satisfactory. In some cases, however, it may not be. Perhaps light from a window that cannot be fully covered will wash out the projected image (sunlight is much brighter than any artificial light), or you might wish to use the chalkboard during your presentation and a screen so positioned will make it difficult or impossible for you to do so. An alternative position is in a front corner of the room. Indeed, the screen should not be at "center stage" when there is danger that it will attract unwanted attention while non-projection activities are going on.

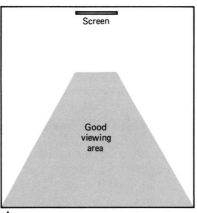
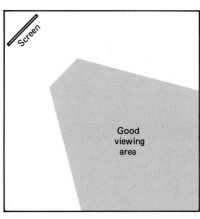

▲ **Figure 10.13**
In a rather square room, placement of the screen in the corner creates a larger good viewing area.

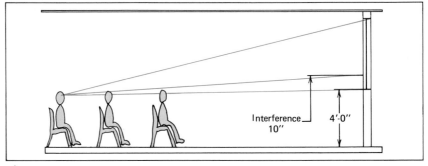

▲ **Figure 10.14**
The bottom of the screen should be above head level to avoid obstruction of the view.

Corner placement is especially advantageous in a room that is square or nearly so. As illustrated by Figure 10.13, placing the screen in one corner allows more viewers to be seated in the good viewing area.

In any case, nowhere is it written in stone that the screen must be placed front and center. Position your screen wherever it will best suit your purpose.

The height of the screen should generally be adjusted so that the *bottom* of the screen is about level with the heads of the seated viewers. The bottom of the screen should be at least four feet above the floor to prevent excessive head interference as illustrated in Figure 10.14. Other inhibiting factors aside, this arrangement will allow reasonably clear sight lines for the most viewers. In general, the higher the screen, the greater the optimal viewing area. Of course, care

must be taken that the screen can be seen without viewers uncomfortably craning their necks.

Lamps

Types. There are three types of projection lamps: incandescent, tungsten halogen, and tungsten halogen with surrounding reflector. The incandescent lamps should be watched because they have a tendency to blister. Such blisters can become so big that the lamp cannot be removed from the projector. If the lamp does blister to the extent that it must be broken for removal, an audiovisual technician should be contacted. In addition to the blistering problem, the incandescent lamps require more wattage for the same light output.

▲ **Figure 10.15**
Projection lamps come in a wide variety of sizes and shapes; when they burn out they must be replaced with a matching type.

▲ **Figure 10.16**
Avoid directly touching both burned-out lamps (because they may be hot) and replacement lamps (because the oil on fingertips can encourage blistering of the lamp).

The first innovative response to incandescent blistering was the tungsten halogen lamp. These lamps do not blister as incandescent lamps do, but they do require the same high wattage and thus have the associated heat problems and fan noise.

The newest type of lamps are the tungsten halogen lamps with surrounding reflectors. These lamps generally operate at one-half the wattage of the incandescent or tungsten halogen lamps.

Coding. Projection lamps are labeled with a three-letter ANSI (American National Standard Institute) code. This code is printed on the lamp and on the box. In addition, many projectors now have stickers in the lamp housing of the projectors with the ANSI code stating which lamp should be used in that projector.

Replacement of Lamps.
When replacing a lamp, the replacement should be a lamp with the same ANSI code or an authorized substitute. Substitutes can be found in replacement guides written by the lamp manufacturers. These guides are available from the manufacturers or from local audiovisual dealers. NOTE: Do *not* use higher wattage lamps than specified. You may burn the materials in the projector!

Handling a Lamp. When handling a lamp, *never* touch the clear glass bulb. The oils from your fingers can shorten the life of the lamp. The lamp should always be manipulated by its base. The incandescent lamps and the tungsten halogen lamp (without exterior reflector) are supplied with a piece of foam or paper around the lamp. This wrap or a cloth should be used to hold the lamp when it is inserted into the projector.

When removing a burned-out lamp, wait until the lamp has cooled to prevent injuring your fingers. It is wise to always use a cloth when removing a lamp. A word of caution— even a lamp that burns out when the

projector is first turned on will be hot enough to burn. So use a cloth!

Expense. Lamps are expensive. They usually cost about twenty times the cost of a household light bulb. Since the average lamp life is fifty hours, projectors should be turned off when not in use. If the projector offers a low-lamp setting, use it if possible to increase the life of the lamp. A projector should not be jarred when the lamp is on as this can cause a premature burnout of the lamp. You should not leave the fan on for cooling after use unless the projector is going to be moved immediately, as this also will shorten the life of the bulb.

Lenses
For everyday media use you do not have to pay much attention to technicalities about lenses. Whatever lens your projector is equipped with is usually sufficient. However, understanding some basic ideas about lenses can help you cope with extraordinary situations.

First, lenses vary in focal length (measured in inches in the United States, in millimeters elsewhere). *The longer the focal length, the smaller the image* at a given distance. Since your objective is to project an image that will fill the screen, this means that the shorter the projection throw, the shorter the lens (in terms of focal length) that will be needed to enlarge the projected image sufficiently. Fortunately, the actual length of most lenses corresponds roughly with their focal length; the longer of two lenses

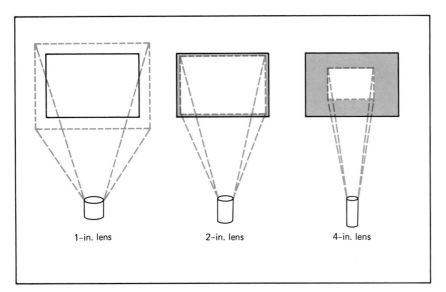

◀ **Figure 10.17**
The longer the focal length of the lens, the smaller the image.

▼ **Figure 10.18**
The varied types of projector carts are suited for different purposes.

will have the longer focal length. Figure 10.17 illustrates the relationship of lens focal length to the size of its projected image.

One type of lens has a variable focal length—the zoom lens. It can, therefore, be adjusted to cast a larger or smaller picture without moving the projector or changing its lens. The most commonly encountered zoom lens (found on many slide projectors) has a focal-length range of 4 to 6 inches.

When precise specifications are needed in selecting lenses for particular conditions, media specialists use calculation devices prepared by manufacturers, such as the *Da-Lite Lens-Projection Screen Calculator* or Kodak's *Projection Calculator and Seating Guide*.

Projection Tables and Carts

Projection tables have legs and are meant to be used in one position. The portable projection table is designed to be folded up and moved to another location and reassembled. Its legs telescope so that the projector can be as high as five feet from the ground. When the table is folded up, the typical package dimension of 30 inches × 12 inches × 3 inches makes

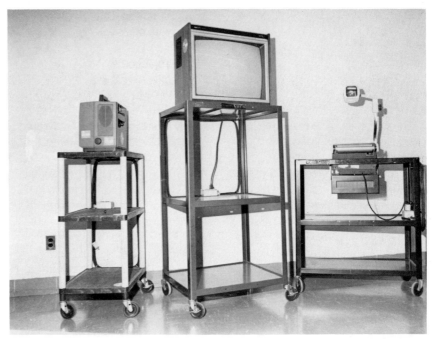

it easily transportable.

Carts come with wheels that allow the equipment to be set up and easily moved. The carts are designed both for inside-only use and inside/outside use. You take a great risk in moving equipment out-of-doors on a cart designed for inside use. The small wheels can catch in cracks in sidewalks and cause the cart to tip over. For this reason, even for exclusive indoor use it is wise to purchase carts with 5-inch casters.

Manufacturers normally offer power outlet cord assemblies for their carts. These are worthwhile investments. You plug your projector

into the outlet on the cart and the cord on the cart into the wall outlet. If someone should trip over the power cord, he or she moves the cart, but does not pull the projector onto the floor. In addition, the cord on the cart is considerably longer than the typical power cord furnished with the equipment. The longer cord can be laid on the floor along the wall, thereby reducing the risk that someone will trip over it.

Features of Carts. Carts have a number of possible features related to location of use, construction materials, degree of enclosure, and type of equipment with which the cart can be used. We have already discussed the location of use—inside or outside.

Projection carts are constructed of both metal and plastic. A metal cart should be welded together instead of bolted. The nuts on the bolts will become loose over time and the cart will become very unstable. Plastic carts, while not as stable as welded metal carts, have a number of advantages. They are much lighter and less expensive than metal carts. Some plastic carts can be disassembled and placed in the trunk of a car.

Projection carts have varying degrees of enclosure. The basic cart has no enclosed cabinets. Cabinets provide for security of materials and protection from dust during storage.

Some carts are designed for specific projectors. For example, overhead projector carts have adjustable-depth wells into which the projectors can be placed. They are 26 inches high for use in seated positions and 39 inches high to be used while standing. Low carts are to be used with opaque projectors. Carts 34 inches and 42 inches high are used with 16-mm, 8-mm, slide, and filmstrip projectors. Video equipment carts have heights of 39 inches, 42 inches, and 54 inches. The lower carts can be used for "production centers" (recorder and monitor mounted on the cart) to be moved from one classroom to another. The 54-inch carts are used to hold large 19-inch, 21-inch, and 25-inch television monitors. Since these carts tend to be somewhat unstable, caution must be exercised when moving them.

Projector Placement

The first requirement in projector placement is to align the projection lens perpendicular to the screen (that is, it must make a 90-degree angle

with the screen). Thus, the lens of the projector should be about level with the middle of the screen. If the projector is too high, too low, or off to either side, a distortion of the image will occur, referred to as the "keystone effect." The effect takes its name from the typical shape of a keystoned image—wide at the top, narrower at the bottom, like a keystone. Figure 10.19 illustrates this problem and its remedy: Move either the projector or the screen to bring the two into a perpendicular relationship.

The keystone effect is especially prevalent with the overhead projector because it is ordinarily set up very close to the screen and far lower than the screen (to allow the instructor to write on its stage). For this reason, many screens used for overhead projection are equipped with a "keystone eliminator," a notched bar at the top that allows the screen to be tilted forward (see Figure 10.20).

Once you have properly aligned the projector and screen, consider distance between projector and screen. If the distance is too long, the image will spill over the edges of the screen. If it is too short, the image will not fill the screen properly. Your goal is to fill the screen as fully as possible with the brightest image possible. The principle to remember here is that the image becomes *larger and less brilliant* with increase in distance between projector and screen. If the projected image is too large for your screen, push the projector closer. If the image is too small, pull the projector back.

Positioning a projector at the proper distance from the screen need not be done solely by trial-and-error. Since classroom-type projectors usually are fitted with certain focal-length lenses, their proper placement can be estimated in advance. Figure 10.21 shows the place-

▼ **Figure 10.19**
The "keystone effect"—its causes and its remedies.

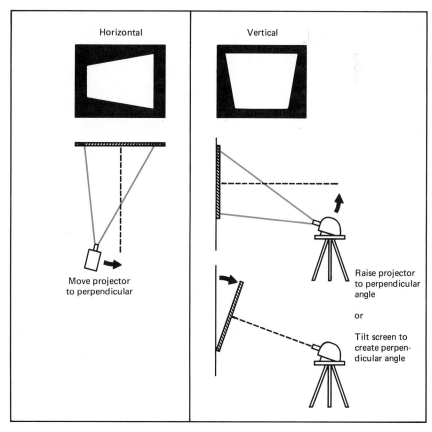

ment of the overhead, slide, and 16-mm film projectors when they are equipped with their most typical lenses.

However, it is best to place all projectors, except the overhead and the opaque, behind the audience to prevent people from tripping over the power cords. For the same reason, extension cords should be used so that the power cords can be run along the wall to the outlet rather than across the center of the room.

The projection distances described here assume appropriate lighting conditions. Where the room light is so bright that it is washing out the screen image and it cannot be dimmed any further, you must move the projector forward. This will give you a brighter image, but also, unfortunately, a smaller one. In some cases, however, it may be possible to compensate for this reduction in image size by having your audience move closer to the screen.

SOUND SYNCHRONIZATION

Cassette player/recorders with sound synchronizing capability allow you to play an audio tape that is coordinated with a set of slides or a filmstrip. As shown in Figure 10.23, the synchronizers designed primarily for use with slide projectors use two tracks on the audio tape, one for the narration and the other to synchronize the material. These units use a 1000 Hertz signal for changing the slide and a 150 Hertz signal to stop the playback of the cassette tape. A button must then be pushed to restart the tape.

The synchronization units designed to be used with filmstrip projectors do not have the "pause" feature. They often are built into a single piece of equipment along with the filmstrip projector. This system uses an *inaudible* 50 Hertz signal to trigger

▲ **Figure 10.22**
A typical sound-slide synchronization setup.

the change from one frame of the filmstrip to another. This signal is "buried" within the narration (see Figure 10.24). Thus, only one track on the tape is needed. Generally, the other track of the tape (which is reached by turning over the cassette) contains a recording of the audio material with an audible signal to tell you when to change to the next frame of the filmstrip if your filmstrip projector lacks an automatic advance mechanism. The tape will be labeled "inaudible signal" or "50 Hz signal" on one side and "audible signal" on the other.

Please note that the 1000 Hz system is NOT compatible with the 50 Hz system. To solve this problem, the manufacturers have produced cassette player/recorders that will record and play back the 1000 Hz system and only play back the 50 Hz system. These units do not come as a single piece of equipment. You must have the appropriate cords to connect the cassette unit to your slide projector or to your filmstrip projector. Your audiovisual equipment dealer can supply the correct cords for your cassette unit with the appropriate plugs for your projectors.

Of course, your show can *stay* in the proper synchronization only if it *starts* in synchronization. Check to be sure the sequence starts on the proper frame.

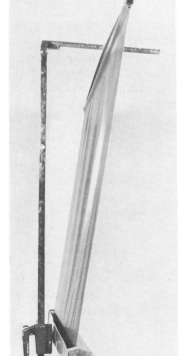

◀ **Figure 10.20**
Portable tripod screen with "keystone eliminator."

▼ **Figure 10.21**
Approximate placement of projectors when equipped with typical lenses.

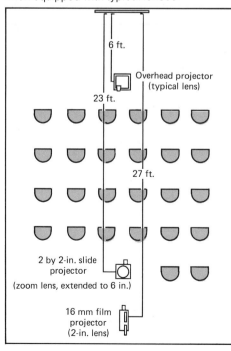

6 ft.

Overhead projector (typical lens)

23 ft.

27 ft.

2 by 2-in. slide projector
(zoom lens, extended to 6 in.)

16 mm film projector
(2-in. lens)

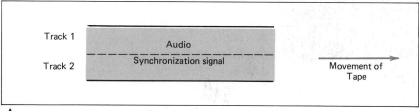

▲ **Figure 10.23**
Tape configuration for cassette sound-slide synchronization.

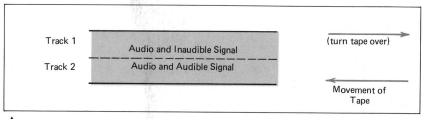

Track 1
Track 2
Audio and Inaudible Signal
Audio and Audible Signal
(turn tape over)
Movement of Tape

▲ **Figure 10.24**
Tape configuration for synchronized sound filmstrips.

Single-Unit Projectors

Most of the single-piece projectors with cassette player and filmstrip unit are for front projection. There are other units that have built-in rear screens for individual viewing. Some of these allow you to open a small door for front projection. Since these projectors have very short focal length lens, you must place the projector close to the screen. This means that the light and sound will "spill" from the machine into the middle of your audience.

Single-piece units also are available for use with slides using the 1000 Hz system. Some units have dissolve-control devices built into them. They allow for a variable rate of dissolve to be used either through digital coding or altering the pitch of the synchronizing signal. Units from different manufacturers are generally not compatible.

Automatic Programmers

All of the aforementioned slide projector units allow for an external control signal to be "written" on the tape by a programmer. However, you do need a programmer or a "reader" to interpret the signals coming from the tape when you play it back. The programmer/reader causes projectors to advance/reverse and to dissolve at various rates, and causes auxiliary units to turn projectors or lights on and off. The programmers include independent units, units combined with a dissolve unit, and units that use microcomputers. If you decide to get involved in this area of multi-image/multi-media, you should work with an expert consultant.

FILM PROJECTORS

Since film projectors and 16-mm films are comparatively expensive instruments of instruction (the typical half-hour educational film costs about $450), it is particularly important for instructors to prolong the life of these items by taking proper care of them.

The average life of an acetate-based film is approximately 100 showings. The newer mylar-based film has the potential for 1,000 showings. Mishandling, however, can greatly reduce this span of service. On the other hand, careful threading, inspection after each use, periodic lubrication of the film, and proper storage (at room temperature, 40 percent humidity) can lengthen the working life of the film.

Proper care of the projector can also help extend the service span of film. It is important to keep the projector's film path clean to prevent undue wear on the film. An aperture brush or other soft-bristled, nonmetalic brush should be used regularly to clean the film path, the film gate, and around the sound drum.

The lens of the projector should be kept free of dust and smudges by periodic cleaning with lens tissue and cleaner. The projector's volume and tone control mechanisms sometimes develop internal carbon buildup, causing crackling sounds when the knobs are turned to adjust audio. This debris can generally be eliminated simply by spraying around the external extensions of the control knobs with an aerosol tuner cleaner while turning the knobs.

Given the electro-mechanical complexity of the film projector, you should not go much beyond these routine cleaning procedures to help keep your projector in good working order.

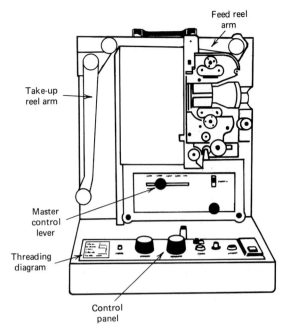

Feed reel arm

Take-up reel arm

Master control lever

Threading diagram

Control panel

Set up (refer to Figure 10.26)

- Unbuckle and separate speaker from projector.
- Swing *feed reel arm* up and into position.
- Raise *take-up reel arm* into position.
- Attach drive belt onto pulley on take-up reel arm.
- Place take-up *reel* on spindle and lock spindle.
- Plug power cord into AC outlet.
- Plug *speaker* or headphones into speaker jack.
- Place *film* on feed reel arm spindle and lock spindle.
- Unwind about 5 feet of film.

Threading

- Check to be sure that "rewind" lever is in raised position.
- Follow threading diagram printed on projector. On the Kodak Pageant projector, the steps are as follows:

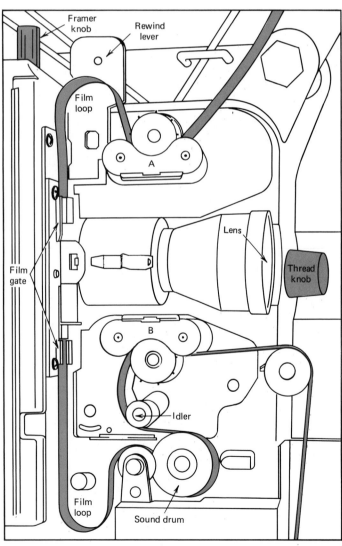

Framer knob

Rewind lever

Film loop

A

Lens

Thread knob

Film gate

B

Idler

Film loop

Sound drum

1. Open clamps around upper and lower drive sprockets. See (A) and (B) on diagram.
2. Turn thread knob until white line faces you.
3. Loop film under *upper sprocket* (A) and engage teeth with sprocket holes in film; then close clamp.
4. Open *film gate* and slide film into channel so that it is flat.
5. Close film gate by pressing in on clamp.
6. Form a loop to match red line on rewind lever or to the top of the lever.
7. Bring film around black *bottom* roller to form loop.
8. Thread film over *pressure roller* and around *sound drum*.
9. Thread film around idler and over lower sprocket (B).
10. Engage sprocket holes with teeth on sprocket (B) and close clamp.
11. Thread film around three remaining *idler rollers*—if more film is needed, turn master control briefly to "motor."
12. Insert end of film leader into slot of empty take-up reel.
13. Double check threading diagram to ensure that film is properly threaded.
14. Rotate threading knob clockwise to check film loops.

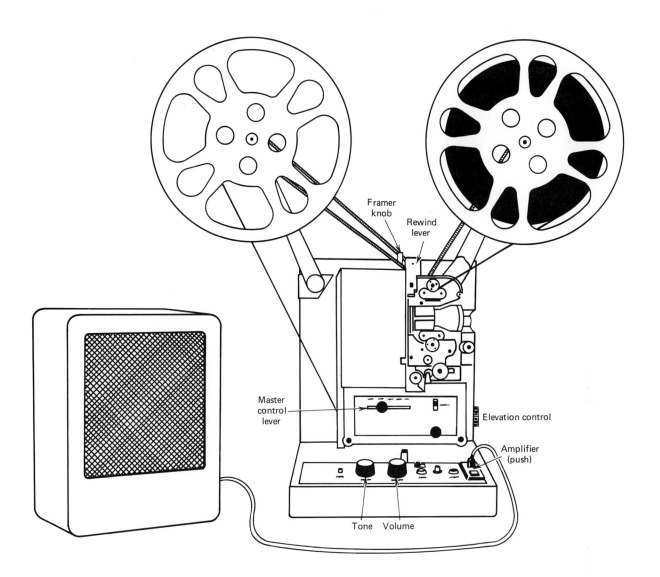

Framer knob

Rewind lever

Master control lever

Elevation control

Amplifier (push)

Tone   Volume

Operate
- Turn amplifier "on."
- Move *master control lever* to "motor," then to "lamp."
- Position image on screen by moving projector and adjusting the elevation control.
- *Focus* image by turning lens.
- Adjust volume and tone.
- Rotate *framer knob* if image is not framed properly.
- You may *reverse* film by pulling master control lever to "off," then "reverse."
- Run film *forward* until all film has run through projector.
- Turn master control lever to "off."

Rewind
- Secure end of film in slot of feed reel, and take up slack.
- Pull *rewind lever* down.
- Move master control to "rewind/forward" position, *not* "reverse."
- When film has been rewound onto feed reel, turn master control lever to "off" and lift rewind lever to "up" position.
- Turn amplifier "off."

Disassemble
- Push rear arm forward to remove belt.
- Lower feed reel arm.
- Press release lever and carefully lower take-up arm.
- Return projector and speaker to storage conformation.

Film Projector Troubleshooting

Problem	Possible Remedy
Projector runs but lamp doesn't light	First, be sure that you have turned the operation lever all the way on. It should be in the "Lamp" position. If the lamp doesn't light after being properly switched on, it is possible that it is burnt out and needs to be replaced.
Projector runs but there is no sound	1. Be sure that the "Amplifier" switch is turned on. 2. Be sure that the speaker is plugged in. 3. Check to see that the film is threaded properly around the sound drum. 4. Check the other switches, such as "Sound/Silent" and "Micro./Film." If there is still no sound after checking all the above steps, it is likely that the exciter lamp is burnt out and needs to be replaced.
Distorted sound	Make sure that the film is wound tightly around the sound drum.
Flowing blur instead of an image	The film is not properly engaged in the gate. Be sure that the sprockets are meshing with the sprocket holes and that the film gate is closed.
Fuzz around edges of projected image	Dirt and lint collect easily around the aperture (due to the static electricity created by moving film). The film gate should be cleaned with a brush before each showing. If dirt is causing distraction during a showing, it can be cleared away by blowing into the aperture area. This is not recommended as a routine cleaning practice (since the moisture in your breath can harm lenses and delicate metal parts), only as a "quick fix" in an emergency.
Projector chatters noisily	Lower loop has been lost. Stop the projector and reform the loop, or press down on the loop restorer while the projector continues running.
Film breaks	Stop the projector. If possible, determine and correct the cause. Then rethread the film. The broken end should be overlapped on the take-up reel. Mark the break by inserting a slip of paper into the reel at this point. Do *not* attempt to repair the break with tape, pins, paper clips, etc.
Voice not synchronized with image (lips)	The lower loop is either too tight or too loose, causing the sound track to pass over the sound drum either before or after the image is projected in the aperture. Adjust the lower loop.

VIDEOTAPE RECORDERS

Video record/playback machines are highly sophisticated electronic instruments. Maintenance and repair, consequently, should generally be left to the specialist. In addition, videotape recording systems are far from standardized in their various mechanisms and modes of operation. You should therefore, refer to the manufacturer's manual for information about the operating principles and procedures of the particular system you happen to be using. The "Troubleshooting" guide included here is limited to general sorts of problems that may occur with virtually any video system and that can be remedied by the nonspecialist.

Videotape Recorder Troubleshooting

Problem	Possible Remedy
Recording. Videotape is running but there is no picture on the monitor	1. Check to see that all components are plugged in and turned on. Make sure the lens cap is off the camera and the lens aperture is open. 2. Check the monitor. Switch it to "TV" and try to tune in a broadcast channel; make sure the brightness and contrast controls are properly set. If you still fail to get a picture, check to see if there is a circuit breaker on the back of the monitor that needs to be reset. If you get a picture while switched to "TV" you should then check the connection between camera and monitor. 3. Check the cable connections from camera to recorder and from recorder to monitor. 4. Check the settings of the switches on the recorder. Is the input selector on "Camera?" Is the "Record" button depressed?
Playback. Videotape is running but there is no picture or sound on monitor	1. Make sure the monitor input selector is set at "VTR" and all units are plugged in. 2. Check connectors between playback unit and monitor (e.g., make sure "Video Out" from playback is connected to "Video In" on monitor). Wiggle the end of the cable to see if there is a loose connection. 3. Check switches on playback unit.
Fuzzy sound and/or snowy picture	1. Video and/or audio heads may be fouled. Clean with approved spray. 2. Brushes under head-drum cover may be fouled or damaged. Have a technician check this possibility.
Picture slants horizontally across screen (the audio may also sound off-speed)	If adjustment of the horizontal hold knob does not clear up the situation, you may have a tape or cassette that is incompatible with your playback unit. Obtain a playback machine that matches the format of the tape or cassette.

Physical Arrangements

Before students can learn from any instructional TV presentation they first have to be able to see it and hear it! Provide proper lighting, seating, and volume control.

Seating and Monitor Placement.

An ideal seating arrangement for ITV may sometimes be difficult to achieve. Because of economic constraints, there are often not enough television sets available to give every student an adequate view. Ideally, one 23-inch-screen TV set should serve no more than 30 students seated at desks in an aisled classroom. If conditions are not ideal, the best you can do is do your best. If feasible, seats may be shared or moved closer together so that all may have at least an adequate view of the screen. If possible, stagger seats to help prevent view blockage.

Here are some basic rules of thumb for good seating arrangement (see Figure 10.25):

- Seat no one closer than 7 feet from the receiver.
- Seat no one farther away (in feet) than the size of the TV screen (in inches).
- Seat no one more than 45 degrees from the center axis of the screen.
- Place the TV set no more than 30 degrees above the normal eye level of any seated viewer to avoid having viewers crane their necks uncomfortably.

▼ **Figure 10.25**
Recommended monitor placement and seating distances for TV viewing.

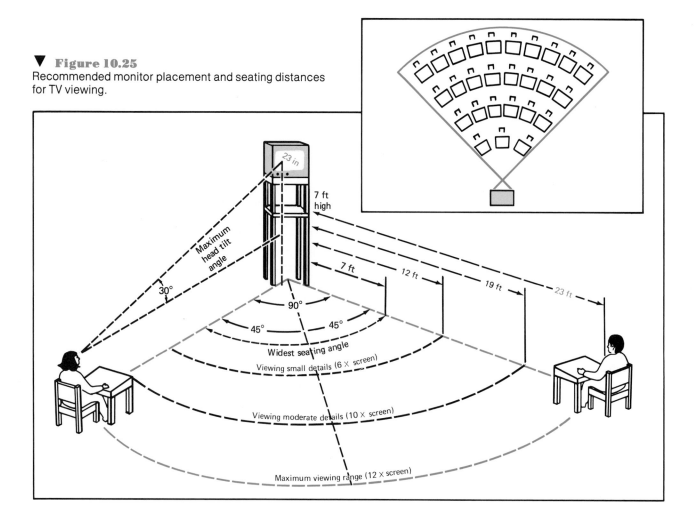

Monitor Placement.

When locating television monitors for instructional viewing, you need to consider the amount of detail to be shown on the screen. As illustrated in Figure 10.25, a distance of no more than six times the size of the monitor is best if *small details* are important. Examples might include studying computer output, reading small captions, and televised viewing through a microscope using a high-resolution camera. For a 23-inch monitor, the acceptable viewing range would be from 7 feet to 12 feet.

Viewers should be no further than ten times the monitor size if *moderate details* are important.

If details are not critical, as in the case of people and landscapes, the farthest viewer can be back as far as twelve times the monitor size. For a 23-inch monitor, the maximum range would be 23 feet (unless details are important).

Sample room arrangements indicating placement of television monitors are shown in Figure 10.26. In addition to the distance of the viewers from the monitor, you must also consider the height of the monitor. For group viewing a 54-inch-high stand or cart works best.

Lighting.
Television should be viewed in normal or dim light, not darkness. Besides being more comfortable to the eye, normal illumination provides necessary light for student participative activities, for referring to handouts, and for occasional note taking.

The television receiver should be located so that harsh light from a window or light fixture cannot strike the screen and cause glare. Do not place the receiver in front of an unshaded window that will compete with light from the television screen and make viewing difficult.

Volume.
For proper hearing, the volume of the receiver should be set loud enough to be heard clearly in the rear of the viewing area, but not so loud that it bowls over those in the front. Normally this happy middle ground is not difficult to achieve—if your seating arrangement is within acceptable bounds and your receiver's speaker mechanism is functioning properly.

Appraisal Checklist: Equipment

Type:_____   Price:_____

Make:_____   Model:_____

Audio

Speaker size:_____   Amplifier output:_____

Inputs	Outputs
_____	_____
_____	_____

Sound controls	Tape
_____	Size:_____ Tracks:_____
_____	Speeds:_____

Other features:

Projector

Lamp:_____   (wattage_____)   Exciter lamp:_____

Power controls	Lamp level control
_____	_____
_____	_____

Lens:_____

Other features:

Rating	High		Medium		Low	**Strong points:**	**Weak points:**
Sound quality	☐	☐	☐	☐	☐		
Picture quality	☐	☐	☐	☐	☐		
Ease of operation	☐	☐	☐	☐	☐		
Price range	☐	☐	☐	☐	☐		
Durability	☐	☐	☐	☐	☐		
Ease to maintain	☐	☐	☐	☐	☐		
Ease to repair	☐	☐	☐	☐	☐		

Accessories: Reviewer_____

                                                                                    Position_____

Recommended action_____   Date_____

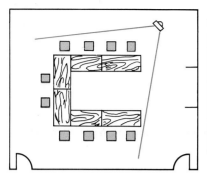
Small Conference Room

Classroom

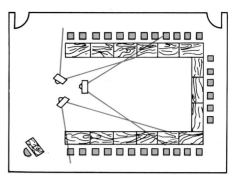
Large Training Room

▲ **Figure 10.26**
TV monitor placements for typical viewing situations.

Obviously, volume should be kept low enough so as not to disturb neighboring classes. Unfortunately, contemporary "open plan" buildings with only movable room dividers as walls provide a poor environment for TV or other audiovisual presentations. Under such conditions cooperation is critical. Teachers in neighboring areas can mutually agree to lower their decibel level to minimize interference (better than escalating the problem by trying to drown each other out!). Sometimes the only alternative is to seek out an enclosed room that can be reserved for audiovisual use.

References

Print References

Alten, Stanley R. *Audio in Media*. (Belmont, Calif.: Wadsworth Publications, 1981).

Bullard, John R., and Mether, Calvin E. *Audiovisual Fundamentals: Basic Equipment Operation, Simple Materials Production*. 3d ed. (Dubuque, Iowa: Wm. C. Brown, 1984).

Crocker, A. H. "Equipment for Individual Learning." *Educational Media International* (March 1977), pp. 2–6.

Educational Products Information Exchange (EPIE). *Videocassette Recorders/Players*, Report no. 89e. (Water Mill, N.Y. EPIE Institute, 1979).

_____. *Audio Cassette Players*, Report no. 91e (Water Mill, N.Y.: EPIE Institute, 1980).

The Equipment Directory of Audio-Visual, Computer and Video Products. (Fairfax, Va.: NAVA, the International Communications Industries Assn., annual).

Johnson, Warren. "Resources for Hardware Selection." *Audiovisual Instruction* (April 1978), pp. 46–47.

King, Kenneth L., et al. *A Systematic Approach to Instructional Media Competency*. 4th ed. (Dubuque, Iowa: Kendall/Hunt, 1981).

Knirk, Frederick G. *Designing Productive Learning Environments*. (Englewood Cliffs, N.J.: Educational Technology Publications, 1979).

Kodak Projection Calculator and Seating Guide (S-16). (Rochester, N.Y.: Eastman Kodak, 1979).

Le Clerq, Angie. "Wide Screen Television Projection Systems." *Library Technology Reports* (July-August 1983), pp. 395–442.

Lord, Kenniston W., Jr. *The Design of the Industrial Classroom*. (Reading, Mass.: Addison-Wesley, 1977).

McVey, Gerald F. "Environments for Effective Media Utilization: Some Design Considerations." *Viewpoints* (September 1975), pp. 59–77.

Magee, John L. "Before You Call for Service, Try These Simple AV Repairs." *American School and University* (May 1981), pp. 126–129.

Meisel, Susan Lee. "A Hard Look at Audiovisual Equipment." *Media and Methods* (October 1983), pp. 9–11, 48.

Minimum Specifications for 16-mm Sound Film Projectors. (The Hague, Netherlands: International Council for Educational Media, 1982).

Minimum Specifications for Slide Projectors. (The Hague, Netherlands: International Council for Educational Media, 1980).

Rosenberg, Kenyon C., *Dictionary of Library and Educational Technology*. 2d ed. (Littleton, Colo.: Libraries Unlimited, 1983).

Rowat, Robert W. "A Guide to the Use of the Overhead Projector." ERIC, 1982. ED 211109.

Sakovich, Vladimir, and Costello, William. "Work Horses or White Elephants: A Guide to Selecting AV Equipment." *Media and Methods* (January 1980), pp. 26–29, 60–61.

Schroeder, Don, and Lare, Gary. *Audiovisual Equipment and Materials: A Basic Repair and Maintenance Manual*. (Metuchen, N.J.: Scarecrow Press, 1979).

Stafford, Carl W. "Standardize Your Adapters." *Instructional Innovator* (May 1980), pp. 26–28.

Sturken, Marita. "Video Systems for Libraries." *Sightlines* (Spring 1983), pp. 25–26.

Sullivan, Sam, and Baker, Bryan. *A Handbook of Operating Information and Simplified Maintenance Instructions for Commonly Used Audio-visual Equipment*." Rev. ed. (Huntsville, Tx.: KBS, Inc., 1982).

Teague, Fred A.; Newhouse, Barbara S.; and Streit, Les D. *Instructional Media Basics*. (Dubuque, Iowa: Kendall/Hunt, 1982).

Wadsworth, Raymond H. *Basics of Audio and Visual Systems Design*. (Indianapolis: Howard W. Sams, 1983).

Waggener, Joe, and Tim Kraft. "Video Troubleshooting for the Technically Butterfingered." *Audiovisual Instruction* (January 1979), pp. 44–45.

Wilkinson, Gene L. "Projection Variables and Performance." *AV Communication Review* (Winter 1976), pp. 413–436.

Wilshusen, John. "How to Prevent Equipment Failures." *Instructional Innovator* (March 1980), pp. 35–36.

Wyman, Raymond. *Mediaware: Selection, Operation, and Maintenance*. 2d ed. (Dubuque, Iowa: Wm. C. Brown, 1976).

Yeamans, George T. *Projectionists' Primer*. (Pullman, Wash.: Information Futures, 1979).

Organizations

EPIE (Educational Products Information Exchange) Institute, P.O. Box 839, Water Mill, New York 11976

EPIE is a nonprofit, consumer-supported agency functioning like a "consumer's union" and providing analytical information about instructional materials and equipment. EPIE conducts workshops on analyzing instructional materials and publishes *EPIE Reports* bimonthly and a newsletter, *EPIEgram*.

International Communications Industries Association (NAVA), 3150 Spring Street, Fairfax, Virginia 22031

Trade association for producers and distributors of audiovisual equipment and materials. Publishes annually *The Equipment Directory of Audio-Visual, Computer and Video Products*.

Possible Projects

10-A. Demonstrate the proper setup, operation, and disassembly of the following pieces of equipment: tape recorder (reel-to-reel and cassette), record player, overhead projector, slide projector, filmstrip projector, opaque projector, 16-mm film projector and video tape recorder.

10-B. Given a piece of equipment from the list in Project 10-A with a "problem," troubleshoot and correct the problem.

10-C. Demonstrate proper care and maintenance for each piece of equipment listed in Project 10-A.

10-D. Set up (or diagram the setup) for a given instructional situation requiring audio, projection, and/or video.

10-E. Demonstrate the proper procedures for replacing lamps in the following types of projectors: overhead, slide, filmstrip, opaque, and film. You will be evaluated on selecting the correct replacement lamp and on handling it properly.

10-F. Procure catalogs illustrating projection tables and carts, identify examples from each of the functions described in the chapter, and compare the examples in terms of versatility of use, advantages, limitations, and cost.

10-G. Synchronize a set of slides and an audio tape. You may use existing slides, but you must record the narrative on the tape and incorporate the advance pulses into the system.

10-H. Evaluate a piece of audiovisual equipment using the "Appraisal Checklist: Equipment" in the chapter.

Technologies
of Instruction

Outline

Objectives

After studying this chapter, you should be able to:

1. Define "technologies of instruction" and identify five characteristics of such a "technology."

2. Identify five examples of "technologies of instruction."

3. Discuss the basic application of reinforcement theory, including a definition of "reinforcer."

4. Describe the relationship between "teaching machines" and "programmed instruction."

5. Identify five attributes of today's programmed instruction and distinguish programmed instruction from other forms of instruction.

6. Distinguish between "linear" and "branching" formats of programmed instruction.

7. Describe an appropriate application of programmed instruction in an instructional setting.

8. Generate five guidelines for using programmed instruction in the classroom.

9. Describe "programmed tutoring," indicating what it is, how it is used, and an instructional situation in which it could be applied.

10. Discuss why the Personalized System of Instruction is a technology for *managing* instruction and compare and contrast PSI with the other technologies of instruction.

11. List the three types of sessions used in the A-T System and briefly describe the purpose of each.

12. Define "instructional module" and identify six components of a module.

13. Justify why instructional simulations and games can be considered as technologies of instruction.

14. Justify why the computer itself is *not* a technology of instruction as defined in this chapter.

15. Synthesize an instructional situation in which *one* of the technologies of instruction could be used effectively. Your description should indicate both *how* and *when* you would use it.

Lexicon

reinforcement theory
programmed instruction
programmed tutoring
Personalized System of Instruction (PSI)
Audio-Tutorial System (A-T)
instructional module
simulation
game
computer-assisted instruction (CAI)

American economist John Kenneth Galbraith defines *technology* as "the systematic application of scientific or other organized knowledge to practical tasks."* This view of the concept of technology correctly focuses on technology as a *process*, an approach to solving problems, rather than on the *products* of technology—computers, transistors, satellites, bionic devices, and the like. Unfortunately, the debate over the role of technology in education has too often been clouded by a tendency to concentrate on the role of artifacts such as audiovisual hardware, television transmission systems, "teaching machines," and so on. Advocates and critics alike have too often assumed that there is some sort of "magic" inherent in these artifacts. The only question seems to have been whether this "magic" was helpful or harmful to students, teachers, and educational institutions.

This is not to denigrate the educational value of the products of technology. Indeed, much of this book is devoted to helping you choose among these products and use them for more effective teaching and learning. But there is nothing magical about the hardware. The magic, if there is to be magic, stems from the selection of materials according to their usefulness in achieving specific learning objectives and their utilization in ways conducive to applying sound learning principles.

---

*John Kenneth Galbraith. *The New Industrial State*. Boston: Houghton-Mifflin, 1967, p. 12.

This chapter, therefore, highlights *technology as a process*. It will extend Galbraith's definition into the realm of education, showing ways in which materials and activities can be combined to allow a "systematic application of scientific knowledge." These special arrangements we will refer to as *technologies of instruction*.

A TECHNOLOGY OF INSTRUCTION: a teaching/learning pattern designed to provide reliable, effective instruction to each learner through application of scientific principles of human learning.

We use this term in the plural because many different arrangements could merit this label. The six examples of technologies of instruction explored in this chapter do not by any means constitute a full listing of all technologies of instruction; they are intended merely to be representative of some of the most common formats in widespread use today. Criterion-referenced instruction, competency-based education, and mastery learning are names given to instructional formats that could be classified as technologies of instruction. They share many features in common with each other and in common with the formats elaborated on in this chapter. The four formats discussed in depth in this chapter are programmed instruction, programmed tutoring, the Personalized System of Instruction, and Audio-Tutorial Systems. Two other technologies of instruction alluded to only briefly here are examined in detail in the two following chapters—simulation and gaming and computer-assisted instruction.

THE ROOTS OF TODAY'S TECHNOLOGIES OF INSTRUCTION

Many of today's methods of instruction have roots in theories that are hundreds or even thousands of years old. Socrates, Comenius, Pestalozzi, and Herbart would find many of their own ideas clearly reflected in contemporary classroom practices. But the body of theory that influenced most strongly the development of today's technologies of instruction is of much more recent origin. In fact, many regard an article published in 1954 in *Harvard Educational Review* as the catalyst that sparked a whole new movement in education. In that article, the author, psychologist B. F. Skinner, challenged educators to modify their traditional practices to put into effect new principles of learning that were emerging from studies in experimental psychology.

Basic Concepts of Reinforcement Theory

Skinner's body of theory, which he referred to as "operant conditioning" but is generally known as reinforcement theory, differs from earlier behaviorist theories in that it applies to voluntary behaviors. He claimed that earlier stimulus-response paradigms were adequate for explaining reflexive responses such as salivation, dilation of the pupil of the eye, the knee-jerk reflex, and the like. However, he was more interested in explaining responses that people emit voluntarily,

---

*B. F. Skinner. "The Science of Learning and the Art of Teaching. *Harvard Educational Review* (Spring 1954), pp. 86–97.

▲ **Figure 11.1**
Psychologist B.F. Skinner whose theory of operant conditioning game impetus to the development of programmed instruction.

Transferring these basic concepts (overt response, followed by reinforcement) to formal human learning requires adding another element to the formula—a *prompt*. Rather than waiting around for a desired response to occur spontaneously or randomly, the instructional material can be structured to hint at or prompt the desired response. The basic formula for applying reinforcement theory to human learning, then, requires a prompt, an overt response, and a reinforcement. For example:

1. PROMPT (e.g., math problem)
   ↓
2. RESPONSE (e.g., correct answer)
   ↓
3. REINFORCEMENT (e.g., knowledge of correct response and/or praise)

such as driving a car, writing a letter, and balancing a checkbook.

The backbone of Skinner's theories was the concept of reinforcement. He hypothesized that the *consequences* of a response determine whether or not it will be learned. That is, a behavior that is followed by a satisfying consequence is more likely to occur in the future. Giving such a satisfying consequence is referred to as *reinforcement*.

A reinforcer is any event or thing that increases the likelihood of a preceding behavior's being repeated: learned. This phrasing is intended to point out that a thing is a reinforcer only if it *works*. An object may be desirable or satisfying to one person at one time but not to another person or at another time. For instance, a chocolate bar might sound quite inviting to you right now, but not if you are a diabetic or are on a diet or have just finished eating a big box of candy.

Also fundamental to reinforcement theory is the notion that complex skills can be broken down into clusters of simpler behaviors. Each behavior bit can be learned one at a time through skillful arrangement for immediate reinforcement after each correct response. These simple behaviors then become links in a longer, more complex behavior chain. Skinner was able to demonstrate this process dramatically by teaching a pigeon to turn a complete circle clockwise within just a single demonstration session. Closely observing the pigeon's behavior, he rewarded every partial movement of the head or feet toward the clockwise direction with a kernel of corn. Counterclockwise movements went unrewarded. Gradually, the pigeon's clockwise movements became less random, until, by the end of the session, counterclockwise movement ceased and the pigeon moved only in a clockwise direction.

▲ **Figure 11.2**
The apparatus used in Skinner's early experiments on the effects of reinforcement.

Emergence of Programmed Instruction

In his 1954 article Skinner pointed out that the elements of his formula were not well represented in traditional classroom instruction. In large-group instruction, students spend much of their time listening, with little opportunity for overt response. Even if an overt response is given, the typical teacher, responsible for large numbers of students at once, has limited opportunity even to observe individual responses, much less to reinforce each one appropriately. How, then, could the principles of response/reinforcement be implemented in the classroom?

Skinner's initial solution to this problem was an innovative method of presenting instructional material printed in small bits or "frames," each of which included an item of information (prompt), an incomplete statement to be completed or question to be answered (response), and provision of the correct answer (reinforcement). A mechanical device—which later came to be referred to as a teaching machine—was used to control the logistics of the process.

This solution—programmed instruction—provided a mechanism for adapting lessons to an individual's pace, thereby circumventing the large-group barrier. Further, it assured that students would be kept actively at work making frequent (and nearly always correct) responses, thus gaining frequent reinforcement. In short, programmed instruction appeared to be a feasible method for putting reinforcement theory into practice in all sorts of real-life classroom situations.

Reinforcement theory has been presented in some detail here not because it is the basis for *all* technologies of instruction but because of its historical primacy in stimulating the concept of a "technology of instruction." And it does lie at the heart of several of the techniques described in the rest of this chapter. The first to be examined in detail is programmed instruction itself.

▲ **Figure 11.3**
This type of early teaching machine required written ("constructed") responses.

▲ **Figure 11.4**
An early teaching machine of the type described by Skinner in his original article; the paper roll advanced only when the correct multiple-choice response was chosen.

▲ **Figure 11.5**
By the mid-1960s the "machine" element had shrunk and most programs required written responses.

PROGRAMMED INSTRUCTION

What It is

Originally, the term *programmed instruction* was used in reference to a particular *format* for presenting printed learning materials to an individual learner. B. F. Skinner's 1954 article, previously mentioned, described a mechanical device consisting of a small box having on its top surface a window through which information printed on a paper roll could be read. The learner responded to a question or blank to be filled by selecting a multiple choice answer. If the right one was chosen, the paper roll would advance to the next question when a knob was turned. Other early devices required written responses. (See Figures 11.4 and 11.5.)

Since reinforcement theory demanded that reinforcement be given only after a correct response, it was originally considered necessary to use a mechanical monitoring device to enforce this requirement. During the infancy of programmed instruction, much creative energy was invested in developing such "teaching machines" to automate the presentation of frames of information to the learner. Research and practical experience soon indicated, however, that students were quite capable of monitoring their own progress without the help of a cumbersome and expensive page-turning machine. So, in many cases, the "teaching machines" were discarded and their learning contents were put into book formats. The earliest programmed instruction texts arranged the frames across the page in horizontal strips. The correct response for each question could be checked only by turning the page. Later, this method was relaxed, allowing the frames to be arranged vertically, just as in conventional printed pages. These programmed texts were meant to be read with a piece of paper covering the rest of the page while a frame was being read. After writing in an answer in the blank on the first frame, for example, the cover was moved down to see the confirmation (correct answer) printed in the box to the left of the second frame. You will have a better idea of how progammed instruction works if you go through the following example.

Programmed Instruction as a Technology of Instruction

It is clear that programmed instruction was developed very consciously as a specific pattern of activities designed to put scientific principles of learning into practice. As such, it fits our definition of a "technology of instruction." However, the translation from the laboratory into the classroom was quite direct and unadorned. By the early 1960s an orthodoxy had developed around the construction of programmed instruction. The elements of this orthodoxy were

An Example Of Linear Programming

	1. Psychologists differ in their explanations about what learning is and precisely how it occurs. The series of statements or "frames" presented here deal with one particular explanation of the process of _____.
learning	2. We cannot observe learning directly, but we can infer that it has occurred when a person consistently makes a *response* that he or she previously was unable to make. For example, if a student says "nine" when asked "What is three times three?" she is making a _____ that was probably learned through practice in school.
response	3. If you reply "kappa" when asked "What Greek letter is represented by K?" you are making a _____ that you learned through some prior experience.
response	4. The word or picture or other sensory stimulation that causes you to make a response is a *stimulus* (plural: stimuli). Therefore, if "kappa" is your response, "What Greek letter is represented by K?" would be the _____.
stimulus	5. To the stimulus "good," the student of Spanish responds "bueno"; the student of Arabic responds "gayid." To the stimulus "silver," the student of Spanish responds "plata"; the student of Arabic responds "fida." They are responding to English words which are serving as _____.
stimuli	6. In these frames the written statements are the stimuli to which you are writing _____ in the blanks.
responses	7. We learn to connect certain verbal responses to certain stimuli through the process of forming *associations*. We say that the student associates "nine" with "three times three"; he learns to associate "kappa" with "K"; and he _____ "plata" with "silver."
associates	8. Much verbal learning seems to be based on the formation of associations between _____ and responses.
stimuli	Etc.

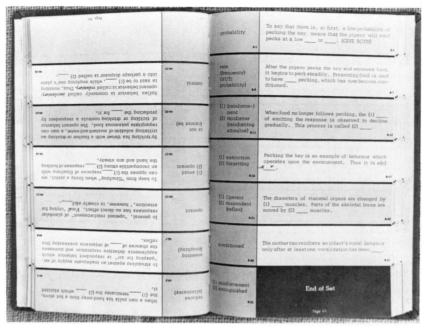

▲ **Figure 11.6**

An early programmed textbook was *The Analysis of Behavior* by James G. Holland and B.F. Skinner (1961); note the "zebra stripe" arrangement of the pages, requiring the reader to turn the page to see the correct answer.

▲ **Figure 11.7**

In contrast to the original teaching machines, those using the branching format provide remedial pathways for students who give incorrect responses.

summarized by Wilbur Schramm follows:

(a) *an ordered sequence of* stimulus items,
(b) *to each of which a student* responds *in some specified way*,
(c) *his response being reinforced by immediate knowledge of results*,
(d) *so that he moves by* small steps,
(e) *therefore making few errors and practicing mostly correct responses*,
(f) *from what he knows, by a process of* successively closer approximations, *toward what he is supposed to learn from the program.*

Although many of the materials which incorporated these elements were found to be successful with students, in a good number of controlled studies the programmed materials failed to live up to the claims made by their adherents. In some experiments it was found that "large steps" worked better than "small steps."

Delayed rather than immediate knowledge of results sometimes yielded just as good results. At times, even scrambling the order of the frames produced better learning than "an ordered sequence." In addition, it was found that some students considered the repetitious pattern of small, easy steps tedious and boring.

Further doubts were raised when Norman Crowder challenged the programmed instruction orthodoxy with a competing technique of program writing—one that ignored all psychological theory and attempted instead simply to present information to readers in a more efficient, individualized form. He called this technique "intrinsic programming." Its basic method was to present a large block of information followed by multiple choice questions requiring application of the facts or principles presented.

Each choice of answer directed the reader to a different page. If the correct choice was made, the learner skipped ahead to new frames of information. Incorrect choices led to explanations of the correct response and to fresh questions. If the learner had additional difficulty he or she would be routed to sequences of remedial instruction. At each step the learner encountered questions testing mastery of the subject matter and was directed onward to new material only after demonstrating a grasp of the prerequisite skills. Because Crowder's pattern of frames resembled the branches of a tree, this programming technique became known as the branching format. The original Skinnerian format is referred to as linear. The two patterns are compared in Figure 11.8. The major advantage of branching over linear programming is that students who catch on quickly can move through the material much more efficiently, following the "prime path." In the linear format, all learners are expected to go through all the steps.

By the late 1960s it had become clear that programmed instruction was not to be confined to the precise formats originally worked out by Skinner. The initial form of programmed instruction was seen to be too literal an application of reinforcement theory to formal learning. For one thing, it was apparent that *knowledge of results* was not consistently reinforcing to all learners all of the time. Its potential for being reinforcing varies with the situation, as is the case with

*Wilbur Schramm. *Programmed Instruction: Today and Tomorrow.* New York: Fund for the Advancement of Education, 1962.

*Norman Crowder. "On the Differences Between Linear and Intrinsic Programming." Phi Delta Kappan (March 1963), pp. 250–254.

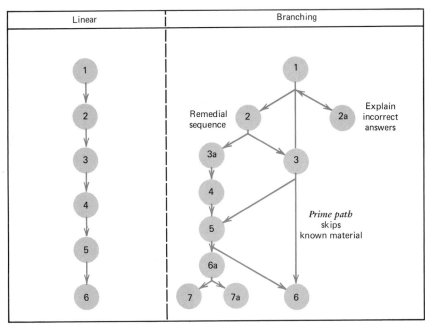

▲ **Figure 11.8**
Comparison of linear and branching formats of programmed instruction.

▼ **Figure 11.9**
A contemporary example of linear programmed instruction, a book on art. This program calls for a variety of types of responses, including painting, as seen at the bottom of the page.

other potential reinforcers such as food, sex, praise, money, and the like. In addition, programmed materials, like any other instructional materials, needed to be made varied and interesting, a need that could not be met by rigid adherence to any single stereotyped "recipe."

In recent years the basic concepts underlying programmed instruction have found expression in a multitude of forms; programmed tutoring, the Personalized System of Instruction, and computer-assisted instruction are three concepts that we will be examining more closely. And printed programs are still being produced and used. In fact, today they are more widely used than ever before. But they are not necessarily labeled as "programmed instruction" and they hardly ever follow the rigid formula of earlier linear programming. Note, for example, the variety of programming formats illustrated in Figures 11.9 and 11.10.

▼ **Figure 11.10**
A review exercise in a programmed book. Previously learned principles are applied to the solving of a hypothetical problem.

Every hue has a tone sequence from its lightest tints to its darkest shades. Through light/dark contrast, color can be controlled to exaggerate form toward three-dimensional effect or to suppress form toward a flattened effect.

Examples

When your hair becomes bleached by summer sun or peroxide, it becomes lighter in value than before. When the bleach grows out, the hair becomes darker in value.

When you roast a marshmallow, it changes in value from white to a very light brown to a darker value of brown. If you are not careful at this point, it will turn black—a still darker value.

Exercise

Indicate the contrasting tones associated with each of the following:

(a) Coffee stain on a white shirt
(b) New blue denim patch on faded denim jeans
(c) Tree shadow on a yellow house
(d) Teeth brushed with "Sparkle-brite" showing through lips with red lipstick

---

(a) Stain is darker in value than white fabric
(b) Patch is darker in value than the jeans
(c) Shadow area is darker in value than the yellow wall
(d) Teeth are lighter in value than lips

You may find it helpful to make a tonal scale of at least one hue. Using blue-colored ink or paint, place the undiluted blue in the center frame. Going to the right of center, add a little water or white paint to dilute the blue for each step of the frame, leaving white in the last frame. Going to the left, add a very little black for each step until you reach black for the last frame. You may even succeed in extending this value scale further than the steps in following the sketch. It is possible to make such a tonal scale for each hue.

black — undiluted blue — white

shades — tints
dark tones — light tones

SELF-TEST

This self-test is designed to show you whether or not you have mastered the objectives of Chapter 2. Answer each question to the best of your ability, based on what you learned in this chapter. Correct answers are given following the test.

Read the following paragraph. Then answer the following questions that refer to the situation.

Mr. Cee, a sixth grade teacher, is concerned about Bill Boneau, a boy in his class. Bill, a natural leader, can command the respect of his fellow students. However, far too often, he uses this leadership ability to distract students from academics. In addition, he seldom pays attention to the teacher presentations or class discussions, and his homework is seldom done—all of which seem to be affecting his test scores. A notable exception to his lack of interest is science. Bill is interested in scientific projects, and he does well on them. His interest and leadership in this area have carried the entire class to levels of scientific inquiry and understanding far beyond those of any of Mr. Cee's previous classes.

1. List three inappropriate behaviors of Bill's which should be reduced in frequency.
   a. _____
   b. _____
   c. _____

2. List two appropriate behaviors to be encouraged.
   a. _____
   b. _____

3. List the rules for Bill that would be included in a behavioral contract.
   _____
   _____
   _____

Appraisal Checklist: Programmed Materials

Series title (if applicable)_____

Individual title_____

Producer/distributor_____   Date_____

Required completion time—range_____ average_____

Intended audience/grade level_____   Subject area_____

Objectives (should be clearly stated in learner performance terms):

Brief description/summary:

Entry capabilities required:

　　—prior subject matter knowledge
　　—reading ability
　　—math ability (or other)

Rating	High		Medium		Low
Likely to arouse student interest (e.g., humor, vivid examples, variety of formats)	☐	☐	☐	☐	☐
Content accurate and timely	☐	☐	☐	☐	☐
Structure is "lean"—sufficient review without unnecessary redundancy	☐	☐	☐	☐	☐
Test (criterion) frames parallel to the stated objectives	☐	☐	☐	☐	☐
Relevant practice is consistently provided	☐	☐	☐	☐	☐
Learner responses require "thought," not just copying given information	☐	☐	☐	☐	☐
Feedback (knowledge of correct response) is well delivered (e.g., consistent, well hidden)	☐	☐	☐	☐	☐
Feedback provides remediation	☐	☐	☐	☐	☐
Validation data are provided (should describe tryout population, time, gains in achievement and attitude)	☐	☐	☐	☐	☐

Strong points:

Weak points:

Reviewer_____

Position_____

Recommended action_____   Date_____

The most comprehensive listing of commercially available programmed materials is *Programmed Learning and Individually Paced Instruction—Bibliography* compiled by Carl Hendershot 5th ed. (Bay City, MI: Hendershot Bibliography. 1983).

Despite the great diversity of styles and formats evident among programmed materials, there are still a number of features shared in common among them. These include performance objectives stated in advance, clear sequence of activities, frequent response (requiring thinking, not just copying), regular feedback, test items that are parallel to the stated objectives, and validation based on actual learner tryouts. Note that these features are among the criteria included here in the appraisal checklist for programmed materials.

Applications of Programmed Instruction

Programmed materials have been used successfully from the elementary school through the adult education levels and in almost every subject area. By itself or in conjunction with other strategies, a program can be used to teach an entire course or a segment of a course. Many teachers use short programmed units to teach simple principles and terminology. Programmed instruction is particularly useful as an enrichment activity. It can help provide highly motivated students with additional learning experiences that the teacher might ordinarily be unable to provide because of classroom time pressures. Programmed materials have proven to be very effective in remedial instruction. The program can function as a kind of tutor for slow learners in situations where more personalized attention may be virtually impossible (in overcrowded classrooms, for example). Such students may even take this particular tutor with them when they leave the classroom! One of the reasons for the success of programmed materials in remedial instruction is their "failure-proof" design. By being broken into small steps, by allowing the student to take as much time as needed for each step, and by being evaluated and revised carefully prior to publication, these materials are more likely to provide the slow learner with a successful experience.

For some students it may be their first encounter with school work that gives them an immediate and continued feeling of success.

Programmed instruction can be an effective means of providing class-wide competencies in skills prerequisite to successful completion of a unit of study. For example, one high school physics teacher used a small programmed text to allow his students to teach themselves the power-of-ten notation, which is a prerequisite for solving physics problems. At the outset, some of the students were even more proficient with power-of-ten operations than their instructor; others had been introduced to the technique but had lost their competence in it because they had not been required to use the skill; still others had never even been introduced to it. The program on power-of-ten notation eliminated devoting class time to a subject that would have bored some and confused others. Instead, the students were allowed to consider the material on their own. Those who knew the technique could ignore the program;

▼ **Figure 11.11**

The wide array of programmed materials that have been published give many options for self-instruction.

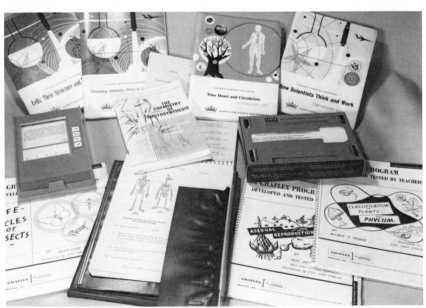

▼ **Figure 11.12**

Through programmed instruction, trainees can begin study when ready, not just when a full class becomes available.

those who had previously learned the skill but were a little rusty could use the program as a review; and those who had never been exposed to power-of-ten notation could master the necessary manipulations on their own and at their own pace. All students were subsequently required to pass a criterion test demonstrating mastery of this skill.

Programmed materials have a wide variety of other more or less specialized uses. They can, for example, be used for make-up instruction by students who have been absent from school for an extended period of time. They can be used to expand curricular offerings when it might be difficult or impossible otherwise to do so—because of too few interested students, for instance, or no qualified instructor. This could be an important consideration for smaller schools and for training programs in business/industry settings.

It is true that programmed materials are often more expensive than ordinary textbooks, mainly because of the time and effort spent in their careful development and in their validation testing. Their increased efficiency as learning tools, however, may compensate for their higher cost (especially in situations in which the cost of student time and failure is taken into account).

Programmed instruction is by its very nature individualized learning, in which the student advances at his or her own pace. However, as with other techniques for individualized instruction, this does not mean that students are always working alone. Group activities can and should be scheduled to supplement the programmed instruction and to meet other desired educational goals. In addition, as with other properly planned individualized activities, programs help release teachers from routine classroom chores in order to interact personally with students and to provide them with human reinforcement.

Utilization of Programmed Instruction

Programmed instruction is basically learner-centered. It focuses on the activities of the student rather than the activities of the teacher. The role of the teacher, however, is as important to the success of programmed instruction as it is to any other type of instruction. It is up to the instructor to arrange and maintain conditions conducive to achievement of the program's learning objectives. Be sure to familiarize yourself with the entire program before implementing it for class use so that you will be in a position to assist students to work through it when and if they need help. Familiarity with the program will also help you coordinate the programmed materials with other instructional activities—lectures, group discussions, etc.

The students' first exposure to programmed materials is particularly important. Be sure to explain the mechanics of using the materials so that the students will not get bogged down with them when they begin to work the program. For example, clarify whether answers are to be recorded directly on the materials or on separate sheets of paper. (Recording answers on separate sheets allows the materials to be used over and over again.) Once the mechanics of the program are understood, the student is free to concentrate on working the program and to experience the immediate success so important in initial exposure to new learning methods.

▼ **Figure 11.13**
As with any other instructional materials, good utilization of programmed instruction begins with "preview" of the materials.

Because programmed materials often have the physical appearance of a test, the fact that the program is not a test should be emphasized. Carefully explain that even though the program confronts the student with a series of questions to be answered, users need not be fearful of making errors. If errors are made, the program automatically helps the learner correct them. Explain that students are never evaluated on the basis of their performance in working through the program. Evaluation is based upon student performance on criterion tests administered *after* using the program. Programs are for teaching, not for testing.

It should be established that students will be working at their own pace, neither pushed faster than they can efficiently perform nor held back if they wish to work rapidly. Under no circumstances should a student be assigned a minimum amount of material to be covered in a single class period.

Students should be encouraged to ask questions about the material as they work, especially if they become confused. Confusion may not only indicate misunderstanding on the part of the student. It may also indicate ambiguities and weaknesses in the program itself which you will want to record for future reference.

Stress the importance of being intellectually honest with oneself when working with programmed materials. Inform your students of the futility of peeking ahead in order to ascertain a correct response rather than thinking it out for themselves. Explain that there is nothing to gain by such actions and much to lose, namely, the opportunity to learn. Human nature being as it is, you will probably find some students unable to resist some initial peeking ahead. But this behavior will likely fade as students discover for themselves that there is no advantage in it and that the program is designed to make certain they can work out the correct responses on their own.

PROGRAMMED TUTORING

What It Is

Programmed tutoring (also referred to as structured tutoring) is a one-to-one method of instruction in which the decisions to be made by the tutor are "programmed" in advance by means of carefully structured printed instructions. In a typical program the tutor and student sit down together to go through the lesson material. The "teacher's book" has the answers to the exercises; the "student's book" does not. An excerpt from a typical programmed tutoring teacher's book is shown here. Note how the tutor's role in the program is set forth, step-by-step, to conform with learner response to the materials.

Since the tutor is continually choosing the next step on the basis of the learner's last response, programmed tutoring is a form of branching programming. As such, it shares the basic advantage for which branching was originally developed: the fast learner may skip quickly through the material without tedious, unnecessary repetition.

Programmed tutoring uses what might be called "brightening," as opposed to the "fading" or gradual reduction of prompts used in conventional linear programmed instruction. In "brightening," the item is first presented in a relatively difficult form. If the learner responds correctly he or she is reinforced and goes on to a new item. If not, a series of increasingly clearer prompts or hints are given. For example, in teaching a beginning reader to follow written instructions, the student's book might say, "Point to your teacher." If the learner does not do so when first shown the instruction, the tutor might follow this sequence of "brightening" prompts:

1. "Read it again." (Wait for response.)
2. "What does it say?"
3. "What does it tell you to do?"
4. "Do what it tells you to do."

▲ **Figure 11.14**
A typical arrangement for a programmed tutoring lesson.

▶ **Figure 11.15**
The directions given in the tutor's guidebook structure the programmed tutoring lesson.

STEP 1 Tell the student that this exercise will help him learn to sound out new words.

STEP 2 Point to the first word and ask the student to *sound* it out.
    a. If the student reads the word correctly, praise him; then go on to the next word.
    b. If the student is unable to read the word or reads it incorrectly, have him make the individual sounds in the word separately and then assist him in blending the sounds.

    Example:
      Word: "THIN"
    Tutor: Place your finger over the last two letters in the word and ask: "What sound does the *th* make?" If the student answers correctly, praise him and go to the next sound. If he answers incorrectly or fails to answer, tell him the sound and have him repeat it. Follow the same procedure for each sound in the word, and then show him how to blend the separate sounds.

STEP 3 Follow step 2 for each word on the sheet.
STEP 4 At the end of the session, praise the student.
STEP 5 Fill out your tutor log.

Source: Grant Von Harrison, *Beginning Reading 1: A Professional Guide for the Lay Tutor.* Provo, Utah: Brigham Young University Press, 1972, p. 101.

The sequence of prompts would continue until the learner gives an acceptable response. Then reinforcement would be given. The idea is to lead the student toward the solution with "brightening" hints but to avoid actually giving the correct answer itself.

Programmed Tutoring as a Technology of Instruction

Programmed tutoring shares with programmed instruction the characteristics of individualized pacing, active learner response, and immediate feedback. The use of a live tutor as a mediator adds immensely to the flexibility of the system, and it adds another major advantage over printed self-instructional material by employing *social reinforcers* in the form of praise ("That's great." "Oh, what a good answer." "You're really on the ball today.") rather than just simple knowledge of results. Administered flexibly and creatively by a live guide, this technology of instruction can overcome the monotonous pattern sometimes associated with other programmed formats.

Applications and Utilization of Programmed Tutoring

Programmed tutoring combines the qualities of programmed instruction with the warmth and personal attention that only a human tutor can add. The tutor may be a teacher aide, a parent, or another student ("peer tutoring"). Almost anyone can be trained as a tutor since the sequencing of the material and the tutor's responses are carefully programmed into the lesson by the designer. As such, it is particularly attractive for areas in which qualified teachers are lacking. Douglas G. Ellson, a principal developer of programmed tutoring, estimates that over a million young people in less-developed countries have learned to read by this method since its origins in 1960.

Reading and mathematics have been the most popular subject areas for application of tutoring. These subjects lend themselves to this method because of their high degree of structure. Also, being very basic skills, they are frequently the targets of remedial or compensatory education programs—the milieu in which volunteer tutoring projects are often

mounted. Indeed, Ellson's tutoring program centered at Indiana University has been recognized by American Institutes for Research and the U.S. Education Department as one of the half dozen most effective compensatory education programs in the United States.

In preparing to utilize programmed tutoring, keep in mind that the research consistently indicates that tutors gain even more than their students. So give everyone a chance to be a tutor, not just the most advanced students. In any case, ensure that the tutors are trained in and do use the correct procedures. The materials are validated for effectiveness only when they are used as directed.

A final utilization hint: Consider using the tutorial method to make productive use of high-absence days. Train those who are present to tutor absentees when they return. Tutors deepen their knowledge; the absentees catch up.

PERSONALIZED SYSTEM OF INSTRUCTION

What It is

The *Personalized System of Instruction* (*PSI*) could be described as a technology for *managing* instruction. It puts reinforcement theory into action as the overall framework for a whole course. In the PSI classroom students work individually at their own pace using any of a variety of instructional materials—a chapter in a book, computer-assisted instruction, a loop film, a sound filmstrip, a programmed booklet, etc. The materials are arranged in sequential order and the student must show *mastery* of each unit before being allowed to move on to the next.

Mastery is determined by means of a test taken whenever the student feels ready for it. The content and emphasis of the test should be no surprise because each unit is accompanied by a study guide that spells out the objective and most important points to be learned in that unit.

Study help and testing are handled by *proctors*—usually more advanced students who volunteer to help others. Proctors are a critical component of PSI for it is their one-to-one tutorial assistance that makes the system *personalized*. After scoring each test the proctor reviews it immediately with the student, asking questions to probe weak points and listening to defenses of alternative answers. If performance is below the

▶ **Figure 11.16**
Psychologist Fred S. Keller, originator of the Personalized System of Instruction, also referred to as the "Keller Plan."

specified mastery level the student returns at another time to take a second form of the test.

Group meetings are rare, being used mainly for "inspirational" lectures, film showings, and review sessions. The instructor acts primarily as a planner, designer, manager, and guide to students and proctors.

PSI as a Technology of Instruction

Like programmed tutoring. PSI strives to implement the learning principles that programmed instruction originally envisioned: (a) the presentation of information appropriate to the student's current ability, (b) frequent opportunities to respond to the material, and (c) immediate feedback/correction. To these principles PSI adds the philosophy of mastery—the student may not tackle new material until the prior skills have been mastered—and the person-to-person contact with a proctor and instructor.

Unlike programmed tutoring and programmed instruction, PSI does not revolve around the design of specially structured materials; it manipulates the *framework* in which instruction occurs. It consciously puts into play a number of "generalized reinforcers," rewards that tend to work

well with humans despite differences in preference or current need. These include grades, diplomas, and other similar tokens of achievement, personal attention, social approval, affection, and deferent behavior of others. The designers of PSI aimed to maximize rewards for conscientious study, minimize frustration, and eliminate the fear connected with not knowing where one is going, how well one is doing, and what surprise the instructor is going to pull on the final exam.

Applications and Utilization of PSI

Since its origins in Fred S. Keller's psychology course at the University of Brasilia in the mid-1960s, PSI has been successfully used at all grade levels and in virtually every subject area. It is also widely known in military training and in business/industry education. The validity of the PSI approach has been attested to by extensive research. Kulik, Kulik, and Smith prepared a review of studies in which PSI had been compared with conventional instruction. Their conclusion was as follows:

In a typical published comparison, PSI and lecture means are separated by about two-thirds of a stan-

dard deviation. How large a difference is this? Let us take an average student, Mary Smith, who may take her introductory physics course, for example, by either a conventional method or by PSI. If she takes a typical lecture course, her achievement in physics will put her at the 50th percentile on a standardized test. She is an average student in an average course. If she takes the same course in PSI format, she will achieve at the 75th percentile on the standardized test. This increment is what PSI has to offer the individual student. . . . In our judgment, this is the most impressive record achieved by a teaching method in higher education. It stands in stark contrast to the inconclusive results of earlier comparisons of college teaching methods.

Specific guidelines for setting up and running courses according to the PSI system can be found in the books and articles listed in the References section at the end of this chapter. A few cautions about implementing a PSI approach are in order. First, PSI involves a great deal of time in planning and developing supplementary materials. Even though less lecture time is involved, instructors should be prepared to spend about half again as many hours conducting a PSI course as conducting a conventional course. Second, a willingness and ability to state objectives specifically is prerequisite. Third, the "mastery" point-of-view built into PSI rejects norm-referenced grading (the "normal curve") and insists on complete mastery as the criterion of success. It aims to elevate all students to the "A" level.

▼ **Figure 11.17**
Interaction with the proctor "personalizes" the Personalized System of Instruction.

*James A. Kulik, Chen-Lin Kulik, and Beverly B. Smith. "Research on the Personalized System of Instruction." *Programmed Learning and Educational Technology* (Spring 1976), pp. 13, 23–30.

▼ **Figure 11.18**
The printed materials used in PSI and Audio Tutorial courses are sometimes published as "minicourses" for widespread use.

A GUIDE TO THE
**MINICOURSES
IN
BIOLOGY**

Flashback: SERENDIPITY AND BOTANY 108

In the fall of 1961, S. N. Postlethwait, a professor of botany at Purdue University, began preparing supplementary lectures on audio tape to provide an opportunity for students with inadequate academic backgrounds to keep up with his introductory botany class. Any student could listen to these recordings at the university audiovisual center. Soon Dr. Postlethwait decided that he could improve the effectiveness of these tapes by having the students bring their botany textbooks to the audiovisual center when they came to listen to the tapes. On the tapes he could refer them to the photographs, diagrams, and drawings in the text as he discussed the concepts and principles under study.

Later, the tapes included instructions that the students check views contained in the recorded lectures against views expressed in the text. Thus the author's point of view could be considered along with the lecturer's. Then Dr. Postlethwait decided to add a new dimension to his instructional approach. He placed plants in the audiovisual center so that students could observe and handle the plants when they were being discussed on the tapes. Ultimately, the students were instructed to bring their laboratory manuals to the center and conduct experiments in conjunction with study of their texts and listening to the tapes. Consciously or unconsciously, Dr. Postlethwait had moved his instructional technique from one focusing on abstract learning experiences (lectures) toward a multimedia system emphasizing concrete experiences—an integrated lecture-laboratory approach.

During the spring of 1962 an experimental group of thirty-six students was chosen to receive all of the instruction via the integrated lecture-laboratory approach. The experimental class met with Dr. Postlethwait only once each week, to take quizzes and for a general discussion of the week's subject matter. They were required to take the same examina-

AUDIO-TUTORIAL SYSTEMS

What They Are

The term *Audio-Tutorial Systems* is used in the plural here to acknowledge that many variations have evolved from the original tape-controlled independent study method developed by S. N. Postlethwait at Purdue University in the early 1960s. Like PSI, this is a technology for *managing* instruction. But it springs from different roots and has a different emphasis from the preceding methods, which derive from programmed instruction.

As described in the accompanying "Flashback," the Audio-Tutorial Sys-

tem had its birth in expediency. It was an intuitive response to a felt problem. It later evolved into an identifiable, systematic method of instruction through years of experimentation and refinement by instructional developers.

The most visible aspect of most Audio-Tutorial (A–T) courses is the study carrel equipped with specially designed audio tapes that direct students to various learning activities. This component is known as the Independent Study Session. The taped presentation is *not* a lecture but a tutorial conversation by the instructor, designed to facilitate effective communication. A live instructor is nearby to assist students when needed. Learners proceed at their own pace; sessions begin and end to suit students' schedules.

Since the students are proceeding individually, there seldom is more than one student at any given point in the study program. So, often only one or two pieces of equipment are necessary to accommodate many students in a laboratory situation. Demonstration materials are set out at a central location; again, one set may be sufficient to serve a large class. Motion and color are provided when necessary by means of 8-mm film and/or videocassette. Instructions on how to perform a laboratory procedure, for instance, can be viewed coincident with handling the apparatus itself. The student can view the first step in a procedure, do that step, view the second step, turn the projector to "hold" while carrying out that step, and so on.

tions given the conventionally taught group. At the end of the semester the experimental group scored just as well on the exam as the group that had received traditional instruction.

The students' reactions to the "supplementary" material were so positive that in the fall of 1962 Postlethwait decided that rather than carrying plants and other materials from the biology greenhouse to the audiovisual center each week, he would set up a botany learning center in the biology building. A conventional science laboratory was converted to a learning center with the addition of twenty-two learning carrels equipped with tape recorders. At this time, Postlethwait was covering the same content in his classroom lectures that was being presented on the tapes in the learning center. By the end of the semester most of the students were going to the learning center instead of coming to the lectures! In spite of the fact that Postlethwait missed their "sitting at his feet" to learn about botany, he candidly admitted that all the students missed by not coming to the lectures were his smiling face and West Virginia jokes.

Eventually, Postlethwait did away with his traditional lectures and restructured his Biology 108 course to give the students maximum freedom for independent study and to pace themselves according to their individual interests and capabilities. Students could come in at their convenience and spend as much time as necessary for them to master the material under study.

A significant aspect of Postlethwait's audio recordings was the conversational tone and relaxed atmosphere he deliberately cultivated. He would sit among the materials gathered for the particular lesson and speak into the recorder as if he were having a conversation with a friend whom he wished to tutor through a sequence of pleasant inquiries. Later, in their carrels, students would examine duplicates of the same materials while they listened to Postlethwait's chat.

Group meetings were later added to the program to supplement the independent study sessions. Students were brought together periodically in small groups (the "small assembly session") to discuss what they had learned in independent study and to present their own "lectures" on the current subject matter. Larger meetings (the "general assembly sessions") were scheduled for guest lectures, films, review sessions, and the like.

Serendipity is the faculty of making fortunate and unexpected discoveries by accident. Dr. Postlethwait turned out to be embarking on a serendipitous journey when he set out to tinker with the traditional format of his botany course. What began simply as audio tapes to supplement his classroom lectures eventually evolved into a full-scale technology of instruction—the Audio-Tutorial System.

In addition to the Independent Study Session, there are two other basic components in most A–T systems: a General Assembly Session and a Small Assembly Session.

The General Assembly Session is a large-group meeting with no fixed format. It may include a presentation by a guest lecturer, a long film, an orientation to subject matter, an opportunity for review or emphasis of critical materials, help sessions, a major exam, or any other activity appropriate to a large-group setting.

▶ **Figure 11.19**
The independent study carrel is the most visibly distinctive feature of the Audio-Tutorial approach.

During the Small Assembly Session, six to ten students and an instructor meet for a modified seminar. Students are seated informally around a table with the instructor. The primary purpose of the session is to exploit the principle that one really learns a subject when one is required to teach it. For this session each student is expected to prepare a little lecture about each of the objectives being covered that session. Each student is asked to discuss at least one of the objectives in turn. The other students then have an opportunity to correct or add comments concerning any item. This session has proven to be an effective feedback mechanism for both the students and the instructor. It lets the students know how they did and often provides clues to the instructor for improving the study program. The miniature seminar enables many students to see relationships and concepts which may not have been evident from the Independent Study Session.

Audio-Tutorial Systems as a Technology of Instruction

Unlike programmed instruction, programmed tutoring, and PSI, A–T did not originate from a particular theory of learning. Its development was pragmatic. What worked was kept; what didn't work was pruned away. The resultant system, though, does fit our definition of a technology of instruction. It takes the form of an indentifiable, unique pattern of teaching/learning. Its procedures provide consistent (replicable), effective instruction on an individualized basis. And, most importantly, A–T puts into action a number of principles of human learning:

1. The conversational audio tapes embody principles of communication theory (source credibility, personalization in the form of address, etc.).

2. The special emphasis on concrete media, such as slides, films, and realia applies what cognitive psychology advocates regarding realistic, meaningful messages.
3. Self-pacing and varied media alternatives cater to individual differences in learning style and rate.
4. The pervasive concern for individual success embodies the "whole person" emphasis of humanistic psychology.

These attributes differentiate A–T from the other systems discussed in this chapter. What unifies all of these systems is their common technological approach, characterized by such qualities as modular units, requirement of active student participation, and provision of rapid feedback and correction.

Applications and Utilization of Audio-Tutorial Systems

The A–T approach is still most prevalent in science education, where it began. But during the two decades since its inception, it has also been successfully applied in many other areas, at many levels, and in both formal and nonformal educational settings. One indication of its widespread diffusion is the existence of a professional association, the International Society for Individualized Instruction, devoted to sharing ideas and research on Audio-Tutorial and other systems of individualized instruction.

As a result of these many and varied experiences with A–T, a number of generalizations can be recommended to anyone considering implementing such a system. First, as is true of PSI, setting up an Audio-Tutorial System requires a great deal of preparation. However, A–T materials need not always be invented locally. Commercial publishers now offer sizable collections of packaged A–T materials.

▲ **Figure 11.20**
Multisensory materials and varied activities help maintain student interest in Audio-Tutorial courses.

Individualization and personalization are critical elements in this sort of system. Self-pacing and frequent corrective feedback must be designed into the system and vigilantly maintained. One aspect of personalization is the conversational tone of the audio materials; "lecture" style is not very appealing on a one-to-one basis.

Active participation by the learner is essential. A varied menu of activities—viewing films, manipulating real objects, field trips—helps keep interest high.

A NOTE ON MODULES

For generations teachers have spoken in terms of "lessons" and "units" when talking about the parts of a course of instruction, but the age of space travel and computer technology has given us a new way of looking at the basic building blocks of instruction: the concept of the module.

In order to create complex electronic systems, engineers had to think in terms of small interchangeable units that could be easily plugged into and detached from the total system. Thus the concept of modules (as in "lunar module" and "modular designed TV") was born and popularized. Carried over into education, *instructional module* has become the generic name for freestanding instructional units. Modules carry a wide variety of labels, including unipack, individualized learning package, and learning activity package.

Modules are usually designed as self-instructional units for independent study. However, group-based modules (for example, built around a simulation, a game, or a field experience) are also found. The Personalized System of Instruction and Audio-Tutorial Systems, discussed in this chapter, are two types of course management systems that are designed around modules.

The reading materials used in a PSI course, for example, may be designed in the module format. If so, those modules become part of the PSI technology of instruction. If a module embodies the prompt/response/reinforcement pattern characteristic of programmed instruction, it becomes part of that technology of instruction. However, it is also possible for modules to be designed in a conventional prose style and to be used in a conventional teaching method. Then they are merely small bits of conventional instruction, not elements of a technology of instruction.

Characteristics of Modules

There are many different formulas for designing instructional modules, but certain components are virtually universally agreed upon:

1. *Rationale.* An overview of the content of the module and explanation of why the learner should study it.
2. *Objective.* What the learner is expected to gain from studying the module, stated in performance terms.
3. *Entry-Test.* To determine if the learner has the prerequisite skills needed to enter the module, and to check whether the learner already has mastered the skills to be taught.
4. *Learning Activities.* Resources to be used in attaining the objectives; materials not contained in the module per se, such as textbooks, audio tapes, filmstrips, and laboratory materials.
5. *Self-Test.* A chance to review and check one's own progress.
6. *Post-Test.* An examination to test whether the objectives of the module have been mastered.

Specific guidelines on selection criteria, design steps, and utilization principles for instructional modules can be found in the References listed at the end of this chapter.

▼ **Figure 11.21**
More and more modular materials are being offered by commercial publishers, including those in machine mediated format.

SIMULATION AND GAMES

What They Are

We will not dwell long on defining simulation and games at this point. These concepts are described in detail in Chapter 12. It will suffice to define *simulation* as any scaled-down representation of some real-life happening. A *game* is an activity in which participants follow prescribed rules that differ from those of reality as they strive to attain a challenging goal. As used in instruction, these two concepts can be applied separately, or together in the form of a *simulation game.* For present purposes the two will be grouped together to allow us to consider simulation/gaming (S/G) in general.

Simulation / Gaming as a Technology of Instruction

Recalling our basic definition of technology of instruction as a teaching/learning pattern that puts into effect scientific understandings about human learning, we find that S/G can embody a number of principles that are fundamental in the psychology of learning.

▼ **Figure 11.22**
Simulation exercises are widely used for developing communication skills.

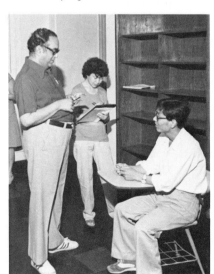

Meaningful Organization of Subject Matter. By placing the learner in a more or less realistic setting, simulation presents the subject matter in context. Facts, principles, and problems are viewed in their interaction rather than presented singly as separate unrelated items.

Repetition. Repetition has always played a major role in school learning. The problem has been to maintain student interest in drill exercises. The game format, with its repetitive cycles of play (e.g., dealing out new hands in a card game), can direct learners through extensive drill-and-practice exercises while keeping interest high by means of variation in the pattern and the excitement of chance.

Reinforcement. S/G can be employed as a framework for reinforcement just as well as printed programmed materials. In a well-designed game the participants are required to make frequent responses related to the instructional objectives; for example, classifying items, making value judgments, making decisions. Each of these responses can be connected with certain preordained consequences—favorable consequences for correct responses and unfavorable consequences for less correct actions. Through such trial-and-error patterns the participant's behavior can be "shaped" toward the desired learning goals. In addition, like programmed tutoring, S/G goes beyond just "knowledge of results" in its array of possible reinforcers. It capitalizes on the social context of game play to incorporate such generalized reinforcers as achievement, dominance, and social approval.

COMPUTER-ASSISTED INSTRUCTION

Any discussion of technologies of instruction would be incomplete and woefully out-of-date if the revolution in computer applications were omitted. Because of the computer's importance, Chapter 13 will be devoted to this topic. Our purpose at this point is to call attention to the computer's unmatched ability to *manage information* with such speed and accuracy that teaching/learning interactions can be handled with much greater efficiency and effectiveness.

The computer *is not in itself a technology of instruction.* It is a physical tool that can be used to present programmed instruction, programmed tutoring, simulation/gaming, and other instructional formats on demand to individual learners without the necessity of a human helper being immediately present. Further, it can take such technologies of *managing* instruction as PSI and A–T and carry out their management functions far more efficiently than human paper shufflers and materials dispensers.

These functions, usually referred to as computer-assisted instruction and computer-managed instruction respectively, will be examined in detail in Chapter 13.

▼ **Figure 11.23**
The popularization of microcomputers has encouraged the development of computer-assisted instruction.

SUMMARY

In this chapter we have examined six teaching/learning formats, analyzing their differences in emphasis and their similarities as examples of technologies of instruction. These characteristics are summarized in Table 11.1. You can see how each of these formats fulfills the requirements of the definition given at the beginning of the chapter. In addition, it should

TABLE 11.1 CHARACTERISTICS OF TECHNOLOGIES OF INSTRUCTION

	Programmed Instruction	Programmed Tutoring	Personalized System of Instruction	Audio-Tutorial Systems	Simulation and Gaming
A teaching/learning *pattern*	Small units of information requiring practice, followed by feedback	Small units of information requiring practice, followed by feedback	Large units of information in sequential order; passing a test is required before proceeding (mastery)	Core of instruction is on audio tape, used in lab setting independently; small group and large group sessions are added	Small group activity, may entail representation of reality and/or competition
designed to provide *reliable,*	Program recorded in printed form	Tutor follows directions; learner uses structured workbook	Course organization is clearly spelled out; based on print materials and standardized tests	Core material recorded on audio tape and other audiovisual materials	Procedures are enforced by means of game directions and play materials
effective instruction	Programs must be learner tested and revised during development process	Programs are learner tested and revised during development process	Materials themselves are not validated, but mastery is assured by testing/correction cycle	Materials themselves are not validated, but mastery is encouraged by small group test/review sessions	May be learner tested for effectiveness
to *each* learner	Allows individual pacing	Allows individual pacing plus highly flexible, responsive branching via human tutor	Allows individual pacing plus one-to-one discussion of test errors and questions	Allows individual pacing in independent study portion of course	Usually group paced, with individuals assigned to compatible groups
through application of *scientific* principles of human learning	Reinforcement theory: verbal response followed by knowledge of results	Reinforcement theory: verbal or other overt response followed by knowledge of results plus social reinforcers Constant personalized human contact Variety	Rather frequent response to tests over content followed by immediate correction Occasional personalized human contact Mastery requirement ensures that learner is working at his level of comprehension	Conversational relationship with instructor via tape High use of audiovisual and other concrete media Occasional personalized human contact Active involvement in challenging tasks	Meaningful organization of content (in simulation) Frequent practice with immediate feedback Social interaction with small group Emotional involvement Repetition of drill-and-practice without tedium High motivation

now be clearer why other teaching/learning formats do not meet these requirements. A conventional lecture, for example, lacks reliability (it is not repeatable unless recorded), ordinarily lacks prior testing, does not accommodate individual differences, and allows little practice/feedback or other instructionally desirable traits. Much the same could be said of a sound-slide presentation or other multi-media show.

A computer or other machine in itself is not a technology of instruction although it can be a contributing element when coupled with a program with certain special qualities.

References

Print References

Programmed Instruction

Bullock, Donald H. *Programmed Instruction.* Volume 8, Instructional Design Library (Englewood Cliffs, N.J.: Educational Technology Publications, 1978).

Center for Vocational Education. *Employ Programmed Instruction.* (Athens, Ga: American Association for Vocational Instructional Materials, 1977).

_____.*Employ Reinforcement Techniques.* (Athens, Ga: American Association for Vocational Instructional Materials, 1977).

Cram, David. *Explaining "Teaching Machines" and Programmed Instruction.* (Belmont, Calif.: Fearon, 1961).

Deterline, W. A. *An Introduction to Programmed Instruction.* (Englewood Cliffs, N.J.: Prentice-Hall, 1962).

Hartley, James. "Programmed Instruction 1954–1974: A Review." *Programmed Learning and Educational Technology* (November 1974), pp. 278–291.

"Instructor Workshop in Print 5: How to Design Programmed Learning Sequences." *Instructor* (February 1978), pp. 124–128.

Kulik, Chen-Lin, Shwarb, B. J., and Kulik, James A. "Programmed Instruction in Secondary Education." *Journal of Educational Research* (1982), pp. 133–138.

Pereira, P. D. *Introduction to Programmed Learning.* (Geneva, Switzerland: International Labor Organization, 1967).

Williams, Robert E. "Programmed Instruction for Creativity." *Programmed Learning and Educational Technology* (February 1977), pp. 50-–4.

Programmed Tutoring

Cohen, P. A., Kulik, James A., and Kulik, Chen-Lin. "Educational Outcomes of Tutorings: A Meta-Analysis of Findings." *American Educational Research Journal* (1982), pp. 237–248.

Ellson, Douglas G. "Tutoring." In *The Psychology of Teaching Methods,* 75th yearbook of the National Society for the Study of Education. (Chicago: NSSE, 1976).

Endsley, William R. *Peer Tutorial Instruction.* Volume 28, Instructional Design Library. (Englewood Cliffs, N.J.: Educational Technology Publications, 1980).

Harrison, Grant, and Guymon, Ronald. *Structured Tutoring.* Volume 34, Instructional Design Library. (Englewood Cliffs, N.J.: Educational Technology Publications, 1980).

Thiagarajan, Sivasailam. "Programming Tutorial Behavior: Another Application of the Programming Process." *Improving Human Performance Quarterly* (June 1972).

_____.*Tutoraids.* Volume 20, Instructional Design Library. (Englewood Cliffs, N.J.: Educational Technology Publications, 1978).

Personalized System of Instruction

Freemantle, M. H. "Keller Plans in Chemistry Teaching." *Education in Chemistry* (March 1976), pp. 50–51.

Johnson, Kent R., and Ruskin, Robert S. *Behavioral Instruction: An Evaluative Review.* (Washington, D.C.: American Psychological Association, 1977).

Keller, Fred S. "Good-Bye, Teacher . . .". *Journal of Applied Behavior Analysis* (Spring 1968), pp. 79-88.

Keller Fred S., and Sherman, J. Gilmour. *The Keller Plan Handbook.* (Menlo Park, Calif.: W. A. Benjamin, 1974).

Keller, Fred S., and Sherman, J. Gilmour. *The PSI Handbook: Essays on Personalized Instruction.* (Lawrence, Ks.: TRI Publications, 1982).

"The Personalized System of Instruction (PSI)—Special Issue." *Educational Technology* (September 1977), pp. 5–60.

Reiser, Robert A. "Reducing Student Procrastination in a Personalized System of Instruction Course."*Educational Communications and Technology Journal* (Spring 1984), pp. 41–49.

Sherman , J. Gilmour, and Ruskin, Robert S. *The Personalized System of Instruction.* Volume 13, Instructional Design Library. (Englewood Cliffs, N.J.: Educational Technology Pubs., 1978).

Terman, Michael. "Personalizing the Large Enrollment Course." *Teaching of Psychology* (April 1978), pp. 72–75.

Audio-Tutorial Systems

Kalmbach, John A. "Successful Characteristics of Students in an AudioTutorial College Course: A Descriptive Study." *NSPI Journal* (February 1980), pp. 43–46.

Postlethwait, S. N. "Principles Behind the Audio-Tutorial System." *NSPI Journal* (May 1978), pp. 3, 4, 18.

Postlethwait, S. N.; Novak, J.; and Murray, H. *The Audio-Tutorial Approach to Learning.* (Minneapolis, Minn.: Burgess Publishing Company, 1972).

Postlethwait, S. N. "Using Science and Technology to Teach Science and Technology." *Engineering Education* (January 1984), pp. 204–209.

Russell, James D. *The Audio-Tutorial System.* Volume 3, Instructional Design Library. (Englewood Cliffs, N.J.: Educational Technology Pubs., 1978).

Smith, Horace G. "Investigation of Several Techniques for Reviewing Audio-Tutorial Instruction." *Educational Communication and Technology Journal* (Fall 1979), pp. 195–204.

Sturgis, A. V., and Grobe, Cary H. "Audio-Tutorial Instruction: An Evaluation." *Improving College and University Teaching* (Spring 1976), p. 81.

Instructional Modules

Fisher, Kathleen M., and MacWhinney, Brian. "AV Autotutorial Instruction: A Review of Evaluative Research." *AV Communication Review* (February 1976), pp. 229–261.

Johnson, Rita B., and Johnson, Stuart R. *Toward Individualized Learning: A Developer's Guide to Self-Instruction.* (Reading, Mass.: Addison-Wesley, 1975).

Moore, David M. "Self-Instruction and Technology: A Review." *Journal of Educational Technology Systems* (no. 1 1976–1977), pp. 51–56.

Radway, Bonnie, and Schroeder, Betty. "Modular Instruction Is the Way of the Future!" *Journal of Business Education* (March 1978), pp. 247, 249–50.

Russell, James D., and Johanningsmeier, Kathleen A. *Increasing Competence through Modular Instruction.* (Dubuque, Iowa: Kendall/Hunt, 1981).

Sussman, Miriam L. "Making Tracks with LAP's." *Florida Vocational Journal* (April 1978), pp. 17–19.

Thiagarajan, Sivasailam. *Grouprograms.* Volume 8, Instructional Design Library. (Englewood Cliffs, N.J.: Educational Technology Publications, 1978).

Audiovisual References

The Audio-Tutorial System—An Independent Study Approach. West Lafayette, Ind.: Purdue University, 1968. 16-mm film. 25 minutes. Color.

Individualized Learning Using Instructional Modules. Englewood Cliffs, N.J.: Educational Technology Publications, undated. Set of 6 audio cassettes. 20 minutes each.

The Personalized System of Instruction. Washington, D.C.: Center for Personalized Instruction, 1974. 16-mm film. 20 minutes. Color.

Programmed Instruction: The Development Process. Austin, Tex.: University of Texas, 1969. 16-mm film. 19 minutes. Color.

PSI. Washington, D.C.: Center for Personalized Instruction, 1976. Sound slide set (cassette), 80 slides. 20 minutes.

Periodicals

British Journal of Educational Technology (quarterly)
Council for Educational Technology
10 Queen Anne Street
London W1, England

Educational Technology (monthly)
Educational Technology Publications
720 Palisade Avenue
Englewood Cliffs, New Jersey 07632

Journal of Educational Technology Systems (quarterly)
Baywood Publishing Company
43 Central Drive
Farmingdale, New York 11735

Performance & Instruction Journal (monthly)
National Society for Performance and Instruction (NSPI)
1126 Sixteenth Street, N.W.
Washington, DC 20036

Organizations

Center for Personalized Instruction
Loyola Hall, Room 29
Georgetown University
Washington, DC 20057

International Society for Individualized Instruction (ISII)
c/o Dr. Charles E. Wales
West Virginia University
Morgantown, W. Virginia 26506

National Society for Performance and Instruction (NSPI)
1126 Sixteenth Street, N.W.
Washington, DC 20036

Programmed Tutoring Center
2805 East Tenth Street
Indiana University
Bloomington, Indiana 47401

Possible Projects

11-A. Appraise a commercially available program using the "Appraisal Checklist" in the chapter, one from another source, or of your own design.

11-B. Construct a short (10 to 15 frame) program on a subject of your choice. Use either the linear or branching style of programming. Describe exactly how you would use your program and under what conditions.

11-C. Submit a bibliography of at least ten titles of commercially available programs which could be used in your subject field.

11-D. Observe a programmed tutoring session and write up your analysis of the session including strengths and weaknesses of the approach as you observed it being used.

11-E. Interview an instructor or students who have used the Personalized System of Instruction. Determine their reaction to using the system and ascertain what they perceive as the advantages and disadvantages of the approach.

11-F. Visit an Audio-Tutorial learning center. Interview students using A–T materials as well as the instructors. Prepare a report describing the center and the reactions of the students and the instructor(s).

11-G. Utilize an instructional module as though you were a student. Be sure to do all the activities and complete the exercises. Prepare an appraisal of the module from your point of view. Submit the module with your appraisal, if possible.

11-H. Take some teaching/learning format not discussed in the chapter and analyze it according to the criteria shown in the summary table at the end of the chapter.

Simulation
and Games

Outline

Objectives

After studying this chapter, you should be able to:

1. Define *game*, *simulation*, *simulation game*, and *instruction* and distinguish among examples of each.
2. Relate games to drill-and-practice learning.
3. Describe an instructional situation appropriate to game use; the description should include objectives, audience, and the nature of the game chosen.
4. Relate the special attributes of simulation to: (a) discovery learning, (b) social interaction, and (c) physical skill learning.
5. Define *role play* and discuss its applications.
6. Give at least two examples of simulators.
7. Describe an instructional situation appropriate to simulation use; the description should include objectives, audience, and nature of the simulation chosen.
8. Define *holistic learning* and relate it to simulation games.
9. Describe an instructional situation appropriate to simulation game use; the description should include objectives, audience, and nature of the simulation game chosen.
10. Identify at least four limitations of instructional games and simulations.
11. State at least three appraisal criteria that apply particularly to simulation/game materials.
12. Appraise one simulation/game using the ''Appraisal Checklist'' given in this chapter.
13. Name two general reference works most useful for locating simulation/game materials.
14. Define *frame game* and give two examples of adaptations of familiar game frames.
15. Outline the eight major steps in designing simulation/games.
16. Define *scenario*, *transaction*, and *consequence* in the context of simulation/game design.
17. Identify the utilization procedures that are emphasized in simulation/game use more than with other media.
18. Paraphrase the four major phases of the group debriefing process.
19. Discuss briefly the evaluation problems that are relatively unique to simulation/game use.

Lexicon

game
simulation
simulation game
drill-and practice learning
inductive/deductive learning
discovery learning
role-play
simulator
holistic learning
frame game
scenario
transaction
consequence
debriefing

The use of gaming and simulation techniques in instruction is by no means a new idea. The simulation of battlefield strategy in the form of games can be traced back to 3000 BC in China. Games such as chess and *go* are the residue of these ancient training exercises. Today's wargaming employs computers to digest vast volumes of data, and the application of gaming techniques to training and instruction has spread into business, higher education, and elementary/secondary education. Experience has shown that simulations and games can make a powerful contribution to learning if they are properly understood and properly used.

The reasons that simulation and game enthusiasts give to explain their interest in these techniques are as varied as the kinds of simulation and game materials. Some express their concern that learning should avoid the drudgery too often associated with the classroom. Others emphasize the sociological point that play is a natural and necessary component of young children's learning; play should be encouraged and melded with academic objectives. Adult educators and trainers are interested in simulation as a cost-effective method of practicing complex skills. Futurists, along with educational psychologists, cite the importance of learning to view problems as a whole. These and other claims need to be appraised critically before deciding whether to use simulation and game materials.

This chapter examines the more conventional applications of simulation/gaming; Chapter 14 takes a deeper look at the emerging technology of video games and other such computer-controlled games.

▲ **Figure 12.1**
Games appeal to all ages.

BASIC CONCEPTS

Game

A *game* is an *activity in which participants follow prescribed rules that differ from those of reality as they strive to attain a challenging goal*.

The distinction between "play" and "reality" is what makes games entertaining. Most people seem to enjoy setting aside the logical rules of everyday life occasionally and entering an artificial environment with different dynamics. For example, in chess the markers each have arbitrarily different movement patterns based roughly on the military potentials of certain societal roles in some ancient time. Players capture each other's markers by observing elaborate rules of play, rather than simply reaching across the board to grab the marker.

Attaining the goal usually entails competition. The competition may be individual against individual, as in chess; group against group, as in basketball; or individual against a standard, as in golf (with "par" as the standard). In playing video games,

players typically are competing against their own previous scores, and ultimately against the designer of the game as they approach mastery of the game.

To be challenging, goals should have a probability of achievement of something in the range of 50 percent. A goal that is always attained or never attainable presents no real challenge; the outcome is too predictable. People exhibit most interest and motivation in a task when the challenge is in the intermediate range.

On the other hand, the "striving to attain a challenging goal" does not necessarily have to involve competition. Communication games, fantasy games, and "encounter" games exemplify a whole array of activities in which participants agree to suspend the normal rules of interpersonal communication in order to pursue such goals as self-awareness, empathy, sensitivity, and leadership development. These activities are considered games but they do not entail competition.

Simulation

A *simulation* is an *abstraction or simplification of some real-life situation or process.* In simulations, participants usually play a role that involves them in interactions with other people and/or with elements of the simulated environment. A business management simulation, for example, might put the participant into the role of production manager of a mythical corporation, provide him or her with statistics about business conditions, and direct him or her to negotiate a new labor contract with the union bargaining team.

Simulations can vary greatly in the extent to which they fully reflect the realities of the situation they are intended to model. A simulation that incorporates too many details of a complex situation might be too complicated and time-consuming for the intended audience. On the other hand, if the model is oversimplified it may fail completely to communicate its intended point. A well-designed simulation provides a faithful model of those elements that are most salient to the immediate objective and it informs the instructor and participants about elements that have been simplified or eliminated completely.

Simulation Game

A *simulation game combines the attributes of a simulation (role-playing, a model of reality) with the attributes of a game (striving toward a goal, specific rules).* Like a simulation, it may be relatively high or low in its modeling of reality. Like a game, it may or may not entail competition.

Instruction

Any of the types of activities described so far may be designed to *help someone learn new skills or values applicable beyond the game itself.* Most commercially developed games intend to provide diversion, not instruction. A person who plays *Clue* or *Thinking Man's Golf* enough times probably learns more and more about the game itself but little in the way of usable skills.

Admittedly, the attribute of being "instructional" is often a matter of degree. The stated intentions of the designer or user would have to be examined closely. For example, basketball—normally a non-instructional game—could be assigned by a football coach to his players as a means of developing agility and faster reflexes. In such a case basketball would be "instructional" for that situation.

Many game activities contain some modeling of reality and the distinction between simulations and games is not always clear. Many role-playing exercises take on game-like qualities as participants maneuver toward a good outcome for themselves. Yet the distinctions are worth making because they have significant implications for when and how these different types of materials are used. Figure 12.2 illustrates how the basic concepts of game, simulation, and instruction may overlap and interact; it shows that seven different classifications can be given. The following sections of the chapter will deal with the three classifications of most direct relevance to our interests: instructional games, instructional simulations, and instructional simulation games.

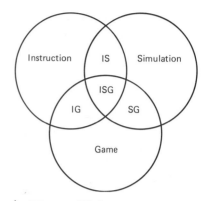

▲ **Figure 12.2**
"Instruction," "Simulation," and "Game" are each separate concepts; a given activity may have attributes of two or more of these concepts, e.g. "instructional simulation game."

INSTRUCTIONAL GAMES

Play in Human Development

Games are, above all, a form of play. As such, they may be looked upon with suspicion by those who think learning and playing are incompatible. But as viewed by developmental psychologists, play can be a useful mechanism indeed; deprivation of play can impede an individual's cognitive and creative growth.

Anthropologists note that primitive societies often use the playing of games to acculturate their members and to teach survival skills. It is certainly reasonable to assume that play in more advanced societies serves similar functions. Freudian interpretations of play see it as a symbolic reenactment of a threatening event, a safety valve for relieving pressures placed on children by the childrearing practices of a culture. Child psychologist Jean Piaget views play as a manifestation of "assimilation," one of the mental processes fundamental

Flashback: GAMING—FROM ANCIENT BATTLEFIELDS TO MODERN CLASSROOMS

It is ironic that educational simulation/gaming, which is now prominently associated with the promotion of mutual understanding and cooperation, traces its ancestry to games designed to teach military tactics and strategies.

One of the earliest known examples of war gaming is *wei-chi* (meaning "encirclement"), the existence of which can be traced back to at least 2000 BC. The game was introduced into Japan around the eighth century AD and survives throughout the world today in the popular game *go*. A variation of the encirclement game evolved in India as *chaturanga*. In this game, representations of foot soldiers, horsemen, chariots, and elephants faced each other on a board representing a battlefield. The Western version of *chaturanga*, chess, evolved into its current form during the Middle Ages. Although chess has long since lost its specific functions as a military training tool, tactics and strategic moves are still at its core, and the object of the game remains a "military" one: to capture (or checkmate) the opponent's king.

Following military defeats in the Napoleonic Wars, the Prussians throughout the nineteenth century invested great ingenuity in the refinement of war games that would allow greater latitude for experimentation at lower cost than actual military exercises. Terrain models of battlefields replaced checkered boards; rules for the value of movement of pieces were more realistically prescribed; teams of opposing forces replaced individual players; judges monitored the observance of rules. The resounding Prussian victory in the Franco–Prussian War of 1870 to 1871 and the subsequent Prussian reputation for military genius may be attributable in part to their preparedness born out of years of practice in *Kriegspiel*.

In the years immediately following the Franco–Prussian War, the competition began to catch up. War gaming took root in England and was introduced soon afterward at the United States Military Academy, where the data from the American Civil War added further precision to the components of war games.

By the early twentieth century, war gaming had spread to all the technologically advanced nations of the world. Germany and Japan raised war-gam-

ing techniques to a high art as part of their preparations for World War II. At Japan's Total War Research Institute, for example, highly elaborate simulation games were used to plot both military and civilian strategies to be employed in the conflict which lay immediately ahead.

A breakthrough in war-gaming technique came toward the end of World War II with the advent of the electronic computer. The high speed calculating power of the computer vastly increased designers' ability to deal with complexity. It became possible to include in the games, with a good deal of precision, social and political variables as well as military data.

An important step in the evolution of war games toward educational games came with the development in the mid-1950s of so-called "crisis games." Growing largely out of experimentation at the RAND Corporation to deal with potential Cold War problems, crisis games are simulations of hypothetical crisis situations, with participants trying to solve or alleviate the crises within a framework of rules structured to reflect the conditions of the simulated crisis situation.

Not long after the original RAND experiments, crisis games were in use at several universities. Gaming became a popular instructional technique in which students of international relations could adopt the roles of government decision makers and play out hypothetical crises.

Business Games

Since economists and business management theorists already possessed well-defined, quantitative models upon which simulation/gaming could be based, it is not surprising that business games were among the first academic games to be developed. The linkage of business games with military games is quite clear. In 1956 the American Management Association (AMA) launched a research project to consider the possibility of developing a simulation that would allow management trainees to experience the same kind of strategic decision-making practice as military officers were then experiencing. Its efforts culminated in the creation of the AMA Top Management Decision Simulation, a computer-assisted simulation game in which teams of players representing officers of companies make business decisions and receive "quarterly reports" on the outcomes of their decisions. Business executives and business educators reacted to the game with great enthusiasm.

By the end of 1959 variations of the AMA game had been developed at IBM and the University of California at Los Angeles, and within three years the development of over 85 such games had been noted in professional journals.

To a great extent, business games and crisis games were an extension of war games into new "battlefronts"—the marketplace and the diplomatic arena. Further development was needed to encourage the use of simulation/gaming for more "peaceful" academic purposes, that is, for the understanding and minimization of conflict rather than simply the achievement of supremacy within the conflict situation. This transition can perhaps best be illustrated by considering the career odyssey of one of the major figures in contemporary simulation gaming.

Clark C. Abt, a systems engineer, became involved in the 1950s with the design of computer simulations of air battles, space missions, disarmament inspection systems, and other military problems. He and his colleagues at the Missile Systems Division of the Raytheon Company began to apply war-gaming techniques to increasingly complex problems—problems that became more and more involved with human factors—the social, eco-nomic, and political causes and consequences of military actions.

Seeking to better understand these human factors, Abt returned to M.I.T. to earn a Ph.D. in the social sciences. He founded his own company, Abt Associates, in 1965.

Classroom Simulation Games

Within the next few years Abt Associates became a major fountainhead of classroom simulation games, some of the better-known examples being *Pollution*, *Neighborhood*, *Empire*, *Manchester*, *Colony*, and *Caribou Hunting Game*.

As Abt Associates was developing the techniques for classroom simulation/gaming, many educators, especially in the social studies, were becoming interested in inquiry-oriented approaches to teaching. Jerome Bruner and other instructional theorists, working in the same vein as John Dewey had a generation earlier, were advocating the importance of active student involvement in learning. Immersion in a problem, informed guessing, and hypothesis testing were the methods best calculated to promote discovery learning.

This theoretical viewpoint activated a number of reform-minded curriculum development projects. Bruner's own contribution was *Man: A Course of Study*, a total curriculum package incorporating the Abt Associates' *Caribou Hunting* and *Seal Hunting*. Other such projects, including the High School Geography Project and the Holt Social Studies Program, yielded several simulation games.

Another historical influence critical to the establishment of the academic respectability of simulation/gaming in the classroom was the Academic Games Program at Johns Hopkins University. Headed by eminent educational sociologist James S. Coleman from 1966 to 1973, the Johns Hopkins group developed a number of ground-breaking games (including *Life Career*, *Democracy*, *Generation Gap*, and *Ghetto*) and conducted many studies of game playing and the learning associated with it. Their general conclusions confirmed the advantages of simulation/gaming and also helped identify some of the problem areas in simulation/game utilization.

▲ **Figure 12.3**
Play is a natural and essential feature of human growth.

▲ **Figure 12.4**
A game can be a motivator of intellectual skill practice.

to intellectual growth. All observers agree that play is an adaptive mechanism important for human development.

Games as Learning Frameworks

Games can provide attractive and instructionally effective frameworks for learning activities. They are attractive because they are fun! Children and adults alike tend to react positively to an invitation to play. Games are a welcome break in the day-to-day routine of the classroom or training program. Novelty reduces boredom for adults as well as for children. The pleasant, relaxed atmosphere fostered by games has proven to be highly conducive to efficient learning.

Games are particularly appropriate for the *drill-and-practice mode* of learning. This mode is employed with skills that require *repetitive practice in order to be mastered*. Multiplication table drills are an example of this mode. Drill-and-practice exercises can become tedious, leading to rapid burnout of interest. But putting this sort of practice into a game format makes it more palatable, thus keeping the learner "on task" for a longer time with greater satisfaction.

Of course, to be instructionally meaningful the game activity must provide actual practice of the intended academic skill. An instructionally fatal shortcoming of poorly designed games is that players spend a large proportion of their time exercising the "skill" of waiting for their turn, throwing dice, moving markers around a board, and similar trivial actions.

The element of competition must be handled very thoughtfully in choosing and using instructional games. Individual-versus-individual competition can be a highly motivating device as long as the contenders are fairly matched and the conflict does not overshadow the educational goal. Group-versus-group competition entails the same cautions, but it

has the added attraction of providing practice in cooperation and teamwork. For instructional purposes, competition versus a standard may be the best option. It allows individualization, setting different standards for different players. In fact, one of the most effective standards can be the student's own past performance, the goal being to continually raise the level of aspirations.

In any event, in cases in which competition is an element, the scoring system provides a clue as to what type of competition is being fostered. Is one individual or group declared the "winner"? Or is it possible for all players to attain equally high scores? For educational purposes, the latter certainly is preferable. An example is the *Planet Management Game* (described in detail later), in which it is possible for all play groups to achieve a similar level of prosperity for the inhabitants of their planet.

Applications of Instructional Games

Instructional games are particularly well suited to:

- Attainment of cognitive objectives in general, particularly those involving recognition, discrimination, or drill and practice, such as grammar, phonics, spelling, arithmetic skills, formulas (chemistry, physics, logic), basic science concepts, place names, terminology, etc.
- Adding motivation to topics which ordinarily attract little student interest, for example, grammar rules, spelling, math drills.
- Small-group instruction; instructional games provide structured activities that students or trainees can conduct by themselves without close instructor supervision.

▲ **Figure 12.5**
A wide range of basic skills are called upon in card games.

- Basic skills such as sequence, sense of direction, visual perception, number concepts, and following rules can be developed by means of card games. A leading advocate of the educational potential of card games is Margie Golick, a psychologist specializing in learning disabilities.*
- Vocabulary building; a number of commercial games such as *Boggle*, *Fluster*, *Scrabble*, and *Probe* have been used successfully by teachers to expand spelling and vocabulary skills although they were designed and are marketed primarily for recreational purposes.

―――――――――

*Margie Golick. *Deal Me In!* New York: Jeffrey Norton Publisher, 1973.

Media File:
"Tuf" Instructional Game

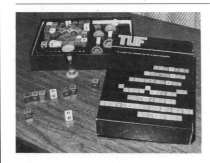

Content area: Mathematics
Age Level: Grade 3 through college

Players roll cubes containing numbers and mathematical symbols, and attempt to form these into equations. "Tuf" might be used throughout a whole course in algebra; it can be played at increasing levels of sophistication.

Source: Avalon Hill.

Media File:
"On-Words" Instructional Game

Content area: Language arts, spelling
Age Level: Grade 4 through adult

In "On-Words" players roll letter and number cubes, then attempt to form words of a specified length. Intersecting words are formed, as in a crossword puzzle. Can be played at Basic, Advanced, or Adventurous levels, progressing from simple spelling and counting through word analysis.

Source: wff 'N Proof.

INSTRUCTIONAL SIMULATIONS

Simulation and Discovery Learning

A particular value of simulation is that it provides a specific framework for implementing what has become known as *discovery learning, the inquiry approach, experiential learning,* and other such terms denoting *inductive* teaching/learning strategies.

The typical conventional classroom teaching/learning approach (we could call it a *deductive* strategy) proceeds something like this:

Presentation of information
(The Point)
▼
Reference to particular examples
▼
Application of the knowledge to the student's experiences

This is an efficient and economical way to learn. One of its weaknesses, though, is its heavy dependence on language for transmission of information, which can be a real handicap for students with limited verbal skills. Another drawback to the deductive method is the difficulty many students have in applying the symbolically coded concept ("The Point") to everyday experience. They may be able to pass a written test (knowledge on a verbal-symbolic level) but they cannot solve real-life problems.

In contrast, the discovery or *inductive* strategy proceeds more like this:

Immersion in a real or contrived problematic situation
▼
Development of hypotheses
▼
Testing of hypotheses
▼
Arriving at conclusion
(**The Point**)

In discovery learning the *learner is led toward "The Point" through trial-and-error grappling with a problem*. Cause-and-effect relationships are discovered by observing the actual consequences of actions. This sort of immersion in a problem is the core of most simulations. Through simulations we can offer learners a laboratory in areas such as social sciences and human relations as well as in areas related to the physical sciences, where laboratories have long been taken for granted. True, it tends to be more time-consuming than the straightforward lecture approach but the payoff is a higher level of comprehension that is likely to be retained longer.

The great advantage of this sort of firsthand immersion in a topic is that students are more likely to be able to apply to real life what they have practiced applying in simulated circumstances. This raises the issue of the degree of realism captured by a simulation. A common defect in poorly designed simulations is an overemphasis on *chance* factors in determining outcomes. Much of the reality is spoiled if "Chance Element" cards cause players to gain or lose great quantities of points or other resources regardless of their strategic decisions. An overemphasis on chance or an overly simplified representation of real relationships might end up teaching lessons quite contrary to what was intended.

Role-Plays

Role-play refers to a *simulation in which the dominant feature is relatively open-ended interaction among people*. In essence, a role-play asks someone to imagine that he or she is himself or herself, or another person, in a particular situation; he or she then behaves as that person would or the way the situation seems to demand. The purpose is to learn something about that sort of person or about the dynamics of that sort of situation. The role descriptions may be very general, leaving great latitude for the participant; for example, in *Actionalysis* (see "Media File") the person playing the role of "teacher" is given only a one-word description of the attitude he or she is supposed to be reflecting. The purpose here is to allow the person's own traits to emerge so that they may be discussed and possibly modified. In other simulations, such as historical recreations, highly detailed roles are described in order to project the realities of life in that period.

As a technology of instruction, the role-play simulation has proven to be a motivating and effective method of developing social skills, especially empathy—putting oneself in someone else's shoes. Our day-to-day social behavior tends to be governed by our assumptions about who we are, who our associates are, and *why* they act the way they do. A potent

way of challenging—and thereby changing—these assumptions is to experience a slice of life from someone else's perspective.

The sorts of tasks that lend themselves especially well to role-playing are counselling, interviewing, sales and customer services, supervision, and management. The settings most often simulated are committee meetings, negotiation sessions, public meetings, work teams, and one-to-one interviews.

Simulators

Competencies in the motor skill domain require practice under conditions of high feedback—giving the learner the feel of the action. Although it might be ideal to practice such skills under real-life conditions, some skills (for example, piloting an airplane or driving a car) can be practiced much more safely and conveniently by means of simulated conditions. The devices employed to represent physical systems in a scaled-down form are referred to as *simulators*.

One familiar example of a simulator is the flight trainer, a mock-up of the interior of the cockpit, complete with controls and gauges. Today the flight crews of most major airlines receive a large proportion of their training in flight simulators, which are often controlled by computers and

---

Media File:
"Principles of Effective Salesmanship"
Instructional Simulation

Content area: Salesmanship
Age Level: Adult
Playing time: Approximately three hours

In groups of three to five, participants play the roles of salespeople. They make decisions related to identification of customer needs, preparation of a needs checklist, and development of an effective sales approach based on needs identified.

Source: Didactic Systems, Inc.

Media File:
"Actionalysis" Instructional Simulation

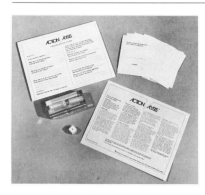

Content area: Education (adaptable to others)
Age Level: College and other adult

"Actionalysis" provides two rather simple and flexible structures for role-playing related to teaching or supervision. Participants break into triads for each round: a "teacher," a "student," and an observer; each follows role instructions on a card. Roles and situations change each round.

Source: Harvey Mette.

Media File:
"Starpower" Instructional Simulation

Content area: Social studies, government
Age Level: High school and above

"Starpower" revolves around the trading of tokens which have been distributed "randomly" at the start. During each round participants try to increase their wealth and move upward in the three-tiered class structure which evolves. Later in play, the "rich" make the rules.

Source: Simile II.

offer highly realistic audiovisual effects. Besides eliminating the possibility of loss of life and aircraft, these simulators allow significant savings of energy—millions of gallons of fuel annually—and other costs.

One recent study estimated that in-air training costs about $4000 per hour compared to only $400 per hour on the flight simulator, with no loss in effectiveness.

Another example, which more people have experienced personally, is the automobile driver-training simulator. One of the best known of such systems is the AEtna Drivotrainer, shown in Figure 12.7. This system typically consists of a number of simulated car-driving units complete with all the controls of a real automobile.

At the front of the room is a screen. At the rear are a film projector and audio console used to simulate the sights and sounds of actual driving conditions. Students "drive" on filmed streets and highways and their individual responses to filmed driving conditions are recorded and scored. Since its inception in 1953, over 10 million students have sharpened their driving skills by means of this particular system.

Simpler simulators are in widespread use in areas such as training workers in a broad range of manual skills. A full discussion of such devices, including a number of examples, can be found in A. J. Romiszowski's *The Selection and Use of Instructional Media.* *

*London: Kogan Page, 1974, p. 305–329.

◀ **Figure 12.6**
An airplane cockpit simulator by Grumman Aerospace.

▲ **Figure 12.7**
Students training on driver education simulators learn to deal with potentially hazardous conditions in the safety of the classroom.

INSTRUCTIONAL SIMULATION GAMES

Simulation Games and Holistic Learning

Since they combine the characteristics of both simulations and games, instructional simulation games have advantages and applications in common with both formats. As such, they exemplify one of the major rationales for the use of simulation and gaming: the provision of *holistic learning*. That is, *through the modeling of reality* and through the players' interactions as they strive to succeed, *learners encounter a whole and dynamic view of the process being studied*. Conventional instruction tends to segment reality into separate packages (biology, mathematics, psychology, etc.), but that is not how the real world is organized. Through participation in simulation games we can see the whole process and its dynamic interrelationships in action. In addition, our *emotions are allowed to get involved along with the thinking process*. Participants commonly experience excitement, elation, disappointment, even anger, as they struggle to succeed. This, of course, is

Applications of Instructional Simulation

Instructional simulations, including role-plays, are particularly well suited for:

- Training in motor skills, including athletic and work skills, and complex skills that might otherwise be too hazardous or expensive to practice in real-life settings.

- Instruction in social interaction and human relations, where empathy and coping with the motivations of other people are major goals.
- Development of decision making skills (e.g., microteaching in teacher education, mock court in law school, management simulations in business administration).

▼ **Figure 12.8**
Role-playing simulation helps service personnel develop their ''people'' skills.

▼ **Figure 12.9**
A well-designed simulation game stirs emotional responses comparable to the reality being modeled.

how learning takes place in the world outside the classroom.

Applications of Instructional Simulation Games

As indicated earlier, instructional simulation games are found in curricular applications that require both the repetitive skill practice associated with games and the reality context associated with simulations. Societal processes (e.g., *Ghetto, Democracy*), cultural conflicts (e.g., *Bafa Bafa*), historical eras (e.g., *Empire, Manchester*), and ecological systems (e.g., *Extinction, Planet Management Game*) are popular topics.

In general, instructional simulation games are frequently used to provide an overview of a large, dynamic pro-

cess. The excitement of play stimulates interest in the subject matter, and the holistic treatment of the game gives students a feel for the total process before approaching parts of it in a more linear form.

Media File:
"Planet Management" Instructional Simulation Game

Content area: Ecology, social planning
Age Level: Junior high school through adult

Participants play in teams, each representing the governing body of a mythical planet. They must decide the annual budget allocations for agriculture, manufacturing, social welfare, etc. An elaborate feedback system shows the effects of their decisions on food, income, population, and environment.

Source: Houghton Mifflin.

Media File:
"The Green Revolution Game," Instructional Simulation Game

Content area: Community development, social studies
Age Level: College and adult

The setting is a village in contemporary India. Players attempt to manage their limited resources to provide subsistence for their families. Pests, drought, crop failures, shortage of cash and credit, and deaths of family members are among the realistic variables with which each player must contend.

Source: Marginal Context Ltd.

Media File:
"Stress Survival" Instructional Simulation Game

Content area: Management, supervision
Age Level: Adult

Players first determine their own stress threshold with a stress tolerance profile. The profile score becomes a "handicap" when dealing with simulated on-the-job stress situations, earning or losing points. Final score reflects the player's personal stress tolerance and ability to diffuse stress.

Source: Education Research.

LIMITATIONS OF INSTRUCTIONAL GAMES AND SIMULATIONS

As with all of the other instructional media and formats discussed earlier, simulations and games have their limitations as well as potential strengths. Any materials-based instruction is only as good as the materials themselves. The simulation/game format is not magical. The effectiveness of the learning depends on the quality of the particular material and its utilization.

The use of simulation/game materials usually demands special grouping arrangements—pairing, for instance, or small groups. Some learners might not be able to exercise the responsibility and self-discipline necessary to the success of self-directed instruction.

Obtaining all the needed materials can be expensive and time-consuming. Sometimes costs can be kept down by making local modifications (e.g., altering the procedures so that consumable materials are not consumed). But effort will still be needed to get all the materials together and keep them together before, during, and after play.

Some simulation/game activities depend heavily on post-game discussion ("debriefing") for their full instructional effect. This debriefing must be skillfully planned and conducted. If the instructor lacks discussion-leading skills the whole learning experience is diminished.

Time can be a significant obstacle. Inductive learning is more time-consuming than straightforward lectures or reading assignments. A principle that can be stated in a single sentence might require an hour of play plus discussion to be conveyed experientially. You have to decide whether the added richness of the learning experience is worth the time.

As discussed earlier, some games entail competition in some form. A cultural setting that discourages competitiveness would not be a very compatible place for using competitive games. Likewise, a culture in which achievement is not valued might not provide the motivation required for students to get "into the spirit" of the game. On an individual level, there will be students for whom competition would be uncomfortable, unfair, or instructionally ineffective. This is true, of course, of every type of instructional treatment. It emphasizes the need to always be prepared to deal with individual differences.

SIMULATION / GAMING AND THE ASSURE MODEL

Putting simulations and games into use can be organized by turning once more to the ASSURE model. Again, it is assumed that you have analyzed the needs, interests, and learning characteristics of your audience and clearly specified your objectives. So we will begin here with the third element of the model: select, modify, or design the materials.

Select Materials

Selection of any particular simulation or game involves the same considerations as selection of media materials in general. How does the material fit your curricular objectives? Does it address those objectives in a way no other media format can? Is the cost in money and time worth the benefit?

Other considerations that apply particularly to simulation and gaming are noted in the "Appraisal Checklist" included here. You will note that emphasis is placed on identifying whether the item really does provide *relevant practice of meaningful skills* within a *valid representation of reality*. These are aspects of simulation/game materials most likely to prove faulty.

Even more than with most other instructional materials, you will not be able to judge the appropriateness and effectiveness of simulation/gaming materials on the basis of superficial examination. You really can't judge a simulation/game by its "cover." A trial run-through by yourself or with friends is the only relatively sure way of determining how the game flows and what it teaches.

One discouraging aspect of simulation/gaming instruction is the difficulty of locating and acquiring simulation/gaming materials. Many such materials are marketed by their individual developers, so they do not get into regular trade distribution channels and are likely to be publicized only by word-of-mouth. Others are distributed by small commercial houses that have an annoying tendency to move and/or go out of business very rapidly. Only a minority are sold through regular publishing outlets. So the prospective simulation/game user may need good detective skills and perseverance to obtain exactly the sort of material required. Fortunately, there are two reference aids that can help you in this task *The Guide to Simulations/Games for Education and Training*, edited by Robert E. Horn and Ann Cleaves, and *Handbook of Simulation Gaming in Social Education*, edited by Ron Stadsklev. (Both books are described in detail in Appendix A.)

Modify Materials

Although the supply of commercially developed simulation and game materials is growing, you might find it necessary or desirable to *modify* some existing materials to fit your instructional objectives more closely.

Role-play and other less structured activities (e.g., communication games) can be modified easily by changing role descriptions, changing the setting of the activity, or simplifying the interaction pattern in the original activity.

Some games are designed for adaptation to varying age or grade levels. Several of the games in the *Wff 'N Proof* series, such as *On-Words* and *Equations*, begin as simple spelling or arithmetic drills. The instruction manual contains directions for progressively raising the objectives and rules to higher cognitive levels, ending with games of transformational grammar and symbolic logic.

Appraisal Checklist: Simulation / Game

Title_____ ☐ Has gaming features
(e.g. competition, scoring)

Publisher/distributor_____ ☐ Has simulation features
(e.g. role playing)

Publication date_____

Number of players   Playing time_____

Intended audience/grade level_____   Subject area_____

Special equipment or facilities needed:

Objectives (stated or implied):

Brief description:

Entry capabilities required:

   —prior knowledge:
   —reading ability:
   —math ability:

Rating	High		Medium		Low
Likely to arouse student interest	☐	☐	☐	☐	☐
Provides practice of meaningful skills	☐	☐	☐	☐	☐
(Game) Winning dependent on player actions (vs. chance)	☐	☐	☐	☐	☐
(Simulation) Validity of game model (realistic, accurate)	☐	☐	☐	☐	☐
Technical quality (durability, attractiveness, etc.)	☐	☐	☐	☐	☐
Evidence of effectiveness (e.g., field-test results)	☐	☐	☐	☐	☐
Clear directions for conducting game	☐	☐	☐	☐	☐
Clear and concise players' instructions	☐	☐	☐	☐	☐
Useful debriefing guide	☐	☐	☐	☐	☐

Strong points:

Weak points:

Reviewer_____

Position_____

Recommended action_____   Date_____

A more substantive type of modification is to take an existing game and change the subject matter while retaining the original game structure. The original game is referred to as a *frame game* because its framework lends itself to multiple adaptations. When one is modifying a frame game, the *underlying structure of a familiar game provides the basic procedures of play*—the dynamics of the process. The designer loads the desired content onto a convenient frame (see Stolovitch and Thiagarajan's *Frame Games* in the References at the end of this chapter).

Familiar parlor games such as tic-tac-toe, rummy, concentration, and bingo, which were intended for recreation rather than instruction nevertheless can be viewed as potential frameworks for carrying your own instructional content. Television game shows often have been modeled after such parlor games; they in turn suggest additional frameworks. Here are some sample adaptations:

Safety tic-tac-toe—A three-by-three grid is used; each row represents a place where safety rules pertain—home, school, street; each column represents the level of question difficulty. Teams take turns selecting and trying to answer safety-related questions, attempting to fill in three squares in a row.

▼ **Figure 12.10**
"Hollywood Squares" is one of the television game shows based on a familiar "frame."

Spelling rummy—Using alphabet cards instead of regular playing cards, players attempt to spell short words following the general rules of rummy.

Reading concentration—This game uses about a dozen matched picture-word pairs of flash cards. Cards are placed face down. On each turn the player turns over two cards, seeking to match a pair. Both reading ability and memorization ability are exercised.

Word bingo—Each player's card has a five-by-five grid with a vocabulary word in each square. The leader randomly selects words; players then seek the words on their boards and if they are found, the square is marked. Winner is first player with five correctly marked squares in a row.

Design Materials

As indicated above, simple simulation/gaming materials may be adapted by an imaginative instructor with little more than pencil and paper. This does not mean, however, that designing simulation/gaming materials is a simple process. A great deal of careful thought is required for the planning and development of *effective* materials. Good simulation/gaming materials do not just happen.

The accompanying "How To . . ." section presents a model for the design of simulation and game materials. As you can see, many individual steps are involved in the process and the relationships between and among these steps can be quite complex.

Utilize Materials

For simulation/gaming, the utilization step of the ASSURE model entails procedures that are quite different at some points from those suggested earlier for other media.

▲ **Figure 12.11**
Successful learning from simulation/gaming is heavily dependent on the instructor's utilization practices, especially being well prepared.

Preview.   Familiarize yourself with the materials, preferably going through a "dry run" with some friends or a few selected students. Acquaint yourself with the rules. Note individual phases of the simulation/game. Be sure you are aware of exactly when and where important instructional points are made. Practice any activities that the game director is responsible for (e.g., providing tokens, computing scores for each round).

Set a time schedule for use of the materials. Your first concern is to have enough time for a successful session. A "good" game squeezed into too short a time can become a "bad" game. Some games—*Starpower*, for example—cannot be broken down to fit into separate class periods; they must be played through continuously. If you have to divide play into separate periods, try to have the breaks come at natural stopping points.

Prepare the Environment.   Check over all the materials to be certain that everything is ready in sufficient quantities. Before the participants arrive count everything again. If any audiovisual equipment is involved, give it a last minute checkout, too. As with any other kind

HOW TO...DESIGN INSTRUCTIONAL SIMULATIONS/GAMES

The process outlined in the above diagram will become clearer when considered step-by-step. Examples of each step are provided in the form of a rough prototype actually developed by participants in recent simulation/game design workshop.

Step 1. Select content and scope

Example: The general subject matter is ecology; more specifically, this activity will center on the sociopolitical conflicts involved in establishing a nature reserve, "Mountain Park Nature Reserve." Emphasis will be on developing the interpersonal skills to deal with such conflict situations. This activity will have both simulation *and* game characteristics. It should be playable within one session (approximately two to three hours). It will not deal with scientific or technical aspects of nature reserves.

Step 2. Specify audience
Example: "Mountain Park Nature Reserve" is meant to be played by environmental educators; that is, adults having previous formal background in some aspect(s) of ecology. The primary audience will be expected to have college level educational background.

Step 3. Specify objectives
Example: The general objectives are that participants will be able to: (a) describe the interactions

and conflicts among the social and political motivations of the major parties involved in establishing a nature reserve, and (b) anticipate and counter the objections raised by critics of the nature reserve.

Step 4. Develop Game Model

A. Create a scenario (for a simulation).

Example: A public hearing will be the setting for the action. This hearing has been set up to air the pros and cons of establishing the "Mountain Park Nature Reserve." The place is the capital city of a state or country with limited financial resources but a rather high degree of technological development. The time is the present.

B. Select roles to be represented and ascribe motives to those roles (for a simulation).

Example: The number of roles represented in the game can vary with the size of the playing group. Role descriptions will be written up for each of the following roles; each description will inform the player what his or her motives are—that is, what values he or she is seeking to promote. Possible roles include: representatives for concerned government agencies—Agriculture, Tourism, Industry, Conservation, etc.; residents of the impacted area; scientific experts; potential users; environmental activists; and others.

C. Describe constraints and resources.

Example: During the public hearing phase of the game, players will be able to address the total group only for specified limited amounts of time. During the prior "lobbying" phase their one-to-one contacts with other players will be limited according to how many "influence" chips they have accumulated. At the beginning of the game, players will have personal information only about those roles that are closely allied to their own positions.

D. Specify *transactions* to be carried out.

In order to achieve productive learning, players must be engaged in actions directly associated with the game's performance objectives. The transactions they carry out with other players or with the game materials should entail planning, discussing, choosing, testing hypotheses, gathering information, and the like. Players should *not* be spending most of their time waiting for turns, throwing dice, spinning spinners, or moving markers around a playing board.

Example: Since the second stated objective calls for countering the objections of critics, one of the main transactions will be listening critically to arguments, followed by the formulation of responses to those arguments. This means that one-to-one discussions will be one major transaction embedded in the game.

E. Arrange appropriate *consequences* for player actions.

Each action taken by the player should result in some feedback about the goodness or badness of that move. The designer wants to reinforce appropriate actions. This feedback can often be handled conveniently with a point system.

Example: Players will receive "influence points" depending on how they perform in each round of discussion in terms of: (a) presenting a logical argument consistent with their role, (b) using data to support their arguments, and (c) paraphrasing accurately the contrary arguments of others.

Step 5. Develop rules

A. Spell out procedures for play.

The aim here is to set up procedures and rules that will channel players into carrying out the sorts of transactions identified earlier. As mentioned previously, an existing game may serve as a "frame," supplying basic procedures for play.

Example: "Mountain Park Nature Reserve" will be played in two major phases—a series of small-group mini-debates and a public hearing that will conclude with a vote being taken. The debates will be carried out in triads consisting of two different roles plus an observer. (This "frame" is borrowed from *Actionalysis*.) The observer will award points to each role player depending on the criteria stated in Step 4E above. Each round of mini-debates lasts five minutes, after which everyone rotates into a new triad. Approximately six rounds will be allowed, after which the public hearing will afford various roles the opportunity to present testimony and to be questioned by others.

B. Devise scoring procedures (for a game).

A point system is often a convenient mechanism for delivering and keeping track of reinforcers.

Example: As described in Step 4E above, points will be allocated by the triad observers according to the given criteria. These "influence points" will be translated into political strength in the public hearing phase of the game. In the public hearing phase the scoring will be based on how many players vote for each position put forth.

Step 6. Construct prototype

At this point the designer constructs the needed player materials (e.g., role sheets and score cards) and a teacher's guide (including a debriefing outline).

Step 7. Try out prototype

The essence of the instructional technology approach is that materials are considered merely as prototypes until they have been tested in actual practice. Ideally, pilot testing would be conducted on a small sample group prior to use with the full group. Both the performance outcomes of the players and their emotional reactions to the prototype are observed and recorded to find clues to needed modifications.

Step 8. Revise

The tryout results may suggest revisions in any of the previous elements. There may be rough edges in the play procedures or scoring system. Playing time may run longer than desired. Additional roles may need to be added for increased realism. The original scope or objectives may even be reexamined.

The revised prototype would in turn be tested for effectiveness.

of teaching, students will judge you harshly if they sense that *you* haven't done *your* homework.

Prepare the Audience.

Inform your audience of the learning objectives of the simulation/game activities. Relate the simulation/game to previous studies. Announce the time schedule for completion of the activities. Run through the rules concisely and clearly. If the procedures are somewhat complex, walk the students through one initial round of activities. Resist the urge to lecture about content or to give hints about strategies. Get into the game as quickly as possible.

Present the Simulation/ Game.

Once the simulation/ game is rolling, your job is to keep the mood and the tempo upbeat. Stay in close touch with the action. Be ready to intervene, but only when intervention is clearly called for.

Some participants in simulation/ game activities may feel a bit confused in the initial stages and be hesitant to get into the swing of things. Reassure such students that initial confusion is not uncommon and that they will soon pick up on rules and procedures.

Watch for individuals or teams who have fallen behind in the activities or even dropped out of them. They may need additional help in mastering the game mechanics. Withdrawal often signals some basic disagreement with the game's approach to the subject matter. Rather than stifling or suppressing the dissent, discuss the disagreement on a one-to-one basis. Ask the dropout to suspend criticism until the end of the activities.

Watch out for personality clashes; they may require switching of partners or teammates for successful completion of the activities.

Keep track of elapsed time. The excitement and fascination of simulation and game activities make it easy to forget that time is passing. If necessary, remind participants of time limitations. Resist the temptation to extend simulation/game play at the expense of debriefing time.

If announcements must be made during utilization, try not to bluntly interrupt the activities by shouting above the hubbub. Dimming room lights or flashing your message on the overhead projector can attract the attention you need.

Record significant participant reactions and comments for discussion during the debriefing period.

Require Learner Response

A unique attribute of simulations and games is that participants are continuously responding *throughout* the activity. Indeed, without response there can be no activity. Why, then, should we be concerned with the response element of our ASSURE model when dealing with simulations and games?

The truth is that attention to learner response is perhaps more important in simulations and games than in any other instructional medium we have discussed in this book. The reason? Learner response in simulation/gaming is of a different order than is response in most other media. During the hurly-burly or determined concentration of intense involvement in simulations and games, there is little opportunity to intellectualize or verbalize what one is learning or failing to learn from the activity. The overlay of emotion inherent in simulation/gaming militates against cognitive awareness. Because conscious awareness of the main instructional points may be very low *during* play it is doubly important to plan for a thorough discussion—a debriefing—*after* play. The debriefing to clarify the instructional goals may be conducted on either an individual or group basis,

◀ **Figure 12.12**
Avoid stifling student eagerness by dwelling too long on rules and play procedures; five minutes is a reasonable rule of thumb for rule explanations.

or a combination of both may be employed, as suggested in the accompanying "How To. . . . Conduct Simulation/Game Defriefing."

Evaluate

The final element of the ASSURE model for teaching/learning is, of course, evaluation. As we have pointed out throughout this text in connection with other instructional media, although full evaluation must await completion of a learning activity, the process begins much earlier.

▲ **Figure 12.13**
For complex simulation/game activities, such as social simulations, the group debriefing is crucial for bringing out the main points of the experience.

HOW TO...CONDUCT SIMULATION/GAME DEBRIEFING

Individual Debriefing

In situations in which participants finish simulation or game activities at different times or in which the schedule prevents immediate group discussion, a form of individual debriefing may be used.

One method developed to help participants reflect on their feelings immediately after play uses a simple sentence-completion form to be filled out individually.* Each participant writes a completion to each of the following sentences:

1. I was _____. (the role you played in the game)
2. I did _____. (actions you performed)
3. I felt _____. (emotions you felt during play)
4. I wish _____. (open response)

The reactions captured on this form can either substitute for group discussion or can supplement the later discussion, with participants referring back to their sheets to remind themselves of their reactions.

Group Debriefing

It is usually preferable to have the debriefing conducted as a group discussion if time and conditions permit. This discussion will be most fruitful if pre-

*Theodore F. Smith " 'Was/Did/Felt/Wish' Bridges Gap When Debriefing Has to Be Delayed," *Simulation/Gaming*, January/February 1978, pp. 5–6.

ceded by careful planning, including formulating key questions in advance. The format suggested here is based on procedures recommended by Ron Stadsklev, an experienced simulation/game leader (see his *Handbook of Simulation Gaming in Social Education*).

Step 1. Releasing Emotions.   Your first step in the group debriefing session should be to relieve any tensions that may have built up during the simulation/gaming activity. Some roles played by participants may engender conflict and anger. Players who feel they did not succeed very well in the game may be experiencing anxiety and feelings of inadequacy. In any event, learners are not likely to be able to think about your questions and concerns until these built-up feelings simmer down to a manageable level.

In order to release some of these pent-up feelings, start with some "safety valve" questions. In many cases the players will have attained some sort of score, so you can start simply by asking for and recording the scores. (You will find it useful to have a chalkboard handy so that you can write down the scores and other comments that participants make. The information on the chalkboard will help build up a "data base" you can refer to in subsequent portions of the debriefing.)

From tabulations of the scores you will be able to declare the winner of the game, if the game calls for winners and losers. Let the winner(s) show off a little

The notes made during utilization and the records kept of student response to the simulation/gaming materials used will contribute to your final evaluation. The debriefing session, however, will probably provide the most precise and useful data upon which your final evaluation will be based.

A frequent criticism of research and evaluation studies of simulation/game products is that paper-and-pencil tests are too often the primary instruments used to assess learning outcomes. Simulations and games ordinarily emphasize different kinds of outcomes than conventional lecture/textbook teaching. Their forte is the promotion of holistic learning, usually including appreciation of and insight into complex processes. These sorts of learnings do not lend themselves to measurement by means of typical multiple-choice tests or other verbal tests that dwell on cognitive—often low level cognitive—outcomes.

A truer test of effectiveness would be the extent to which the simulation/game experience has changed the student's or trainee's approach to real-world problems. Short of following the learner out into the field, the next best means of evaluation would be performance on simulated problems with relatively open-ended opportunities to respond physically, mentally, and emotionally. If these are the goals of the material, logic requires that the method of evaluation be parallel.

---

bit by asking them how they managed to score so highly. Then the lowest scorers should have a chance to explain their tale of woe—what went wrong for them?

At this point be sure to explain any hidden agendas or "dirty tricks" the designer may have built into the game to influence certain scores unfairly. In many simulations modeled on the social class structure, for instance, certain players start out as "disadvantaged" and are consistently impeded from advancing. Obviously, in simulations such as these the final scores are not meant to reflect player skills. Also, you may want to point out that chance plays some part in the scoring—as it does in real life—so that two players might have followed the same strategy and have come out with different scores.

To deal further with the emotional residue, ask one or two players how they felt while playing the game. Did anyone else feel that way too? Let all those who want to chime in freely.

Step 2. Description. The nature and purpose of the activity will, of course, have been explained before the beginning of play. But some students may not have fully appreciated or fully understood the symbolic intent of the activity at this initial stage. Others may have lost track of it in the heat of participation. For example, players of *Triangle Trade* might need to be reminded that they have simulated the experiences of British colonists of the seventeenth century. Make certain that all participants are fully conscious of the real-world situation or experience that the activity was intended to represent or simulate. Ask basic questions such as "What real-life situation was represented in this activity?" "What real-life experiences?" "What was so-and-so or such and such intended to symbolize?"

Step 3. Transfer. Help the participants transfer the lessons learned in the game to reality. Encourage them to compare and contrast the activities of the simulation or game with the actual dynamics of the real-life situation or experience symbolized by the simulation game. Ask questions such as "How does the scoring system compare with real-world rewards?" "What elements of reality were missing from or muted in the simulation or game?" "Were some elements of reality given more weight than they would have in real life?" "Were some given less weight?"

Step 4. Drawing Generalizations. You are now ready to hit paydirt in your post-activity debriefing session. Get the participants to intellectualize and verbalize exactly what they have learned from the activity. Verbalization will reinforce what has been learned in the activity and strengthen insights that have been gained. Sample questions: "What conclusions can you draw from the simulation/game experience?" "What did you learn about what specific real-life problems?" "Did the simulation/game change any of your previous attitudes or opinions?"

References

Print References

General

Abt, Clark C. *Serious Games*. (New York: Viking Press, 1970).

Bell, I. W. *Gaming in the Media Center Made Easy*. (Littleton, Colo.: Libraries Unlimited, 1982).

Byrne, Michael, and Johnston, Alex. "Interactive Units for the Development of Critical Attitudes." *Simulation/Games for Learning* (Autumn 1983), pp. 95–103.

Center for Vocational Education. *Employ Simulation Techniques*. (Athens, Ga.: American Association for Vocational Instructional Materials, 1977).

Coleman, James, et al. "The Hopkins Games Program: Conclusions from Seven Years of Research." *Educational Researcher* (August 1973), pp. 3–7.

Dalke, Connie. "Life-size Learning Games." *Teaching Exceptional Children* (Winter 1984), pp. 106–109.

Dormant, Diane. *Rolemaps*. Volume 33, Instructional Design Library. (Englewood Cliffs, N.J.: Educational Technology Publications, 1980).

Dukes, Richard L, and Seidner, Constance J. eds. *Learning with Simulations and Games*. (Beverly Hills, Calif.: Sage Publications, 1978).

Ellington, Henry; Addinal, Eric; and Percival, Fred. *A Handbook of Game Design*. (New York: Nichols, 1982).

Evans, David R. *Games and Simulations in Literacy Training*. (Amersham, Bucks, England: Hulton Educational Publications, 1979).

Felder, B. Dell, and Hollis, Loye K. "Using Games to Teach Social Studies." *Georgia Social Science Journal* (Spring 1983), pp. 18–21.

Glickman, Carl D. "Problem: Declining Achievement Scores, Solution: Let Them Play!" *Phi Delta Kappan* (February 1979), pp. 454–455.

Golas, Katharine C. "Separating Simulation from Instruction." *Training and Development Journal* (December 1983), pp. 72–73.

Greenblat, Cathy S., and Duke, Richard D. *Principles and Practices of Gaming/Simulation*. (Beverly Hills, Calif.: Sage, 1981).

Heyman, Mark. *Simulation Games for the Classroom*. (Bloomington, Ind.: Phi Delta Kappa, 1975).

Hoper, Claus, et al. *Awareness Games*. (New York: St. Martin's Press, 1975).

Jones, Ken. *Simulations: A Handbook for Teachers*. (New York: Nichols, 1980).

Krulik, Stephan, and Rudnick, Jesse A. "Strategy Gaming and Problem Solving—An Instructional Pair Whose Time Has Come." *Arithmetic Teacher* (December 1983, pp. 26–29).

Krupar, Karen R. *Communication Games*. (New York: Free Press, 1973).

Malehorn, Hal. *Complete Book of Illustrated Learning Aids, Games, and Activities for the Early Childhood Teacher*. (Englewood Cliffs, N.J.: Parker, 1982).

Metzner, Seymour. *One-Minute Game Guide*. (Belmont, Calif.: Pitman Learning, 1968).

Michaelis, Bill, and Michaelis, Dolores. *Learning through Noncompetitive Activities and Play*. (Belmont, Calif.: Pitman Learning, 1977).

Molloy, William F. "Making Role Plays Pay Off in Training." *Training* (May 1981), pp. 59–63.

Reiser, Robert A. "Increasing the Instructional Effectiveness of Simulation Games." *Instructional Innovator* (March 1981), pp. 36–37.

Saegesser, François. "The Introduction of Play in Schools: A Philosophical Analysis of the Problems." *Simulation and Games* (March 1984), pp. 75–96.

Stadsklev, Ron. *Handbook of Simulation Gaming in Social Eduation, Part One*. (Asheville, N.C., University of North Carolina at Asheville, 1976). (University, Ala.: Institute of Higher Education Research and Services, University of Alabama, 1974).

Stolovitch, Harold D., and Thiagarajan, Sivasailam. *Frame Games*. Volume 24, Instructional Design Library. (Englewood Cliffs, N.J.: Educational Technology Publications, 1980).

Sullivan, Dorothy. *Games as Learning Tools: A Guide for Effective Use*. (New York: McGraw-Hill, 1978).

Taylor, John, and Walford, Rex. *Learning and the Simulation Game*. (Beverly Hills, Calif.: Sage Publications, 1978).

Thiagarajan, Sivasailam. "Keep That Delicate Balance." *Simulation/Gaming* (September-October 1977), pp. 4–8.

———, and Stolovitch, Harold D. *Instructional Simulation Games*. Volume 12, Instructional Design Library. (Englewood Cliffs, N.J.: Educational Technology Publications, 1978).

van Ments, Morry. *The Effective Use of Role-Play: A Handbook for Teachers and Trainers*. (New York: Nichols, 1983).

Wiekert, Jeanne, and Bell, Irene Wood. *Media/Classroom Skills: Games for the Middle School*. (Littleton, Colo.: Libraries Unlimited, 1981).

Wohlking, Wallace, and Gill, Patricia J. *Role Playing*. Volume 32, Instructional Design Library. (Englewood Cliffs, N.J.: Eduational Technology Publications, 1980).

Curricular Applications

Barker, J. A. "Simulation and Gaming, without Computers, for School Biology Courses." *Journal of Biological Education* (Autumn 1982), pp. 187–196.

Calculator Activities and Games to Play at Home. (Washington, D.C.: National Council of Teachers of Mathematics, 1981).

Clark, Todd. "Reality in the Classroom." *Social Education* (April 1977), pp. 353–368.

Creamer, Robert C.; Cohen, Richard B.; and Escamilla, Manuel. "Simulation: An Alternative Method for Bilingual-Bicultural Education." *Contemporary Education* (Winter 1977), pp. 90–91.

Ellington, H. I.; Addinall, E.; and Percival, F. *Games and Simulations in Science Education*. (New York: Nichols, 1980).

Hoffman, Thomas R. "Training Games Corporations Play." *Audio-Visual Communication* (January 1977), pp. 32, 34.

Hotchkiss, Gwen, and Athey, Margaret. "Music Learning Grows with Games." *Music Educators Journal* (April 1978), pp. 48–51.

Keller, Clair W. "Role Playing and Simulation in History Classes." *History Teacher* (August 1974), pp. 573–581.

Kiser, Michael, and Stuart, Larry. "Putting Games into English and English into Games." *Media and Methods* (April 1974), pp. 26–29.

Spencer, Jan. "Games and Simulations for Science Teaching." *School Science Review* (March 1977), pp. 397–413.

Steiner, Karen. "Child's Play: Games to Teach Reading." *Reading Teacher* (January 1978), pp. 474–477.

Wertlieb, Ellen. "Games Little People Play." *Teaching Exceptional Children* (Fall 1976), pp. 24–25.

Design

Gillespie, Perry. "A Model for the Design of Academic Games." In Loyda M. Shears and Eli M. Bower, eds., *Games in Education and Development.* (Springfield, Ill.: C. C. Thomas, 1974).

Greenblat, Cathy S. "The Design of Gaming Simulations." *Improving Human Performance Quarterly* (Fall 1975), pp. 115–121.

Maidment, Robert, and Bronstein, Russell H. *Simulation Games: Design and Implementation.* (Columbus: Charles E. Merrill, 1973).

Olmo, Barbara G. "Simulations—Do It Yourself." *Social Studies* (January/February 1976), pp. 10, 14.

Rausch, Erwin, "30,000 Ways to Invent Your Own Group Games." *Successful Meetings* (March 1976), pp. 533–536.

Audiovisual Reference

Finding Values through Simulation Games. Hollywood, Calif.: Media Five, 1977. 16-mm film. 20 minutes. Color.

Periodicals

Journal of Experiential Learning and Simulation (quarterly)
Elsevier North-Holland,Inc.
52 Vanderbilt Avenue
New York, New York 10017

Simgames: The Canadian Journal of Simulation and Gaming (quarterly)
Champlain Regional College
Lennoxville, Quebec
Canada

Simulation & Games: an International Journal of Theory, Design, and Research (quarterly)
Sage Publications, Inc.
275 S. Beverly Drive
Beverly Hills, California 90212

Organizations

International Simulation and Gaming
   Association (ISAGA)
c/o Prof Jan H. G. Klabbers
Department of Educational Sciences
P.O. Box 80.140
3508 TC Utrecht, Netherlands

North American Simulation and Gaming
   Association (NASAGA)
c/o B. Farzanegan, Executive Director
University of North Carolina at Asheville
Asheville, NC 28814

Possible Projects

12-A. Using the sources and references provided in the chapter, identify games and simulations that you could use for your own instructional objectives.

12-B. Appraise an instructional simulation/game using the "Appraisal Checklist" given in the chapter.

12-C. Play an instructional simulation/game and describe your own reaction to the experience; suggest objectives for which it might be appropriate.

12-D. Utilize an instructional simulation/game in an actual instructional situation. Describe the game, its objectives, and the actual results (performance outcomes and reactions) obtained with your group.

12-E. Design a simulation/game prototype. Include a description of the audience, objectives, the game materials (player materials and teacher's guide), and rules for play.

omputers

Outline

Objectives

After studying this chapter, you should be able to:

1. Distinguish between "computer-assisted instruction" (CAI) and "computer-managed instruction" (CMI).

2. Describe the development of computer technology and its applications to instruction over the past three decades.

3. Explain how the modern computer can assist in the individualization of instruction.

4. Describe a concomitant learning (unintended side effect) that may be developed through interaction with computer programs.

5. Discuss six different aspects of computer literacy as described in this chapter.

6. Discuss five advantages and five limitations of computers.

7. Generate examples of the use of the computer: (a) as an object of instruction and (b) as a tool during instruction.

8. Compare and contrast the six modes of computer-assisted instruction in terms of the role of the teacher, the role of the computer, and the role of the learner, including a specific example of courseware in each mode.

9. Generate examples of the use of the computer for computer-managed instruction to: (a) individualize learning, (b) provide computer-based testing, and (c) prescribe media, materials, and activities.

10. Identify three instructional applications of computers in education and/or training other than CAI or CMI.

11. Outline the process (steps) and materials needed to select computer-based materials.

12. Apply the "Appraisal Checklist" to a sample CAI program.

13. Identify and briefly describe the seven common components of a computer system, given a generalized schematic diagram.

14. Distinguish between "ROM" and "RAM."

15. Discuss two common storage media formats used with microcomputers.

16. Compare microcomputers, minicomputers, and mainframes with regard to cost and capability.

17. Suggest five criteria besides cost that might be important considerations in purchasing a computer for instructional purposes.

Lexicon

microprocessor
courseware
software
hardware
peripherals
ROM (Read Only Memory)
RAM (Random Access Memory)
bit
byte
mainframe

The computer with its virtually instantaneous response to student input, its extensive capacity to store and manipulate information, and its unmatched ability to serve many individual students simultaneously is becoming more and more widely used as an aid to instruction. The computer has the ability to control and manage a wide variety of media and learning material—films, filmstrips, slides, audio tapes, and printed information. The computer can also record, analyze, and react to student responses that are typed on a keyboard or indicated with a "light pen" on a cathode ray tube (video display screen). Some display screens even react to the touch of a student's finger.

There are two types of computer-based instruction: computer-assisted instruction (CAI) and computer-managed instruction (CMI). In CAI the student interacts directly with the computer which stores the instructional material and controls its sequence. In CMI the computer helps teachers administer and guide the instructional process. The student is not "on-line" (directly connected) with the computer system, and the instructional material is not stored in the computer. The computer does, however, store information about students and about relevant instructional materials that can be retrieved rapidly. The learner may be "on-line" to take tests. In addition, the computer can diagnose the learning needs of students and prescribe optimal sequences of instruction for them. We will take a closer look at each of these forms of computer-based instruction later in this chapter.

In addition, the computer can be an object of instruction, as in computer science and computer literacy. It also is a tool that can be used during instruction to do complex calcula-

▲ **Figure 13.1**
The computer has become a feasible means of individualizing instruction.

tions, data manipulations, and word processing. Other educational and training applications will also be described here.

THE ROLES OF COMPUTERS IN EDUCATION AND TRAINING

Development of the Technology
The introduction of computers is considered by many to be the third revolution in education; the first was the printing of books, the second the introduction of libraries. The computers developed in the 1950s were awesome creations. Their vacuum tubes and miles of wiring filled several large rooms, dwarfing the sizable crew of attendants needed to keep them working. Not highly reliable but fabulously expensive, they were designed for carrying out complicated mathematical manipulations and did this very efficiently for those who were able to speak their highly specialized mathematical language.

▼ **Figure 13.2**
The "mainframe" computer with its massive components was the norm before the advent of microcomputers.

The possibility of educational applications was mainly conjectural at that time, although important instructional experiments were conducted throughout the 1950s and 1960s. These experiments were spurred by the development of FORTRAN, a more easily learned computer language, and B.F. Skinner's research in programmed instruction. It was seen that the step-by-step format of linear programmed instruction lent itself well to the logical "mentality" of the computer. The factors of cost, hardware reliability, and the availability of adequate materials remained major barriers to the widespread adoption of computers for instruction.

The advent of the *microcomputer* in 1975 altered this picture dramatically. The microcomputer was made possible by the invention of the *microprocessor*, a tiny chip of silicon that contains within itself all the information processing ability of those roomfuls of original computer circuitry. The development of the silicon chip reduced the cost of computers to a truly remarkable degree. The microcomputer was an immediate success in the marketplace, especially for use in small businesses and in the home.

The acceptance of microcomputers by the schools has been unusually rapid compared with other educational innovations. By 1984, figures compiled by Market Data Retrieval* indicated that over 86 percent of the public senior high schools in the United States had one or more microcomputers, more than doubling the number from two years earlier. Junior high schools were not far behind with over 80 percent having at least one microcomputer, while only 25 percent had had microcomputers two years earlier. The biggest growth rate was in the elementary schools, from 11 percent to 62 percent in just two years. At this rate of adoption, virtually every public school in the United States can be expected to have at least one microcomputer by 1986. And by 1987 the National Institute of Education predicts that there will be a computer for every 23 students in school in the United States.**

The Computer and Individualization

The recent emergence of computer technology coincides with a heightened awareness among educators of the importance of individualization. Research into new instructional methods consistently indicates that certain treatments work for certain

---

*John Pepe. *Microcomputers in Schools, 1983–84: A Comprehensive Survey and Analysis*. Westport, Conn.: Market Data Retrieval, 1984. p. 5.

**Lawrence P. Grayson. "An Overview of Computers in American Education." *T.H.E. Journal* (August 1984), pp. 78–87.

▼ **Figure 13.3**
The tiny microprocessor fostered the microcomputer revolution. Chips like this one are being built into home appliances, automobile components, and dozens of other machines in addition to computing machines, giving each a "brain" of its own.

▼ **Figure 13.4**
Innovative microcomputer systems such as the Macintosh have helped popularize the use of micros in businesses and homes.

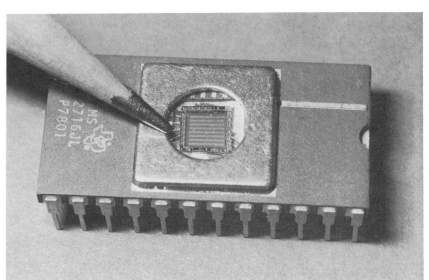

people under certain conditions. There are no panaceas.

The great quest in the field of media and technologies of instruction is to find ways of matching individual learners with the appropriate subject matter, pitched at the right level, and presented in a compatible medium at the optimal pace in the most meaningful sequence.

True individualization imposes a tremendous burden of decision making and resource management. One instructor might approach an ideal level of individualization with a handful of students. But when dealing with twenty, thirty, forty, or more students the logistics of individualization overwhelm any single teacher's capacity.

The computer gives promise of overcoming these and other logistic barriers to individualization of instruction. Its electronic circuitry can accurately make the myriad decisions necessary to the planning and implementation of an individualized program of instruction on a mass basis in a fraction of the time required by the human mind.

Concomitant Skills

"Reading," said seventeenth-century philosopher Francis Bacon, "maketh a full man, conference a ready man, and writing an exact man." If Bacon were alive today he might well add that "writing a computer program maketh an even more exact man." One serendipitous effect of working with computers is that they literally force us to communicate with them in an orderly and logical way. The computer user must learn to communicate with explicit, exact instructions and responses. Any departure from precision is rejected by the computer.

▲ **Figure 13.5**
Computer literacy, particularly programming ability, builds basic intellectual skills of logic, organization, and systematic thinking.

Observers who have watched the development of young people as they work with computers, particularly in computer programming, note a tendency for orderly, logical thinking to be carried over into other areas of the students' work. Deductive reasoning thus becomes the "hidden curriculum" or concomitant learning—an unintended but welcome side-effect of contact with computers.

Computer users also learn keyboarding or typing skills. Now very young children as well as adults are developing these skills in order to communicate with computers. Specific computer games, such as "Type Attack" (see the Media File on p. 000), have been developed to teach and/or improve keyboarding skills.

THE CONCEPT OF COMPUTER LITERACY

Literacy once implied exclusively the ability to read and write, i.e., verbal literacy. In the mid-1970s, however, we began to hear about a different kind of literacy—visual literacy—as described in Chapter 3. It resulted from the realization that specific skills are needed to "read" (interpret) and "write" (create) visual messages, just as certain skills are needed to read and write printed ones. Visual literacy is the learned ability to interpret messages accurately and to create these messages. Thus, interpretation and creation in visual literacy may be said to parallel reading and writing in verbal literacy.

With the rapid spread of computer use in the late 1970s and early 1980s came an equally rapid flowering of public awareness of the emergent importance of computers in society.

▲ **Figure 13.6**
Intense absorption is a common reaction to early computer experiences.

▲ **Figure 13.7**
By 1982 the computer's impact had become so pervasive that TIME magazine named it "Machine of the Year." Schools have mirrored the national fascination closely.

Out of this heightened popular awareness emerged yet another type of literacy—computer literacy—referring to the ability to understand and to use computers. Analogous to reading, the computer puts out messages that require the user to do something, i.e., respond to a question or to a computer command. Analogous to writing, the user generates messages that tell the computer what to do—*if* the "vocabulary," "grammar," and

"sentence structure" are correct.
Our discussion thus far has focused on the two most fundamental aspects of computer literacy. However, actual computer literacy exists along a continuum from general awareness to the ability to write computer programs. Also involved are ethical issues related to how and when computers should be used.

▼ **Figure 13.8**
The development of computer literacy can be laid out along a continuum.

COMPUTER LITERACY CONTINUUM							
What is a computer?	What can computers do?	How are computers used?	How do computers work?	Can I operate a computer?	Can I think about a problem?	Can I program a computer?	How should a computer be used?
Knowledge	Knowledge	Comprehension	Comprehension	Application	Analysis	Synthesis	Evaluation
Discuss the characteristics of computers and their historical development	State the capabilities of computers (advantages/	Describe applications of computers	Describe how computers and their components function	Use computers (respond to computer questions and commands)	Analyze a practical task for possible computer solution	Develop computer programs (produce new programs to perform tasks)	Make value judgements regarding proper use of computers
	Talk about computers (terminology)				Examine or modify existing programs		Impact on society— privacy, legal, ethical, and security issues

There is at least one microcomputer in each of the 163 institutions in the Fairfax, Virginia public school system. As part of a coordinated computer literacy program, these machines are used to teach elementary students how computers will affect their lives, as well as how to use computers. The high school students use them in business and data processing courses. Word processing software is used to teach composition, and music synthesizers let students compose their own songs. Learning-disabled students use computers to improve their eye-hand coordination.

The program in Fairfax was cited in 1984 by AECT's Project BEST (Basic Education Skills through Technology) for exemplary use of computers "to enhance the efforts of teachers and stimulate student creativity."

Computer literacy focuses on integrating computers into the existing curriculum rather than using them as a stand-alone program. Now the program is extending into the uses of computers for instruction. For example, one foreign language teacher uses a program in which his students "visit" a French restaurant and must use French to order from the menu.

As the teachers' computer literacy expands, the computers are used more and more for the management of instruction. Teachers can call up questions from a test-item bank, have them printed, and administer them to students. The computer then collects the student answers through an optical scanner, analyzes the results, provides test scores, and updates student records.

(See Figure 13.8.) Most students start at the left of the continuum and move further along toward the right. Computer literacy involves knowledge, attitudes, and skills. Knowledge of hardware, software, and data-processing concepts is necessary as well as of the applications of computers. Attitudes include a willingness to use computers where appropriate in everyday situations without fear and an awareness of the social implications of abusive uses as well as beneficial uses. Skills include operating computers, modifying existing programs, and programming new applications.

ADVANTAGES OF COMPUTERS

The computer can be viewed generally as a tool for enhancing the various technologies of instruction (through CAI) and of instructional management (through CMI). It is the *interactive* nature of computer-based instruction that underlies most of its advantages. As an active mode of instruction, it requires learner response (the R of the ASSURE model). Specific advantages are:

- Simply allowing students to learn at their own pace produces significant time savings over conventional classroom instruction. Computer-based instruction allows students some control over the rate and sequence of their learning (individualization).

- High speed personalized responses to learner actions yield a high rate of reinforcement.
- The patient, personal manner that can be programmed provides a more positive affective climate, especially for slower learners.
- Color, music, and animated graphics can add realism and appeal to drill exercises, laboratory activities, simulations, etc.
- The record-keeping ability of the computer makes individualized instruction feasible; individual prescriptions can be prepared for all students (particularly mainstreamed special students) and their progress can be monitored.

- Memory capacity allows students' past performance to be recorded and used in planning next steps.
- The teacher's "span of control" is enlarged as more information is put easily at his or her disposal, helping to keep control close to the point of direct contact with the learner.
- The novelty of working with a computer raises student motivation.
- The computer provides reliable instruction from learner to learner regardless of the teacher/trainer, the time of the day, or the location.
- Computer-based training (CBT) can improve efficiency and effectiveness. Effectiveness refers to improved learner achievement, while efficiency means achieving objectives in less time or at lower cost. Efficiency is very important to business and industrial applications and is becoming increasingly important in educational settings. According to Kearsley,* the "time savings (an average of 30 percent compared with conventional training) with CBT is almost completely due to the individualization of instruction, not the use of the computer itself. However, it is virtually impossible to run a large individualized instructional program without the use of a computer to manage the activity."

---

*Greg Kearsley. *Computer-Based Training: A Guide to Selection and Implementation*. Reading, Mass.: Addison-Wesley, 1983.

LIMITATIONS OF COMPUTERS

As we have seen with all the other media and technological innovations, there are always trade-offs to be made and limitations to consider. Some of the major limitations of computers in instruction are:

- Despite the dramatic reduction in cost of computers and computer use, computerized instruction is still relatively expensive. Careful consideration must be given to the costs and benefits of computers in education and training. Maintenance can also be a problem, especially if equipment is subjected to heavy use.
- Design and production of computers specifically for instructional purposes has lagged behind design and production for other purposes.
- There is a lack of high-quality direct-instruction materials for use with computers, especially for use with microcomputers. There is also a compatability problem. Software developed for one computer system usually cannot be used with another. (The ease with which software can be duplicated without permission has inhibited commercial publishers and private entrepreneurs from producing and marketing instructional software.)
- Design of instructional materials for use with computers is a laborious task, even for instructors with courseware design skills.
- Creativity may be stifled in computerized instruction. The computer is slavish in its obedience to its program. Creative or original learner responses will be ignored or even rebuked if the program's designer has not anticipated such possibilities.

- Some learners, especially adult learners, may resist the linear, lock-step control of the learning process typical of run-of-the-mill computer instruction materials.
- The "novelty effect" associated with CAI in its earlier days seems to be decreasing. As learners become more familiar with computers in the home and the workplace the newness of the stimulus wears off and has less motivational value.

APPLICATIONS OF COMPUTER-BASED INSTRUCTION

The potential uses of computers in educational settings go far beyond the provision of direct instruction. There is the obvious administrative role of keeping school records, scheduling classes, making out paychecks, and the like. Guidance programs use computers to deliver career planning assistance. In the domain of instruction, though, there are four broad classes of applications: computer as object of instruction, computer as tool, computer-assisted instruction, and computer-managed instruction. Each of these areas, especially the latter two, will be explored here in some depth.

Object of Instruction

The computer can itself be the *object* of instruction. For example, in computer literacy students learn "about" computers, and in vocational training trainees learn to use computers on the job for data processing and analysis purposes. In this role, the computer is treated like any other machine one is learning to use.

When a learner is studying computer programming, the computer and the associated software are the objects of instruction. The various programming languages and the techniques for constructing a program using these languages are beyond the scope of this book. More and more high schools and vocational schools are teaching courses in computer technology. Some even have entire curricula in this expanding field.

Tool during Instruction

The computer can also serve as a *tool* during instruction. It can be used by the learner to solve complex mathematical calculations as a slide rule or pocket calculator was once used, but with increased power and speed. Even a small microcomputer can an-

▲ **Figure 13.9**
The computer serves as a tool in carrying out design tasks.

alyze data, perform repeated calculations, or even gather data when hooked to laboratory equipment or subjects.

Today microcomputers are being used increasingly for word processing and composition. More and more students have access to computers with word processing programs upon which to do term papers and assignments. Some of the programs even check spelling, grammatical structure, and word use. Studies have shown that students are more willing to modify their original compositions when the papers do not have to be completely retyped. The students can devote more time to creative writing and less to the mechanics of "getting it on paper." In these roles the computer serves as a fancy calculator or typewriter.

Computer-Assisted Instruction

Computer systems can deliver instruction directly to students by allowing them to *interact with lessons programmed into the system*; this is referred to as *computer-assisted instruction (CAI)*. The various utilization possibilities can best be discussed in terms of the various instructional modes that the computer can facilitate most effectively: drill and practice, tutorial, gaming, simulation, discovery, and problem solving. Utilization of each of these modes is summarized in Table 13.1.

Drill-and-Practice Mode.
Use of this mode assumes that a concept, rule, or procedure has already been taught to the learner. The program leads the learner through a series of examples to increase dexterity and fluency in using the skill. The key is to reinforce constantly all correct responses. The computer can display infinite patience, going ahead only when mastery is shown. Drill and practice is predominantly used for math drills, foreign language translating practice, vocabulary building exercises, and the like. Other drill-and-practice programs, such as *Sentences*, let the learners practice sentence constructions.

Drill-and-practice programs provide a variety of questions with varied formats. The trainee is usually given several tries before the computer presents the correct answer. Several levels of difficulty can be available within the same drill-and-practice program. Positive and negative feedback as well as reinforcement can be included.

Tutorial Mode.
In this mode the pattern followed is basically that of branching programmed instruction (see Chapter 11); that is, information is presented in small units followed by a question. The student's response is analyzed by the computer (compared with responses plugged in by the author) and appropriate feedback is given. A complicated network of pathways or "branches" can be programmed. The more alternatives available to the computer, the more adaptive the tutorial can be to individual differences. The extent to which a skilled live tutor can be approximated depends on the creativity of the author.

In the tutorial role, the computer acts as the teacher. All interaction is between the computer and the learner. One example of the tutorial mode is *Welding*, which presents the basic concepts and terminology to would-be welders.

Media File:
"Wordwright" Drill and Practice

Wordwright is one of a series of courseware packages developed by The Encyclopaedia Britannica Corporation. The *Wordwright* package includes a drill-and-practice lesson on word definitions, as well as a range of other word games and tests. The vocabulary drill and practice lesson presents a sequence of ten vocabulary questions. If a student's answer is correct, the machine presents the next question. If a student's answer is incorrect, the machine responds with the correct definition as well as with examples of correct usage. After presenting the ten questions, the computer gives a summary of both the words defined correctly and the words incorrectly defined.

Source: Encyclopaedia Britannica.

Media File:
"MIT8" Tutorial

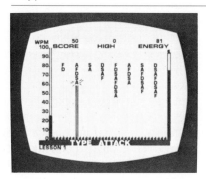

Trainees learn about the design and utilization of steam traps in heating systems. The program presents concepts, principles, and techniques needed for the understanding of the operation of steam traps. Questions are then presented to provide tutorial interaction and promote understanding of the content. The program can be used to train new employees or as a refresher for building and mechanical engineers.

Source: Plato/CDC.

Media File:
"Type Attack" Game

Type Attack is a touch-typing instructional game modeled after the *Space Invaders* game. The program presents columns of letters marching across and down the screen. The student's task is to match the lowermost "invading" letters by typing those letters on the keyboard. Once an invading letter has been matched, that invader is zapped, exposing the letter directly above it. The object of the game is to stop the invading horde of letters from reaching the bottom of the screen. *Type Attack* has 39 different lessons for the student to choose from, all of which are presented at the speed selected by the student.

Source: Sirius Software.

Gaming Mode. In Chapter 12 we discussed the distinction between gaming and simulation. A game activity may or may not entail simulation elements. Likewise, a game may or may not be instructional. It depends on whether or not the skill practiced in the game is an academic or training one, that is, related to a specified instructional objective.

At the moment, recreational games of the *Space Invaders, Battleship,* and *Blackjack* variety are major attractions to home computer buyers and young school-age users. They can serve a useful purpose in building up computer literacy in an enjoyable, nonthreatening manner. But the ultimate goal of useful learning must be kept in mind. Instructors experienced in computer utilization recommend rationing purely recreational game use, using it as a reward for completing other assignments.

Still, when applied to *instructional* tasks, gaming can be a highly motivating framework, especially for repetitious drills. Another common instructional game application is in management training. Participants form management teams making decisions regarding a mythical corporation. The winning team is the one reaping the highest corporate profits.

Simulation Mode. The simulation mode of instruction is described in detail in Chapter 12. In this mode, the learner confronts a scaled-down approximation of a real-life situation. It allows realistic practice without the expense or risks otherwise involved. A well-known computer simulation, *Hammurabi*, puts the player in charge of economic decisions for a small agrarian country in pre-Biblical times.

Business management problems and laboratory experiments in the physical sciences are other popular subjects for computer simulations. In other simulations, the learner manipulates mathematical models to see the effect of changing certain variables, as in the case of controlling a

TABLE 13.1 Utilization of Various CAI Modes

Modes	Description	Role of Teacher	Role of Computer	Role of Student	Applications/Examples
Drill and Practice	Content already taught Review basic facts and terminology Variety of questions in varied formats Question/answer drills repeated as necessary	Arranges for prior instruction Selects material Matches drill to student Checks progress	Asks question "Evaluates" student response Provides immediate feedback Records student progress	Practices content already taught Responds to questions Receives confirmation and/or correction Chooses content and difficulty level	Parts of a microscope Completing balance sheets Vocabulary building Math facts Product knowledge
Tutorial	Presentation of new information Teaches concepts and principles Provides remedial instruction	Selects material Adapts instruction Monitors	Presents information Asks questions Monitors responses Provides remedial feedback Summarizes key points Keeps records	Interacts with computer Sees results Answers questions Asks questions	Clerical training Bank teller training Science Medical procedures Bible study
Gaming	Competitive Drill and practice in a motivational format Individual or small group	Sets limits Directs process Monitors results	Acts as competitor judge score keeper	Learns facts/strategies/skills Evaluates choices Competes with computers	Fraction games Counting games Spelling games Typing (arcade-type) games
Simulation	Approximates real-life situations Based upon realistic models Individual or small group	Introduces subject Presents background Guides "debriefing"	Plays role(s) Delivers results of decisions Maintains the model and its database	Practices decision making Makes choices Receives results of decisions Evaluates decisions	Trouble-shooting History Medical diagnosis Simulators (pilot/driver) Business management Laboratory experiments
Discovery/ Inquiry	Inquiry into data base Inductive approach Trial and error Tests hypotheses	Presents basic problem Monitors student progress	Presents student with source of information Stores data Permits search procedures	Makes hypotheses Tests guesses Develops principles/rules	Social science Science Food intake analysis Career choices
Problem Solving	Works with data Systematizes information Performs rapid and accurate calculations	Assigns problems Checks results	Presents problem Manipulates data Maintains database Provides feedback	Defines the problem Sets up the solution Manipulates variables Trial and error	Business Creativity Troubleshooting Mathematics Computer programming

nuclear power plant. A similar simulation deals with weather forecasting.

A large number of civilian and military occupations involve the operation or maintenance of complex equipment such as aircraft, manufacturing machines, weapons systems, nuclear power plants, and oil rigs. Major airlines and the military use computer-based simulators to reduce the amount of actual flying time required for training. The Navy has reduced pilot training costs from $4,000 per hour, to $400 per hour in one of its programs through the use of computer-based simulation.

United Airlines is planning to do all of its flight training for the Boeing 767 via a computer-simulation system, eliminating the need for any special-purpose trainers or actual flying time.

A number of open-ended simulations that do not have stated objectives are available. Instructors and/or learners must determine their own objectives. Some of these simulations do not provide instruction within the programs. The instructor must provide this information before the simulation or let the learners discover the effect of changing certain variables for themselves. These simulations can be used in a variety of ways to suit the needs of the instructional situation.

Discovery Mode. *Discovery* is a general term to describe activities using an inductive approach to learning; that is, presenting *problems* which the student solves through trial and error. It approximates laboratory learning outside the classroom.

The opposite of rote or drill learning, the aim of the discovery approach is the deeper understanding that results from grappling with a puzzling problem. Through the complex branching and data storage capabilities of the computer, more students will be exposed to "laboratory" learning in such areas as math, social sciences, and other science areas.

Close-Up:
Cardiac Arrest Simulation Program

Interns and medical students can study cardiac arrest and resuscitation techniques with a program entitled "Cardiac Arrest Simulation Program."* As a teaching tool in the intensive care unit of Childrens Hospital in Los Angeles, J. M. Dean's program lets the learner practice cardiac resuscitation at the computer terminal before encountering the actual situation. Dean reports that those using his computer program as a "practice patient" agree this simulation has enhanced their performance in emergencies.

*J. M. Dean. "Microcomputer Applications in Clinical Media Education: Cardiac Arrest and Resuscitation." *Creative Computing* 7 (1981), pp. 156–159.

In CAI using the discovery mode the learner employs an information retrieval strategy to get information from a database. For example, a salesperson interested in learning about competitors' products can select from a set of critical product features, display them on the computer, and draw conclusions about the comparisons of the products.

Some discovery lessons such as *Inquir* analyze large databases of election information, population statistics, or other user-built databases. OIC (Occupational Information Systems) provides a large database of information about careers to assist the user with exploration of various careers.

Problem-Solving Mode.
Problem-solving programs fall into two categories, those the learner writes and those written by someone else to help the learner solve problems. In learner-written programs, the student defines a problem logically and writes a computer program to solve it. The computer will do the necessary calculations and/or manipulations to provide the answers. In this case the computer aids the learner in attaining problem-solving skills by doing complex calculations and manipulations.

In the second category, the computer is the problem solver. The computer makes the calculations while

Media File:
"Lemonade" Simulation

Students can work individually, compete in pairs, or work in small groups to learn the basics of business. They are the proprietors of a neighborhood lemonade stand. They decide how many glasses of lemonade to make, how much to charge per glass, and how many advertising signs to put up for each simulated day. There are random occurrences such as changes in the weather and street construction that affect the computer-generated outcome, so chance does intrude to a significant extent on the underlying economic model. By studying the outcomes of their decisions, students can make inferences about the economic model used in the simulation and gain insight into its real-world counterpart.

Source: Apple Computers.

Media File:
"Health Hazard Appraisal" Discovery Program

By asking a variety of questions, this discovery program apprises you of your current health status and risks. Of course, the accuracy of the assessment depends on the accuracy of your responses to the questions. The questions relate to current blood pressure, history of serious illness in the family, number of miles driven, use of seat belts, diet, etc. The computer program analyzes the answers to the questions. The results compare your current chronological age with with the age at which you are living your life (health equivalent) and othe age at which you could be living your life. Recommendations for improving your life expectancy are also provided.

Source: Pillsbury.

the student manipulates one or several variables. A learner may wish to factor a certain trinomial so that a mathematical problem involving rectangles can be solved. The issue is not whether the learner can factor, but whether the learner can solve a problem involving rectangles. Factoring is a tedious task that can be done quickly by the computer. A previously written program can be used to factor as many trinomials as are supplied by the learner.

One commercially available simulation for the computer is *Odell Lake*. Marketed through the Minnesota Educational Computing Consortium, it combines simulation, instructional gaming, and problem-solving strategies by modeling plant and animal life in a lake in the Cascade Mountains of Oregon. Users of this CAI program learn ecological relationships by role playing one of six fish swimming in Odell Lake and by making survival decisions. Although designed for students at a third to fourth grade reading level, *Odell Lake* has been used successfully with learners from second grade through adult.*

Computer-Managed Instruction

Computer-managed instruction (CMI) refers to the use of a computer system to manage information about learner performance and learning resource options in order to prescribe and control individualized lessons.

There is considerable impetus for using CMI these days because of the increasing emphasis being placed on individualized instruction. Both in formal education and in settings such as the military, business/industry, and government, there is recognition that greater efficiency, effectiveness, and equal opportunity can be reached in instruction only to the extent that teachers can accommodate the individual differences that cause each

*O. Calabrese. "Another View of Problem Solving." *Apple Journal of Courseware Review* 1 (1982), pp. 39–42.

Media File:
"The Factory" Problem-Solving Program

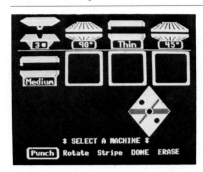

The Factory focuses on several strategies used in problem solving: working backward, analyzing a process, determining a sequence, and applying creativity. The learners are given a square on the computer and three types of machines. The "punch" machine can punch squares or circles, with one, two, or three of each. The "rotation" machine can be programmed to rotate the square 45, 90, 135, or 180 degrees. And the "stripe" machine paints a thin, medium, or thick stripe.

The program has three types of activities. The learners can "test a machine" to see what each option does. They can "build a factory" composed of up to eight machines to make a product of their own design. The most difficult task is to assemble and program a variety of machines in the proper sequence to "duplicate a product" shown on the screen.

Source: Sunburst Communications.

▲ **Figure 13.10**
In computer-managed instruction the computer provides automated test scoring.

student to have different learning patterns.

Individualized instruction means that students will be moving through the checkpoints in the educational process at different times via different paths. You can imagine the management problem this entails if you think of one teacher responsible for teaching 5 subjects or major topics, with 20 objectives in each subject, to 30 students. This adds up to a minimum of 3000 checkpoints.

The computer can help solve this management problem by administering diagnostic tests, scoring them, prescribing appropriate next steps,

monitoring the progress of the student all the way along the route, and keeping records. This is essentially what CMI attempts.

One of the largest CMI systems in use today was developed by the U.S. Navy.* This system manages the daily instruction of about 10,000 students in twenty-four courses in nine schools, and it represents about 28 percent of the Navy technical training. The system generates detailed progress reports that indicate where each student currently is and how long it will be before he or she is finished.

Over the years a number of different CMI systems have been developed and tried out, among them PLAN developed by Westinghouse (in Iowa City schools), TIPS (at the University of Wisconsin), CISS (at New York Institute of Technology), Advanced Instructional System (for the U.S. Air Force), Plato Learning Management (Control Data Corp.), and TICCIT (developed by Mitre Corp. and Brigham Young University). Each of

*J. D. Davis. "The Navy CMI System: A Brief Overview." *Journal of Educational Technology Systems* 2 (1978), pp. 143–150.

▲ **Figure 13.11**
A well-designed CMI program keeps track of individual students, prescribing remedial activities as needed.

these systems is designed for a different environment, makes different assumptions about the instructional setting, and emphasizes different strengths. Finding the right match with your own institutional needs demands a careful analysis of the available products on a number of dimensions, including computer system compatibility.

Whatever the merits of the various CMI systems, they generally suffer from a lack of adequate instructional materials (referred to as "courseware"). The instructional materials controlled by the CMI system may, of course, consist of standard textbooks or workbooks as well as CAI courseware. A notable exception to the general lack of courseware is Plato Learning Management. Since PLATO began as a CAI system, it is rich in courseware. Time-sharing mainframe systems like Plato also tend to offer more courseware because the expense of developing such materials can be spread out over a larger number of users. The key, though, is that you can't have computer-managed instruction without *instruction* to manage.

Hardware cost is another factor to bear in mind. Because microcomputers trade off speed for smaller size, current models are not capable of processing efficiently all the data needed to serve large numbers of students. Access to a mainframe computer or a mini-computer is still

desirable for efficient CMI. This picture is changing as storage techniques improve and more efficient programming languages are developed for the microcomputer.

Computer-based testing.

Computers can be used to store and file banks of test items. The test items can be filed by subject content, objective measured, and/or level of difficulty. Items in the bank can be readily updated and modified, new items added, and old items deleted with minimal effort. From the pool of test items the instructor can choose the items to include on an examination or the computer can be programmed to select the items, either randomly or according to specified parameters. The computer can be programmed to select items based upon variables in each category used to classify test items.

The computer also can be used to print out a copy of the test in as many different forms as desired or to administer the test to the student who is sitting at the computer. In the latter case, the computer can provide immediate feedback regarding right and wrong responses and keep a permanent record of the learner's achievement on the test.

Test scoring and analysis can be computerized by typing the student responses at the keyboard, by using mark-sensed sheets during the test that can be "read" by the computer, or by having the student take the test at the computer. The computer can display the number of students selecting each alternative, as well as the raw scores and standard scores of each student. In addition, group data such as means and standard deviations can be calculated.

Record Keeping.   Records

of student scores on tests can be stored by the computer. The student record can be updated each time a test is taken. The computer serves as as "electronic gradebook." At the end of the grading period, the scores can be manipulated (i.e., the lowest

score can be dropped, the highest score doubled, etc.), the average calculated, the final grade determined, and the composite student performance printed out by the computer.

Computer Prescription of Media/Materials/Activities.   Based upon student data (background, interest, test scores, etc.) and instructor input (available materials, alternative sequences, time available, etc.), the computer (particularly a minicomputer or mainframe) can develop a learning prescription for each student or trainee. Often traditional instruction is lock-step because the teacher or trainer cannot keep all the alternatives as well as each student's characteristics and background in mind. The computer with its extensive storage capacity can perform the countless manipulations necessary to assign instructional activities and learning materials based on a wide variety of decision parameters programmed into it.

Other Education/ Training Applications
Computers, even microcomputers, are being used for a wide variety of applications in education and training beyond the CAI and CMI examples described above. The scheduling of students, rooms, and instructional equipment (real objects, projectors, and carrels) is a greater logistics problems with individualized instruction whether computer-based instruction is used or not. Depending upon how the program is written, the students, rooms, and equipment can be scheduled by the instructors or by the students themselves.

As instructional activities employ a wider variety of media and printed materials (other than full-length textbooks), the task of keeping track of the ever-increasing supply of materials becomes more demanding. Many courses of instruction in formal and especially nonformal education use booklets and worksheets. The computer can keep a record of the number of such items on hand and signal the operator when additional copies are necessary. In some cases the text of the booklets and worksheets are stored in the computer and copies can be printed upon demand.

The computer can be used to generate materials. Computer-generated materials (CGM) are becoming more popular and commonly used. Such programs can produce one or more copies of a maze, a test (as described above), a puzzle, worksheet, illustration, diagram, or other trainer/teacher-developed items. With their increased graphics capabilities, microcomputers are being used to generate masters for overhead transparencies.

With increased concern for efficient allocation of limited funds and other resources, the computer is a handy tool for developing budgets and keeping records of expenditures. Many instructors store an expanding list of desired materials and equipment for purchase in the computer. If funds become available at the end of the fiscal year, a request for these materials, along with necessary purchasing information, can be generated quickly.

SELECT, MODIFY, OR DESIGN COMPUTER-BASED MATERIALS

In the context of computer-based materials, the term "software" refers in general to any computer programs and their accompanying documentation. It is customary to refer to software which teaches the actual subject matter as "courseware."

As has happened before in the field of instructional media, the development of hardware for CAI has exceeded the pace of courseware development. It is clear that the ability to compose computer programs is not synonymous with the ability to design effective instruction. Reviewers who have had the opportunity to appraise critically a portion of the flood of CAI programs being offered in the marketplace dismiss a large percentage of them as "junk."

Select Materials

Before selecting courseware for purchase, you should establish the need, determine the objectives, and characterize the audience that will be using the material as described in Chapter 2. Then search the sources, listings, and reviews to find the courseware that might meet your specific need. Preview the courseware using the "Appraisal Checklist." Finally, select the one that appears to meet your needs best.

Sources. There are numerous types of sources for educational and training courseware. They include educational institutions and consortia that develop new courseware, businesses that develop courseware to train their employees, software companies, and textbook publishers. In addition, clearinghouses such as CONDUIT and MECC are nonprofit organizations that sell courseware for minimal cost. CONDUIT, located at the University of Iowa, specializes in materials for higher education,

while MECC, the Minnesota Educational Computing Consortium, provides courseware for elementary and secondary applications. (Addresses for these organizations are given in the References at the end of this chapter. Additional review sources are given in Appendix A.)

Listings. In addition to catalogs from the sources listed above, there are numerous indices, on-line databases, and printed directories listing courseware available by subject headings. The comprehensive directory of computer-based instructional programs is *Index to Computer-Based Learning*, edited by Anastasia C. Wang. This nonevaluative index is published annually on microfiche at the University of Wisconsin—Milwaukee. Additional listings of computer courseware sources are included in Appendix A.

Reviews. Several agencies are attempting to help teachers and trainers cope with the courseware selection task by conducting independent reviews and evaluations of materials. These include MicroSIFT at the Northwest Regional Education Lab and the EPIE Institute. (Addresses for these and other review selection sources are included at the end of this chapter and in Appendix A.) In addition, many educational magazines and training journals include courseware reviews. Numerous such periodicals are listed in the Reference section at the end of this chapter.

Previews. You can use the review and selection sources to identify those computer programs that might meet your educational and training needs. However, you should preview the materials yourself to see if they are likely to meet your specific needs. You should request a copy of the courseware from the distributor

Appraisal Checklist: Computer-Based Instruction

Series title (if applicable)_____

Individual title_____

Distributor_____

Format: ☐ cassette   ☐ disk   ☐ other_____

Designed for what system?_____

Language?_____ Memory size?_____

Length of lesson_____ Cost_____

Intended audience/grade level_____ Subject area_____

Objectives (stated or implied)

Brief description:

Entry capabilities required
    —prior subject matter knowledge
    —reading ability
    —math/computer skill

Rating	High		Medium		Low
Focuses clearly on objectives relevant to instructional needs	☐	☐	☐	☐	☐
Quality of documentation (clear and complete)	☐	☐	☐	☐	☐
User-friendly, simple interactions	☐	☐	☐	☐	☐
Error-free (no infinite loops or dead ends)	☐	☐	☐	☐	☐
Learner control of pace and sequence	☐	☐	☐	☐	☐
Frequent interaction and positive reinforcement/feedback	☐	☐	☐	☐	☐
Branches to adapt to varying aptitude levels	☐	☐	☐	☐	☐
Handling of user errors	☐	☐	☐	☐	☐
Motivating presentation format and screen displays	☐	☐	☐	☐	☐
Appropriate graphics, sound, and color	☐	☐	☐	☐	☐
Clear and concise adjunct materials	☐	☐	☐	☐	☐
Evidence of effectiveness (e.g., field tests)	☐	☐	☐	☐	☐

Strong points:

Weak points: Reviewer_____

                                                              Position_____

Recommended action_____ Date_____

with return privileges. Some companies will provide preview/demo disks which include samples of a variety of their courseware. These disks allow you to preview the programs but avoid the possibility that the companies' programs will be illegally copied. There may be a clearinghouse or local site where you can preview materials. Many of these preview sites are operated by local school districts and universities. Some local computer stores sell instructional materials and will allow you to preview the courseware within the store. In all cases, use the "Appraisal Checklist: Computer-Based Instruction" when you preview courseware.

As we have pointed out in reference to the other media and technologies of instruction, each format of media/technology has particular attributes that contribute to a unique set of criteria by which to judge the associated materials. In the case of CAI materials, we find many of the same concerns that affect programmed instruction materials—active participation, consistent reinforcement, and field test data. To these we add criteria based on the special capabilities of computers—branching, use of graphics, and random variations to allow repeated use. Finally, there are descriptive data related to the different physical variations among computer systems. What language is it coded in? What size memory is required? Is the software on cassette, disk, or some other storage device?

Modify Materials

Modification is not possible with most commercial courseware. Even when it is possible to obtain a program listing, revising is a very difficult task and is usually against the copyright law. You can modify the *uses* of the courseware and the associated (adjunct) materials, such as handouts and study guides. For noncommercial programs that are obtained from other teachers and trainers the procedures for making modifications to meet specific needs are beyond the scope of this book; you should consult a textbook on the programming language used to develop the courseware.

Design Materials

Some instructors design their own courseware. However, most teachers and trainers do not have the time or expertise to do so. It can take up to 300 hours to design, code (program), and "debug" (correct) one hour of computer-based instruction. There are books written on courseware design for those who have the time and are interested. (See References at the end of this chapter.)

COMPUTER HARDWARE

Basic Computer Components

Regardless of the size of the computer or complexity of the system, computers have a number of standard components. The core element is the *central processing unit* (CPU). The other components needed for input, output, and memory storage are referred to as *peripherals*. All of the physical equipment of which the computer is composed is referred to as the hardware. The basic hardware components are diagrammed in Figure 13.12.

CPU (Central Processing Unit).
This is the "brain" that carries out all the calculations and controls the total system. In a microcomputer the CPU is just one of the tiny chips inside the machine.

Memory.
This stores information for manipulation by the CPU. The memory contains the *control* function, that is, the programs (detailed sequential instructions) that are written to tell the CPU what to do in what order. Memory and CPU are part of the microcomputer and usually are built into the machine.

▼ **Figure 13.12**
Basic elements of a microcomputer system.

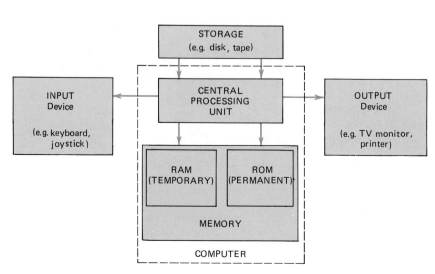

In microcomputers, control instructions are stored in two types of memory.

ROM (Read-Only Memory)— control instructions which have been "wired" *permanently* into the memory. Usually stores instructions that the computer will need constantly, such as the programming language(s) and internal monitoring functions.

RAM (Random Access Memory)— the flexible part of the memory. The particular program or set of data being manipulated by the user is *temporarily* stored in RAM, then erased to make way for the next program.

Storage.　This is a way of keeping all the programs that you are not using. In microcomputers, the computer can process only one program at a time, so you need some place to store the other programs and sets of data for future use. These programs and data are stored outside the computer. There are two common storage media:

Cassette tape— is used to "record" (save) computer programs, to store data, and to "input" the information into the computer. A standard audio cassette is used. The information is stored magnetically, just as on an audio recording. Also, as on an audio tape, the user has to play through the whole tape to get to any single portion of it.

▼　**Figure 13.13**
Audio cassette tape is a common form of mass storage for microcomputers.

Disk— may be of two types and several sizes. The basic types are "floppy" (flexible) and "hard" (rigid). A floppy disk is a thin, circular piece of plastic with a magnetic recording surface, enclosed in a cardboard jacket for protection. The computer "reads" the information through an oval-shaped hole in the top of the jacket. The two standard sizes of diskettes are 5¼ inches and 8 inches. The disk has the advantage of fast access to programs stored on different bands of the disk. The device that allows the computer to read information from and "write" information to disks is called a disk drive.

Hard disks are similar to phonograph records, have the capacity to store more information, and usually are used with a network of many computers. They are made of aluminum and coated with a magnetic recording surface. Hard disks are a common form of storage for large computer systems and with networks up to several hundred computers. A large amount of information can be stored on a hard disk, and as they operate at very high speeds the information can be accessed quickly.

▼　**Figure 13.14**
The "floppy disk" method of microcomputer mass storage.

Input.　This is a means of getting information into the computer. The most commonly used input device is a typewriter-like keyboard. Other input devices include joysticks, paddles, and graphics tablets. Joysticks and paddles are associated primarily with games. Graphics tablets can be used by students or teachers to incorporate drawings into their programs. Science laboratory monitoring devices can also be connected directly to a microcomputer with the proper interface device.

Output.　This is a means of displaying the results of your program. A television monitor, referred to as a CRT (cathode ray tube), is the usual output device for a microcomputer. It may be built into the total package, or be a separate component.

Microcomputers designed primarily for home use can be plugged into TV sets. Large computers and minicomputers commonly provide output in the form of data printed on paper sheets ("hard copy"). This option is also available on most microcomputer systems by adding a printer as a peripheral.

Computer Languages

As mentioned before, instructions are relayed to and throughout the computer via programs. Originally, since computers were used basically as high-powered calculators, the programs were written strictly in mathematical terms. But over the years, as a broader variety of business and educational applications have sprung up, new computer languages have been developed. Certain of these languages have incorporated terminology more and more resembling the English language. The language used by most microcomputers is BASIC. A newer language, Pascal, permits more sophisticated programming using less memory.

HOW TO... HANDLE AND STORE FLOPPY DISKS

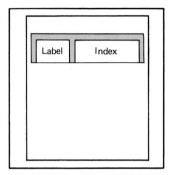

Keep disk in its protective envelope when not in use. Protect it from excessive heat and magnetized objects.

Disks should be stored vertically in their box, not laid flat, especially not with heavy objects set on them.

Marking on the disk label should be done only with felt-tip pen, not with sharp pencil or ballpoint pen. Avoid paper clips, which also could scratch the disk.

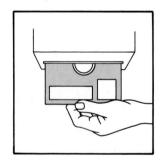

Protect the delicate surface from fingerprints by grasping the disk only by the edge to place it into the disk drive. Do not bend, fold, or warp by using rubber bands.

A popular programming language for use with elementary-aged children, Logo, was developed by Seymour Papert at MIT. The visual language centers around commands to move a ''turtle'' around the screen and draw its path. Seeing the graphic change as the program runs helps children visualize and understand what their instructions to the computer (program) have done. The focus of learning Logo is on the process of programming rather than the product. The process is discovered by the child rather than taught by the teacher.

Types of Computers

Although there are no hard and fast boundaries to classify the different types of computer systems, most users base the classification on the size of the machine's computing ability. To understand the comparisons, a little technical jargon is necessary. The term *bit* (*bi*nary dig*it*) refers to the smallest unit of information. The bit can be thought of as a 1 or a 0. Actually it is an indication of the direction of magnetism (clockwise or counterclockwise) within the memory and magnetic storage devices (tape and disk).

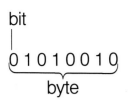

▲ **Figure 13.15**
Representation of a letter A in ASCII (American Standard Code for Information Interchange) code when 8 bits represents 1 byte.

A *byte* is the number of bits required to store/represent one character of text (letter or number). A byte is most commonly, but not always, made up of eight bits in various combinations of 0s and 1s. See Figure 13.15 for the relationship between bits and bytes.

A computer's memory size is usually described in terms of how many bytes it can store at one time. A "kilobyte," usually abbreviated "K," refers to approximately 1000 bytes (1024 to be exact). Thus, if a computer can store 16,384 bytes it is said to have a 16K memory capacity.

Note that the more powerful machines are capable of using a larger word size (more bits per byte), thus increasing their processing capacity. Most mini-computers have 16-bit RAM memory, double the 8-bit RAM memory of the microcomputer.

Computers can be classified into three main groups according to their general capabilities: mainframes, mini-computers, and microcomputers. Table 13.2 compares the three types of computers in terms of their general descriptions, capabilities, costs, and limitations.

Selecting Hardware

The term "hardware" refers to the physical equipment that makes up a computer system. It is becoming increasingly common for instructors to be involved in the selection of hard in-

Media File:
Apple IIe Microcomputer

One of the most popular microcomputers used for instruction, the Apple IIe (for *expanded*) is built around a low-cost starter system that can be expanded by adding memory capacity and peripherals, such as a printer. The IIe comes with 64K bytes of memory with the possibility of adding an additional 64K

The computer has a full ASCII keyboard with 63 keys (96 printable characters and special-purpose keys). Its major special features include built-in capability for color graphics and sound effects—from computer music to synthesized human speech.

The manufacturer, Apple Computer Inc., has shown a commitment to educational and training applications by funding an Apple Education Foundation and by publishing a sizable amount of supporting literature, including a newsletter, *Apple Education News*.

Media File:
Plato Computer System

Plato represents a special breed of computer system especially designed for and dedicated to instructional applications. Plato falls into the category of the large mainframe system. Individual terminals are connected to a powerful main CPU by means of telephone lines.

Begun in 1960 at the University of Illinois, Plato (originally known as PLATO—Programmed Logic for Automatic Teaching Operation) pioneered in CAI research and development. Today more than 10,000 hours of Plato courseware cover the span from kindergarten through graduate school levels in every conceivable subject area, including business/industry training.

Control Data now owns and sells Plato services. The Control Data 110 microcomputer represents a lower-cost level of Plato instruction. Lessons are delivered independently of a central computer by using a microprocessor in the terminal and off-line disk drives. The Control Data 110 microcomputer uses courseware contained on disks and can be hooked up to the central system for additional "computer power," other program applications, and more extensive testing and record retention abilities.

TABLE 13.2 COMPARATIVE ATTRIBUTES OF THREE MAIN COMPUTER TYPES

	General Description	Capabilities	Hardware Costs	Limitations
Microcomputers (e.g., Apple IIe, Commodore 64, Radio Shack TRS-80 Model 4, IBM-PC)	Microprocessor as CPU, originally, 8-bit per byte memory, now often 16-bit or even 32-bit. TV set for display output. Cassette or disk for add-on memory. May be self-contained or have separate components. Size of a typewriter.	Handles drill and practice and simple branching programs well. Game playing is a major strength. Music and motion graphics (usually in color). Designed to use simple languages such as BASIC.	About $1,000 to $5,000 can buy basic package. (Per learner hour cost under $1)	Relatively slow speed makes them unsuitable for "number-crunching" or handling voluminous records needed for CMI. 10,000 operations/second
Mini-Computers (e.g., Digital Equipment, Data General, Wang, Hewlett Packard)	Between micro and mainframe in size; 16-bit per byte memory. Size of a desk.	Can support up to several dozen terminals. Larger memory means higher speed and accommodation of higher power CAI author languages like Pascal.	Costs about $10,000 depending on number of peripherals. (Per learner hour cost, about $2)	Between micros and mainframes in terms of capacity. 100,000 operations/second
Mainframes (e.g., IBM, Control Data, Sperry Univac, Cyber)	High-speed, flexible machines for business and scientific computing; 32 to 64 bit per word memory. Designed for processing huge amounts of numerical data. Size of a room.	Great computing capability. High speed permits many simultaneous users. Large memory allows extensive data bases and complex programs to be stored.	Cost usually in multi-million dollar range. (Per learner hour cost about $4 per hour)	Sharing time with multiple users can mean inconvenience. Machine failure wipes out *all* users. 1,000,000 operations/second

Media File:
IBM Personal Computer

A recent entrant into the microcomputer field, but with a long history in computers, IBM has a significant number of users in the education and training areas. Their Personal Computer (the PC) has a separate keyboard that can be moved around on a table or desk or held in the user's lap. The microprocessor is a high-speed, 16-bit chip. The basic system has 64K of user memory that is expandable to 640K.

For applications, such as CMI, requiring immediate access to a large quantity of stored data, two 360K capacity floppy disk drives and two additional 10 megabyte (1 megabyte = 1,000K) hard disk drives can be added. The total storage capacity becomes 20,720K.

IBM offers a wide variety of business, communications, and educational programs.

structionally related computer hardware for their institution. This section is meant to give you at least some general guidelines for participating intelligently in such a selection process.

The general rule of computer selection is to begin by specifying what you want the computer to do. Select the software in advance. Table 13.2 allows you to compare capabilities with costs and arrive at a rough estimate, at least, of the type of system you ought to be considering. Once that is established you can begin to look at specific models of equipment.

In comparing models, many different criteria may be considered. The "Appraisal Checklist: Microcomputers" includes the most important criteria for selecting microcomputers for instructional purposes. Which criteria will be most salient to you depends on the specifics of your situation. Certain of the rating criteria may need some further explanation:

- Expandability. Can additional output and input devices be added? Can internal memory be expanded? Can peripherals (add-on devices) such as a hard-copy printout device or a modulator/demodulator device (modem) that allows computer signals to be transmitted via telephones be added to the basic system?
- Local Service and Support. Does the supplier have a local representative to answer user's questions and to take care of maintenance problems?

Appraisal Checklist: Microcomputers

Manufacturer_____

Model_____

Price_____

Memory size: RAM_____K, expandable to_____K; ROM_____K

Languages available_____

Peripherals available_____

Monitor: Size_____; Built -in   yes_____   no_____; Color_____   Green Screen_____.

Graphics available   yes_____   no_____   Sound available   yes_____   no_____

Rating	Excellent				Poor	Comments
Ease of operation	☐	☐	☐	☐	☐	
Durability/reliability	☐	☐	☐	☐	☐	
Availability of software	☐	☐	☐	☐	☐	
Video display quality	☐	☐	☐	☐	☐	
Keyboard layout and "touch"	☐	☐	☐	☐	☐	
Expandability	☐	☐	☐	☐	☐	
User documentation	☐	☐	☐	☐	☐	
Local service support	☐	☐	☐	☐	☐	
Portability	☐	☐	☐	☐	☐	

Other Features:

Strong points:

Weak points:

Reviewer_____

Position_____

Recommended action_____   Date_____

Media File:
Radio Shack TRS-80 Model 4 Microcomputer

The TRS-80 Model 4 microcomputer has its keyboard, monitor, and input devices built into the cabinet with the microprocessor. The purchaser can obtain the machine with cassette tape input, or one or two disk drives.

The Model 4 will run the thousands of programs written for its predecessor, the Model III, as well as CP/M software. It can be hooked up to a number of different peripherals including up to four disk drives, a hard disk system, hard copy (paper) printer, voice synthesizer, and multiplexer (to feed several terminals from the same CPU).

Within the lowest price range, Radio Shack is a leader in software development and in hardware service through its thousands of local electronics supply dealers.

Media File:
Commodore 64 Microcomputer

As the name implies, the Commodore 64 has 64K of internal memory. The "Sprite Graphics" feature allows the user to design pictures in four colors. The Commodore 64 has built-in music and sound effects. Available peripherals include "DATASETTE" (a special cassette recorder for storage), disk drive storage units, dot matrix printer, and "VICMODEM" to connect the 64 with larger computers through a telephone.

One of the least expensive 64K microcomputers, the Commodore 64 is widely used in schools. The *Commodore Software Encyclopedia* (available for a nominal charge from authorized Commodore dealers) describes the various programs currently available for use on Commodore microcomputers.

References

Print References

Baker, F. B. *Computer Managed Instruction: Theory and Practice.* (Englewood Cliffs, N.J.: Educational Technology Publications, 1978).

Bradley, Buff. "Let's Do More with Computers than Study Computers." *Learning* (October 1984), pp. 21–44.

Bunderson, C. V. "Courseware." In H. F. O'Neill, ed., *Computer-Based Instruction: The State of the Art.* (New York: Academic Press, 1981).

Coburn, Peter, et al. *Practical Guide to Computers in Education.* (Reading, Mass.: Addison-Wesley, 1982).

Dennis, J. Richard, and Kansky, Robert J. *Instructional Computing: An Action Guide for Educators.* (Glenview, Ill.: Scott Foresman, 1984).

DucQuy, N., and Covington, J. "The Microcomputer in Industry Training." *T. H. E. Journal* (March 1982), pp. 65–68.

Educational Products Information Exchange. *Microcomputer Courseware/ Microcomputer Games.* (Water Mill, N.Y.: EPIE Institute, 1982).

_____. *Microcomputer Hardware/Interactive Videosystems.* (Water Mill, N.Y.: EPIE Institute, 1982).

Frederick, Franz J. *Guide to Microcomputers.* (Washington, D.C.: Association for Educational Communications and Technology, 1980).

A Guide to the Selection of Microcomputers. (London: Council for Educational Technology for the United Kingdom, 1980).

Harper, Dennis O., and Stewart, James H. *Run: Computer Education.* (Monterey, Calif: Brooks/Cole Publishing, 1983).

Hopper, Grace, M., and Mandell, Steven L. *Understanding Computers.* (St. Paul, Minn.: West Publishing, 1984).

Judd, Dorothy H., and Judd, Robert C. *Mastering the Micro: Using the Microcomputer in the Elementary Classroom.* (Glenview, Ill.: Scott Foresman, 1984).

Kearsley, Greg. *Computer Based Training.* (Reading, Mass.: Addison-Wesley, 1983).

_____; Hillelsohn, M. J.; and Seidel, R. J. "Microcomputer-Based Training in Business and Industry: Present Status and Future Prospects." *Journal of Educational Technology Systems* 10 (1981), pp. 101–108.

_____; Hunter, B.; and Hillelsohn, M. J. "Computer Literacy in Business and Industry: Three Examples Using Microcomputers." *Educational Technology* (July 1982), pp. 9–14.

Merrill, David. *TICCIT.* (Englewood Cliffs, N.J.: Educational Technology Publications, 1980).

Metzcus, Richard. *The PDK Guide: An Introduction to Microcomputer Literacy for Educators.* (Bloomington, In.: Phi Delta Kappa, 1983).

"Microcomputers." *Instructional Innovator* (September 1980).

Milner, Stuart D. "Teaching Teachers about Computers: A Necessity for Education." *Phi Delta Kappan* (April 1980), pp. 544–546.

Nickles, Herbert L., and Culp, George. *Instructional Computing with the TRS-80.* (Monterey, Calif.: Brooks/Cole Publishing, 1984).

O'Neil, Harold F. *Computer-Based Education: A State-of-the-Art Assessment.* (New York: Academic Press, 1981).

Orlansky, J., and String, J. "Computer-Based Instruction for Military Training." *Defense Management Journal* (2d quarter 1981), pp. 46–54.

Radin, Stephen, and Lee, Fayvian. *Computers in the Classroom*. (Chicago: Science Research Associates, 1984).

Rahmlow, H.; Fratine, R.; and Ghesquiere, J. *PLATO*. (Englewood Cliffs, N.J.: Educational Technology Publications, 1980).

Richman, Ellen. *Spotlight on Computer Literacy*. (New York: Random House, 1982).

Seaman, J. "Microcomputers Invade the Executive Suite." *Computer Decisions* (February 1981), pp. 68–172.

Sleeman, D., and Brown, J. S. *Intelligent Tutoring Systems*. (New York: Academic Press, 1982).

Smith, C., ed. *Microcomputers in Education*. (Chicester, West Sussex, England: Elliss Horwood Limited, 1982).

Sniederman, B. *Software Psychology: Human Factors in Computer and Information Systems*. (Cambridge, Mass.: Winthrop Publishers, 1980).

Solomon, C. "Introducing Logo to Children." *Byte* 7 (1982), pp. 196–208.

Terry, Colin, ed. *Using Microcomputers in Schools*. (New York: Nichols Publishing, 1984).

Troutner, Joanne. *The Media Speclialist, the Microcomputer, and the Curriculum*. (Littleton, Colo.: Libraries Unlimited, 1983).

Vockell, Edward L., and Rivers, Robert H. *Instructional Computing for Today's Teachers*. (New York: MacMillan, 1984).

Watt, D. "Logo in the Schools." *Byte* (1982), pp. 116–134.

Williams, Frederick, and Williams, Victoria. *Microcomputers in Elementary Education: Perspectives on Implementation*. (Belmont, Calif.: Wadsworth Publishing, 1984).

Courseware Design

Burke, Robert L. *CAI Sourcebook*. (Englewood Cliffs, N.J.: Prentice-Hall, 1982).

Dean, Christopher, and Whitlock, Quentin. *A Handbook of Computer Based Training*. (New York: Nichols Publishing, 1983).

DeBloois, M. L. *Videodisc/Microcomputer Courseware Design*. (Englewood Cliffs, N.J.: Educational Technology Publications, 1982).

Eisele, J. "Lesson Design for Computer-Based Instructional Systems." *Educational Technology* 18 (1978), pp. 14–21.

Galitz, W. *Handbook of Screen Format Design*. (Wellesley, Mass.: Q.E.D. Information Sciences, 1981).

Heines, Jesse M. *Screen Designs for Computer-Assisted Instruction*. (Bedford, Mass.: Digital Press, 1984).

Jenkin J. "Some Principles of Screen Design and Software for Their Support." In P. R. Smith, ed., *Computer Assisted Learning*. (Oxford: Pergamon Press, 1981).

Nievergelt, J. "A Pragmatic Introduction to Courseware Design." *IEEE Computer* (September 1980), pp. 7–21.

Walker, Decker F., and Hess, Robert D. *Instructional Software: Principles and Perspectives for Design and Use*. (Belmont, Calif.: Wadsworth Publishing, 1984).

Audiovisual References

Adventures of the Mind. Bloomington, Ind.: Indiana University Audio-Visual Center, 1980. Series of 16-mm films (or videocassettes) about microcomputers. 20 minutes each. Individual titles are:
Data Processing Control Design
Extending Your Reach
For Better or For Worse
Hardware and Software
Speaking the Language

The Audio-Visual Library of Computer Education. Mill Valley, Calif.: Prismation Productions, 1983. 15-part, 345-minute series of materials dealing with computer literacy. Available as sound/filmstrip, sound/slide, or videocassette.

Computer Basics. (Los Angeles: AV Systems, 1981. Series of 6 sound/filmstrips and computer diskette titled:
What Is a Computer?
Do You Need a Computer?
How to Use a Computer
How Do Computers Work?
How to Program a Computer
What Do Computers Mean?

Computer Hardware: What It Is and How It Works. Mount Kisco, N.Y.: Center for the Humanities, 1982. 2 sound filmstrips or sound/slide sets, also available on videocassette.

Computer History. Stamford, Ct: Educational Dimensions Group, 1982. 4 sound filmstrips with teacher's guide.

Computer Literacy: The First Step. (Stamford, Ct: Educational Dimensions Group, 1982. 4 sound filmstrips with teacher's guide.

The Computer Programme. Wilmette, Ill.: Films, Inc., 1981. Films/videocassettes on the workings and applications of computers.

Computer Series 1: An Introduction to Computers. Bedford Hills, N.Y.: Educational Enrichment Materials, 1983. 5 sound filmstrips with teacher's guide.

Computer Software: What It Is and How It Works. Mount Kisco, N.Y.: Center for the Humanities, 1982. 2 sound filmstrips or sound/slide sets, also available on videocassette.

Computer-Rage. Morristown, N.J.: Creative Computing, 1980. Game.

Computers for Kids. Ormond Beach, Fla.: Camelot Publishing, 1979. Kit including slides, cassette, and teacher's manual.

Computers: From Pebbles to Program. White Plains, N.Y.: Guidance Associates, 1975. 3 sound filmstrips or sound/slide sets on the history of computers and their applications.

Don't Bother Me, I'm Learning—Adventures in Computer Education. New York: CRM/McGraw-Hill, 1980. 16-mm film/videocassette on the use of computers in the classroom.

Don't Bother Me, I'm Learning—Computers in the Community. New York: CRM/McGraw-Hill, 1982. 16-mm film/ videocassette on the use of computers in the community.

Making It Count: An Introduction to Computers. Seattle, Wash.: Boeing Aerospace, 1982. Videotape course on how computers work and their application.

Making the Most of the Micro. Wilmette, Ill.: Films Inc., 1982. Series of 10 films or videocassettes produced by the British Broadcasting Company.

Microcomputer Courseware. Sioux Falls, S.D.: United Education and Software, 1983. Kit with 2 student workbooks, project kit, and computer diskette designed for personal or professional computer users.

Visual Masters for Teaching about Computers. Ormond Beach, Fla.: Camelot Publishing, 1978. Overhead transparency master set.

Welcome to the Future: Computers in the Classroom. Wilmette, Ill.: Films, Inc., 1982. 16-mm film/videocassette. 28 min.

Organizations

Association for Educational Data Systems (AEDS)
1201 Sixteenth Street, N.W.
Washington, D.C. 20036
The largest of the organizations dedicated to the use of computers in education. Its emphasis is on the secondary-school level and its interests include both administrative and instructional uses of computers.

Association for the Development of Computer-Based Instructional Systems (ADCIS)
Computer Center
Western Washington University
Bellingham, Washington 98225
Organization for persons interested in research and development of computer-based instruction.

CONDUIT
PO Box 388
Iowa City, Iowa 52244
Evaluates and distributes computer-based instructional materials and publishes a periodical, *Pipeline.*

Education Products Information Exchange Institute (EPIE)
Box 839
Water Mill, New York 11976
Publishes reviews of microcomputer courseware/hardware and procedures for their evaluation, including the *EPIE Annotated Courseware Provider List.*

International Council for Computers in Education
Department of Computer and Information Science
University of Oregon
Eugene, Oregon 97403
Collects and distributes information concerning computer applications in education and publishes *The Computing Teacher.*

Minnesota Educational Computing Consortium (MECC)
2520 Broadway Drive
St. Paul, Minnesota 55113
Develops and disseminates courseware and computer-related materials, especially for elementary and secondary schools.

Northwest Regional Educational Laboratory
300 S.W. Sixth Avenue
Portland, Oregon 97204
Clearinghouse for catalogs and review guides, publishes evaluations of courseware including *Microcomputer Software Catalog List.*

Computer Hardware Manufacturers

Acorn Computers Corporation
400 Unicorn Park Drive
Woburn, Massachusetts 01801

Apple Computer, Inc.
20525 Mariana Avenue
Cupertino, California 95014

Atari, Inc.
P.O. Box 50047
60 E. Plumeria Drive
San Jose, California 95150

Commodore Business Machines
487 Devon Park Road
Wayne, Pennsylvania 19087

Franklin Computer Corp.
7030 Colonial Highway
Pennsauken, New Jersey 08109

IBM Corporation
P.O. Box 1328
Boca Raton, Florida 33432

Kaypro Corporation
P.O. Box N
Del Mar, California 92014

Radio Shack
One Tandy Center
Fort Worth, Texas 76102

Plato/CDC
Control Data Corporation
P.O. Box 0
Minneapolis, Minnesota 55440

Periodicals

Classroom Computer Learning
Pitman Learning, Inc.
5615 West Cermak Road
Cicero, Illinois 60650
10 issues/yr.

Classroom Computer News: The Magazine for Teachers & Parents
Intentional Educations
Box 266
Cambridge, Massachusetts 02138
8 issues/yr.

The Computing Teacher
International Council for Computers in Education
University of Oregon
1787 Agate St.
Eugene, Oregon 97403-1923
9 issues/yr.

Creative Computing
Ahl Computing
PO Box 789-M
Morristown, New Jersey 07960
12 issues/yr.

Electronic Education
Electronic Communications
Suite 220
1311 Executive Center Dr.
Tallahassee, Florida 32301
8 issues/yr.

Electronic Learning: The Magazine for Educators of the 80s
Scholastic, Inc.
PO Box 644
Lyndhurst, New Jersey 07071-9985
10 issues/yr.

Teaching and Computers: Scholastic's Magazine for Today's Elementary Classroom
Scholastic Magazine
730 Broadway
New York, New York 10003-9538
8 issues/yr.

TLC (Teaching, Learning, Computing): The Educator's Guide to Personal Computing
Seldin Publishing
1061 S. Melrose, Suite D
Placentia, California 92670-7180
10 issues/yr.

Possible Projects

13-A. Read and summarize an article on the use of computers in education or training.

13.B. Interview a student and/or teacher who has used computers for instruction. Report on how the computer was used, including the user's perceptions as to strengths and limitations.

13.C. Develop a list of topics you would include if you were to conduct a one-day computer literacy workshop for teachers/trainers in your subject area.

13.D. Describe how you could use a computer as an object of instruction or as a tool during instruction in your instructional field.

13.E. Synthesize a situation in which you could use computer-based materials. Include a description of the audience, the objectives, the role of the computer, and the expected outcomes (or advantages) of using the computer.

13.F. Locate computer programs suitable for your subject area using the information sources available to you.

13.G. Appraise an instructional computer program using the "Appraisal Checklist: Computer-Based Instruction" provided in the chapter.

13.H. Evaluate a microcomputer using the "Appraisal Checklist: Microcomputers" in the chapter.

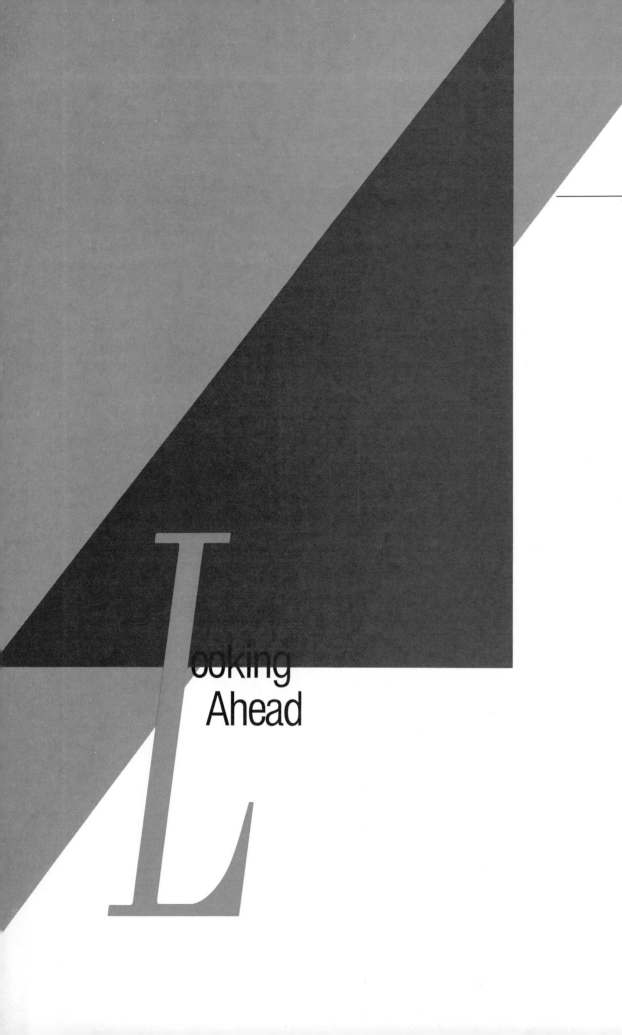

Looking Ahead

Outline

Objectives

After studying this chapter, you should be able to:

1. Give two examples of the effect of miniaturization on instruction and explain how these increase access to learning.
2. Give two examples of electronic delivery systems that have had a major impact on increasing access to learning.
3. Describe two electronic distribution methods of displaying text on the screen of a video terminal.
4. Relate the multiplication of electronic delivery systems to the decentralization of education.
5. List at least three information-processing skills that are exercised in pinball-type video games.
6. Appraise the educational value of adventure-type video games in general.
7. Discuss the instructional strengths and weaknesses of drill-and-practice games and hand-held microprocessor games.
8. Relate "altered states of consciousness" to improved learning.
9. Give two examples of how "bionic extensions of the brain" could in the future enhance communication and/or learning.
10. Critique the conventional self-contained classroom as an organizational arrangement for incorporating technology.
11. Critique the "craft approach" of public education as a system for incorporating technology.
12. Relate the accountability movement to the increased use of technology in education.
13. Relate the lifelong-learning movement to the increased use of technology in education.
14. Describe three areas of specialization within the educational technology career field.
15. Name at least three major professional associations in educational technology; characterize the membership of each.
16. Name at least three journals published by professional associations and one not published by an association; characterize the emphases of each.

Lexicon

biochip
videotex
teletext
pinball-type game
adventure game
microprocessor game
suggestive-accelerative learning and teaching
emgor
economy of scale
division of labor
low-cost learning technology
craft
accountability

The previous chapters of this book have focused on the various media and technologies of instruction—what they are, their advantages and limitations, and their potential applications to improving learning.

This final chapter attempts to give a broader perspective of how media and technology fit into the overall scheme of education and training. The emphasis is on change: what trends have brought us to where we are now, what new developments hold promise for improving learning productivity, what impediments limit the implementation of these developments, and what avenues may exist for getting around these impediments. The chapter concludes with consideration of the professional organizations and journals devoted to further implementation of media and technology in education and training, since these may be the tools by which you become further involved in the efforts of this field.

TRENDS IN MEDIA AND TECHNOLOGY

Two major trends in communications technology have paralleled each other over the past half century: the miniaturization of the media of communication and the multiplication of electronic delivery systems. These trends have combined to increase our *access* to instructional media. As will be discussed later, however, the mere availability of media has not necessarily led to a proportionate increase in the *use* of these tools.

Miniaturization: Making Instruction Portable

Perhaps the most important single technological trend affecting the use of instructional media has been the movement toward miniaturization of mediaware formats and equipment. This trend has led to lower cost, increased ease of operation and portability of equipment, and hence to increased availability of instructional media in the formal and nonformal learning situation.

Even 16-mm film equipment has become more portable and easier to operate. For example, many such projectors now on the market feature automatic threading, whereas two decades ago all machines had to be manually threaded. The machines have become smaller because mechanical parts have become more re-

liable and smaller. Reduction in amplifier size has been made possible by the introduction of, first, transistors and printed circuits, and, more recently, integrated circuits. Standard reel-to-reel tape recorders also have gotten progressively smaller. To take but one further example, many schools and colleges now use small-screen television viewers in individualized and small-group instructional situations, an impossibility two decades ago because small-screen television monitors for classroom use were not available.

Very few technological innovations have been more quickly or universally adapted to instructional purposes than the cassette tape recorder. The advantages of the cassette were immediately obvious. First, the whole cassette is considerably smaller than a comparable reel-to-reel tape and its box. The principal reason for this reduction in size is that the tape itself is half the width of the standard ¼-inch recording tape. The next obvious difference between the cassette and reel-to-reel format is convenience of operation. No longer does the user have to thread the tape into the machine. Finally, the machine is considerably smaller than reel-to-reel tape recorders. The most widely sold form of cassette tape recorder today can be carried in one hand. This is a vast change from the earlier 15- to 30-pound reel-to-reel tape recorders.

In the early days of cassette development, recording quality left a good deal to be desired. Even so, teachers were quite willing to trade quality for miniaturization. But, as the cassette format became widely adopted, making further technological improvements economically feasible for producers of cassettes, the quality of the

▶ **Figure 14.1**
Miniaturization in audio can be seen in the progression from an early open reel tape recorder to a cassette recorder to a microcassette recorder.

recording improved. With today's high-fidelity systems, it is difficult to tell the difference between the audio quality of a well-recorded cassette tape and a well-recorded reel-to-reel tape with similar quality speakers.

Miniaturization of electronic components has today resulted in videotape recorders portable enough to be carried on a shoulder strap, a development that has contributed immensely to the use of videotaped materials for instructional purposes. Videotape itself also has been improved remarkably in recent years. When it was first introduced, the tape had to travel at a very high speed in order to record with any degree of fidelity. However, today's videotape recorders record at a relatively slow speed, allowing much more recording time per standard reel. Today, videocassette machines can record up to six hours per reel. When video tape was originally introduced the tape was 2 inches wide; today ½-inch tape is very common for school

and home, with little discernible difference in quality. The ½-inch videocassette system is rapidly becoming the standard format in both education and training. Recording in this format is simple and of acceptable quality.

The videodisc represents another step toward compressing the size of the software needed for the storage and playback of moving pictures. The collapse in 1984 of RCA's effort to market its line of videodisc equipment to the home consumer dictates caution in assuming that this new format will replace completely the existing means of magnetic tape recording. Many home and instructional users of video want a system on which they can record their own programming as well as play back mass-distributed programs. Until an erasable videodisc is proven feasible for general use, we can expect to see tape and disc continue to coexist. The fascinating potentials of laser videodiscs when combined with computer control—discussed in Chapter 7 under "Interactive Video" and later in this chapter—make this a most promising technology of the future.

Miniaturization has also had its effect on the print medium, making the printed word more easily and widely

available for instructional and other purposes than the developers of movable type could have imagined. Perhaps the most universally used micro-form for reducing the size of the printed word so that it can be more widely disseminated is microfiche. In different microfiche formats, dozens, even hundreds, of pages of print can be recorded on a single piece of film. The contents of the entire *Encyclopaedia Britannica,* for example, can be reduced to a stack of microfiches small enough to be thrust into one's pocket.

Recent advances in the photographic quality of microfiche have raised the possibility of using microfiches as still projection media. Microfiches containing color transparent images and the projectors to show them are now available, suggesting a new format for future packaging of filmstrips and slide sets. Up to ninety-eight images fit on one 4 by 6 inch fiche, making production, mailing, storing, and handling easier and less expensive than ever before.

Another striking manifestation of miniaturization is to be seen in the area of computer technology. Mainly because of advances in microchip technology, computers, which used to be obtainable only in extremely

▼ **Figure 14.2**
The latest in portable video recording—an integrated camera and ½-inch recorder weighing under five pounds.

▼ **Figure 14.3**
The videodisc is a highly compact format for storage of still or motion pictures.

▼ **Figure 14.4**
One volume of a typical encyclopedia can be reduced to a small handful of microfiches, as shown here.

cumbersome form and at extremely high cost, are now available in formats taking up no more space than a television set and costing about the same amount of money. The educational importance of this development was discussed in Chapter 13. Schools and small training organizations that only a few years ago could not have dreamed of using computer technology for administrative and instructional purposes are now finding this tool logistically and economically feasible. We can certainly expect that computer-based instruction will continue to grow rapidly in the years to come.

The degree of miniaturization that has evolved in the realm of microprocessors is truly staggering. The wiring in the integrated circuits of the pre-1980 era could be inspected with the naked eye. The next generation of integrated circuits required a magnifying glass. Today you need a microscope, or even an electron microscope. The tiny integrated circuits of today are etched in silicon using optical lithography or electron beams. The emerging development is to apply the techniques of genetic engineering—recombinant DNA—to construct tiny biological microprocessors of protein, or "biochips." Biochips measuring in the 10 to 25 nanometer range (a nanometer is

▼ **Figure 14.5**
Microprocessor chips visible only under a magnifying glass are common components of today's computers.

one-billionth of a meter) would represent about two orders of magnitude smaller than the current silicon chips. Protein circuits as small as a single molecule are being envisioned. The implications of such biotechnology are discussed later in this chapter.

Multiplication of Electronic Delivery Systems

Another technological innovation that has already had tremendous impact on education and undoubtedly will have even greater impact in the future is the use of electronic systems for the delivery of instruction. Just a few years ago, the individual instructor was practically the sole "distributor of instruction" on the educational scene. Today we have instruction via open broadcast by radio and television stations, microwave systems, satellite, and closed-circuit systems such as cable television and the telephone.

Although instruction via open broadcast by radio and television, especially television, has been and will continue to be a significant force in education, there is presently a trend toward wider applications of closed distribution systems to the instructional situation. Closed distribution systems—microwave, closed-circuit, satellite—unlike open systems, have the advantage of being able to transmit a number of instructional programs simultaneously. In addition, they have the significant advantage

▼ **Figure 14.6**
Satellite distribution systems make television available even in remote Eskimo village schools in Alaska.

of being able to overcome broadcast television's inherent limitation in coverage area. For example, satellite signals can be sent to virtually any spot on the face of the earth and, once received, can be carried by cable and/or microwave systems to any instructional setting, including the home. Direct reception of satellite transmissions by schools, business and industrial facilities, hospitals, or any other likely instructional setting is now a reality with the proper receiving equipment, eliminating the need for redistribution by cable. Satellite signals can now also be received and transmitted via telephones equipped with optical fibers capable of transmitting hundreds of messages simultaneously. Appropriate equipment attached to such telephones permits local display of the signals. A recent survey disclosed that telecommunications networks of the type described here are already in widespread use throughout all parts of the United States. *Looking only at educational networks within individual states, researchers found ninety-eight organizations operating networks in forty-four of the fifty states.

The successful operation of the Space Shuttle signals another breakthrough in the cost of providing the satellites that are the backbone of these electronic delivery systems covering broad geographic areas. With the lowered costs of the recyclable Shuttle and its ability to carry multiple satellites into orbit on a single trip, the cost of placing and maintaining satellites will be cut many times.

Computer technology is adding yet another dimension to electronic distribution of instruction. Along with the instructional capabilities of localized computers, we can expect the growing use of large centralized computer

*Jerold Gruebel, W. Neal Robison, and Susan Rutledge. "Intrastate Educational Telecommunication Systems: A National Survey," *Educational Technology*, (April 1981), pp. 33–36.

▲ **Figure 14.7**
Regular Space Shuttle flights have routinized the process of launching new communication satellites.

▲ **Figure 14.8**
A videotex home information system display.

facilities offering instructional programming to be used in "real time" or stored in microcomputer systems for delayed use.

Electronic distribution systems have also given rise to the technique of *teleconferencing* for instructional purposes. Pioneered in the Scandinavian countries, teleconferencing can provide an interactive learning experience between instructor and students without the instructor (or other resource person) having to leave his or her home base. For example, an instructor may videotape a lesson for transmission via a closed-circuit distribution system and after it is shown, or even while it is being shown, engage in a dialogue with the audience through a telephonic communication system specially designed for this purpose.

Interest in this technique has grown with the high cost and growing inconvenience of travel due to energy shortages in many parts of the world. The Center for Interactive Programs and Instructional Communications at the University of Wisconsin, for example, has been offering seminars in teleconferencing since 1975. Even without assuming that energy resources will remain in short supply in much of the world, teleconferencing and similar telecommunication instructional techniques are likely to grow in use in the coming years. Applications of teleconferencing were explored at some length in Chapter 6.

The multiplication and recombination of different means of electronic information distribution has broken down and will continue to break down the previously clear distinctions among, for instance, television, telephone, computer, and print media. For example, we now find verbal information, once the domain of print, being distributed regularly via wired and through-the-air transmission. The current terms to describe this phenomenon are *videotex* and *teletext*. Videotex involves two-way transmission of print information through either telephone lines or coaxial cable. Teletext, on the other hand, is transmitted on a broadcast television signal using the "vertical blanking interval," a portion of the signal not used to carry visual or auditory information. These technical distinctions, of course, are of no interest to the viewer. As we use video terminals it is of little consequence whether the words we see on the screen are generated inside the microcomputer linked to the screen or transmitted to that screen via telephone or broadcast channels. The point is that there are now many ways of doing the same job.

Economies of Scale. In the long run the development of electronic systems for the distribution of instruction will have a profound effect on the organization and administration of our educational facilities. For the last half-century educators and the public have been assuming that in order to increase access of each child to a full range of instruction and in order to make better use of personnel and to increase cost efficiency (economy of scale), smaller schools had to be replaced by larger ones. However, advances in technology have now made it administratively and economically feasible to educate smaller groups of students in a larger number of instructional settings. Pro-ponents of "decentralization" as a step toward greater public participa-tion in the control of public education may well have found an unexpected and powerful ally in technological ad-vances such as electronic systems for the distribution of instruction.

▼ **Figure 14.9**
This Tennessee one-room schoolhouse of 1936 was designed primarily for lecture instruction but had to accommodate individual and small-group study for children at different grade levels.

▼ **Figure 14.10**
This Toronto classroom of the 1970s contains only one grade level but is easily adaptable to a variety of learning modes. The impact of technology is visible in terms of the role of instructional materials, the use of space, and the richness of stimuli.

FUTURE TECHNOLOGIES OF INSTRUCTION

The possibilities of technological de-velopments that could lead to major impacts on education and training are infinite. For our purposes here we will look at examples from three realms of development—hardware/software technology, psychological technology, and biological technol-ogy—as examples of the sorts of in-novations that are here or coming soon.

Hardware/Software Technology: Computer-Based Games

Video arcades seemed to spring up like mushrooms in the early 1980s. In 1981 more money was spent in the United States playing video arcade games—some $5 to $7 billion—than the total take of all the Nevada gam-bling casinos and the movie industry combined. Just as quickly, contro-versy flourished regarding the educa-tional desirability of playing such games. Today, both the popularity of the arcade games and the contro-versy seem to have plateaued. The issue remains, though, as to the in-structional usefulness of computer-based games in general.

There is still not enough objective evidence available to make confident judgments about the overall effects of particular microprocessor-con-trolled games, much less about these games as a whole. But some pat-terns have emerged and, interest-ingly, they parallel what educators have discovered about each of the previous waves of new technological marvels: that is, that the pedagogical merit varies with the features of the particular game. As was stated in Chapter 1, seven decades of instruc-tional media research have taught us to ask, "What attributes are needed for proper communication of this idea, and does this material have those attributes?" We can examine those attributes more easily if similar

▲ **Figure 14.11**
The sudden burst of popularity of video games and video arcades in the early 1980s raised questions about their effect on young people's behavior.

materials are clustered together. For discussion purposes we will use four categories: *pinball-type arcade games, adventure games, drill-and-practice games,* and *hand-held microprocessor games.*

Pinball Games.   Most visible because of their broad popularity are the pinball-type arcade games such as *Pac Man, Space Invaders,* and *Donkey Kong.* The player controls a joystick or paddle, making rapid hand movements in response to a moving pattern of threatening situations on a

display screen. Successful play requires eye-hand coordination, quick reflexes, concentration, and visual perception skills. It is arguable to what extent these skills transfer to real-world utility. One realm of immediate application is military training. U.S. Air Force trainers feel that the rapid information processing skills re-

quired in the pinball type games are similar to those used by fighter pilots with video displays in their cockpits. Several commercial arcade games have been adapted for Air Force training and research purposes. The attention of U.S. Army trainers was caught by *Battlezone,* a shooting gallery game which uses realistic silhouettes of enemy tanks and helicopters as its targets. It, too, is being adapted for formal training use.

The rapid movement, visual and auditory stimulation, and immediate feedback aspects of the pinball-type games also hold great attraction for special education and remedial education. The eye-hand coordination practice, for instance, allows a brain-injured individual with a manual dexterity handicap the chance to gain through practice capabilities that are "wired-in" from birth in normal, uninjured brains. For those with sensory handicaps due to brain injury, games can be developed to target the specific auditory or visual skills for which they need practice. Experience to date indicates at least that novel computer games provide intrinsic motivation to persist at a learning task, increasing attention span as well as time on task.

▼ **Figure 14.13**
Fast-action video games provide motivating practice in hand-eye coordination, especially valuable for those with motor handicaps.

▼ **Figure 14.12**
Atari's *PacMan* became the most famous of the early pinball-type arcade games.

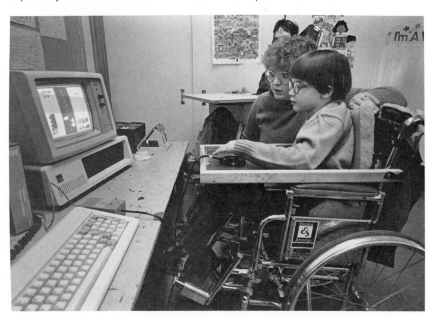

For those with less dramatic learning disabilities, other adaptations of the animated graphics and interactivity of video games hold promise for remedial education. Neuro Linguistic Programming, a technique of visualization for improving memory and learning in general, is the basis for *Spelling Strategy* and *Math Strategy*. Another game, *Speed Reader*, uses a moving cursor on the display screen to train for faster, smoother eye movements—one of the fundamental reading skills.

The most ambitious claim for this class of video games is that basic information-processing skills are flexed in solving these fast-moving puzzles. Concentration, scanning the display for useful information, employing peripheral vision, separating relevant from irrelevant information, deciding, and acting must be integrated in order for the player to succeed. And the gradual improvement of most players' scores indicates that "something" is being learned along these lines. Whether that "something" is a generic cognitive skill transferable to other situations is yet to be established.

Adventure Games.

A more recent development in commercial video games is the adventure game. Introduced around 1983 as the pinball-type games began to slacken in popularity, these games have rapidly established a large following. Adventure games such as *Dragon's Lair*

and *Eon and the Time Tunnel* combine the huge visual storage capabilities of videodisc with the branching and interactive abilities of microprocessors. Each game consists of a series of action scenes stored on videodisc. Each action sequence has several possible continuations, each of which in turn has several branches of its own. The player periodically must make split-second decisions and communicate them by means of an 8-position joystick. Correct decisions lead ahead to further episodes enroute to the goal (*Dragon's Lair* requires 200 correct decisions to win); slow or mistaken responses lead to early demise of the game character.

The addition of the videodisc gives these games another dimension of visual sophistication. The simulation possibilities are impressive, as are the potentials for escapist entertainment. The educative potential would appear to be limited, though, to rather specific problem-solving abilities. It remains to be seen whether the deductive reasoning applied to finding the "prime path" in a specific adventure game is transferable to real-world application.

Drill-and-Practice Games.

More pedestrian than the above games but more commonplace in school use are drill-and-practice games. These are designed for instructional uses and aimed at the

home and school personal computer market. *Word Attack, Math Blaster, Flight Vector*, and *MasterType* are a few examples of the many drill-and-practice microcomputer programs that have game-type features built in. The majority so far are clustered around the obvious curricular applications: drill of math skills and spelling/vocabulary drill. Reviews complain that most materials of this type fail either by overemphasizing the game at the expense of curricular learning or by doing the opposite—grafting trivial "bells and whistles" onto basically tedious drills. Programs that simply allow students to move a flashing cursor through a maze display or around a baseball diamond as a reward for correct answers will lose quickly whatever motivational appeal they may start with.

Hand-Held Microprocessor Games.

Another major class of "educational" games includes the inexpensive, limited-purpose, calculator-type toys such as *Dataman, Little Professor*, and *Speak & Spell*. These are small hand-held instruments costing from $10 to $50 and marketed primarily to the mass

▼ **Figure 14.16**
Little Professor is a hand-held game that presents math drill items at varying difficulty levels.

▼ **Figure 14.14**
Dragon's Lair was the first adventure game to gain mass popularity.

▼ **Figure 14.15**
Drill-and-practice games such as *Math Blaster* borrow the "target shooting" format to maintain interest in repetitive drills, such as multiplication tables.

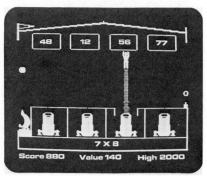

▲ **Figure 14.17**
Speak & Spell is another hand-held microprocessor game; it has several game modes, all based around spelling practice.

▲ **Figure 14.18**
Touch & Tell by Texas Instruments asks questions by means of a voice synthesizer and requires pressing the correct square; it provides discrimination practice and builds literacy skills without requiring literacy as a prerequisite.

home market for arithmetic or spelling practice. The EPIE Institute in 1981 conducted field tests of eight of the most widely distributed models in elementary schools. The findings were negative to say the least. The summary judgment was that "The actual 'instructional' function of these games was found to be nil."* The problem is that these devices provide only for drill of *previously learned skills*. As the EPIE report concluded regarding the spelling games:

> *...students either knew or did not know how to spell the words. . . . Those who did know appeared to find the positive "beep" of the reinforcement encouraging, but clearly became bored rather quickly. Students, on the other hand, who did not know, did not, without exception, learn the correct spelling even after two to three repetitions and were, additionally, bored when not frustrated.†*

*Microcomputer Courseware/Microprocessor Games. EPIE Materials Report 98/99m. Stony Brook, N.Y.: EPIE Institute, 1981 p. 42.

†Ibid., p. 40.

At the same time, there are other compact microprocessor-controlled educational game systems that hold considerably more promise. For example, Texas Instruments' *Touch & Tell* device adds two features which add immensely to its instructional potential: a voice synthesizer and a complex branching program. The compact *Touch & Tell* system consists of a flat touch-sensitive keyboard in rugged plastic case that also holds the complete hardware and software. Different plastic templates can be placed on the keyboard to allow practice of many different alphabet, number, shape, and other visual discrimination skills. The voice synthesizer is employed to ask questions, to state correct answers, and to play lively musical salutes for a series of correct answers. The program keeps track of the correctness of responses and passage of time, and it goes ahead to more challenging items or goes back to rehearse missed items depending on the child's response.

Since the mode of response is simply touching an image (letter, number, shape, picture, or the like) on a flat board, it is accessible to children of a very wide range of ages or handicapping conditions. The use of interchangeable overlays and plug-in command modules gives *Touch & Tell* great flexibility.

A device similar to the *Touch & Tell* is Mattel's *TLC* (*Teach and Learn Computer*). It, too, uses a touch-sensitive keyboard and voice synthesizer as its main features. The *TLC* employs a hard disc for the branching program memory. Examples of two of the available programs illustrate the variety of learning tasks possible on compact, relatively inexpensive systems of this type:

"Sounds of Musical Instruments" (ages 3 +). Thirty different instruments introduce children to the sound of music. The child presses the button on any of the pictures and hears the name of the instrument, something about it, and the way it sounds. To help hold a child's interest, there are five comments and suggestions, one of which occurs after every five responses.

"Find the Lost Dog" (ages 5 +).

A game that helps children learn to listen, look, and follow directions as they track the trail of the little lost dog. Children hear clues directing them to one of the six houses shown on the overlay. If they find the right house, they're given a new clue. A wrong choice brings a "try again" message. They have three chances to find the right answer before the TLC asks a new question. When they have followed all the clues, they find the missing dog. They're learning about colors as they play.

In summary, computer games—even supposedly educational ones—vary widely both in their proven instructional merit and in their theoretical potential. Objectives are often obscure. Supposed reinforcers may fail to evoke motivation in actual users. Sorting the wheat from the chaff requires careful previewing. Some games may yield a side effect of development of certain generic cognitive skills related to concentration, visual scanning, and high-speed information processing. But the actual effects of any particular computer game depend on the specific attributes built into that game.

Psychological Technology: Using Altered States of Consciousness

Shifting our attention from "technology as product" to "technology as process" we can recognize that new scientific understanding of human learning will also be contributing to changes in how instruction is carried out in the future. Conventional educational research and development has already yielded the sorts of technologies of instruction described in Chapter 11: programmed instruction, programmed tutoring, Audio-tutorial methods, and the like. Looking into the future, though, breakthroughs in improved learning may well be coming from less conventional sources.

Meditation has long been associated with religious practices and religious training in India and the Orient. In the 1960s these religious influences began to attract popular attention in North America. Experimentation since that time has built up a sizable body of evidence that meditative techniques can have physiological and psychological effects on humans, and that these effects can have instructional consequences. For example, some studies have shown that meditation reduces anxiety, thereby facilitating complex problem solving by groups under stress. Individuals often report that the relaxation and fresh perspective lent by meditation heighten their study abilities.

▲ **Figure 14.19**
The benefits of meditation have become accepted widely and are being explored for educational potentials.

The meditative state and other "altered states of consciousness" are already being integrated into new teaching/learning approaches being developed in North America and elsewhere. One of the most advanced—known as "suggestive-accelerative learning and teaching"—is described in detail in Volume 36 of the Instructional Design Library.* This approach has grown out of earlier research done by Georgi Lozanov in Bulgaria. Lozanov found that by inducing a state of conscious relaxation prior to a lesson, and by using special techniques involving music and drama during a lesson, adults could learn foreign languages with unusual ease and high rates of retention. Similarly impressive results have been reported by experimenters in Eastern and Western Europe, Canada, and the United States. In the References at the end of the chapter there are further readings that provide additional information on what may become new technologies of instruction of the future.

▲ **Figure 14.20**
The "Boston arm" responds to signals from the wearer's own nervous system.

Biological Technology: Bionic Extensions of the Brain

The possibility of constructing various sorts of electronic extensions of our brains and central nervous systems has advanced greatly in the past several years. One of the indications of a breakthrough in this area was the appearance in 1969 of the "Boston arm," an artificial limb that could be manipulated by signals from an individual's own nervous system. Nowadays a number of *emgors* (electro*myogram* sens*ors*) are available. These prosthetic devices use the brain's own natural impulse, the myoelectric signal or electromyogram, to control electromechanical devices in the artificial limb.

These bionic developments moved closer to educational interests with the development of cerebellar stimulators or "brain pacemakers." These implanted devices are being used to regulate brain waves in patients whose afflictions are caused by irregular functioning of the brain's electro-

---

*Owen L. Caskey. *Suggestive-Accelerative Learning and Teaching.* Englewood Cliffs, N.J.: Educational Technology Publications, 1980.

chemistry. Some success has been found in cases of severe depression, certain psychoses and neuroses, and cerebral palsy.

The convergence of developments such as these and the "biochips" mentioned earlier in the chapter raises the possibility of interfacing the brain with external electronic devices either indirectly, by detecting brain waves with external sensors, or directly, by employing implanted electrodes. The implications of these possibilities for instruction were explored in a 1983 paper by Glenn F. Cartwright.* He envisions as aspects of the "symbionic mind":

- Memory enhancement by means of "add-on brains" to expand storage capacity.
- Controlling electronic appliances merely by thinking about them, employing "thought switches;" such appliances could help in monitoring or detecting blood alcohol levels, blood sugar levels, stress factors, and impending heart attacks.
- Plugging into the telephone network without phones; carrying on long distance conversations in a seemingly telepathic fashion. It has been reported that the U.S. Air Force has trained subjects to control their alpha waves in order to send Morse code messages that could be picked up by a scalp-monitoring machine and fed into a computer.
- Artificial senses, replacing or simply bypassing damaged receptor organs such as the eye or ear.*

Cartwright sees these developments as contributing to the decentralization of education and as changing the role of conventional teachers and trainers.

---

*Glenn F. Cartwright. "Symbionic Technology and Education." Paper presented at the Annual Meeting of the American Educational Research Association, Montreal, April 1983.

ORGANIZATIONAL IMPEDIMENTS

Any casual observer of the daily go-ings-on in schools, higher education institutions, corporate training sites, and other organized instructional settings will notice that the tools and techniques discussed throughout this book are not actually employed to any extent remotely resembling the extent to which they are talked about and advocated by bystanders. Of course, there is considerable variance. Some corporations make extensive use of advanced media and technology systems, but fewer schools and colleges do. Why is the adoption rate of technology so low, especially among public formal education systems?

The 1983 report of the National Commission on Excellence in Education pointed out a number of shortcomings in the American public education system, among them: inadequate academic content, low standards and expectations, insufficient time spent on learning, poor quality of teaching, and lack of leadership. Similar observations could be made regarding the situation in higher education as well. Many feel that such shortcomings are symp-

toms of a more fundamental problem—the very structure of public educational institutions. The case is stated succinctly by Charles Reigeluth:

*Just as the one-room schoolhouse, which was so appropriate for an agricultural society, proved to be inadequate for an industrial society, so our present system is proving to be inadequate for an information society. It is the fundamental structure of our educational system that is at the heart of our current problems. For example, it is our group-based, lock-stepped, graded, and time-oriented system that has the dubious distinction of effectively destroying the inherent desire to learn in all but a small percent of our children. Also, microcomputers are accelerating the trend toward increased use of nonhuman resources in the education of our children, but the current structure of our educational system cannot adequately accomodate the effective use of these powerful tools. ***

---

*Charles M. Reigeluth. "Restructuring: The Key to a Better Educational System for an Information Society." IDD&E Working Paper No. 16. Syracuse, N.Y.: School of Education, Syracuse University, September 1983, p. 1.

▼ **Figure 14.21**
The lecture and textbook, not the newer media and technology, still dominate formal education.

The sorts of structural problems that Reigeluth is referring to exist at two levels: first, the structure of the classroom as a learning environment, and second, the organizational structure of the school, college, or corporation attempting to deliver instruction. We will look at these two levels separately.

Structure of the Classroom

The typical setup of the classroom—almost everywhere in the Western world and at virtually every level—has the fundamental weakness of being organized around a single adult who attempts to orchestrate more or less diverse activities for a generally large group of learners. This one person typically is expected to be responsible for selecting and organizing the content of lessons; designing materials; producing materials; diagnosing individual needs; developing tests; delivering instruction orally to the group and/or through other media individually or in different groupings; administering, scoring, and interpreting tests; prescribing remedial activities; and coordinating the number-

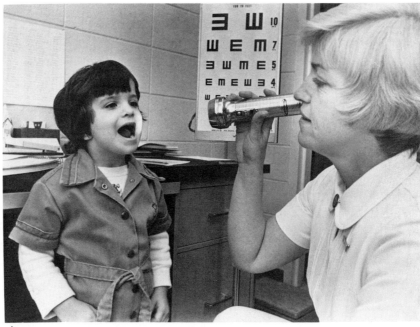

▲ **Figure 14.23**
Division of labor has helped extend health care without a proportionate increase in the number of physicians.

less logistical details that hold the whole enterprise together. Other sectors of society have long since recognized that improvements in effectiveness and productivity require division of labor, but this concept has not yet

been accepted in the preindustrial world of formal education.

An example of a profession in which division of labor has been accepted is that of medicine. Physicians have tended toward the practice of specializations, enabling each to keep better abreast of innovations in practice. Second, physicians have adopted differentiated staffing within their offices and clinics so that less critical functions can be delegated to paraprofessionals and technicians, reserving to the physicians the function of diagnosing and treating conditions that merit their attention. Physicians have incentive to accept this restructuring in those societies in which there exists a free market place for their services. In this environment, embracing division of labor increases their profits. Educators work in a very different environment—but there will be more about those factors a bit later.

Alternative classroom structures do exist and, in fact, have been adopted in many places. In Chapter 11 you encountered programmed tutoring, PSI, and Audio-Tutorial systems, each of which provides a total

▼ **Figure 14.22**
How can one person provide individualized instruction *and* take care of the thousand-and-one details of classroom management?

▲ **Figure 14.24**
The low-cost learning technology project in Indonesia, Project PAMONG, makes extensive use of students as peer group teachers.

and radically different pattern for setting up a learning environment.

More recently, a plan that incorporates virtually all of the technologies of instruction but centers on the notion of division of labor has been field tested in a number of countries, among them Indonesia, Liberia, and the Philippines. The classroom teacher, who may not be a fully certified teacher-training institution graduate, uses materials that are centrally designed and rather fully "scripted" to lead participatory lessons. Parents, volunteers, and student tutors share other teaching and logistical tasks. Thus there is a division of labor both for the design and for the implementation of instruction. The plan takes a somewhat different shape in each locale and is known by a different name in each country, but the generic name and concept is "low-cost learning technology."* It is essentially a systematic method for implementing a variety of managerial and

instructional innovations; it focuses on improving student learning outcomes while reducing overall costs, especially labor costs (hence the name "low-cost"). This concept has shown sufficient promise that the U.S. Agency for International Development (AID) has made a major commitment to implementing it in some thirty additional countries.

Structure of the Organization*

The underlying reason why teachers and trainers teach the way they do, embracing the methods they do—however inefficient or ineffective they may be—is that they are following the "rules of the game" that their daily environment reinforces. A useful way of analyzing this situation is to compare teaching as a *craft* with instruction as a *technology.** In a craft activity the emphasis is on the use of tools by the skilled craftsman. In a

*Robert Heinich. "Instructional Technology and the Structure of Education." *Educational Communication and Technology Journal* (Spring 1985).

technology the emphasis is on the design of tools that produce replicable, reliable results. In a craft, ad-hoc decision making is valued, while in a technology value is placed on incorporating those decisions into the design of the tools themselves (e.g., the "scripted" lesson plan used in low-cost learning technology).

The organizational structures that evolve due to craft thinking are fundamentally different from those that evolve from engineering or technological thinking. Because a craft makes a virtue of the use of tools, the power and the discretion of a craftsman in any given situation are very high, while the power and the discretion of management in the same situation are relatively low. However, in an engineering operation, the power and discretion of the individual operator are low while the power and discretion of the team designing the required tools are extremely high. It is inadvisable to attempt to place the products developed by an engineering team into the organizational structure of a craft. The craftsmen will have a natural tendency to modify arbitrarily the engineered products.

This is precisely what happens in traditional education and training. The organizational structures are built around a craft model, a model that gives considerable discretion to

▼ **Figure 14.25**
The "craft" tradition of teaching leads teachers to prefer materials that *they* control according to their spontaneous decisions.

▲ **Figure 14.26**
The approach of technology is to develop prestructured modules that can be used independent of a live teacher.

FORCES TENDING TOWARD CHANGE

The preceding argument leads to the conclusion that major restructuring of education both at the classroom level and at the highest organizational level will be required in order for media and technology to deliver the benefits on a massive basis that they already deliver on a piecemeal basis and in selected cases. This is a long-term process and one not sure of success. However, there are forces working in the direction of change.

Accountability in Education and Instruction

For almost two decades there has been a trend in education toward what has come to be referred to as *accountability*. Basically, account-ability is a demand for some form of public demonstration that schools do what they are supposed to do and do it effectively. But beyond that, each teacher is accountable for the progress or lack of progress in his or her class.

each instructor in the classroom. When engineered products (e.g., fully "scripted" lesson plans) are placed in this environment, the individual instructor constantly second-guesses decisions that have already been built into the instructional system. The instructor tends to reduce such systematic products to separate bits of material to be used at his or her own discretion.

The craft tradition of education leads to a structure that stops short of developing specific instructional products centrally because it assumes that such specific decisions are made by the person in face-to-face contact with learners. It is expected that any products that are developed may be used or ignored by the instructor in the classroom. In this structure, technological products represent an *added cost*, serving only to aid the teacher when he or she deems it appropriate. Solutions that increase overall costs besides demanding special effort to produce and implement are not likely to flourish.

If this analysis is correct, if the "rules of the game" do determine how educators act, reforms must be made in the rules of the game. History shows that changes in performance do follow changes in the rules. Consider the following rule changes in public education: *Brown* vs. *Topeka Board of Education* (racial desegregation of schools), the inclusion of questions on "new math" in the national college entrance exams (adoption of "new math" into the curriculum), and state-legislated consolidation of schools (reforms in school organization and curriculum).

Much of the impetus toward accountability has come from increasing competition for the tax dollar of the American public—a general social and political phenomenon certain to continue in the foreseeable future. Taxpayers hard pressed for money to support schools want to be assured that their taxes are being well spent. They are concerned both with the cost-benefit of instruction (whether or not we are getting the right kinds of benefit from instruction for the money that is being spent on it) and with the cost-effectiveness of instruction (whether or not these benefits are being achieved as effectively as possible at the lowest possible cost).

Not only a large segment of the public but also many educators support the idea that the schools should be held accountable for the learning progress of students. These educators claim that some teachers are too

▲ **Figure 14.27**
Technology tends to make instruction visible. As parents and other community members get involved in the schools as reading tutors, volunteer aides, and the like, structured materials make their help more effective. By the same token, teachers' use of well-designed materials heightens their credibility in the eyes of the general public.

working with low-ability students who will naturally have far greater difficulty achieving specific predetermined objectives than will high-ability students.

These and other objections to accountability have a certain validity, and we hope the concept will develop in such a manner that legitimate qualms will be allayed. In any case, it seems reasonable to assume that the educational establishment, and individual teachers within the establishment will become more and more publicly accountable for the outcome of the educational enterprise.

Perhaps the most widely known and highly publicized manifestation of the trend toward accountability has been the National Assessment of Educational Progress (NAEP) program. Under this program, general achievement tests are given periodically at various grade levels throughout the country. The tests are intended for long-range comparisons between groups of students at various periods of time. They compare how well students do on standard measures of learning in different parts of the country and in various kinds of schools. So far the results have been used simply to determine whether the schools in general are achieving what they are supposed to achieve. No attempt has yet been made to use NAEP to compare specific schools for instructional effectiveness, but many educators are naturally apprehensive that the program may in the future come to be used for this purpose. Despite opposition from the organized teaching profession, some form of national assessment is likely to continue on the educational scene.

A number of states have developed similar assessment mechanisms. In 1977, for example, the state of California inaugurated its own educational assessment program. In March 1977, all students at designated grade levels took the same

easily diverted from concentration on the learning tasks at hand to unnecessary and unrelated class activities. Some educators further claim that society has asked the schools to do so many jobs that the main purpose, instruction, is lost, or at least lessened, in the process.

This demand by the public and by concerned educators for some sort of accountability seems reasonable. Accountability has, however, met with considerable resistance from many members of the education profession. They argue that the really

vital outcomes of the educational process cannot be quantified or measured, that the only learning outcomes that can be measured are trivial ones—dates, names of historical personages, rules of grammar, multiplication tables, etc. They further argue that accountability requires rigid determination of goals in advance of instruction, thus ruling out serendipitous opportunities that arise during instruction to teach material not specifically covered by predetermined goals. Opponents also claim that accountability will lead to public onus being put upon dedicated teachers

achievement tests in reading, arithmetic, social science, and science. The reports were processed and distributed in April 1977, not only to the schools and school districts but also to the parents of each child taking the test. Parents received a computer printout that indicated where their children stood in relation to other members of their grade levels throughout the state of California. While, again, this assessment movement was resisted by professional educators in California, parents of California school children responded favorably to the program. A number of other states that do not yet have assessment programs are currently considering establishing them.

Other states have developed minimum competency tests to determine promotion from one cluster of grades to another and/or graduation from high school. Although some of these efforts have been challenged in the courts (most notably in Florida), the assessment and minimum competency movements will probably continue to gain strength.

During the National Forum on Excellence in Education, held in 1983, many states revealed plans requiring accountability of teachers and schools. Many planned to use merit pay as an incentive to teachers to change their behaviors.

The trend toward accountability and public disclosure of educational achievement will result in closer ties between the general public and the educational enterprise. Educators will be called upon to explain their selection of instructional methods and materials in terms of attainment of instructional objectives. They will also be called upon to defend their selections in terms of cost-benefit and cost-effectiveness. Education and evaluation of education will become public processes rather than purely private ones between teachers and students. It behooves all instructors, then, to be prepared to defend their

choices of materials and methods. If they are not prepared to do so, they run the increasing risk that those materials and methods will be publicly judged as dispensable frills.

Fortunately for those particularly concerned with the use of media in the schools, instructional technology allows instructors to construct flexible yet structured designs for achievement of specific educational objectives that can be laid out for public inspection. As pointed out throughout this text, such designs, when properly planned and adhered to, can be demonstrated to result in consistent and readily apparent learning experiences—readily apparent to the teacher, the student, and the public. Accountability need not necessarily make us apprehensive. We can, rather, look upon it as an opportunity to further the trend toward partnership between home and school in the educational enterprise, a trend that innovative technology itself has done so much to foster.

Lifelong Learning Systems

Lifelong learning has long been an ideal of professional educators. Advances in the products and processes of instructional technology have brought us to the verge of making that ideal attainable for millions of our citizens. Indeed, we might say that in this respect, at least, our society has "lucked out." Never before in our development as a people have we had a greater need for life-long learning.

Fifty years ago, it was possible for a doctor, a teacher, a scientist, or, for that matter, an electrician or a typewriter repairperson to be trained in a field and remain reasonably competent in it with little or no updating for the rest of his or her life. However, scientific and technological knowledge is increasing at such a rapid pace that this is no longer possible. Indeed, for millions of us, lifelong education is something more than an ideal—it has become a necessity.

In our mobile society today, many people switch from the field in which they were trained to another, or to several others, during their working lives. Early retirement systems in some professions and businesses have contributed to this trend, and many people in our present-day economic system become what economists call "structurally unemployed" and must seek new jobs and careers outside the fields of their expertise and/or training. For all these people, access to an educational system geared to lifelong education is virtually a necessity.

Then there are the rest of our people—millions of ordinary members of our society who wish to keep up with a rapidly changing world, many of whom are beyond the age of formal schooling. These people, too, will more and more be demanding access to lifelong learning; and, indeed, there will be more and more such people as the average age of the population continues to climb.

Obviously, the products and processes of instructional technology are destined to play a major role in the development of lifelong learning systems. Audio and video cassettes and discs, electronic learning devices, electronic systems for delivery of instruction to wherever the lifelong learner may be (the formal learning institution, the factory, the business office, the community center, the home), and numerous other kinds of instructional technology will necessarily be in the forefront in society's efforts to establish such systems. Without the products and processes of instructional technology, lifelong learning would likely be destined to remain an ideal. With them, we at least have reason to hope that it will soon become a reality for the millions of people who need and desire it.

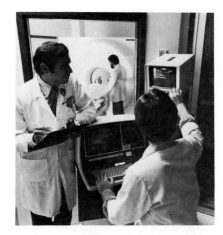

▲ **Figure 14.28**
Jobs at all societal levels, from neurosurgery to police work to auto mechanics, are being affected by technological advances. People will have to change as jobs change; life-long learning becomes a practical necessity, not just a utopian ideal.

PROFESSIONAL CAREERS IN EDUCATIONAL TECHNOLOGY

This book has been dedicated to helping you become a more effective instructor (manager of instruction, if you will) through application of instructional media and technology to your teaching tasks. You may, however, wish to specialize in this fascinating and fast-growing field. (A directory of graduate programs in instructional technology is available from the Association for Educational Communications and Technology.) If so, what opportunities for professional employment are likely to be open to you? Unlike some education areas, instructional technology is becoming more and more pervasive in formal and nonformal education with each passing year, and, correspondingly, an ever larger number of people is being employed in this specialty.

Traditionally, the areas in which the growth of instructional technology has created career opportunities are the various media programs at school, district, regional, and state levels. At all of those levels, media professionals are employed to run programs and, depending on the size of the organization, produce materials for use in schools. As school districts and regional media centers have built up their collections of audiovisual materials for distribution, they have employed instructional media professionals as selectors of these materials. In formal education, media selection specialists determine not only what materials will be added to collections but also how well collections of materials are serving the curricular and instructional needs of the institution. In training programs, media specialists frequently evaluate the effectiveness of the programs as well as determine the materials to be used in them. Another major career area at all education levels is the professional management—classification, storage, distribution—of media collections.

Instructional product design—the development of validated and reliable instructional materials—has been an important specialty in the field of instructional technology for some time. Publishers and producers of instructional materials, along with school districts, community colleges, and colleges and universities, are constantly on the alert for specialists trained in the skills of product design. Computer-assisted instruction, interactive video, and other emerging forms of individualized instruction constitute an important growth area within the instructional product design field.

And we must not overlook fields other than education that require specialists in educational technology. The health sciences, for example, are heavily involved with instructional technology and have been employing an increasing number of professionals to help develop the instruction used in those programs. Industrial training also presents a growing area of employment. In this area, skills in developing instructional materials are very advantageous. As service industries have increased in importance in our economy, training programs for service personnel have correspondingly increased. Aside from employment opportunities within such industries, organizations that design programs for training service personnel employ, both on a permanent and a freelance basis, people skilled in designing instructional media.

Training programs in fields other than formal education require teachers. Most teacher trainees in schools

of education tend to focus on formal educational institutions, public, private, or parochial, as their locus of future employment. However, training programs in business and industry and in government and private institutions have been employing an ever-growing number of professionally trained teachers in recent years. Many if not most of these programs rely heavily on instructional media. Consequently, specialists in instructional technology are in considerable demand as teachers in these programs, as are nonspecialists who have secured for themselves some academic background in the basic principles and techniques of instructional technology.

PROFESSIONAL ORGANIZATIONS IN EDUCATIONAL TECHNOLOGY

Whether your interest in instructional technology is general or whether you intend to specialize in this area of education, you should be familiar with some of the major organizations dedicated to its advancement.

The Association for Educational Communications and Technology (AECT)

AECT is an umbrella organization intended to encompass all the substantive areas of instructional technology. These various areas are expressed as divisions within the organizational structure of the Association. For example, the Division of Educational Media Management is concerned with the administration of media programs and media collections. The Industrial Training and Education Division is concerned with the application of instructional technology to training programs. The Division of Instructional Development is concerned with analysis of instructional problems, and the design of effective solutions. The Division of Telecommunications is concerned with instruction delivered via radio, television, and other telecommunications media. Other divisions of AECT reflect other professional concerns

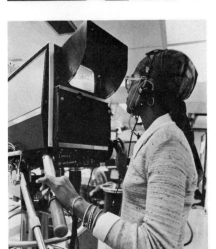

◀ **Figure 14.29**
The field of educational technology offers many and varied career opportunities in activities such as managing media centers; designing and producing film, television, and computerized programs; selecting and evaluating audiovisual materials; and implementing innovative programs with groups of learners. These activities may be based in schools, colleges, medical centers, government agencies, businesses, industries, or wherever there are people who need to learn.

▲ **Figure 14.30**
Professional conventions, such as those sponsored by AECT, help practitioners keep in touch with new developments.

within instructional technology. AECT publishes a monthly journal, *Instructional Innovator*, and a research quarterly, *Educational Communication and Technology Journal*. Its annual convention features a major exhibition of audiovisual hardware and software in addition to a broad-ranging program of educational seminars and workshops.

American Library Association (ALA)

The ALA is an organization of professionals concerned with the organization, classification, storage and retrieval, and distribution of print and nonprint materials. The ALA has divisions for particular interests. The American Association of School Librarians, for example, is concerned with management of materials collections at the school level.

American Society for Training and Development (ASTD)

ASTD is an association composed primarily of professionals engaged in training programs in business and industry.

ASTD is by far the predominant association for people working in training and management development programs in business, industry, government, and similar institutions. Between 1970 and 1980 its membership grew fourfold to more than 20,000 individuals. During this period the original name, American Society of Training Directors, was changed to reflect the broadened base of interests of its members. The society publishes a monthly journal, *Training and Development Journal*; sponsors studies of problems in the training field; and conducts an annual convention that includes a varied and significant educational program. ASTD is organized into divisions; the Media Division is of primary interest to professionals working in instructional media production.

National Society for Performance and Instruction (NSPI)

This organization originally was called the National Society for Programmed Instruction, but its name was changed to reflect broadened interests. NSPI members are interested in the study and application of performance and instructional technologies. NSPI membership includes a mixture of people in business, in-

dustry, the military, allied health professions, government, and formal education. The society publishes a monthly journal, *Performance and Instruction Journal*.

The International Visual Literacy Association (IVLA).

The IVLA is an organization dedicated to exploring the concept of visual literacy—how we use visuals for communication and how we interpret these visuals. As such, it is particularly concerned with the development of instructional materials designed to foster skills in interpreting visuals.

State Organizations

Several of the national organizations cited above have state affiliates (e.g., AECT, ALA), or local chapters (e.g., NSPI). By joining one or more of these, you will be brought quickly into contact with nearby professionals who share your particular concerns.

PROFESSIONAL JOURNALS IN EDUCATIONAL TECHNOLOGY

All of the above organizations publish journals of interest to their members. There are a number of other periodicals of special interest to teachers interested in using instructional media. *Media & Methods*, for example, highlights new software and hardware. *Booklist* will keep you current on the availability of new instructional materials. *Learning* gives practical ideas for improving instruction. *Educational Technology* addresses both teachers and media specialists with articles on a broad range of topics from the theoretical to the practical. For the business/industry setting, *Training* covers new developments in training techniques in a lively, popular style.

By this time we hope that you have made the acquaintance of all these journals—and many more. But if you haven't, take the opportunity to browse through them in the periodical room of your university or public library. It will be time well spent.

As you work with instructional media and technology and as you gain experience in whatever instructional position you find yourself, you may want to explore the possibility of deepening your professional interest in one of the specialities in instructional technology. Through regular reading of one or more of the journals in the field, you will be kept informed about developments in instructional technology. You will find it a fascinating area within education and one with exciting career possibilities.

References

Print References

Carnegie Commission on Higher Education. *The Fourth Revolution: Instructional Technology in Higher Education.* (New York: McGraw-Hill, 1972).

Caskey, Owen L. *Suggestive-Accelerative Learning and Teaching.* Volume 36, Instructional Design Library. (Englewood Cliffs, N.J.: Educational Technology Publications, 1980).

Communications Tomorrow: The Coming Information Society. (Bethesda, Md.: World Future Society, 1982).

Daniel, John S. "Independence and Interaction in Distance Education: New Technologies for Home Instruction." *Programmed Learning and Educational Technology* (August 1983), pp. 155–160.

Dayton, Deane K. "Future Trends in the Production of Instructional Materials: 1981–2001." *Educational Communication and Technology Journal* (Winter 1981), pp. 231–249.

Dede, Christopher J. "Educational Technology: The Next Ten Years." *Instructional Innovator* (March 1980), pp. 17-23.

Ely, Donald P. *Information Technology in Education: The Best of ERIC.* (Syracuse, N.Y.: ERIC Clearinghouse on Information Resources, 1982).

Gordon, Jack; Lee, Chris; and Zemke, Ron. "Remembrance of Things Passé." *Training* (January 1984), pp. 22–39.

Harrison, Shelley A., and Stolurow, Lawrence M., eds. *Improving Instructional Productivity in Higher Education.* (Englewood Cliffs, N.J.: Educational Technology Publications, 1975).

Hawkins-Sager, Susan. "The 'School without Schools': What It Really Taught Us." In *National Conference on Professional Development and Educational Technology Proceedings.* (Washington, D.C.: Association for Educational Communications and Technology, 1980).

Hawthorne, Elizabeth M.; Libby, Patricia A.; and Nash, Nancy S. "The Emergence of Corporate Colleges." *Journal of Continuing Higher Education* (Fall 1983).

Heinich, Robert. "Instructional Technology and Decision Making." *Educational Considerations* (Spring 1983), pp. 25–26.

———. "The Proper Study of Educational Technology." *Educational Communication and Technology Journal* (Summer 1984), pp. 67–87.

Heyman, Mark. *Places and Spaces: Environmental Psychology in Education.* (Bloomington, Ind.: Phi Delta Kappa, 1978).

Holmberg, Borje. *Status and Trends of Distance Education.* (London: Kogan Page, 1981).

Information Technology and Its Impact on American Education. (Congress of the United States, Office of Technology Assessment, Washington, DC, 1982).

Jenkins, Janet. "New Technologies and Distance Learning." *Media in Education and Development* (September 1983), pp. 106–108.

Lazar, Ellen A., ed. *The Teleconferencing Handbook: A Guide to Cost Effective Communication.* (White Plains, NY: Knowledge Industries, 1983).

Lozanov, Georgi. *Suggestology and the Outlines of Suggestopedy.* (New York: Gordon and Breach Science Publishers, 1978).

◀ **Figure 14.31**
A sampling of journals in educational technology.

Macken, E. et al. *Home-Based Education: Needs and Technological Opportunities*. (Washington, D.C.: U.S. Government Printing Office, 1976).

Monson, Mavis; Parker, Lorne; and Riccomini, Betsy, eds. *A Design for Interactive Audio*. (Madison, Wis.: University of Wisconsin—Extension, 1977).

Naisbitt, John. *Megatrends: Ten New Directions Transforming Our Lives*. (New York: Warner Books, 1982).

Neuman, Susan B. "Teletext/Videotex: The Future of the Print Media." *Journal of Reading* (January 1984), pp. 340–344.

Nichols, Daryl G. "Low-Cost Learning Systems: The General Concept and Specific Examples." *NSPI Journal* (September 1982), pp. 4–8.

Oettinger, Anthony G., and Zapol, Nikki. "Will Information Technology Help Learning?" *Teachers College Record* (September 1972), pp. 116–126.

Olgren, Christine H. and Parker, Lorne A. *Teleconference Technology and Applications*. (Dedham, Mass.: Artech House, 1983).

Ostrander, Sheila, and Schroeder, Lynn. *Superlearning*. (New York: Dell, 1979).

Polcyn, Kenneth A. *An Educator's Guide to Communication Satellite Technology*. (Washington, D.C.: Academy for Educational Development, 1973).

Project IMPACT: Low-Cost Alternative for Universal Primary Education in the Philippines. Project Impact Evaluation No. 38. (Washington, D.C.: U. S. Agency for International Development, 1982).

"Satellites Will Be Flying High in the 1980s." *Educational & Industrial Television* (January 1980), pp. 31–33.

Toffler, Alvin. *The Third Wave*. (New York: Morrow, 1979).

Tunstall, Jeremy, ed. *The Open University Opens*. (Amherst, Mass.: University of Massachusetts Press, 1974).

Van Horn, Royal W. "Environmental Psychology: Hints of a New Technology?" *Phi Delta Kappan*, (June 1980), pp. 696–697.

Williams, Frederick. *The Communications Revolution*. Rev. ed. (Beverly Hills, Calif.: Sage Publications, 1984).

Possible Projects

14-A. For one week collect reports of new developments in electronic media from newspapers, news magazines, and other popular media sources. Write a two to three page report describing potential educational impacts of these new developments.

14-B. Play several different types of computer-based games at a video arcade or on a microcomputer. Compare and contrast their possible educational uses.

14-C. Compile your own list of trends in the uses of media and technology in instruction. In your two to three page report be specific about what learning tasks could be facilitated by which developments.

14-D. If you work in a school or other organization offering instruction, analyze the structural/organizational factors that impede your full use of media/technology.

14-E. Prepare a documented profile on the status of your state or province in regard to the enforcement of accountability in public education.

14-F. Compile the copy for a brochure that would explain to newcomers to your community the nonformal educational opportunities (lifelong learning) available locally.

14-G. Interview two or more professionals working in educational technology; compare and contrast their duties in a two to three page written report or five-minute cassette recording.

14-H. Survey the content of several different educational technology journals and write a one to two page report summarizing the types of articles and information covered in each.

Information Sources

Instructors ordinarily begin their search for needed audiovisual materials in the media collection at their own facility. School people would turn next to the catalogs of media collections housed at the school district or regional educational service center. But where can you turn to *beyond* your own organization? This appendix will help you gain access to the wealth of audiovisual resources available for rental or purchase from commercial and noncommercial sources. (Appendix B focuses on sources that give away or loan materials for free or for a nominal cost.)

COMPREHENSIVE INFORMATION SOURCES

Assuming that you had identified an instructional need for which audiovisual materials were not available within your organization or from a free loan source, where might you begin searching for another supplier? The most comprehensive information source is the set of indexes published by the National Information Center for Educational Media (NICEM). NICEM provides indexes for each media format and for several popular subject areas plus a producer/distributor index. All are revised periodically and are updated by a supplement service. Arranged by subject as well as by title, these annotated indexes give a comprehensive view of what is available in the marketplace.

In 1984, NICEM was acquired in a joint venture by the Association for Educational Communications and Technology (AECT) and Access Innovations, Inc. The new address is: NICEM, P.O. Box 40130, Albuquerque, New Mexico 87196.

The NICEM data base can also be accessed through computerized search services, for example, Lockheed's DIALOG. Any library subscribing to such a search service would have a terminal by means of which you could sift through the NICEM references on-line.

NICEM indexes covering still-picture formats are:

Index to Educational Overhead Transparencies
Index to Educational Slides
Index to 35mm Educational Filmstrips

Audio materials are indexed in:

Index to Educational Audio Tapes
Index to Educational Records

Films are covered by two indexes:

Index to 16mm Educational Film
Index to 8mm Motion Cartridges

Video tapes appear in:

Index to Educational Video Tapes

NICEM indexes covering multiple types of media on a given topic are:

Index to Environmental Studies
Index to Health and Safety Education
Index to Vocational and Technical Education
Index to Producers & Distributors
NICEM Index to Non-Print Special Education Materials: Multimedia (Learner Volume)
NICEM Index to Non-Print Special Education Materials: Multimedia (Professional Volume)

The University of Southern California maintains the nation's largest and most comprehensive bibliographic information retrieval system for special education, the National Information Center for Special Education Materials (NICSEM). NICSEM provides information on the content of materials and their applicability to specific handicaps. The NICSEM material is helpful in the construction of individualized programs for handicapped children. Current publications include:

NICSEM Master Index to Special Education Materials

NICSEM Mini-index to Special Education Materials: Functional Communication Skills

NICSEM Mini-index to Special Education Materials: Family Life and Sex Education

NICSEM Mini-index to Special Education Materials: High Interest, Controlled Vocabulary Supplementary Reading Materials for Adolescents and Young Adults

NICSEM Mini-index to Special Education Materials: Independent Living Skills for Moderately and Severely Handicapped Students

NICSEM Mini-index to Special Education Materials: Personal and Social Development for Moderately and Severely Handicapped Students

NICSEM Source Directory

NICSEM Special Education Thesaurus

Special Education Index to Assessment Materials

Special Education Index to Parent Materials

Other reference works covering a broad range of media and content areas are:

Brown, Lucy Gregor. *Core Media Collection for Elementary Schools*. 2d ed. (New York: R. R. Bowker, 1978).

———. *Core Media Collection for Secondary Schools*. 2d ed. (New York: R. R. Bowker, 1979).

Elementary School Library Collection: A Guide to Books and Other Media. Annual. Edited by Lois Winkel. (Williamsport, Pa.: Bro-Dart Foundation).

A Multimedia Approach to Children's Literature: A Selective List of Films (and Videocassettes), Filmstrips, and Recordings Based on Children's Books. 3d ed. Edited by Mary Alice Hunt. (Chicago: American Library Association, 1983).

Selected Audiovisual Materials Produced by the United States Government, 1984. (Washington, D.C.: National Audiovisual Center, 1984.)

SPECIALIZED INFORMATION SOURCES

Many information sources are restricted to a particular media format, content area, or audience.

Filmstrip

Educational Sound Filmstrip Directory. Annual. (St. Charles, Ill.: Dukane Corp., Audiovisual Division).

Audio

Schwann Record and Tape Guide. Updated periodically. (Boston: ABC Schwann Publications). Available from many record and tape stores.

Film

AAAS Science Film Catalog. (Washington, D.C.: American Association for the Advancement of Science, 1975).

American Folklore Films and Videotapes: A Catalog. 2d ed. (New York: R.R. Bowker, 1982).

Collier, Marilyn. *Films for 3 to 5's*. (Berkeley: California University Department of Education, Instructional Laboratories, 1975). Cover title: *Films for Children Ages 3 to 5*.

Feature Films on 8-mm and 16-mm and Videotape. 6th edition. Edited by James Limbacher. (New York: R. R. Bowker, 1979).

Film Resources for Sex Education. (New York: Sex Information and Education Council of the United States, distributed by Human Sciences Press, 1976).

Films for Children: A Selected List. 4th ed. (New York: Children's and Young Adult Section of the New York Library Association, 1977).

More Films Kids Like. Edited by Maureen Gaffney. (Chicago: American Library Association, 1977).

Movies for Kids: A Guide for Parents and Teachers on the Entertainment Film for Children. Edited by Edith Zornow and Ruth M. Goldstein. (New York: Frederick Ungar, 1980).

Parlato, Salvatore J. *Films—Too Good for Words: A Director of Non-Narrated Films*. (New York: R. R. Bowker, 1973). _____. *Films Ex Libris: Literature in 16-mm and Video*. (Jefferson, N.C.: McFarland, 1980).

Positive Images: A Guide to Non-Sexist Films for Young People. (San Francisco: Booklegger Press, 1976).

Selected Films for Young Adults, 1980. Media Selection and Usage Committee, Young Adults Services Division, ALA. (Chicago: American Library Association, 1980).

Video

Chicorel Index to Video Tapes and Cassettes. Annual. Edited by Marietta Chicorel. (New York: Chicorel Library). An annotated index of more than 4000 commercially available video recordings. Emphasis is on entertainment rather than educational items.

Videolog. Three volumes: "Programs for Business and Industry," "Programs for General Interest and Entertainment," "Programs for the Health Sciences" (Edison, N.J.: Esselte Video, Inc.). Program information on over 15,000 videotapes and videocassettes in a broad range of categories.

Video Source Book. Annual. (Syosset, N.Y.: National Video Clearinghouse). Computer-generated catalog of 18,000 video programs, encompassing entertainment, sports, fine arts, business/industry, and education.

T.H.E. Catalog, Televised Higher Education: Catalog of Resources. (Boulder, Colo.: Western Interstate Commission for Higher Education, 1984).

Programmed Instruction

Programmed Learning and Individually Paced Instruction—Bibliography. Complied by Carl H. Hendershot. (Bay City, Mich.: Hendershot Bibliography, 1983). Supplements are issued periodically.

Simulation / Games

The Guide to Simulations/Games for Education and Training. 4th ed. Edited by Robert E. Horn and Anne Cleaves. (Beverly Hills: Sage, 1980). Aims for comprehensive coverage of formal education and the business/industry training sector. All listings carry full descriptions including, in some instances, evaluations and/or testimonials of users.

Handbook of Simulation Gaming in Social Education. 2d ed. Edited by Ron Stadsklev. (s.l. : Institute of Higher Education Research and Service, University of Alabama, 1979). Published in two volumes—the first an introductory textbook on simulation/gaming, particularly as it relates to objectives in the social sciences arena, and the second a directory of individual materials with extensive descriptive annotations. Coverage is limited to "social education," interpreted quite broadly.

Computer Courseware

Apple Education Software Directory. Annual. (Chicago: WIDL Video).

EPIE Annotated Courseware Provider List. Annual. (Water Mill, N.Y.: EPIE Institute).

Index to Computer Based Learning. Edited by Anastasia C. Wang. Annual. (Milwaukee: Educational Communications Division, University of Wisconsin-Milwaukee). Available in microfiche and printed format, this index lists programs available for CAI, CMI, computer-generated tests, and other educational applications. Each entry contains a full program description covering twelve elements. Cross-referenced by source, central processor, program language, and subject-matter content. All levels of education are covered.

International Microcomputer Software Directory. Annual. (Fort Collins, Colo.: Imprint Software).

Microcomputer Index. Annual. (Santa Clara, Calif.: Microcomputer Information Services).

Microcomputer Market Place. Annual. (New York: R. R. Bowker).

Microcomputer Software Catalog List. Annual. (Portland, Ore.: Northwest Regional Laboratory).

Micro Software Solutions. Annual. (Chatsworth, Calif.: Career Aids, Inc.)

Swift Directory. Annual. (Austin, Tex.: Sterling Swift Publishing Co.)

RENTAL SOURCES

The media formats that are generally available for rental for a fee are 16-mm films and videotapes. Several universities maintain large libraries of educational films (some of them are also available as videotapes). Indiana University, the University of Illinois, Syracuse University, and the University of Southern California are among these libraries. Each publishes a catalog of titles available and their rental prices. But there is one "umbrella" publication that pulls together rental information as well as purchase information on each of 40,000 current films:

The Educational Film Locator of the Consortium of University Film Centers and R. R. Bowker Co. 2d ed. (New York: R. R. Bowker, 1980).

COMMERCIAL INFORMATION SOURCES

Commercial producers and distributors of audiovisual materials publish promotional catalogs of their wares. Companies often assemble a special "school and library" catalog, arranged by subject or medium, to display their offerings more effectively. When you use these catalogs keep in mind the bias of the seller. The descriptions given and the claims made do not pretend to be objective. Any purchases should be guided by objective evidence such as field test results, published reviews, and local appraisals based on previews.

A sampling of major audiovisual producers and distributors is given below. The alphabetical lists of companies are grouped roughly according to the media format(s) with which they are identified.

Nonprojected Visuals

Educational Insights, 150 W. Carob Street, Compton, CA 90220.

Encyclopaedia Britannica Educational Corporation, 425 North Michigan Avenue, Chicago, IL 60611.

Silver Burdett Company, 250 James Street, Morristown, NJ 07690.

Society for Visual Education (SVE), Inc., 1345 Diversey Parkway, Chicago, IL 60614.

Overhead Transparencies

Allyn & Bacon, Inc., AV Dept., 7 Wells Avenue, Newton, MA 02159

Denoyer-Geppert Audiovisuals, 5235 Ravenswood Avenue, Chicago, IL 60640.

Encyclopaedia Britannica Educational Corporation, 425 North Michigan Avenue, Chicago, IL 60611.

Hammond, Inc., 515 Valley Street, Maplewood, NJ 07040.

Instructo Products Company/McGraw-Hill, 18 Great Valley Parkway, Malvern, PA 19355.

Lansford Publishing Company, P.O. Box 8711, San Jose, CA 95155.

McGraw-Hill Film Division, 1221 Avenue of the Americas, New York, NY 10020.

Milliken Publishing, 1100 Research Boulevard, St. Louis, MO 63132.

Rand McNally & Co., P.O. Box 7600, Chicago, IL 60657.

3M Audio Visual, Bldg. 225-3NE, 3M Center, St. Paul, MN 55144.

United Transparencies, P.O. Box 688, Binghamton, NY 13902.

Filmstrips

Argus Communications, 7440 Natchez Avenue, Niles, IL 60648.

Audio Visual Narrative Arts, Inc., Box 398, Pleasantville, NY 10570.

BFA Educational Media, 468 Park Avenue South, New York, NY 10016.

Communacad, The Communications Academy, Box 541, Wilton, CT 06897.

Coronet Perspective Centron Films & Video, 65 East South Water Street, Chicago, IL 60601.

Denoyer-Geppert Audiovisuals, 5235 Ravenswood Avenue, Chicago, IL 60640.

EMC Productions, 300 York Avenue, St. Paul, MN 55101.

Educational Images, P.O. Box 367, Lyons Falls, NY 13368.

Encyclopaedia Brittanica Educational Corporation, 425 North Michigan Avenue, Chicago, IL 60611.

Eye Gate Media Inc., 3333 Elston Avenue, Chicago, IL 60611.

International Film Bureau, 332 South Michigan Avenue, Chicago, IL 60614.

January Productions, 124 Rea Avenue, Hawthorne, NJ 07506.

McGraw-Hill Film Division, 1221 Avenue of the Americas, New York, NY 10020.

National Film Board of Canada, 1251 Avenue of the Americas, New York, NY 10020.

Paramount Communications, 1136 N. Las Palmas Avenue, Hollywood, CA 90038.

The Reading Laboratory, Inc., Content Materials Division, 55 Day Street, South Norwalk, CT 06584.

Society for Visual Education (SVE), Inc., 1345 Diversey Parkway, Chicago, IL 60614.

Sunburst Communications, 39 Washington Avenue, Pleasantville, NY 10570.

Time-Life Multimedia, Time-Life Building, 1271 Avenue of the Americas, New York, NY 10020.

Weston Woods Studio, 389 Newton Turnpike, Weston, CT 06883.

Slides

American Museum of Natural History, Central Park West at 79th Street, New York, NY 10024.

Art Now, Inc., 144 North 14th Street, Kenilworth, NJ 07033.

The Center for Humanities, Inc., Communications Park, Box 1000, Mt. Kisco, NY 10549.

Clay-Adams 229 Webro Road, Parsippany, NJ 07054.

Harcourt Brace Jovanovich, 757 Third Avenue, New York, NY 10017.

Harper & Row Media, 2350 Virginia Avenue, Hagerstown, MD 21740.

Hester and Associates, 11422 Harry Hines Boulevard, Suite 212, Dallas, TX 75229.

Instructional Resources Corp., 351 E. 50th Street, New York, NY 10022.

Metropolitan Museum of Art, Educational Marketing, 6 East 82nd Street, New York, NY 10028.

Museum of Modern Art, 11 West 53rd Street, New York, NY 10019.

National Audubon Society, 950 Third Avenue, New York, NY 10022.

National Geographic Educational Services, 17th and M Street, N.W., Washington, DC 20036.

Sandak, Inc., 18 Harvard Avenue, Stamford, CT 06902.

Society for Visual Education (SVE), Inc., 1345 Diversey Parkway, Chicago, IL 60614.

United Scientific Co., 216 South Jefferson Street, Chicago, IL 60606.

Ward's Natural Science Establishment, Inc., P.O. Box 1712, Rochester, NY 14603.

Wilson/Lund, Inc., 1830 Sixth Avenue, Moline, IL 61265.

Audio Materials

Audio Book Company, Box 7111, Pasadena, CA 91109.

Bilingual Educational Services, Inc., 2514 South Grand Avenue, Los Angeles, CA 90007.

Books on Tape, P.O. Box 7900, Newport Beach, CA 92060.

Bowmar Records, 4563 Colorado Boulevard, Los Angeles, CA 90039.

Broadcasting Foundation of America, 52 Vanderbilt Avenue, New York, NY 10017.

Caedmon, 1995 Broadway, New York, NY 10023.

Capitol Records, 1750 North Vine, Hollywood, CA 90028.

Columbia Records, 51 West 52nd Street, New York, NY 10019.

Coronet Instructional Media, 65 East South Water Street, Chicago, IL 60601.

Decca Records, 445 Park Avenue, New York, NY 10022.

Walt Disney Educational Media Company, 500 South Buena Vista Street, Burbank, CA 91521.

Educational Corp. of America/Rand McNally, P.O. Box 7600, Chicago, IL 60680.

Grolier Educational Corp., Sherman Turnpike, Danbury, CT 06816.

Imperial International Learning, Box 548, Kankakee, IL 60901.

Information Management Institute, The Hill, Portsmouth, NH 03801.

Language Master Systems, Bell & Howell, 7100 N. McCormick Road, Chicago, IL 60645.

Listening Library, Inc., 1 Park Avenue, Old Greenwich, CT 06870.

Miller-Brody Productions, 342 Madison Avenue, New York, NY 10017.

Pacifica Foundation, 5316 Venice Boulevard, Los Angeles, CA 90010.

RCA Educational Division, Front and Cooper Streets, Camden, NJ 08102.

Scholastic Records, 730 Broadway, New York, NY 10003.

Science Research Associates (SRA), 155 North Wacker Drive, Chicago, IL 60606.

Society for Visual Education (SVE), Inc., 1345 Diversey Parkway, Chicago, IL 60614.

3M Company, 3M Center, St. Paul, MN 55144.

Variable Speech Control (VSC) Corporation, 185 Berry Street, San Francisco, CA 94107.

Films

BFA Educational Media, 468 Park Avenue South, New York, NY 10016.

Bullfrog Films, Olney, PA 19547.

CFM Films, American Management Associations, 85 Main Street, Watertown, MA 02172.

CRM/McGraw-Hill Films, 110 15th Street, Del Mar, CA 92014.

Churchill Films, 662 North Robertson Boulevard, Los Angeles, CA 90069.

Coronet Perspective Centron Films and Video, 65 East South Water Street, Chicago, IL 60601.

Walt Disney Educational Media, 500 South Buena Vista Street, Burbank, CA 91521.

Encyclopaedia Britannica Educational Corporation, 425 North Michigan Avenue, Chicago, IL 60611.

Films, Inc., 1144 Wilmette Avenue, Wilmette, IL 60091.

Indiana University, Audio-Visual Center, Bloomington, IN 47405.

International Film Bureau, 332 South Michigan Avenue, Chicago, IL 60604.

Learning Corporation of America, 1350 Avenue of the Americas, New York, NY 10019.

Modern Learning Aids, P.O. Box 1712, Rochester, NY 14603.

National Audiovisual Center, General Services Administration, Washington, DC 20409.

National Film Board of Canada, 1251 Avenue of the Americas, New York, NY 10020.

Perspective Films: see Coronet.

Phoenix/BFA Films and Video, Inc., 468 Park Avenue South, New York, NY 10016.

Pyramid Film and Video, P.O. Box 496, Media, PA 19063.

Time-Life Video, Time & Life Building, 1271 Avenue of the Americas, New York, NY 10020.

Wombat Films, Little Lake, Glendale Road, Box 70, Ossining, NY 10562.

Zipporah Films, 54 Lewis Wharf, Boston, MA 02110.

Video

Agency for Instructional Technology (AIT), P.O. Box A, Bloomington, IN 47402.

The Annenberg/CPB Collection, 1213 Wilmette Avenue, Wilmette, IL 60091.

Central Educational Network (CEN), 4300 West Paterson, Chicago, IL 60646.

Coast Telecourses, 11460 Warner Avenue, Fountain Valley, CA 92708.

Dallas Community College District, Center for Telecommunications, 4343 North Highway 67, Mesquite, TX 75150.

Eastern Educational Network (EEN), 120 Boylston Street, Boston, MA 02116.

Great Plains National Instructional Television Library (GPN), Box 80669, Lincoln, NE 68501.

National Video Clearinghouse, Inc. (NVC), 100 Lafayette Drive, Syosset, NY 11791.

Pacific Mountain Network (PMN), Suite 170-13, 248 West 26th Avenue, Denver, CO 80211.

Public Broadcasting Service (PBS) Video, 475 L'Enfant Plaza, S.W., Washington, DC 20024.

Southern Educational Communications Association (SECA), P.O. Box 5966, Columbia, SC 29250.

Time-Life Video, Time-Life Building, 1271 Avenue of the Americas, New York, NY 10020.

TVOntario, P.O. Box 200, Station Q, Toronto, Ontario M4T 2T1, Canada.

University of Mid-America, P.O. Box 82006, Lincoln, NE 68501.

Video-Forum, Division of Jeffrey Norton Publishers, 145 East 49th Street, New York, NY 10017.

Western Instructional Television, Inc. (WIT), 1438 N. Gower Street, Los Angeles, CA 90028.

Simulations and Games

Avalon Hill Co., 4517 Harford Road, Baltimore, MD 21214.

Denoyer-Geppert, Inc., 5235 Ravenswood Avenue, Chicago, IL 60640.

Didactic Systems, Inc., Box 457, Cranford NJ 07016.

Educational Research, P.O. Box 4205, Warren, NJ 07060.

Edu-Game, P.O. Box 1144, Sun Valley, CA 91352.

Houghton-Mifflin Co., 2 Park Street, Boston, MA 02107.

Interact Co., P.O. Box 262, Lakeside, CA 92040.

Management Research Systems, Ltd., Suite 201, Executive Center, P.O. Box 1585, Ponte Vedra Beach, FL 32082.

Marginal Context Ltd., 36 St. Andrew's Road, Cambridge CB4 1DL, England

Harvey Mette, School of Education, Long Island University, Greenvale, NY 11548.

Simile II, P.O. Box 910, Del Mar, CA 92014.

Simulations Publications Inc., 44 East 23rd Street, New York, NY 10010.

Teaching Aids Co., 925 South 300 West, Salt Lake City, UT 84101.

Wff 'N Proof, 1490-TZ South Boulevard, Ann Arbor, MI 48104.

John Wiley & Sons, Inc., 605 Third Avenue, New York, NY 10158.

Computer Courseware

Atari, Inc., 1312 Crossman Avenue, P.O. Box 61657, Sunnyvale, CA 94086.

Avalon Hill Microcomputer Games, 4517 Harford Road, Baltimore, MD 21214.

C-4 Computer Company, 115 N. Neil Street, P.O. Box 1408, Champaign, IL 61820.

Classroom Consortia Media, 28 Bay Street, Staten Island, NY 10301.

COMPress, Division of Van Nostrand Reinhold, P.O. Box 102, Wentworth, NH 03282.

Conduit, 100 Lindquist Center, The University of Iowa, P.O. Box 388, Iowa City, IA 52244.

Harcourt Brace Jovanovich, 1250 Sixth Avenue, San Diego, CA 92101.

Houghton-Mifflin, P.O. Box 683, Hanover, NH 03755.

IBM, Electronic Communications, Inc., Suite 220, 1311 Executive Center Drive, Tallahassee, FL 32301

Instructional Software Inc., 131 Clarendon Street, Boston, MA 02116.

Intellectual Software, 798 North Avenue, Bridgeport, CT 06606.

Milliken Publishing Co., 1100 Research Blvd., P.O. Box 21579, St. Louis, MO 63132.

Minnesota Educational Computing Consortium (MECC), 2520 Broadway Drive, St. Paul, MN 55113.

Opportunities for Learning, Inc., 8950 Lurline Avenue, Chatsworth, CA 91311.

Plato Educational Courseware, Control Data Corp., P.O. Box O, Minneapolis, MN 55440.

Scholastic, Inc., P.O. Box 7502, 2931 E. McCarty Street, Jefferson City, MO 65102.

Sirius Software, Inc., 10364 Rockingham Drive, Sacramento, CA 95827.

Society for Visual Education, Inc. (SVE), 1345 Diversey Parkway, Chicago, IL 60614.

Softswap, San Mateo County Office of Education, 333 Main Street, Redwood, CA 94063.

Sunburst Communications, 39 Washington Avenue, P.O. Box 40, Pleasantville, NY 10570.

John Wiley & Sons, Inc., 605 Third Avenue, New York, NY 10158.

REVIEW SOURCES

Your search-and-sift process can be aided greatly by drawing on the evaluative judgments made by other professionals. A number of periodicals are devoted to reviewing audiovisual materials; others publish reviews in addition to their other editorial content. These periodicals are listed below.

Audiovisual Media

Booklist. American Library Association, 50 East Huron Street, Chicago, IL 60611.

Choice. Association of College and Research Libraries, 100 Riverview Center, Middletown, CT 06457. Reviews college-level instructional materials.

EFLA Evaluations. Educational Film Library Association, Inc., 43 West 61st Street, New York, NY 10023.

EPIE reports. EPIE (Educational Products Information Exchange) Institute, P.O. Box 839, Water Mill, NY 11976, publishes several series of evaluative reports on instructional materials. Those covering conventional audiovisual and print materials are:

- *Textbook PRO/FILES* (biennial, K–12 textbooks)
- *EPIEgram: Materials* (monthly, K–12 textbooks and related materials)
- *EPIE Report: Materials* (biennial, trends in instructional materials)
- *A-V/V PRO/FILES* (biennial, audiovisual and video products)
- *EPIEgram: Equipment* (monthly, audiovisual and video equipment)
- *EPIE Report: Equipment* (biennial, trends in media and microcomputer hardware)

Film Library Quarterly. Film Library Information Council, Box 348, Radio City Station, New York, NY 10101.

Film News. Open Court Publishing Company, Box 619, LaSalle, IL 61301.

Media & Methods. American Society of Educators, 1511 Walnut Street, Philadelphia, PA 19102.

Media Review. Key Productions, 346 Ethan Allen Highway, Ridgefield, CT 06877. Monthly; carries objective reviews of all types of audiovisual materials; available in three editions: K–Col lege complete, K–Grade 8, Grade 9–College.

Rockingchair. Cupola Productions, 966 North Randolph Street, Philadelphia, PA 19123. A review newsletter for librarians and popular music fans who purchase records.

School Library Journal. R. R. Bowker, 205 East 42d Street, New York, NY 10017.

School Library Media Quarterly. American Association of School Librarians, American Library Association, 50 East Huron Street, Chicago, IL 60611.

Science Books and Films. Variant title: *AAAS Science Books and Films*. American Association for the Advancement of Science, 1776 Massachusetts Avenue, N.W., Washington, DC 20036.

Sightlines. Educational Film Library Association, 43 West 61st Street, New York, NY 10023.

Computer Courseware

Courseware Report Card. 150 W. Carob Street, Compton, CA 90220.

EPIE reports. EPIE (Educational Product Information Exchange) Institute, P.O. Box 839, Water Mill, NY 11976, publishes several series of evaluative reports on instructional materials. Those covering computer courseware are:

- *MICROgram* (monthly, educational computing products)
- *Micro PRO/FILES* (bimonthly, indepth analyses of microcomputer hardware and software)
- *The Educational Software Selector—TESS* (definitive information source on availability of all types of microcomputer educational software, including many evaluative comments; published jointly with Teachers College Press, Columbia University)

Journal of Courseware Review. Apple Education Foundation, 20525 Mariani Avenue, Cupertino, CA 95014.

Microcomputers in Education. Queue, Inc., 5 Chapel Hill Drive, Fairfield, CT 06432.

Micro-Scope. JEM Research, Discovery Park, University of Victoria, P.O. Box 1700, Victoria, BC V8W 2Y2, Canada.

MicroSIFT. Northwest Regional Educational Lab, 300 SW Sixth Street, Portland, OR 97204.

Pipeline. Conduit Clearinghouse, P.O. Box 388, Iowa City, IA 52244.

Purser's Magazine. P.O. Box 466, El Dorado, CA 95623.

School Microware Reviews. Dresden Associates, P.O. Box 246, Dresden, ME 04342.

Software Review. Meckler Publishing, 520 Riverside Avenue, Westport, CT 06880.

OTHER REFERENCE TOOLS

For more extensive, annotated guides to media reviews or descriptions of other audiovisual information sources, consult:

Chisholm, Margaret E. *Media Indexes and Review Sources*. (College Park, Md.: School of Library and Information Services, University of Maryland, 1972).

Multi-Media Indexes, Lists and Review Sources. A Bibliographic Guide. Edited by Thomas L. Hart, Mary A. Hunt, and Blanche Woolls. (New York: Marcel Dekker, 1975).

Media Review Digest. Annual. (Ann Arbor, MI: Pierian Press).

Rufsvold, Margaret I. *Guides to Educational Media*. 4th ed. (Chicago: American Library Association, 1977).

Sive, Mary Robinson, *Selecting Instructional Media*. 3d ed. (Littleton, Colo.: Libraries Unlimited, 1983).

Free and Inexpensive Materials

With the ever-increasing costs of instructional materials, teachers and trainers should be aware of the wide variety that can be obtained for classroom use at little or no cost. These free and inexpensive materials can supplement instruction in many subjects, or they can even be the main source of instruction on certain topics. For example, many films are available for loan without a rental fee; the only expense is the return postage. By definition, any material that you can borrow or acquire permanently for instructional purposes without a significant cost (usually less than a couple of dollars) can be referred to as "free and inexpensive."

The types of free and inexpensive materials are almost endless. The more commonly available items include posters, games, pamphlets, brochures, reports, charts, maps, books, filmstrips, audiotapes, films, videotapes, multimedia kits, and realia. The more costly items, such as films and videotapes, are usually sent only on a free-loan basis and must be returned to the supplier after use. In some instances, single copies of audio cassettes and filmstrips will be donated to your organization to be shared among many users.

ADVANTAGES

Free and inexpensive materials can provide up-to-date information that is not contained in textbooks or other commercially available media. In addition, they often provide more in-depth treatment of a topic. If classroom quantities are available, printed materials can be read and discussed by the learners as textbook material would be. If quantities are limited, they can be placed in a learning center for independent or small-group study. Audiovisual materials lend themselves to classroom presentation by the instructor. Individual students who want to explore a subject of interest can use the audiovisual materials for self-study or for presentation to the class. Posters, charts, and maps can be combined to create topical displays. These can be motivational, as in the case of a safety poster, or can be used for direct instruction, as in studying the solar system. Materials that do not have to be returned can be modified and adapted for varied instructional or display purposes.

Materials that are expendable have the extra advantage of allowing learners to get actively involved with them. Students can cut out pictures for notebooks and displays. They can assemble printed information and visuals in scrapbooks as reports of group projects. Of course, when treating free materials as raw materials for student projects, you will have to develop your own objectives and plan appropriate learning activities to go along with the materials.

LIMITATIONS

Several potential limitations of free and inexpensive materials must be taken into consideration. First, many free and inexpensive materials can be described as sponsored materials because their production and distribution are sponsored by particular organizations. These organizations—whether private corporations, non-profit associations, or government agencies—often have a message to convey. That message might be in the form of outright advertising. If so, you will have to be aware of your own organization's policies on the use of advertising matter. You may consider covering or removing the advertisement, but that, too, raises ethical questions in view of the effort and expense that the sponsor has incurred in providing the materials to you. In addition, you are removing the identification of the source of the material and that prevents disclosure of any vested interests by which one might judge the information presented.

What may be even more troublesome to deal with is sponsored material that does not contain outright advertising but does promote some special interest in a less obvious way. For example, a "fun in the sun" poster may subtly promote the eating of junk food without including the name or logo of any manufacturer. As discussed in Chapter 8 in regard to sponsored films, a recent study by the Center for the Study of Responsive Law* disclosed a persistent tendency for privately-sponsored materials to convey self-serving messages. Propagandistic or more subtly biased materials can thus enter the curriculum through the "back door." Careful previewing and caution are advisable when considering sponsored materials. Teachers should solicit informational materials on the same subject from several points of view. Thereby, students are afforded a balance and diversity of opinions.

The Center for Study of Responsive Law (P.O. Box 19367, Washington, D.C. 20036) provides a free annotated bibliography, *Alternative Resources for Curriculum Balance*, upon receipt of a self-addressed, stamped envelope. It lists selected informational and educational resources in subject areas predominant in corporate educational efforts. The intent is to help provide a balance of resources and perspectives on controversial issues.

---

*Sheila Harty, *Hucksters in the Classroom: A Review of Industry Propaganda in the Schools*. Washington, D.C.: Center for Study of Responsive Law, 1980.

LOCAL SOURCES

Many local government agencies, community groups, and private businesses provide informational materials on free loan. Public libraries often make films, prints, and filmstrips available. Even libraries in small communities may have access to films through a statewide network. These materials usually can be loaned to local organizations. However, public library collections are often entertainment-oriented, as would be expected in a service designed for the general public, so you will probably not find in them a great many strictly instructional materials. Other government agencies, such as the Cooperative Extension Service, public health departments, and parks departments, make materials available for use in schools, churches, hospitals, and companies.

Community organizations, such as the Red Cross, League of Women Voters, medical societies, and the like welcome opportunities to spread information about their special interests. Films, slide-tapes, printed material, and guest speakers are frequently offered.

Among business organizations, utilities—telephone, electric, gas and water companies—are most likely to employ education specialists who can inform you about what instructional services they offer. Chambers of commerce often can suggest private corporations that might supply materials of interest to you.

NATIONAL AND INTERNATIONAL SOURCES

Nationally, one of the most prolific sources of free and inexpensive materials is the federal government. In the United States, two federal agencies offer special access to materials, the U.S. Government Printing Office and the National Audiovisual Center. Your key to the tremendous wealth of posters, charts, brochures, books, and other printed government documents that are available to the general public is "Selected U.S. Government Publications," a monthly catalog of all new listings. You can have your name added to the free mailing list by sending a request to: Superintendent of Documents, U.S. Government Printing Office, Washington DC 20402.

The National Audiovisual Center is the central clearinghouse for all federal government-produced audiovisual materials. Its catalog, *Selected Audiovisual Materials Produced by the United States Government*, 1984 is issued every four years, with a supplement every two years. It lists more than 12,000 titles of films, videotapes, slide sets, audiotapes, and multimedia kits that have been produced by or for government agencies. All are available for purchase; the 16-mm films (constituting 80 percent of the collection) can be rented; some of the materials are made available for free loan from regional sources. For further information, write to: National Audiovisual Center, Information Services/RN, General Services Administration, Washington DC 20409.

Trade associations and professional associations also aim to acquaint the general public with their own fields of interest and the causes they promote. Some examples are the American Society of Civil Engineers, the National Diary Council, the American Petroleum Institute, National Wildlife Federation, American Heart Association, and National Association for the Advancement of Colored People.

Private corporations that operate on the national or even international basis offer sponsored materials, as discussed earlier in this appendix. Examples of these businesses include: Goodyear Tire and Rubber Company, Exxon, US Steel, and AT&T.

Most foreign governments disseminate information about their countries to promote trade, tourism, and international understanding. They typically offer free posters, maps, and informational booklets plus films on a free-loan basis. To find out what is available for any particular country, write to the embassy of that country in Washington, DC. International organizations such as the Organization of American States (OAS), United Nations, and the North Atlantic Treaty Organization (NATO) also operate information offices. Popular sources of posters of foreign countries are the airline and cruise ship companies. Consult your local travel agent for possible materials and addresses.

COMPREHENSIVE INFORMATION SOURCES

It would be impractical to list here all the thousands of suppliers of free and inexpensive materials, much less to offer up-to-date addresses. Instead, we recommend that you consult one of the many books and catalogs devoted specifically to free and inexpensive materials. They are updated regularly and contain full name, address, and cost information.

The most comprehensive information source on free and inexpensive materials is the series of guides published by Educators Progress Service, 214 Center Street, Randolph, Wisconsin 53956. There is a cost for the guides themselves; the materials listed in the guides are free and inexpensive. Revised annually, the titles in this series include:

Educators Index of Free Materials
Educators Guide to Free Films
Educators Guide to Free Filmstrips
Educators Guide to Free Teaching Aids
Educators Guide to Free Audio and Video Materials
Educators Guide to Free Social Studies Materials
Educators Guide to Free Science Materials
Educators Guide to Free Guidance Materials
Educators Guide to Free Health, Physical Education and Recreation Materials
Elementary Teachers Guide to Free Curriculum Materials
Guide to Free Computer Materials

Books that list sources of free and inexpensive materials are:

Aubrey, Ruth H. *Selected Free Materials for Classroom Teachers*. (Belmont, CA: Pitman Learning). Updated periodically.

Cardozo, Peter. *The Third Whole Kids Catalog* (New York: Bantam Books, 1981).

Feinman, Jeffrey. *Freebies for Kids* (New York: Wanderer Books, 1979).

Free Stuff Editors. *Free Stuff for Kids* (Deephaven, MN: Meadowbrook Press, 1984).

Moore, Norman R., ed. *Free and Inexpensive Learning Materials* (Nashville: George Peabody College; Incentive Publishers, Inc., distributor). Updated biennially.

Weisinger, Thelma. *1001 Valuable Things You Can Get Free* (New York: Bantam Books). Updated periodically.

National level services for free-loan films are:

Association-Sterling Films, which provides free-loan films from its twelve offices in the United States and Canada.

Modern Talking Picture Service (5000 Park Street North, St. Petersburg, FL 33709), which provides sponsored films for free loan from its twenty-two offices in major cities throughout the United States and Canada.

HOW TO OBTAIN FREE AND INEXPENSIVE MATERIALS

When you have determined what you can use and where you can obtain it, correspond on school or company stationery; some agencies will not supply free and inexpensive materials unless you do. For classroom quantities (when they are available), send just one letter. Do not have each student write individually. If a single student is requesting one copy of something for a class project, the student can write the letter, but you should also sign it. We recommend that you request a preview copy of the material before requesting multiple copies. Don't send a request for "anything you have!" Be specific and at least specify the subject area and the grade level. Only ask for what you need. Don't stockpile materials or take advantage of a "free" offer. Somebody is paying for those materials, so don't waste them. Follow up with a "thank you" note to the supplier and let them know how you used the materials and what the students' reaction was to them. Be courteous, but be honest. Many suppliers attempt to improve free and inexpensive materials on the basis of user comments.

APPRAISING FREE AND INEXPENSIVE MATERIALS

As with any other type of material, appraise the educational value of these materials critically. Some are very "slick" (technically well presented) but are not educationally sound. The "Appraisal Checklist: Free and Inexpensive Materials" is intended to help you make these judgments.

The final potential limitation is a logistical one. With the increasing expense of producing both printed and audiovisual materials, your supplier may have to impose limits on the quantities of items available at one time. You may not be able to obtain a copy of the material for every student in the class.

Appraisal Checklist: Free and Inexpensive Materials

Topic_____   **Type of Material**_____

Source_____   (booklet, filmstrip, tape, film, etc.)

Cost_____ Date_____

Objectives (stated or implied):

Brief Description:

Rating	High		Medium		Low
Free from undesirable advertising and/or bias	☐	☐	☐	☐	☐
Accurate, honest, and up-to-date	☐	☐	☐	☐	☐
Useful in meeting objectives	☐	☐	☐	☐	☐
Appropriate level for the audience	☐	☐	☐	☐	☐
Potential uses (alone or with other media)	☐	☐	☐	☐	☐
Readability	☐	☐	☐	☐	☐
Illustration quality (well done and eye-catching)	☐	☐	☐	☐	☐
Durability (if to be re-used)	☐	☐	☐	☐	☐

Strong points:

Weak points:

Reviewer_____

Position_____

Recommended action_____   Date_____

Copyright Guidelines

BACKGROUND: COPYRIGHT LAW

To protect the financial interests of the creators, producers, and distributors of original works of information and/or art, nations adopt what are referred to as copyright laws. These laws set the conditions under which anyone can copy, in whole or in part, original works transmittable in any medium. Without copyright laws, writers, artists, film makers, and the like, would not "receive the encouragement they need to create and the remuneration they fairly deserve for their creations" (from the legislative 1976 Omnibus Copyright Revision Act). The flow of creative work would be reduced to a trickle, and we would all be the losers.

The first copyright law in the United States was passed by Congress in 1790. In 1976, Congress enacted the latest copyright law, taking into consideration technological developments that had occurred since the passage of the previous Copyright Act of 1909. For example, in 1909, anyone who wanted to make a single copy of a literary work for personal use had to do so by hand. The very process imposed a limitation on the quantity copied. Today, a photocopier can do the work in seconds; the limitation has disappeared. Nor did the 1909 law provide full protection for films and sound recordings, nor anticipate the need to protect ra-dio and television. As a result, violations of the law, and abuses of the intent of the law, have made serious inroads on the financial rewards of authors and artists. We are all aware (and probably guilty) of photocopy abuse, but did you know that more than one out of three 8-track cartridges of pop music sold in the open market are pirated copies of the original production? Or that under-the-counter video tapes of new feature films are available *before* general distribution of the films to theaters takes place? Abuses such as these were not even contemplated in the 1909 law. Clearly, corrections were in order. The 1976 Copyright Act has not prevented these abuses fully but it has clarified the legal rights of the injured parties and given them an avenue for redress.

If you have been reading about the copyright law in the professional literature, you are aware of the confusion about interpretation of the act caused by claims, counterclaims, and, frankly, righteous breast-beating by both copyright holders and consumers. We must remember that the fine points of the law will have to be decided by the courts and by acceptable common practice over an extended period of time. As these decisions and agreements are made, we can modify our behavior accordingly. As of now, then, we need to interpret the law and its guidelines as accurately as we can, and to act in a fair, judicious manner.

INTERPRETING THE COPYRIGHT ACT

Although detailed examination of the law is beyond the scope of this text, here we describe the basic framework of the law and present examples of violations and examples of reasonable interpretation of "fair use" to help guide you in the decisions you need to make about copying protected works for class use. The law sets forth in section 107 four basic criteria for determining the principle of fair use:

1. The purpose and character of the use, including whether such use is of a commercial nature or is for nonprofit educational purposes.
2. The nature of the copyrighted work.
3. The amount and substantiality of the portion used in relation to the copyrighted work as a whole.
4. The effect of the use on the potential market for or value of the copyrighted work.

The following interpretations are based on several sets of guidelines issued to spell out the criteria in section 107.

For educational use, an instructor may make a single copy of a chapter from a book; an article from a periodical or newspaper; a short story, short essay, or short poem whether or not from a collective work; an illustration from a book, periodical, or newspaper. The context in which the term "teacher" is used seems to be broad enough to include support personnel working with teachers.

The guidelines further stipulate the amount of material that may be copied and the special circumstances that permit multiple copies. Fair use is defined as one illustration per book or periodical, 250 words from a poem, and 10 percent of a prose work up to 1000 words. Multiple copies cannot exceed the number of students in a class, nor can there be more than nine instances of multiple copying for one course during one class term. No more than one short poem, article, story, essay, or two excerpts may be copied from the same author. The limitations of nine instances and one item or two excerpts do not apply to current news periodicals, newspapers, and current news sections of other periodicals.

However, multiple copies must meet a "spontaneity" test. The copying must be initiated by the individual teacher, not directed or suggested by any other authority. The decision to use the work, *and* the "inspiration" for its use, must be close enough to the moment of use to preclude waiting for permission from the copyright holder. This means, of course, that the same "inspiration" cannot occur the same time next term.

The last guideline, market value, means that copying must not substitute for purchase of the original, or create or replace an anthology or a compilation of works protected by copyright. It also prohibits copying works intended to be consumable, for example, workbooks or standardized tests.

If a work is "out of print," that is, no longer available from the copyright holder, then you are not affecting the market value of the work by copying it. The market value guideline can act in favor of the user as we will see from the examples given below.

Unfortunately, neither the law nor the guidelines spell out fair use of media other than print. Eventual fair use criteria, therefore, may evolve more out of acceptable common practice than out of the law and guidelines.

As for music, the new copyright law protects the performance of the work as well as the work itself. For example, Beethoven's Fifth Symphony may be in the public domain but the recorded performance by the Chicago Symphony Orchestra is protected.

The term, or period of time, of the copyright has been changed by the new act. For an individual author, the copyright term continues for his or her life and for 50 years after death. If a work is made for hire, that is, by an employee or by someone commissioned to do so, the term is 100 years from the year of creation or 75 years from the year of first publication or distribution, whichever comes first. Works copyrighted prior to January 1, 1978 are protected for 28 years and then may have their copyrights renewed. The renewal will protect them for a term of 75 years after their original copyright date.

Congress amended the copyright act in 1980 to clear up some questions about computer courseware. The important changes are: (1) computer programs are defined as literary works and are to be treated as such under the law; (2) the purchaser of a computer program may copy it for archival purposes as protection against accidental damage; (3) the purchaser may adapt the program if necessary for effective use; and (4) the purchaser (whether individual or agency) may add features to the program for personal or internal use.

As stated before, final interpretation of the provisions of the 1976 Copyright Act will have to wait for future court decisions to define the language and to resolve internal contradictions or conflicts in the law. For example, under the 1976 law, a suit was brought against Sony to prohibit the company from stating in its ads that videotape recorders may be used to record television programs for future viewing. In 1984, the Supreme Court decided that the copyright law does not prohibit an individual from videotaping a television program for personal viewing at a later time.

Until the courts decide otherwise, it would seem reasonable that teachers (and media professionals) can use the fair use criteria to copy materials that would seem otherwise to be protected. Some examples follow:

1. If the school media center subscribes to a journal or magazine to which you refer students and you want to make slides of several graphics or photos to help students understand an article, it would seem that this is fair use based on the following:
   a. The nature of the work is general, its audience (and market) is not predominantly the educational community.
   b. The character of use is nonprofit.
   c. The amount copied is small.
   d. There is no intent to replace the original, only to make it more useful in a class in conjunction with the copyrighted words.
2. If *you* subscribe to a journal and want to include several pictures from it in a presentation in class, it would seem reasonable to do so for the same reasons.

3. Suppose a film you frequently use drops out of the distributor's catalog; it is "out of print." To protect the print you have, it would seem reasonable, after unsuccessful attempts to reach the copyright owner to get permission, to videotape the film and use the videotape in class. If, at a later date, the film is put back on the market by the same or another distributor, you must go back to using the film. This is not uncommon. For example, *Pacific 231*, an effective film to demonstrate editing, was originally distributed by Young America Films. After Young America Films was purchased by another company, *Pacific 231* was dropped from the catalog. It was not available for almost twenty years. Then Pyramid Films secured the distribution rights and it is now available for purchase. During the long period of unavailability, it would have been reasonable to use a videotape copy.

4. From experience you know that recordings of literary works put out by major record labels may disappear from their catalogs in a few years. For example, RCA Victor once made available a recording of Shakespeare's *Midsummer Night's Dream* with Mendelsohn's incidental music inserted at the appropriate place. It is no longer available. If you had taped the records, put the tapes on the shelf as a contingency, and used the records in class, you would at least now have the tape available if your records were damaged. You would not have intended to deprive anyone of income; you would simply have used the technology to guarantee availability to yourself.

5. You have rented a film for a specific date but circumstances beyond your control prevent your using it before it is due back. It would seem reasonable, after requesting permission (a telephone call could clear it), to videotape the film, use the videotape, and then erase the tape after use. Again, you have not deprived anyone of income. (This should **never** be done if the film is in on a preview basis!)

6. You are a consumer education teacher and you have advance notice that a documentary series on TV is going to deal with a young married couple in financial trouble due to excessive use of credit cards. The "spontaneity" section of the guidelines would seem to cover videotaping the program for use in class within the next few days after the broadcast. Much of the "common law" of fair use comes about by general agreement among affected parties. The general agreement among broadcasters and representatives of users is that a videotaped TV program may be used several times in class during ten school days following the telecast and may be retained for an additional forty-five calendar days but then must be erased. Remember that, while an agency such as a media center may do the actual taping, the initiative to do so must come from the teacher. This permission does *not* extend to pay TV services such as HBO.

There are not any guidelines in regard to nonprint material in contrast to printed matter. Until the courts decide otherwise, it would seem reasonable to extend the print guidelines to nonprint material in judicious fashion.

We are not advocating deliberate violation of the law. On the contrary, we support the intent of the copyright law to protect the financial interests of copyright holders. What we are saying is that the proper balance in the application of the guidelines eventually has to be decided by the courts and by accepted common practice. In the meantime, reasonable interpretations of fair use may permit you to do copying that might seem on the face of it to be prohibited.

Primacy of First Sale

Have you ever wondered why public libraries, book rental businesses, and video rental clubs are not in violation of the copyright law when they do not pay royalties to copyright owners on the items they circulate or rent? They come under the protection of what is referred to as the *primacy of first sale*. This means that the purchaser of a copyrighted work may loan or rent the work without having to pay a second royalty. At the present time, great pressure is being brought to bear on Congress to amend the law to require anyone who rents a copyrighted work to pay a royalty to the copyright owner. As you might expect, the television and motion picture industries are putting on the pressure and video rental agencies are resisting the change.

While it is not likely that *free* circulation of material from public libraries and regional media centers will be affected by a change such as this, college and university *rental* of films and videotapes certainly will be. Educators need to keep on the alert for any possible changes in the first sale doctrine that could adversely affect access to materials.

SEEKING PERMISSION FOR USE OF COPYRIGHTED MATERIALS

Aside from staying within the guidelines that limit but recognize our legal right to free use of copyrighted materials, what else can we do to assure our students access to these materials? We can, obviously, seek permission from the copyright owners and, if required, pay a fee for their use. Certain requests will ordinarily be granted without payment of fee—transcripts for the blind, for example, or material to be tried out once in an experimental program. (Use of materials in the public domain—materials on which copyright protection has run out, for instance, or materials produced by federal government employees in the course of their regular work—need no permission.)

In seeking permission to use copyrighted materials, it is generally best to contact the producer or publisher of the material rather than its creator. Whether or not the creator is the holder of the copyright, the producer or publisher generally handles permission requests and sets fees. The address of the producer (if not given on the material) can be obtained from various reference sources, including the *Literary Market Place*, the *Audio-Visual Market Place*, and *Ulrich's International Periodicals Directory*.

Be as specific as possible in your request for permission. Give the page numbers and exact amount of print material you wish to copy. (If possible, send along a photocopy of the material.) Describe nonprint material fully. State how you intend to use the material, where you intend to use it, how you intend to reproduce it, your purpose in using it, and the number of copies you wish to make.

Remember that fees for reproduction of copyrighted materials are sometimes negotiable. If the fee seems to you to be too high or otherwise beyond your budget, do not be hesitant about asking that it be lowered.

If for *any* reason you decide not to use the requested material, make this fact known to the publisher or producer. Without this formal notice it is likely to be assumed that you have in fact used it as requested, and you may be dunned for a fee you do not in fact owe.

Keep copies of all your correspondence and records of all other contacts that you made relevant to seeking permission for use of copyrighted instructional materials.

THE TEACHER AND VIOLATION OF THE COPYRIGHT LAW

What happens if an educator knowingly and deliberately violates the copyright law? The 1976 Act contains both criminal and civil sanctions. The criminal penalty can be a fine up to $1000 and a year in jail. Copyright owners may recover up to $50,000 in civil court for loss of royalties due to infringement. Furthermore, in any infringement lawsuit, the employing institution can be held liable along with the instructor.

The producers of materials for the education market are just as serious about seeing the copyright act enforced as are the companies serving the general public. In 1982, a high school home economics teacher in San Diego was brought into court by a publisher for copying substantially more than 10 percent of a copyrighted book. This really was a test of the legality of the guidelines. Because the guidelines are not part of the law, and the law treats fair use only in general terms, the courts are not required to consider them. The district court agreed with the teacher but was overruled by the appellate court and the teacher was found guilty. Unfortunately, the case was not carried to the Supreme Court by the teacher so we do not have as definitive a ruling as we do in the video case that follows.*

---

*"Appeals Court Cites 'Fair Use' Guidelines in Copyright Ruling" *Chronicle of Higher Education* (9 February 1983), p. 28.

A Board of Cooperative Educational Services was taken to court and found guilty of distributing videotapes of copyrighted material. The media personnel in this case flagrantly violated the law.† Punitive damages aside, in a profession devoted to promoting ethical behavior, deliberate violation of the copyright law is unacceptable.

---

†Enclyclopaedia Britannica Education Corporation v. The Board of Cooperative Educational Services (BOCES)

REFERENCES

We have concentrated here on the problem of copying copyrighted materials for educational purposes and on the guidelines set up under the 1976 Act to help assure that such duplication does not violate the law or otherwise infringe on copyright ownership. The Act itself contains hundreds of these provisions covering all aspects of copyright law and ownership. Some of these other provisions are of particular interest to educators—provisions covering copying by libraries, for example, or use of copyrighted materials for instruction of the visually handicapped and the hearing impaired. Other provisions may be of interest to those who have authored or plan someday to author or produce instructional materials. In any case, it behooves each of us to be familiar at least with those aspects of the law likely to affect our own special activities and interests.

Copyright and Educational Media: A Guide to Fair Use and Permission Procedure. (Washington, D.C.: Association for Educational Communications and Technology, 1977).

Explaining the New Copyright Law. (Washington, D.C.: Association of American Publishers, 1977).

Gary, Charles L. *The New Copyright Law and Education.* (Arlington, Va.: Educational Research Services, 1977).

General Guide to the Copyright Act of 1976, L. C.-3.7/2:C79. Available from the Copyright Office Library of Congress, Washington, D.C. 20559. The following pamphlet materials are also available from the Copyright Office: *Copyright and the Librarian, Reproduction of Copyright Works for the Blind and Physically Handicapped, Highlights of the New Copyright Law.*

Johnston, Donald. *Copyright Handbook.* (New York: R.R. Bowker, 1981).

Librarian's Copyright Kit: What You Must Know Now. (Chicago: American Library Association, 1978).

Lieb, Charles H. *New Copyright Law: Overview.* (Washington, D.C.: Association of American Publishers, 1976).

Sturdevant, Rosemary, "Microcomputers and Copyright in Education." *Phi Delta Kappan* (January 1982), pp. 316–317.

Talab, Rosemary Sturdevant. "Copyright, Fair Use, and the School Microcomputer Lab." *Educational Technology* (February 1984), pp. 30–32.

Troost, F. William. "Students—The Forgotten People in Copyright Considerations." *Educational-Industrial Television* (June 1983), pp. 70–74.

The Visual Artist's Guide to the New Copyright Law. (New York: Graphic Artists Guild, 1978).

Glossary

accountability. The idea that a person or agency should be able to demonstrate publicly the worth of the activities carried out.

acetate. A transparent plastic sheet, associated with overhead projection.

advance organizer. Outlines, "previews," and other such pre-instructional cues used to promote retention of verbal material, as proposed by David Ausubel. Also referred to as pre-instructional strategies.

adventure game. An arcade video game that combines a visualized fantasy story stored on videodisc with microprocessor-controlled interaction with the player.

affective domain. The domain of human learning that involves changes in interests, attitudes, and values, and the development of appreciations and adequate adjustment.

animation. A film technique in which the artist gives motion to still images by creating and juxtaposing a series of pictures with small incremental changes from one to the next.

aperture. The lens opening that determines the amount of light that enters a camera. Also, the opening through which light travels from the lamp to the lens in a projector.

articulation. The highest level of motor skill learning. The learner who has reached this level is performing unconsciously, efficiently, and harmoniously, incorporating coordination of skills. See *motor skill domain.*

aspect ratio. Length/width proportions or format of an audiovisual material, such as 3 × 4 for a filmstrip or motion picture frame.

audio card reader. A device for recording and reproducing sound on a card with a magnetic strip. The card may contain verbal and/or pictorial information. Separate tracks may provide for a protected master and erasable student responses.

audio head. A magnetic element in a tape recorder that records or plays back sound.

Audio-Tutorial system. A technology for managing instruction that employs a study carrel equipped with specially designed audio tapes that direct students to various learning activities. This component is known as an Independent Study Session. Large-group and small-group assemblies are also major components of this system.

automatic level control (ALC). (audio recorders) A circuit used to control the volume or level of the recorded signal automatically to provide uniform level without distortion due to overloading. Sometimes called automatic gain control (AGC) or automatic volume control (AVC).

automatic programmer. See *programmer.*

bar graph. A type of graph in which the height of the bar is the measure of the quantity being represented.

bass. See *frequency.*

Beta. (video) A 1/2-inch video cassette format not compatible with the VHS format, which is also 1/2-inch but differs electronically.

bidirectional. A microphone that picks up sound in front of and behind itself and rejects sound from the sides.

biochip. A (hypothetical) miniature microprocessor constructed of organic matter, such as a protein molecule.

bit. An acronym for *bi*nary digi*t.* The smallest unit of digital information. The bit can be thought of as a 1 or a zero—a circuit on or off.

byte. The number of bits required to store/represent one character of text (a letter or number). Most commonly, but not always, made up of eight bits in various combinations of zeros and ones.

cable television. A television distribution system consisting of a closed-circuit, usually wired, network for transmitting signals from an origination point (see *head-end*) to members of the network. Typically, the origination point receives and retransmits broadcast programs, adding recorded programs and/or some live originations.

capstan. A rotating shaft or spindle that moves the tape at a constant speed during recording or playback in tape recorders. A pressure roller squeezes or pinches the tape tight against the capstan to provide traction.

cardioid microphone. A microphone that picks up sound primarily in the direction it is pointed, rejecting sounds at the rear of microphone; a undirectional microphone.

carrel. A partially enclosed booth that serves as a clearly identifiable enclosure for learning center activities.

cassette. A self-contained reel-to-reel magnetic tape system with the two reels permanently intalled in a rugged plastic case. The tape is permanently fastened to each of the reels.

cathode ray tube (CRT). The video display tube used in video monitors and receivers, radar displays, and computer terminals.

CCTV. See *closed circuit television.*

characterization. The highest level of affective learning. The learner who has reached this level will demonstrate an internally consistent value system, developing a characteristic lifestyle based upon a value or value system. See *affective domain.*

cinéma vérité. A film-making technique in which the camera becomes either an intimate observer of or a direct participant in the events being documented.

circle graph. A graphic form in which a circle or "pie" is divided into segments, each representing a part or percentage of the whole.

closed-circuit television (CCTV). A television distribution system that limits reception of a signal to those receivers or monitors directly connected to the origination point by coaxial cable or microwave link.

close-up. In motion or still photography, a shot in which the camera concentrates on the subject or a part of it, excluding everything else from view.

cognitive domain. The domain of human learning involving intellectual skills, such as assimilation of information or knowledge.

communication model. A mathematical or verbal representation of the key elements in the communication process.

composition. The creative process of manipulating a camera to frame a picture to suit some contemplated purpose.

comprehension. The level of cognitive learning that refers to the intellectual skill of "understanding"; this includes translating, interpreting, paraphrasing, and summarizing. See *cognitive domain.*

computer-assisted instruction. Instruction delivered directly to learners by allowing them to interact with lessons programmed into the computer system.

computer literacy. The ability to understand and to use computers, paralleling reading and writing in verbal literacy. Actual computer literacy exists along a continuum from general awareness to the ability to create computer programs.

computer-managed instruction. The use of a computer system to manage information about learner performance and learning resources options in order to prescribe and control individual lessons.

concrete-abstract continuum. The arrangement of various teaching methods in a hierarchy of greater and greater abstraction, beginning with "the total situation" and culminating with "word" at the top of the hierarchy. In 1946 Edgar Dale used the same construct to develop his "Cone of Experience."

condenser microphone (also referred to as electrostatic or capacitor). A microphone with a conductive diaphragm that varies a high-voltage electric field to generate a signal. May be any pattern (uni-, bi-, or omni-directional). Requires a miniaturized amplifier and power supply.

condenser lens. Lens(es) between the projection lamp and slide or film aperture to concentrate light in the film and lens apertures.

consequence. In psychology, the result of a particular behavior. Learning may be facilitated by arranging positive consequences to follow desired behaviors.

copy stand. A vertical or horizontal stand for accurately positioning a camera when photographing flat subjects very close to the lens.

courseware. Lessons delivered via computer, consisting of content conveyed according to an instructional design controlled by programmed software.

covert response. A learner response that is not outwardly observable.

craft. In a craft approach to problem solving the emphasis is on the use of tools by a skilled craftsman. Such ad hoc decision making contrasts with the approach of technology.

criterion. As part of a performance objective, the standard by which acceptable performance will be judged; may include a time limit, accuracy tolerance, proportion of correct responses required, and/or qualitative standards.

debriefing. Discussion conducted among simulation/game participants after play in order to elucidate what has been learned.

decoder. In electronics, the device in a synchronizer or programmer which reads the encoded signal or pulse and turns it into some form of control. In human communication, the element that translates any signal into a form decipherable by the receiver.

deductive learning. The typical classroom teaching approach that proceeds as follows: presentation of information (the Point), reference to particular examples, application of the knowledge to the students' experiences.

degausser. See *head demagnitizer or eraser.*

depth of field (photography). The region of acceptably sharp focus around the subject position, extending toward the camera and away from it. Varies with the distance of the camera from the subject, the focal length of the lens, and the F/stop.

differentiation. The intellectual skill of separating items into different classes.

digital recording. Advanced method of recording which involves a sequence of pulses or on-off signals rather than a continuously variable or analog signal; advantages are increased frequency range and lower tape noise. May be used for control, audio, and video purposes.

discovery learning. See *inductive learning*.

dissolve. An optical effect in film and video involving a change from one scene to another in which the outgoing and incoming visual images are superimposed or blended together for a discernible period of time as one scene fades out while the other fades in. Also applicable to sequential slides.

dissolve control. A device that controls the illumination from one, two, or more projectors in such a manner that the images fade from one into another at a fixed or variable rate.

division of labor. In economics, the reorganization of a job so that some tasks are performed by one person or system and other tasks by others for purposes of increased efficiency and/or effectiveness.

documentary film. A film that deals with fact, not fiction or fictionalized versions of fact.

dolly. The movement of a camera toward or away from the subject while shooting.

drill-and-practice game. A game format that provides repetitive drill exercises in an interactive mode and that has game-type motivational elements.

drill-and-practice learning. A mode of learning that presents a lengthy series of items to be rehearsed; employed with skills that require repetitive practice for mastery.

dry mounting. A method of mounting visuals on cardboard or similar sheet materials in which a special tissue impregnated with a heat-sensitive adhesive is placed between the visual and mount board and is softened by the heat of a dry-mounting press to effect the bond.

economy of scale. In economics, the principle that certain functions decline in cost as they are expanded to encompass a larger population.

EIAJ standards. Electronic equipment standards, notably involving videotape recorders, promoted by the Electronic Industry Association of Japan; they allow for the compatibility of the equipment of all affected manufacturers.

electrostatic copying (xerography). A method of making overhead transparencies. Similar to the thermal process, this process requires specially treated film that is electrically charged and light sensitive.

emgor. An acronym for *electromyogram sensor*. A prosthetic device that uses the brain's own natural impulse, called the myoelectric signal or electromyogram, to control electromechanical devices in an artificial limb.

encoder. In electronics, a device used with a tape recorder or other information storage device to produce the synchronizing signals or pulses for later decoding required to operate combinations of devices (projectors) in synchronizatrion. In human communication, the element that converts the thoughts of the source into visible or audible messages.

exciter lamp. The small lamp that projects its single-coil illumination through the optical sound track on 16-mm film; the varying light intensity is "read" by the projector's photoelectric cell, which converts the light impulses into electronic signals amplified and made audible by a loudspeaker (or earphones).

fade in/out. In motion pictures and video, an optical effect in which a scene gradually appears out of blackness or disappears into blackness.

feedback. 1. In electronics, the regeneration of sound caused by a system's microphonic pickup of output from its own speakers causing a ringing sound or squeal. 2. In communication, signals sent from the destination back to the source which provide information about the reception of the original message.

filmstrip. A roll of 35-mm film containing a series of related still pictures intended for showing one at a time in sequence.

flip chart. A pad of large-sized paper fastened together at the top and mounted on an easel.

F/number. See *lens speed*.

f/stop. Numerical description of the relative size of the aperture that determines the amount of light entering a camera.

focal length. Loosely, the focal distance when the lens is focused on infinity; more accurately, the distance from the focal point of the lens to the image plane when the lens is focused on infinity.

format. The physical form in which a medium is incorporated and displayed. For example, motion pictures are available in 35-mm, 16-mm, and 8-mm formats.

frame 1. An individual picture in a filmstrip or motion picture. 2. The useful area and shape of a film image. 3. A complete television picture of 525 horizontal lines. 4. In programmed instruction, one unit in a series of prompt-response-reinforcement units; a block of verbal/visual information.

frame game. An existing game that lends its structure to new subject matter.

freeze frame. A film technique in which a film maker selects an image in a motion sequence and prints that image over and over again, so that one moment is held frozen on the screen.

frequency. The rate of repetition in cycles per second (Hertz) of musical pitch or electrical signals. Low frequencies are bass; high frequencies are treble.

fresnel lens. A flat glass or acrylic lens in which the curvature of a normal lens surface is collapsed into small steps in an almost flat plane, resulting in concentric circle forms impressed or engraved on the lens surface. Because of lower cost, less weight, and compactness, it is often used for the condenser lens in overhead projectors and in studio lights.

front screen projection. An image projected on the "audience side" of a light-reflecting screen.

game. An activity in which participants follow prescribed rules that differ from those of reality as they strive to attain a challenging goal.

Gestalt learning. A theory of learning based on analysis of the unified whole, suggesting that the understanding of an entire process is better than the study of individual parts or sequences of the whole.

goal. A desired instructional outcome that is broad in scope and general with regard to criteria and performance indicators.

gothic lettering. A style of lettering with even width of strokes and without serifs (the tiny cross strokes at the end of a line).

hardware. Mechanical/electronic components that make up a computer; the physical equipment that makes up a computer system. By extension, any audiovisual equipment.

head-end. The origination point of a cable television system.

head demagnetizer (degausser). A device that provides an alternating magnetic field used during routine maintenance to remove the residual magnetism from recording or playback heads.

headphone. A device consisting of one or two electro-acoustic receivers attached to a headband for private listening to audio sources; sometimes called earphone.

hearing. A physiological process in which sound waves entering the outer ear are transmitted to the eardrum, converted into mechanical vibrations in the middle ear, and changed in the inner ear into nerve impulses that travel to the brain.

Hertz (Hz). The frequency of an alternating signal. Formerly called *cycles per second* (cps).

holistic learning. In the modeling of reality learners encounter a whole and dynamic view of the process being studied. Emotions are involved along with the thinking process.

Hz. See *Hertz*.

iconic. Pertaining to an image that resembles a real object.

inductive learning. A teaching strategy that proceeds as follows: immersion in a real or contrived problematic situation, development of hypotheses, testing of hypotheses, arrival at conclusion (the Point).

input. Information or a stimulus that enters a system.

instruction. Deliberate arrangement of experience(s) to help a learner achieve a desirable change in performance; the management of learning, which in education and training is primarily the function of the instructor.

instructional development. The process of analyzing needs, determining what content must be mastered, establishing educational goals, designing materials to help reach the objectives, and trying out and revising the program in terms of learner achievement.

instructional module. A free-standing instructional unit, usually used for independent study. Typical components are: (1) rationale, (2) objective, (3) pre-test, (4) learning activities, (5) self-test, and (6) post-test.

instructional technology. "A complex, integrated process involving people, procedures, ideas, devices, and organization, for analyzing problems and devising, implementing, evaluating, and managing solutions to those problems in situations in which learning is purposive and controlled."*

instructional television. Any planned use of video programs to meet specific instructional goals regardless of the source of the programs (including commercial broadcasts) or the setting in which they are used (e.g., including business/industry training).

---

*Association for Edcuational Communications and Technology (AECT). *The Definition of Educational Technology*. Washington, D.C.: AECT, 1977.

integration. The intellectual skill of relating parts to a whole, which includes drawing inferences about the whole from a part.

interactive video. An instructional delivery system in which recorded video material is presented under computer control to viewers who not only see and hear the pictures and sound, but also make active responses, with those responses affecting the pace and sequence of the presentation.

internalization. The degree to which an attitude or value has become part of an individual. The affective domain is organized according to the degree of internalization. See *affective domain*.

IPS. Inches per second; more properly written in/s. Standard method for measuring the speed of tape movement.

ITFS. Instructional Television Fixed Service; a portion of the microwave frequency spectrum (2500–2690 mHz) reserved by law in the United States for educational use.

ITV. See *instructional television*.

jack. Receptacle for a plug connector for the input or output circuits of an audio or video device. There are several common sizes and formats of plugs, including:

Standard Phone	0.25″ or 6.35 mm diameter
Small Phone	0.206″ or 5.23 mm
Mini	0.140″ or 3.6 mm
Micro	0.097″ or 2.5 mm

keystone effect. The distortion (usually of a wide top and narrow bottom effect) of a projected image caused when the projector is not aligned at right angles to the screen.

lamination. A technique for preserving visuals that provides them with protection from wear and tear by covering them with clear plastic or similar substances.

lantern slide. A once common slide format of 3¼ × 4 inch dimensions.

lavalier mike. A small microphone worn around the neck.

learning. A general term for a relatively lasting change in performance caused directly by experience; also, the process or processes whereby such change is brought about. Learning is inferred from performance.

learning center. An individualized environment designed to encourage the student to use a variety of instructional media, to engage in diversified learning activities, and to assume major responsibility for his or her own learning.

lens speed. Refers to the ability of a lens to pass light expressed as a ratio—the focal length of the lens divided by the (effective) diameter. A fast lens (which passes more light) might be rated f/1.1 or 1.2; a much slower lens (which passes less light) might be designated f/3.5.

$$\text{f/\# or F/number} = \frac{\text{focal length}}{\text{aperture}}$$

line graph. The most precise and complex of all graphs based on two scales at right angles. Each point has a value on the vertical scale and on the horizontal scale. Lines (or curves) are drawn to connect the points.

listening. A psychological process that begins with someone's awareness of and attention to sounds or speech patterns, proceeds through identification and recognition of specific auditory signals, and ends in comprehension.

low-cost learning technology. An approach to implementing instructional technology in formal education featuring systematic selection and implementation of a variety of managerial, instructional, motivational, and resource utilization strategies to increase student learning outcomes while decreasing or maintaining at a constant level the recurrent educational costs.

mainframe computer. A high-speed, multiple purpose computer intended primarily for business and scientific computing; designed for processing huge amounts of numerical data.

material. An item of a medium format; in the plural, a collection of items of a medium format or of several media formats.

medium; media. A means of communication. Derived from the Latin *medium*, ''between,'' the term refers to anything that carries information between a source and a receiver.

microfiche. A sheet of microfilm (usually 4×6'') containing multiple micro-images in a grid pattern. It usually contains a title that can be read without magnification.

microfilm. A film in which each frame is a miniaturized image of a printed page or photograph. May be 16-, 35-, 70-, or 105-mm.

microform. Any materials, film or paper, printed or photographic, containing micro-images that are units of information, such as a page of text or drawing, too small to be read without magnification.

micro/mini cassette. One of several audio cassettes much smaller than the compact cassette; used principally for note taking and dictation.

microphone. A device that converts sound into electrical signals usable by other pieces of audio equipment. Microphones vary in sound quality, generating system used, directional patterns, and impedance.

microprocessor. The brain of the microcomputer; the electronic chip (circuit) that does all the calculations and control of data. In larger machines, it is called the Central Processing Unit (CPU).

microprocessor game. Inexpensive, limited-purpose calculator-type toy, such as *Dataman*, *Little Professor*, *Speak & Spell*, and *Teach & Tell*. Marketed primarily to the mass home market for arithmetic, spelling, or discrimination practice.

microwave transmission. A television distribution system using the ultra high and super high frequency ranges (2000-13,000 mHz). Includes ITFS in the United States (2500-2690 mHz).

monitor. A TV set without broadcast receiving circuitry that is used primarily to display video signals.

motor skills domain. The category of human learning that involves athletic, manual, and other physical action skills.

multi-image. The use of two or more separate images, usually projected simultaneously in a presentation. Multiple images are often projected on adjacent multiple screens.

multimedia. Sequential or simultaneous use of a variety of media formats in a given presentation or self-study program.

multimedia kit. A collection of teaching/learning materials involving more than one type of medium and organized around a single topic.

multimedia system. A combination of audio and visual media integrated into a structured, systematic presentation.

multipurpose board. A board with a smooth white plastic surface with which special marking pens rather than chalk are used. Sometimes called ''visual aid panels,'' these usually have a steel backing and can be used as a magnetic board for display of visuals. May also be used as a screen for projected visuals.

multi-screen. The use of more than one screen in a single presentation. Multiple images are often projected on adjacent multiple screens.

noise. 1. In audio systems, electrical interference or any unwanted sound. 2. In video, it refers to random spurts of electrical energy or interference. In some cases it will produce a ''salt-and-pepper'' pattern over the televised picture. 3. In communication, any distortion of the signal as it passes through the channel.

nonformal education. Purposeful learning that takes place outside the boundaries of formal educational institutions.

omnidirectional. A microphone that picks up sound from all directions.

opaque projection. A method for projecting opaque (nontransparent) visuals by reflecting light off the material rather than transmitting light through it.

open reel. Audio or video tape or film mounted on a reel that is not enclosed in a cartridge or cassette.

optical sound. Sound that is recorded by photographic means on motion picture film. The sound is reproduced by projecting a narrow beam of light from an exciter lamp through the sound track into a photoelectric cell which converts it to electrical impulses for amplification.

oral history. Historical documentation of a time, place, or event by means of recording the spoken recollections of participant(s) in those events.

output. In electronics, the signal delivered from any audio or video device; also a jack, connector, or circuit that feeds the signal to another piece of equipment such as a speaker or headphones. In communication, information or a stimulus leaving a system.

overhead projection. Projection by means of a device which produces an image on a screen by transmitting light through transparent acetate or similar medium on the stage of the projector. The lens and mirror arrangement in an elevated housing creates a bright projected image cast over the head or shoulder of the operator.

overlay. One or more additional transparent sheets with lettering or other information that can be placed over a base transparency.

overt response. A learner response which is outwardly observable (e.g., writing or speaking). See *covert response.*

patch cord. An electrical wire used to connect two pieces of sound equipment (e.g., tape recorders and record players) so that electrical impulses can be transferred between the two units in order to make a recording.

performance objective. A statement of the new capability the learner should possess at the completion of instruction. A well-stated objective names the intended audience, then specifies: (1) the performance or capability to be learned, (2) the conditions under which the performance is to be learned, and (3) the criterion or standard of acceptable performance.

peripheral. A device, such as a printer, mass storage unit, or keyboard, that is an accessory to a microprocessor and that transfers information to and from the microprocessor.

persistence of vision. The psycho-physiological phenomenon that occurs when an image falls on the retina of the eye and is conveyed to the brain via the optic nerve; the brain continues to "see" the image for a fraction of a second after the image is cut off.

Personalized System of Instruction (PSI). A technology for managing instruction that puts reinforcement theory into action as the overall framework for a whole course. Students work individually at their own pace using a variety of instructional materials. The materials are arranged in sequential order and the student must show mastery of each unit before being allowed to move on to the next.

pictorial graph. An alternate form of the bar graph, in which a series of simple drawings is used to represent the value.

pinball-type game. A microprocessor-controlled arcade game in which the player controls a joystick or paddle, and makes rapid hand movements in response to a moving pattern of threatening situations on a display screen.

playback. A device to reproduce a previously recorded program for hearing and/or viewing.

portable video. The several methods of playing back video programs in the classroom by means of video recorders. The distribution system itself—the record/playback machine—is portable and can be set up wherever needed.

programmed instruction. A method of presenting instructional material printed in small bits or "frames," each of which includes an item of information (prompt), an incomplete sentence to be completed or a question to be answered (response), and provision of the correct answer (reinforcement).

programmed tutoring. A one-to-one method of instruction in which the decisions to be made by the tutor are "programmed" in advance by means of carefully structured printed instructions.

programmer. A multi-channel, multi-function device used with a tape recorder or microprocessor to perform certain predetermined functions when called upon to do so by the synchronizer. In addition to controlling projectors, dissolve controls, etc., it can be arranged to perform other functions (often via interfaces) such as operating a motorized screen, turning on room lights, etc. It may contain the functions of a synchronizer and/or a dissolve control.

projected visual. Media formats in which still images are projected onto a screen.

projection lens. A convex lens or system of lenses that recreates an enlarged image of the transparency, object, or film on a screen.

public access channels. Cable channels that are outlets for use by community and special interest groups.

RAM. See *random access memory.*

random access. The ability to retrieve in any sequence slides, filmstrip frames, or information on audio or video tapes or video discs regardless of original sequence.

random access memory (RAM).
The flexible part of the computer memory. The particular program or set of data being manipulated by the user is temporarily stored in RAM, then erased to make way for the next program.

rangefinder camera.   A camera featuring a built-in, optical rangefinder, usually incorporated into the viewfinder and linked mechanically with the focusing mount of the lens so that bringing the rangefinder images into coincidence also focuses the lens.

rate-controlled audio playback.
An audio tape system that can play back recorded speech either at a faster or slower rate than the rate at which it was recorded—without loss of intelligibility. See *speech compression and expansion.*

read only memory (ROM).   Control instructions that have been "wired" permanently into the memory of a computer. Usually stores instructions that the computer will need constantly, such as the programming language(s) and internal monitoring functions.

realia.   Real things; objects such as coins, tools, artifacts, plants, animals, etc.

rear screen.   A translucent screen of glass or plastic with a specially formulated coating on which the image is transmitted through the screen for individual or group viewing. The screen is between the projector and the viewer.

reel-to-reel.   Film or tape transport in which separate supply and take-up reels are used; they may be open or enclosed.

referent.   That which is referred to.

reinforcement theory.   A body of psychological theory revolving around the role of reinforcement (consequences that follow responses) in learning.

responder.   A device used with some audiovisual equipment to allow a student to respond to the program; e.g., by answering multiple choice questions.

role-play.   A simulation in which the dominant feature is a relatively open-ended interaction among people.

ROM.   See *read only memory.*

roman lettering.   A style of lettering resembling ancient Roman stone carved lettering: vertical strokes are broad and horizontal strokes are narrower; curved strokes become narrower as they turn toward the horizontal.

rule of thirds.   A principle of photographic and graphic composition: divide an area into thirds both vertically and horizontally; the center(s) of interest should be near the intersection of the lines.

scenario.   Literally, a written description of the plot of a play. In simulation/game design, it refers to a description of the setting and events to be represented in a simulation.

sequencing.   Arranging ideas in logical order.

shot.   The basic element of which motion pictures are made: each separate length of motion-picture footage exposed in one "take."

showmanship.   Techniques that an instructor can use to direct and hold attention during presentations.

simulation.   An abstraction or simplification of some real-life situation or process.

simulation game.   An instructional format that combines the attributes of simulation (role-playing, model of reality) with the attributes of a game (striving toward a goal, specific rules).

simulator.   A device that represents a real physical system in a scaled-down form; it allows the user to experience the salient aspects of the real-life process.

single-lens reflex (SLR) camera.
A camera in which the viewfinder image is formed by the camera lens and reflected to a top-mounted viewing screen by a hinged mirror normally inclined behind the camera lens. During exposure of the film, the mirror flips up allowing light to pass through onto the film.

slide.   A small-format (e.g., 35-mm) photographic transparency individually mounted for one-at-a-time projection.

slow motion.   A film technique that expands time by photographing rapid events at high speeds (many exposures per second) and then projecting the film at normal speed.

software.   Computer program control instructions and accompanying documentation; stored on diskettes or cassettes when not being used in the computer. By extension, refers to any audiovisual materials.

speech compression and expansion.   A method of maintaining intelligibility of normally recorded speech when it is played back at speeds greater than (compression) or less than (expansion) normal; the effect is attained by electronically correcting the pitch to approximate the pitch of normal speech. Variable speeds of playback may be set, from 50 percent of normal to 250 percent of normal speed.

spirit duplicating.   An inexpensive duplicating-printing process using master sheets that release color through type indentations when a colorless alcohol fluid ("spirits") is applied; images can be imprinted on paper, card stock, or acetate.

sponsored film.   A film produced by a private corporation, association, or government agency, usually with the purpose of presenting a message of interest to the sponsor for general public consumption.

storyboard(ing).   An audiovisual production planning technique in which sketches of the proposed visuals and/or verbal messages are put on individual cards; the cards then are arranged into the desired sequence on a display surface.

study print.   A photographic enlargement printed in a durable form for individual or group examination.

stylus.   The "needle" assembly of a phonograph cartridge.

suggestive-accelerative learning and teaching (SALT). A U.S. adaptation of suggestopedy as proposed by Lozanov; major features are conscious relaxation, visual imagery, positive suggestions, multisensory inputs and presentation of information to be learned in meaningful units, often to musical accompaniment.

synchronizer. A single-function device that, together with a tape recorder or other type of playback, operates other equipment, for example, signalling slide changes.

tacking iron. A small thermostatically controlled heating tool used to tack or attach dry-mounting tissue to the back of a print or to the mount board, so as to hold it in place while the print is trimmed and heated in the dry-mount press.

take-up reel. The reel that accumulates the tape or film as it is recorded or played.

technology. 1. A process—"the systematic application of scientific or other organized knowledge to practical tasks;" the process of devising reliable and repeatable solutions to tasks. 2. A product—the hardware and software that result from the application of technological processes. 3. A mix of process and product—used in instances where: (a) the context refers to the combination of technological processes and resultant products; (b) process is inseparable from product.

technology of instruction. A teaching/learning pattern designed to provide reliable, effective instruction to each learner through application of scientific principles of human learning.

teleconference. A communications technique in which groups at separate geographic locations use microphones and special amplifiers that are linked together to allow everyone to actively participate in one large meeting.

telelecture. An instructional technique in which an individual, typically a content specialist or a well-known authority, addresses a group listening by means of a telephone amplifier; the listeners may ask questions of the resource person, with the entire group able to hear the response.

teletext. Print information transmitted on a broadcast television signal using the "vertical blanking interval," a portion of the signal not used to carry visual or auditory information.

thermal film. Specially treated acetate used to make overhead transparencies. In this process infrared light passes through the film onto a prepared master underneath. An image is "burned into" the film wherever it contacts carbonaceous markings.

threading. Inserting or directing a film or tape through a projector or recorder mechanism.

tilt. The swivelling of a motion picture or video camera upward or downward.

time-lapse. A film technique that compresses the time that it takes for an event to occur. A long process is photographed frame by frame, at long intervals, then projected at normal speed.

transaction. In simulation/game design, the specific actions and interactions carried out by the players as they engage in the activity.

transparency. The large-format (typically 8 by 10 inch) film used with the overhead projector.

treble. See *frequency*.

"2-by-6" rule. A general rule of thumb for determining screen size: No viewer should be seated closer to the screen than two screen widths or farther away than six screen widths.

UHF (ultra high frequency). Television transmission on channels 14 through 83 (300-3000 mHz).

ultra violet (UV). Rays just beyond (shorter than) the visible spectrum; ordinarily filtered or blocked to prevent eye damage and dye fading.

U-matic. A particular video cassette system offered by several manufacturers in which ¾ inch tape moves at 7½ ips between two enclosed hubs.

unidirectional microphone. See *cardioid microphone*.

variable motion programming. An 8-mm film-audio cassette system in which the audio cassette moves at a constant speed, but the film can be programmed to move at variable speeds from still (stop action) up to 24 frames per second. The film and sound are synchronized by inaudible pulses recorded on the audio cassette.

VHF (very high frequency). Television transmission on channels 2 through 13 (30-300 mHz).

VHS. A ½ inch video cassette format. Not compatible with the beta format, which is also ½ inch but differs electronically.

videocassette. Video tape that has been enclosed in a plastic case. Available in one ¾ inch format (U-matic) and two ½ inch formats, Betamax and VHS (Video Home System).

videodisc. A video recording and storage system in which audiovisual signals are recorded on plastic discs, rather than on magnetic tape.

videotex. Two-way transmission of print information through either telephone lines or coaxial cable.

visual literacy. The learned ability to interpret visual messages accurately and to create such messages.

volume unit meter (VU-meter). A device to indicate the relative levels of the various sounds being recorded or played. Usually calibrated to show a point of maximum recording level to avoid tape saturation and limit distortion.

wide-angle lens. A camera lens that permits a wider view of a subject and its surroundings than would be obtained by normal lens from the same position.

P H O T O   C R E D I T S

Chapter 1

Fig. 1.1: David S. Strickler/Picture Cube. Fig. 1.2: Frank Siteman/ Picture Cube. Fig. 1.3: Children's Television Workshop. Fig. 1.4: Drawing by Berke Breathed © Washington Post Writer's Group. Fig. 1.5: Jeff Miller and Bill Hinds © 1982 Universal Press Syndicate. Fig. 1.6: Alan Carey/Image Works. Fig. 1.7: Donald Dietz/ Stock Boston. Fig. 1.8: Ira Berger/Woodfin Camp. Fig. 1.9: Suzanne Szasz. Fig. 1.10, Fig. 1.11, Fig. 1.12: Michal Heron. Fig. 1.13: Michael Molenda. Page 13: Elyse Rieder. Fig. 1.4: Peter Menzel/Stock Boston. Fig. 1.17: Michael Neff. Fig. 1.18: Paul Fortin/Picture Group. Fig. 1.20, Fig. 1.21: William Vandervert. Fig. 1.22: Shirley Zeiberg/Taurus Photos. Fig. 1.23: Michael Neff. Fig. 1.24: Deane Dayton. Fig. 1.25: New York University Education Quarterly. Fig. 1.26: Michael Molenda. Fig. 1.27: Rhoda Sidney/Monkmeyer. Fig. 1.28: Eric Neurath/Stock Boston. Page 23: Jim Owens. Fig. 1.29: Deane Dayton. Fig. 1.30: Sybil Shackman/ Monkmeyer. Fig. 1.31: Norm Hurst/Stock Boston. Fig. 1.32: Research for Better Schools, Inc. Fig. 1.33: Response Systems Corp. Fig. 1.34 (left): © 1982 American Broadcasting Companies, Inc. Fig. 1.34 (right): Kurzweil Computer Products. Fig. 1.35: Peter Menzel/Stock Boston. Fig. 1.36: Michael Molenda. Fig. 1.37: David Strickler/Monkmeyer. Fig. 1.38: Paul S. Conklin/ Monkmeyer.

Chapter 2

Page 34 (left): Ellis Herwig/Stock Boston. Page 34 (center): Ken Karp. Page 34 (right): Jim Anderson/Woodfin Camp. Page 35 (left): David Strickler/Picture Cube. Page 35 (center): Russell Abraham/Stock Boston. Page 35 (right): Hugh Rogers/Monkmeyer. Fig. 2.1: Laimute Druskis/Taurus Photos. Fig. 2.3: © 1971 United Feature Syndicate, Inc. Fig. 2.4: Alan Carey/Image Works. Page 44: Pitman Learning, Inc. Fig. 2.5: Michael Molenda. Fig. 2.7: Jim Owens. Fig. 2.8: Michal Heron. Fig. 2.9: Laimute Druskis. Fig. 2.10: Michael Molenda. Fig. 2.11: Michael Hayman/Stock Boston. Fig. 2.21: Richard Wood/Picture Cube. Fig. 2.22: Laimute Druskis/Taurus Photos. Fig. 2.23, Fig. 2.24: Michal Heron. Page 60: Michael Molenda.

Chapter 3

Fig. 3.1 (all): Michal Heron. Fig. 3.2: © 1983 by NEA, Inc. Fig. 3.3: Karsh, Ottawa/Woodfin Camp. Fig. 3.5: Richard Kalvar/Magnum. Fig. 3.7: The Bettmann Archive. Fig. 3.8, Fig. 3.9: Michael Molenda. Fig. 3.10: Konica Corporation. Fig. 3.11: Pentax Corporation. Fig. 3.12: Eastman Kodak. Fig. 3.13: Olympus Camera Corporation. Fig. 3.14, Fig. 3.15: Michael Molenda. Page 73 (top): John Soudah. Page 73 (center): Peter Menzel/Stock Boston. Page 73 (bottom): John Soudah. Page 74 (top): Peter Vandermark/Stock Boston. Page 74 (center): Florida Division of Tourism. Page 74 (bottom): John Soudah. Fig. 3.19: Michael Molenda. Page 76, Page 77, Page 78: Thomas Cecere.

Chapter 4

Fig. 1.1, Fig. 1.2: Jim Owens. Fig. 4.3: Michael Neff. Page 91: Jim Owens. Fig. 4.4: Department of Psychology, Duke University. Fig. 4.6: Denoyer-Geppert Audio-Visuals. Fig. 4.8: Mike Mazzaschi/Stock Boston. Page 98: Jim Owens. Fig. 4.9: Paul Fortin/Picture Group. Fig. 4.10: John Soudah. Fig. 4.11: Mike Mazzaschi/

Stock Boston. Fig. 4.12: Laimute Druskis/Taurus Photos. Fig. 4.13: John Soudah. Fig. 4.14: Jim Owens. Fig. 4.15: Michal Heron. Page 105: Michael Neff. Fig. 4.16, Fig. 4.17: Michal Heron. Fig. 4.18, Fig. 4.19: John Soudah. Fig. 4.20: Gabor Demjen/Stock Boston. Fig. 4.21: Joseph P. Schuyler/Stock Boston. Fig. 4.24: David Strickler/Monkmeyer. Fig. 4.25: Jim Owens. Fig. 4.26: John Soudah. Fig. 4.27: AT&T Communications. Fig. 4.28: Sandra Johnson/Picture Cube. Fig. 4.29: American Museum of Natural History.

Chapter 5

Fig. 5.2: Swan Pencil Company. Fig. 5.4: 3M Company. Fig. 5.5: Suhl Industry, Inc. Fig. 5.6: John Soudah. Page 122: Milliken Publishing Company. Page 123: Denoyer-Geppart Audio-Visuals. Fig. 5.7: Ken Robert Buck/Stock Boston. Fig. 5.8, Fig. 5.9: John Soudah. Page 127: Indiana University Audio-Visual Center. Fig. 5.11: Michael Neff. Fig. 5.12, Fig. 5.13: Eastman Kodak. Page 131: Adopted permission of the publisher, from *Concepts in Science 5: Experiences, A Workbook* by Paul F. Brandwein, et al © 1966 by Harcourt Brace Jovanovich, Inc. Page 132: © 1979 Art Now, Inc. Fig. 5.14: Jack Spratt/Picture Group. Page 134 (bottom): Michael Neff. Page 134 (top), Page 135: Dennis Short. Fig. 5.15: Indiana University Audio-Visual Center. Fig. 5.17: Bell & Howell Company. Fig. 5.18: Jim Owens. Fig. 5.19: Singer Educational Division. Fig. 5.20: Dukane Corporation. Fig. 5.21: Indiana University Audio-Visual Center. Page 138 (top): Society for Visual Education, Inc. Page 138 (bottom): Denoyer-Geppert Audio-Visuals. Fig. 5.23, Fig. 5.24: Michael Neff.

Chapter 6

Fig. 6.1 (left): Ken Heyman. Fig. 6.1 (right): Martha Stewart. Fig. 6.4: Xerox Learning Systems. Page 149 (top): Stuart Rosner/ Stock Boston. Page 149 (bottom): Frank Siteman/Picture Cube. Fig. 6.5: Courtesy Folkways. Page 150: U.P.I. Fig. 6.8: Michael Neff. Fig. 6.9: Audiotronics. Fig. 6.10: Voxcom. Fig. 6.11: American Printing House for the Blind, Inc. Fig. 6.12: Ellis Herwig/Picture Cube. Page 155 (top): Julie O'Neil/Stock Boston. Page 155 (bottom): Ira Kirschenbaum/Stock Boston. Page 156 (a): Audiotronics. Page 156 (b): Eastman Kodak. Page 156 (c): P & H Electronics, Inc. Page 156 (d): Michael Molenda. Page 157 (a): Michael Neff. Page 157 (b, c, d): Michal Heron. Fig. 6.13: Bruce Roberts/Photo Researchers. Fig. 6.14: Michael Neff. Fig. 6.20: Telex Communications, Inc. Fig. 6.21: VSC Corporation. Fig. 6.22: Michael Neff. Fig. 6.23: AT&T Communications.

Chapter 7

Fig. 7.1: Singer Educational Division, Society for Visual Education. Fig. 7.2: © 1979 King Features Syndicate, Inc. Fig. 7.3: Visual Horizons. Fig. 7.6: Hugh Rogers/Monkmeyer. Fig. 7.7, Fig. 7.9: Michael Neff. Fig. 7.11: Eastman Kodak. Fig. 7.13: Indiana University Audio-Visual Center. Fig. 7.15: John Soudah. Fig. 7.16, Page 182: Beseler Company. Fig. 7.17: Synsor Corporation. Fig. 7.18, Fig. 7.19: Indiana University Audio-Visual Center. Page 185: Clark Equipment Company. Page 186: Jim Sheldon. Page 187: Frank Siteman/Taurus Photos. Fig. 7.20: Encyclopedia Britannica Educational Corporation. Fig. 7.21: Dennis Short. Page 189: Michael Neff. Page 190: Kit developed at the Boston Children's Museum. Fig. 7.22: Hugh Rogers/Monkmeyer. Fig. 7.23: F. Bernstein/Leo de Wys. Fig. 7.24: Will McIntyre/Photo Researchers. Page 192: Dennis Short. Fig. 7.25: Peter Vandermark/Stock Boston.

Chapter 8

Page 201 (left): The Bettmann Archive. Page 201 (right), Page 202: From ''Teaching with Films'' by George H. Ferns and Eldon Robbins. The Bruce Publishing Company © 1946. Fig. 8.5: National Film Board of Canada. Fig. 8.6: Jen and Des Bartlett/Photo Researchers. Fig 8.7: Ira Kirschenbaum/Stock Boston. Fig. 8.8: Pyramid Film & Video. Fig. 8.9: National Film Board of Canada. Fig. 8.10: International Film Bureau, Inc. Fig. 8.11: David Powers/Stock Boston. Fig. 8.12: Roger Wirth/Woodfin Camp. Fig. 8.13: Phil Ellin/Picture Cube. Fig. 8.14: ''The Pilgrims'' from the Encyclopedia Britannica Educational Corporation. Fig. 8.15: Produced by CRM Productions, Distributed by CRM/McGraw Hill Films. Fig. 8.16: Dean Williams/American Broadcasting Companies, Inc. Fig. 8.17: Agency for Instructional Television. Fig. 8.18: Museum of Modern Art—Film Stills Archives. Fig. 8.19: ''U.S. Congress,'' from the Encyclopedia Britannica Educational Corporation. Fig. 8.20: Agency for Instructional Technology. Fig. 8.21: Michael Molenda. Fig. 8.22: ''Images of Einstein'' courtesy IBM. Fig. 8.23: International Film Seminars, Inc. Fig. 8.24, Fig. 8.25, Fig. 8.26: Museum of Modern Art—Film Stills Archives. Fig. 8.27: Films, Inc. Fig. 8.28: Museum of Modern Art—Film Stills Archives. Fig. 8.29: Zipporah Films, Inc. Fig. 8.30: McGraw Hill Films. Fig. 8.31: Wombat Productions. Fig. 8.32: ''Death of a Princess,'' WGBH Educational Foundation. Fig. 8.33, Fig. 8.34, Fig. 8.35, Fig. 8.36: Laimute Druskis. Page 217: Janus Classic Collection/Films, Inc. Page 218 (top): Bureau of Reclamation, U.S. Department of the Interior. Page 218 (bottom): Encyclopedia Britannica Educational Corporation. Fig. 8.37: William Orisich. Page 219 (top): Aimes Media, Inc. Page 219 (center): CRM/McGraw Hill. Fig. 8.38: Frank Siteman/Stock Boston. Page 199–211: Ballet dancer photo sequence from the film, ''Movement in Classical Dance,'' Indiana University, Audio Visual Center.

Chapter 9

Fig. 9.1: Teri Leigh Stratford/Photo Researchers. Page 225: The School Board of Broward County, Florida. Instructional Television Center. Fig. 9.2: Jack Spratt/Picture Group. Page 226 (top), Page 226 (bottom): Agency for Instructional Television. Page 227: Public Broadcasting Service. Funded by the Corporation for Public Broadcasting & Kellog Company. Page 228 (top): University of Mid-America. Page 228 (bottom): An Annenberg/CPB Project produced by theDallas County Community College District. Page 229 (top): WETA/26, The Annenberg/CPB Collection. Page 229 (bottom): Coast Telecourses, 1984. Fig. 9.4, Fig. 9.5: Children's Television Workshop. Page 232 © 1984 National Broadcasting Company, Inc. Fig. 9.6: Agency for Instructional Television. Fig. 9.8: Warner Amex Qube. Fig. 9.9: Purdue University Continuing Engineering Education. Fig. 9.10: Laimute Druskis/Taurus Photos. Fig. 9.12: Michael Molenda. Fig. 9.13: JVC Company of America. Fig. 9.14: Kodak, Fig. 9.15: Pioneer Corp. Fig. 9.16: JVC Company of America. Page 240 (a, b): Sony Video Products Company. Page 240 (c): Shure Brothers, Incorporated. Page 240 (d, e): Audiotronics. Page 241: JVC Company of America. Page 244 (a, b, c, top): Michael Heron. Fig. 9.17: Ellis Herwig/Stock Boston.

Chapter 10

Fig. 10.2: Shure Brothers, Inc. Fig. 10.3, Fig. 10.4: John Soudah. Fig. 7: Eastman Kodak. Fig. 10.8: John Soudah. Fig. 10.9: Indiana University Audio-Visual Center. Fig. 10.15, Fig. 10.16, Fig. 10.18: John Soudah. Fig. 10.20: Michael Neff. Fig. 10.22: John Soudah.

Chapter 11

Fig. 11.1: Kathy Bendo. Fig. 11.2: B. F. Skinner. Fig. 11.3, Fig. 11.4: from *Teaching Machines & Programmed Learning*, published by Association for Educational Communications & Technology. Fig. 11.5: Indiana University Audio-Visual Center. Fig. 11.6: John Soudah. Fig. 11.7: Hugh Rogers/Monkmeyer. Fig. 11.11: Indiana University Audio-Visual Center. Fig. 11.12, Fig. 11.13: Elyse Rieder. Fig. 11.14, Fig. 11.15: Michael Neff. Fig 11.16: J. S. Keller, Kalamazoo, 1968. Fig. 11.17: Donald Dietz/Stock Boston. Fig. 11.18: John Soudah. Page 296, Fig. 11.19: Dennis Short. Fig. 11.20: Hugh Rogers/Monkmeyer. Fig. 11.21: Jean-Claude Lejune/Stock Boston. Fig. 11.22, Fig. 11.23: John Soudah.

Chapter 12

Fig. 12.1: Owen Franken/Stock Boston. Page 308: The Bettmann/ Archive. Fig. 12.3: Alan Carey/Image Works. Fig. 12.4: Richard Hutchings/Photo Researchers. Fig. 12.5: Michael Molenda. Page 311: Deane Dayton. Page 312: Indiana University Audio-Visual Center. Page 313 (top, center): Thomas Cecere. Fig. 12.6: Grumman Aircraft. Fig. 12.7: Doron Precisions Systems, Inc., Drivotrainer System. Fig. 12.8: Bell Labs. Fig. 12.9: John Soudah. Page 315 (top): Thomas Cerece. Page 315 (center): Jean-Claude Lejune/Stock Boston. Page 315 (bottom): Arthur Tress/Photo Researchers. Fig. 12.10: National Broadcasting Company, Inc. Fig. 12.11: Thomas Cecere. Fig. 12.12: Rick Friedman/Picture Cube. Fig. 12.13: Donald Dietz/Stock Boston.

Chapter 13

Fig. 13.1: John Soudah. Fig. 13.2: Deane Dayton. Fig. 13.3: Michael Neff. Fig. 13.4: John Soudah. Fig. 13.5: David Strickler/Picture Cube. Fig. 13.6: Deane Dayton. Fig. 13.7: Richard Sobol/Stock Boston. Page 332: Fairfax County Public Schools. Fig. 13.9: Lockheed California Company. Page 335 (top): © Encyclopedia Britannica. Page 335 (center): Ellis Herwig/Stock Boston. Page 335 (bottom): Sirius Software. Page 337 (center): Apple Computer Company. Page 337 (top): P. Dameen/Click. Page 337 (bottom): Eric Neurath/Stock Boston. Page 338 (top): Sunburst Communications. Fig. 13.10, Fig. 13.11: Michael Neff. Fig. 13.13: Radio Shack, a Division of Tandy Corporation. Fig. 13.14: Deane Dayton. Page 345: John Soudah. Page 346: IBM. Page 348: Commodore Computer. Page 348: Radio Shack, a Division of Tandy Corporation.

Chapter 14

Fig. 14.1: Association for Educational Communications & Technology/University of Iowa. Fig. 14.2: JVC VideoMovie. Fig. 14.3: North America Philips Corporation. Fig. 14.4: Michael Neff. Fig. 14.5: RCA. Fig. 14.6: Pro Pix/Monkmeyer. Fig. 14.7: NASA. Fig. 14.8: AT&T. Fig. 14.9: The Bettmann Archive. Fig. 14.10: Gene S. Zimbel/Photo Researchers. Fig. 14.11: Alan Carey/Image Works. Fig. 14.12: Atari, Inc. Fig. 14.13: Alan Carey/Image Works. Fig. 14.14: John Soudah. Fig. 14.15: Davidson and Associates. Fig.